Thru-Hikers' Companion

WITHDRAWN

2020

The Appalachian Long Distance Hikers Association

Appalachian Trail
Thru-Hikers' Companion
2020

Robert Sylvester

Editor

Harpers Ferry

Cover: Hikers gather at Mountain Crossings, Neel Gap, Georgia, © *Gary Monk*

Elevation profiles © *2019 Appalachian Trail Conservancy. Derived from the 2020* Appalachian Trail Data Book *and other ATC sources.*

Maps developed or revised by Robert Sylvester.

Twenty-seventh edition   FEB 2 6 2020

Published by the Appalachian Trail Conservancy
    799 Washington Street (P.O. Box 807)
    Harpers Ferry, West Virginia 25425-0807
    <www.appalachiantrail.org>

ISBN 978-1-944958-14-5

Contents

Foreword

Welcome to the twenty-seventh edition of the *Appalachian Trail Thru-Hikers' Companion*. The 2020 *Companion* is a carefully conceived, diligently compiled and designed book that belongs in the possession of every Appalachian Trail hiker. Our hope is that the *Companion*, used in conjunction with official Trail maps, will lead the reader into making informed decisions about towns and services for resupply options.

This book is the culmination of the volunteer efforts of nearly forty ALDHA field editors and ATC staff members who worked to make this edition as accurate and up-to-date as possible. The newly structured tables include more than 2,080 waypoints and are keyed to the ATC maps and the AMC White Mountain trail system. Separate columns show northbound and southbound mileages, distance to the next waypoint, and elevation, as well as a features column with towns, road crossing, water sources, and distances to the next shelter, both north and south.

Thanks also go to Brian King, who, no doubt, worked long and hard putting all the pieces together. And, to everyone else who contributed in some way to the publication of this book, many heartfelt thanks!

A guidebook, like the Trail, is not static. Each hiker may discover something previously unknown. Your contributions are vital to this process. Your comments are most welcome—and requested! We rely on hikers' feedback to help us update future editions. Please send your comments on this book to ALDHA at <companion@aldha.org>, along with any corrections to maps or Trail, shelter, or town descriptions.

Robert "Sly" Sylvester
Editor

Additional Thru-Hikers' Companion content (and a PDF of the entire book) is on line at <www.aldha.org/companion/online>: waypoints and maps to Trailhead parking; maps of post offices, hostels, and other lodging; The A.T. Mailing-Label maker; and much more, including periodic updates, can be found there.

CHECKING THE WEATHER: A highly recommended Web site, truly keyed to Trail landmarks, is <atweather.org>.

HIKING TO KATAHDIN?
THERE ARE SOME THINGS YOU SHOULD KNOW.

Katahdin is in Baxter State Park.

Baxter is different from anywhere else on the AT. Wilderness comes first. Recreation comes second.

Katahdin is sacred to Maine's native people. It is a fragile and special place to finish a thru-hike.

In Baxter State Park and on Katahdin, plan to:
- ✔ Hike in small groups
- ✔ Celebrate quietly
- ✔ Save alcohol for later
- ✔ Share the summit with other hikers

You need to get a free AT hiker permit from Baxter State Park.

Visit the AT Visitor Center in Monson for the latest updates and help planning a great finish to your hike.

The future of the AT in Baxter State Park depends on partnership and good ethics from AT hikers.

DON'T JUST FINISH THE AT.
FINISH WELL. www.friendsofbaxter.org

v. 2018

Between Springer Mountain and the entrance to Shenandoah National Park above Waynesboro, Va., and again from the Massachusetts–Vermont line to the New Hampshire–Maine line, the A.T. runs mostly through national-forest lands. While ATC offers the official A.T. hiking maps (at <www.atctrailstore.org>), the U.S. Forest Service offers digital maps of the whole forests for iPhone and Android devices at iTunes and the Android Play Store. Prices range from 99¢ to $4.99.

About the *Companion*

The *Companion* is compiled, written, and edited by volunteers of the Appalachian Long Distance Hikers Association (ALDHA) and published by the Appalachian Trail Conservancy (ATC) as a service to those seeking to explore the Trail. It is intended for those making thru-hikes but is also valuable for those taking shorter section-hikes or overnight backpacking trips. The *Companion* provides you with details on shelters, water sources, post offices, hostels, campgrounds, lodging, groceries, restaurants, outfitters, and other related services along the Trail. In addition, the *Companion* offers information of historical significance about places you pass through while hiking the A.T. Unlike commercial guides, this book benefits from the latest information from volunteers who measure, maintain, and manage the Trail and those who hike it regularly.

Due to publication deadlines, we cannot guarantee that the information in this book will not change by the time you arrive in an area, despite the efforts of volunteers to acquire the most up-to-date information. Businesses close or change hours, hostels change rates and policies, and the Trail itself is subject to relocation. This edition was produced in the fall of 2019.

As you walk, talk to other hikers, and read shelter registers. The Conservancy's Web site periodically posts updates at <www.appalachiantrail.org/home/explore-the-trail/trail-updates>.

Inclusion in this book is not an endorsement by ALDHA or ATC, but rather a listing of services available and contacted by field editors. Likewise, the businesses listed do not pay for "advertisements" but are listed because of their proximity to the Trail.

ALDHA members do field research for each section of the Trail and are instrumental in gathering information. Without the hard work of the following ALDHA field editors, other volunteers, and ATC staff members, this book would not have been possible: **Georgia and North Carolina**—Scott Dowling (Pilgrim), Ann W. Thomas (Timberpixie); **North Carolina and Tennessee**—Deb and Charlie Tucker (Mawee & Pawee), Jim Chambers (Just Jim), Tim Steward (Mountain Squid); **Southwest Virginia**—Ken & Nora Ann Bennett (Big Cranky & Dragonfly), Charles Davidson (Chase); **Central Virginia**—Ken Bunning (Nimbus), Pat and Mike Ohleger, Leonard Adkins (Habitual Hiker); **Northern Virginia**—David and Sue Hennel (Gourmet Dave and The Real Gourmet), Jill Byrd (IWOX); **West Virginia**—ATC Information Services Manager Laurie Potteiger (Mountain Laurel) and Visitors Center Coordinator Jeff Metzger; **Maryland**—Mike Wingeart (Wingheart); **Southern Pennsylvania**—Roger Hahn (Samurai Blue); **Central and Northern Pennsylvania**—ATC's Boiling Springs regional office, Mary Parry (Trailangelmary); **New Jersey & New York**—Debbie Melita (Baby Carrots); **Connecticut**—Daryl Byrne (Wormwood); **Massachusetts**—Jim Niedbalski (High Octane); **Vermont**—Jeff Taussig, Kathy Krevetski (Ma Buddha); **New Hampshire**—Stephen King (Kinga), Art Cloutman (Gabby); **Maine**—Kevin Reardon (Slider) & Terrie Kee, Tammy Meserve (AT Gracie). Also, special thanks to Cameron Root (Zorro), who thru-hiked the Trail in 2019 and sent updates along the way. Mileage figures are based on information from the 2020 edition of the *Appalachian Trail Data Book*, edited by volunteer Daniel Chazin since 1983.

TRAIL-MAINTAINING CLUBS AND REGISTERS

Trail-maintaining clubs are listed throughout the book. You may use the addresses provided to contact the clubs with any comments, suggestions, or feedback. Although often a thru-hiker will leave an additional one, the official shelter registers are the property of the maintaining club and should not be removed by hikers. The register is a useful tool for information on Trail conditions and other things that are happening in its section of the A.T. It may also help locate a hiker in case of an emergency. If you wish to donate a register (assuming that one doesn't already exist), you should include a note asking the maintaining club to forward it to you when it's filled.

GETTING TO THE TRAIL

Section-hikers looking for shuttle services should check the business and individual listings for the area in which they plan to hike. (See page 1 for an important note on shuttles.) The ATC Web site on public transportation will link to information on Trailhead parking.

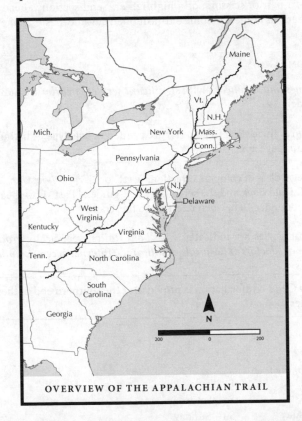

OVERVIEW OF THE APPALACHIAN TRAIL

Plan by registering: ATC strongly encourages would-be northbound thru-hikers to use its voluntary, on-line registration system to help determine their starting date. The system lets you see how many are planning to start on a given date, in the hope that people will spread the crunch out more—to relieve pressure on themselves and the Trail's resources. To check it out, go to <www.appalachiantrail.org/thruhikeregistration>.

Something else to consider: Increasingly, hikers are choosing to start somewhere in the middle of the Trail. Generally, these alternative itineraries offer a gradual progression from easier to more difficult terrain and more frequent resupplies. You can also avoid crowds and the party atmosphere, follow favorable weather conditions, reduce shelter overflow, and minimize damage to the Trail. More details can be found at <www.appalachiantrail.org/home/explore-the-trail/thru-hiking/alternative>.

Reading the *Companion*

MAKING THE COMPANION YOUR OWN

Do not be afraid to abuse your paper *Companion*. While it has considerable information, it has been suggested that it could be made smaller. Unfortunately, no one agrees on what should be left out. So, here is an idea—do your own editing. Rip out what you don't want, use a hole-punch, a pair of scissors, or a highlighter. Send sections ahead to mail drops; mail completed sections home. Do some old-fashioned cut-and-paste. Make this book your own.

READING THE COMPANION

 Road-crossings and Trailheads with significant services nearby are indicated in south-to-north order.

Towns and post offices (including P.O. hours) are printed in **bold type**. A listing of post offices can also be found on page 258.

East and West—Regardless of compass direction, "**east**" or "E" and "**west**" or "W" are used as they are in the *A.T. Data Book* and the series of 11 A.T. guides: "East" is to the northbounder's right and the southbounder's left, when referring to the Trail.

Services—Major categories are indicated with ***bold italics***, specifically ***groceries, lodging, hostels, campgrounds, doctors or hospitals, restaurants, Internet access, laundries, veterinarians,*** and ***outfitters***.

Trail-Maintaining Clubs—Information is provided at the southern end of their sections and is offset by two rules.

Abbreviations—

In the body of the text:

M—Monday	F—Friday
Tu—Tuesday	Sa—Saturday
W—Wednesday	Su—Sunday
Th—Thursday	

FedEx—Federal Express	PP—per person
USPS—U.S. Postal Service	EAP—each additional person
UPS—United Parcel Service	D—double
AYCE—all-you-can-eat	S—single
B/L/D—breakfast/lunch/dinner	T—triple
CATV—cable television	a/c—air conditioning

In the tables at beginning of each chapter:

B—bus	O—outfitter
C—campground, campsites	P—parking
cl—coin laundry	P.O.—post office
D—doctor, medical	R—road access
f—fuel	S—shelter
G—groceries, supplies	sh—shower
g—short-term resupply	T—train
H— hostels	nw—no potable water
L— lodging	V—veterinarian
m—miles	w—water
M—meals; restaurants	

Shaded features mean they are explored in more detail in the text.

Elevation—This column refers to the approximate elevation (in feet) of the landmark.

Comma—Services separated by commas are in the same location. For example, E–1.5m P.O., G means that the post office and grocery store are both located 1.5 miles east.

Parentheses—Services separated by parentheses are not all in the same location. For example, (E–0.2m C, S) (W–0.1m w) means that the campsite and shelter are east 0.2 mile, and the water source is west 0.1 mile from the Trailhead.

Shelters—May also be referred to as lean-tos. Shown in **bold print**, with distance and direction off Trail, water-source location, and distance to the next shelter (in italics, both north and south). **The distance to the next north and south shelter shown in the *Companion* includes the side-trail(s) distance from one to the other.**

 Indicates a designated Appalachian Trail Community™ in the text (several more communities participate but are outside the distance scope of the *Companion*). Towns and counties participating in this Appalachian Trail Conservancy program agree to help promote, preserve, and maintain the A.T. in various ways while ATC helps them with economic development.

Symbols on the Elevation Profiles

🛣 **22**	Interstate highway	▫	Water: undeveloded
⬡	Federal highway	◈	Shelter
⬭	State highway	▲	Campsite
▢	Local or forest road	◣	Campground
		🅟	Parking

Issues on the Trail

2,000-MILER CERTIFICATES

ATC recognizes anyone who reports completion of the entire Trail as a "2,000-Miler" with a certificate. The term "2,000-Miler" is a matter of tradition and convenience, based upon the original estimated length of the Trail. ATC operates on the honor system, assuming that those who apply for 2,000-Miler status have hiked all of the A.T. between Katahdin and Springer. In the event of an emergency, such as a flood, forest fire, or an impending storm on an exposed high-elevation stretch, blue-blazed trails or officially required roadwalks are considered viable substitutes for the white-blazed route. Issues of sequence, direction, speed, length of time, or whether one carries a pack or not are not considered. ATC assumes that those who apply have made an honest effort to *walk* the entire Trail. (P.S. The Shenandoah River is not the official Trail route.)

HUNTING SEASONS

Hunters are rarely an issue for northbound thru-hikers, but southbounders need to be aware of the hunting seasons, which may begin as early as mid-Oct, as you progress south toward Springer. Hunting is legal along many parts of the Trail, and ATC's Web site lists local hunting seasons. Wearing bright ("blaze") orange is a necessity in fall, winter, and spring.

SAFETY—OTHER HUMANS

If you tell friends you are planning a long-distance hike on the A.T., one of the first questions is likely to be, "Aren't you afraid? What will you do to protect yourself?" There are dangers in the backcountry, but, because of mass-media publicity and the popularity of backpacking, your friend was likely speaking of the dangers posed by other humans. Violent crimes have occurred on the Trail, with a frequency rate of less than two every *ten* years, on a footpath more than three million people use *each* year.

The difference on the A.T. and in any wilderness setting—other than people's expectations—is that you only have yourself and your instincts for protection. That means you must use common sense to avoid potential dangers. It is best not to hike alone. If you choose to, a few precautions can help keep you safe:

- Don't tell strangers where you are headed or plan to camp for the night; *don't post plans in real time on on-line journals or blogs.*
- If you run into a suspicious person, consider moving on to another location.
- Avoid camping or staying at shelters that are within a mile of a road crossing.
- Leave an itinerary of your trip with family or friends.
- If you use a Trail name, make sure the folks back home know what it is.
- Even with a partner, don't be lulled into a false sense of security. Two or more can also be vulnerable.
- Eliminate opportunities for theft. Don't bring jewelry. Keep wallets and money on your person rather than in your pack or tent. Leaving a pack unattended at trailheads or shelters is risky, even when it is hidden.
- Trust your gut. Always.

ATC and most long-distance hikers strongly discourage the carrying of a gun on the Trail. Guns are restricted (you can carry with all the proper permits but not legally discharge) on national park lands (40 percent of the route) and in many other jurisdictions through which the Trail passes. Report any crime or harassment immediately to the local police *and* ask the dispatcher to contact the National Park Service 24-hour communications center at (866) 677-6677. Further advice can be found at <www.appalachiantrail.org/explore-the-trail/hiking-basics/safety>.

SAFETY—MOTHER NATURE

While natural dangers are inherent to backpacking, many are misunderstood. For some, a hike in the woods conjures images of snakebites and bear attacks—both rare.

BEARS

Black bears live along many parts of the Trail and are particularly common in Georgia, the Shenandoah and Great Smoky Mountains national parks, and north of Shenandoah on into New York. While attacks on humans are rare, a startled bear or a female with cubs may react aggressively. The best way to avoid an encounter while you are hiking is to make noise by whistling, talking, *etc.*, to give the bear a chance to move away before you get close enough to make it feel threatened. If you encounter a bear and it does not move away, you should back off, and avoid making eye contact. Do not run or "play dead," even if a bear makes a "bluff charge."

The ATC strongly recommends using a bear-resistant canister between Springer Mountain and Damascus, Va., due to a rising number of bear encounters in the region. USFS-approved canisters: <www.sierrawild.gov/bears/food-storage>.

The best preventive defense is preparing and storing food properly:

- Cook and eat meals away from your tent or shelter so food odors do not linger.
- Hang food, cookware, toothpaste, personal hygiene items, water bottles with drink mixes in a sturdy bag from a strong tree branch 10 feet off the ground, 6 feet from the tree, and away from your campsite.
- Use bear boxes, poles, or cable systems where provided.
- *Never* feed bears or leave food behind for them.
- A bear entering a campsite should be considered predatory. Yelling, making loud noises, and throwing rocks may frighten it away, but be prepared to fight back.
- If attacked, fight for all you are worth with anything at hand—rocks, sticks, fists.

Less dramatic threats to safety, such as contaminated water, dehydration, and hypothermia, afflict far more hikers—particularly those who are unprepared.

If you are unfamiliar with backcountry travel, ask questions, and read and learn about backpacking safely. Learn about dehydration, heat exhaustion, and hypothermia; learn safe ways of fording rivers and purifying water; learn how to avoid lightning, rabies, and Lyme disease—the most common threats to a hiker's well-being. A good resource for learning more about these topics is the ATC publication *Step by Step: An Introduction to Walking the A.T.* Before starting an end-to-end hike, take shorter backpacking trips until you feel confident in the backcountry. Finally, information and experience are useless if you forget one thing—common sense.

LYME DISEASE

In the Northeast, the heightened risk for Lyme disease (LD) is Apr to Jul and Oct to Nov, which coincide with the time frame thru-hikers pass through the states with the highest reported cases of the disease. Cases have been reported in all fourteen Trail states.

LD is a bacterial infection transmitted to humans by the bite of infected blacklegged ticks (formerly called "deer" ticks). Hikers should watch carefully for symptoms of LD, which may include "flu-like" reactions of fever, headache, chills, and fatigue and a characteristic "bulls-eye" skin rash, called *erythema migrans,* at the site of the tick attachment. Hikers should seek immediate medical attention for treatment.

Steps hikers can take to prevent LD include using insect repellent with Deet for exposed skin; spraying clothing items with the insecticide permethrin; removing ticks promptly; conducting a daily full-body tick check, including the head, underarms, and groin area; minimizing contact with high grass, brush, and woody shrubs; wearing long pants tucked into your socks; and wearing long sleeves, tucking your shirt into your pants to keep ticks off your torso.

LEAVE NO TRACE

With the millions who enjoy this place each year, the chances are great that any of us may inadvertently damage the natural environment along the Trail and mar the experience for others. Those negative effects can be minimized by adopting sound hiking and camping techniques which, while simple to learn, require some committed effort—think of LNT, wholly endorsed by ATC and ALDHA, as an educational and ethical program for responsible enjoyment of the outdoors, not a set of rules. If we are successful, the Trail will retain its essential natural qualities and continue to be a place where an extraordinary outdoor experience is available. Everyone's help is important. Please do your part by committing to these practices, and encourage others to learn about techniques that "Leave No Trace" on the Appalachian Trail. More information can be found at <www.LNT.org> and <www.appalachiantrail.org/lnt>.

PLAN AHEAD AND PREPARE

- Check Appalachian Trail guidebooks and maps for guidance and note that camping regulations vary considerably along the Trail. Travel in groups of 10 or fewer. If in a group of more than five, leave shelters for lone hikers and smaller groups.
- Bring a lightweight trowel or wide tent stake to dig a hole for burying human waste.
- Bring a piece of screening to filter food scraps from your dishwater and pack them out.
- Bring a waterproof bag and at least 50 feet of rope to hang food and scented articles.
- Repackage food in resealable bags to minimize waste.
- Prepare for extreme weather, hazards, and emergencies—especially the cold—to avoid impacts from searches, rescues, and campfires.
- Try to avoid areas when they are most crowded. If you are planning a northbound thru-hike, avoid starting on March 1, March 15, the first day of spring, or April 1.

TRAVEL AND CAMP ON DURABLE SURFACES

- Stay on the trail; never shortcut switchbacks. Take breaks off-trail on durable surfaces, such as rock or grass.
- Restrict activities to areas where vegetation is already absent.
- Avoid expanding existing trails and campsites by walking in the middle of the trail, and using the already-impacted core areas of campsites.
- If tree branches block the trail, move them off if possible, rather than going around and creating new trails.
- Wear gaiters and waterproof boots, so you can walk through puddles instead of walking around them and creating a wide spot in the trail.

CAMPING

- Camping at designated sites is required in many areas of the Appalachian Trail, including (but not limited to) the Smokies, some areas in Virginia, and much of the A.T. from Harpers Ferry, West Virginia, north to Katahdin. Even where dispersed camping (sometimes called "stealth camping") is allowed, camping at designated sites helps conserve the Trail.
- A list of camping and campfire regulations can be found at <www.appalachiantrail.org/camping>.
- Planning your hike to avoid the most popular times, such as the southern end of the A.T. in March and April, will allow you to stay at designated sites and still avoid crowded conditions.

DISPOSE OF WASTE PROPERLY

- "Pack it in, Pack it out." Don't burn, bury, or leave litter or extra food. That includes cigarette butts, fruit peels, and hygiene articles. Keep your trash bag handy, so you can pick up litter left by others.
- Use the privy for human waste only (feces). Do not add trash. If there is no privy, dispose of human waste by burying it in a "cathole," a hole 6-8 inches deep, 4-6 inches wide, at least 200 feet (80 steps) from campsites, water sources, and shelters, and well away from trails. Add dirt to the

hole, and stir with a stick to promote decomposition. Push toilet paper to the bottom of the hole, and leave your stick in the hole. Don't hide your waste under a rock; this slows decomposition.

- Note that most "disposable wipes" are made from nonbiodegradable material that must be carried out rather than buried, burned, or left in privies. For those willing to go the extra mile, consider packing out your toilet paper, too. Animals' curiosity often brings toilet paper and other trash to the surface.
- Wash dishes, bodies, and clothing 200 feet away from water sources. Use biodegradable soap sparingly, or not at all. Avoid polluting the water by rinsing off at a distance to remove your excess sunscreen, bug repellent, *etc.*, before swimming in a lake or stream.
- Disperse dishwater and toothpaste, and urinate well away (at least 100 feet) from shelters and popular campsites. In that way, wildlife is not attracted close to camp. Animals sometimes defoliate plants to consume the salt in urine, so urinate on rocks or bare ground rather than on vegetation. Where water is plentiful, consider diluting the urine by adding water to the site.
- If you wish to donate items to other hikers (food, extra gear, clothing, books, *etc.*), don't leave them at shelters—use the hiker boxes at motels and hostels.

LEAVE WHAT YOU FIND

- Leave plants, artifacts and natural objects where you found them, for others to enjoy.
- Don't build structures or dig trenches around tents.
- Do not damage live trees or plants; green wood burns poorly. Collect only firewood that is dead, down, and no larger than your wrist. Leave dead standing trees and dead limbs on standing trees for the wildlife.
- Consider using rubber tips on the bottom of your trekking poles to avoid scratch marks on rocks, "clicking" sounds, and holes along the Trail.

MINIMIZE CAMPFIRE IMPACTS

- Use stoves for cooking—if you *need* a fire, build one only where it's legal and in an existing fire ring. Leave hatchets and saws at home. Burn all wood to ash.
- Do not try to burn trash, including foil, plastic, glass, cans, tea bags, food, or anything with food on it. These items do not burn thoroughly. They create noxious fumes, attract wildlife like skunks and bears, and make the area unsightly.
- Where campfires are permitted, leave the fire ring clean by removing others' trash and scattering unused wood, cold coals, and ashes 200 feet away from camp after the fire is cold and completely out.

RESPECT WILDLIFE

- Bears inhabit or travel through nearly every part of the A.T. Sightings have increased at shelters and campsites and even small food rewards teach bears to associate humans with food. When that happens, they often have to be killed to protect human safety. Dropped, spilled, or improperly stored food also attracts rodents. Even a few noodles are a large meal for mice. Clean up spills completely, and pack out all food scraps.
- Store your food according to local regulations. Store all food, trash, and scented articles (toothpaste, sunscreen, insect repellent, water-purification chemicals, balm, *etc.*) out of reach of bears and other animals. A safe distance is 12 feet from the ground and 6 feet from a limb or trunk.
- Keep a respectful distance. If hiking with a dog, keep it on a short leash. Do not follow or approach animals. Particularly avoid wildlife during sensitive times, *i.e.,* when they are mating, nesting, or raising young.

BE CONSIDERATE OF OTHER VISITORS

- Let nature's sounds prevail. Respect others by keeping loud voices and noise to a minimum. Do not use cell phones or audio equipment within sight or sound of other hikers, and turn ringers off.
- A.T. shelter space is available on a first-come, first-served basis in most (but not all) areas, regardless of the type of hiker or length of their hike.
- Limit-of-stay is generally two nights at any one shelter or campsite.

- If you are hiking with a dog, be aware of its potential impact on animals and other hikers. Keep your dog leashed and under control at all times, and learn where dogs are prohibited. Ask permission before bringing your dog into a shelter. If you find the shelter is crowded, be considerate and tent with your dog. Keep your dog away from springs and other water sources. Bury your dog's waste as you would your own.

TOWN CONDUCT

As a result of tension between hikers and some communities along the Trail, ALDHA started an "Endangered Services Campaign" to educate hikers to be responsible for their actions. In town, consider yourself a walking, talking billboard for all backpackers and the Trail. Your actions have a direct impact on the businesses that provide services for the long-distance hiking community.

The success of a thru-hiker's journey depends on Trail towns and the services they provide. Remember that you are a guest of the community, no matter how large or small, even though you may be pumping money into

The Endangered Services Campaign

the local economy. Be courteous to those who earn their livelihood there, and remember that your conduct will have a bearing on how well—or badly—the next hiker is treated. As with so many other things in life, we are never truly alone. You are an ambassador for all those who follow you on the Trail. Nothing can turn a person or town against backpacking and the Trail quicker than an arrogant, smelly, and ill-behaved hiker.

Some business owners have reduced services or closed their doors to hikers simply because some hikers wouldn't respect their rules. Be a part of a movement that will reverse this practice and ensure that no one closes another door because of bad hiker behavior.

DONATIONS

Many hostels listed in this book suggest donations for the services provided. This means that the service should not be considered a gift or that it costs the provider nothing. The honor system of the Trail requires that you leave something.

GIVING BACK

If you would like to give back what was freely given to you by those who maintain the Trail or while you stayed in Trail towns, volunteer your time, effort, or money to the services and people who supported you. Consider contacting a Trail-maintaining club and working with them to organize or participate in a work trip, Trail-construction project, or regular maintenance. Every year, ALDHA sponsors work trips to Trail establishments. The Konnarock and other ATC crews seek volunteers during the summer, and you often will pass a Trail club working busily as you head along the path. Be sure to acknowledge their work with your thanks and respect. Giving back to the Trail and community helps keep the Trail safe and services available.

HITCHHIKING

Hitchhiking is illegal in certain states. It is your responsibility to know the motor-vehicle law as it applies to hitchhiking where you are hiking, to avoid being fined or hitching into worse trouble. Hitchhiking poses the risk of being picked up by an unsafe driver or someone who is personally dangerous. Hitchhiking is prohibited on interstate highways, the Blue Ridge Parkway, and Skyline Drive in Shenandoah National Park.

HIKING WITH DOGS

If you choose to hike with your canine companion, treat your dog as another backpacker. That means bury its waste as you would your own, and carry a water bowl so your dog won't drink directly from

Trailside water sources. You are responsible for your dog, and you will be held accountable if it decides to steal another hiker's food or flop its wet body on another hiker's equipment. Keep your pet under control in camp, on the Trail, and in towns. Many hostels and other accommodations don't allow dogs, and, in those that do, a dog does not belong in the communal kitchen and sleeping areas. Closely monitor your pet's feet for torn flesh, bleeding, and other sores. After the weather warms up, check for ticks. It is best to keep your dog on a leash at all times; on national-park lands (40 percent of the Trail), regulations require it. Most post offices allow only guide dogs inside. Carry current rabies-vaccine certification papers in addition to a tag on the dog's collar. Dogs are prohibited in the Great Smoky Mountains National Park, the zoo area of Bear Mountain State Park in New York, and Maine's Baxter State Park. (For information on kennels near GSMNP and BSP, see entries for those sections.)

APPALACHIAN TRAIL MUSEUM SOCIETY

The Appalachian Trail Museum opened in June 2010 in Pine Grove Furnace State Park near the Trail's midpoint after years of work by the Appalachian Trail Museum Society (ATMS), formed in 2002. The group includes representatives of ATC and ALDHA and works with the National Park Service. The society is collecting items for eventual display in the museum and monetary donations. They are also in need of volunteers to help in many areas. Please contact ATMS, if you'd like to help, at <www.atmuseum.org>.

APPALACHIAN LONG DISTANCE HIKERS ASSOCIATION

The Appalachian Long Distance Hikers Association (ALDHA) is a nonprofit organization founded in 1983 to promote the welfare of the Appalachian Trail and the Trail community. ALDHA conducts work weekends on the Trail, speaks out on issues concerning the A.T. and its environs, and collects the information for this book. It has worked with various clubs and hostels to maintain areas widely used by hikers. ALDHA is open to anyone. A membership form is included at the back of this book. Annual dues are $10 per family (or individual). Benefits include the *Thru-Hikers' Companion* in pdf format, a membership directory, and a quarterly newsletter. For more information, visit our Web site, <www.aldha.org>.

THE GATHERING

Folks who want to learn what it takes to thru-hike the Appalachian Trail can find out everything they need to know at the fall Gathering. If you are already thru-hiking the Trail this year, the Gathering is also the place to receive an "ALDHA Way" certificate and patch for your accomplishment and find out what's next for your worn-in hiking boots. Slide shows and how-to workshops on the Pacific Crest Trail, Continental Divide, and other major foot trails help fill the weekend event. The 39th Gathering will be Oct. 9–12, 2020, at the southwest Higher Education Center, Abingdon, Va. For more information, visit <www.aldha.org/gathering>. **Special notice to 2020 thru-hikers and 2000-Milers: Bring your Trailworn 2020 A.T. Thru-Hikers' Companion (or the Maine section in its entirety) and a completed-trail form to the registration desk, and your gathering fee is on ALDHA!**

AN INVITATION

This is the twenty-seventh edition of the *A.T. Thru-Hikers' Companion,* and ALDHA will again depend on comments, suggestions, and volunteers to update it in the fall of 2020. If you see information that needs correcting or come across information that should be included, or would like to be a volunteer field editor, please contact the editor at <companion@aldha.org>.

THE APPALACHIAN TRAIL CONSERVANCY

For additional information about the Appalachian Trail and a complete list of guidebooks, maps, and thru-hiking publications, contact the Appalachian Trail Conservancy at P.O. Box 807, Harpers Ferry, WV 25425-0807, or call (304) 535-6331, Monday through Friday except federal holidays, between 9 a.m. and 5 p.m. Eastern time. Its visitors center at Harpers Ferry is open year-round except Thanksgiving, Christmas, and New Year's Day. The e-mail address is <info@appalachiantrail.org>; the Web address is <www.appalachiantrail.org>. For direct access to the Ultimate A.T. Store, e-mail <sales@appalachiantrail.org>, call (888) 287-8673 weekdays between 9 a.m. and 4:30 p.m. Eastern time, or visit <www.atctrailstore.org>.

2020 Calendar and Key Dates to Remember

JANUARY
S	M	T	W	T	F	S
			1	2	3	4
5	6	7	8	9	10	11
12	13	14	15	16	17	18
19	20	21	22	23	24	25
26	27	28	29	30	31	

FEBRUARY
S	M	T	W	T	F	S
						1
2	3	4	5	6	7	8
9	10	11	12	13	14	15
16	17	18	19	20	21	22
23	24	25	26	27	28	29

MARCH
S	M	T	W	T	F	S
1	2	3	4	5	6	7
8	9	10	11	12	13	14
15	16	17	18	19	20	21
22	23	24	25	26	27	28
29	30	31				

APRIL
S	M	T	W	T	F	S
			1	2	3	4
5	6	7	8	9	10	11
12	13	14	15	16	17	18
19	20	21	22	23	24	25
26	27	28	29	30		

MAY
S	M	T	W	T	F	S
					1	2
3	4	5	6	7	8	9
10	11	12	13	14	15	16
17	18	19	20	21	22	23
24	25	26	27	28	29	30
31						

JUNE
S	M	T	W	T	F	S
	1	2	3	4	5	6
7	8	9	10	11	12	13
14	15	16	17	18	19	20
21	22	23	24	25	26	27
28	29	30				

JULY
S	M	T	W	T	F	S
			1	2	3	4
5	6	7	8	9	10	11
12	13	14	15	16	17	18
19	20	21	22	23	24	25
26	27	28	29	30	31	

AUGUST
S	M	T	W	T	F	S
						1
2	3	4	5	6	7	8
9	10	11	12	13	14	15
16	17	18	19	20	21	22
23	24	25	26	27	28	29
30	31					

SEPTEMBER
S	M	T	W	T	F	S
		1	2	3	4	5
6	7	8	9	10	11	12
13	14	15	16	17	18	19
20	21	22	23	24	25	26
27	28	29	30			

OCTOBER
S	M	T	W	T	F	S
				1	2	3
4	5	6	7	8	9	10
11	12	13	14	15	16	17
18	19	20	21	22	23	24
25	26	27	28	29	30	31

NOVEMBER
S	M	T	W	T	F	S
1	2	3	4	5	6	7
8	9	10	11	12	13	14
15	16	17	18	19	20	21
22	23	24	25	26	27	28
29	30					

DECEMBER
S	M	T	W	T	F	S
		1	2	3	4	5
6	7	8	9	10	11	12
13	14	15	16	17	18	19
20	21	22	23	24	25	26
27	28	29	30	31		

January 17–19	Southern Ruck, Vogel State Park, Blairsville, Ga.
January 24–26	Northern Ruck, Bears Den Trail Center, Bluemont, Va.
March 6–8	Appalachian Trail Kick-Off, Amicalola Falls State Park, Ga.
April 18	ALDHA Steering Committee Meeting, Ironmasters Mansion, Pa.
April 25–26	ATC's Flip-Flop Festival, Harpers Ferry, W.Va.
May 2	Appalachian Trail Hall of Fame Induction, Boiling Springs, Pa.
May 2	Hiker Festival at Appalachian Trail Museum
May 15–17	Trail Days, Damascus, Va.
June 6	National Trails Day
September 5	ATC Annual Meeting, on line (see appalachiantrail.org)
September 11–13	Trails End Festival, Millinocket, Maine
October 9–12	39th ALDHA Gathering, Southwest Higher Education Center, Abingdon, Va.

Getting to the Termini

An important note about shuttle services

Beginning in 1995, USDA Forest Service law-enforcement rangers in the South—who report to the regional office rather than the supervisor of an individual forest—began enforcing agency regulations on "special-use permits." The regulations say anyone taking money for a service involving Forest Service lands (including roads) must obtain a permit to do so; profit is not a factor. Permit-holders must pay a fee (up to $75) and, more prohibitively, carry high-premium insurance. Some A.T. shuttlers have been fined. Responding to questions from ATC and its Park Service partners, regional officials made it clear they will continue to enforce the policy and cited directives stating that it is to be enforced consistently and nationally. The A.T. crosses six national forests in the South and two in New England. Some state and local law-enforcement agencies also are regulating shuttle services that charge a fee.

Getting to Baxter State Park, Maine

No public transportation is available to or from Baxter State Park, but arrangements can be made to conclude or begin your journey with little difficulty. This usually means going through Boston, Portland, and/or Bangor, then to Medway, and then to Millinocket, still 20 miles southeast of the park. The nearest airport is in Bangor; the Portland airport is said to have more competitive rates, and Boston more so. Bus transportation is available from Portland to Medway and also from Boston to Portland.

LEAVING BANGOR

Cyr Bus Lines of Old Town, Maine, (207) 827-2335 or (800) 244-2335, <www.cyrbustours. com>, serves northern Maine. A bus leaves Bangor/Hermon Greyhound bus station at 6:00 p.m. and Concord–Trailways bus station at 6:30 p.m. and arrives at Medway at 7:40 p.m. A bus leaves Medway at 9:30 a.m. and arrives at Concord-Trailways station at 10:50 a.m. and at Bangor/Hermon Greyhound station at 11:10 a.m. ($12 fare). The A.T. Lodge in Millinocket, (207) 723-4321, shuttles.

MEDWAY TO MILLINOCKET

From Medway, in the past, you would have to hitch on Maine 157 or call a taxi to go to either Millinocket, 10 miles to the west, or Baxter State Park, about 30 miles away. Today, however, transportation is available to and from BSP *via* shuttle from Maine Quest Adventures, (207) 746-9615, <www.mainequestadventures.com>, from Medway bus stop to BSP or Abol Bridge, $55 couple, $5EAP. Bull Moose Taxi, (207) 447-8070, charges $55 to Katahdin Stream Campground or to the A.T. Lodge in Millinocket. The A.T. Lodge also offers a SOBO special: pick-up in Medway, bed in the bunkroom, breakfast at the A.T. Café, and shuttle to Katahdin Stream Campground..

Baxter State Park—The park, (207) 723-5140, has 10 campgrounds available May 15–Oct 22 by reservation on a first-come, first-served basis—$30 per night per 4-person lean-to or 6-person-max-tentsite, except at the Birches long-distance hiker site, where the fee is $10PP/night. The Birches campsite, near Katahdin Stream Campground, is intended for northbound long-distance hikers who have hiked 100 miles or more contiguous with the park on their current trip. Hikers staying at the Birches must sign up at the information kiosk just north of Abol Bridge. Please see the entry for Baxter on page 252 for more information and details about camping and regulations near Katahdin. Southbound hikers should reserve a regular lean-to or tentsite at Katahdin Stream or Abol campgrounds. Reservations may be made four months in advance of the date you wish to stay in the park and can be made by mail or in person using a credit card. More information and a chart outlining real-time availability of sites is available at <www.baxterstate-parkauthority.com>. Inside the park, ranger stations do NOT accept credit cards. Every hiker must register *with a ranger* upon entering Baxter. Information kiosks are located at Abol Stream and Katahdin Stream campgrounds.

Pets—No dogs or other pets are allowed; see Medway and Millinocket entries for kennels.

Parking—No long-term parking is available, and parking at all trailheads and campgrounds is at a premium and is managed at the entrance gates. Check the park Web site, <www.bax-terstatepark authority.com>, for information on how to reserve a parking space. Advance reservations for day-use parking May 15–Oct 22 become available for Maine residents Apr 1; two weeks in advance of the day for nonresidents. When the spaces for a particular day have been reserved, that specific parking lot is closed. Plan ahead!

APPROACH TO KATAHDIN

A note for would-be southbounders—Katahdin is no stroll in the park. The profile and topo on the MATC's maps only give you a hint of what to expect—the single greatest sustained climb on the A.T. Get yourself physically prepared before you start at Baxter State Park (you will be on your own once you get past the ranger station). Northbounders routinely leave their full packs on the ranger's porch and hike up with daypacks provided there for that purpose. Every year, several stubborn southbounders, invariably much less-conditioned than seasoned northbound-ers, insist on carrying their fully loaded packs up the A.T. beyond Katahdin Stream Campground. This results in knee injuries and aborted climbs or even entire A.T. hiking plans. Take a hint from the northbound veterans: Hike Katahdin with a day pack, and pick up your full pack on your way back through the campground—you will still be a thru-hiker, and you will enjoy your day, rather than suffer the entire time and predispose yourself to any number of injuries or the need for a rescue on your first Trail day. The footpath below treeline is more rocks and roots than soil—no problem for the hikers who have been rock-hopping for 2,000 miles, but not a pleasant journey straight from the desk chair. Above treeline, you pull yourself over rocks in a few places and walk across slanted, roof-sized boulders in others. The climb is tough, even without a pack. The park recommends you bring or borrow a day pack (plenty of water, lots of snacks, sunscreen, a first-aid kit, gloves, hat, and extra layers of clothing). If you don't want to retrace your steps, you might consider going up the Abol Trail (part of which is referred to as the "Abol Slide," because of the loose rocks and steepness formed by a nineteenth-century land-slide) and down the Hunt Trail (A.T.). That requires a two-mile walk or ride from Katahdin Stream along the Perimeter Road to Abol Campground before starting your hike. The Abol Trail usually opens after the Hunt Trail; until the sandy, gravelly soils dry out, the trail is unstable, and boulders can become dislodged.

"Weather permitting," you can begin a southbound hike as early as May 31. Before then, trails are so wet, even without snow and ice, that foot traffic would irreparably harm the alpine and subalpine areas. However, even for the following few weeks, the tiny, biting blackflies can drive you out of the woods in agony and frustration, leaving behind a contribution of your blood to the North Woods ecosystem. Overnight camping season in Baxter is May 15–Oct 22.

Baxter Park will provide information on weather and conditions and recommendations regarding climbing but will remind hikers that your safety and good decision-making are your responsibility. The park is largely wilderness, and hikers should *not* expect timely rescue or assistance and *should* be prepared to self-rescue. Each morning, rangers at Chimney Pond (elev. 2,914 feet) make observations of conditions to determine both the safety of hiking con-ditions and the need to protect fragile alpine areas. At times, trails are closed for safety con-siderations and to protect the rare and endangered alpine plants, animals, and their habitat, as well as protecting unstable soils. Trail statuses and alerts then are posted at campgrounds throughout the park to provide hikers a guideline for planning their day's hike. Any park-wide alerts will be listed, including, for example, high heat index, blowdowns, thunderstorms, high water, snow, ice, *etc*. Be sure to check the posted weather report before embarking on your day's hike. Change plans if warranted.

Hikers who hike closed trails are subject to a court summons and fine and having park visitation privileges revoked. Those daily weather reports and trail alerts are posted at the trailheads at 7 a.m. during the hiking season.

Getting to Amicalola Falls State Park, Georgia

No public transportation is available to or from Amicalola Falls State Park, but hikers have several options from Atlanta, Gainesville (located 40 miles southeast of the park), and the mountain town of Dahlonega (located 16 miles east of Amicalola Falls).

LEAVING ATLANTA

If you fly into Atlanta, you can take Atlanta's rapid-transit trains (MARTA) from the airport to either the Greyhound bus station or the Amtrak station. To reach either station, take the MARTA train north from MARTA's airport station ($2.50 fare). To reach the Greyhound bus station, exit the train at Garnett Station. The bus station is located at 232 Forsyth Street, within sight of the entrance to the MARTA station. To get to the Amtrak station, continue north on the train to the Arts Center Station. From the Arts Center Station, bus No. 23 (departing the station every 10 minutes) will take you to the Amtrak station, located about 10 blocks north on Peachtree. If you wish to walk to the Amtrak station, follow Peachtree Street approximately one mile north; the station is on the left (west) at 1688 Peachtree NW. For more information, call MARTA, (404) 848-4711. Other options from the airport to the bus and train stations include taxis and the Atlanta Airport Shuttle, (404) 941-3440, a privately owned bus service. Superior Transportation, (770) 457-4794, leaves Atlanta airport every two hours on the odd hour; $85 one way, by appointment only.

ATLANTA TO GAINESVILLE

Two buses and one Amtrak train leave daily from Atlanta for Gainesville. At publication time, Greyhound buses, (800) 229-9424, <www.greyhound.com>, departed the Atlanta station for Gainesville at 9:10 a.m. and 4:30 p.m. ($20) and arrived in Gainesville at 10:45 a.m. and 6:10 p.m. Buses departed Gainesville at 11:45 a.m. ($20) and arrived in Atlanta at 1:05 p.m. However, Greyhound routinely revises its schedule; call for current information. Amtrak's train was scheduled to depart from Atlanta daily at 8:04 p.m. and arrive in Gainesville at 8:59 p.m. ($14). A train is scheduled to depart Gainesville for Atlanta daily at 6:58 a.m., arriving at 8:13 a.m. Reservations are required. Call (800) 872-7245, or visit <www.amtrak.com>. Donald Ballard, (772) 321-9005, (706) 745-3306, <www.thefurthershuttleappalachian.com>, shuttles from the North Springs MARTA station or Gainesville to Amicalola Falls State Park or Springer and as far as Davenport Gap. Brett "Suches" Eady, (404) 569-8776, <beady2727@gmail.com>, also shuttles from the North Springs MARTA, Amicalola Falls, Springer, *etc*., to as far as Fontana Dam; pets welcome.

Gainesville—*Lodging:* Motel 6, (770) 532-7531, $75 weekdays, $85 weekends, $3EAP, WiFi, pet-friendly; Lanier Center Holiday Inn, (770) 531-0907, $85–100D, no dogs, hot B, WiFi; Country Hearth and Suites, (770) 287-3205, $68.27–$72.99D weekdays, $69.57–$84D weekends, B buffet, pets $15; Hampton Inn, (770) 503-0300, $140–160, WiFi, no pets, hot B; Best Value Inn, (770) 534-0303, $65S–$75D, WiFi, no pets. All are within four miles of the bus and train stations.

GAINESVILLE TO AMICALOLA FALLS STATE PARK

Donald Ballard, (772) 321-9095, (706) 745-3306, <www.thefurthershuttleappalachian.com>, shuttles from Gainesville to Amicalola Falls State Park and Springer. Appalachian Adventure Company, Tom Bazemore, (706) 265-9454 or (865) 209-1827, offers service to Amicalola Falls State Park; transports dogs and accepts cash (deposit may be required). Service to the Trailhead at USFS 42 available at an additional cost. Tom also shuttles regionally as far north as Gatlinburg, Tenn.

GAINESVILLE TO DAHLONEGA

Some hikers choose to stay in Dahlonega rather than Gainesville. The site of the country's first gold rush, in the 1830s, Dahlonega sits 16 miles east of Amicalola Falls and offers all major services. Don Ballard offers service to Dahlonega.

Dahlonega—■ *Lodging:* Hotel rates in Dahlonega vary with the season. After May 1 and on weekends, expect listed rates to increase. Barefoot Hills, 7693 Hwy. 19N, Dahlonega, (770) 312-7342, <www.barefoothills.com>, thru-hiker experience package $35–$120 T–Th includes bunk-cabin-room and B, pick-ups at North Springs MARTA in Atlanta T, Th 2:30 or Gainesville on W at 4 for a fee, next-day shuttle to Springer or Amicalola for a fee; Holiday Inn Express, (706) 867-7777, $99–$239, $5EAP, includes hot B, no pets or smoking allowed; Super 8, (706) 864-4343, $60D, includes B, $10 for pets, WiFi; Days Inn, (706) 864-2338, $70–$150, B, WiFi; Quality Inn, (706) 864-6191, $70–$150, includes B, limited room for pets <20 pounds $10 fee, Internet access and WiFi; Smith House, (706) 867-7000, <www.smithhouse.com>, $109–$359, no dogs, no smoking. The Smith House Restaurant, in operation since 1922, is famous for its family-style AYCE fare (beginning in April): Tu–F 11–3 & 3:30–7:30, Sa–Su 11–8. Hours are seasonal and may vary. Call ahead. ■ *Outfitter:* Woodlands Edge, 36 N. Park St., (706) 864-5358, <woodlands. dahlonega@gmail.com>, M–Su 10:30–5, boots and apparel, gear.

ALTERNATIVES

Several Trail enthusiasts in the Atlanta area offer shuttles from Atlanta to the park and Springer Mountain. Many people who offer shuttles do so on their time off; arrangements are best made at least a week or two in advance. See page 1 for shuttle services.

AMICALOLA FALLS APPROACH TRAIL

Miles from Springer	Miles to Next Point	Features & Services		Elevation	Miles from AFSP	M A P
8.8	0.5	Amicalola Falls State Park Visitors Center Archway AFSP "Max Epperson" Shelter...*0.0mS; 7.3mN* *East–20m to* **Dahlonega, Ga., P.O. 30533** *West–25m to* East Ellijay, Ga	R, P, C, sh, cl, w S G, M, L, O, cl O	1,700'	0.0	
8.3	0.6	Base of Amicalola Falls...*604 steps*		2,150'	0.5	
7.7	0.1	Wide Trail to Amicalola Lodge *(E–0.1m)* privy	P, L, M, w	2,540'	1.1	
7.6	0.2	Amicalola Lodge Rd, paved *(E–0.1m lodge)*	R, P, L, M, w	2,550'	1.2	
7.4	0.1	+Len Foote Hike Inn Trail *(E–5m)*	L, M, w	2,600'	1.4	
7.3	1.6	USFS 46...*log steps on north side*	R	2,580'	1.5	
5.6	1.6	High Shoals Road	R	2,800'	3.2	
4.0	0.3	Frosty Mountain...*former fire tower site*	C, w	3,382'	4.8	
3.7	0.3	Frosty Mountain Road, USFS 46	R	3,192'	5.1	

ATC N.C.–Ga. Map 4

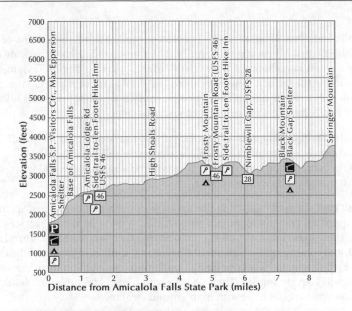

Distance from Amicalola Falls State Park (miles)

3.4	0.3	+Len Foote Hike Inn Trail, *blazed lime-green (E–1m)*	L, M, w	3,310'	5.4	
3.1	0.3	Woody Knob		3,400'	5.7	N.C.–Ga. Map 4
2.8	0.8	Nimblewill Gap, USFS 28	R	3,100'	6.0	
2.0	0.5	Black Mountain		3,600'	6.8	
1.5	1.5	**Black Gap Shelter...*7.3mS; 1.9mN***	S, C, w	3,300'	7.3	
0.0		Springer Mtn, *bronze plaque, register in rock,* **southern terminus**		3,782'	8.8	

+ Fee charged

Amicalola Falls State Park—Its facilities nestled almost nine miles southwest of Springer Mountain, the park is the gateway to the southern terminus of the A.T. Scales to weigh packs and showers are located near the center entrance, as well as a rest room, snack machines, and water fountain. The visitors center sells guidebooks, maps, and gift items. The park holds UPS and USPS packages sent c/o Amicalola Falls State Park, 240 Amicalola Falls State Park Rd., Dawsonville, GA 30534. Indicate on the box to hold the package at either the visitors center or the lodge. The visitors center, (706) 265-4703, is open 8:30–5 daily. While at the park, sign the hiker register inside the visitors center. Look for new thru-hike registration area in visitors center Mar 1–Apr 15. A $5/vehicle user fee is charged to all park visitors. Long-distance hikers may leave vehicles only in the parking area opposite the visitors center for up to 14 days before an annual pass is needed. Dogs must be on a leash within the park. ■ *Camping:* The park also offers campsites and cabins: campsites $30 with shower, coin laundry, 1- to 3-bedroom cabins (2-night minimum), call for pricing. ■ *Lodging:* The desk at Amicalola Lodge, (706) 265-8888, (800) 573-9656, <www.gastateparks.org>, is staffed around the clock; call for pricing on rooms, B included. Reservations suggested for cabins, campsites, and the lodge. ■ *Restaurant:* The lodge houses the Maple Restaurant, daily buffets, full-buffet B 7–10:30, L 11:30–3, D 5–8.

West 25 miles to *Outfitters:* North Georgia Mountain Outfitters, Travis/Shirley/ Whitney Crouch, (706) 698-4453, fax (706) 698-4454, <www.hikenorthgeorgia.com>, <info@hikenorthgeorgia.com>, 14244 Highway 515N, Suite 1200, East Ellijay, GA 30536, Tu–Sa 10–6; full-service outfitter, Coleman and alcohol fuels by the ounce, canister fuels, short-term food resupply; will hold packages without fee; possible shuttles to Atlanta airport, Amicalola, Springer, and Neel Gap; call for possible delivery of packages and store items.

Amicalola Falls State Park Shelter (1993)—Located 50 yards behind the visitors center, sleeps 12, and available to thru-hikers at no charge. Built by a group of Trail backpacking enthusiasts from nearby Canton in memory of their friend, Max Epperson. The "A.T. Gang" spent 800 hours constructing the facility. Epperson hiked the Trail as far north as Connecticut before his health failed. Afterward, he continued to offer shuttles and support for his hiking friends. Water source and rest room 50 yards away at visitors center.

Approach Trail to Springer Mountain—From the park visitors center, it is an 8.8-mile trek to the first white blaze, most of it uphill. To cut off the steep, one-mile ascent of the falls, catch a ride to the top of the falls, and pick up the blue blazes there. The southern end was recently relocated just past its start at the visitors center.

Approach Trail *via* Nimblewill Gap—This alternative puts you 2.2 miles south of Springer Mountain on the Approach Trail but requires a bumpy, muddy drive up Forest Service roads. From the park entrance, go east 9.5 miles on Ga. 52 to abandoned Grizzles Store. Turn left on Nimblewill Road, and continue past Nimblewill Church at 6.6 miles. Just beyond the church, pass a road on the left where the pavement ends. Continue to the right on the unpaved road, and reach Nimblewill Gap at 14 miles. This is a very rough road and probably should not be attempted unless you have a vehicle with high ground clearance.

From Amicalola Falls to Springer Mountain *via* Forest Service roads—The easiest and quickest route takes you within one mile of the Springer summit; it is clearly outlined on ATC's map for the area (item #135 at <www.atctrailstore.org>). From the park, go west on Ga. 52 for 13.6 miles to Roy Road, at Cartecay Church and Stanley's Store. Turn right, and proceed 9.5 miles to the second stop sign at the junction with Doublehead Gap Road. At the stop sign, bear right, and go 2.3 miles to Mt. Pleasant Church on the left. Across from the church, turn right onto unpaved Forest Service Road 42. This well-graded gravel road, suitable for all vehicles, winds 6.6 miles to the A.T. crossing at Big Stamp on the north side of the road. To reach the summit of Springer Mountain, walk 0.9 mile south. If you don't want to retrace your steps on the A.T., an alternative is to continue 1.7 miles past the A.T. crossing to USFS 42's intersection with the Benton MacKaye Trail (BMT). The BMT leads 1.5 miles up Springer and joins the A.T. just north of the southern terminus.

Len Foote Hike Inn—(800) 581-8032, <www.hike-inn.com>. This $1-million lodge is similar to huts in New Hampshire's White Mountains. The 40-bed, 20-room inn is approximately 5.0 miles north of Amicalola Falls State Park facilities and 4.5 miles south of the Springer Mountain summit. The yellow-blazed Hike Inn Trail creates a loop with the blue-blazed Approach Trail that leads from the park to Springer. Overnight stays, which include family-style B/D, are $117S, $170D, rates subject to change; no dogs allowed. Amenities include linens, hot showers, composting toilets, and electricity (outlets in bath house only). Owned by the Georgia Department of Natural Resources, the inn is operated by the Appalachian Education and Recreation Services, Inc., a nonprofit corporation affiliated with the Georgia Appalachian Trail Club. Walk-ins are allowed, subject to availability. Registration is at the Amicalola Falls State Park visitors center, where you can check on room availability. Open year-round, guest rooms in the bunkhouse are heated. Sleeping bags recommended Nov–Mar.

Black Gap Shelter (1953/1995)—Sleeps 8. Privy. Once the Springer Mountain Shelter, dismantled and moved to this location in 1995. This shelter is 1.5 miles south of the summit of Springer Mountain on the Approach Trail. Water is located 300 yards downhill to the right of the shelter.

Georgia

Miles from Springer	Miles to Next Point	Features	Services	Elev	Miles from Katahdin	M A P
0.0	0.2	Springer Mountain …bronze plaque, register in rock	southern terminus	3,782'	2,193.0	
0.2	0.1	**Springer Mountain Shelter** (E–0.2m) …1.9mS; 3mN	S, C, w	3,730'	2,192.8	
0.3	0.7	Benton MacKaye Trail (southern terminus)		3,710'	2,192.7	
1.0	0.3	USFS 42, Big Stamp Gap	R, P	3,350'	2,192.0	
1.3	0.3	Benton MacKaye Trail		3,370'	2,191.7	
1.6	0.3	Davis Creek	w	3,220'	2,191.4	
1.9	0.7	Rich Mountain, Benton MacKaye Trail		3,430'	2,191.1	
2.6	0.2	Stover Creek	w	2,850'	2,190.4	
2.8	0.1	**Stover Creek Shelter** (E–0.2m) …3mS; 5.7mN	S, C, w	2,870'	2,190.2	
2.9	0.9	Stover Creek	w	2,850'	2,190.1	
3.8	0.4	Stover Creek	w	2,660'	2,189.2	
4.2	0.1	Benton MacKaye Trail		2,580'	2,188.8	
4.3	0.9	USFS 58, Three Forks	R, P, C, w	2,530'	2,188.7	
5.2	1.0	Side trail to Long Creek Falls …waterfalls (W–0.1m) Benton MacKaye and Duncan Ridge Trails Jct.	w	2,800'	2,187.8	ATC N.C.–Ga. Map 4
6.2	1.2	USFS 251, Hickory Flats …picnic pavilion, cemetery	R	3,000'	2,186.8	
7.4	0.6	Hawk Mountain Campsite (W–0.2m)	C, w	3,250'	2,185.6	
8.0	0.1	Stream	w	3,225'	2,185.0	
8.1	0.5	**Hawk Mountain Shelter** (W–0.2m S; 0.4m stream) …5.7mS; 7.9mN	S, C, w	3,200'	2,184.9	
8.6	1.9	Hightower Gap, USFS 42/69	R, P	2,854'	2,184.4	
10.5	1.0	Horse Gap	R, P	2,673'	2,182.5	
11.5	0.7	Sassafras Mountain		3,336'	2,181.5	
12.2	0.6	Cooper Gap, USFS 42/80	R, P	2,828'	2,180.8	
12.8	0.3	Justus Mountain		3,224'	2,180.2	
13.1	0.5	Brookshire Gap		2,936'	2,179.9	
13.6	0.6	Old logging road		2,920'	2,179.4	
14.2	0.1	Justus Creek	C, w	2,564'	2,178.8	
14.3	0.9	Justus Creek Tentpads	C	2,590'	2,178.7	
15.2	0.5	Blackwell Creek	w	2,600'	2,177.8	
15.7	0.9	**Gooch Mountain Shelter** (W–0.1m) …7.9mS; 12.3mN	S, C, w	2,778'	2,177.3	
16.6	0.3	Spring	w	2,850'	2,176.4	
16.9	0.1	Gooch Gap, USFS 42 (E–0.1m campsite) West–3.3m to **Suches, Ga., P.O. 30572**	R, P, C, w g, f	2,821'	2,176.1	
17.0	0.9	Marked trail to water (E–230 yds.)	w	2,815'	2,176.0	
17.9	0.3	Cross abandoned old road		3,000'	2,175.1	

Miles from Springer	*Miles to Next Point*	Features	Services	Elev	Miles from Katahdin	MAP
18.2	0.6	Liss Gap ...*poplar tree stand*		3,028'	2,174.8	
18.8	0.2	Jacks Gap		3,000'	2,174.2	
19.0	0.5	Ramrock Mountain ...*views south*		3,260'	2,174.0	
19.5	1.0	Tritt Gap		3,050'	2,173.5	
20.5	1.2	Woody Gap, Ga. 60...*picnic area, privy, spring (W–0.1m)* *West–2m* to **Suches, Ga., P.O. 30572** *East–7m* to Barefoot Hills *East–15m* to **Dahlonega, Ga. P.O. 30533**	R, P, C, w g, f L G, M, L, O, cl	3,173'	2,172.5	
21.7	0.2	"Preaching Rock" ...*views east and south*		3,700'	2,171.3	
21.9	0.5	Big Cedar Mountain ...*rock ledges*		3,737'	2,171.1	
22.4	0.4	Augerhole Gap ...*spring*	w	3,560'	2,170.6	
22.8	0.1	Small stream	w	3,120'	2,170.2	
22.9	0.8	Dan Gap		3,261'	2,170.1	
23.7	0.8	Miller Gap, Dockery Lake Trail ...*spring (E–100 yds)*	w	**2,995'**	2,169.3	
24.0	0.8	Lance Creek Campsite ...*tentpads*	C, w	2,880'	2,169.0	
24.8	0.9	Henry Gap		3,100'	2,168.2	
25.7	0.6	Burnett Field Mountain		3,480'	2,167.3	ATC N.C.–Ga. Map 4
26.3	0.4	Jarrard Gap...*unpaved private road (W–0.3m stream)* *West–1m* to USFS Lake Winfield Scott Recreation Area	w C, sh	3,250'	2,166.7	
		Bear Canisters required if camping from here to Neel Gap				
26.7	0.7	Gaddis Mountain		3,410'	2,166.3	
27.4	0.3	Turkey Stamp Mountain		3,740'	2,165.6	
27.7	0.3	Bird Gap, **Woods Hole Shelter** *(W–0.4m)* ...*12.3mS; 1.6mN* Freeman Trail (1.8m) rejoins A.T. north	S, C, w	3,650'	2,165.3	
28.0	0.1	Slaughter Creek Trail at Slaughter Creek Gap ...*spring*	w	3,790'	2,165.0	
28.1	0.8	Slaughter Creek Campsite ...*tentpads*	C	3,800'	2,164.9	
28.9	1.4	Blood Mountain ...*views* **Blood Mountain Shelter** ...*1.6mS; 10.3mN*	S, nw	4,461'	2,164.1	
30.3	0.1	Flatrock Gap; Freeman Trail (1.8m) rejoins A.T. south *West–0.2m* to spring; *1m* to Byron Reece Memorial picnic area	P, w	3,420'	2,162.7	
30.4	0.9	Balance Rock		3,410'	2,162.6	
31.3	1.1	Neel Gap, U.S. 19 & 129 On A.T.–Mountain Crossings at Walasi-Yi Center *East–0.3m* to Blood Mountain Cabins *East–14m* to Barefoot Hills *East–22m* to Dahlonega, Ga., P.O. 30533 *West–3m* to Vogel State Park *West–13m* to **Blairsville, Ga., P.O. 30512**	R, P H, O, cl, sh, f L, g L G, L, M, cl C, G, cl, sh G, L, M, cl	3,125'	2,161.7	Map 3
32.4	0.4	Bull Gap	C, w	3,644'	2,160.6	

Miles from Springer	Miles to Next Point	Features	Services	Elev	Miles from Katahdin	M A P
32.8	0.7	Levelland Mountain ...open rocky area		3,942'	2,160.2	
33.5	0.8	Swaim Gap		3,450'	2,159.5	
34.3	0.7	Rock Spring Top ...west to spring	w	3,526'	2,158.7	
35.0	0.5	Wolf Laurel Top ...views		3,766'	2,158.0	
35.5	0.8	Baggs Creek Gap ...west to spring	C, w	3,591'	2,157.5	
36.3	1.0	Cowrock Mountain ...views		3,842'	2,156.7	
37.3	0.7	Tesnatee Gap, Ga. 348	R, P	3,138'	2,155.7	
38.0	0.2	Crest of Wildcat Mountain **Whitley Gap Shelter** (E–1.2m S; 1.5m spring) ...10.3mS; 6.1mN	S, w	3,600'	2,155.0	
38.2	0.9	Hogpen Gap, Ga. 348 ...A.T. plaque	R, P, w	3,450'	2,154.8	
39.1	1.1	White Oak Stamp		3,470'	2,153.9	
40.2	0.6	Poor Mountain		3,650'	2,152.8	
40.8	1.2	Wide Gap		3,150'	2,152.2	
42.0	0.8	Sheep Rock Top		3,575'	2,151.0	
42.8	1.4	**Low Gap Shelter** (E–0.1m) ...6.1mS; 7.4mN NoBo cross several small streams	S, C, w	3,050'	2,150.2	
		Bear Canisters required if camping from here to Jarrad Gap				ATC N.C.–Ga. Map 3
44.2	2.4	Poplar Stamp Gap	C, w	3,350'	2,148.8	
46.6	1.2	Cold Springs Gap SoBo cross several small streams	nw	3,450'	2,146.4	
47.8	0.7	Chattahoochee Gap ...spring (E–0.2m) West–2.4m on Jacks Knob Trail to Ga. 180	w R	3,500'	2,145.2	
48.5	0.7	Red Clay Gap		3,450'	2,144.5	
49.2	0.2	Spaniards Knob Campsite	C	3,600'	2,143.8	
49.4	0.2	Spring	w	3,500'	2,143.6	
49.6	0.1	Rocky Knob	w	3,590'	2,143.4	
49.7	0.3	Henson Gap		3,550'	2,143.3	
50.0	0.1	Spring ...water for Blue Mountain Shelter	w	3,890'	2,143.0	
50.1	0.9	**Blue Mountain Shelter** ...7.4mS; 8.3mN	C, S, w	3,900'	2,142.9	
51.0	1.5	Blue Mountain		4,025'	2,142.0	
52.5	0.6	Unicoi Gap, Ga. 75 ...A.T. plaque East–9m to **Helen, Ga., P.O. 30545** East–17m to Cleveland, Ga. West–4.8m to Enota Mountain Retreat West–11m to **Hiawassee, Ga., P.O. 30546**	R, P G, L, M, cl O, D C, L, g, cl, f G, L, M, O, D, V, cl	2,949'	2,140.5	
53.1	0.3	Stream	w	3,300'	2,139.9	
53.4	0.5	Rocky Mountain Trail (W–1m USFS 283)		3,700'	2,139.6	
53.9	1.3	Rocky Mountain ...views	C	4,017'	2,139.1	
55.2	0.7	Indian Grave Gap, USFS 283 East–1.9m blue blaze to USFS Andrews Cove CG	R, P C, w	3,113'	2,137.8	
55.9	0.3	Tray Mountain Road, USFS 79	R	3,580'	2,137.1	
56.2	0.7	Cheese Factory Site ...campsites (W–0.1m spring)	C, w	3,590'	2,136.8	

Miles from Springer	Miles to Next Point	Features	Services	Elev	Miles from Katahdin	M A P
56.9	0.8	Tray Gap, Tray Mountain Road, USFS 79/698	R, P	3,847'	2,136.1	
57.7	0.5	Tray Mountain ...*views*		4,430'	2,135.3	
58.2	1.2	**Tray Mountain Shelter** (*W–0.2m S; 0.3m spring*) ...*8.3mS; 7.9mN*	S, C, w	4,200'	2,134.8	
59.4	0.6	Wolfpen Gap		3,550'	2,133.6	
60.0	0.5	Steeltrap Gap		3,500'	2,133.0	
60.5	1.3	Younglick Knob		3,800'	2,132.5	
61.8	1.1	Swag of the Blue Ridge		3,400'	2,131.2	
62.9	0.9	Sassafras Gap (*E–190 yds. spring*)	w	3,500'	2,130.1	
63.8	1.0	Addis Gap *East–0.5m on Old Fire Road to USFS 26-2 and stream*	C R, C, w	3,304'	2,129.2	
64.8	0.8	Kelly Knob		4,085'	2,128.2	
65.6	1.0	**Deep Gap Shelter** (*E–0.3m*) ...*7.9mS; 8.6mN*	S, C, w	3,550'	2,127.4	ATC N.C.–Ga. Map 3
66.6	0.2	Campsite ...*east on blue blaze with view*	C, nw	3,625'	2,126.4	
66.8	0.2	McClure Gap	C	3,650'	2,126.2	
67.0	1.0	Powell Mountain		3,850'	2,126.0	
68.0	0.6	Moreland Gap		3,050'	2,125.0	
68.6	0.6	Snake Mountain ...*cross small streams*	w	2,650'	2,124.4	
69.2	1,1	Dicks Creek Gap, U.S. 76 ...*picnic area, stream* *West–0.5m to Top of Georgia Hostel and Hiking Ctr* *West–11m to* **Hiawassee, Ga., P.O. 30546**	R, P, w H, f G, L, M, O, D, V, cl	2,675'	2,123.8	
70.3	0.7	Little Bald Knob Campsite	C, w	3,160'	2,122.7	
71.0	1.1	Cowart Gap		2,920'	2,122.0	
72.1	0.4	Buzzard Knob		3,680'	2,120.9	
72.5	1.2	Bull Gap		3,550'	2,120.5	
73.7	0.7	**Plumorchard Gap Shelter** (*E–0.2m*) ...*8.6mS; 7.5mN*	S, C, w	3,050'	2,119.3	
74.4	0.6	As Knob		3,460'	2,118.6	
75.0	1.0	Blue Ridge Gap, USFS 72 ...*dirt road*	R, P	3,020'	2,118.0	
76.0	0.2	Wheeler Knob ...*campsite, spring*	C, w	3,560'	2,117.0	
76.2	1.9	Rich Cove Gap		3,400'	2,116.8	
78.1	0.1	Georgia–North Carolina State Line ...*tree register*		3,825'	2,114.9	

The Trail in Georgia begins at Springer Mountain and follows a rugged, often rocky terrain, reaching a height of more than 4,461 feet and never dipping below 2,500 feet. It passes through five major gaps and more than 25 smaller ones. Thru-hikers starting their journey in March or April will probably see snow, which can add to the difficulty. Spring melts give way to many of the wildflowers common throughout the mountains, including bloodroot, trillium, and azalea. Forests are mostly second-growth hardwoods of hickory, oak, and poplar. Half of the Trail lies within five designated wilderness areas in the forest.

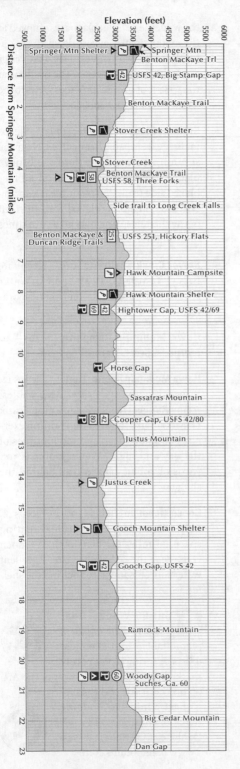

Georgia Appalachian Trail Club—GATC maintains the 78.3 miles from Springer Mountain to the North Carolina line. Correspondence should be sent to GATC, P.O. Box 654, Atlanta, GA 30301; (404) 494-0968; <www.georgia-atclub.org>; <trails_supervisor@georgia-atclub.org>.

Chattahoochee National Forest—The Trail in Georgia winds through the Chattahoochee National Forest, created by Congress in 1936. By that time, much of the land had been laid bare from intensive timber harvesting. Today, little virgin timber remains, but the hardwoods have reestablished themselves with the help of 77 years of management and protection.

Bear problems—With the loss of habitat from development in the mountains, black bears are roaming farther in search of food. To combat this problem, the GATC and the USFS are placing bear cables for hanging food at the shelters most affected. If bear cables are not available, secure food using bear-proof techniques. *See page xiii.*

U.S. Forest Service rules require using a bear canister while camping overnight between Jarrard and Neel gaps, a five-mile stretch that includes Woods Hole and Blood Mountain shelters and Slaughter Gap Campsite. **Plan accordingly.**

Springer Mountain—Springer has served as the A.T.'s southern terminus since 1958. Before that, Mt. Oglethorpe, to the southwest, was the southern terminus. In 1993, GATC members and the Forest Service installed a new plaque marking the Trail's southernmost blaze. The hiker register is located within the boulder on which the plaque is mounted. The original bronze plaque marking the southern terminus, one of three intended for road crossings, was created in 1934 by GATC member and amateur sculptor George Noble at a cost of $20—a hefty amount in those days. Warner Hall, the club's second president, served as Noble's model and coined the phrase, "A footpath for those who seek fellowship with

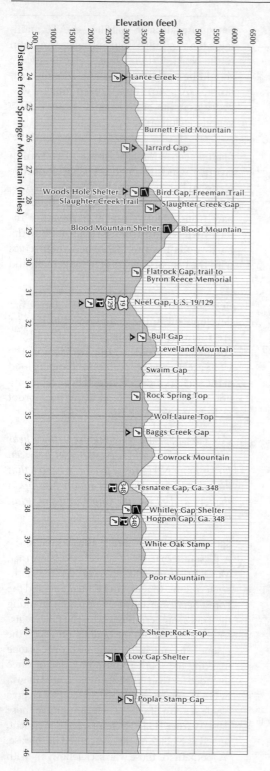

Elevation (feet)

Distance from Springer Mountain (miles)

Lance Creek

Burnett Field Mountain

Jarrard Gap

Woods Hole Shelter
Slaughter Creek Trail   Bird Gap, Freeman Trail
                            Slaughter Creek Gap

Blood Mountain Shelter   Blood Mountain

Flatrock Gap, trail to
Byron Reece Memorial

Neel Gap, U.S. 19/129

Bull Gap
Levelland Mountain

Swaim Gap

Rock Spring Top

Wolf-Laurel-Top

Baggs Creek Gap

Cowrock Mountain

Tesnatee Gap, Ga. 348

Whitley Gap Shelter
Hogpen Gap, Ga. 348

White Oak Stamp

Poor Mountain

Sheep-Rock-Top

Low Gap Shelter

Poplar Stamp Gap

the wilderness." That plaque was moved to the mountain in May 1959; keep an eye out for the other two plaques at road crossings along the Trail in Georgia. The overlook at the 3,782-foot summit provides views to the west—a nice sunset spot.

Springer Mountain Shelter (1993)—Sleeps 12. Privy. Tentpads. Bear cables. Near the summit, 250 yards north of the bronze plaque, then east 200 yards on a blue-blazed side trail. Water source is a spring 80 yards on a blue-blazed trail in front of the shelter; spring may go dry in times of drought.

Stover Creek Shelter (2006)—Sleeps 16. Privy. Tentpads. Bear cables. Water source is the creek. No tenting near water.

Hawk Mountain Campsite (2016)—30 tentpads, privy, water.

Hawk Mountain Shelter (1993)—Sleeps 12. Limited camping. Privy. Bear cables. Army Rangers from nearby Camp Frank D. Merrill use the area for training exercises and have been spotted all times of the day and night. Water source is 300 yards on a blue-blazed trail behind the shelter.

Gooch Mountain Shelter (2001)—Sleeps 14. Privy. Bear cables. Additional tenting space 1.6 miles farther north at Gooch Gap, near the old shelter site. Excellent water source is 100 yards behind the shelter.

Ga. 60/Woody Gap/ Suches—Parking area, picnic tables, and chemical toilets. A spring is on a poorly marked side trail 0.1 mile west of the A.T. on northern side of the gap.

East 7 miles to *Lodging:* Barefoot Hills, 7693 Hwy 19N, Dahlonega, GA, (404) 736-9431, <www.barefoothills.com>, thru-hiker experience package $35–$120 T–Th includes bunk-cabin-room and B. Next-day shuttle to Springer or Amicalola for a fee.

West 2 miles to **Suches, Ga. [P.O. ZIP 30572: M–F 12:15–4:15; (706) 747-2611].** ■ *Groceries:* Wolfpen Gap Country Store (short-term resupply), 411 Wolf Pen Gap Rd., Suches, GA 30572 ; (706) 747-2271; fuel, hot L; WiFi. Store open M–F 6:30–10, Su 7–10. ■ *Other services:* Jim Ann Miner, (706) 747-5434, lives in town and is available if you need help.

Lance Creek—Campsite with 4 tent platforms, built by the ATC Konnarock crew. Good water.

Jarrard Gap—**West** 1 mile on blue-blazed trail to USFS Lake Winfield Scott Recreation Area; tentsites, showers, $15; dogs must be leashed. *Bear canisters for food storage are required if you plan to camp between here and Neel Gap; see page xiii.*

Woods Hole Shelter (1998)—Sleeps 7. Privy. Bear cables. Located 0.4 mile west on a blue-blazed side trail, this "Nantahala design" shelter is named in honor of the late Tillie and Roy Wood, original owners of the Woodshole Hostel near Pearisburg, Virginia. Water source is an unreliable spring along the trail to the shelter.

Bird Gap—From here, the Freeman Trail leads 1.7 miles around the south slope of Blood Mountain and rejoins the A.T. 1.1 miles from Neel Gap. Those who choose this blue-blazed route miss the climb to the Trail's high point in Georgia; it serves as a foul-weather route around Blood Mountain.

Slaughter Gap—Slaughter Creek Trail leads to tentsites near Slaughter Creek that ease the load on Blood Mountain. *In an effort to counter visitor impact, fires have been banned along a 3.3-mile section between Slaughter Gap and Neel Gap.*

Blood Mountain—According to tales of the Creek and Cherokee, a battle here between the two nations left so many dead and wounded that the ground ran red with blood. Blood Mountain is the most-visited spot on the A.T. south of Clingmans Dome, and the impact of more than 40,000 visitors a year has taken its toll. Vandalism in and around the shelter is a chronic problem.

Blood Mountain Shelter (1934)—Sleeps 8. Privy. Located atop the highest peak on the A.T. in Georgia (4,461 feet), this historic two-room stone structure was last refurbished in 2012. No water or firewood available; no fires permitted. Northbounders can get water from a stream 0.3 mile north of Bird Gap or on a blue-blazed side trail at Slaughter Gap, 0.9 mile from the shelter. Southbounders can get water at Neel Gap or at a spring located on the blue-blazed trail to Byron Reece Memorial, 0.2 mile from where the trail joins the A.T., 2.4 miles south of Neel Gap.

U.S. 19 & 129/Neel Gap—Mountain Crossings at Walasi-Yi Center, 12471 Gainesville Hwy., Blairsville, GA 30512; (706) 745-6095, <www.mountaincrossings.com>. A full-service ■ *Outfitter* with all stove fuels and gift shop (short-term resupply). Expert footwear and pack fitters, also offer free pack shakedown service. UPS, FedEx, and USPS packages held, $1 donation. ■ *Hostel:* Walasi-Yi, open year-round, $20PP, with shower.

East 0.3 mile to *Lodging:* Blood Mountain Cabins, (706) 745-9454, <www.bloodmountain.com>, store with snacks and pizza, 9–5 M, Tu, Th–Sa. Cabins with showers, kitchens, and satellite TV sleep 4; thru-hiker rate $72, free laundry, Internet access, no pets. A trail leads from the Walasi-Yi Center to the resort office.

West 3 miles to *Camping:* Vogel State Park, (800) 864-7275, <www.gastateparks.org>.

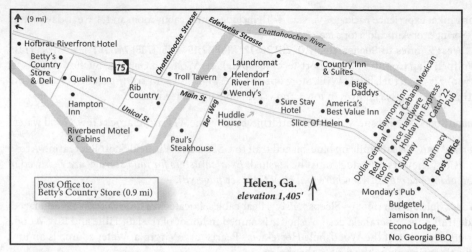

Helen, Ga.
elevation 1,405'

Post Office to:
Betty's Country Store (0.9 mi)

Tentsites with shower $25–$30, showers only $2. Camp store (limited resupply) has snacks; coin laundry (detergent $1); and cabins, reservations suggested. Leash dogs inside the park.

Whitley Gap Shelter (1974)—Sleeps 6. Privy. Bear cables. This shelter is located 1.2 miles east of the A.T. down a steep side trail. Water source is a spring 0.3 mile beyond the shelter.

Low Gap Shelter (1953)—Sleeps 7. Privy. Bear cables. Water source is crossed at the shelter; a second source can be found 30 yards in front of the shelter.

Chattahoochee Gap—A blue-blazed side trail leads east to Chattahoochee Spring, source of the Chattahoochee River, which supplies drinking water to Atlanta and almost half of the state's population. Some 500 miles from this point, the river empties into the Gulf of Mexico.

Blue Mountain Shelter (1988)—Sleeps 7. Privy. Bear cables. Located on a short side trail. Water source is a spring on the A.T. 0.1 mile south of the shelter.

Ga. 75/Unicoi Gap—**East** 9 miles to **Helen, Ga. [P.O. ZIP 30545: M–F 9–12:30, 1:30–4, Sa 9–12; (706) 878-2422].** ■ *Lodging:* Helendorf River Inn, (800) 445-2271, $44–$84 Su–Th, coin laundry, pets $20 in designated rooms only, B, WiFi, heated pool; Econo Lodge, (706) 878-8000, $45–$180, $10EAP, WiFi, B, $20/pets under 20 lbs. in selected rooms; Baymont Inn, (706) 878-2111, $70–$150, WiFi, hot B, no pets, free possible shuttles to Trail M–F; America's Best Value Inn, (706) 878-4079, $80–$129, $10EAP, pets ($20) under 30 lbs., WiFi, B; Jamison Inn, (706) 878-1451, $80-150D, B, no pets; Quality Inn, (706) 878-2268, $70–$120, $75 hiker rate, B, $20/pet up to 40 lbs., WiFi; RiverBend, (706) 878-2155, hiker rate $49–$169, $10EAP, rooms and cabins up to 4 people $80–$300, no smoking, WiFi, B, pets $20 ea.; Budgetel, (706) 878-2141, $40–$70 in off-season, $5EAP, B, pets $20; Red Roof Inn, (706) 878-8888, $70–$250, $5EAP, pets al-lowed, B, WiFi. ■ *Groceries:* Betty's Country Store and Deli (long-term resupply), ATC books, open daily 7–8, free shuttles 8 a.m.–6 p.m. ■ *Restaurants:* numerous. ■ *Internet access:* White County Library, Helen Branch. ■ *Other services:* bicycle rentals available at Woody's Mountain Bikes, (706) 878-3715, <www.woodysmtb.com>, Tu–Sa 10–5; pharmacy. ■ *Shuttles:* Woody's.

East 17 miles to **Cleveland, Ga.** ■ *Outfitter:* Smoky Mountain Outfitter, 18 W. Jarrard St., (706) 865-7296, <www.smokymountaintrader.com>, open M–F 10–6, Sa 9–5, full-service outfitter, can-ister fuels. ■ *Medical:* Urgent Care, (706) 348-4280, M–Su 8–8; Northeast Georgia Physicians Group, (706) 865-1234, M–F 10–6, Sa 9–5.

West 2.3 miles, then left 2.5 miles on Ga. 180 to *Lodging:* Enota Mountain Retreat, 1000 Hwy.

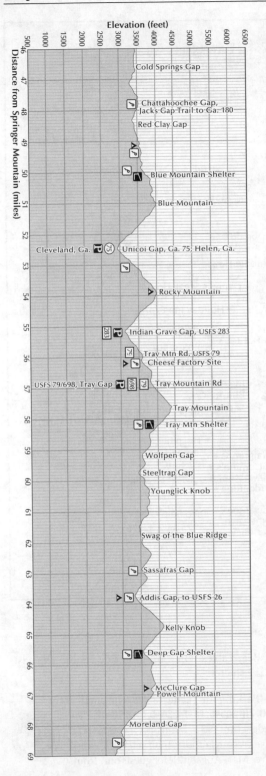

180, Hiawassee, GA 30546; (800) 990-8869, <www.enota.com>; waterfalls, organic gardens, and an animal sanctuary; $10 membership per visit and $5 campfire fee; tentsites (1 tent only) $30D, $10EAP, with access to bathhouse, motel-type room $80D, cabins $135–$165, dogs $5. Free long-distance phone, coin laundry with soap, video library, possible shuttle to Trail for fee. Holds packages for guests only.

West 11 miles to **Hiawassee, Ga**. (see below).

USFS 283, Indian Grave Gap—USFS Andrews Cove Campground, open seasonally, $12.

Cheese Factory Site—In the mid-1800s, a New Englander established a dairy near Tray Mountain, about 15 miles from the nearest farmhouse. Other Georgians, who received parcels in the mountains after a government survey of former Indian lands in the 1830s, opted to sell their land to speculators rather than tame the untamable. For years, the man reportedly produced a superior cheese that won several awards. Little evidence of the dairy remains today, although the spot is a designated campsite with a spring.

Tray Mountain—Spectacular views from the 4,430-foot summit and probably the southernmost breeding area in the United States for Canada warblers. These small, active songbirds may be spotted in the rhododendron thickets along the southern approach to the summit. Males are blue-gray above and yellow throughout the chest. Look for the distinctive "necklace" on both the males' and females' chests. The Canada warbler's song is an irregular burst of beautiful notes.

Tray Mountain Shelter (1971)—Sleeps 7. Privy. Bear cables. Excellent spot for taking in the sunset and sunrise from the summit or from viewpoints along the 0.2-mile trail to the shelter. Water source is a spring located 260 yards behind the shelter.

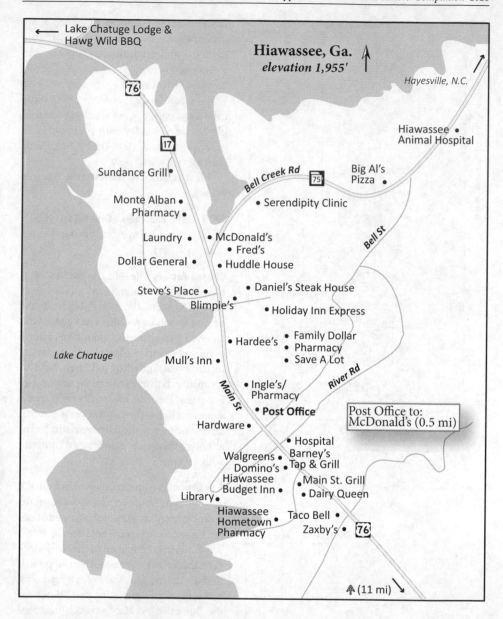

← Lake Chatuge Lodge &
Hawg Wild BBQ

Hiawassee, Ga. ↑
elevation 1,955'

Hayesville, N.C.

[76]

Hiawassee •
Animal Hospital

[17]

Sundance Grill •

Bell Creek Rd [75]

Big Al's
Pizza •

Monte Alban •
Pharmacy •

• Serendipity Clinic

Bell St

Laundry •   • McDonald's
                 • Fred's

Dollar General •   • Huddle House

Steve's Place •   • Daniel's Steak House
      Blimpie's •
                     • Holiday Inn Express

Lake Chatuge

                  • Hardee's   • Family Dollar
                              • Pharmacy
Mull's Inn •   • Save A Lot

                 • Ingle's/   River Rd
                 Pharmacy
Main St   • **Post Office**

      Hardware •

                              ┌─────────────────────┐
                              │ Post Office to: │
                              │ McDonald's (0.5 mi)   │
                              └─────────────────────┘

                        • Hospital
       Walgreens • Barney's
         Domino's • Tap & Grill
       Hiawassee
       Budget Inn •   • Main St. Grill
Library •   • Dairy Queen

       Hiawassee   Taco Bell •
       Hometown •
       Pharmacy   Zaxby's •   [76]

                              ⚑ (11 mi) ↘

Addis Gap—**East** 0.5 mile to stream at USFS 26.

Deep Gap Shelter (1983)—Sleeps 12. Privy. Bear cables. On a 0.3-mile side trail to the east.
Water source is on the blue-blazed trail to the shelter.

U.S. 76/Dicks Creek Gap/Hiawassee—Parking lot, picnic tables, and small creek.
       West 11 miles to **Hiawassee, Ga. [P.O. ZIP 30546: M–F 8:30–5, Sa 8:30–12; (706)
896-3632]**. *See map.* ■ *Lodging:* Hiawassee Budget Inn, 193 S. Main St., (706) 896-4121,
<www.hiawasseebudgetinn.com>, $44.95S, $5EAP, coin laundry, Internet/WiFi access,
short-term resupply, small in-house outfitter, free Mar–Apr shuttle for guests only from/

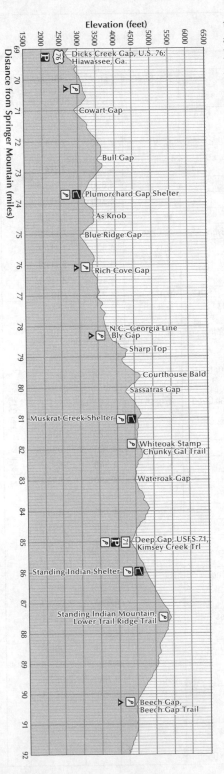

to Trail at Dicks Creek or Unicoi gaps at 9 and 11 a.m. (fee for nonguests), $5 per person other months, holds packages only for guests. Mull's Inn, 213 N. Main St., (706) 896-4196, $55 and up, pets allowed (fee), holds packages for guests only. Holiday Inn Express, 300 Big Sky Dr., (706) 896-8884, <www.hiexpress.com/hiawasseega>, $89.99–$159, $6–$10EAP, no pets, coin laundry with free detergent, indoor whirlpool, WiFi/Internet access, will hold UPS packages. ■ *Groceries:* Saves-A-Lot, Ingles (ATM), both long-term resupply. ■ *Restaurants:* Steve's Place, AYCE; Main Street Grill, B/L; Monte Alban Mexican, L/D; Daniel's Steakhouse, L/D AYCE; various fast-food places. ■ *Internet access:* Towns County Public Library. ■ *Other services:* Western Union; coin laundry; Chatuge Regional Hospital, (706) 896-2222, known for treatment of blisters; Serendipity Clinic (urgent care), (706) 970-1154, M 9–5, T 9–3, W 9–5 with appointment, F 10–6 and Su 12–4 walk-ins, credit-card fees apply; pharmacy; dentist; banks with ATM; hardware store; Hiawassee Animal Hospital, (706) 896-4173. ■ *Shuttles:* Hiawassee Budget Inn, (706) 896-4121; Henry Carter, (678) 525-3497.

Plumorchard Gap Shelter (1993)—Sleeps 14. Privy. Bear cables. The stump in front has been home to copperheads. Water source is a creek that crosses the trail to the shelter or a spring located 200 yards west of the A.T., opposite the shelter trail. Food-hoisting cables.

North Carolina

Miles from Springer	Miles to Next Point	Features	Services	Elev	Miles from Katahdin	M A P
78.1	0.1	Georgia–North Carolina State Line ...*tree register*		3,825'	2,114.9	
78.2	0.7	Bly Gap...*gnarly oak tree (spring 250 ft. south and east)*	C, w	3,840'	2,114.8	
78.9	0.7	Sharp Top...*vista*		4,338'	2,114.1	
79.6	0.5	Courthouse Bald		4,690'	2,113.4	
80.1	0.6	Sassafras Gap		4,300'	2,112.9	
80.7	0.6	Stream	w	4,625'	2,112.3	
81.0	0.8	**Muskrat Creek Shelter** ...*7.5mS; 4.9mN*	S, C, w	4,600'	2,112.0	
81.8	0.2	Whiteoak Stamp	C, w	4,620'	2,111.2	
82.0	0.9	Chunky Gal Trail *(W–5.5m to U.S. 64)*		4,700'	2,111.0	
82.9	2.1	Wateroak Gap		4,460'	2,110.1	
85.0	0.9	Deep Gap, USFS 71 ...*campsite (W–0.1m)* *West–3.7m on Kimsey Creek Trail to* USFS Standing Indian Campground	R, P, C, w C, g, sh	4,341'	2,108.0	
85.9	1.5	**Standing Indian Shelter** ...*4.9mS; 7.6mN*	S, C, w	4,760'	2,107.1	
87.4	2.9	Lower Ridge Trail; Standing Indian Mountain (5,498') *South–100ft. of jct.–unmarked spring trail (W–0.2m)* *East–to* campsite; 0.2m to summit *West–4.2m to* USFS Standing Indian Cpgd	w C C, g, sh	5,410'	2,105.6	A T C N . C . – G a . M a p 2
90.3	1.8	Beech Gap, Beech Gap Trail	C, w	4,460'	2,102.7	
92.1	1.0	Coleman Gap		4,220'	2,100.9	
93.1	0.4	Timber Ridge Trail		4,700'	2,099.9	
93.5	1.4	**Carter Gap Shelter** ...*7.6mS; 8.7mN*	S, C, w	4,540'	2,099.5	
94.9	0.3	Ridgepole Mountain		4,990'	2,098.1	
95.2	2.0	Little Ridgepole Vista		4,800'	2,097.8	
97.2	0.9	Betty Creek Gap, Betty Creek Trail	C, w	4,300'	2,095.8	
98.1	0.3	Mooney Gap, USFS 83	R, P	4,400'	2,094.9	
98.4	0.6	Log Steps ...*spring*	w	4,500'	2,094.6	
99.0	0.4	Bearpen Gap ...USFS 67 nearby		4,700'	2,094.0	
99.4	0.3	Bearpen Trail, USFS 67, Albert Mtn Bad Weather Bypass	R	4,790'	2,093.6	
99.7	0.2	Albert Mountain ...*firetower*	P	5,250'	2,093.3	
99.9	0.4	Albert Mountain Bad Weather Bypass Trail		5,020'	2,093.1	
100.3	1.9	Big Spring Gap		4,940'	2,092.7	
102.2	0.9	**Long Branch Shelter** ...*8.7mS; 3.4mN*	S, C, w	4,503'	2,090.8	
103.1	2.5	Glassmine Gap, Long Branch Trail		4,400'	2,089.9	
105.6	0.1	**Rock Gap Shelter** ...*3.4mS; 8mN*	S, C, w	3,760'	2,087.4	
105.7	0.6	Rock Gap, USFS 67 *West–1.5m to* USFS Standing Indian Campground	R, P C, g, sh	3,750'	2,087.3	
106.3	3.1	Wallace Gap, "Old U.S. 64, Old Murphy Road", S.R. 1448	R	3,738'	2,086.7	
		West–1.5m to USFS Standing Indian Cpgd				

Miles from Springer	Miles to Next Point	Features	Services	Elev	Miles from Katahdin	M A P
109.4	0.2	Winding Stair Gap, U.S. 64 ...piped spring *East–10m to* **Franklin, N.C., P.O. 28734**	R, P, w H, all	3,770'	2,083.6	
109.6	0.7	East Fork Moore Creek ...*bridge, waterfall*	w	3,780'	2,083.4	
110.3	0.2	Moore Creek Campsite	C, w	3,970'	2,082.7	
110.5	0.9	Swinging Lick Gap		4,100'	2,082.5	
111.4	1.7	Panther Gap		4,480'	2,081.6	
113.1	0.5	**Siler Bald Shelter** *(E–0.5m on loop trail)* ...*8mS; 7.8mN*	S, C, w	4,700'	2,079.9	
113.6	1.7	Snowbird Gap, **Siler Bald Shelter** *(E–0.6m)* *West–0.2m to Siler Bald Summit (5,216')*	S, C, w	4,980'	2,079.4	
115.3	1.3	Wayah Gap, S.R. 1310 ...*picnic area* Aquone Hostel at Nantahala Mountain Lodge ...*pick-up*	R, P H	4,180'	2,077.7	
116.6	0.5	Wilson Lick Ranger Station ...*historic site*		4,650'	2,076.4	
117.1	0.5	USFS 69 ...*log steps, piped spring*	R, w	4,900'	2,075.9	
117.6	1.8	Wine Spring, Bartram Trail *(E–campsite; W–water)*	C, w	5,360'	2,075.4	
119.4	0.1	Latrines, USFS 69 Parking Area	R, P	5,320'	2,073.6	
119.5	0.4	Wayah Bald ...*stone observation tower*		5,342'	2,073.5	ATC N.C.–Ga. Map 2
119.9	0.1	Spring *(west)*	w	5,250'	2,073.1	
120.0	0.4	Bartram Trail ...*campsite, spring (E–200 yds)*	C, w	5,200'	2,073.0	
120.4	1.3	**Wayah Shelter** ...*7.8mS; 4.8mN*	S, C, w	4,480'	2,072.6	
121.7	2.3	Licklog Gap ...*logging road (W–0.1m C; 0.5m stream)*	C, w	4,440'	2,071.3	
124.0	1.2	Burningtown Gap, S.R. 1397 Aquone Hostel at Nantahala Mountain Lodge ...*pick-up*	R, P H	4,236'	2,069.0	
125.2	0.7	**Cold Spring Shelter** ...*4.8mS; 5.8mN*	S, C, w	4,920'	2,067.8	
125.9	1.2	Copper Ridge Bald Lookout		5,080'	2,067.1	
127.1	0.3	Rocky Bald Lookout Side Trail *(E–0.2m)*		5,030'	2,065.9	
127.4	1.4	Big Branch Campsite	C, w	4,900'	2,065.6	
128.8	1.4	Tellico Gap, Otter Creek Road, S.R. 1365 ... *powerline* Aquone Hostel at Nantahala Mountain Lodge ...*pick-up*	R, P H	3,850'	2,064.2	
130.2	0.7	Wesser Bald Observation Tower *(E–100 feet)*		4,627'	2,062.8	
130.9	0.1	Spring ...*water for Wesser Bald Shelter (east)*	w	4,100'	2,062.1	
131.0	1.8	**Wesser Bald Shelter**, Wesser Creek Trail ...*5.8mS; 4.9mN*	S, C, w	4,115'	2,062.0	
132.8	3.1	Jump-up Lookout		4,000'	2,060.2	
135.9	0.8	**A. Rufus Morgan Shelter** ...*4.9mS; 7.7mN*	S, C, w	2,300'	2,057.1	
136.7	0.1	U.S. 19, U.S. 74, Nantahala River, N.O.C., Wesser, N.C. *East–1m to* Nantahala Food Mart *East–13m to* **Bryson City, N.C., P.O. 28713**	R, P, H, G, L, M, O, cl, sh, f G G, L, M, D, cl	1,723'	2,056.3	N.C.–Ga. Map 1
136.8	1.2	Railroad Tracks		1,795'	2,056.2	
138.0	0.3	Powerline		2,030'	2,055.0	
138.3	0.7	Wright Gap ...*dirt road*	R	2,390'	2,054.7	

Miles from Springer	Miles to Next Point	Features	Services	Elev	Miles from Katahdin	M A P
139.0	0.4	Tyre Knob ...*skirt southeast side*		2,760'	2,054.0	
139.4	0.4	Campsite and Spring	C, w	2,940'	2,053.6	
139.8	0.4	Grassy Gap		3,050'	2,053.2	
140.2	1.4	Grassy Top		3,290'	2,052.8	
141.6	0.6	Spring ...*at trail switchback*	w	3,690'	2,051.4	
142.2	0.7	The Jump-up ...*trail switchback*		3,780'	2,050.8	
142.9	0.9	Swim Bald ...*views of the Smokies*		4,720'	2,050.1	
143.8	1.2	**Sassafras Gap Shelter** ...*7.7mS; 9.1mN*	S, C, w	4,330'	2,049.2	
145.0	0.4	Cheoah Bald ...*vistas, Bartram Trail northern terminus*	C	5,062'	2,048.0	
145.4	2.0	Bartram Trail		4,830'	2,047.6	
147.4	1.0	Locust Cove Gap ...*spring (west)*	C, w	3,690'	2,045.6	
148.4	1.4	Simp Gap		3,700'	2,044.6	
149.8	0.7	Ridge High Point (*W–0.1m to spring on logging road*)	w	3,520'	2,043.2	
150.5	1.0	Stecoah Gap, N.C. 143, Sweetwater Creek Road ...*table* *West–2m to* Cabin in the Woods *West–9m to* **Robbinsville, N.C., P.O. 28771**	R, P, w L G, L, M	3,165' 2,470'	2,042.5	
151.5	1.4	Sweetwater Gap		3,220'	2,041.5	
152.9	0.4	**Brown Fork Gap Shelter** ...*9.1mS; 6.1mN*	S, C, w	3,800'	2,040.1	
153.3	1.8	Brown Fork Gap (*E–35 yds. spring*)	w	3,580'	2,039.7	
155.1	0.8	Hogback Gap		3,500'	2,037.9	
155.9	2.0	Cody Gap	C, w	3,600'	2,037.1	
157.9	0.4	Stream	w	3,560'	2,035.1	
158.3	0.9	Yellow Creek Gap, N.C. 1242, Yellow Creek Mountain Road	R, P	2,980'	2,034.7	
159.2	1.4	**Cable Gap Shelter** ...*6.1mS; 6.7mN*	S, C, w	2,880'	2,033.8	
160.6	1.4	Black Gum Gap		3,400'	2,032.4	
162.0	0.4	Walker Gap, Yellow Creek Trail *West–2.8m to Fontana Village*	PO, G, L, M, O, cl, f	3,450'	2,031.0	
162.4	0.1	Campsite ...*stream*	C, w	3,200'	2,030.6	
162.5	1.5	Crest of Bee Cove Lead		2,620'	2,030.5	
164.0	0.4	Spring	w	2,470'	2,029.0	
164.4	0.3	Benton Mackaye Trail *West–3m to Fontana Village*	PO, G, L, M, O, cl, f	2,070'	2,028.6	
164.7	0.1	N.C. 28 ...*stone steps* *East–6m to* The Hike Inn *West–2m to* **Fontana Dam, N.C., P.O. 28733**	R, P L, f G, L, M, O, cl, f	1,810'	2,028.3	
164.8	1.1	S.R 1245, Fontana Lake Marina ...*restrooms*	P	1,170'	2,028.2	
165.9	0.3	**Fontana Dam Shelter** ...*6.7mS; 11.8mN*	R, P, S, C, sh, w	1,775'	2,027.1	
166.2	0.1	Fontana Dam Bypass Trail ...*TVA maintenance area*		1,725'	2,026.8	
166.3	0.4	Fontana Dam Visitor Center ...*showers*	R, P, sh, w	1,700'	2,026.7	

ATC N.C.–Ga. Map 1

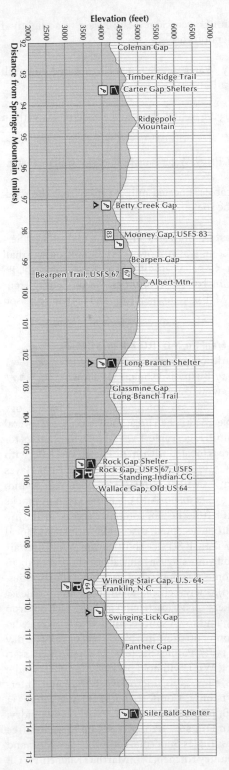

Elevation (feet)

Distance from Springer Mountain (miles)

Coleman Gap

Timber Ridge Trail
Carter Gap Shelters

Ridgepole Mountain

Betty Creek Gap

Mooney Gap, USFS 83

Bearpen Gap

Bearpen Trail, USFS 67
Albert Mtn.

Long Branch Shelter

Glassmine Gap
Long Branch Trail

Rock Gap Shelter
Rock Gap, USFS 67, USFS
Standing Indian CG
Wallace Gap, Old US 64

Winding Stair Gap, U.S. 64;
Franklin, N.C.

Swinging Lick Gap

Panther Gap

Siler Bald Shelter

At Bly Gap, northbounders enter the Nantahala National Forest with 4,000-foot gaps and 5,000-foot peaks. Nantahala is Cherokee for "land of the noonday sun." Long climbs between the Stecoah–Cheoah Mountain area and Cheoah Bald offer panoramic views of western North Carolina. Don't rush; enjoy the landscape from an observation tower or two.

Nantahala Hiking Club—NHC maintains the 58.5 miles between the Georgia line and the Nantahala River. Correspondence should be sent to NHC, 173 Carl Slagle Rd., Franklin, NC 28734; <www.nantahalahikingclub.org>.

No road access to the A.T. is available between Bly Gap and Rock Gap during Jan, Feb, and part of Mar. The Forest Service closes USFS 71 to all vehicular traffic until Mar 1 and USFS 67 until Mar 15. Frequently used Trailheads at Deep Gap, and others, are inaccessible.

Bly Gap—If you are thru-hiking, it is time to celebrate your first (or last) state line. When you see the gnarled oak in a clearing, you're officially in North Carolina. The gap, with its grassy area and views to the northwest, makes a good campsite. Water from a spring about 100 yards south on the A.T.

Muskrat Creek Shelter (rebuilt 1995)—Sleeps 8. Moldering privy. This shelter uses the "Nantahala design." Water source is just south and visible from the shelter.

Deep Gap—From here, the Kimsey Creek Trail leads 3.7 miles west to the Forest Service's Standing Indian Campground (see next page).

Standing Indian Shelter (1996)—Sleeps 8. Privy. "Nantahala design" shelter. Water source is a stream opposite the side trail to the shelter. Recent bear sightings; *use bear-proofing techniques.*

Standing Indian Mountain—The 5,498-foot summit of the mountain 0.2 mile east is reached *via* a blue-blazed side trail. Cliff-top views to the south gave it the nickname, "Grandstand of the Southern Appalachians." At the top are flat areas for camping and views south toward Blood Mountain. A spring is located 0.2 mile downhill on an unmarked trail near the A.T. junction with Lower Ridge Trail. Please tread lightly if you choose to camp here; the area receives tremendous use.

Carter Gap Shelter (1998)—Shelter sleeps 8. Privy. Water source is a spring located downhill behind the old shelter, on the west side of the Trail.

Mooney Gap—This gap has been identified as among the wettest places in the eastern U.S., with an estimated annual precipitation of 93.5 inches.

Long Branch Shelter (2012)—Timber frame, sleeps 8. Privy. Water is on right of side trail to shelter.

Rock Gap Shelter (1965)—Sleeps 8. Privy. Bear cables. Located only 0.1 mile from the road. Water source is a spring to the left and behind the shelter.

Rock Gap/Standing Indian Campground—West 1.5 miles on a paved road to the Forest Service campground with tentsites $20, restroom, warm showers ($2 shower only); small campstore with snacks open M–Sa 10–12, 1–5, Su 1–5 Apr–Nov; will hold packages shipped UPS to 2037 Standing Indian Campground Rd., Franklin, NC 28734. *Shuttles:* Macon County Transit, (828) 349-2222, $3PP from Rock Gap to Franklin, M–F 9:15 a.m., 12:15 p.m., and 3:15 p.m. in season (Feb–May).

U.S. 64/Winding Stair Gap—East 10 miles to **Franklin, N.C. [P.O. ZIP 28734: M–F 8:30–5, Sa 9–12; (828) 524-3219].** *See map.* Although a bit spread out, most major services are within walking distance along Business U.S. 441. The town runs several Trail-related events in Mar and Apr; <www.discoverfranklinnc.com/at110>. ■ *Hostels:* "Baltimore Jack" Tarlin Hostel, (828) 524-2064, open Mar 1–May 1, $20PP includes clean bunk with linens and shower, cable TV, kitchen area; shower only, $5; several private rooms $45PP, $5EAP, with microwave, minifridge, cable TV, WiFi. Daily shuttles to/from Trail. A Three Eagles Outfitters satellite store is located within the hostel; WiFi, PC with printer available for GSMNP permits. Gooder Grove A.T. & Adventure Hostel, 130 Hayes Circle, (828) 332-0228, <goodergrove@gmail.com>; owner Colin Gooder, open year-round, private and semiprivate rooms with queen beds $30–$50, bunk $23, tenting $15, hammocks $13, dogs welcome, lodging includes shower, WiFi, full kitchen, computer access, grills, fire pit; laundry $6, check-in 10 a.m.–8 p.m., mail drops accepted, discounts with stay to local restaurants and stores; M–F, take Macon County Transit Service shuttle from Winding Stair or Rock gaps to Gooder Grove to get the $3 cost off your stay; Sa–Su, call for shuttle; in-town shuttles available; parking for section hikers; some resupply; slackpacking opportunities. Chica & Sunsets, (715) 315-0876 (text preferred), <www.chicaandsunsets.com>, <chica@chicaandsunsets.com>, operated by 2017 thru-hikers; $45PP (cash only) includes pick up/drop off at Winding Stair Gap, full breakfast, laundry, and town shuttle; limited to 4 hikers who will have full use of apartment, 2 twin beds per room; no drop-ins; please text or call one day ahead to secure a spot. ■ *Lodging:* Budget Inn, 433 E. Palmer St., (828) 524-4403, $45S $55D $10EAP, no pets, microwave, refrigerator, Internet, WiFi, will hold packages for guests only; The Sapphire Inn, 761 E. Main St., (828) 524-4406, $49S, $59D, microwave, refrigerator, Internet, WiFi, pets $10, will hold packages for guests only; Comfort Inn, (828) 369-9200, 313 Cunningham Rd., starting at $89.99 including B, pets $25 each, pool, WiFi, coin laundry; Microtel Inn & Suites, (828) 349-9000, 81 Allman Dr., $67–$120, pets $25 up to 35 lbs., free long-distance phone (U.S.), B, WiFi. ■ *Groceries:* Ingles Supermarket, BiLo, Sav-Mor, and Walmart (long-term resupply). ■ *Restaurants:* Kountry Kitchen, B/L; Martha's Kitchen, AYCE

L; Shoney's, AYCE; Sunset Restaurant, (828) 524-4842, M–Sa, 6 a.m.–8 p.m., B/L/D, daily specials, 10% hiker discount; Rock House Lodge, (828) 349-7676, M–Sa 10–7, quality craft beers on tap, 10% hiker discount, Internet access; Rathskeller Coffee Haus & Pub, Tu–Th 8 a.m.–9 p.m., F–Sa 8 a.m.–11 p.m., Internet access; and various other restaurants. ■ *Outfitters:* Three Eagles Outfitters, 78 Siler Rd., (828) 524-9061, open M–Sa 10–6, Su 12–4, full-service outfitter and coffee house with WiFi and Internet kiosk, Coleman and alcohol fuel by the ounce, Esbit and canisters, will ship and hold packages; Outdoor 76, 35 East Main St., (828) 349-7676, <www.outdoor76.com>, full-service outfitter, lightweight gear, food, fuel, footwear experts with trained staff, M–Sa 10–7, Su 12–5, 10% thru-hiker discount, $10 local-restaurant gift card with $50 purchase, Internet access, mail drops accepted. ■ *Internet access:* Macon County Library, open T–Th 10–7, F–Sa 10–5. ■ *Other services:* Franklin First Baptist Church, free B daily Mar 14–Apr 10; UPS Store, (828) 524-9800; coin laundry; Mission My Care Now clinic, (828) 369-4427, 190 Riverview St., M–F 7–7, Sa 9–4; Franklin Health & Fitness, (828) 369-5608, yoga, massage therapy, pool, hiker discount; Currahee Brewery, open daily, WiFi, printer, charging outlets, library, food cart; Lazy Hiker brewery, food cart; pharmacy; veterinarian. ■ *Shuttles:* Macon County Transit, (828) 349-2222, $3PP from Winding Stair, Wallace, and Rock gaps to Franklin, M–F 9 a.m., noon, and 3 p.m. in season (Feb 26–May 25), $1 town shuttle; Zen Shuttles, (828) 332-0228.

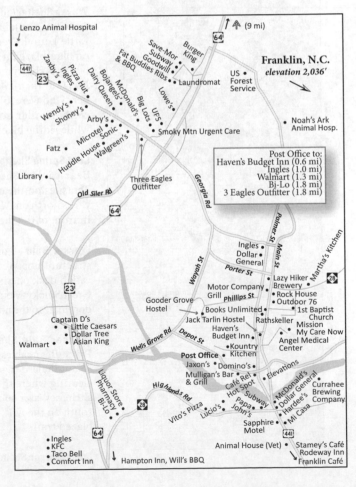

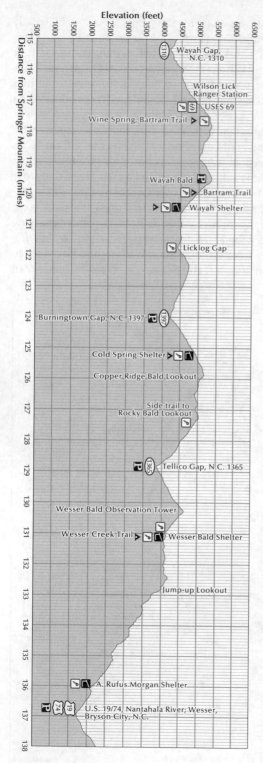

Aquone Hostel at Nantahala Mountain Lodge—(828) 321-2340, 63 Britannia Dr., Aquone (or Topton), NC 28781. Call owner Steve Bennett for pick-up from Wayah, Burningtown, or Tellico gaps, $20PP. Hot food and hiker supplies available. Mail drops only for guests with reservations.

Siler Bald Shelter (1959)—Sleeps 8. Privy. Bear cables. Located 0.5 mile on a blue-blazed loop. Water source is 80 yards down a blue-blazed trail from the shelter.

Wayah Bald—The stone observation tower at the summit of Wayah Bald (5,342 ft.) was built in 1937 by the CCC and renovated in 1983. Wayah is Cherokee for "wolf."

Wayah Shelter (2007)—Sleeps 8. Privy. Five tentsites. Nantahala-style. Water source is Little Laurel Creek, 600 feet west of A.T. on blue-blazed trail. This shelter was built by the NHC in memory of Ann and Larry McDuff, thru-hikers and ALDHA members who were killed about a year apart in eerily similar accidents, hit by vehicles while riding bikes near home.

Cold Spring Shelter (1933)—Sleeps 6. Privy. Bear cables. Shelter built by the CCC. Tentsites on the east side of the Trail 200 yards north on A.T. Water source is 5 yards in front of the shelter.

Wesser Bald—Formerly a fire tower, the structure atop Wesser Bald is now an observation deck offering panoramic views. The Great Smoky Mountains and Fontana Lake dominate to the north.

Wesser Bald Shelter (1994)—Sleeps 8. Privy. Bear cables. This was the first of the "Nantahala design" shelters. Tentsites in clearing where the blue-blaze leads to the shelter. Water source is a spring 0.1 mile south on the A.T., then 75 yards on a blue-blazed trail.

Rufus Morgan Shelter (rebuilt 1989)—Sleeps 6.

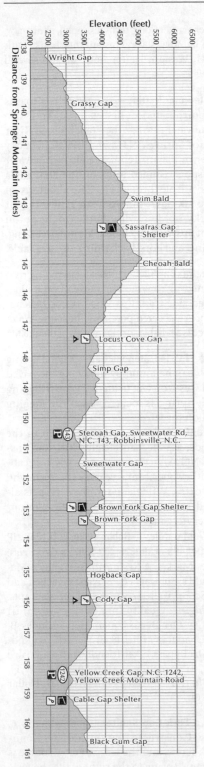

Elevation (feet)

Distance from Springer Mountain (miles)

Wright Gap

Grassy Gap

Swim Bald

Sassafras Gap Shelter

Cheoah Bald

Locust Cove Gap

Simp Gap

Stecoah Gap, Sweetwater Rd, N.C. 143, Robbinsville, N.C.

Sweetwater Gap

Brown Fork Gap Shelter
Brown Fork Gap

Hogback Gap

Cody Gap

Yellow Creek Gap, N.C. 1242, Yellow Creek Mountain Road

Cable Gap Shelter

Black Gum Gap

Privy. Located in a small cove, this shelter is named after the Nantahala club's founder. The water source is a stream across the A.T. from the shelter.

Smoky Mountains Hiking Club—SMHC maintains the 102.4 miles between the Nantahala River and Davenport Gap. Correspondence should be sent to the SMHC, P.O. Box 51592, Knoxville, TN 37950; <www.smhclub.org>.

U.S. 19/Nantahala River/Nantahala Outdoor Center—At U.S. 19, the A.T. passes through the Nantahala Outdoor Center (NOC), (828) 488-2175 or (800) 232-7238, <www.noc.com>, an outdoor-adventure center with many services for backpackers; call ahead for shuttles. Between the outfitter and River's End Restaurant, the A.T. crosses a pedestrian bridge over the Nantahala River. *Please note that NOC could be closed during inclement weather in Feb and Mar.* ■ *Lodging:* NOC, 9–5; call ahead for reservations and for after hours arrival; check in at Wesser General Store; winterized hostel with rooms that may be full on weekends, $27.69s bunk, $40 two twin beds/room, $80 four twin beds/room; motel room, $70–$120D; NOC cabins $200 and up with cleaning fee; limited rooms for pets ($10). Reservations recommended. ■ *Groceries:* Wesser General Store (short-term resupply), open 7–9 Mar–Sep. ■ *Restaurants:* River's End Restaurant, open 11–6 Nov–Feb L/D, 8–7 Mar–Oct B/L/D, WiFi; Big Wesser Mexican, open May 1, 10 a.m.–11 p.m., snacks, light meals, drinks, open seasonally. ■ *Outfitter:* NOC Outfitters (short-term resupply), 9–5 (varies with season), offers backpacking gear, ability to print your GSMNP permit, Coleman and alcohol fuel by the ounce, Esbit and canisters, ATM, stamps, coin laundry detergent, ATC publications, WiFi. Coin laundry with detergent at outfitter; restroom and coin showers are located on the southern side of U.S. 19. NOC accepts USPS, UPS, and FedEx packages sent to 13077 Hwy. 19W, Bryson City, NC 28713. Check with the front desk; packages must be marked "Hold for A.T. Hiker." NOC can ship packages *via* USPS up to 10 lbs. max (add $1 processing fee); extra charge on weekends.

East 1 mile to *Groceries:* Nantahala Food Mart (short-term resupply), daily 7 a.m.–8 p.m., pizza.

East 13 miles on U.S. 19 to **Bryson City, N.C. [P.O. ZIP 28713: M–F 9–4:30, Sa 10–12; (828) 488-3481].** Bryson City is a large town with many services, including Ingles

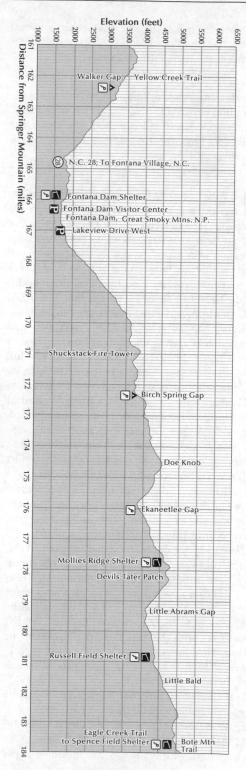

Elevation (feet)

Distance from Springer Mountain (miles)

- Walker Gap; Yellow Creek Trail
- N.C. 28; To Fontana Village, N.C.
- Fontana Dam Shelter
- Fontana Dam Visitor Center
- Fontana Dam, Great Smoky Mtns. N.P.
- Lakeview Drive West
- Shuckstack Fire Tower
- Birch Spring Gap
- Doe Knob
- Ekaneetlee Gap
- Mollies Ridge Shelter
- Devils Tater Patch
- Little Abrams Gap
- Russell Field Shelter
- Little Bald
- Eagle Creek Trail to Spence Field Shelter
- Bote Mtn Trail

Supermarket (long-term resupply), pharmacy, coin laundry, several restaurants, banks with ATM, Western Union, hospital, and several hotels.

Whitewater Rafting—The Nantahala marks the northbounder's first chance at Trail-side whitewater rafting. The French Broad River in Hot Springs, N.C., and the Nolichucky River in Erwin, Tenn., are also whitewater hot-spots. Guided tours on the Nantahala are available through NOC for about $25 on nonpeak days, but you can rent a raft or "ducky" for less, with shuttles to the put-in point upstream included. Mountain biking, zipline, and horseback riding also available.

Sassafras Gap Shelter (2002)—Sleeps 14. Privy. Located in a ravine 100 yards in on a blue-blazed side trail, this wood-framed shelter features a covered porch and benches. Water source is a reliable spring in front of the shelter.

N.C. 143/Stecoah Gap—A good spring can be found by following the paved road west 200 feet to an overgrown logging road. Spring is located down the logging road on the left.

East 2 miles to *Lodging:* Cabin in the Woods, 301 Stecoah Heights Rd., Robbins-ville, NC 28771; (828) 735-1930, <www.thecab-insinthewoods.com>, 3 cabins $25–$95/night; B/D extra, WiFi, laundry, showers, pets allowed; area shuttles and slackpacking/resupply service; mail drops accepted.

West 9 miles to **Robbinsville, N.C. [P.O. ZIP 28771: M–F 9–4:30; (828) 479-3397].** ■ *Groceries*: Ingles Market. ■ *Restaurants*: Wendy's; Mc-Donald's; Subway; Pop & Nana's Kitchen and The Scoop, B all day; various other restaurants. ■ *Lodging*: Quality Inn, (828) 479-6772, 111 Rodney Orr Bypass, $89-$119D includes B, WiFi; San Ran Motel, (828) 479-3256, 253 Rodney Orr Bypass, hiker-friendly with reasonable rates, kitchenettes in all rooms, A/C, WiFi. ■ *Other:* Walgreens, Family Dollar, Dollar General.

Brown Fork Gap Shelter (1996)—Sleeps 6. Privy. Constructed by the SMHC, Konn-arock Crew, and the USFS. Water source is a reliable spring to the right of the shelter.

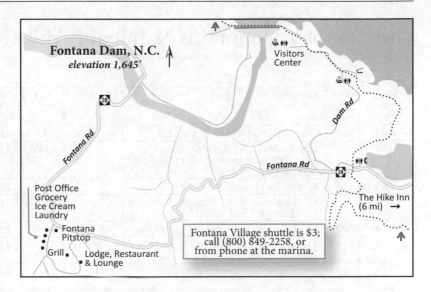

Fontana Dam, N.C. elevation 1,645'

Visitors Center

Dam Rd

28

Fontana Rd

Fontana Rd

28

The Hike Inn (6 mi) →

Fontana Rd

Post Office
Grocery
Ice Cream
Laundry

Fontana Pitstop

Grill   Lodge, Restaurant
& Lounge

Fontana Village shuttle is $3;
call (800) 849-2258, or
from phone at the marina.

Cable Gap Shelter (1939/1988)—Sleeps 6. Privy. Shelter originally built by the CCC. The water source is a reliable spring in front of the shelter.

Walker Gap—The Yellow Creek Trail leads 2.5 miles west to Fontana Village. However, it is a poorly marked, difficult short-cut to the resort.

N.C. 28/Fontana Dam—East 6 miles to *Lodging:* The Hike Inn, 3204 Fontana Rd. Fontana Dam, N.C. 28733, (828) 479-3677, <www.thehikeinn.com>, <hikeinn@graham.main.nc.us>. open Mar–Oct. A hikers-only motel and shuttle service, run by Nancy Hoch since 1993, now joined by 2014 thru-hiker Tom "High Loon" Barrett. Private room with bath, TV, WiFi, and coffee-maker, $50 (2 max); laundry $5. Thru/long-distance-hiker package, $75S–$100D, includes laundry, dinner/resupply trip to Robbinsville, and shuttle from/to Stecoah Gap, Yellow Creek Gap, Fontana Dam. Free slackpacking between Stecoah Gap, Yellow Creek Gap, and Fontana Dam with 2-night stay; free parking for section-hikers with stay and shuttle; printing of Smokies permit; and mail drops held free for guests only. Shuttles available between Atlanta and Damascus.

West 2 miles to **Fontana Dam, N.C. [P.O. ZIP 28733; M–F 11:45–3:45, closed Sa; (828) 498-2315],** which is located 2 miles from Fontana Dam within the Fontana Village Resort. *Please note: Some services may close or be under reduced hours during off-season, and supplies are limited; most services available by late Mar.* ■ *Lodging:* Fontana Lodge, Fontana Village, 300 Woods Rd., Fontana Dam, NC 28733; (800) 849-2258, <www.fontanavillage. com>; cabins or lodge rooms $79D; tentsites $15–$20; reservations recommended; will hold packages at lodge. ■ *Groceries:* Fontana General Store (short-term resupply). ■ *Other services:* minimart, restaurant, coin laundry, ice cream/soda fountain (open in May) with Internet access, disc golf, mountain-bike rentals, and fitness center.

Fontana Dam Shelter (1982)—Sleeps 24. Restroom with water, showers, USB chargers at shelter. Known as the "Fontana Hilton," this spacious shelter is located 0.3 mile south of the dam on TVA land. Shower facilities also are located at the dam; see below.

Fontana Dam—At 480 feet, Fontana Dam is the highest dam in the eastern United States. This facility offers a visitors center with restrooms and shower that is normally open 9–7 Apr–Aug and 9–6 Sep–Oct (last Su).

Great Smoky Mountains National Park

Miles from Springer	Miles to Next Point	Features	Services	Elev	Miles from Katahdin	M A P
166.3	0.4	Fontana Dam Visitor Center ...*showers*	R, P, sh, w	1,700'	2,026.7	
166.7	0.1	Little Tennessee River, Fontana Dam; southern boundary, Great Smoky Mountains National Park	R	1,740'	2,026.3	
166.8	0.6	Fontana Dam Bypass Trail		1,755'	2,026.2	
167.4	3.6	Lakeview Drive West, Benton MacKaye Trail, Lakeshore Trail	R, P	1,800'	2,025.6	
171.0	0.3	Shuckstack Fire Tower *(E–0.1m)* ...*on old road*		3,800'	2,022.0	
171.3	1.0	Sassafras Gap, Lost Cove Trail, Twentymile Trail Jct.		3,653'	2,021.7	
172.3	2.2	Birch Spring Gap Campsite ...*tentpads, spring*	C, w	3,834'	2,020.7	
174.5	0.5	Doe Knob, Gregory Bald Trail		4,520'	2,018.5	
175.0	1.0	Mud Gap		4,260'	2,018.0	
176.0	1.7	Ekaneetlee Gap ...*spring (west 300 ft.)*	w	3,842'	2,017.0	
177.7	0.5	Gant Lot (Rich Gap) **Mollies Ridge Shelter** ...*11.8mS; 3.1mN*	S, w	4,570'	2,015.3	
178.2	1.1	Devils Tater Patch		4,775'	2,014.8	
179.3	0.3	Little Abrams Gap		4,120'	2,013.7	
179.6	1.2	Big Abrams Gap		4,080'	2,013.4	
180.8	0.3	Russell Field Trail Jct. **Russell Field Shelter** *(W–150 yds. stream)...3.1mS; 3.1mN*	S, w	4,360'	2,012.2	
181.1	2.6	McCampbell Gap		4,328'	2,011.9	
183.7	0.4	Eagle Creek Trail to **Spence Field Shelter** *(E–0.2m)* ...*3.1mS; 6.3mN* Bote Mountain Trail *(W–0.2m spring)*	S, w w	4,915'	2,009.3	
184.1	0.7	Jenkins Ridge Trail		4,950'	2,008.9	
184.8	0.6	Rocky Top ...*vista*		5,441'	2,008.2	
185.4	1.1	Thunderhead *(east peak)* ...*vista*		5,527'	2,007.6	
186.5	0.6	Beechnut Gap *(W–75 yds.)* ...*spring*	w	4,920'	2,006.5	
187.1	0.3	Mineral Gap		5,030'	2,005.9	
187.4	0.6	Brier Knob ...*vista*		5,215'	2,005.6	
188.0	0.8	Starkey Gap		4,500'	2,005.0	
188.8	1.0	Sugar Tree Gap		4,435'	2,004.2	
189.8	0.3	**Derrick Knob Shelter** ...*6.3mS; 5.7mN*	S, w	4,880'	2,003.2	
190.1	2.1	Sams Gap, Greenbrier Ridge Trail *(W–100 yds.)* ...*spring*	w	4,840'	2,002.9	
192.2	0.3	Cold Spring Knob		5,240'	2,000.8	
192.5	3.0	Buckeye Gap, Miry Ridge Trail *(E–200 yds.)...spring*	w	4,817'	2,000.5	
195.5	0.2	**Silers Bald Shelter** ...*5.7mS; 1.7mN*	S, w	5,460'	1,997.5	
195.7	0.2	Silers Bald ...*vistas*		5,607'	1,997.3	
195.9	0.8	Welch Ridge Trail		5,430'	1,997.1	
196.7	0.5	Jenkins Knob		5,550'	1,996.3	

Miles from Springer	Miles to Next Point	Features	Services	Elev	Miles from Katahdin	M A P
197.2	0.6	**Double Spring Gap Shelter** ...*1.7mS; 6.1mN*	S, w	5,507'	1,995.8	
197.8	1.8	Goshen Prong Trail		5,750'	1,995.2	
199.6	0.1	Mt. Buckley ...*vista*		6,582'	1,993.4	
199.7	0.3	Clingmans Dome Bypass Trail		6,550'	1,993.3	
200.0	0.5	Clingmans Dome *(E–0.5m)...observation deck*	R, P, w	6,643'	1,993.0	
200.5	1.0	Mt. Love		6,446'	1,992.5	
201.5	0.9	Collins Gap		5,886'	1,991.5	
202.4	0.4	Mt. Collins		6,188'	1,990.6	
202.8	0.2	Sugarland Mountain Trail **Mt. Collins Shelter** *(W–0.5m) ...6.1mS; 8.5mN*	S, w	5,900'	1,990.2	
203.0	3.0	Fork Ridge Trail, Mountains to the Sea Trail *(E–35 yds.)*	R	5,890'	1,990.0	
206.0	0.4	Indian Gap, Road Prong Trail	R, P	5,317'	1,987.0	
206.4	1.3	Mt. Mingus Lead ...*feral hog barrier*		5,460'	1,986.6	
207.7	1.7	Newfound Gap, U.S. 441, Tenn. 71 Rockefeller Memorial ...*restrooms* *East–18m to* **Cherokee, N.C., P.O. 28719** *West–15 m to* **Gatlinburg, Tenn., P.O. 37738**	R, P, w all all	5,045'	1,985.3	
209.4	0.8	Sweat Heifer Trail		5,820'	1,983.6	
210.2	0.3	Mt. Ambler		6,000'	1,982.8	
210.5	0.3	Boulevard Trail to Mt. LeConte *(W–5.3m L, M)*		5,695'	1,982.5	
210.8	0.1	**Icewater Spring Shelter** ...*8.5mS; 7.8mN*	S, w	5,920'	1,982.2	
210.9	0.7	Spring	w	5,900'	1,982.1	
211.6	0.1	Charlies Bunion ...*southern loop trail jct to view from Fodder Stack*		5,500'	1,981.4	
211.7	0.4	Charlies Bunion ...*northern loop trail jct to view from Fodder Stack*		5,500'	1,981.3	
212.1	0.1	Dry Sluice Gap		5,375'	1,980.9	
212.2	0.9	Dry Sluice Gap Trail		5,310'	1,980.8	
213.1	1.3	Porters Gap, the Sawteeth		5,500'	1,979.9	
214.4	1.8	False Gap		5,400'	1,978.6	
216.2	2.0	Bradley's View ...*vistas*		5,200'	1,976.8	
218.2	1.7	Hughes Ridge Trail to **Peck's Corner Shelter** *(E–0.4m) ...7.8mS; 5.6mN* *Intermittent spring 100 feet north on A.T.*	S, w w	5,280'	1,974.8	
219.9	0.7	Copper Gap		5,478'	1,973.1	
220.6	1.0	Mt. Sequoyah		6,003'	1,972.4	
221.6	0.7	Chapman Gap		5,801'	1,971.4	
222.3	1.1	High Point on Mt. Chapman		6,218'	1,970.7	
223.4	0.3	**Tri-Corner Knob Shelter** ...*5.6mS; 7.7mN*	S, w	5,920'	1,969.6	
223.7	1.1	Balsam Mountain Trail		6,000'	1,969.3	
224.8	0.6	Guyot Spur		6,360'	1,968.2	
225.4	0.1	Guyot Spring ...*on A.T.*	w	6,150'	1,967.6	
225.5	0.4	Mt. Guyot Side Trail		6,395'	1,967.5	
225.9	0.5	Cross Pinnacle Lead, NoBo enter Hell Ridge		6,260'	1,967.1	
226.4	0.7	Deer Creek Gap		6,020'	1,966.6	

National Geographic Smokies Park Map

Miles from Springer	*Miles to Next Point*	Features	Services	Elev	Miles from Katahdin	MAP
227.1	*0.3*	Yellow Creek Gap		5,900'	1,965.9	National Geographic Smokies Park Map
227.4	*1.3*	Snake Den Ridge Trail, Inadu Knob		5,491'	1,965.6	
228.7	*0.9*	Camel Hump Knob		5,250'	1,964.3	
229.6	*1.1*	Camel Gap, Camel Gap Trail		4,645'	1,963.4	
230.7	*0.4*	Cosby Knob, State-Line Ridgecrest, SoBo enter Hell Ridge		5,150'	1,962.3	
231.1	*0.7*	**Cosby Knob Shelter** ...*7.7mS; 6.9mN*	S, w	4,700'	1,961.9	
231.8	*2.1*	Low Gap, Low Gap Trail *West–2.5m to* NPS Cosby Campground	 C, w	4,242'	1,961.2	
233.9	*0.4*	Mt. Cammerer side trail to fire tower *(W–0.6m)*		5,000'	1,959.1	
234.3	*1.5*	Spring *(west)*	w	4,300'	1,958.7	
235.8	*0.2*	Spring *(E–50 yds.)*	w	3,700'	1,957.2	
236.0	*1.0*	Lower Mt. Cammerer Trail *West–7.8m to* NPS Cosby Campground	 C, w	3,465'	1,957.0	
237.0	*1.0*	Chestnut Branch Trail *East–2m to* Big Creek Ranger Station *East–2.3m to* Big Creek Country Store *East–2.5m to* NPS Big Creek Campground	 G P, C, w	2,900'	1,956.0	
238.0	*1.1*	**Davenport Gap Shelter** ...*6.9mS; 10.9mN*	S, w	2,600'	1,955.0	
239.1	*0.7*	Davenport Gap, Tenn. 32, S.R. 1397 (Old N.C. 284/Cove Creek Road) Eastern boundary, Great Smoky Mountain National Park *East–1m to* Big Creek Country Store *East–1.3m to* Big Creek Ranger Station *East–2.3m to* NPS Big Creek Campground	R, P G C, w	1,975'	1,953.9	

Established in 1934, the Smokies is the most visited of the traditional national parks; for that reason, it is especially important to practice Leave No Trace here. The highest elevation on the A.T. is here at Clingmans Dome at 6,643 feet. The Smokies also has the most rainfall and snowfall on the A.T. in the South, and many hikers are caught off-guard by the snow and cold temperatures that the high elevation means.

Great Smoky Mountains National Park—<www.nps.gov/grsm>. The Trail through the park officially begins for northbounders on the northern side of Fontana Dam; for southbounders, Davenport Gap is the beginning. In recent years, the park has hosted more than nine million visitors annually. Home to the most diverse forest in North America, the park includes more than 100 species of trees, 1,570 species of flowering plants, 60 species of mammals, more than 25 different salamanders, and 2,000 varieties of mushrooms.

Seasonal and temporary closures can be found at <www.nps.gov/grsm>.

Backcountry Permits—Backcountry permits <u>must be obtained</u> before entering the park—the thru-hiker fee is $20 for a seven-night permit. Purchase permits on-line <u>up to 38 days</u> before your planned entry of the park at <smokiespermits.nps.gov> or by telephone at (865) 436-1297. You will need a paper copy; don't count on finding a computer and printer on the way. Anyone caught without a permit may be issued a ticket! Additional rangers are being deployed in the backcountry to enforce this fee.

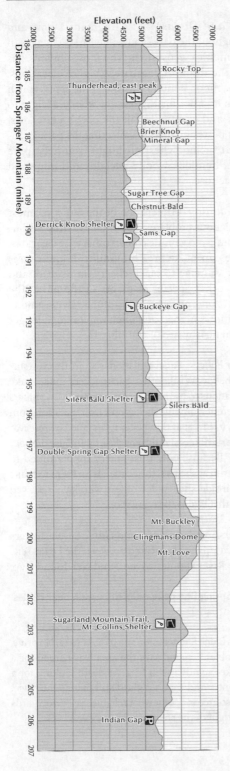

Elevation (feet)

Distance from Springer Mountain (miles)

184
185 — Rocky Top
186 — Thunderhead, east peak
187 — Beechnut Gap / Brier Knob / Mineral Gap
188
189 — Sugar Tree Gap / Chestnut Bald
190 — Derrick Knob Shelter / Sams Gap
191
192
193 — Buckeye Gap
194
195
196 — Silers Bald Shelter / Silers Bald
197 — Double Spring Gap Shelter
198
199
200 — Mt. Buckley / Clingmans Dome / Mt. Love
201
202
203 — Sugarland Mountain Trail, Mt. Collins Shelter
204
205
206 — Indian Gap
207

Human Waste and Privies—In past years, the park's administration shunned privies at backcountry facilities. Instead, "toilet areas" were designated where backpackers are supposed to dig cat holes and bury their waste. A privy-building campaign, underwritten by ATC and SMHC, resulted in new facilities at the shelters by 2010. Although privies mainly provide an aesthetically acceptable way to deal with many hikers' refusal to use proper Leave No Trace methods, they are costly to maintain and a management last resort. The best decision is to do your business away from the shelter area before you get to camp or after you leave. Pick a spot far from any trails and 200 feet or more from any water, and practice Leave No Trace methods.

Horses—Within the park, half of the A.T. is open to horseback riding; horse users may also share A.T. shelters. SMHC and ATC have made a concerted effort to resolve issues with the horse users, who have helped with major rehabilitation and other projects along the Trail in that half.

Bears—Between 400 and 600 bears reside in the park. They become more active in the early spring and remain active through the fall. Following a few simple guidelines can help keep bears and other animals away from people and safe within the park. Be sure to hang food on the provided bear-bag system, and do not feed or leave food for these wild creatures to eat. Shelters no longer have chain-link fences to keep bears out. Whenever possible, eat away from the shelters.

Dogs—Dogs are not permitted on trails in the park. Hikers violating this rule will be fined up to $500. Those hiking with dogs should arrange to board their pets. Several kennels provide this service: Standing Bear Farm Hiker Hostel, (423) 487-0014; contact for details. Loving Care Kennels, (865) 453-2028, <www.lovingcarekennels. net>, in Pigeon Forge, Tenn.; owner Lida O'Neill will pick up and/or drop off your dog at Fontana Dam and Davenport Gap for $300 for one dog, $450 for two dogs; also holds mail drops, will shop for delivery.

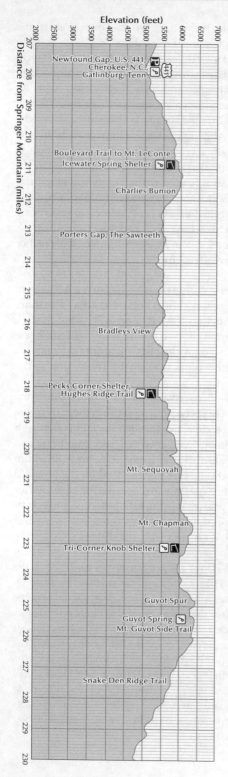

Pests and Disease—At Clingmans Dome and throughout the park, you will witness changes in the Smokies' ecosystem. The most obvious has been the death of conifers at higher elevations. Atmospheric pollution weakens the trees, which makes it easier for the balsam woolly adelgid to attack and eventually kill the park's Fraser firs. Other pests and diseases affecting the park's ecosystem include chestnut blight, southern pine beetle, hemlock woolly adelgid, and dogwood anthracnose.

Air Pollution—This is one of the Smokies' most conspicuous problems. Pollution can drop visibility from 93 to 22 miles on an otherwise clear day. Ozone can make breathing difficult and causes visible damage to black cherry, milkweed, and thirty other species of plants in the park. The park's ozone, nitrogen, and sulfur levels are among the nation's highest and often remain high longer than in nearby urban communities.

Shelter Policy—Park regulations require that you stay in a shelter. While other backpackers must make reservations to use backcountry shelters, thru-hikers are exempt from this shelter-specific regulation from Mar 15 to Jun 15. If the shelter is occupied by reservation, thru-hikers should tent close by and use the bear cables. Because only thru-hikers are permitted to tent-camp at shelters, the burden is on them to make room inside shelters for others who have reserved space; that is also the regulation.

Shelters South of Newfound Gap—Seven shelters and a campsite are located between the Little Tennessee River (Fontana Dam) and Newfound Gap.

Birch Spring Campsite—Spring water, bear cables, and tentpads.

Mollies Ridge Shelter (1961/2003)—Sleeps 12. No privy. Bear cables. Legend says the area was named for a Cherokee maiden who froze to death looking for a lost hunter and that her ghost still haunts the ridge. Water source is a somewhat reliable spring 200 yards to the right of the shelter.

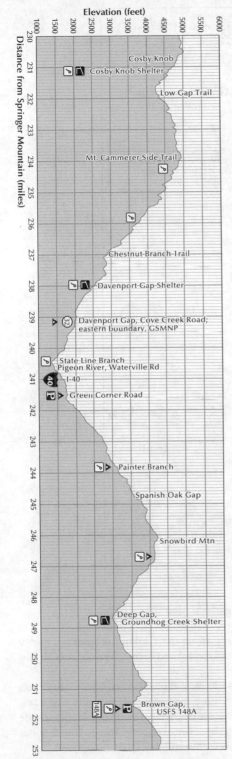

Elevation (feet)

Distance from Springer Mountain (miles)

Cosby Knob
Cosby Knob Shelter
Low Gap Trail
Mt. Cammerer Side Trail
Chestnut-Branch-Trail
Davenport-Gap-Shelter
Davenport Gap, Cove Creek Road; eastern boundary, GSMNP
State Line Branch
Pigeon River, Waterville Rd
I-40
Green Corner Road
Painter Branch
Spanish Oak Gap
Snowbird Mtn
Deep Gap, Groundhog Creek Shelter
Brown Gap, USFS 148A

Russell Field Shelter (1961)—Sleeps 14. No privy. Bear cables. This section of Trail is popular with riders. Water source is a spring 150 yards down the Russell Field Trail toward Cades Cove. A short walk beyond the spring is an open, grassy area with views into Cades Cove; the Russell Gregory family grazed stock here in the 1800s.

Spence Field Shelter (1963/2005)—Sleeps 12. Privy. Bear cables. Shelter is located 0.2 mile east on the Eagle Creek Trail. This section of Trail is popular with riders and bears. Spence Field, to the north of the shelter, offers azaleas, blueberries, and open views into North Carolina and Tennessee from the largest grassy bald in the Smokies. Water source is a reliable spring 150 yards down the Eagle Creek Trail.

Derrick Knob Shelter (1961)—Sleeps 12. No privy. Bear cables. Water source is a reliable spring near the shelter.

Silers Bald Shelter (1961/2001)—Sleeps 12. No privy. Bear cables. The increasingly overgrown bald 0.3 mile north of the shelter offers views of Clingmans Dome and sunsets over Cove Mountain. Water source is to the right; a trail leads 75 yards to a reliable spring.

Double Spring Gap Shelter (1963)—Sleeps 12. Privy. Bear cables. Gap was named to indicate the existence of two springs, one on each side of the state line and both now unreliable. The better water source is on the North Carolina side, 15 yards from the crest; second source is on the Tennessee side, 35 yards from the crest.

Clingmans Dome—At 6,643 feet, this is the highest point on the A.T. There are no feet-on-the-ground views from the tree-clad summit, but the observation tower provides 360-degree views. The summit is usually busy; a park road leads to within 0.5 mile of the tower. From here to the northern end of the park, Fraser firs and red spruce are now dying *en masse*—a dramatic change from the southernmost 30 miles of the park.

Mt. Collins Shelter (1960)—Sleeps 12. Privy. Bear cables. Nestled in spruce thicket. Water source is a

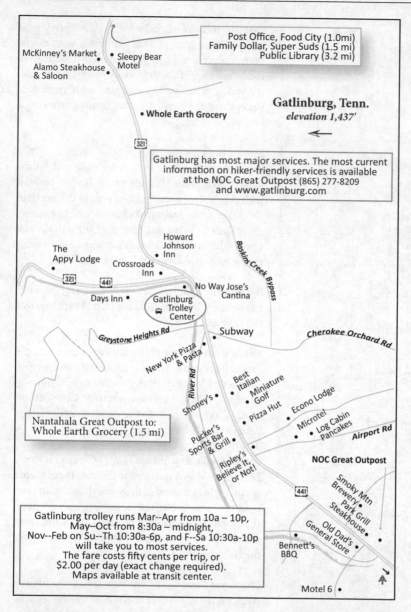

McKinney's Market
Alamo Steakhouse & Saloon
Sleepy Bear Motel

Post Office, Food City (1.0mi)
Family Dollar, Super Suds (1.5 mi)
Public Library (3.2 mi)

Whole Earth Grocery

Gatlinburg, Tenn.
elevation 1,437'
←

321

Gatlinburg has most major services. The most current information on hiker-friendly services is available at the NOC Great Outpost (865) 277-8209 and www.gatlinburg.com

The Appy Lodge
Howard Johnson Inn
Crossroads Inn
Baskins Creek Bypass
321   441
Days Inn
No Way Jose's Cantina
Gatlinburg Trolley Center
Greystone Heights Rd
Subway
Cherokee Orchard Rd
New York Pizza & Pasta
River Rd
Best Italian
Miniature Golf
Shoney's
Pizza Hut
Econo Lodge
Microtel
Log Cabin Pancakes
Airport Rd

Nantahala Great Outpost to:
Whole Earth Grocery (1.5 mi)

Pucker's Sports Bar & Grill
Ripley's Believe It, or Not!
NOC Great Outpost
441
Smoky Mtn Brewery
Park Grill Steakhouse
Old Dad's General Store
Bennett's BBQ

Gatlinburg trolley runs Mar--Apr from 10a – 10p, May--Oct from 8:30a – midnight, Nov--Feb on Su--Th 10:30a-6p, and F--Sa 10:30a-10p will take you to most services. The fare costs fifty cents per trip, or $2.00 per day (exact change required). Maps available at transit center.

Motel 6

small spring 200 yards beyond the shelter on the Sugarland Mountain Trail.

U.S. 441/Newfound Gap—The only road crossing along the Trail in the Smokies. Plenty of traffic goes through the gap with its large parking lot and scenic overlook; usually an easy hitch into Gatlinburg.

East 18 miles to **Cherokee, N.C., [P.O. ZIP 28719: M-F 9-4:30; (828) 497-3891]**, <www.visitcherokeenc. com>, home of the Eastern Band of the Cherokee, with more than 40 motels and most major services. Attractions include the Museum of the Cherokee Indian, Unto These Hills Mountainside Theatre, Qualla Arts & Crafts center, and Harrah's Hotel & Casino. *Lodging:* Microtel Inn & Suites (828) 497-7800, contact for rates; free phone, WiFi, B, pool; coin laundry.

West 15 miles to the resort town of **Gatlinburg, Tenn.** [P.O. ZIP 37738: M–F 9–5, Sa 9–11; (865) 436-3229]. *See page vii.* ■ *Lodging:* Motel 6, (865) 436-7813, near edge of town closest to the park, hiker rate, B, Internet access, coin laundry. Nearly 100 other hotels and motels, including the new A.T.-centric Appy Lodge, an ATC partner, 168 Parkway, (865) 430-3659, <www.theappylodge.com>. ■ *Restaurants:* More than 70, including Shoney's, with AYCE B and soup/salad bar. ■ *Groceries:* Food City *et alia* (see map). ■ *Outfitter:* NOC's Great Outpost, 1138 Parkway, (865) 277-8209; full-service outfitter, free showers for thru-hikers, Internet access, white gas and alcohol fuel by the ounce. Mail drops accepted; may ship as well. ■ *Other services:* Banks with ATM; doctor; A Walk in the Woods kennel, <www.awalkinthewoods.com>, (865) 436-8283, hiker shuttles, dog-shuttling and boarding; Appalachian Adventure Co., (865) 456-7677, shuttles.

Boulevard Trail—This side trail, located 2.7 miles north of Newfound Gap, leads 5 miles to the summit of Mt. LeConte. A shelter and LeConte Lodge, (865) 429-5704, <www.lecontelodge.com>, are located at the top (reservations required; $145PP includes B/D). The round-trip to this spectacular peak is worth it, if you have the time.

Shelters North of Newfound Gap—GSMNP has five shelters between Newfound Gap and Davenport Gap.

Icewater Spring Shelter (1963/1999)—Sleeps 12. Privy. Bear cables. Water source for this heavily used shelter is 50 yards north on the A.T.

Charlies Bunion—Views of Mt. LeConte to the west. It got its name on a hike in 1929, when Charlie Conner and Horace Kephart, an A.T. pioneer and famed writer/conservationist of the period, discovered this feature, created by a landslide after a disastrous rain that year. The two decided the rocky outcropping stuck out like a bunion on Charlie's foot. The narrow path was blasted out by the Park Service.

Pecks Corner Shelter (1958/2000)—Sleeps 12. Privy. Bear cables. Follow the Hughes Ridge Trail 0.4 mile to a junction with the side trail to the shelter. Water source is in front of the shelter 50 yards.

Tri-Corner Knob Shelter (1961/2004)—Sleeps 12. Privy. Located on the North Carolina side of the A.T., this is the most remote shelter in the GSMNP. The water source for this shelter is a reliable spring 10 yards in front of the shelter.

Cosby Knob Shelter (1959)—Sleeps 12. Privy. Bear cables. Shelter is located 100 yards east down a side trail. Water source is a reliable spring 35 yards downhill and in front of the shelter.

Mt. Cammerer Side Trail—This trail to the west leads 0.6 mile to the Mt. Cammerer firetower, a historic stone-and-timber structure originally built in 1939 by the CCC and rebuilt in 1994. Panoramic views from its platform.

Davenport Gap Shelter (1961/1998)—Sleeps 12. No privy. Your last, or first, GSMNP A.T. shelter, dubbed the "Smokies Sheraton." Water source is a spring to the left of the shelter.

Tenn. 32, Cove Creek Rd. (Old N.C. 284)/Davenport Gap—East 1 mile to *Groceries:* The Big Creek Country Store, 67 Mt. Sterling Rd., Waynesville, N.C., (828) 476-4492, Th–M 9–6 (limited hours Jan–Feb); packaged food, hiking and camping supplies; dog-friendly.

East 1.3 miles to Big Creek Ranger Station, (828) 486-5910; 1 mile farther to the station's seasonal campsites, $14/site, no showers. The Chestnut Branch Trail leads out from the ranger station and, in two miles, meets the A.T. one mile south of Davenport Gap Shelter.

North Carolina & Tennessee Border

Miles from Springer	Miles to Next Point	Features	Services	Elev	Miles from Katahdin	M A P
239.1	0.7	Davenport Gap, Tenn. 32, S.R. 1397 (Old N.C. 284/Cove Creek Road) Eastern boundary, **Great Smoky Mountain National Park** *East–1m to* Big Creek Country Store *East–1.3m to* Big Creek Ranger Station *East–2.3m to* NPS Big Creek Campground	R G C, w	1,975'	1,953.9	
239.8	0.6	Powerline		1,840'	1,953.2	
240.4	0.2	State Line Branch ...*blue blaze to spring (W–60 yds.)*	C, w	1,600'	1,952.6	
240.6	0.4	Pigeon River; Tobes Creek Rd, Waterville Rd	R	1,400'	1,952.4	
241.0	0.5	I-40 ...*underpass and 150 yds. north to Green Corner Road steps in rock cut*	R	1,500'	1,952.0	
241.5	2.3	Green Corner Road *West 0.15m to* Standing Bear Farm Hiker Hostel	R, P H, g, cl, sh, f	1,800'	1,951.5	
243.8	0.9	Painter Branch Campsite ...*blue-blaze*	C, w	3,100'	1,949.2	
244.7	1.5	Spanish Oak Gap ...*sharp switchback*		3,730'	1,948.3	
246.2	0.5	Snowbird Mountain ...FAA tower		4,263'	1,946.8	
246.7	0.2	Campsite ...spring	C, w	4,100'	1,946.3	
246.9	1.8	*Wildcat Spring*	w	4,000'	1,946.1	
248.7	2.3	Deep Gap **Groundhog Creek Shelter** *(E–0.2m)* ...*10.9mS; 8.5mN*	S, C, w	2,900'	1,944.3	
251.0	0.1	Harmon Den Mountain, Rube Rock Trail		3,800'	1,942.0	
251.1	0.5	Hawk's Roost	C, nw	3,800'	1,941.9	
251.6	0.6	Brown Gap, USFS 148A	R, P, w	3,500'	1,941.4	
252.2	1.9	Spring ...*steep ravine (W–100 yds.)*	w	4,320'	1,940.8	
254.1	0.2	Cherry Creek Trail		4,250'	1,938.9	
254.3	0.8	Max Patch Road, S.R. 1182 ...*stile*	R, P	4,280'	1,938.7	
255.1	1.4	Max Patch Summit ...*1933 benchmark*		4,629'	1,937.9	
256.5	0.5	Stream ...*dense rhododendron*	w	4,050'	1,936.5	
257.0	0.3	**Roaring Fork Shelter** ...*8.5mS; 4.8mN*	S, C, w	3,950'	1,936.0	
257.3	0.7	Footbridge		3,940'	1,935.7	
258.0	2.3	Footbridge over creek, cross road		3,840'	1,935.0	
260.3	0.2	Stream, campsite, and woods road	C, w	3,590'	1,932.7	
260.5	0.7	Lemon Gap, S.R. 1182, Tenn. 107, USFS 3505	R, P	3,550'	1,932.5	
261.2	0.6	Stream(s)	w	3,940'	1,931.8	
261.8	0.8	**Walnut Mountain Shelter** *(W–0.1m)*... *4.8mS; 9.9mN*	S, w	4,260'	1,931.2	
262.6	0.7	Kale Gap ...*woods road*		3,700'	1,930.4	
263.3	0.2	Catpen Gap ...*views*		4,130'	1,929.7	
263.5	0.7	Brooks	w	4,160'	1,929.5	
264.2	0.8	Bluff Mountain		4,686'	1,928.8	
265.0	0.8	Spring ...*blue blaze (W–50 yds.)*	w	4,360'	1,928.0	
265.8	0.3	Big Rock Spring ...*base of log steps (E–50 yds)*	w	3,730'	1,927.2	
266.1	0.9	Cross Old Road		3,360'	1,926.9	

Miles from Springer	Miles to Next Point	Features	Services	Elev	Miles from Katahdin	MAP
267.0	0.8	Small brook ...*cascades*	C, w	2,520'	1,926.0	Map 4
267.8	0.5	Vista (E–0.1m) ...*blue-blaze*		2,640'	1,925.2	
268.3	1.8	Garenflo Gap, Garenflo Gap Road	R, P	2,500'	1,924.7	
270.1	0.3	Lamb Knob		2,880'	1,922.9	
270.4	1.3	Little Bottom Branch Gap		2,700'	1,922.6	
271.7	2.8	Gragg Gap, **Deer Park Mountain Shelter** ...*9.9mS; 14.2mN*	S, C, w	2,330'	1,921.3	
274.5	0.1	Serpentine Street ...*kiosk*	R, P, H	1,408'	1,918.5	
274.6	0.3	N.C. 209	R	1,340'	1,918.4	
274.9	0.4	U.S. 25 & 70, N.C. 209 **Hot Springs, N.C., P.O. 28743**	R, P G, L, M, O, cl, f	1,326'	1,918.1	
275.3	0.5	Highway Bridge, French Broad River, Spring Creek, Hot Springs Spa	R, C, g, sh	1,320'	1,917.7	
275.8	0.5	Bank of French Broad River		1,320'	1,917.2	
276.3	1.9	Lovers Leap Rock		1,820'	1,916.7	
278.2	1.6	Pump Gap		2,100'	1,914.8	
279.8	0.2	Campsite near pond dam ...*boxed spring*	C, w	2,490'	1,913.2	
280.0	0.8	Mill Ridge ...*piped spring on gated USFS Road (W–50 ft.)*	P, w	2,800'	1,913.0	
280.8	1.4	Tanyard Gap, U.S. 25 & 70 overpass, Lookout Mountain Road	R, P	2,278'	1,912.2	
282.2	0.5	Cross foot log ...*below is a good spring*	w	3,020'	1,910.8	ATC Tenn.–N.C. Map 3
282.7	0.4	Roundtop Ridge Trail		3,250'	1,910.3	
283.1	0.1	Rich Mountain fire tower side trail *(W–0.1m)*		3,600'	1,909.9	
283.2	0.5	*Campsite and spring*	C, w	3,550'	1,909.8	
283.7	0.3	Spring	w	3,380'	1,909.3	
284.0	0.2	Gated USFS 3514	R	3,160'	1,909.0	
284.2	1.7	Hurricane Gap, USFS 467	R, P	2,900'	1,908.8	
285.9	1.5	**Spring Mountain Shelter** ...*14.2mS; 8.6mN*	S, C, w	3,300'	1,907.1	
287.4	0.2	Spring *(west)*	w	3,190'	1,905.6	
287.6	2.0	Deep Gap, Little Paint Creek Trail		2,930'	1,905.4	
289.6	1.6	Allen Gap, N.C. 208, Tenn. 70, Paint Creek ...*spring (E–200 ft.)*	R, P, w	2,234'	1,903.4	
291.2	3.3	Log Cabin Drive *West–0.7m to* Hemlock Hollow Farm Shop and Cafe	R C, G, L, M, sh, f	2,560'	1,901.8	
294.5	1.8	**Little Laurel Shelter** ...*8.6mS; 7.3mN*	S, C, w	3,300'	1,898.5	
296.3	1.7	Bald Mountain Road, Camp Creek Bald firetower trail *(W–0.2m)*	R	4,844'	1,896.7	
298.0	0.1	Spring, creek ...*blue-blaze trails both sides of A.T.*	w	4,390'	1,895.0	
298.1	0.2	White Rock Cliffs *(E–0.1m)*		4,450'	1,894.9	
298.3	0.2	Blackstack Cliffs *(W–0.1m)*		4,420'	1,894.7	
298.5	0.8	Bad weather trail *(1.5m)* ...*rejoins A.T. to north*		4,425'	1,894.5	
299.3	0.8	Big Firescald Knob	w	4,360'	1,893.7	
300.1	0.6	Bad weather trail *(1.5m)* ...*rejoins A.T. to south*		4,280'	1,892.9	
300.7	0.9	Round Knob Trail		4,200'	1,892.3	

Miles from Springer	Miles to Next Point	Features	Services	Elev	Miles from Katahdin	M A P
301.6	0.2	USFS Fork Ridge Trail		4,210'	1,891.4	
301.8	1.6	**Jerry Cabin Shelter** ...*7.3mS; 6.7mN*	S, C, w	4,150'	1,891.2	
303.4	0.3	Dirt road		4,690'	1,889.6	
303.7	1.1	Big Butt; Squibb Creek Trail	C	4,750'	1,889.3	
304.8	0.5	Spring ...*seasonal*	w	4,480'	1,888.2	
305.3	1.1	Shelton Graves (E–80 yds.)		4,500'	1,887.7	
306.4	0.5	Snake Den Ridgecrest ...*old logging road*		4,520'	1,886.6	
306.9	0.8	Seasonal water source	w	4,240'	1,886.1	
307.7	0.8	Flint Gap ...*old logging railroad grade*		3,425'	1,885.3	
308.5	0.9	**Flint Mountain Shelter** ...*6.7mS; 8.9mN*	S, C, w	3,570'	1,884.5	
309.4	1.8	Campsite ...*water west in ravine*	C, w	3,400'	1,883.6	
311.2	0.5	Devil Fork Gap, Tenn.352/N.C. 212	R, P	3,107'	1,881.8	
311.7	0.3	Rector Laurel Road	H, R, w	2,960'	1,881.3	
312.0	0.3	Pass small cemetery, cross stream	w	3,060'	1,881.0	
312.3	0.3	Cross stream and woods road	w	3,210'	1,880.7	
312.6	0.4	Cross stream at waterfall	w	3,990'	1,880.4	
313.0	0.4	Sugarloaf Gap		4,000'	1,880.0	
313.4	0.8	Spring ...*big rocks*	w	4,280'	1,879.6	
314.2	0.3	Cross summit Frozen Knob		4,570'	1,878.8	
314.5	0.6	Lick Rock		4,579'	1,878.5	
315.1	1.0	Big Flat	C	4,160'	1,877.9	
316.1	1.2	Rice Gap ...*rough gravel road impassable by car*		3,800'	1,876.9	
317.3	0.6	**Hogback Ridge Shelter** (E–0.1m S; 0.3m spring) ...*8.9mS; 10.3mN*	S, C, w	4,255'	1,875.7	
317.9	1.8	High Rock (E–150 ft.)		4,460'	1,875.1	
319.7	0.7	Sams Gap, U.S. 23, I-26, Flag Pond Road Mother Marian's Hostel, call for ride	R, P H	3,760'	1,873.3	
320.4	1.6	Springs	w	4,000'	1,872.6	
322.0	0.1	Street Gap Road, Street Gap Mother Marian's Hostel, call for ride	R, P	4,100'	1,871.0	
322.1	1.1	Powerline		4,180'	1,870.9	
323.2	0.2	Spring ...*blue blaze (E–20 yds.)*	w	4,240'	1,869.8	
323.4	0.6	Low Gap ... *campsite, spring*	C, w	4,300'	1,869.6	
324.0	1.4	Spring	w	4,660'	1,869.0	
325.4	0.1	Spring (W–100 yds.)	w	4,850'	1,867.6	
325.5	0.4	Blue-blazed bypass trail southern jct.		5,001'	1,867.5	
325.9	0.3	Slipper Spur		5,160'	1,867.1	
326.2	0.3	Big Bald Mother Marian's Hostel, call for ride		5,516'	1,866.8	
326.5	0.9	Big Stamp, bypass trail northern jct., spring (W–0.3m)	C, w	5,298'	1,866.5	
327.4	0.2	**Bald Mountain Shelter** (W–0.1m) ...*no tent camping* ...*10.3mS; 10.7mN*	S, w	5,100'	1,865.6	
327.6	0.2	Spring and stream	w	5,000'	1,865.4	
327.8	1.0	Blue-blaze to campsite (W–0.2m spring)	C, w	4,890'	1,865.2	
328.8	2.0	Little Bald ...*wooded summit*		5,185'	1,864.2	

ATC Tenn.–N.C. Map 3

Miles from Springer	Miles to Next Point	Features	Services	Elev	Miles from Katahdin	M A P
330.8	0.3	Whistling Gap ...small clearing, campsite, spring (W–0.1m)	C, w	3,650'	1,862.2	
331.1	1.5	Blue-blaze trail to High Rocks ...east to views		4,280'	1,861.9	
332.6	0.5	Campsite and stream	C, w	3,490'	1,860.4	
333.1	0.6	Spivey Gap, U.S. 19W	R, P, w	3,200'	1,859.9	
333.7	0.7	Oglesby Branch ...plank bridge	w	3,800'	1,859.3	
334.4	0.2	Stream	w	3,815'	1,858.6	
334.6	0.8	USFS 278	R	3,770'	1,858.4	
335.4	2.4	Devils Creek Gap ...overgrown logging road		3,400'	1,857.6	
337.8	0.2	Spring ...hemlock grove, water for No Business Knob Shelter (west)	w	3,300'	1,855.2	
338.0	2.4	**No Business Knob Shelter** ...10.7mS; 10.5mN	S, C, nw	3,251'	1,855.0	
340.4	0.7	Temple Hill Gap ...old logging road		2,850'	1,852.6	
341.1	3.2	Access road ...to former Temple Hill firetower	R	3,250'	1,851.9	
344.3	0.1	River Road, Chestoa Bridge, Nolichucky River West–1.3m to Mountain Inn & Suites West–3.8m to **Erwin, Tenn., P.O. 37650**	R, P, H, C, sh, cl, f L G, L, M, D, V, cl, f	1,700'	1,848.7	
344.4	0.1	Chestoa Pike ...East 1.2m to NOC and Nolichucky Gorge Campground West–0.9m to Cantarroso Farm	C, L, g R, L	1,700'	1,848.6	ATC Tenn.–N.C. Map 3
344.5	0.8	CSX Railroad Track ...caution		1,715'	1,848.5	
345.3	0.3	Nolichucky River gorge view		1,760'	1,847.7	
345.6	0.7	Nolichucky River Valley ...sidetrail to private Nolichucky Gorge Campground	C, L, g	1,760'	1,847.4	
346.3	0.7	Two bridges over Jones Branch	w	1,720'	1,846.7	
347.0	0.2	Bridge over Jones Branch	w	1,780'	1,846.0	
347.2	0.2	Bridge over Jones Branch ...hemlock tree stand	w	1,810'	1,845.8	
347.4	0.9	Jones Branch	w	2,480'	1,845.6	
348.3	0.2	Jones Branch	w	2,280'	1,844.7	
348.5	0.1	**Curley Maple Gap Shelter** ...10.5mS; 12.8mN	S, w	3,900'	1,844.5	
348.6	1.0	Curley Maple Gap ...abandoned USFS road		3,080'	1,844.4	
349.6	0.2	Small stream	w	3,280'	1,843.4	
349.8	2.8	Spring	w	3,280'	1,843.2	
352.6	0.7	Indian Grave Gap, Tenn. 395, N.C. 197 West–7m to **Erwin, Tenn., P.O. 37650**	R, P, C G, L, M, D, V, cl, f	3,360'	1,840.4	
353.3	0.4	Powerline		3,760'	1,839.7	
353.7	1.0	Cross USFS 230	R	3,770'	1,839.3	
354.7	0.8	Beauty Spot ...grassy bald		4,437'	1,838.3	
355.5	1.0	USFS 230 ...spring	R, C, w	4,300'	1,837.5	
356.5	0.6	Beauty Spot Gap ...spring across road at gate	C, w	4,100'	1,836.5	
357.1	1.0	USFS 230, Unaka Mountain Road	R	4,660'	1,835.9	
358.1	2.2	Unaka Mountain		5,180'	1,834.9	

Miles from Springer	Miles to Next Point	Features	Services	Elev	Miles from Katahdin	M A P
360.3	1.1	Low Gap	w	3,900'	1,832.7	Map 3
361.4	0.4	**Cherry Gap Shelter** *...12.8mS; 9.2mN*	S, w	3,900'	1,831.6	
361.8	2.7	Cherry Gap		3,900'	1,831.2	
364.5	1.2	Iron Mountain Gap, Tenn. 107, N.C. 226 *East–3m to* convenience store *West–10.3m to* **Unicoi, Tenn., P.O. 37692**	R, P G f M, D, g	3,723'	1,828.5	
365.7	0.2	Campsite *...northern end of orchard*	C, w	3,950'	1,827.3	
365.9	0.9	Weedy Gap		4,000'	1,827.1	
366.8	1.1	Large rock formation *...granite gneiss and schist*		4,426'	1,826.2	
367.9	0.7	High point near summit of knob		4,332'	1,825.1	
368.6	0.8	Greasy Creek Gap *...old roadbed to Greasy Creek Road (W–0.2m spring)* *East–0.6m to* Greasy Creek Friendly	C, w R, H, C, M, g, sh, f	4,034'	1,824.4	
369.4	1.1	Campsite, spring *...gnarled maple trees*	C, w	4,110'	1,823.6	
370.5	1.2	**Clyde Smith Shelter** *(W–0.1m)...9.2mS; 8.6mN*	S, C, w	4,400'	1,822.5	
371.7	2.2	Little Rock Knob		4,918'	1,821.3	
373.9	0.4	Hughes Gap, Hughes Gap Road, N.C. 1330	R, P, C	4,040'	1,819.1	
374.3	2.1	Spring *...piped (W–65 yds.)*	w	4,440'	1,818.7	
376.4	0.5	Beartown Mountain		5,481'	1,816.6	
376.9	1.4	Ash Gap *...spring (E–0.1m)*	C, w	5,340'	1,816.1	
378.3	0.2	Trail to Roan High Bluff USFS Cloudland Rhododendron Garden Road Parking Area*...former Cloudland Hotel Site*	R, P, w	6,200'	1,814.7	ATC Tenn.–N.C. Map 2
378.5	0.5	Pass old chimney		6,220'	1,814.5	
379.0	1.1	**Roan High Knob Shelter** *(E–0.1m)...8.6mS; 5.2mN*	S, w	6,285'	1,814.0	
380.1	0.3	Hack Line Road *...old carriage route*		5,640'	1,812.9	
380.4	0.1	Northernmost board bridge *...piped spring*	w	5,560'	1,812.6	
380.5	0.7	Carvers Gap, Tenn. 143, N.C. 261 *...picnic area, spring*	R, P, w	5,512'	1,812.5	
381.2	0.3	Skirt west side of Round Bald		5,826'	1,811.8	
381.5	0.4	Engine Gap		5,640'	1,811.5	
381.9	0.5	Jane Bald		5,807'	1,811.1	
382.4	0.1	Side trail to Grassy Ridge		5,770'	1,810.6	
382.5	1.7	Springs	w	5,800'	1,810.5	
384.2	0.4	Low Gap; **Stan Murray Shelter** *...5.2mS; 19.9mN*	S, C, w	5,050'	1,808.8	
384.6	0.7	Elk Hollow Ridge		5,180'	1,808.4	
385.3	0.8	Buckeye Gap		4,730'	1,807.7	
386.1	1.2	Yellow Mountain Gap *(E–0.2m spring; 0.3m C)*	C, w	4,682'	1,806.9	
387.3	0.4	Saddle in open field *...spring (E–100 yds.)*	w	5,180'	1,805.7	
387.7	1.3	Little Hump Mountain *...exposed campsites*	C	5,459'	1,805.3	
389.0	0.9	Bradley Gap *...campsites and springs*	C, w	4,960'	1,804.0	
389.9	2.4	Hump Mountain *...Stan Murray plaque*		5,587'	1,803.1	

Miles from Springer	Miles to Next Point	Features	Services	Elev	Miles from Katahdin	M A P
392.3	0.4	Doll Flats northern end; North Carolina–Tennessee State Line	C, w	4,600'	1,800.7	
392.7	0.1	Crest of Rocky Spur ...*overlook to east*		4,400'	1,800.3	
392.8	1.8	Overhanging rock above the Trail ...*cliff*		4,820'	1,800.2	ATC Tenn.–N.C. Map 2
394.6	0.1	Wilder Mine Hollow Group Campsite			1,798.4	
394.7	0.4	Apple House Campsite and spring *(west)*	C, w	3,060'	1,798.3	
395.1	0.2	Old Mine Road in Wilder Mine Hollow		2,860'	1,797.9	
395.3	0.2	U.S. 19E, Buck Creek *East–2.5m to* **Elk Park, N.C., P.O. 28622** *West–0.3m to* Mountain Harbour B&B and Hostel *West–2m to* Restaurant (Pizza/Subs) *West–2.5m to* Dollar General *West–3.4m to* **Roan Mountain, Tenn., P.O. 37687** *West–7.5m to* Roan Mountain State Park	R, P G, M H, C, L, sh, f M G G, H, M, D, V C, L, sh	2,880'	1,797.7	

This section has plentiful 360-degree views and ever-changing scenery flowing from rich mountain coves, boreal forests, and heath balds. Highlights are Max Patch, Big Bald, Beauty Spot, Unaka Mountain, Roan Mountain at 6,285 feet, and the open, grassy bald of Hump Mountain.

Carolina Mountain Club—CMC maintains the 94 miles between Davenport Gap and Spivey Gap. Send correspondence to CMC, P.O. Box 68, Asheville, NC 28802; <www.carolinamountainclub. org>.

Due to trailhead vandalism, the supervisor of trails for the CMC advises, "We do not recommend leaving cars at trailheads for anything more than a day trip." **Water sources**—*Several water sources are located between Davenport Gap and Deep Gap. State Line Branch may be polluted.*

Green Corner Road—**West** 0.15 mile to *Hostel:* Standing Bear Farm Hiker Hostel, 4255 Green Corner Rd., Hartford, TN 37753; (423) 487-0014; <www.standingbearfarmhostel. com>; owner Maria Guzman; bunkhouse $25PP, tenting or hammock $15PP, creek cabin or tree house $40S, $70D, 4-bed cabin $30PP (do a chore, save $5; see staff), free WiFi, campstore with beer, trail food, fuel; overnight parking $5; leashed dogs $5PN, kennel services (shuttle and boarding during GSMNP traverse) $275; credit/debit cards accepted. Holds packages ($3 for nonguests). *Directions:* After walking under I-40, go about 30 yards on gravel road to rock steps on left, continue north on the A.T. 1.0 mile to the first gravel road (Green Corner Rd.), turn left, walk 200 yards to hostel on right.

Groundhog Creek Shelter (1939)—Sleeps 6. Privy. Stone shelter located 0.2 mile on a blue-blazed side trail. Water source is a reliable spring to the left of the shelter.

Max Patch—The site of an old homestead and logging camp, Max Patch was originally forested, but early inhabitants cleared the mountaintop to graze sheep and cattle. The summit also has been used as a landing strip for small planes. In 1982, the USFS purchased the 392-acre grassy-top mountain for the A.T. and now uses mowing and controlled burns to maintain its bald appearance. The wide summit, at 4,629 feet, offers panoramic views of the Smokies to the south and a glimpse east to Mt. Mitchell (at 6,684 feet, the highest peak east of the Mississippi).

Roaring Fork Shelter (2005)—Sleeps 8. Privy. Bear cables. Two water sources, both located on the A.T., 800 ft. north and south of side trail to shelter.

Walnut Mountain Shelter (1938)—Sleeps 6. Privy. Bear cables. An old shelter, with a water source located down the blue-blazed trail to the left of Rattlesnake Trail; difficult to locate, may be seasonal. The neighborhood bears show no fear of hikers.

Deer Park Mountain Shelter (1938)—Sleeps 5. Privy. Bear cables. A former farmstead; the water source is located on the trail to the shelter.

N.C. 209/Hot Springs, N.C. [P.O. ZIP 28743: M–F 9–11:30 & 1–4, Sa 9–10:30; (828) 622-3242]. The A.T., now marked by special A.T. diamonds in the sidewalk, passes through the center of Hot Springs on Bridge Street, and most services are located on the Trail. ■ *Hostel:* The Hostel at Laughing Heart Lodge, 289 NW U.S. Hwy 25/70, (828) 206-8487, a stone's throw from the A.T. as you exit the woods at south Trailhead parking lot. Open year-round. Cash-only prices including tax: $20 bunks ($5 linens), $25 semiprivate, $35S private, $50D private (one full bed). All rooms include shower & towel, movies, hiker kitchen, morning coffee service, WiFi. Pet-friendly but no pets in bunk rooms. Tenting with shower $10 one person/one tent, $15 two/one tent. Shower only, $5; laundry, $5 includes wash/dry/soap. Quiet time 10 p.m.–7 a.m.; massage therapist on site. Blue Ridge Hiking Co., Appalachian Trail-er, 200 Lance Ave, Hot Springs, NC 28743, (828) 622-3319 or (828) 713-5451, bunkhouse, cottage, gear sales and rentals, shuttles, guided backpacking trips.

■ *Lodging:* The Sunnybank Inn, 26 Walnut St. (P.O. Box 233), (828) 622-7206, <www.sunnybankretreatassociation.org>, owned by Elmer Hall, located at the white Victorian house across the street from the Dollar Store; thru-hiker rates $25PP, private rooms available, all with shared bath, pillows and linens; hot showers (towel, soap, shampoo); legendary AYCE organic vegetarian meals, $6 B, $12 D; work exchange is possible; 10 p.m. quiet hours; no pets, no smoking, no tents; holds packages for guests. Alpine Court Motel, (828) 215-1261, hiker discounts, call for rates; credit/debit cards accepted; pet-friendly, satellite TV. Creekside Court Motel, (828) 206-5212, hiker and multinight discounts, call for rates; some pet-friendly rooms. Hot Springs Resort and Spa, (828) 622-7676, <www.nchotsprings.com>, thru-hiker cabin rate $50–$72, $6EAP up to 5; primitive tentsites $10PP up to 4; shower only, $5. Iron Horse Inn, (828) 622-0022, <www.theironhorsestation.com>, bunkroom with special hiker rate $70D/night. Little Bird Cabins, 49 S. Serpentine Ave. on the A.T., (828) 206-1487, <www.littlebirdcabinrentals.com>, owner Natalie Hesed, two cabins each with an efficiency kitchen; one cabin sleeps seven $85–$95 Su–Th, $105–$115 F–Sa: WiFi; pet-friendly with $25 fee. Mountain Magnolia Inn, 204 Lawson St., (800) 914-9306; discount hiker rates $100S, $125D when rooms available, includes AYCE B; D Th–M open to all; mail drops accepted. Springbrook Cottages, (828) 622-7385, 94 S. Andrews St., <www.springbrookcottages.com>,

Laughing
Heart
Lodge

Newport, Tenn.

Hostel at
Laughing Heart
Lodge

Little
Bird
Cabins

25

Hot Springs, N.C.
elevation 1,330'

← The Appalachian Trail-er (hostel)

209

70

Surpentine Ave

Mountain
Diner

Dollar
General

Sunnybank
Inn (Elmer's)

Hillbilly
Market

Mountain
Magnolia
Inn

Walnut St

Tobacco
Road

Bridge St

Alpine
Court
Motel

**Post
Office**

Creekside
Court
Motel

Welcome
Center

Spring Creek
Tavern

Gentry
Hardware

Mosiac
Gourmet

Spring St

Bluff Mountain
Outfitter

Library

Iron Horse
Station

ArtiSun
Gallery

S. Andrews Ave

Springbrook
Cottages

Hot Springs Resort
& Campground

70

25

Post Office to:
Hostel at Laughing
Heart Lodge   (0.4 mi)

French Broad River

Weaverville
& Asheville

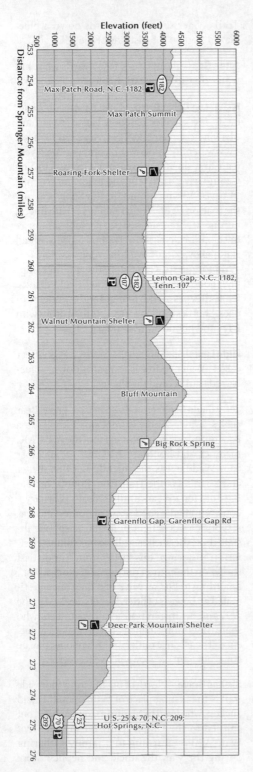

owner Carolyn Ammons; cabin rates (subject to change) $65D-$85D, $10EAP (up to four). Spring Creek Tavern, 145 Bridge St., (828) 622-0187, no pets. ■ *Groceries:* Bluff Mountain Outfitters and Hillbilly Market (both long-term resupply). ■ *Restaurants:* Smoky Mountain Diner, B/L/D; Mountain Magnolia Inn, D Th–M; Spring Creek Tavern; Ironhorse Station, open weekdays 'til 9 p.m., F–Sa 'til 10, occasional live music; Mosaic Gourmet; ArtiSun Gallery, (828) 539-0030, open 8–8 daily, espresso/coffee bar, Ultimate ice cream, wine bar, free WiFi. ■ *Outfitter:* Bluff Mountain Outfitters, 152 Bridge St. (P.O. Box 114), (828) 622-7162, <www.bluffmountain.com>; owner Wayne Crosby; a full-service outfitter including full resupply, ATM, SoBo GSMNP permits; mail drops accepted. ■ *Internet access:* Library, 170 Bridge St., <www.madisoncountylibrary.net>, (828) 622-3584, 10–6 M–F, 10–2 Sa, $1 computer fee. ■ *Other services:* Hiker laundry service, drop off (behind Mosaic gourmet) or call robin or Joe for pick-up at (828) 206-1799, 10 lbs minimum ($11), $1 for each additional lb.; ATM; Dollar General; Gentry Hardware; massage therapist Glenda Dolbeare, (603) 204-7893.

Southbound permits for Smokies—*Southbounders must have a backcountry permit before entering Great Smoky Mountains National Park (see page 30 for details). Permits can be obtained at Bluff Mountain Outfitters, (828) 622-7162, Sa–Su 9–5.*

Whitewater Rafting—Rafting companies offer guided trips on the French Broad River: Nantahala Outdoor Center, (800) 232-7238; Hot Springs Rafting Co., (877) 530-7238; Blue Ridge Resort, (800) 303-7238.

Hot Springs Spa—(828) 622-7676. At the northern end of town, on the southern bank of the French Broad River, the spa offers baths and massages at the famous therapeutic mineral baths for which the town was named.

Rich Mountain—The firetower was been rehabilitated and is open for viewing.

Spring Mountain Shelter (1938)—Sleeps 5. Privy. Bear cables. The shelter is on the west side of the

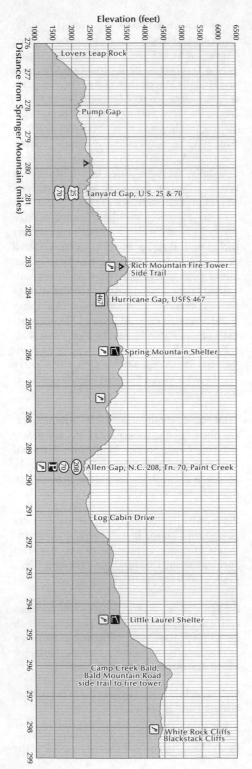

Trail. Water source is 75 yards down a blue-blazed trail on the east side of the A.T.

Allen Gap—Paint Creek is 350 yards west, but water quality is questionable.

Log Cabin Drive—West 0.7 mile to *Lodging:* Hemlock Hollow Hostel, 645 Chandler Circle, Greenville, TN 37743; (423) 787-1736, <www.hemlockhollowinn.com>; open all year (call first during off-season). Go west to Log Cabin Drive. Turn left, and follow for 0.6 mile to paved Viking Mountain Rd. Shop is across the road on right. Heated cabins $55 with linens; bunks, $22; tentsite $15 per person; shower & towel and ride back to Trail included with all stays; shower only, $5; hiker dogs $5/day; free WiFi for guests. Campstore (long-term resupply); good variety of hiker foods, cold drinks, fruit; all types of fuel; first-aid and outfitter supplies. Shuttles available. Accepts mail drops with ETA and phone number on package.

Little Laurel Shelter (1967)—Sleeps 5. Privy. Bear cables. Water source is 100 yards down a blue-blazed trail behind the shelter.

Jerry Cabin Shelter (1968)—Sleeps 6. Privy. Bear cables. Water source is on a small knoll, up a path found on the opposite side of the A.T. CMC member and honorary ALDHA life member Sam Waddle was the caretaker of this shelter and 2.9 miles of the Trail, from Round Knob to Big Butt, for 26 years until his death February 1, 2005. Sam had a good sense of humor and was responsible for a light bulb and telephone installed on the shelter wall. Sam's volunteer efforts transformed this shelter from "the dirtiest shelter on the entire Trail to one of the cleanest," according to Ed Garvey, by hauling out an estimated 20 bushels of litter. He was devoted to the A.T. and an inspiration to all volunteers who share the commitment it takes to make a difference. The electric outlet and telephone may be gone, but Sam's legacy will live forever.

Shelton Grave—North of Big Butt on a short side trail is the resting place of William and David Shelton, who lived in Madison County, N.C., but enlisted in the Union Army during the Civil War. While returning to a family gathering during the war, the uncle and nephew were

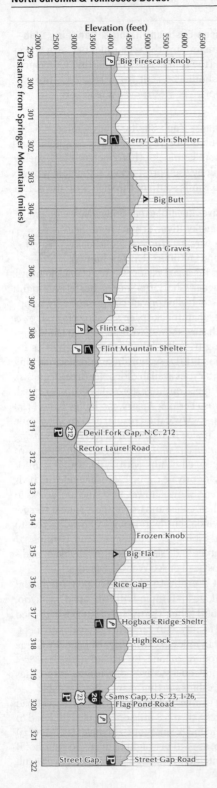

ambushed near here and killed by Confederates. It's a single grave.

Flint Mountain Shelter (1988)—Sleeps 8. Privy. Bear cables. Water source is on the A.T. north of the shelter.

Hogback Ridge Shelter (1986)—Sleeps 6. Privy. Water source is a spring 0.3 mile on a side trail near the shelter.

Sams Gap—*Hostels:* Mother Marian's, owner Marian Smartt, (828) 680-9944, or hostel manager Fred, (828) 231-2736; limited space, 4–6 hikers on first-come basis; free pick-up/return from Big Bald or Sams Gap, $5, bunk $30PP, private room $50D, WiFi, TV with NetFlix, laundry $5 or shower $4 each, area shuttles available, credit/debit cards accepted. Nature's Inn Hostel and Cabins, 4872 Old Asheville Hwy., Flag Pond, TN 37657, (828)-216-1611 or (423)-270-0540, owners Taft and Sara Ring; pet-friendly with dogs leashed at all times; 2 bunkhouses, one sleeps 8, one sleeps 5; creekside cabins, each with 1 queen and 1 twin bunk; private rooms in main hostel, 2 queen rooms, 1 king room; hilltop cabin available; tenting; hammock lodge; tiled bath house; common area with hot food available; short-term resupply; laundry service; call for details and pricing (best after 3 p.m.); credit cards accepted; free shuttle to and from Sam's Gap; quiet time 10 p.m. –7 a.m.; mail drops accepted.

Big Bald—Big Bald offers 360-degree views at an elevation of 5,516 feet. From 1802 to 1834, the bald was inhabited by a cantankerous hermit named David Greer. Spurned by a woman, he retreated to the mountaintop where he lived in a small, cave-like structure (no longer visible). He declared himself sovereign of the mountain and eventually killed a man, only to be acquitted on grounds of insanity. The life of "Hog Greer," called so by the neighbors because he lived like one, ended when a local blacksmith shot him in the back (but was never charged). Greer Bald eventually became known as Big Bald. A golf and ski resort, Wolf Laurel, is clearly visible from the summit. A spring and campsite can be found by following the A.T. 0.2 mile north of the summit to a dirt road and then walking west 0.3 mile down the dirt road.

Bald Mountain Shelter (1988)—Sleeps 10. Privy. One of the highest on the A.T. (5,100 feet). The surrounding area is too fragile for tenting. Water source is a spring on the side trail to the shelter.

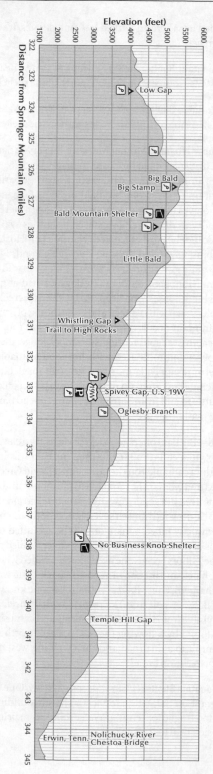

Tennessee Eastman Hiking & Canoeing Club—
TEHC maintains the 133.8 miles between Spivey
Gap and the Tennessee–Virginia line. Correspon-
dence should be sent to TEHC, P.O. Box 511,
Kingsport, TN 37662; <www.tehcc.org>.

No Business Knob Shelter (1963)—Sleeps 6. No
privy. Surrounded by large Fraser magnolias and
mammoth hemlocks, this concrete-block shelter
was built by the Forest Service. Reliable water is
found 0.2 mile south of the shelter on the A.T.

**River Road/Chestoa Bridge/Noli-
chucky River/Erwin, Tenn.** *See
map on page 47.* **Hostels:** Nolichucky
Hostel and Outfitters (Uncle Johnny's);
151 River Rd.; (423) 735-0548, <www.unclejohnnys.
net>; owner Charlotte Shores; hostel $22/night;
climate-controlled private cabins $40–$105, camping $15PP; hammock space $15, showers and towel
free with stay, shower without stay $5; laundry $5
load; dog-friendly; WiFi; free town shuttles for
guests for B/L/D; section-hike and slackpacking
shuttles; bicycles available for $2 fee (free for guests),
fully equipped outfitter store; mail drops accepted.
Cantarroso Farm & Apiary, 777 Bailey Lane, (423)
833-7514, <www.cantarrosofarm.com>, 0.9 mile
west of Chestoa Bridge; open all year *but only taking
in section-hikers and AirBnB guests in 2020.* Two
fully equipped cabins with WiFi, $30PP (2-6) or
$45–$65 for private cabin; cabins include full beds
with linens, shower, towel, heat, and a/c, access to
full kitchen, coffee and tea; upstairs suite, $75–$90;
stays include shuttle to/from Trailhead, access to
river and fishing gear; laundry $5/load, parking $2/
day, shuttles and slackpacking available at additional cost (call or see Web site); no dogs.

West 1.0 mile to Unicoi County Memorial
Hospital, 2030 Temple Hill Rd., (423) 735-4700,
<www.balladhealth.org>, full-service 10-bed
medical facility with 24/7 emergency department.

West 1.3 miles to *Camping:* Nolichucky Gorge
Campground, 101 Jones Branch Rd., (423) 743-8876,
<www.nolichucky.com>, day use $4, campsites
$11.50PP, cabins starting at $95 when available.

West 1.3 miles to *Lodging:* 0.5 mile on River Road
(best hitch), then 0.8 mile on Temple Hill Road to
Mountain Inn & Suites, 2002 Temple Hill Rd.; (423)
743-4100; $79.95D per night (4 max), no pets, hot B
buffet, Internet in lobby, guest coin laundry, hot tub

and swimming pool (both seasonal), parking for section-hikers, mail drops accepted.

West 3.8 miles to **Erwin, Tenn. [P.O. ZIP 37650: M–F 8:30–4:45; Sa 10–12; (423) 743-9422].** ■ *Lodging:* Best Southern Motel, 1315 Jackson Love Hwy., (423) 743-6438, $39.95S, no pets, mail drops accepted; Super 8 Motel, 1101 N. Buffalo St., (423) 743-0200, $56.99S, $64.99D includes B, Internet, no pets, accepts mail drops. ■ *Restaurants:* many: *See map.* ■ *Groceries:* Food Lion, IGA (both long-term resupply); Dollar General (2 locations); and Family Dollar. ■ *Outfitter:* Mahoney's, (423) 282-8889, in Johnson City, 13 miles north. ■ *Internet access:* library; Chamber of Commerce, (423) 743-3000, M–F 8–5, Sa 9–1, also has information on shuttles. ■ *Other services:* banks; ATM; barber; coin laundries; thrift stores; hardware; dentists; 24-hour emergency center; Walgreens; Walmart (4.5 mi. off I-26); shoe repair; movie theater; art gallery; veterinarian.

Whitewater Rafting—Rafting companies offer guided trips on the scenic, free-flowing Nolichucky River: NOC, (800) 232-7238; USA Raft, (800) USA-RAFT; High Mountain Expeditions, (800) 262-9036; Wahoo's Adventures, (800) 444-RAFT, which also provides rafting on Watauga River near Hampton–Elizabethton.

Map labels: Asheville, N.C. (42 mi); River Rd to Temple Hill Rd to Jackson Love Hwy is the best route to Erwin; NOC Nolichucky River Outpost; Nolichucky Hostel; Cantarroso Farm & Apiary; APPCO; Mountain Inn & Suites; Chestoa Pike; Jackson Love Hwy; Post Office to: Best Southern (1.8 mi) Hardee's (1.3 mi); Priceless Foods; Dollar Store; Pizza Plus; Best Southern Motel; ID's Market; Dari Ace; Food Store; River's Edge; Ohio Ave; Elm Ave; Main St; 23; Cherokee Adventures; Hawg-N-Dog; Library; Clinchfield Drug; Visitors Center; Capital Cinema; Shoe Repair; Roller Drug; Love St; Taco Bell; Bojangles; Pal's; Elm Ave; 2nd St; Post Office; McDonald's; Huddle House; Super 8; Walgreens; Laundry; CVS; Food Lion; Family Dollar; 10th St; Laundromat; China Kitchen; Little Caesars; Pizza Hut; KFC; Azteca Mexican; Rocky's; Subway; Dollar General; Rite Aid; ATM; Hardee's; Erwin, Tenn. elevation 1,679'; 26; Walmart (3 mi), Johnson City (16 mi); Wendy's; 107

Curley Maple Gap Shelter (1961, renovated 2010)—Sleeps 12. No privy. Water source is a spring south on the A.T.

Unaka Mountain—With a large stand of red spruce atop its 5,180-foot summit, Unaka will remind southbounders of the Maine woods. Unaka is the Cherokee word for "white."

Cherry Gap Shelter (1962)—Sleeps 6. No privy. Water source is a spring found 80 yards on a blue-blazed trail from the shelter. *Cherry Gap Shelter will be rebuilt in 2021 in partnership with TEHCC and Elizabethton High School; new shelter will accommodate 14.*

Tenn. 107, N.C. 226/Iron Mountain Gap—**East** 3 miles to *Groceries:* Buladean Shell Gas & Grocery (short-term resupply), (828) 628-4850, Su–Sa 7 a.m.–8 p.m., with made-to-order sandwiches, ice cream, and Coleman fuel; Mountain Grill, (828) 688-9061, M–Sa L/D 11 a.m.-8 p.m., closed Sunday; Dollar General, (828) 688-4473, open daily 7–10.
West 10.3 miles to **Unicoi, Tenn. [P.O. ZIP 37692: M–F 8:45–12 & 1–3:45 Sa 8:30–10:30; (423) 743-4945]**, with Clarence's Restaurant B/L/D, Maple Grove Restaurant, minimarts, and a doctor.

Greasy Creek Gap—**East** 0.6 mile to *Hostel:* Greasy Creek Friendly (short-term resupply), 1827 Greasy Creek Rd., Bakerville, NC 28705; (828) 688-9948; <greasycreekfriendly.com>; bunkhouse $15PP, one room (twin beds) $20PP, camping $7.50PP, includes shower/towel/soap for guests; nonguest shower $3; pup shed $15, bed on front porch from Apr 15 to Oct 15 $15, limited use of kitchen; shuttle, laundry

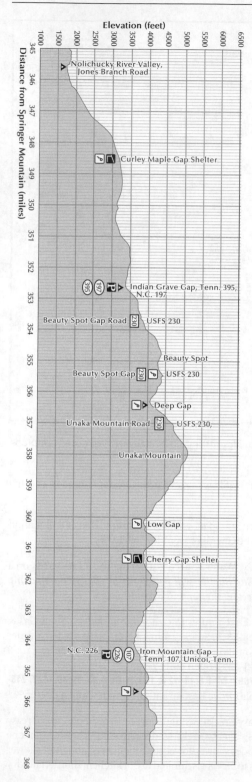

for guests, prepared meals, ice cream, fuel, Internet; no dogs inside. Free evening shuttle for guests to Dollar General, M–Sa. Accepts credit cards and mail drops. *Directions*: At gap, opposite blue-blaze, go through campsite "down" old dirt road past old barns through service gate to first house on right.

Clyde Smith Shelter (1976)—Sleeps 10. No privy. Water source is a spring 100 yards behind the shelter on a blue-blaze. New roof and porch.

Roan Mountain—For northbounders, this will be the last time the A.T. climbs above 6,000 feet until Mt. Washington in New Hampshire. At the top is a parking area, with restroom and running water (May–Oct). Roan Mountain is arguably the coldest spot, year-round, on the southern A.T. Upon reaching the top of the main climb (for northbounders), enter a clearing, and pass the foundation of the former Cloudland Hotel. The state line ran through the center of the hotel's ballroom when Cloudland was a thriving resort during the late 1800s and early 1900s. It was demolished in 1915, after loggers harvested the fir and spruce on the mountaintop. Much of the Catawba rhododendron was dug up and sold to ornamental nurseries. The remaining rhododendron flourished and covered the slopes of Roan, hence the famous rhododendron gardens. The peak blooming time is usually around Jun 20. The gardens can be reached by taking the Forest Service road (visible from the hotel foundation) west, uphill, along the top of the mountain, where an information station is located.

Roan High Knob Shelter (1980)—Sleeps 15. No privy. The highest shelter on the A.T. (6,275 feet). Originally a firewarden's cabin. The loft is known to leak. An unreliable water source can be found on a 100-yard blue-blaze near the shelter. More reliable sources are south on the A.T. at the Roan Mountain restroom, when open, or a spring at Carvers Gap picnic area, 1.3 miles north.

Gray's lily—A protected, red, nodding lily can be seen blooming on the slopes of Round Bald, Grassy Ridge, and Hump Mountain in Jun–

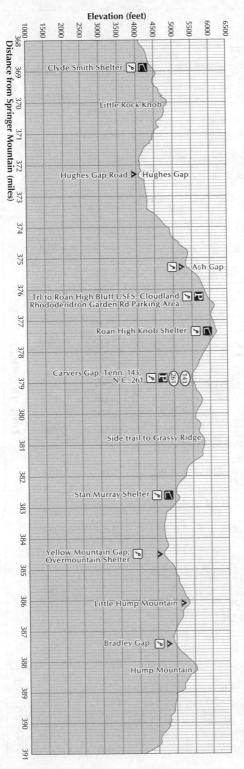

early Jul. Named for botanist Asa Gray, who found it in the 1840s. He called the Roan, "without a doubt, the most beautiful mountain east of the Rockies."

Roan Mountain to Hump Mountain—Between Roan Mountain and Hump Mountain, the Trail crosses several balds. Round Bald (5,826 feet) is the site of a USFS experiment in which goats were used to keep briars and brambles from encroaching on the bald. Although the southern Appalachians do not rise above treeline, they have many balds, the origins of which remains a mystery. Some point to the harsh conditions at high elevations, while others claim Indians cleared the mountains for religious ceremonies. Many cite extensive grazing and cropping. The 6,189-foot summit of Grassy Ridge is reached by following a side trail east before the A.T. begins its descent off the ridge to Stan Murray Shelter. It is the only natural 360-degree viewpoint above 6,000 feet near the Trail. (Clingmans Dome has its observation tower, and Mt. Washington's summit in New Hampshire is covered with buildings.) To avoid potential damage to endangered species, please do *not* camp between the summit and the southern peak. For northbounders, the A.T. veers west from the state line into Tennessee at Doll Flats, where it remains until crossing into Virginia south of Damascus.

N.C. 261/Tenn. 143/Carvers Gap—Picnic area and parking area with restrooms; piped spring beyond restrooms. North out of Carvers Gap, the Trail has been relocated with switchbacks to control erosion and heal the scar of the old treadway. Please stay on the treadway to allow this area time to recover.

Stan Murray Shelter (1977)—Sleeps 6. No privy. Formerly the Roan Highlands Shelter, this shelter was renamed for the former ATC chair and originator of the Appalachian Greenway concept. Water source is a spring on a blue-blazed trail opposite the shelter.

Overmountain Shelter—The shelter is closed this year for structural-safety reasons. Camping is still allowed at least 40' feet away from the building. Privy. Water source is a spring found to the left once you reach the old road before the shelter.

Tennessee

Miles from Springer	Miles to Next Point	Features	Services	Elev	Miles from Katahdin	M A P

395.3	0.2	U.S. 19E, Buck Creek
		East–2.5m to **Elk Park, N.C., P.O. 28622**
		West–0.3m to Mountain Harbour B&B and Hostel
		   West–2m to restaurant (pizza/subs)
		   West–2.5m to Dollar General
		   West–3.4m to **Roan Mountain, Tenn., P.O. 37687**
		   West–7.5m to Roan Mountain State Park
			R, P
			G, M
			H, C, L, sh, f
			M
			G
			G, M, D, V
			
			C, L, sh
				2,880'	1,797.7	

395.5	2.7	Bear Branch Road ...*bridge*	R	2,900'	1,797.5	
398.2	0.4	Isaacs Cemetery		3,600'	1,794.8	
398.6	0.3	Buck Mountain Road	R	3,340'	1,794.4	
398.9	0.7	Campbell Hollow Road	R, P	3,393'	1,794.1	
399.6	1.1	Spring	w	3,430'	1,793.4	
400.7	0.7	Side trail to Jones Falls *(E–0.1m)*	w	2,997'	1,792.3	
401.4	0.3	Elk River ...*southern junction*	w	2,703'	1,791.6	
401.7	0.4	Sugar Hollow Stream Campsite	C, w	3,590'	1,791.3	
402.1	1.8	Elk River ...*northern junction*	w	2,675'	1,790.9	ATC Tenn.–N.C. Map 2
403.9	0.2	Mountaineer Falls Campsite ...*west on blue blaze*	C, w	3,137'	1,789.1	
404.1	0.8	**Mountaineer Falls Shelter** ...*18.3mS; 9.6mN*	S, w	3,470'	1,788.9	
404.9	0.8	Campsite ...*east on blue blaze*	C	3,260'	1,788.1	
405.7	1.2	Walnut Mountain Road ...*gravel*	R, P	3,583'	1,787.3	
406.9	0.5	Stream	w	3,400'	1,786.1	
407.4	0.5	Viewpoint ...*memorial bench (W–0.2m to Vango Solar Hostel)*	H	3,350'	1,785.6	
407.9	1.0	Upper Laurel Fork ...*footbridge (W–0.3m to Vango Solar Hostel)*	H, w	3,290'	1,785.1	
408.9	0.8	USFS 293 at "Bitter End"		3,590'	1,784.1	
409.7	0.9	Stream	w	3,840'	1,783.3	
410.6	2.4	Stream and campsite ...*100 yards south of large rock*	C, w	3,920'	1,782.4	
413.0	0.7	White Rocks Mountain		4,121'	1,780.0	
413.7	1.2	**Moreland Gap Shelter** ...*9.6mS; 8.2mN*	S, C, w	3,813'	1,779.3	
414.9	0.9	Crest of White Rocks Mountain	R	4,206'	1,778.1	
415.8	0.3	Campsite ...*west on blue-blaze to water*	C, w	3,700'	1,777.2	
416.1	0.1	Forest Road to Lacy Trapp Trail/USFS 36 *(E–0.1m); (W–4m to U.S. 19E)*	R	3,800'	1,776.9	
416.2	2.1	Powerline		3,760'	1,776.8	
418.3	1.7	Trail to Coon Den Falls		2,660'	1,774.7	

420.0	0.1	Dennis Cove, USFS 50
		   East–0.4m to Kincora Hiking Hostel
		
		   West–0.2m to Black Bear Resort
			R, P, w
			H, C, G, L, cl, f
			H, C, G, L, cl, f
				2,510'	1,773.0	Tenn.–N.C. Map 1

420.1	0.2	Campsite near "Wye" ...*two small bridges*	C, w	2,510'	1,772.9	
420.3	0.5	Pond Mountain Wilderness Boundary		2,440'	1,772.7	

Miles from Springer	Miles to Next Point	Features	Services	Elev	Miles from Katahdin	M A P
420.8	0.3	Koonford Bridge over Laurel Fork	w	2,420'	1,772.2	
421.1	0.1	High water bypass to Laurel Fork Shelter (E-0.5m) ...southern junction	S	2,200'	1,771.9	
421.2	0.7	Laurel Fork Falls, Laurel Fork Gorge	w	2,120'	1,771.8	
421.9	0.3	Laurel Fork Shelter (E-300 ft.) ...8.2mS; 15.8mN High water bypass northern junction	S, w	2,450'	1,771.1	
422.2	0.1	Waycaster Spring ...footbridge	w	1,900'	1,770.8	
422.3	0.2	Footbridge over stream	w	1,900'	1,770.7	
422.5	0.2	Footbridge over stream	w	1,900'	1,770.5	
422.7	2.5	Hampton Blueline Trail to U.S. 321 West-0.8m to **Hampton, Tenn., P.O. 37658**	w G, L, M, D, f	2,000'	1,770.3	
425.2	0.3	Spring	w	3,650'	1,767.8	
425.5	2.6	Pond Flats ...campsite, east to "pond"	C, w	3,700'	1,767.5	
428.1	0.4	Pond Mountain Wilderness Boundary ... campsite	C	2,200'	1,764.9	
428.5	0.1	Shook Branch Road ...gravel, campsite West 0.1m to Boots Off Hostel & Cmpgrnd	R, C H	2,000'	1,764.5	
		BEAR CLOSURE AREA **North to Wilbur Dam Road**				
428.6	1.5	U.S. 321, Shook Branch Picnic Area West-1.2m to Dividing Ridge Hiker Campground West-2m to **Hampton, Tenn., P.O. 37658** West-9m to **Elizabethton, Tenn.**	R, P, w C, sh G, L, M, D, f G, L, M, D, V, cl	1,990'	1,764.4	A T C Tenn.–N.C. Map 1
430.1	0.4	Griffith Branch	w	2,100'	1,762.9	
430.5	0.9	Stream	w	2,091'	1,762.5	
431.4	0.3	Watauga Dam water inlet tower		2,000'	1,761.6	
431.7	0.3	Watauga Dam (north end), Lookout Road		1,915'	1,761.3	
432.0	0.5	Side Trail To Watauga Dam Visitor Center (E-0.5m)	w	2,100'	1,761.0	
432.5	0.5	Minor Summit ...view of Watauga Lake		2,480'	1,760.5	
433.0	1.0	Wilbur Dam Road (E-0.9m to Dam Visitor Center) Big Laurel Branch Wilderness ... southern boundary	R, P, w	2,240'	1,760.0	
434.0	2.0	Knob ...follow narrow crest of Iron Mtn		3,000'	1,759.0	
436.0	1.7	Spring	w	3,360'	1,757.0	
437.7	1.4	**Vandeventer Shelter** (W-0.3m spring) ...15.8mS; 6.8mN	S, w	3,510'	1,755.3	
439.1	2.4	Big Laurel Branch Wilderness ...northern boundary		3,600'	1,753.9	
441.5	1.4	Spring ...tentsites 175 yards north	C, w	3,900'	1,751.5	
442.9	0.6	Turkeypen Gap		3,970'	1,750.1	
443.5	0.3	Iron Mountain high point		4,190'	1,749.5	
443.8	0.5	Powerlines		4,100'	1,749.2	
444.3	0.2	Spring ...water for Iron Mountain Shelter	w	4,000'	1,748.7	
444.5	1.3	**Iron Mountain Shelter** ...6.8mS; 7.6mN	S, C, nw	4,125'	1,748.5	

Miles from Springer	Miles to Next Point	Features	Services	Elev	Miles from Katahdin	M A P
445.8	0.1	Nick Grindstaff Monument		4,090'	1,747.2	
445.9	0.4	Spring *(W–100 yds.)*	w	4,090'	1,747.1	
446.3	1.0	High Point		4,120'	1,746.7	
447.3	1.0	Top of rise in ridge		3,750'	1,745.7	
448.3	0.9	Cross two streams *...100 yards apart on bog bridges*	w	3,500'	1,744.7	
449.2	0.8	Tenn. 91, Cross Mountain Road *...ridgecrest*	R, P	3,450'	1,743.8	
		East–2.5m to Switchback Creek Cmpgrnd	C, L, cl			
450.0	1.3	Edge of woods on old Osborne Farm		3,600'	1,743.0	
451.3	0.9	Campsite *...spring*	C, w	3,990'	1,741.7	
452.2	0.5	**Double Springs Shelter** *...7.6mS; 8.3mN* Holston Mountain Trail Jct.	S, C, w	4,080'	1,740.8	ATC Tenn.–N.C. Map 1
452.7	2.9	Locust Knob		4,020'	1,740.3	
455.6	0.1	Campsite *...near old homesite*	C	3,480'	1,737.4	
455.7	1.0	Low Gap, U.S. 421 *...picnic table, spring* *East–2.7m to* **Shady Valley, Tenn., P.O. 37688**	R, P, w G, M	3,384'	1,737.3	
456.7	0.9	Minor summit		3,643'	1,736.3	
457.6	1.4	Double Spring Gap *...unreliable water source*	w	3,650'	1,735.4	
459.0	0.1	McQueens Knob *...former fire tower site*		3,885'	1,734.0	
459.1	0.3	McQueens Knob Shelter *...**emergency use only***		3,900'	1,733.9	
459.4	1.1	McQueens Gap, USFS 69	R	3,653'	1,733.6	
460.5	5.4	**Abingdon Gap Shelter** *(E–0.2m spring)* *...8.3mS; 20mN*	S, C, w	3,773'	1,732.5	
465.9	1.1	Backbone Rock Trail *(E–3m to USFS Recreation Area)*		3,466'	1,727.1	
467.0	1.0	Tennessee–Virginia State Line *...Mt. Rogers N.R.A. sign*		3,300'	1,726.0	

Here, you will stroll along the Elk River, pass Jones and Mountaineer falls, see the impressive 50-foot Laurel Falls in the Pond Mountain Wilderness, look over the 16-mile-long Watauga Reservoir, and climb Iron Mountain. *Water sources between Wilbur Dam Road and Tenn. 91 often are unreliable in late summer.*

U.S. 19E—Numerous incidents of vandalism have been reported at this parking area. Overnight parking not recommended.

East 0.7 mile to *Hostel:* The Station @ 19E, 9369 U.S. 19E, Roan Mountain, TN 37687, (423) 250-3700, <www.thestationat193.com>, <thestationat19e@gmail.com>, open year-round, serving B/L/D, outfitter and resupply, $30PP, 3 private rooms and 28 bunks, includes clean linens, shower, laundry, shuttle to/from trail (call/text), slackpack options, mail drops accepted.

East 2.5 miles to **Elk Park, N.C. [P.O. ZIP 28622: M–F 9–12:30 & 1:30–4, Sa 8–11:30; (828) 733-5711].** ■ *Restaurants:* Betty & Carol's Place, cash & take-out only, Tu Th–Sa 11–7:30, W 11–6; Sissy's Country House, M–Sa 6:30–11, Su 7:30–2. ■ *Other services:* Hardware store with Coleman fuel, fuel canisters, and denatured by the ounce; Dollar General; mini-mart.

West 0.3 mile to *Lodging:* Mountain Harbour B&B and Hiker Hostel, 9151 Highway 19E, Roan Mountain, TN 37687; (866) 772-9494; <www.mountainharbour.net>. Hostel open year-round; hiker cabin/hostel over barn $25PP, semiprivate king bed $55; includes linens, shower with towel, microwave and fridge, and long-term resupply available at general store. Tent sites $10 includes shower, B&B rooms $125–$165; private treehouse with queen bed, $75. Shower

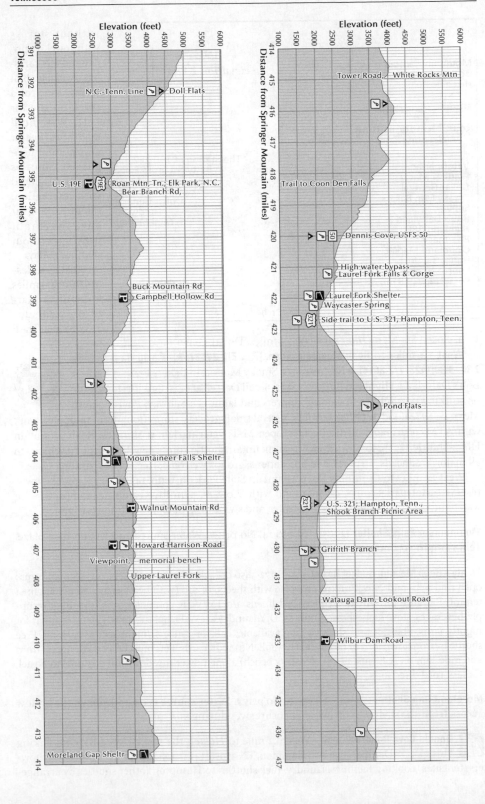

Elevation (feet)

Distance from Springer Mountain (miles)

N.C.-Tenn. Line — Doll Flats

U.S. 19E — Roan Mtn, Tn.; Elk Park, N.C.
Bear Branch Rd,

Buck Mountain Rd
Campbell Hollow Rd

Mountaineer Falls Sheltr

Walnut Mountain Rd

Howard Harrison Road
Viewpoint, memorial bench
Upper Laurel Fork

Moreland Gap Sheltr

Elevation (feet)

Distance from Springer Mountain (miles)

Tower Road, White Rocks Mtn

Trail to Coon Den Falls

Dennis Cove, USFS 50

High water bypass
Laurel Fork Falls & Gorge

Laurel Fork Shelter
Waycaster Spring
Side trail to U.S. 321; Hampton, Teen.

Pond Flats

U.S. 321; Hampton, Tenn.,
Shook Branch Picnic Area

Griffith Branch

Watauga Dam, Lookout Road

Wilbur Dam Road

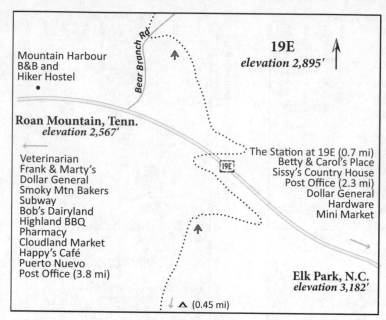

Mountain Harbour
B&B and
Hiker Hostel
•

Bear Branch Rd.

19E
elevation 2,895'

Roan Mountain, Tenn.
elevation 2,567'

←————

Veterinarian
Frank & Marty's
Dollar General
Smoky Mtn Bakers
Subway
Bob's Dairyland
Highland BBQ
Pharmacy
Cloudland Market
Happy's Café
Puerto Nuevo
Post Office (3.8 mi)

[19E]

The Station at 19E (0.7 mi)
Betty & Carol's Place
Sissy's Country House
Post Office (2.3 mi)
Dollar General
Hardware
Mini Market

Elk Park, N.C.
elevation 3,182'

↓ ▲ (0.45 mi)

without stay $5 with towel. Laundry and fuel canisters available; B at times, $12; food truck on site for L/D. Will hold mail drops (free for guests, $5 for non-guests). Shuttles priced by trailhead with reservation, shuttle parking $2/day; overnight parking without shuttle, $10/day.

West to ■ *Restaurant:* 2.0 miles to Frank & Marty's, pizza/subs T–W Sa 4–9, Th–F

11–9, closed Su–M. ■ *Other services:* 2.5 miles, Dollar General.

West 3.4 miles to **Roan Mountain, Tenn. [P.O. ZIP 37687: M–F 8:00–12 & 1–4, Sa 7:30–9:30; (423) 772-3014].** ■ *Restaurants:* Smoky Mountain Bakers Pizza, T–Sa 8–8; Bob's Dairyland; Highland BBQ, W–Sa 11–8, call Darrell at (423) 895-3013 for shuttle or bunking possibilities (including showers and laundry); Subway; Puerto Nuevo Mexican & Seafood. ■ *Other services:* several small grocery stores (long-term resupply); bank with ATM; pharmacy; medical center, open M–F; veterinarian. ■ *Shuttles:* Roan Mountain Hiker Shuttle, (423) 250-3700, <www.roanmountainshuttle.com>; new, fully insured vehicles to all major Trailheads, airports, and bus stations; groups welcome; free, secure parking.

West 7.5 miles to *Camping:* Roan Mountain State Park on Tenn. 143, (423) 772-0190; <www.reserve.tnstateparks.com>, campground with showers, primitive campsite, campsites with water and electricity, cabins; visitors center, and swimming pool. Reservations suggested.

Mountaineer Falls Shelter (2005)—Sleeps 14. No privy. Water source 200 feet on blue-blaze. Tent camping 0.2 mile south of the shelter.

Scotty's Roan Mountin Budget Hostel—(423) 772-3450 or (423) 772-5589, <hikerscotty@gmail.com>; open mid-Feb–mid-Nov. Bunkroom $5 ($6 with sheets) or $10 (with heat) suggested donation; $1 tenting. Private room with deck, queen bed, linens, a/c, TV/VCR, computer, $30S–40D. Basic resupply, beverages, stove fuels; showers only $3, DIY laundry $5, WiFi, hot tub, porch piano & guitar for nightly jams. Shuttles and slackpacking available; call for rates; $1/night secure parking. Free shuttle to/from town for 3 or more and Hwy 19E. No credit cards. Pets must be leashed. Access from 406 mile sign on A.T. (just north of vista & bench) along powerline, downhill 0.25 mile to hostel. Call for road directions.

Moreland Gap Shelter (1960)—Sleeps 6. No privy. Water source is 0.2 mile down the hollow across from the shelter. Northwest exposure; wet during storms.

 Dennis Cove Road/USFS 50—West 0.2 mile to *Hostel:* the never-closed Kincora Hiking Hostel, 1278 Dennis Cove Rd., Hampton, TN 37658; (423) 725-4409, with bunkroom, showers, tentsites, cooking facilities, laundry, fuel, shuttles to Hampton (other shuttles by arrange-

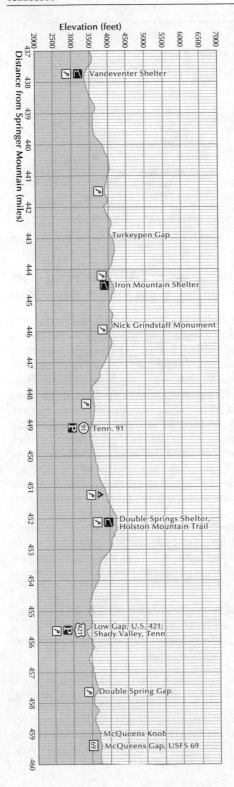

Elevation (feet)

Distance from Springer Mountain (miles)

Vandeventer Shelter

Turkeypen Gap

Iron Mountain Shelter

Nick Grindstaff Monument

Tenn. 91

Double Springs Shelter;
Holston Mountain Trail

Low Gap, U.S. 421;
Shady Valley, Tenn.

Double Spring Gap

McQueens Knob
McQueens Gap, USFS 69

ment), $5/night donation; owner Bob Peoples holds packages for guests ($5 nonguests). No dogs, alcohol, or drugs allowed. Plan to arrive before 10 p.m.

East 0.4 mile to *Lodging:* Black Bear Resort, 1511 Dennis Cove Road, Hampton, TN 37658; (423) 725-5988, <www.blackbearresorttn.com>. Creekside resort with bunkroom $25 includes shower, towel and laundry; tent or hammock starting at $10PP; rustic cabins $60–$76 for up to 4, $15–$19EAP (6 max). Courtesy phone, Internet access, movies (DVD), free morning coffee for guests. Camp store with long-term resupply items, snacks, pizza, beer, sodas, ice cream, and food that can be prepared on-site with microwave or stove. Laundry and showers only, $5. Fuel by ounce & canister. Pet-friendly, accepts credit cards ($5 minimum). Parking $3/night for nonguests. Shuttles. Mail drops (nonguest fee $5) accepted. Prices subject to change.

Laurel Fork Falls—The Trail passes within sight of this waterfall, under which two hikers, father and son, drowned in 2012. Be careful if swimming or wading; the undertows are dangerous.

Laurel Fork Shelter (1977)—Sleeps 8. No privy. Constructed from native rocks, shelter is located on the blue-blazed high-water route above the Laurel Fork. Water source is a stream 50 yards behind the shelter.

Shook Branch Road—**West** 0.1 mi to *Hostel:* Boots Off Hostel & Campground, 142 Shook Branch Rd., (239) 218-3904., owner Jim Gregory. Bunkhouse $25+tax, tent/hammock $12. Cabin up to 3, $60+ tax, $10EAP. All stays include AC/heat, continental B, shower ($5 w/o stay), use of kitchen, WiFi, evening town shuttle ($5 w/o stay). Other shuttles from Sams Gap to Damascus for a fee. Pet friendly; call ahead (before coming up driveway). Mail drops accepted ($5 w/o stay). Lake recreational equipment available. Inquire about aqua-blaze.

BEAR CLOSURE NOTICE

National forest lands around Watauga Lake are closed to most recreation from north of Shook Branch (U.S. 321) to Wilbur Dam Rd., including former site of Watauga Lake Shelter. No picnicking, lingering, or overnight camping. Only hiking is allowed on this 4-mile section of Trail. Please use

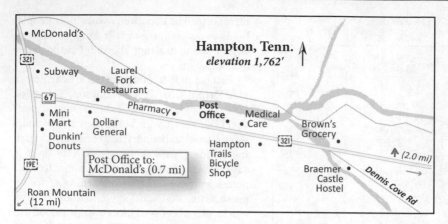

caution while hiking through and do not stop. This closure is effective until further notice. See page xiii.

U.S. 321— West 1.2 miles to Dividing Ridge Hiker Campground, 1219 Highway 321, (423) 957-0821. Open only in May. Tenting by donation, includes shower and local transportation. Outdoor pavilion with WiFi.

West 2 miles to **Hampton, Tenn. [P.O. ZIP 37658: M–F 7:30–11:30 & 12:30–4:00, Sa 8–10; (423) 725-2177].** ■ *Lodging:* Braemar Castle Hostel and Guest House, (423) 725-2411 or 725-2262. Sutton and Beverly Brown offer hiker space ($15), kitchen, showers, WiFi, laundry ($5), and private single rooms ($25). Iron Mountain Inn B&B, (423) 768-2446, <www.ironmountaininn.com>; private room and bath $100D, includes B. Creekside Chalet, same phone as Iron Mountain Inn, <www.creeksidechalet.net>, $50PP includes hot tub on deck, pet-friendly, call from Hampton or Tenn. 91 for pick-up, inquire about slackpacking. ■ *Restaurants:* Laurel Fork Restaurant, M–Sa 7–7, Su 7–4; Dunkin' Donuts, McDonald's; Subway. ■ *Groceries:* Brown's Grocery, 613 U.S. 321, (423) 725-2411, long-term resupply, closed Su; check with Sutton at the grocery store for accommodations; Coleman fuel, denatured alcohol, and canisters; holds USPS and UPS packages. ■ *Other services:* Dollar General, convenience stores, health clinic, banks, and ATM. **Shuttles:** Hampton Trails Bicycle Shop, (423) 725-5000 or (423) 957-9847, owner Brian White, <www.hamptontrails.com>, <brian@hamptontrails.com>. *Note: Best access to Hampton from the A.T. is the 0.8-mile blue-blaze in Laurel Gorge, 1.5 miles downstream from Laurel Falls.*

West 9 miles to **Elizabethton, Tenn.** ■ *Lodging:* Travelers Inn, (423) 543-3344, $59.99, continental B, coin laundry, pool (seasonal); Americourt Hotel, (423) 542-4466, <americourthotels.com>, located on U.S. 19E, $60 hiker rate (except black-out days) includes B, WiFi, Internet. ■ *Groceries:* Food City, Walmart. ■ *Internet access:* library. ■ *Other services:* restaurants, convenience stores, hospital, bank, veterinarian, laundry, and ATM.

Shook Branch Recreation Area—This developed area on Watauga Lake offers picnic tables, a restroom, and a beach for swimming. This is a fee area, and water is turned on after the last freeze of spring (usually by late Apr). Please be considerate of rules and regulations when entering the recreation area. Regulations are posted at the information board near the fee tube.

Watauga Lake Shelter (1980)—*Dismantled and removed due to bear activity.* Water source is on A.T., south of the former shelter area (if dry, follow stream up to small pool). No camping.

Watauga Dam—The A.T. crosses the Watauga River on this dam at Watauga Lake. Hiking north, as the Trail leaves the road, a side trail leads 0.5 mile to a visitors center with restroom, often closed during cold-weather months. It also can be reached by following Wilbur Dam Road 0.9 mile east.

Vandeventer Shelter (1961)—Sleeps 6. No privy. Water source is 0.3 mile down a steep, blue-blazed trail south of the shelter.

Iron Mountain Shelter (1960)—Sleeps 6. No privy. Water source is a spring 500 yards south on A.T.

Nick Grindstaff Monument—Nick Grindstaff traveled west to win his fortune but was robbed of all his money during the journey. He then returned to Iron Mountain, where he lived for more than 40 years as one of the region's most famous hermits. He died in 1923, and the plaque on the chimney was erected in 1925.

Tenn. 91/Cross Mountain Road—East 1.9 miles to The Rabbit Hole, A Home for Hikers, 391 Hopper Road, Shady Valley, TN 37688, (423) 739-3391, < homeforhikers@gmail.com>. Owners Rabbit and Kat welcome you to this family-friendly campground. Free pick-up and drop off from Tenn. 91 trailhead. Tents $10PP, bunkhouse $25PP, private cabin $50 for first person $10EAP. Laundry $4/load, showers $3 w/o stay. Day pass available for $10, includes shower, laundry, charging ports, all hostel grounds, and a milkshake (day pass expires at 8 p.m.). Shuttles to local restaurant $5 per carload, includes pickup. Milkshakes starting at $3 (vanilla, chocolate, cookies 'n cream, *etc.* Parking $2 a day w/ stay, $4 a day w/o stay. Slackpack options available from Hampton to Damascus. Shuttles available to destinations within 100 miles. Pets welcomed; $5 cleaning fee for pets kept in bunkhouse. For more info: <www.facebook.com/homeforhikers>.

East 2.5 miles to Switchback Creek Campground, (407) 484-3388. Open Apr 1–late Oct. Tenting $10, cabin $40D, $10 for 1 extra person. Shower included; laundry $5. Call for directions. Credit cards accepted. Can pick up from Cross Mountain Rd. or U.S. 421/Low Gap or Shady Valley Country Store.

East 10 miles on Va./Tenn. 91 to Mountain City, Tenn., and **Appalachian Folk School**, (423) 341-1843, <www.warrendoyle.com>. Warren Doyle (ALDHA founder; 18 A.T. traverses) offers work-for-stay for hikers who have a spiritual/poetic connection to the entire white-blazed Trail (M–Th only), Mar 23–Apr 8, May 11–17 (Trail Days), Jun 18–Jul 6, Sep 26–Nov 8; 2-3 hours of work for each night. Kitchen privileges, shower, WiFi. Rides to and from the Trail for work-for-stays between U.S. 321 (Watauga Lake) and Va. 603 (Fox Creek). No smoking, alcohol, drugs, or pets.

Double Springs Shelter (1960)—Sleeps 6. No privy. Water source is a spring located 100 yards in the draw beyond the shelter.

U.S. 421/Low Gap—A piped spring is located in the gap, on the A.T. **East** 2.7 miles to **Shady Valley, Tenn.** [P.O. ZIP 37688: M–F 8–12, Sa 8–10; (423) 739-2073]. ■ *Groceries:* Shady Valley Country Store & Deli, (423) 739-2325, open daily Apr 21–Thanksgiving Eve, short-term resupply. ■ *Restaurant:* Raceway, (423) 739-2499, open daily, closes W & Su at 2.

McQueens Knob Shelter (1934)—Sleeps 2 (if that). No privy. This shelter is one of the A.T.'s oldest. Not up to current standards, it is intended *for emergency use only,* and, even then, the unchinked walls allow for the weather to easily enter. No water at this site.

Abingdon Gap Shelter (1959)—Sleeps 5. No privy. Water source is a spring 0.2 mile east on a steep, blue-blazed side trail, downhill behind the shelter.

Tennessee/Virginia State Line—You're entering or leaving Virginia when you see the Mt. Rogers National Recreation Area sign, which is on the state line.

Virginia—Part 1 (Southwest)

Miles from Springer	Miles to Next Point	Features	Services	Elev	Miles from Katahdin	M A P
467.0	1.0	Tennessee–Virginia State Line ...*Mt. Rogers N.R.A. sign*		3,300'	1,726.0	
468.0	0.6	Campsite	C		1,725.0	
468.6	1.6	Spring ... *downhill (E–250 yds.)*	w	2,600'	1,724.4	
470.2	0.1	Mock Ave. and Water St.		1,975'	1,722.8	
470.3	0.3	Gravel path ...*through town park*		1,960'	1,722.7	
470.6	0.1	Beaverdam Creek ...*bridge*	P	1,928'	1,722.4	
470.7		U.S. 58, Laurel Ave., Damascus Town Hall On A.T.–**Damascus, Va., P.O. 24236** *East–10m on* Va./Tenn. 91 to Appalachian Folk School *West–2m to* veterinarian *West–12m to* Abingdon, Va.	R, P H, G, L, M, O, D, cl, sh, f work for stay V all	1,928'	1,722.3	
471.7	1.9	U.S. 58/Va. 91, Virginia Creeper Trail ... *steps*	R	1,928'	1,721.3	
473.6	0.6	Cuckoo Knob		2,920'	1,719.4	
474.2	1.5	Iron Mountain Trail, Feathercamp Ridge		2,850'	1,718.8	
475.7	0.5	Beech Grove Trail		2,490'	1,717.3	
476.2	0.1	Feathercamp Trail, Feathercamp Branch	w	2,330'	1,716.8	
476.3	1.4	U.S. 58 at Straight Branch Creek ...*picnic area, privy*	R, P, w	2,310'	1,716.7	
477.7	0.6	Creek ...*log bridge above small falls*	w	2,490'	1,715.3	
478.3	1.4	Taylors Valley Side Trail *East–0.7m on* Virginia Creeper Trail	M, w	2,400'	1,714.7	
479.7	0.2	South side trail to **Saunders Shelter** *(W–0.3m)* ...*20mS; 0.8mN*	S, w	3,310'	1,713.3	
479.9	0.3	Straight Mountain		3,440'	1,713.1	
480.2	2.3	North side trail to **Saunders Shelter** *(W–300 yds.)* ...*0.8mS; 6.5mN*	S, w	3,310'	1,712.8	
482.5	0.2	Beartree Gap Trail ... *to USFS Beartree Recreation Area* *West–0.6m to* bathouse, lake, swimming area *West–3.6m to* campground	P, w, sh C, w, sh	3,050'	1,710.5	
482.7	1.5	Campsite ...*small pond, spring*	C, w	3,020'	1,710.3	
484.2	0.1	Junction with Virginia Creeper Trail		2,700'	1,708.8	
484.3	0.6	Creek Junction Station to Va. 728 ...*old railroad bed (E–0.5m P, privy)*	R	2,720'	1,708.7	
484.9	0.6	Virginia Creeper Trail, Whitetop Laurel Creek ...*Luther Hassinger Memorial Bridge*	R, P	2,690'	1,708.1	
485.5	0.2	Va. 859, Grassy Ridge Road	R	2,900'	1,707.5	
485.7	0.6	Streams	w	3,040'	1,707.3	
486.3	0.4	Lost Mountain		3,400'	1,706.7	
486.7	1.1	**Lost Mountain Shelter** ...*6.5mS; 12.4mN*	S, w	3,360'	1,706.3	
487.8	0.4	U.S. 58; Summit Cut, Va.	R	3,160'	1,705.2	
488.2	0.9	Campsites near stream	C, w	3,300'	1,704.8	

Miles from Springer	Miles to Next Point	Features	Services	Elev	Miles from Katahdin	MAP
489.1	2.5	Va. 601, Beech Mountain Road ...*reliable boxed spring*	R, P, w	3,530'	1,703.9	
491.6	0.8	Buzzard Rock on Whitetop Mountain		5,080'	1,701.4	
492.4	0.1	Spring ...*piped (east)*	w	5,100'	1,700.6	
492.5	2.4	Whitetop Mountain Road, USFS 89 to summit (5,520')	R, P, C	5,150'	1,700.5	
494.9	0.5	Va. 600, Elk Garden, Whitetop, Va.	R, P, privy	4,458'	1,698.1	
495.4	1.4	Lewis Fork Wilderness Boundary		4,640'	1,697.6	
496.8	0.1	Campsite ...*blue blaze (east)*	C	4,850'	1,696.2	
496.9	0.1	Deep Gap ...*no camping zone, piped spring (E–0.2m)*	w	4,900'	1,696.1	
497.0	1.0	Mt. Rogers Trail *West–4m to* USFS Grindstone Campground at Va. 603	R, C, w, sh	5,200'	1,696.0	
498.0	0.9	Brier Ridge Saddle ...*views in meadow*		5,125'	1,695.0	ATC Southwest Va. Map 4
498.9	0.2	Spur trail *West–0.5m to* summit of Mt. Rogers (5,729')		5,490'	1,694.1	
499.1	1.0	**Thomas Knob Shelter** ...*12.4mS; 5.1mN*	S, w	5,400'	1,693.9	
500.1	0.5	Rhododendron Gap, Pine Mountain Trail	C	5,400'	1,692.9	
500.6	0.1	Wilburn Ridge Trail ...*southern jct.*		5,440'	1,692.4	
500.7	0.6	Fatman Squeeze ...*narrow rock tunnel*		5,300'	1,692.3	
501.3	0.3	Wilburn Ridge Trail ...*northern jct.*		4,900'	1,691.7	
501.6	0.5	Grayson Highlands State Park ...*cross fence*		4,880'	1,691.4	
502.1	0.7	Park service road to Massie Gap *East–0.5m to* Grayson Highlands State Park ...*day parking* *East–2m to* campground	R, P C, g, sh	4,800'	1,690.9	
502.8	0.5	A.T. spur trail on Wilburn Ridge (E–0.8m)	R, P	4,920'	1,690.2	
503.3	0.9	Quebec Branch	w	4,200'	1,689.7	
504.2	0.1	**Wise Shelter** ...*5.1mS; 6mN*	S, w	4,460'	1,688.8	
504.3	0.2	Big Wilson Creek ...*footbridge*	C, w	4,300'	1,688.7	
504.5	0.1	Wilson Creek Trail ...*footbridge (E–1.3m to CG)*	R, C, sh	4,300'	1,688.5	
504.6	1.0	Scales Trail Junction		4,650'	1,688.4	
505.6	1.2	Spring ...*unreliable*	w	4,610'	1,687.4	
506.8	0.4	Stone Mountain		4,800'	1,686.2	
507.2	0.7	The Scales, USFS 613 ...*livestock corral, privy*	P, R	4,620'	1,685.8	ATC Southwest Va. Map 3
507.9	0.7	Stream	w	4,700'	1,685.1	
508.6	1.6	Pine Mountain Trail		4,960'	1,684.4	
510.2	0.1	**Old Orchard Shelter** ...*6mS; 4.9mN*	S, C, w	4,050'	1,682.8	
510.3	0.7	Upper Old Orchard Trail		4,020'	1,682.7	
511.0	0.9	Old Orchard Trail One		3,750'	1,682.0	
511.9	0.1	Va. 603, Fairwood Road, Fox Creek ...*Fox Creek Horse Camp* *East–4m to* **Troutdale, Va., P.O. 24378** *West–1.9m to* USFS Grindstone Cpgrd	R, P, C, w H C, w, sh	3,480'	1,681.1	
512.0	1.9	Fox Creek ...*footbridge*		3,450'	1,681.0	

Miles from Springer	Miles to Next Point	Features	Services	Elev	Miles from Katahdin	M A P
513.9	0.3	Hurricane Mountain; Tennessee–New River Divide		4,325'	1,679.1	
514.2	0.9	Iron Mountain Trail, Chestnut Flats		4,240'	1,678.8	
515.1	0.6	**Hurricane Mountain Shelter** ...*4.9mS; 9.3mN*	S, w	3,850'	1,677.9	
515.7	0.8	Hurricane Creek Trail ...*old logging road*		3,300'	1,677.3	
516.5	2.1	Stream	w	3,000'	1,676.5	
518.6	0.4	Dickey Gap Trail *West–0.4m to* USFS Hurricane Cpgrnd	C, w, sh	3,090'	1,674.4	
519.0	1.2	Comers Creek Falls Trail, Comers Creek ...*footbridge is unsafe; ford creek, or follow marked detour signs if water is high*; *waterfalls*	w	3,120'	1,674.0	
520.2	0.8	Dickey Gap, Va. 650, Comers Creek Road *East 180 ft. to Va. 16–from Va. 16:* *East–2.6m to* **Troutdale, Va., P.O. 24378** *East–3.6m to* Fox Creek General Store *East–4.3m to* Grayson Highlands Clinic *West–5m to* **Sugar Grove, Va., P.O. 24374** *West–5.6m to* Sugar Grove Food Mart	R, P H G, M, f D G, M, f, ATM	3,310'	1,672.8	
521.0	0.7	Virginia Highlands Horse Trail		3,480'	1,672.0	
521.7	0.5	Bobby's Trail to campsite and spring (E–0.2m) *East–3.3m to* USFS Raccoon Branch Campground	C, w C, w, sh	3,570'	1,671.3	
522.2	2.1	High point		4,040'	1,670.8	
524.3	1.2	Slabtown Trail Jct., **Trimpi Shelter** (E–0.1m) ...*9.3mS; 9.9mN*	S, w	2,900'	1,668.7	
525.5	0.7	Va. 672, Slabtown Road ...*gravel*	R	2,700'	1,667.5	
526.2	0.2	Slabtown Trail		2,600'	1,666.8	
526.4	1.5	Va. 670, Teas Road, South Fork Holston River ...*bridge*	R, P	2,470'	1,666.6	
527.9	0.1	Campsite	C	2,720'	1,665.1	
528.0	2.2	Stream ...*intermittent*	w	2,780'	1,665.0	
530.2	1.6	Va. 601, Pugh Mountain Road ...*gravel*	R, P	3,250'	1,662.8	
531.8	0.9	Powerline		3,300'	1,661.2	
532.7	1.4	Creek ...*footbridge*	w	3,010'	1,660.3	
534.1	0.2	**Partnership Shelter** ...*9.9mS; 7mN*	S, w, sh	3,360'	1,658.9	
534.3	0.7	Va. 16, Mt. Rogers NRA Headquarters *East–3.2m to* **Sugar Grove, Va., P.O. 24375** *West–6m to* **Marion, Va., P.O. 24354**	R, P, w G, M, f G, L, M, D, B, cl, f	3,240'	1,658.7	
535.0	1.9	Va. 622, Nick's Creek Road	R	3,250'	1,658.0	
536.9	1.0	Brushy Mountain ...*northern end*		3,700'	1,656.1	
537.9	0.4	Locust Mountain		3,900'	1,655.1	
538.3	1.3	USFS 86, Glade Mountain Road ... *campsite, spring*	R, P, C, w	3,530'	1,654.7	
539.6	1.5	Glade Mountain		4,093'	1,653.4	

ATC Southwest Va. Map 3

Miles from Springer	Miles to Next Point	Features	Services	Elev	Miles from Katahdin	M A P
541.1	0.3	**Chatfield Shelter** ...*7mS; 19.3mN*	S, w	3,150'	1,651.9	
541.4	1.5	USFS 644	R	3,100'	1,651.6	
542.9	0.5	Va. 615, Rocky Hollow Road, Settlers Museum, Lindamood Schoolhouse	R, P	2,590'	1,650.1	
543.4	0.4	Va. 729, Kegley Lane ...*gravel*	R	2,540'	1,649.6	
543.8	1.0	Kegley Trail ...*old road*	R	2,540'	1,649.2	
544.8	0.9	Middle Fork of Holston River Bridge ... *active railroad tracks*	w	2,420'	1,648.2	
545.7	1.0	U.S. 11, I-81 (exit 54), Va. 683, Grose-close, Va. *West–3.2m to* **Atkins, Va., P.O. 24311** *West–10.2m to* **Marion, Va., P.O. 24354**	R, P, G, L, M, B, sh, cl, f G, L, M, cl B, G, L, M, D, cl	2,420'	1,647.3	ATC SW Va. Map 3
546.7	0.7	Va. 617, Davis Valley Road	R, P	2,580'	1,646.3	
547.4	1.1	Spring ...*blue-blaze*	E–300 yds w	2,610'	1,645.6	
548.5	2.8	Davis Path Campsite	C, nw	2,840'	1,644.5	
551.3	1.1	Little Brushy Mountain, Crawfish (Channel Rock) Trail		3,300'	1,641.7	
552.4	0.1	Reed Creek, Crawfish Valley	w on A.T. (E–0.3m C, w)	2,600'	1,640.6	
552.5	1.8	Crawfish (Channel Rock) Trail		3,300'	1,640.5	
554.3	1.5	Tilson Gap, Big Walker Mountain		3,500'	1,638.7	
555.8	1.5	Va. 610, Old Rich Valley Road *West–0.3m to* Quarter Way Inn, Ceres, Va.	R H, C, g, sh	2,700'	1,637.2	
557.3	0.4	Va. 742, Shady Grove Road, North Fork of Holston River, Tilson's Mill ...*low-water bridge*	R, w	2,460'	1,635.7	
557.7	0.6	Spring ...*25 yds. downhill*	w	2,550'	1,635.3	
558.3	0.9	Va. 42, Ceres, Va. *(E–0.2m small creek)* *West–2.5m to* Appalachian Dreamers Hiker Hostel	R, P, w H, C, g, sh	2,500'	1,634.7	
559.2	1.2	Brushy Mountain		3,200'	1,633.8	
560.4	0.5	**Knot Maul Branch Shelter** ...*19.3mS; 9.4mN*	S, nw	2,800'	1,632.6	ATC Southwest Va. Map 2
560.9	0.6	Campsite and creek ...*water for Knot Maul Branch Shelter*	C, w	2,810'	1,632.1	
561.5	1.1	Lynn Camp Creek ...*footbridge*	w	2,400'	1,631.5	
562.6	1.2	Lynn Camp Mountain		3,000'	1,630.4	
563.8	1.4	Lick Creek ...*footbridge*	C, w	2,250'	1,629.2	
565.2	2.8	USFS 222, Va. 625 ...*dirt*	R, P	2,310'	1,627.8	
568.0	1.1	Spring-fed pond ...*spring box NE end of pond water for Chestnut Knob Shelter*	w	3,800'	1,625.0	
569.1	0.5	Chestnut Ridge ...*views*		3,700'	1,623.9	
569.6	0.2	Spring ...*intermittent on old jeep road (E–0.1m)*	w	4,300'	1,623.4	
569.8	1.4	**Chestnut Knob Shelter** ...*9.4mS; 10.7mN* Burkes Garden Overlook ...*"God's Thumbprint" view*	S, nw	4,409'	1,623.2	
571.2	4.8	Walker Gap ...*water for Chestnut Knob Shelter, blue blaze to spring (E–130 yds.)*	R, P, w	3,520'	1,621.8	

Miles from Springer	*Miles to Next Point*	Features	Services	Elev	Miles from Katahdin	M A P
576.0	*1.0*	Va. 623, Burkes Garden Road, Garden Mountain *West–2m to* St. Luke's Hostel	R, P H	3,880'	1,617.0	
577.0	*2.6*	Davis Farm Campsite *(W–0.4m)*	C, w	3,850'	1,616.0	
579.6	*0.9*	Stream	w	3,700'	1,613.4	
580.5	*0.1*	**Jenkins Shelter** *...10.7mS; 13.8mN*	S, w	2,470'	1,612.5	
580.6	*3.3*	Hunting Camp Creek	w	2,450'	1,612.4	
583.9	*0.2*	High-water trail		2,950'	1,609.1	
584.1	*0.8*	Brushy Mountain		3,080'	1,608.9	
584.9	*2.1*	Va. 615, Suiter Road, Laurel Creek	R, P, C, w	2,450'	1,608.1	
587.0	*4.3*	Trail Boss Trail		3,100'	1,606.0	
591.3	*0.5*	USFS 282 (Wyrick Road) *...gravel*	R	2,950'	1,601.7	
591.8	*0.4*	U.S. 52 *East–2.7m to* **Bland, Va., P.O. 24315** *East–3.3m to* services *West–2.5m to* **Bastian, Va., P.O. 24314** *West–3.5m to* services *West–20m to* Bluefield, W. Va.	R, P G, M, f G, L, M, D D, M, g B, all	2,910'	1,601.2	ATC Southwest Va. Map 2
592.2	*0.4*	Va. 612, I–77 overpass	R	2,750'	1,600.8	
592.6	*1.4*	Va. 612, Kimberling Creek	R, P, w	2,600'	1,600.4	
594.0	*6.6*	**Helveys Mill Shelter** *(E–0.3m)...13.8mS; 10mN*	S, w	3,090'	1,599.0	
600.6	*1.4*	Va. 611, Slide Mountain Road *...gravel*	R, P	2,720'	1,592.4	
602.0	*1.7*	Brushy Mountain		3,101'	1,591.0	
603.7	*1.2*	**Jenny Knob Shelter** *...10mS; 14.5mN*	S, w	2,800'	1,589.3	
604.9	*3.4*	Va. 608, Lickskillet Hollow *East–0.8m to* Lickskillet Hostel	R, P H	2,200'	1,588.1	
608.3	*1.8*	Brushy Mountain		2,680'	1,584.7	
610.1	*0.1*	Kimberling Creek *...suspension bridge*	C, w	2,090'	1,582.9	
610.2	*1.9*	Va. 606, Wilderness Road *West–0.5m to* Trent's Grocery	R C, G, M, cl, sh, f	2,040'	1,582.8	
612.1	*1.1*	Dismal Creek Falls Trail *...waterfalls (W–0.3m)*	w	2,320'	1,580.9	
613.2	*0.8*	Bridge *...over deep gully*		2,390'	1,579.8	
614.0	*2.0*	Bridge, trail to Walnut Flats Campground *(W–0.4m)*	C, w	2,400'	1,579.0	
616.0	*0.1*	Lion's Den Road		2,400'	1,577.0	
616.1	*0.3*	Ribble Trail south junction *...USFS White Cedar Horse Campground (W–0.5m)*	C, w	2,400'	1,576.9	
616.4	*0.8*	Creek *...bridge*	w	2,500'	1,576.6	ATC Southwest Va. Map 1
617.2	*0.8*	Creek *...two bridges*	w	2,550'	1,575.8	
618.0	*0.2*	Levee and pond		2,570'	1,575.0	
618.2	*0.6*	**Wapiti Shelter** *...14.5mS; 9.5mN*	S, w	2,600'	1,574.8	
618.8	*2.0*	Dismal Creek	w	2,700'	1,574.2	
620.8	*2.9*	Sugar Run Mountain *...rocky outcrop*		3,870'	1,572.2	
623.7	*0.1*	Ribble Trail north junction	w	3,800'	1,569.3	
623.8	*1.2*	Big Horse Gap, USFS 103	R	3,752'	1,569.2	
625.0	*0.4*	Nobusiness Creek Road *...closed road*		3,500'	1,568.0	

Miles from Springer	Miles to Next Point	Features	Services	Elev	Miles from Katahdin	M A P
625.4	1.4	Sugar Run Gap, Sugar Run Gap Rd, Va. 663 *East–0.5m to* Woodshole Hostel	R, P H	3,382'	1,567.6	ATC Southwest Va. Map 1
626.8	0.9	Rock Cliff Overlook ...*blue-blaze (E–60 yds.)*		3,850'	1,566.2	
627.7	5.7	**Doc's Knob Shelter** ...*9.5mS; 16.1mN*	S, w	3,555'	1,565.3	
633.4	0.2	Rock-ledge view on Pearis Mountain		3,770'	1,559.6	
633.6	0.5	Campsite and spring *(W–300 yds.)*	C, w	3,750'	1,559.4	
634.1	1.0	Angels Rest on Pearis Mountain ...*vista*		3,550'	1,558.9	
635.1	1.0	Abandoned powerline tower		2,740'	1,557.9	
636.1	1.0	Va. 634, Cross Ave. *(E–0.8m Pearisburg, Va.)*	R, PO, all	2,200'	1,556.9	

The state's highest mountain, Mt. Rogers, an area of spectacular highland meadows, routinely receives snowfall from October to May, making it considerably colder, wetter, and snowier than other areas of Virginia. Northbounders may be tempted to mail home their cold-weather gear, only to see spring flavored by winter.

Caution: According to Mt. Rogers National Recreation Area officials, hikers should use caution when leaving vehicles at any local trailhead. Safer hiker parking is available at some locations in Damascus, as well as the Mt. Rogers NRA headquarters.

Mt. Rogers Appalachian Trail Club—MRATC, with maintenance responsibility for the A.T. from the Tennessee line north to Teas Road (59.4 miles), maintains trails in the Mt. Rogers NRA, Jefferson National Forest, Grayson Highlands State Park, and other areas. Send correspondence to MRATC Box 789, Damascus, VA 24236-0789; <www.mratc.org>.

U.S. 58/Damascus, Va. [P.O. ZIP 24236: M–F 8:30–1 & 2–4:30, Sa 9–11; (276) 475-3411]— Called "the friendliest town on the Trail" and the home of Trail Days (to be held this year May 15–17). First held in '87 as a commemorative event for the 50th anniversary of the A.T., the festival's activities and crowds have grown each year since. Activities include a hiker reunion and talent show, hiking-related exhibits, arts-and-crafts exhibits, street dances, live music, and the popular hiker parade through downtown. If you are unable to walk into Damascus for the weekend, rides are easy to find from all points along the Trail. Be aware that state open-container laws that restrict drinking in public places are enforced. Hiker camping during Trail Days is at the south edge of town on Shady Avenue. Camping is prohibited everywhere else. Please keep quiet in the late evening and early morning, and, upon departure, leave your campsite clean. Leave No Trace camping principles apply in town as well as on the Trail. You'll find all major services, except veterinary, in Damascus. ■ *Hostels:* The Place, (276) 206-0440, <www.facebook.com/theplacehostel>, open mid-Mar–mid-Jun, closed 'til Labor Day, closes mid-Nov or when the pipes are in danger of freezing. Check in 2–9 p.m. Stays are limited to two days (unless sick or injured). A large house for hikers and TA cyclists only, with bunk space, showers (towels/soap), and pavilion/picnic tables. Eight-dollars-per-night donation is requested, but larger donations are appreciated in addition to cleaning chores. Seasonal caretaker. No vehicle-assisted hikers except during Trail Days. No dogs, drinking, or smoking are allowed on the property of the First United Methodist Church, its parking lot, or pavilion. **Crazy Larry's B&B**, 209 Douglas Dr., <www.facebook.com/crazylarryshostel>, (276) 475-7130, rates vary according to services and accommodations, includes shower, B, laundry, use of kitchen, WiFi. **Song Peddlar Rest** (formerly Woodchuck Hostel), 533 Docie St., (276) 475-5888 or (276) 739-8863. Beds w/ linens $45, priavte cabin $75-$125, not B w/stay, free shuttle for resupply (others by arrangement). **Broken Fiddle Hostel,** 104 Damascus Dr., (276) 274-4827 or (276) 608-6220 (text); bunk $30, private room $75D $10EAP; includes shower, laundry, tent/ hammocking $10; shower/ laundry $5; WiFi and kitchen available; dog-friendly.

■ *Lodging:* Hikers Inn, 216 E. Laurel Ave., (276) 475-3788, owned and operated by Paul (Skink of 2010) and Lee, bunks in hostel $25, private room $50, private room in house or Airstream

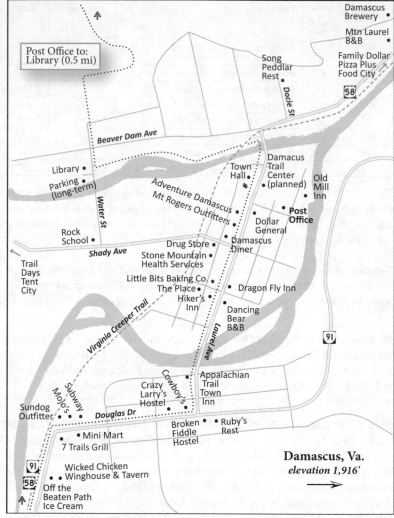

Post Office to: Library (0.5 mi)

Damascus Brewery
Mtn Laurel B&B
Song Peddlar Rest
Family Dollar Pizza Plus Food City
58
Docie St
Beaver Dam Ave
Damacus Trail Center (planned)
Old Mill Inn
Town Hall
Library
Parking (long-term)
Adventure Damascus Mt Rogers Outfitters
Post Office
Dollar General
Water St
Rock School
Drug Store
Damascus Diner
Shady Ave
Stone Mountain Health Services
Trail Days Tent City
Little Bits Baking Co.
The Place
Dragon Fly Inn
Hiker's Inn
Dancing Bear B&B
91
Virginia Creeper Trail
Laurel Ave
Cowboy's
Appalachian Trail Town Inn
Crazy Larry's Hostel
Subway
Mojo's
Sundog Outfitter
Douglas Dr
Broken Fiddle Hostle
Ruby's Rest
Mini Mart
7 Trails Grill
Damascus, Va.
elevation 1,916'
91
58
Wicked Chicken Winghouse & Tavern
Off the Beaten Path Ice Cream

$75/night or $65/multiple nights, a/c and WiFi, laundry $5 for guests, dogs allowed only in hostel and Airstream, closed in winter, credit cards accepted; Mountain Laurel Inn, (276) 475-5956, 0.5 mile west of town on U.S. 58, 2-night minimum; Ruby's Rest, 719 E. 2nd St., (276) 475-3914, $40S, $10EAP, dogs free in fenced yard; Outdoors Inn, (276) 475-3611, rent the entire space for groups of 10 for $150/ night including full kitchen. ■ *Groceries:* Food City (long-term resupply). ■ *Restaurants:* Subway; Cowboy's Deli and convenience store, with ATM; Wicked Chicken Winghouse; Off-the-Beaten-Path Ice Cream Shoppe; Mojoe's Trailside Coffee House; Damascus Diner; 7 Trails Grill; Little Bits Baking. ■ *Outfitters:* Mt. Rogers Outfitters (MRO), 110 Laurel Ave. (P.O. Box 546), (276) 475-5416, <mtrogersoutfitters.com>, owned and operated by Mike Price (Lumpy), backpacking gear and supplies, stove fuel, shuttles, accepts mail drops, open M–Sa 9–6; Adventure Damascus Outdoor Co., 128 W. Laurel Ave., open 7 days/week, full line of backpacking gear and clothing, denatured alcohol and other fuels available, $3 shower; Sundog Outfitter, 331 Douglas Dr., (276) 475-6252, <www. sundogoutfitter.com>, backpacking gear and clothing, repairs, hiker food, denatured alcohol and other fuels, will hold USPS and UPS mail drops, call ahead for shuttles, open 7 days a week. ■ *Internet access:* Damascus Public Library & Visitors Center, WiFi/Skype, M–W–F 9–5, T–Th 11–7, Sa

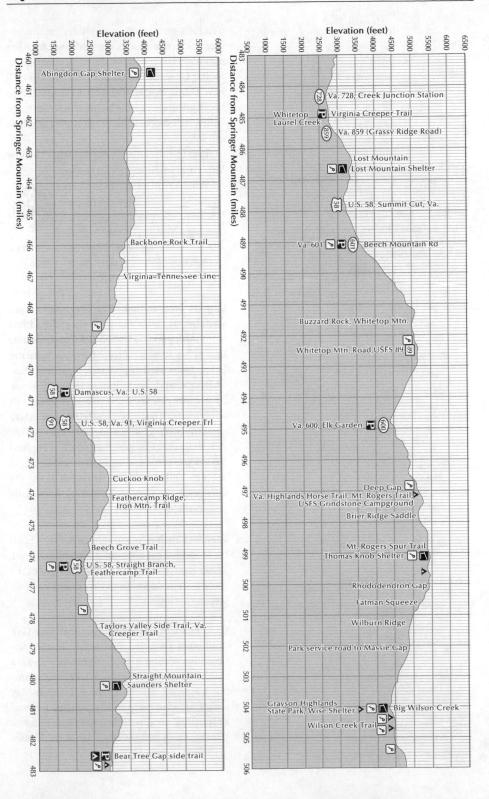

Elevation (feet) (left chart)

Distance from Springer Mountain (miles)

- Abingdon Gap Shelter
- Backbone Rock Trail
- Virginia–Tennessee Line
- Damascus, Va., U.S. 58
- U.S. 58, Va. 91, Virginia Creeper Trl
- Cuckoo Knob
- Feathercamp Ridge, Iron Mtn. Trail
- Beech Grove Trail
- U.S. 58, Straight Branch, Feathercamp Trail
- Taylors Valley Side Trail, Va. Creeper Trail
- Straight Mountain Saunders Shelter
- Bear Tree Gap side trail

Elevation (feet) (right chart)

Distance from Springer Mountain (miles)

- Va. 728, Creek Junction Station
- Whitetop Laurel Creek — Virginia Creeper Trail
- Va. 859 (Grassy Ridge Road)
- Lost Mountain
- Lost Mountain Shelter
- U.S. 58, Summit Cut, Va.
- Va. 601 — Beech Mountain Rd
- Buzzard Rock, Whitetop Mtn.
- Whitetop Mtn. Road, USFS 89
- Va. 600, Elk Garden
- Deep Gap
- Va. Highlands Horse Trail, Mt. Rogers Trail, USFS Grindstone Campground
- Brier Ridge Saddle
- Mt. Rogers Spur Trail
- Thomas Knob Shelter
- Rhododendron Gap
- Fatman Squeeze
- Wilburn Ridge
- Park service road to Massie Gap
- Grayson Highlands State Park, Wise Shelter — Big Wilson Creek
- Wilson Creek Trail

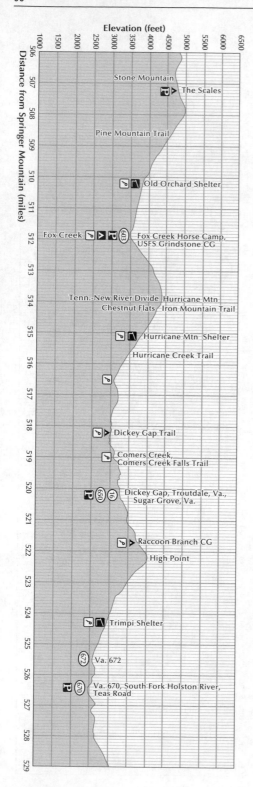

Elevation (feet)

Stone Mountain

The Scales

Pine Mountain Trail

Old Orchard Shelter

Fox Creek 603 Fox Creek Horse Camp, USFS Grindstone CG

Tenn.-New River Divide Hurricane Mtn
Chestnut Flats Iron Mountain Trail

Hurricane Mtn Shelter

Hurricane Creek Trail

Dickey Gap Trail

Comers Creek,
Comers Creek Falls Trail

650 16 Dickey Gap, Troutdale, Va.,
Sugar Grove, Va.

Raccoon Branch CG

High Point

Trimpi Shelter

672 Va. 672

670 Va. 670, South Fork Holston River,
Teas Road

9–1; long-term parking available, inquire on-line at <visitdamascus.org/parking>. ■ *Other services:* Town-wide WiFi; clinic; pharmacy; Dollar General; two banks with ATM. ATC's new Damascus Trail Center to scheduled to break ground in spring 2020 across from town hall; watch <appalachiantrail.org> for developing information.

West 2 miles on U.S. 58 to Fisher Hollow Veterinary Clinic, (276) 475-5397.

West 12 miles on U.S. 58 to Abingdon, Va., a large town near I-81 with all major services, including a Walmart, veterinarian, movie theater, and Highlands Ski & Outdoor Center, (276) 628-1329, open M–F 10–7, Sa 9–7, Su 12–6.

Virginia Creeper Trail—The Virginia Creeper stretches 33 miles along an old railroad bed from Abingdon to the North Carolina state line. It began as a native-American footpath. Later, it was used by pioneers, including Daniel Boone, and, beginning in the early 1900s, by a quintessential mountain railroad, its namesake, with 100 trestles and bridges, as well as many steep grades and sharp curves. The A.T. shares the Creeper route north of Damascus for 300 yards and again 10 miles north. [In Taylors Valley, east of Damascus along the Creeper, is the Creeper Trail Café, open daily 11–5 in season, (276) 475-3918.]

Saunders Shelter (1987)—Sleeps 8. Privy. Shelter is located on a 0.2-mile blue-blazed trail. Water source is behind and to the right of the shelter, then down an old road to a reliable, seeping spring.

USFS Beartree Campground on Bear Tree Gap Trail **west** 3.6 miles. Part of Mt. Rogers National Recreation Area, (276) 388-3642, with a bathhouse (hot showers $4), lake, and swimming area 0.6 mile from the A.T. Open May 1–Oct 31. Campground is 3 miles beyond swimming area, with tentsites $20 and hot showers $4. Parking $5/day. Cash or check only.

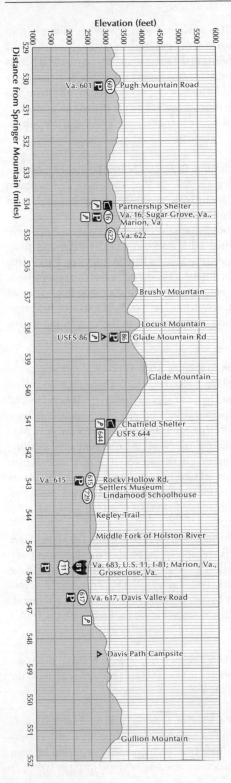

Lost Mountain Shelter (1994)—Sleeps 8. Privy. Bear box. Water source is on a trail to the left of the shelter.

Whitetop Mountain—At 5,520 feet, this is Virginia's second-highest peak, but the A.T. does not go to the top. The nearby town of Whitetop is home to a ramp festival the weekend after Memorial Day. The festival includes a ramp-eating contest thru-hikers have won in past years. Ramps emerge from the forest floor in early spring. The two-leafed greens sprout from an onion-like tuber that can be used to spice up meals. Other plants have a similar look; ramps are identified easily by their smell and taste, which are akin to onions and garlic.

Va. 600, Elk Garden—Elk Garden is named after the extinct eastern elk that once roamed throughout this area, along with timber wolves, mountain lions, and bison. Today, none of those exist here, but black bear, white-tailed deer, and wild turkey are common.

In 2019, an active bear problem in the High Country led to bear-resistant storage boxes being installed at shelters and campsites. Pay attention to any informational signs, and use the food boxes provided.

USFS Grindstone Campground—*via* Mt. Rogers Trail **west** 4 miles. Open May 1–Nov 30. Tentsites including shower $24; hot shower $4; parking $5/day. Cash or check only.

Mt. Rogers—Virginia's highest peak, at 5,729 feet; the Trail does not go to the viewless summit, but it can be reached *via* a side trail, going west 0.5 mile. Camping is prohibited in the area from the A.T. to the summit due to fragile plant life and the endangered Wellers salamander. The Wellers, a dark blue-black salamander with gold splotches on its back, can be found only in coniferous forests above 5,000 feet. You may also see or hear northern birds, such as the hermit thrush and winter wren. Such species nest here because of the favorable altitude at the summit area.

Thomas Knob Shelter (1991)—Sleeps 16. Moldering privy. This two-level shelter was built by the

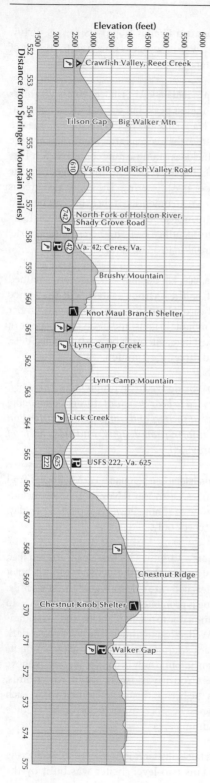

MRATC and Konnarock Crew. Water source is in an enclosed area in a pasture behind the shelter; lock the gate leading to the water source to keep the feral ponies in the area from polluting the water. Be aware those ponies like to chew on packs and other salty items. No tenting near shelter. *Hikers are strongly encouraged to store all food in the metal bear-box located just past the shelter.*

Rhododendron Gap—Just below the highest point on the Virginia A.T. on Pine Mountain and Wilburn Ridge. Many large, established campsites are located between Thomas Knob and Rhododendron Gap, with a bear box just south of the gap. This section extremely popular with weekend and day-hikers. In June, rhododendron blooms here in full force. Panoramic views of the rhododendron thickets can be seen from a rock outcropping. Watch your step from Thomas Knob through the Grayson Highlands State Park area; cattle and feral ponies roam the area. In the spring, you will see mares tending their foals.

Grayson Highlands State Park—(276) 579-7092. At Massie Gap, a blue-blaze leads **East** 0.5 mile to a parking area, then 1.5 miles farther on roads or horse trail to campground. Park is open year-round from dawn to 10 p.m. The campstore and showers are open May 1–Oct 31; may use phone at camp store with a calling card; tentsite $21, shower only $5. Camp store is usually open on weekends during the season, but hours vary; call for details and hours. The park hosts Appalachian music festivals on summer weekends.

Wise Shelter (1996)—Sleeps 8. Privy. Bear box. Water source is a reliable spring south of the shelter on a trail east of the A.T. No tenting around the shelter or in the state park. Tentsites are in the Mt. Rogers NRA, across Wilson Creek, 0.3 mile north. Grayson Highlands State Park is accessible *via* the Seed Orchard Trail, 2 miles.

Old Orchard Shelter (1970)—Sleeps 6. Privy. Bear box. Water source is 100 yards on a blue-blazed trail to the right of the shelter.

Va. 603/Fox Creek—Parking. **East** 100 yards to Fox Creek Horse Camp, $5/night, no water. Multiple bear incidents were reported in 2019, and bears were able to grab food hung in trees.

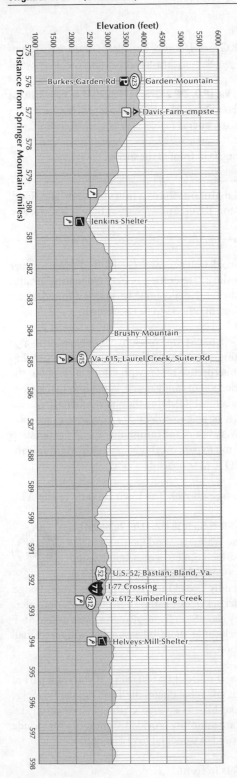

Elevation (feet)

Distance from Springer Mountain (miles)

West 2.5 miles to USFS Grindstone Campground (see above).

Hurricane Mountain Shelter (2004)—Sleeps 8. Moldering privy. Bear box. Water source is a nearby stream.

USFS Hurricane Campground—West 0.5 mile *via* side trail to Hurricane Campground, (276) 783-5196, one of nine USFS campgrounds within the George Washington and Jefferson National Forests. The campground charges $16 per site; $2 shower 10-2; parking $3/day. Open Apr 15–Oct 31, depending on weather. Cash or check only.

Va. 650, East 100 yards to **Va. 16/Dickey Gap**—New parking lot for 5 cars. Turn right **(compass south)** on Va. 16 2.6 miles to **Troutdale, Va. [P.O. ZIP 24378: M–F 8–12, Sa 8:30–11:30; (276) 677-3221].**
■ *Hostels:* Troutdale Baptist Church, Pastor Ken Riggins, (276) 677-4092, located at 66 Sapphire Lane, offers a place to tent or use of a hiker bunkhouse, shower, pets welcome, donations accepted; Sufi Lodge, 67 High Country Ln., (276) 677-0195, <www.sufilodge.org>, 3 private hiker rooms start at $45, twin beds in one shared room $39, includes B, shower/towel/toiletries. Full Mediterranean B, L/D veg and vegan meals; massage, sauna, cupping therapy; shuttles available. Free Epsom-salt foot bath; mail drops for guests, non-guests $10, Attn: mail drop service.
■ *Other*

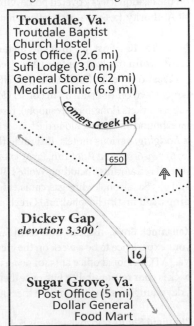

Troutdale, Va.
Troutdale Baptist
Church Hostel
Post Office (2.6 mi)
Sufi Lodge (3.0 mi)
General Store (6.2 mi)
Medical Clinic (6.9 mi)

Comers Creek Rd

650

↑ N

Dickey Gap
elevation 3,300´

16

Sugar Grove, Va.
Post Office (5 mi)
Dollar General
Food Mart

services: ATM, bank.

Continue on Va. 16 3.6 miles to Sarah's Fox Creek General Store & Restaurant (short-term resupply), 7116 Troutdale Hwy, (276) 579-6033, open M–F 7–7, Sa 7–6; canister and alcohol fuel, beer, wine, and BBQ.

From gap, left on Va. 16 5 miles to **Sugar Grove, Va. [P.O. ZIP 24375: M–F 8:30–12 & 1:30–3:30, Sa 8:15–10:30; (276) 677-3200].** *Groceries:* Sugar Grove Food Mart (short-term resupply), (276) 377-3037, M–Sa 6–9, Su 7–9, snack bar, ice cream, ATM. Dollar General, (276) 521-2110, open daily 8-10.

Trimpi Shelter (1975)—Sleeps 8. Privy. A reliable spring is in front of the shelter.

Piedmont Appalachian Trail Hikers (PATH)—PATH maintains the 65.4 miles between Teas Road, a mile north of Va. 670, South Fork of the Holston River, and U.S. 52 at Bland, Va.; <www.path-at.org>.

Partnership Shelter (1998)—Sleeps 16. Privy and cold-water shower (available during warmer months; single-use towel for sale in headquarters during operating hours). No tenting around the shelter. Water source is a faucet behind the shelter. No alcoholic beverages allowed. For a week or more after Trail Days, expect law-enforcement officers to be checking in.

Mt. Rogers National Recreation Area Headquarters—(276) 783-5196 or (800) 628-7202, M–F 8–4:30 year-round, Sa–Su 9–4 May–Oct (weather permitting). Two hundred yards north of Partnership Shelter, the headquarters houses a bookshop and interpretive center with information about the area's natural history. A soda machine and small selection of candy inside. Water is available from a spigot outside. Restroom outside (closes 15 minutes before HQ). From the outside phone (free local calls, calling card needed for long distance), you may be able to order pizza from several area pizzerias, to be delivered to gate (subject to limited delivery hours and minimum orders). Do not sleep on the headquarters' covered porch. Obtain free permit to park overnight or weekly. Marion Transit Authority, (276) 782-9300, offers shuttles from HQ to Marion (call for ride).

 Va. 16—East 3.2 miles to **Sugar Grove, Va.** (see above). The town is home to the ATC Konnarock Volunteer Crew (see below).

West 6 miles to **Marion, Va. [P.O. ZIP 24354: M–F 9–5 Sa 9:30–12; (276) 783-5051]**, a larger town on I-81 with all major services, including Walmart, Food Lion, and Ingles supermarkets (long-term resupply), restaurants, fast-food outlets, a coin laundry, and Greyhound bus service along the I-81 corridor, (276) 783-7114 (closed Sa, Su, and holidays). ■ *Lodging:* various motels, including the hiker-friendly Travel Inn, (276) 783-5112; Econo Lodge, (276) 783-6031; Red Roof Inn, (276) 378-0481. ■ *Other services:* Historic downtown Marion offers several restaurants, including Wolfe's BBQ; an Army Navy Store, (276) 783-3832, open 9–5:30 M–F and 9–5 Sa (alcohol, white gas, canister fuel, outdoor clothing, shoes, hiker supplies, will accept mail drops, call first); a hospital; and Greyhound bus station.

Konnarock Crew—Based 1 mile from Sugar Grove post office at USFS facility. If you want part of your experience to be a week on the crew that builds and rehabilitates the Trail, call the Roanoke, Va., ATC regional office at (540) 904-4393 before your hike to arrange. Getting to base camp and back is your responsibility, but, once there, food and amenities are provided. Commitments include 5 days/4 nights along the Trail in the South. Be prepared to work and have a lot of fun.

Chatfield Shelter (1970s)—Sleeps 6. Privy. A creek is in front.

Va. 615, Settlers Museum—On USFS lands adjacent to the Trail, the farmstead and visitors center include exhibits of rural life at the time the valley was settled. Admission free to hikers. Picnic pavilion. Closed M. No camping.

Va. 683, U.S. 11, I-81—At Groseclose, Va. (no post office), this is the southernmost Trail crossing of I-81. *See map.* ■ *Groceries:* Village Truck Stop (Sunoco station open 24 hours), (276) 783-5775, ATM, snack bar (M–F 11–7), showers $10, Heet fuel (in season), and short-term resupply; E-Z Stop (Exxon), open 7–11 (short-term resupply, has Heet, WiFi, ATM), Burrito Loco restaurant adjacent, Tu–Sa 11–9, Su 11:30–8. ■ *Lodging:* The Relax Inn, 7253 Lee Hwy, Rural Retreat, VA 24368, (276) 783-5811, $45S, $50D, $5EAP, $10 per pet; long-term hiker parking $3/day; coin laundry; call for info on reservations and possible shuttle; free mail drop for guests (nonguests $5, must have ID), will hold 30 days max. Long Neck Lair Alpaca Farm, east 0.3 mile on U.S. 11, (276) 698-2079, offers bunkhouse accommodations $35PP, private room with bath $78D, tentsites $18, stays include B, shower, and laundry, WiFi, farm store w/

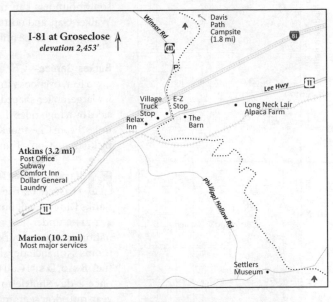

I-81 at Groseclose ⬆
elevation 2,453'

Winsor Rd
Davis Path Campsite (1.8 mi)
81
683
P
Lee Hwy 11
Village Truck Stop
E-Z Stop
Long Neck Lair Alpaca Farm
Relax Inn
The Barn
Atkins (3.2 mi)
Post Office
Subway
Comfort Inn
Dollar General
Laundry
11
Phillippi Hollow Rd
Marion (10.2 mi)
Most major services
Settlers Museum

limited resupply, shuttle service, and mail drops. ■ *Shuttles* and area info: Marion Transit Authority runs a bus from the Exxon station to Marion in season; call (276) 782-9300 for pick-up.

West 10.2 miles (on U.S. 11 south) to **Marion, Va.** (see above), a larger town.

Davis Path Campsite—Tent platform, table, and privy. Water source is a spring 0.9 mile south of the campsite. Southbounders can carry water from Crawfish Valley, 3.5 miles north.

Va. 610, Old Rich Valley Road—**West** 0.3 mile to *Hostel:* Quarter Way Inn, 4083 Old Rich Valley Rd., Ceres, Va., 24318, (276) 522-4603, <www.quarterwayinn.com>, renovated 1910 farmhouse, open Apr–Jun, run by '09 thru-hiker Tina "Chunky" and husband Brett; $30PP includes bunk, shower, towel, laundry, loaner clothes, and morning coffee; $55S/$75D for private room or $18PP tenting also includes the same. Gourmet breakfast available for $12 when 3 or more request it. Resupply (includes snacks, canister fuel, mountain house, pasta sides, oatmeal, *etc.*), pizza, pop, and ice cream. Slackpacking often available—call in advance. Parking $3/day. Credit cards accepted. No dogs. Outgoing mail and mail drops accepted for guests (ID required).

Va. 42—**East** 0.1 mile to *Hostel:* Bear Garden Hiker Hostel, 306 W Blue Grass Trail, Ceres, Va. 24318, (248) 249-1951, owned by Bob and Roberta Lingham. Open year 'round. Bunkhouse $20PP (WiFi) or small house, sleeps up to 6, $100. Includes cold breakfast. Laundry $5, shuttles available. Accepts mail drops (30 days with ETA).

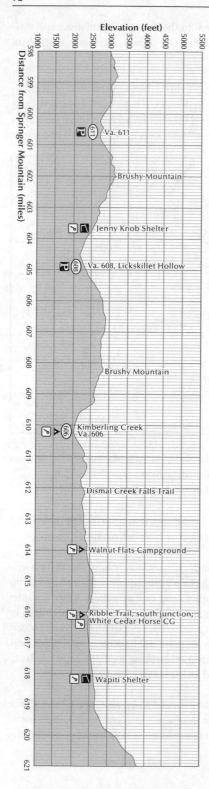

Knot Maul Branch Shelter (1980s)—Sleeps 8. Privy. Water source is 0.2 mile north on A.T.

Chestnut Knob Shelter (renovated 1994)—Sleeps 8. Privy. A former firewarden's cabin; plexiglass windows to let in some light. No water at this shelter, but water is sometimes found 0.2 mile south on the A.T., then 50 yards east on an old Jeep road. Otherwise, southbounders can find water 1.3 miles north in Walker Gap, and northbounders can find water at a spring-fed pond 1.8 miles south.

Burkes Garden—Chestnut Knob Shelter, elevation 4,410 feet, overlooks this unusual geologic feature. It is a large, crater-shaped depression surrounded on all sides by a high ridge that the A.T. follows for nearly 8 miles. From Chestnut Knob, you can see how it got its nickname, "God's Thumbprint."

Va. 623, Garden Mountain— West 2.0 miles to *Hostel:* Garden Mountain Hostel, 1404 Banks Ridge Road, Burkes Garden, VA 24651, (276) 472-2150; under new management. Suggested donation $15-$30 or work for stay (bunks $25, private rooms $50), includes shower, laundry, kitchen, and fuel. B $10, D $15. Call for shuttle, $7.50 round-trip; once-a-day shuttle to store/town, $1/mile. Open year-round, accepts mail drops.■ *Groceries:* Burke's Garden General Store (short-term resupply), (423) 762-2853, fuel, sandwiches, ice cream, snacks, *etc.*

Jenkins Shelter (1960s)—Sleeps 8. Privy. Water source is stream 100 yards north on blue-blazed trail.

U.S. 52—Brushy Mountain Outpost, (276) 266-0537, M–F 8–4, Sa 7–2, short-term resupply, sandwiches, burgers, breakfast, fuel.
    East 2.7 miles to **Bland, Va. [P.O. ZIP 24315: M–F 8:30–11:30 & 12–4, Sa 9–11; (276) 688-3751].** ■ *Grocery:* Grant's Grocery. ■ *Restaurant:* Bland Square Grill (in Bland Square Citgo), 8870 S. Scenic Hwy, first block west of Main on U.S. 52 in downtown, B/L/D, 7 days. ■ *Internet access:* townwide WiFi; library, (276) 688-3737, M F 10–5, Tu–Th 10–7, Sa 10–2, Tu, Th 10–7:30. ■ *Other services:* Napa Auto; banks, ATM.

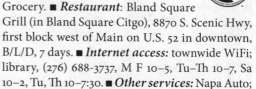

    East 3.3 miles to ■ *Lodging:* Big Walker Motel, 70 Skyview Lane, (276) 688-3331, $74.95S, $79.95D, $5EAP,

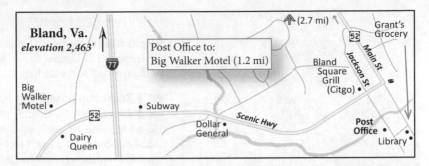

pets OK, WiFi, will hold packages for guests. Call motel or Bubba, (276) 730-5869, for shuttle possibilities. ■ *Other services:* Bland Family Clinic, (276) 688-0500, M–Tu 9–6, W–Th 9–5, F 10–2; Dairy Queen/gas station (short-term resupply) with ATM; Subway; Dollar General. *There is no place to camp in Bland.*

West 2.5 miles to **Bastian, Va. [P.O. ZIP 24314: M–F 8–12, Sa 9:15–11:15; (276) 688-4631]**. P.O. is **West** 1.9 miles, left on Railroad Trail, right on Walnut Drive. Two miles farther down U.S. 52 to *Other services:* medical clinic, after hours call (276) 688-4331, M 8–6, Tu Th 8–8, F 8:30–5; pharmacy next door, (276) 688-4204, M W–F 9–5, Tu 9–8, Sa 9–12; Kangaroo Express, 24-hour ATM; Greyhound bus, (304) 325-9442, available for the I-77 corridor in Bluefield, W.Va., about 10 miles beyond Bastian on U.S. 52 (closed Su, holidays); Pizza Plus, (276) 688-3332, will deliver to U.S. 52 Trailhead and Bland.

Outdoor Club of Virginia Tech—OCVT maintains the 8.8 miles between U.S. 52 and Va. 611 and 18.9 miles in central Virginia between U.S. 460 and Pine Swamp Branch Shelter. Correspondence should be sent to OCVT Box 538, Blacksburg, VA 24060; <www.outdoor.org.vt.edu>.

Helveys Mill Shelter (1960s)—Sleeps 6. Privy. Water source is down a switch-backed trail in front of the shelter.

Jenny Knob Shelter (1960s)—Sleeps 6. Privy. Water source (unreliable) is a seasonal spring near shelter.

Roanoke Appalachian Trail Club—RATC maintains the 36.9 miles between Va. 611 and U.S. 460 and 87.0 miles in the next section between Pine Swamp Branch Shelter and Black Horse Gap. Correspondence should be sent to RATC Box 12282, Roanoke, VA 24024; <www.ratc.org>.

Va. 608—East 0.8 mile to *Hostel:* Lickskillet Hostel, 35 Price Ridge Road, Bland, VA 24315 (corner of 608/42), (276) 779-5447. WiFi, laundry, slackpacking, daily shuttle to Bland. Not a party place. Holds packages for guests.

Va. 606— East 0.5 miles to *Hostel:* Weary Feet Hostel, 13152 E Bluegrass Trail, Bland, VA 24315, (276) 617-8434, <wearyfeethostel@gmail.com>, historic home with big porch, creek, and room for tenting. Check-in 2–9, check-out by 11 a.m. Bunk inside $25, private room $60, outdoor bunkhouse $15, tenting $10; includes shower; laundry $5. Home-cooked B $8, D $12, also burgers, dogs, and fries. Pet friendly. Free shuttle to trailhead on Va. 606 or Trents grocery, slackpacking available. Nonguest day pass $8, includes shower, laundry, and coffee. Mail drops accepted.

West 0.5 mile to *Groceries:* Trent's Grocery, 900 Wilderness Rd., Bland, VA 24315; (276) 928-1349; with ATM, deli, and pizza; possible shuttles. Open M–Sa 7–8, Su 8–8, Coleman and denatured alcohol by the ounce, canister fuel, and soda machines. Camping, shower, and laundry $6, or shower and laundry $3. Room with 2 beds, $40–$50, includes fridge, microwave,

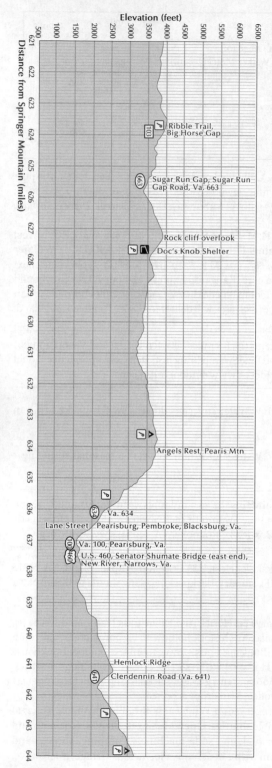

Elevation (feet)

Distance from Springer Mountain (miles)

Ribble Trail,
Big Horse Gap

Sugar Run Gap, Sugar Run
Gap Road, Va. 663

Rock cliff overlook
Doc's Knob Shelter

Angels Rest, Pearis Mtn

Va. 634
Lane Street Pearisburg, Pembroke, Blacksburg, Va.

Va. 100, Pearisburg, Va.
U.S. 460, Senator Shumate Bridge (east end),
New River, Narrows, Va.

Hemlock Ridge
Clendennin Road (Va. 641)

laundry. Accepts packages.

Wapiti Shelter (1980)—Sleeps 8. Privy. Water source is Dismal Creek, just south of the turn-off to the shelter.

Sugar Run Road/Sugar Run Gap— East 0.5 mile to *Hostel:* Woodshole Hostel & Mountain B&B, 3696 Sugar Run Rd., Pearisburg, VA 24134; (540) 921-3444, <www.woodsholehostel.com>. Isolated 1880s chestnut-log cabin was discovered in 1940 by Roy & Tillie Wood, who opened the hostel in 1986. Their granddaughter, Neville, continues the legacy with husband Michael, with emphasis on sustainable living through organic farming, gardening, yoga, and massage therapy. Heated bunkhouse $22PP; camping $16PP. Indoor rooms/safari tents, $33PP shared/$66 private (thru-hiker rate, normally $98). Farm-fresh B $9, D $14. Smoothies, home-roasted coffee, and goods. Laundry, fuel, shuttles, and slackpacking. Pet-friendly, work-for-stay available. Mail drops for guests. *Directions:* Turn east at Sugar Run Gap/dirt road, left at fork to hostel.

Doc's Knob Shelter (1971)—Sleeps 8. Privy. A reliable spring is to left of the shelter.

Virginia—Part 2 (Central)

Miles from Springer	*Miles to Next Point*	Features	Services	Elev	Miles from Katahdin	M A P
636.1	*1.0*	Va. 634, Cross Ave. *(E—0.8m Pearisburg, Va.)*	R, PO, all	2,200'	1,556.9	
637.1	*0.4*	Va. 100, Narrows Road East—1m to **Pearisburg, Va., P.O. 24134** East—2.9m to Holy Family Church Hostel East—6m to Pembroke, Va. East—20m to Blacksburg, Va. West—3.9m to **Narrows, Va., P.O. 24124**	R H, G, L, M, D, V, cl, f H O all C, G, L, M, cl		1,555.9	
637.5	*3.4*	U.S. 460, Senator Shumate Bridge *(east shore)* over New River East—1.5m to **Pearisburg, Va., P.O. 24134** West—4.3m to **Narrows, Va., P.O. 24124**	R all C, G, L, M, cl	1,600'	1,555.5	
640.9	*0.5*	Hemlock Ridge		2,470'	1,552.1	
641.4	*0.1*	Va. 641, Clendennin Road	R, P	2,220'	1,551.6	
641.5	*1.1*	Pocahontas Road ...*reenter woods*	R, P	2,230'	1,551.5	
642.6	*1.0*	Stream	w	2,600'	1,550.4	
643.6	*0.6*	Campsite and springs	C, w	3,200'	1,549.4	
644.2	*1.5*	**Rice Field Shelter** *(E—0.5m spring)* ...16.1mS; 12.6mN	S, C, w	3,400'	1,548.8	
645.7	*3.5*	Campsite (west) and spring (east)	C, w	3,450'	1,547.3	
649.2	*1.0*	Symms Gap Meadow	C, w	3,480'	1,543.8	
650.2	*1.6*	Groundhog Trail ...*(W—1.9m to USFS parking area on W. Va. 219/24)*		3,400'	1,542.8	
651.8	*2.2*	Dickenson Gap		3,300'	1,541.2	
654.0	*0.2*	Peters Mountain ridgecrest		3,860'	1,539.0	
654.2	*2.5*	Allegheny Trail Junction		3,740'	1,538.8	
656.7	*0.3*	**Pine Swamp Branch Shelter** ...12.6mS; 3.9mN	S, C, w	2,530'	1,536.3	
657.0	*1.1*	Va.635, Big Stony Creek Road, Stony Creek Valley ...*USFS parking area (E—200 ft.)*	R, P	2,370'	1,536.0	
658.1	*1.0*	Dismal Branch ...*bridge*	w	2,480'	1,534.9	
659.1	*1.1*	Va. 635, Big Stony Creek Road, Stony Creek	R, P, w	2,524'	1,533.9	
660.2	*0.2*	Va. 734, Seven Mile Road ...*gravel fire road*		3150'	1,532.8	
660.4	*0.2*	Spring ...*water for Bailey Gap Shelter (E—125 yds.)*	w	3,490'	1,532.6	
660.6	*3.7*	**Bailey Gap Shelter** ...3.9mS; 8.8mN	S	3,525'	1,532.4	
664.3	*0.2*	Va. 613, Mountain Lake Road, Salt Sulphur Turnpike East—5m to **Mountain Lake Lodge and Conservancy**	R, P L	3,950'	1,528.7	
664.5	*1.2*	Wind Rock ...*vista*		4,121'	1,528.5	
665.7	*3.7*	Campsite and piped spring	C, w	4,000'	1,527.3	
669.4	*0.8*	**War Spur Shelter** ...8.8mS; 5.8mN	S, C, w	2,340'	1,523.6	
670.2	*1.0*	Johns Creek Valley, USFS 156, Va. 632	R, P, w	2,102'	1,522.8	

Miles from Springer	Miles to Next Point	Features	Services	Elev	Miles from Katahdin	MAP
671.2	1.0	Stream	w	2,700'	1,521.8	
672.2	0.5	Va. 601, Rocky Gap	R, P	3,159'	1,520.8	
672.7	0.1	Johns Creek Mountain Trail			1,520.3	
672.8	1.2	Former firetower site		3,788'	1,520.2	
674.0	0.3	White Rock *(E–100 yds.)*			1,519.0	
674.3	0.9	Kelly Knob		3,742'	1,518.7	
675.2	0.1	**Laurel Creek Shelter** *(E–100 ft.)* ...5.8mS; 6.8mN	S, w	2,720'	1,517.8	ATC Cen. Va. Map 4
675.3	1.1	Laurel Creek	w		1,517.7	
676.4	1.2	Spring	w	2,400'	1,516.6	
677.6	0.9	Sinking Creek Valley, Va. 42	R	2,150'	1,515.4	
678.5	0.5	Va. 630, Sinking Creek ...*road bridge*	R, P, w	2,100'	1,514.5	
679.0	1.2	Keffer Oak		2,240'	1,514.0	
680.2	1.6	Sinking Creek Mountain *(south)*		3,490'	1,512.8	
681.8	3.6	**Sarver Hollow Shelter** *(E–0.4m)* ...6.8mS; 6.4mN	S, w	3,000'	1,511.2	
685.4	1.7	Sinking Creek Mountain *(north)*		3,490'	1,507.6	
687.1	0.7	Cabin Branch	C, w	2,490'	1,505.9	
687.8	1.3	**Niday Shelter** ...6.4mS; 10.4mN	S, w	1,800'	1,505.2	
689.1	3.4	Craig Creek Valley, Va. 621	R, P	1,560'	1,503.9	
692.5	0.4	Brushy Mountain		3,100'	1,500.5	
692.9	2.2	Audie Murphy Monument *(W–50 yds.)*		3,100'	1,500.1	
695.1	1.6	Brushy Mountain ...*vistas*		2,600'	1,497.9	
696.7	1.2	Va. 620, Miller Cove Road, Trout Creek	R, P, w	1,525'	1,496.3	
697.9	4.2	**Pickle Branch Shelter** *(E–0.3m)* ...10.4mS; 13.9mN	S, w	1,845'	1,495.1	
702.1	1.0	Cove Mountain, Dragons Tooth *(E–0.1m)*		3,020'	1,490.9	
703.1	0.5	Lost Spectacles Gap *(W–1.5m to Va. 311)*		2,550'	1,489.9	
703.6	0.6	Rawies Rest		2,350'	1,489.4	
704.2	0.4	Scout Trail			1,488.8	ATC Central Va. Map 3
		Camping Restrictions northbound to U.S. 220				
704.6	1.6	Va. 624, Newport Rd., North Mountain Trail *East–0.4m to* 4 Pines Hostel *West–0.4m to* Catawba Grocery	R, P H G, M	1,790'	1,488.4	
706.2	3.7	Va. 785, Blacksburg Road ...*between two stiles*	R	1,790'	1,486.8	
709.9	0.6	Catawba Greenway			1,483.1	
710.5	0.3	Va. 311, Catawba Valley Drive *West–1m to* **Catawba, Va., P.O. 24070** *West–1.3m to* Homeplace Restaurant	R, P G M	1,980'	1,482.5	
710.8	0.7	Fire Road Connector Trail south junction			1,482.2	
711.5	1.0	**Johns Spring Shelter** ...13.9mS; 1mN	S, w	1,980'	1,481.5	
712.5	0.1	**Catawba Mountain Shelter** ...1mS; 2.4mN	S, w	2,580'	1,480.5	
712.6	0.3	Campsites *(east)*	C		1,480.4	
712.9	1.3	Fire Road Connector Trail north junction			1,480.1	
714.2	0.6	McAfee Knob ...*vista*		3,199'	1,478.8	
714.8	0.1	Pig Farm Campsite ...*spring (E–0.1m)*	C, w	3,000'	1,478.2	

Miles from Springer	Miles to Next Point	Features	Services	Elev	Miles from Katahdin	M A P
714.9	1.9	**Campbell Shelter** *(E–0.2m spring) ...2.4mS; 6mN*	S, w	2,580'	1,478.1	
716.8	1.2	Snack Bar Rock *...two large rocks*			1,476.2	
718.0	1.8	Brickey's Gap *(Tinker Cliff bypass E–1.7m to Lamberts Meadow Campsite)*		2,250'	1,475.0	
719.8	0.5	Tinker Cliffs		3,000'	1,473.2	
720.3	0.6	Scorched Earth Gap, Andy Layne Trail *(W–3.1m to Va. 779)*		2,360'	1,472.7	
720.9	0.3	**Lamberts Meadow Shelter** *...6mS; 14.4mN*	S, w	2,080'	1,472.1	
721.2	4.0	Lamberts Meadow Campsite, Sawmill Run *(Tinker Cliff bypass E–1.7m to Brickey's Gap)*	C, w	2,000'	1,471.8	
725.2	1.1	Angels Gap *...gas-line right of way*		1,800'	1,467.8	
726.3	1.9	Hay Rock, Tinker Ridge *...view of Carvins Cove Reservoir*		1,900'	1,466.7	
728.2	1.0	Tinker Ridge *...crest*			1,464.8	
729.2	0.6	Trail register *...kiosk*			1,463.8	
729.8	0.5	Tinker Creek *...concrete bridge*		1,165'	1,463.2	
		Camping Restrictions southbound to Va. 624				
730.3	1.2	U.S. 220 *East–0.8m to services near I-81 on U.S. 11* *East–12m to Roanoke, Va.* *West–0.3m to Botetourt Commons Shopping Plaza* *West–1m to* **Daleville, Va., P.O. 24083**	R, P, G, L, M G, L, M, cl, sh O G, M, O, f G, D, V	1,350'	1,462.7	Central Va. Map 3
731.5	0.3	U.S. 779, I-81 underpass	R, P	1,400'	1,461.5	
731.8	0.5	U.S. 11, Norfolk Southern Railway *West–0.8m to* **Troutville, Va., P.O. 24175** *West–1.3m to* fire station	R, P C, G, M	1,300'	1,461.2	
732.3	1.6	Va. 652, Mountain Pass Road	R	1,450'	1,460.7	
733.9	1.4	Tollhouse Gap			1,459.1	
735.3	2.8	**Fullhardt Knob Shelter** *...14.4mS; 6.2mN*	S, w	2,676'	1,457.7	
738.1	0.8	USFS 191, Salt Pond Road	R, P	2,260'	1,454.9	
738.9	1.9	Curry Creek, Curry Creek Trail	w	1,680'	1,454.1	
740.8	0.7	Wilson Creek	w	1,690'	1,452.2	
741.5	0.4	**Wilson Creek Shelter** *(W–150 ft.) ...6.2mS; 7.5mN*	S, w	1,830'	1,451.5	
741.9	2.0	Spring *...unreliable*	w	2,050'	1,451.1	
743.9	0.8	USFS 186/Old Fincastle Road at Black Horse Gap, BRP mp 97.7	R, P	2,402'	1,449.1	
744.7	1.1	Taylors Mountain Overlook; BRP mp 97.0	R, P	2,365'	1,448.3	
745.8	0.6	Montvale Overlook; BRP mp 95.9	R, P	2,456'	1,447.2	
746.4	1.6	Harveys Knob Overlook; BRP mp 95.3	R, P	2,540'	1,446.6	
748.0	0.8	Hammond Hollow Trail		2,300'	1,445.0	
748.8	0.7	**Bobblets Gap Shelter** *(W–0.2m) ...7.5mS; 6.7mN*	S, w	1,920'	1,444.2	
749.5	0.7	Peaks of Otter Overlook; BRP mp 92.5	R, P	2,354'	1,443.5	
750.2	1.7	Mills Gap Overlook; BRP mp 91.8	R, P	2,448'	1,442.8	

Miles from Springer	Miles to Next Point	Features	Services	Elev	Miles from Katahdin	M A P
751.9	1.6	Bearwallow Gap, Va. 43; BRP mp 90.9 *East–4.4m to* Peaks of Otter Area *West–5m to* **Buchanan, Va., P.O. 24066** *West–7m to* Wattstull Motel & Restaurant on I-81	R, P C, L, M G, M L, M	2,228'	1,441.1	
753.5	0.4	Cove Mountain		2,707'	1,439.5	
753.9	1.4	Little Cove Mountain Trail *(E–2.8m to Va. 614)*		2,563'	1,439.1	
755.3	1.7	**Cove Mountain Shelter** ...*6.7mS; 7mN*	S, nw	1,996'	1,437.7	
757.0	1.5	Buchanan Trail *(W–0.2m spring)*	w	1,780'	1,436.0	
758.5	1.6	Va. 614, Jennings Creek Road, Panther Ford Bridge, Jennings Creek *East–1.4m to* Middle Creek Campground *West–4.5m to* Wattstull Motel & Restaurant	R, P, C, w G, C, cl, sh, f L, M	987'	1,434.5	
760.1	2.2	Fork Mountain		2,042'	1,432.9	
762.3	1.4	**Bryant Ridge Shelter** ...*7mS; 4.9mN*	S, w	1,330'	1,430.7	
763.7	2.9	Bryant Ridge		2,394'	1,429.3	
766.6	0.6	Floyd Mountain		3,560'	1,426.4	
767.2	0.9	**Cornelius Creek Shelter** ...*4.9mS; 5.3mN*	S, w	3,145'	1,425.8	
768.1	0.6	Black Rock		3,420'	1,424.9	
768.7	1.1	Cornelius Creek Trail		3,179'	1,424.3	
769.8	0.1	Apple Orchard Falls Trail		3,364'	1,423.2	
769.9	1.4	Parkers Gap Road, USFS 812; BRP mp 78.4	R, P	3,410'	1,423.1	
771.3	0.3	Apple Orchard Mountain ...*FAA radar dome*		4,206'	1,421.7	
771.6	0.6	The Guillotine ...*large boulder suspended overhead*		4,090'	1,421.4	
772.2	0.3	Upper BRP crossing mp 76.3	R	3,900'	1,420.8	
772.5	1.0	**Thunder Hill Shelter** ...*5.3mS; 12.4mN*	S, w	3,960'	1,420.5	
773.5	0.6	Lower BRP crossing mp 74.9	R, P	3,650'	1,419.5	
774.1	1.7	Thunder Hill Overlook; BRP mp 74.7	R, P	3,525'	1,418.9	
775.8	1.4	Harrison Ground Spring	w	3,200'	1,417.2	
777.2	1.2	Petites Gap, USFS 35; BRP mp 71.0	R, P	2,369'	1,415.8	
778.4	1.2	Highcock Knob		3,054'	1,414.6	
779.6	0.5	Marble Spring *(W–330 ft. spring)*	C, w	2,300'	1,413.4	
780.1	1.8	Sulphur Spring Trail *(2.3m) rejoins A.T.*		2,415'	1,412.9	
781.9	0.5	Hickory Stand, Gunter Ridge Trail		2,650'	1,411.1	
782.4	0.8	Sulphur Spring Trail *(2.3m) rejoins A.T.*		2,588'	1,410.6	
783.2	1.9	Big Cove Branch	w	1,853'	1,409.8	
785.1	0.8	**Matts Creek Shelter** ...*12.4mS; 3.9mN*	S, w	835'	1,407.9	
785.9	1.2	Campsites	C, w	700'	1,407.1	
787.1	0.2	James River Foot Bridge		678'	1,405.9	
787.3	0.1	U.S. 501, Va. 130 ...*jct. with USFS 36/Va. 812 (Hercules Rd.)* *East–5m to* **Big Island, Va., P.O. 24526** *West–6.1m to* **Glasgow, Va., P.O. 24555**	R, P G, M, D S, G, M, D, cl	680'	1,405.7	
787.4	0.9	Lower Rocky Row Run bridge	w	740'	1,405.6	
788.3	0.1	Rocky Row Run ...*campsites along creek*	C, w	760'	1,404.7	
788.4	0.6	Va. 812, USFS 36 (Hercules Rd.)	R, P	825'	1,404.6	

ATC Central Va. Map 2

Miles from Springer	Miles to Next Point	Features	Services	Elev	Miles from Katahdin	M A P
789.0	2.0	**Johns Hollow Shelter** *(E–400 ft.)* ...*3.9mS; 9mN*	S, w	1,020'	1,404.0	
791.0	0.1	Rocky Row Trail *(W–2.8m to U.S. 501)*		2,431'	1,402.0	
791.1	1.0	Fullers Rocks, Little Rocky Row		2,486'	1,401.9	
792.1	1.5	Big Rocky Row		2,974'	1,400.9	
793.6	1.1	Saddle Gap, Saddle Gap Trail *(E–2.5m to Va. 812, USFS 36, Hercules Rd.)*		2,590'	1,399.4	
794.7	1.5	Saltlog Gap (south)		2,573'	1,398.3	
796.2	1.1	Bluff Mountain ...*Ottie Cline Powell memorial*		3,391'	1,396.8	
797.3	0.5	Punchbowl Mountain		2,841'	1,395.7	
797.8	0.4	**Punchbowl Shelter** *(W–0.2m) ...9mS; 9.7mN*	S, w	2,500'	1,395.2	
798.2	0.1	Punchbowl Mountain Crossing; BRP mp 51.7	R, P	2,170'	1,394.8	
798.3	0.2	Spring (E–150 ft.) ...*piped*	w		1,394.7	
798.5	1.9	Va. 607, Robinson Gap Road ...*jct. with Little Irish Creek Rd. (USFS 311)*	R	2,100'	1,394.5	
800.4	0.7	Rice Mountain		2,169'	1,392.6	
801.1	0.4	Spring *(west)*	w		1,391.9	ATC Central Va. Map 2
801.5	0.8	USFS 311A ...*log steps both sides*	R		1,391.5	
802.3	0.1	USFS 39	R, P	990'	1,390.7	
802.4	2.5	Pedlar River Bridge	w	970'	1,390.6	
804.9	0.4	Swapping Camp Creek	w		1,388.1	
805.3	1.0	Swapping Camp Road, USFS 38	R, P	1,000'	1,387.7	
806.3	1.0	Brown Mountain Creek ...*footbridge*	w		1,386.7	
807.3	0.2	**Brown Mountain Creek Shelter** ...9.7mS; 6.2mN	S, w	1,395'	1,385.7	
807.5	1.6	Joseph Richeson Spring *(E–15 yds.)... walled*	w		1,385.5	
809.1	0.9	U.S. 60, Lexington Turnpike, Long Mountain Wayside ...*picnic tables* *West–9.7m to* **Buena Vista, Va., P.O. 24416** *West–16.2m to* **Lexington, Va., P.O. 24450**	R, P, C C, G, L, M, D, V, sh, cl, f all	2,060'	1,383.9	
810.0	1.9	USFS 507 ...*campsite and spring (E–0.5m)*	C, w		1,383.0	
811.9	1.0	Bald Knob ...*wooded summit*		4,059'	1,381.1	
812.9	1.2	Old Hotel Trail to **Cow Camp Gap Shelter** *(E–0.6m) ...6.2mS; 10.8mN*	S, w	3,428'	1,380.1	
814.1	1.3	Cole Mountain		4,022'	1,378.9	
815.4	0.9	Hog Camp Gap, USFS 48, Wiggins Spring Rd	R, P, C, w	3,522'	1,377.6	
816.3	1.3	Tar Jacket Ridge		3,840'	1,376.7	
817.6	1.2	Salt Log Gap (north), USFS 63, Va. 634	R, P	3,290'	1,375.4	
818.8	0.5	USFS 246	R	3,500'	1,374.2	
819.3	1.0	Greasy Spring Road, USFS 1176A	R	3,600'	1,373.7	Map 1
820.3	0.9	Wolf Rocks *(W–50 yds.)*		3,893'	1,372.7	
821.2	1.2	North Fork of Piney River	C, w	3,500'	1,371.8	
822.4	0.7	Elk Pond Branch	C, w	3,750'	1,370.6	

Miles from Springer	Miles to Next Point	Features	Services	Elev	Miles from Katahdin	M A P
823.1	1.1	**Seeley–Woodworth Shelter** *(E–120 yds.)* *...10.8mS; 6.6mN*	S, w	3,770'	1,369.9	
824.2	1.2	Porters Field *...campsites, spring (W–100 ft. down old road)*	C, w	3,650'	1,368.8	
825.4	0.5	Spy Rock Road *...gravel* *West–2.5m to* **Montebello, Va., P.O. 24464**	R, C C, G, L, cl, sh, f	3,454'	1,367.6	
825.9	0.8	Spy Rock *(E–400 ft.) ...vista*		3,680'	1,367.1	
826.7	1.3	Cash Hollow Rock		3,556'	1,366.3	
828.0	0.8	Cash Hollow Road *...dirt*	R	3,280'	1,365.0	
828.8	0.9	Shoe Creek Gap, Va. 826, Crabtree Farm Rd *West–0.5m to* Crabtree Meadows and Crabtree Falls Trail	C, w	3,319'	1,364.2	
829.7	0.5	**The Priest Shelter** *...6.6mS; 7.6mN*	S, w	3,840'	1,363.3	
830.2	3.0	The Priest		4,063'	1,362.8	
833.2	1.3	Cripple Creek	w	1,800'	1,359.8	
834.5	0.1	Va. 56, Crabtree Falls Highway *West–3.9m to* Crabtree Falls Campground	R, P C, G, sh	997'	1,358.5	
834.6	1.8	Tye River, Three Ridges Wilderness *... suspension bridge*	C, w	970'	1,358.4	
836.4	0.9	Mau-Har Trail *(3m) rejoins A.T. at* Maupin Field Shelter		2,090'	1,356.6	
837.3	2.0	**Harpers Creek Shelter** *...7.6mS; 6.2mN*	S, w	1,800'	1,355.7	
839.3	1.7	Chimney Rocks		3,190'	1,353.7	
841.0	0.5	Three Ridges		3,970'	1,352.0	
841.5	1.6	Hanging Rock *...vista*		3,750'	1,351.5	
843.1	0.4	Bee Mountain		3,034'	1,349.9	
843.5	1.7	**Maupin Field Shelter** *...6.2mS; 15.8mN* *West–1.5m on fire road (USFS 306) to* BRP at Love Gap	S, w R	2,720'	1,349.5	
845.2	0.5	Reids Gap, Va. 664; BRP mp 13.6	R, P	2,645'	1,347.8	
845.7	3.8	Three Ridges Parking Overlook; BRP mp 13.1	R, P	2,700'	1,347.3	
849.5	0.5	Cedar Cliffs *...vista*		2,800'	1,343.5	
850.0	1.2	Dripping Rock Parking Area; BRP mp 9.6	R, P, w	2,950'	1,343.0	
851.2	1.6	Humpback Rocks Picnic Area (W–0.3m)	R, P, w	3,200'	1,341.8	
852.8	1.0	Humpback Mountain		3,606'	1,340.2	
853.8	1.5	Side Trail to Humpback Rocks *(W–0.3mviews; 1.3m VC)*	R, w	3,250'	1,339.2	
855.3	2.2	Bear Spring (west)	w	3,200'	1,337.7	
857.5	0.3	Glass Hollow Overlook *(E–0.2m)*		2,750'	1,335.5	
857.8	0.1	Side Trail to Humpback Visitors Center *(W–2m BRP; 2.2m VC)*	R, w	2,150'	1,335.2	
857.9	1.4	Jack Albright Trail to Humpback Visitors Center *(W–2m)*	R, w	2280'	1,335.1	
859.3	1.7	Mill Creek, **Paul C. Wolfe Shelter** *... 15.8mS;13mN*	S, w	1,700'	1,333.7	
861.0	3.3	Former Mayo Cabin *...hearth, chimney*			1,332.0	

ATC Central Va. Map 1

Miles from Springer	Miles to Next Point	Features	Services	Elev	Miles from Katahdin	M A P
864.3	0.1	Rockfish Gap, U.S. 250, I-64, Crozet Tunnel *West–500 yds. to* Rockfish Gap Visitor Ctr *West–1m to* Colony House Motel *West–4.5m to* **Waynesboro, Va., P.O. 22980**	R, P, L, M all	1,902'	**1,328.7**	Cen Va. 1

BRP=Blue Ridge Parkway, mp=milepost

Central Virginia's treadway is well-graded and includes several 2,000- to 3,000-foot climbs. You will traverse some of the northernmost balds on the Trail. Unusual rock formations offer up views to the valley below from the peaks of Humpback Rocks, Three Ridges, The Priest, McAfee Knob, and Dragons Tooth. This section, more rugged and remote than Shenandoah to the north, parallels the Blue Ridge Parkway for 90 miles.

Va. 100/East 1.0 miles to **Pearisburg, Va. [P.O. ZIP 24134: M–F 9–4:30, Sa 10–12: (540) 921-1100].** ■ *Lodging:* Plaza Motel, 415 N. Main St., (540) 921-2591, $50S $5EAP, stay 3 nights $120S $5EAP, WiFi, laundry, no pets, will hold packages whether guest or not, e-mail available in office; Holiday Motor Lodge, 401 N. Main St., (540) 921-1551, $55D $10EAP; May 1–Sep 15 hostel $20 (shower, TV, fridge, microwave); Internet access, seasonal swimming pool, pet-friendly, accepts packages. ■ *Hostel:* Angels Rest Hiker's Haven, 204 Douglas Lane, Pearisburg, VA 24134, (540) 787-4076, <www.angelsresthikershaven.com>, open all year. Bunks $25, private rooms $35-$75, tent/hammock $12PP. Military discount. Leashed dogs $5 with stay, WiFi, computer, printer, full kitchen. Laundry $5; $7 day pass includes shower, laundry, and all amenities until 6 p.m. Cash or credit, limited work-for-stay. Responsible drinking, no drunks, no drugs, no drama. Accepts mail drops. ■ *Groceries:* Food Lion and Grant's Grocery (long-term resupply). ■ *Restaurants:* Pizza Plus, buy one pizza, get one free, AYCE salad/pizza buffet, and free delivery; Pizza Hut with AYCE L buffet. ■ *Internet access:* Pearisburg Public Library, (540) 921-2556. ■ *Other services:* Pearis Mercantile, (540) 921-2260, large selection of hiking supplies, holds hiker packages, may shuttle; Community Health Center, (540) 921-3502, M-W-F 8–4:30, T-Th 8–12:30 ($20 walk-ins without insurance); Rite Aid with one-hour photo service; automotive and hardware stores; Walmart; coin laundry; ATM; hospital; dentist; veterinarian; municipal swimming pool open to the public Memorial Day to Labor Day (fee). ■ *Shuttles:* Tom Hoffman, (540) 921-1184, <gopullman@aol.com>; Don Raines, (540) 921-7433, <ratface20724@aol.com>.

East 2.9 miles, follow blue-blaze to *Hostel:* Holy Family Church Hostel is located in a peaceful

setting on a hill, hidden by trees beyond the church parking lot. Refrigerator, microwave, and loft with sleeping pads, $10 suggested donation per night; additional

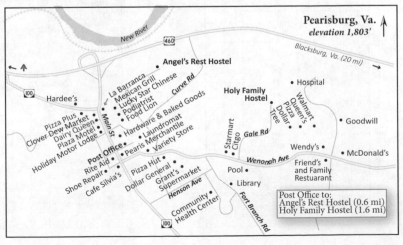

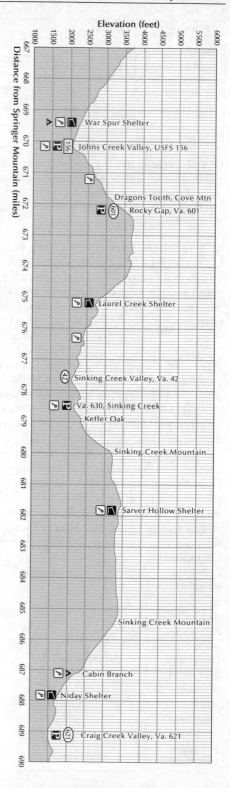

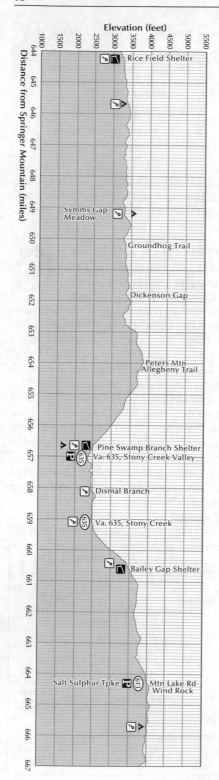

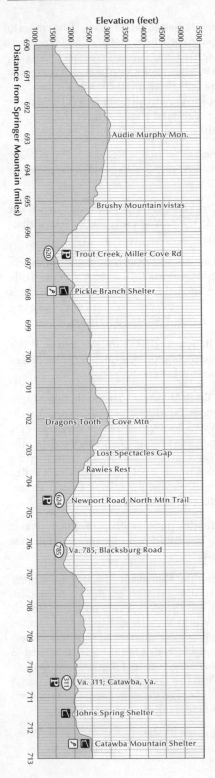

Elevation (feet)

Distance from Springer Mountain (miles)

Audie Murphy Mon.

Brushy Mountain vistas

Trout Creek, Miller Cove Rd

Pickle Branch Shelter

Dragons Tooth   Cove Mtn

Lost Spectacles Gap
Rawies Rest

Newport Road, North Mtn Trail

Va. 785, Blacksburg Road

Va. 311; Catawba, Va.

Johns Spring Shelter

Catawba Mountain Shelter

donations and cleaning appreciated. Stays are limited to two nights. Open Mar–Nov. Alcoholic beverages and drugs are prohibited. Pets allowed if well taken care of. Call caretaker Pat Muldoon, (540) 626-3337.

East 6 miles on U.S. 460 to *Outfitter:* Tangent Outfitters, 201 Cascade Dr., Pembroke, VA 24136; (540) 626-4567, <www.newrivertrail.com>, primarily oriented to rafters.

East 20 miles *via* U.S. 460 to Blacksburg, Va., home of Virginia Tech, with all services. *Outfitter:* Back Country Ski & Sports, (800) 560-6401 or (540) 552-6400, open M–Sa 10–8, Su 1–5.

West 4.3 miles *via* U.S. 460 to Va. 61 to **Narrows, Va. [P.O. ZIP 24124: M–F 9:30–1:15 & 2–4:15, Sa 9–11, (540) 726-3272].** ■ *Lodging:* MacArthur Inn, 117 MacArthur Lane, (540) 726-7510, <www.macarthur-inn.com>; renovated hotel, 26 rooms; hiker rates start at $45, private room with shared bath, full B; shower $8; laundry; no pets; WiFi; free long-distance phone; fuel; shuttle to and from Trail $5 round-trip (call from Pearisburg); accepts mail drops; old-time music and country dinner Th. ■ *Other services:* town campground on river, $2; restaurant; deli; groceries; coin laundry.

Rice Field Shelter (1995)—Sleeps 7. Privy. Shelter has an excellent viewing area for sunsets and clouded valleys in the morning. Water is on a steep, 0.5-mile downhill hike behind and to the left of the shelter.

Symms Gap Meadow—The traverse of Peters Mountain on the Virginia–West Virginia state line is a dry one. At this mountain meadow, with views into West Virginia, a small pond , which might be dry in summer and fall, is downhill from the A.T. on the West Virginia side, with camping nearby.

Allegheny Trail—2.5 miles south of Pine Swamp Branch Shelter is the A.T.'s junction with the southern end of the Allegheny Trail, which extends about 300 miles across West Virginia to Pennsylvania. The trail is maintained by the West Virginia Scenic Trails Association, <www.wvscenictrails.org>. Portions are being incorporated into the Great Eastern Trail, <www. greateasterntrail.net>.

Pine Swamp Branch Shelter (1980s)—Sleeps 8. Privy. Stone shelter. Water is from the stream 75 yards down a blue-blazed trail west of the side trail to the shelter.

Bailey Gap Shelter (1960s)—Sleeps 6. Privy. Water is 0.2 mile south on the A.T., then east down a blue-blazed trail.

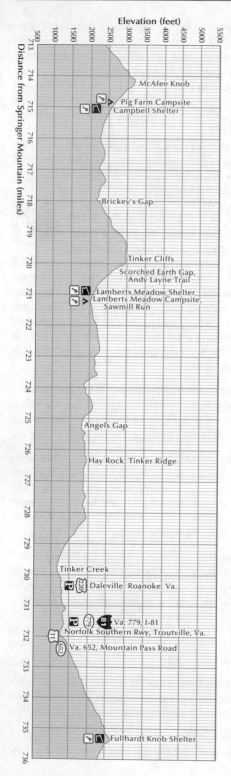

Elevation (feet)

Distance from Springer Mountain (miles)

McAfee Knob

Pig Farm Campsite
Campbell Shelter

Brickey's Gap

Tinker Cliffs

Scorched Earth Gap,
Andy Layne Trail

Lamberts Meadow Shelter
Lamberts Meadow Campsite,
Sawmill Run

Angels Gap

Hay Rock, Tinker Ridge

Tinker Creek

Daleville; Roanoke, Va.

Va. 779, I-81
Norfolk Southern Rwy, Troutville, Va.

Va. 652, Mountain Pass Road

Fullhardt Knob Shelter

Va. 613, Salt Sulfur Turnpike— East 5 miles to *Lodging:* Mountain Lake Lodge and Conservancy, 115 Hotel Circle, Pembroke, VA 24136; (800) 346-3334, <www.mtnlakelodge.com>; site of one of only two natural lakes in Virginia; reservations required; call for rates. Will hold packages for registered guests. One of the locations where the movie "Dirty Dancing" was filmed.

War Spur Shelter (1960s)—Sleeps 6. Privy. Water source is a stream 80 yards north of the shelter on the A.T.

Laurel Creek Shelter (1988)—Sleeps 6. Privy. Water is west on the A.T., 45 yards south of the shelter-trail junction.

Keffer Oak—Located about 0.2 mile north of Va. 630, this is the largest oak tree on the A.T. in the South. Last measured, the girth was 18 feet, 3 inches; it is estimated to be 300 years old. The Dover Oak along the A.T. in New York is slightly larger.

Sarver Hollow Shelter (2001)—Sleeps 6. Privy. Water source is a spring located on a blue-blazed trail near the shelter.

Sinking Creek Mountain—The northernmost spot where the A.T. crosses a notable "continental divide." Waters flowing down the western side of the ridge drain into Sinking Creek Valley and the Mississippi River to the Gulf of Mexico. Waters flowing on the eastern side empty into Craig Creek Valley, the James River, and the Atlantic Ocean. Terrain can be difficult in this area.

Niday Shelter (1980)—Sleeps 6. Privy. Water source is 75 yards down a blue-blazed trail west of the A.T.

Audie Murphy Monument—located on a blue-blazed trail to the west on Brushy Mountain. Murphy was the most decorated American soldier of World War II, and his single-handed capture of a large number of German soldiers made him a legend. After the war, he starred in many Hollywood war and B-grade western movies. He died in a 1971 plane crash near this site. A trail leads beyond the monument to a view from a rock outcropping.

Pickle Branch Shelter (1980)—Sleeps 6. Privy. Water from stream below the shelter.

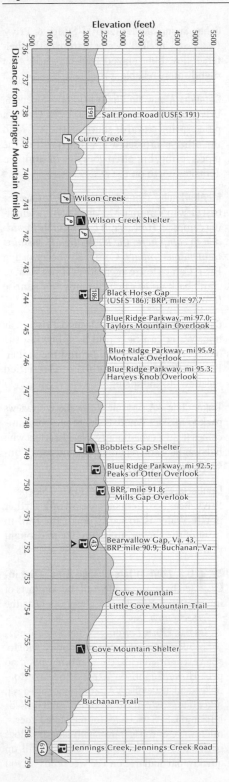

Elevation (feet)

Distance from Springer Mountain (miles)

191 Salt Pond Road (USFS 191)

Curry Creek

Wilson Creek

Wilson Creek Shelter

186 Black Horse Gap
(USFS 186), BRP, mile 97.7

Blue Ridge Parkway, mi 97.0;
Taylors Mountain Overlook

Blue Ridge Parkway, mi 95.9;
Montvale Overlook

Blue Ridge Parkway, mi 95.3;
Harveys Knob Overlook

Bobblets Gap Shelter

Blue Ridge Parkway, mi 92.5;
Peaks of Otter Overlook

BRP, mile 91.8;
Mills Gap Overlook

43 Bearwallow Gap, Va. 43,
BRP mile 90.9; Buchanan, Va.

Cove Mountain

Little Cove Mountain Trail

Cove Mountain Shelter

Buchanan Trail

614 Jennings Creek, Jennings Creek Road

Dragons Tooth—Named by Tom Campbell, an early RATC member and prime mover in the 1930s–1950s in locating the A.T. here. He also named Lost Spectacles Gap, north of Dragons Tooth, after his glasses disappeared on a scouting/ work hike.

Camping Restrictions—Between Va. 624 and U.S. 220, camping and fires are allowed only at the following designated sites of this heavily used section: Johns Spring, Catawba Mountain, Campbell, and Lamberts Meadow shelters and Pig Farm and Lamberts Meadow campsites. *Adherence to this regulation, as well as the one banning consumption of alcohol on this section of the Trail, is being vigorously monitored due to increased use and abuse. This is one the most heavily used areas of the A.T.; please honor these regulations so that all may continue to enjoy it.*

Va. 624/North Mountain Trail—West 0.3 mile to Va. 311, then left 0.1 mile to Catawba Grocery, (540) 384-8050 (short-term resupply), open 5:30–10, Sa–Su 6–10. Nearby North Mountain Trail was once the A.T. route. A 30-mile loop is possible.

East 0.4 mile to *Hostel:* 4 Pines Hostel, 6164 Newport Rd., Catawba, VA 24070; (540) 309-8615; donations accepted; tenting, washing machine; shuttles (fee). Will hold UPS and USPS packages.

Va. 311—West 1 mile to **Catawba, Va. [P.O. ZIP 24070: M–F 9–12 & 1–4, Sa 8–10:30; (540) 384-6011]**. *Groceries:* Catawba Valley Farmers Market, held at the Catawba Community Center in the village of Catawba; open Th, May–Oct, 3:30–7 p.m.

West 1.3 miles to the Homeplace Restaurant, (540) 384-7252; AYCE meals $15 for two meats, $16 for three meats, less if you're vegetarian ($13); desserts, $2–$3. Open Th–F 4–8, Sa 3–8, Su 11–6 (closed the week of Jul 4 and two weeks in late Dec); Th is Southern-barbeque night. No public restroom.

Plans are in the works for a blue-blazed trail from the Va. 311 parking lot to Catawba through a 400-acre Virginia Tech farm; watch for updates along the Trail and in the Trail-updates section of <www.appalachiantrail.org>. Note the new Catawba Greenway 0.6 mile south of Va. 311 that ends near the Homeplace.

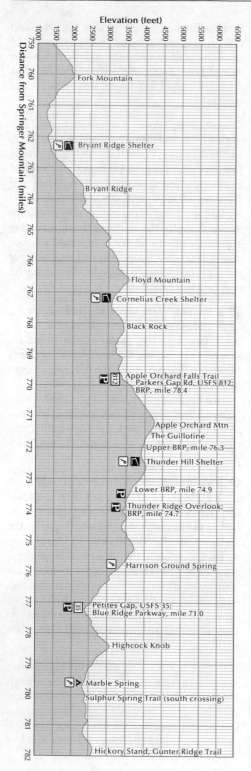

Johns Spring Shelter (2003)—Sleeps 6. Privy. Bear box. Unreliable water in front of the shelter; follow blue-blazed trail 0.25 mile to a slightly more reliable spring.

Catawba Mountain Shelter (1984)—Sleeps 6. Privy. Bear box. Two water sources: One is a piped spring 50 yards south on the A.T., and the other is crossed a few feet north of the piped spring, but often goes dry in summer. Tentsites north on the A.T.

McAfee Knob—Considered by many to have the best view in Virginia, McAfee Knob is a tempting campsite. *However, it is absolutely forbidden to camp here; the knob already sustains tremendous impact.* Campbell Shelter or Pig Farm Campsite are alternatives if you want to climb back up to catch the sunset or sunrise from the cliff.

Campbell Shelter (1989)—Sleeps 6. Privy. Bear box. Water can be found by following the blue-blazed trail left and behind the shelter. Follow the trail through the "electrified meadow" to the spring.

Tinker Cliffs—A 0.5-mile cliff-walk, with views back to McAfee Knob. Folklore says the name comes from Revolutionary War deserters who hid near here and repaired pots and pans ("tinkers"). *No camping here.*

Lamberts Meadow Shelter (1974)—Sleeps 6. Privy. Bear box. Tentsites are 0.3 mile farther north. Water is 50 yards down the trail in front of the shelter; may run dry in drought years.

U.S. 220/I-81 Interchange Area—The interchange area offers all the comforts of interstate travel, with most services near the A.T. *(See map below.)*

On U.S. 220. ■ *Lodging:* Super 8, (540) 992-3000, hiker rates subject to availability, $60S/D, $6EAP, continental B, coin laundry, pool, no pets; Howard Johnson Express Inn, 437 Roanoke Road, Daleville, VA 24083, (540) 992-1234, hiker rate $50S/D, includes continental B, holds UPS and USPS packages for registered guests, microwave & refrigerator, coin laundry, dogs permitted, $10 per pet. Both motels fill up quickly, particularly on the weekends. If you wish to stay there, make reservations during an earlier town stop. ■ *Restaurants:* Mexican restaurant; Pizza Hut with AYCE salad bar. ■ *Other services:* Several convenience stores.

West 0.3 mile to Botetourt Commons Shopping Plaza. ■ *Restaurants:* Mill Mountain Coffee House, 3 Little Pigs BBQ, Wendy's, Bojangles, Little Caesars. ■ *Groceries:* Kroger Super Store, with pharmacy (long-term resupply). ■ *Outfitter:* Outdoor Trails, Botetourt Commons, 28 Kingston Dr., Daleville, VA 24083; (540) 992-5850; M–F 10–8, Sa 10–6, closed Su; a full-service outfitter, sells fuel by the ounce and accepts mail drops ($5 to hold commercial packages); make reservation for shuttle or slackpacking. ■ *Other services:* UPS Store, (540) 966-0221, M–F 8–6:30, Sa 9–2:30; bank with ATM.

West 1 mile to **Daleville, Va. [P.O. ZIP 24083: M–F 8–5, Sa 8–12 (540) 992-4422]**. Convenience stores, Food Lion (long-term resupply), CVS, and bank are nearby. *Other services:* Medical center fits in hikers as schedule permits; veterinarian.

East 0.8 mile to U.S. 11. ■ *Lodging:* Motel 6, 2619 Lee Hwy., Troutville, VA 24175, (540) 992-6700, $41D, $3EAP (hiker rates), pets permitted; Best Western, 2545 Lee Hwy, Troutville, VA 24175, (540) 992-5600, ask for the "hiker-corporate" rates of $55S/D, $10EAP, includes continental B, pets $25,

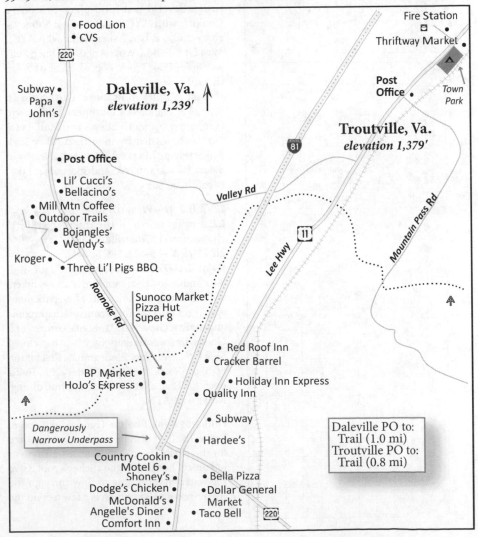

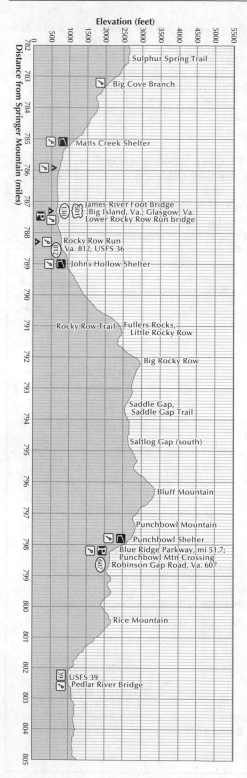

seasonal pool, and Internet access; Red Roof Inn, (540) 992-5055, $50S/$65D $3EAP, limited continental B, pets permitted; Quality Inn, 3139 Lee Hwy. South, Troutville, VA 24175, (540) 992-5335, hiker rate of $65S/D is significantly higher during special events, pets permitted with one-time $15 fee, hot and cold continental B, pool, exercise room, microwave and refrigerator, accepts mail drops; Holiday Inn Express, 3200 Lee Hwy. South, Troutville, VA 24175, (540) 966-4444, $120S/D, weekends add $10 (and may be much higher on "special event" weekends), microwave and refrigerator in rooms, hot and cold B, pool, holds UPS and USPS packages for registered guests. ■ *Restaurants:* Several fast-food places; Country Cookin', with AYCE buffet $7.99; Shoney's, $9.99–$10.99 B bar; Italian Bella, with AYCE $7.79 L M–F; Best Wok; Angelle's Diner; Subway inside Pilot Truck Stop, which also has $12 shower.

East 12 miles to **Roanoke.** *Outfitters:* In Roanoke, Walkabout Outfitters, downtown, (540) 777-2727, and Valley View Mall, (540) 777-0990, owned by 1999 thru-hiker Kirk Miller (Flying Monkey), open daily. Nearby in **Salem**: Backcountry Ski and Sports, (540) 389-8602, closed Su.

 U.S. 11—West 0.8 mile (1.5 miles north of the interchange area) to **Troutville, Va. [P.O. ZIP 24175: M–F 9–12 & 1–5, Sa 9–11; (540) 992-1472].** Town hall, (540) 992-4401, M–F 8–12 and 12:30–4:30, sometimes allows hikers to camp at the city park; call or find park manager, (540) 293-4548, for permission; bathrooms and water. ■ *Groceries:* Troutville Grocery and Goods (long-term resupply), M–Sa 8–7, closed Su. ■ *Other services:* Pomegranate Restaurant, (540) 966-6052, 106 Stoney Battery Rd., Tu–Sa open for D at 4 p.m., casual and fine dining; banks with ATMs.

Fullhardt Knob Shelter (1960s)—Sleeps 6. Privy. The (not-always-reliable) water source for this shelter is an elaborate cistern system of run-off hooked to the shelter's roof. Give the water enough time to flow through the freeze-proof valve, which is a few feet up the pipe toward the cistern. Please make sure spigot is off when you have finished getting water.

Wilson Creek Shelter (1986)—Sleeps 6. Privy. Water source is reliable stream 200 yards in front of the shelter.

Blue Ridge Parkway—Black Horse Gap is the A.T.'s southernmost encounter with the Blue Ridge Parkway (BRP). The A.T. parallels BRP, and later Skyline Drive, for approximately 200 miles. Much of the original A.T. route along the Blue Ridge south of Roanoke was displaced by the parkway when it was built. Hitchhiking is not permitted on the BRP. ■ *Hostel:* Duck-N Hut Hiker's Hostel, 11597 Stewartsville Rd., Vinton, Va. 24179, (540) 819-2164. Donation-based, free shuttle to and from the hostel, other shuttles $1.50 per mile. Short and long-term resupply nearby. Many animals on site and pet-friendly.

Natural Bridge Appalachian Trail Club—NBATC maintains the 90.7 miles between Black Horse Gap and the Tye River. Correspondence should be sent to NBATC Box 3012, Lynchburg, VA 24503; <www.nbatc.org>.

Bobblets Gap Shelter (1961)—Sleeps 6. Privy. Water source is a spring to the left of the shelter that is prone to go dry after prolonged rainless periods. Look farther downstream if the first source is dry.

Va. 43/Bearwallow Gap—**East,** then north 4.4 miles on the BRP to Peaks of Otter Area, (540) 586-1081. Lodge and restaurant open daily Mar 17–Nov and F–Su noon–3:30 Dec–Mar 17. Mail drops: 85554 Blue Ridge Parkway, Bedford, VA 24523. Rates $129 weekdays, $149 weekends (F–Su), $199 in Oct; B buffet Su, B/L/D daily, WiFi. Campsites, (877) 444-6777, <www.nps.gov/blri>, open early May–late Oct, $20–23.

    West 5 miles on Va. 43 to **Buchanan, Va. [P.O. ZIP 24066: M–F 8:30–1 & 1:30–4:30, Sa 10–12; (540) 254-2178].** ■ *Lodging:* Wattstull Inn & Restaurant, 130 Arcadia Rd., (540) 254-1551, <www.wattstul-linn.com>, is 2 miles north of town on I-81, rates $60–$120, pet-friendly, free WiFi, shuttles available, accepts packages. Anchorage House B&B and hostel, 19391 Main St. Buchanan, (540) 425-5239, bunks $25, private room with bath $68. Short-term resupply, shuttle to/from Bearwallow Gap possible. ■ *Internet access:* Buchanan Library. ■ *Other services:* bank with ATM, restaurants.

Cove Mountain Shelter (1981)—Sleeps 6. Privy. No convenient water source at this shelter. A steep, unmarked trail to left of the shelter leads 0.5 mile downhill to a stream.

Va. 614/Jennings Creek—Jennings Creek is a popular swimming hole for both hikers and local residents.

    East 0.2 mile to Va. 618, then 0.1 mile to the USFS Middle Creek Picnic Area with covered picnic pavilions; 1.1 miles farther on Va. 618 to *Camping:* Middle Creek Campground, 1164 Middle Creek Rd., Buchanan, VA 24066; (540) 254-2550, <www.middlecreekcampground.com>, tentsites with shower start at $10PP; bunkhouse $25PP, cabins start at $46 for 2; showers $5, leashed dogs allowed. Campstore (short-term resupply), Coleman fuel, canister and denatured alcohol by the ounce, coin laundry; mail drops accepted; when available, shuttle to the A.T.

    West 4.5 miles to Wattstull Inn & Restaurant (see Buchanan entry above).

Bryant Ridge Shelter (1992)—Sleeps 20. Privy. This trilevel, timber-frame shelter is one of the largest. Water source is a stream 25 yards in front of the shelter, also crossed on the trail to the shelter.

Cornelius Creek Shelter (1960)—Sleeps 6. Privy. A blue-blazed trail leads to the shelter, but just north of the turn-off is a branch of Cornelius Creek where you can find water. Water can also be found on the trail to the shelter. An unmarked trail behind the shelter leads 0.1 mile to a fire road and then left 0.2 mile to the BRP, where it is then 6 miles south to the Peaks of Otter Area.

Apple Orchard Falls Trail—Located 2.6 miles north of Cornelius Creek Shelter. When the water is high, these falls are impressive, making the 3-mile round-trip worth the effort.

Apple Orchard Mountain—When you reach the top, you will be at 4,225 feet. Once an Air Force radar base, the meadows were covered with barracks and support-service buildings for 250 people. On the northern side of the mountain, the A.T. leads you under The Guillotine—an impressively large boulder stuck over the Trail between rock formations. No camping is permitted on top of the mountain, the highest point on the A.T. between Chestnut Knob and Mt. Moosilauke in New Hampshire.

Thunder Hill Shelter (1962)—Sleeps 6. Privy. Bear box. Water source is a walled-in spring south of the shelter, prone to go dry by late summer. A larger, reliable spring can be found by going south on the A.T. to the BRP. At the BRP, turn left, walk 0.3 mile to a gated road on the left; 500 feet down the gated road, where the road turns left, angle right to a spring basin.

Matts Creek Shelter (1961)—Sleeps 6. Privy. Several small swimming holes are nearby. The rocks you will find in this area are 500 million years old. Tentsites north 1.0 mile, where Matts Creek flows into the James River, with river views and the sound of trains across the river. Water source is Matts Creek, in front of the shelter.

James River Foot Bridge—This bridge, the longest foot-use-only bridge on the A.T., is dedicated to the memory of Bill Foot, a 1987 thru-hiker and ALDHA honorary life member (Trail-named "The Happy Feet" with his wife, Laurie) whose efforts in securing the existing piers, applying for grants, and gaining numerous agencies' cooperation made it a reality.

U.S. 501/James River—**East** 5.0 miles to **Big Island, Va. [P.O. ZIP 24526: M–F 8:15–12 & 1–4, Sa 8–10; (434) 299-5072].** ▪ *Groceries:* H&H Market, (434) 299-5153, open daily 5:30–9 (long-term resupply), short-order restaurant, B/L/D. ▪ *Other services:* bank with ATM and medical center, (434) 299-5951.

West 6.1 miles to **Glasgow, Va. [P.O. ZIP 24555: M–F 8–11:30, 12:30–4:30, Sa 8:30–10:30; (540) 258-2852].** ▪ *Hostel:* Stanimal's 328 Hostel and Shuttle, 1131 Rockbridge Rd., (540) 480-8325, $30PP includes pick-up at Foot Bridge (call for pick-up from ridgetop; no service at bridge), a/c, Internet access, laundry, and showers; slackpacking; private-room options. ▪ *Shelter:* Glasgow Hiker's Shelter, 9th St., sleeps 12, camping, water, showers, electricity, microwave, fire pit, and Little Free Library. ▪ *Groceries:* Glasgow Grocery Express (long-term resupply), (540) 258-1818, open M–Sa 6–11:30, Su 8–11:30, has Coleman fuel by the ounce, denatured alcohol, and Heet. ▪ *Restaurants:* Scotto's, (540) 258-2500, Tu–Sa 10:30–9, Su 11–8, closed M; Petro's

Stop & Go, (540) 258-2012, deli and convenience store. ▪ *Internet access:* library, (540) 258-2509; M, Th 10–7; T, W 10–5:30, Sa 10–1. ▪ *Other services:* Dollar General, coin laundry, doctor. ▪ *Shuttles:* See Buena Vista below for lengthy listing.

Map: Glasgow, Va. elevation 736'
Library •
Blue Ridge Rd
Dollar General •
Post Office •
Stop & Go
Grocery Express •
• Scotto's Pizza
[30] • Laundry
Stanimal's Hostel
9th St
Glasgow Hiker Shelter
Buena Vista (9.1 mi)
Maury River
[501]
[130]
Post Office to:
Hiker Shelter (0.5 mi)
Stanimal's Hostel (0.5 mi)
(5.5 mi)

Johns Hollow Shelter (1961)—Sleeps 6. Privy. Water source is a spring to the left of the shelter or a stream to right 25 yards from the shelter.

Bluff Mountain—Site of a monument to four-year-old Ottie Cline Powell. In the fall of 1890, Ottie went into the woods to gather firewood for his schoolhouse and never returned. His body was found five months later on top of this mountain. NBATC members erected a permanent gravestone for his final resting place, seven miles from the monument.

Punchbowl Shelter (1961)—Sleeps 6. Privy. Some believe this shelter is haunted by Little Ottie's ghost. Tentsites nearby if the shelter is full, which it often is. Water source is a spring by a tree next to the pond drainage in front and to the left of the shelter. An alternative water source is a spring in the ravine north 0.4 mile, shortly after crossing the BRP.

Brown Mountain Creek Valley—Community of freed slaves lived here from the Civil War until about 1918; remains of cabins and interpretive signs tell of life in the valley then.

Brown Mountain Creek Shelter (1961)—Sleeps 6. Privy. Water source is a spring in front of, and uphill from, the shelter. In dry conditions, get water from Brown Mountain Creek, crossed on the trail south of the shelter.

U.S. 60—West 9.7 miles to **Buena Vista [P.O. ZIP 24416: M–F 8:30–4:30, closed Sa; (540) 261-8959].** ▪ *Lodging:* Buena Vista Motel, (540) 261-2138, $55.99–$89.99, $10 pet fee; Budget Inn, (540) 261-2156, $59.95S, $64.95S/D, $10EAP, $5 charge for early check-in, pet fee $10 (allowed in smoking rooms only), laundry, WiFi, possible shuttle to and from the Trail. ▪ *Camping:* Glen Maury Campground, (540) 261-7321, hiker specials, tentsites with shower, $5+tax per tent, free shower without stay, pool $2 for guests (closes mid-Aug). ▪ *Groceries:* Food Lion (long-term resupply); Sheltman's Gas & Grocery (short-term resupply). ▪ *Restaurants:* Original Italian Pizza, 10% discount to hikers; Mexican, Italian, BBQ, Chinese, seafood, ice cream, and fast-food choices. ▪ *Shuttles:* Rockbridge Taxi Service, (540) 261-7733; E's-Y Rider Taxi, (540) 461-2467; Buddy Johnson, (540) 817-9168; Gary Serra, (757) 681-2254; Aubrey Taylor, (540) 460-3527. An hourly fixed-rate service (Maury Express) runs between Lexington and Buena Vista M–F 8–6 and Sa 10–4 for 50¢ each way. ▪ *Other services:* Regional Visitors Center, (540) 261-8004; library with Internet access; Michael Ohleger, (540) 460-0236, may be able to arrange shuttles and other support; Advanced Auto (Heet); Buena Vista Hardware, gas canisters, thru-hiker discount; coin laundry; banks with ATM; hardware store; doctor; dentist; pharmacy; and veterinarian. ▪ *Other attractions:* The annual Maury River Fiddlers Convention, popular with hikers, is held at Glen Maury Park, the second weekend in Jun; Beach Music Festival, last Sa in Jul; Nothin' Fancy Bluegrass Festival, last weekend in Sep; annual Mountain Day street festival, second Sa in Oct.

West 16.2 miles to **Lexington [P.O. ZIP 24450: M–F 9–5, Sa 10–12; (540) 463-6449].** A larger town with groceries, motels, doctors, vets. ▪ *Outfitter:* Walkabout Outfitter, (540) 464-HIKE, 21 S. Main St., M–W 10–5:30, Th 10–5:30, F–Sa 10–7, Su 12–5, owned by Kirk Miller (Flying Monkey '99), full-service outfitter, MSR and Jetboil canisters. ▪ *Other services:* Maury Express, from Buena Vista to Lexington & back hourly, M–F 8–6, Sa 10–4, closed holidays, 50¢; Enterprise Car Rental, (540) 463-4679, 33 Quarry Ln.; Rockbridge Taxi, (540) 261-7733; E'S-Y Rider, (540) 461-2465; Cassie's Cab, (540) 784-3785; Uber; Cobblestone Show & Leather Repair, 121 W. Nelson St., (540) 461-8248.

Cow Camp Gap Shelter (1986)—Sleeps 8. Privy. Water source is on blue-blazed trail to the left of the shelter;

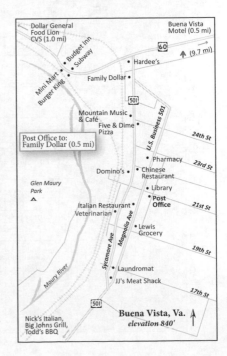

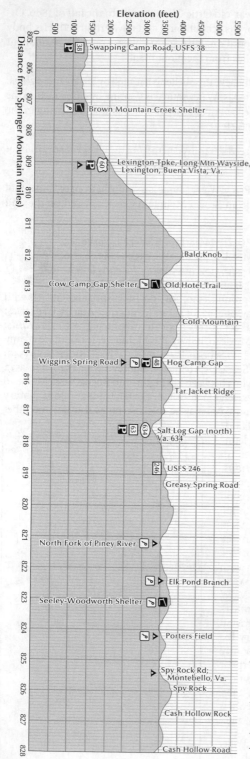

if you have crossed a small stream, you missed the spring.

Cole Mountain—Bald Knob, south of Cole Mountain, isn't a bald, but Cole Mountain and Tar Jacket Ridge are. A mowing project was undertaken by NBATC and the Forest Service to preserve the open views and habitat for northern cottontail rabbits, various raptors, turkey, and grouse.

Seeley–Woodworth Shelter (1984)—Sleeps 8. Privy. A blue-blaze leads 100 yards to shelter and 0.1 mile beyond to piped spring.

Porters Field—West to a spring and campsite 300 feet down the second of two dirt roads.

Spy Rock Road—This "private road"— formerly known as Fish Hatchery Road—is a gated, one-lane dirt road with no traffic. Check with USFS Glenwood–Pedlar District office to see if foot traffic is permitted. **West** 1.5 miles to the fish hatchery, 0.7 mile farther to **Montebello, Va. [P.O. ZIP 24464: M–F 10–2, Sa 10–1; (540) 377-9218]**, on Va. 56. Turn west, and reach town in 0.3 mile, with post office, grocery store, and campground. *Lodging:* Montebello Camping and Fishing, (540) 377-2650, <www.montebellova.com>, special thru-hiker-rate tentsites with shower $15S, $22D, $30 for 3+, furnished efficiency cabin $90–$165, bed-only camping cabin $50–$60, shower, laundry, short-term resupply, leashed dogs allowed.

Crabtree Farm Road—**West** 0.5 mile to campsite and spring; 2 miles farther on the Crabtree Falls Trail to Crabtree Falls, one of the highest cascades in the East. High-clearance vehicle may be needed.

The Priest Shelter (1960)—Sleeps 8. Privy. Named for the massif dominating the area; near a busy access for backpackers and often full. Water source is a spring to left of the shelter.

Tidewater Appalachian Trail Club—TATC maintains the 10.6 miles between the Tye River and Reids Gap. Correspondence should be sent to P.O. Box 8246, Norfolk, VA 23503; <president@tidewateratc.com>; <www.tidewateratc.com>.

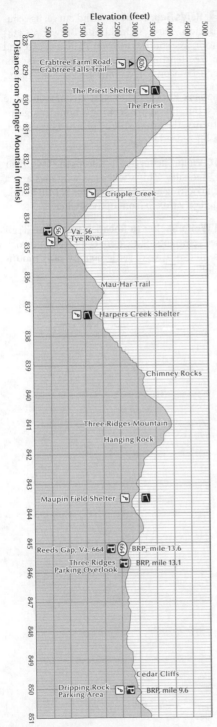

Elevation (feet)

Distance from Springer Mountain (miles)

Crabtree Farm Road,
Crabtree Falls Trail

The Priest Shelter

The Priest

Cripple Creek

Va. 56
Tye River

Mau-Har Trail

Harpers Creek Shelter

Chimney Rocks

Three Ridges Mountain

Hanging Rock

Maupin Field Shelter

Reeds Gap, Va. 664   BRP, mile 13.6

Three Ridges   BRP, mile 13.1
Parking Overlook

Cedar Cliffs

Dripping Rock
Parking Area   BRP, mile 9.6

Va. 56/Tye River—West 3.9 miles to *Camping:* Crabtree Falls Campground (short-term resupply), 11039 Crabtree Falls Hwy., Tyro, VA 22976; (540) 377-2066, <www.crabtreefallscampground.com>; reservations recommended, tentsites with shower $28D, cabins $60D; M–Th 10–5, F–Sa 10–10, Su 10–2. Accepts mail drops for guests. *Northbound directions:* Take Route 826 (Shoe Creek Rd.) west 0.5 mile to Crabtree Meadows parking lot, then down Crabtree Falls Trail 2.9 miles to Va. 56, then east 0.5 mile to campground. *Southbound:* Va. 56 west 2.5 miles to campground.

Mau-Har Trail—Traversing an area with a waterfall, this 3-mile blue-blaze goes around Three Ridges and connects with the A.T. at Maupin Field Shelter.

Harpers Creek Shelter (1960)—Sleeps 6. Privy. Designated low-impact tentsites, which campers are requested to use. Water source is Harpers Creek, in front of the shelter. In extreme droughts, go upstream, and find water in the spring-fed ponds.

Maupin Field Shelter (1960)—Sleeps 6. Privy. Designated low-impact tentsites, which campers are requested to use. The Mau-Har Trail begins behind the shelter and rejoins the A.T. 3 miles south. Water source is a dependable spring behind the shelter.

Fire Road to Blue Ridge Parkway— From Maupin Field Shelter, turn left on fire road (just north of shelter), 1.2 miles to BRP. South on BRP 1.3 miles to *Hostel:* Rusty's Hard Time Hollow. Rusty Nesbitt's gravel driveway with gray pipe gate is on the left at BRP mile 16.7. Section-hikers, thru-hikers, long-distance cyclists, and weekenders are welcome (no groups). From 1982 to 2010, Rusty hosted more than 14,000 hikers and cyclists. The Hollow is a primitive, 19-acre, back-to-basics, Appalachian mountain farm and includes bunkhouses, springhouse, outhouse, and rainwater shower. No tenting allowed during peak season. Limited stay; exceptions for medical conditions. No dogs. Trips to nearby Sherando Lake for swimming on hot days. Rides back to the Trail. Keep in mind that the Hollow is Rusty's home. Donations are needed and appreciated, since Rusty has no other means to keep the it going. No illegal drugs allowed. Mail drops not accepted.

Old Dominion Appalachian Trail Club—ODATC maintains the 19.1 miles between Reids Gap and Rockfish Gap. Correspondence should be sent to P.O. Box 25283, Richmond, VA 23260; <odatc. president@gmail.com>; <www.odatc.net>.

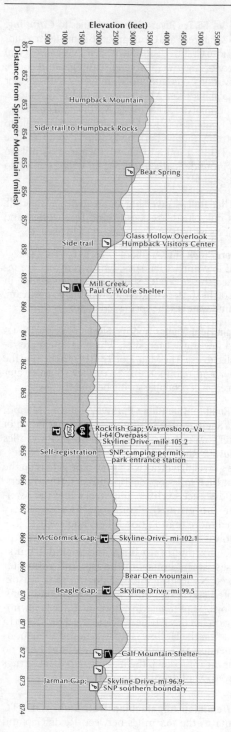

Reids Gap, Va. 664—Blind curve; use caution. Devil's Backbone Brewery, (434) 361-1001; free shuttles to/from Trail at 9, 3:30, and 5:30; free tenting/showers for hikers, B ($5 for hikers), D; N on A.T. 0.1 mile to kiosk with maps.

Humpback Rocks—The Trail circumvents the rocks, but, if you are seeking a bouldering opportunity, they may still be reached by a short, blue-blazed side trail.

Paul C. Wolfe Shelter (1991)—Sleeps 10. Privy. Bear pole. Tentsites. This shelter has windows and a porch cooking area. Water source is Mill Creek, located 50 yards in front of the shelter.

Paul Wolfe Shelter to Rockfish Gap—The Trail passes remnants of a cabin, cemetery, and rock piles, all evocative of settlement by early mountain folks.

Virginia—Part 3
(Shenandoah National Park)

Miles from Springer	Miles to Next Point	Features	Services	Elev	Miles from Katahdin	M A P
864.3	0.1	Rockfish Gap, U.S. 250, I-64, Crozet Tunnel *West–500 yds. to* Rockfish Gap Visitors Center *West–1m to* Colony House Motel *West–4.5m to* **Waynesboro, Va., P.O. 22980**	R, P, L, M L all	1,902'	1,328.7	
864.4	0.2	I-64 overpass	R	1,902'	1,328.6	
864.6	0.5	Skyline Drive mp 105.2	R, P	1,902'	1,328.4	
865.1	2.9	Self-registration for SNP camping permits; park entrance station *(W–0.2m R)*	Kiosk on Trail	2,200'	1,327.9	
868.0	1.3	McCormick Gap; Skyline Drive mp 102.1	R, P	3,450'	1,325.0	
869.3	0.5	Bear Den Mountain *...old tractor seats, vista*		2,885'	1,323.7	
869.8	2.2	Beagle Gap; Skyline Drive mp 99.5	R, P	2,550'	1,323.2	
872.0	0.6	**Calf Mountain Shelter** *(W–0.3m) ...13mS; 13.5mN*	S, w	2,700'	1,321.0	
872.6	0.4	Spring	w	2,200'	1,320.4	
873.0	0.2	Jarman Gap; Skyline Drive mp 96.9; SNP southern boundary	R	2,173'	1,320.0	
873.2	1.6	Spring	w	2,150'	1,319.8	
874.8	1.6	Sawmill Run Overlook; Skyline Drive mp 95.3	R, P	2,200'	1,318.2	
876.4	2.0	Turk Gap; Skyline Drive mp 94.1	R, P	2,600'	1,316.6	
878.4	4.1	Skyline Drive mp 92.4	R, P	3,100'	1,314.6	
882.5	1.8	Skyline Drive mp 88.9	R, P	2,350'	1,310.5	
884.3	0.2	Blackrock Gap; Skyline Drive mp 87.4	R, P	2,321'	1,308.7	
884.5	0.5	Skyline Drive mp 87.2	R	2,700'	1,308.5	
885.0	0.6	**Blackrock Hut** *(E–0.2m) ...13.5mS; 13.5mN*	S, w	2,645'	1,308.0	
885.6	1.0	Blackrock *...open rocky summit*		3,100'	1,307.4	
886.6	1.3	Skyline Drive mp 84.3	R, P	2,800'	1,306.4	
887.9	0.2	Dundo Group Campground *(W–0.1m)*	w	2,700'	1,305.1	
888.1	0.9	Browns Gap; Skyline Drive mp 82.9	R, P	2,600'	1,304.9	
889.0	0.4	Skyline Drive mp 82.2	R	2,800'	1,304.0	
889.4	0.9	Doyles River Parking Overlook; Skyline Drive mp 81.9	R, P	2,800'	1,303.6	
890.3	2.1	Doyles River Cabin *(locked) (spring E–0.3m)*; Skyline Drive mp 81.1	R, P, w	2,900'	1,302.7	
892.4	1.1	+Loft Mountain Campground *(W–0.2m)* *West–1.2m to* Loft Mountain Wayside	C, G, cl, sh R, M	3,300'	1,300.6	
893.5	0.7	Frazier Discovery Trail to Loft Mountain Wayside *(W–0.6m)*	R, M	2,950'	1,299.5	
894.2	0.3	Loft Mountain		3,200'	1,298.8	
894.5	2.1	Spring *(W–0.1m)*	w	2,950'	1,298.5	
896.6	1.6	Ivy Creek Overlook; Skyline Drive mp 77.5	R, P	2,800'	1,296.4	

PATC Map 11

Miles from Springer	Miles to Next Point	Features	Services	Elev	Miles from Katahdin	M A P
898.2	0.2	**Pinefield Hut** (E–0.1m) ...13.5mS; 8.4mN	S, C, w	2,430'	1,294.8	
898.4	1.9	Pinefield Gap; Skyline Drive mp 75.2	R	2,590'	1,294.6	
900.3	3.3	Simmons Gap; Skyline Drive mp 73.2 East–0.2m to water pump at ranger station	R, P w	2,250'	1,292.7	
903.6	0.4	Powell Gap; Skyline Drive mp 69.9	R	2,294'	1,289.4	PATC Map 11
904.0	1.2	Little Roundtop Mountain		2,700'	1,289.0	
905.2	1.2	Smith Roach Gap; Skyline Drive mp 68.6	R, P	2,600'	1,287.8	
906.4	0.5	**Hightop Hut** (W–0.1m S; 0.2m spring) ...8.4mS; 12.6mN	S, C, w	3,175'	1,286.6	
906.9	0.1	Spring	w	3,450'	1,286.1	
907.0	1.5	Hightop Mountain		3,587'	1,286.0	
908.5	1.3	Skyline Drive mp 66.7	R, P	2,650'	1,284.5	
909.8	3.0	Swift Run Gap; U.S. 33; Skyline Drive mp 65.5; Spotswood Trail; self-registration kiosk for SNP camping permits West–2.9m to Country View Motel West–3.2m to Swift Run Campground; store West–7.5m to **Elkton, Va., P.O. 22827**	R, w L C, G, M, cl G, M	2,367'	1,283.2	
912.8	3.3	South River Picnic Grounds (W–0.1m)	P, w	3,200'	1,280.2	
916.1	0.3	Pocosin Cabin (locked) (W–0.1m spring)	w	3,150'	1,276.9	
916.4	1.7	Spring	w	3,100'	1,276.6	
918.1	0.7	+Lewis Mountain Campground and Cabins; Skyline Drive mp 57.6 (W–0.1m)	R, C, G, L, cl, sh	3,500'	1,274.9	
918.8	2.6	**Bearfence Mountain Hut** (E–0.1m) ...12.6mS; 11.8mN	R, P, S, C, w	3,110'	1,274.2	
921.4	0.9	Bootens Gap; Skyline Drive mp 55.1	R, P	3,243'	1,271.6	
922.3	1.9	Hazeltop		3,812'	1,270.7	
924.2	0.9	Milam Gap; Skyline Drive mp 52.8	R, P	3,300'	1,268.8	
925.1	0.8	Spring	w	3,380'	1,267.9	
925.9	0.9	Lewis Spring; Big Meadows Wayside; Harry F. Bird, Sr., Visitors Center (E–0.4m)	R, P, G, M, w	3,390'	1,267.1	PATC Map 10
926.8	0.6	Big Meadows Lodge (E–0.1m); +Big Meadows Campground East–0.9m to Big Meadows Wayside	R, P, C, L, M, cl, sh G. M	3,490'	1,266.2	
927.4	1.0	David Spring (W–50 ft.)	w	3,490'	1,265.6	
928.4	1.9	Fishers Gap; Skyline Drive mp 49.3	R	3,050'	1,264.6	
930.3	0.3	**Rock Spring Hut** (W–0.2m) and (locked) cabin ...11.8mS; 11.1mN	S, C, w	3,465'	1,262.7	
930.6	1.0	Trail to Hawksbill Mountain, Byrd's Nest #2 Picnic Shelter (E–0.9m)	R	3,600'	1,262.4	
931.6	0.4	Hawksbill Gap; Skyline Drive mp 45.6	R, P	3,361'	1,261.4	
932.0	2.1	Side Trail to Crescent Rock Overlook; Skyline Drive mp 44.4		3,450'	1,261.0	
934.1	0.8	Skyland Service Road (south); horse stables	R, P	3,550'	1,258.9	
934.9	0.4	Skyland Service Road (north) ...best access to Skyland Resort (W–0.2m)	R, P, L, M	3,790'	1,258.1	
935.3	1.6	Side trail to Stony Man Mountain Summit	R, P	3,837'	1,257.7	
936.9	2.2	Hughes River Gap; Trail to Stony Man Mountain Overlook; Skyline Drive mp 38.6	R, P, w	3,097'	1,256.1	
939.1	0.1	Pinnacles Picnic Ground; Skyline Dr. mp 36.7	R, w	3,390'	1,253.9	

Miles from Springer	Miles to Next Point	Features	Services	Elev	Miles from Katahdin	M A P
939.2	1.0	Side Trail to Jewell Hollow Overlook; Skyline Drive mp 36.4	R	3,350'	1,253.8	
940.2	1.0	The Pinnacle		3,730'	1,252.8	
941.2	0.7	**Byrds Nest #3 Hut** *(E–0.3m spring)* *…11.1mS; 4.6mN*	S, C, w	3,290'	1,251.8	
941.9	0.6	Meadow Spring *(E–0.3m)*	w	3,100'	1,251.1	PATC Map 10
942.5	1.9	Mary's Rock *…vista*		3,514'	1,250.5	
944.4	1.2	Thornton Gap, Panorama *(W–0.1m)*; U.S. 211; Skyline Drive mp 31.5 *West–4.6m to* Brookside Cabins *West–5.6m to* motels and campground *West–8m to* **Luray, Va., P.O. 22835**	R, P, w L, M C, G, L, cl all	2,307'	1,248.6	
945.6	0.8	**Pass Mountain Hut** *(E–0.2m) …4.6mS; 13.5mN*	S, w	2,690'	1,247.4	
946.4	1.1	Pass Mountain		3,052'	1,246.6	
947.5	0.3	Skyline Drive mp 28.6	R	2,490'	1,245.5	
947.8	0.1	Beahms Gap; Skyline Drive mp 28.5	R, P	2,490'	1,245.2	
947.9	4.6	Byrds Nest #4 Picnic Shelter *(E–0.5m)*	w	2,600'	1,245.1	
952.5	0.5	Spring	w	2,600'	1,240.5	
953.0	0.8	Elkwallow Gap; Elkwallow Wayside Skyline Drive mp 23.9 *(E–0.1m)*	R, P, G, M	2,480'	1,240.0	
953.8	0.7	Range View Cabin *(locked) (E–0.1m spring)*	w	2,950'	1,239.2	
954.5	0.6	Rattlesnake Point Overlook Skyline Drive mp 21.9	R, P	3,100'	1,238.5	
955.1	0.4	Tuscarora Trail *(southern terminus)* to +Mathews Arm Campground *(W–0.9m)*	C, w	3,400'	1,237.9	
955.5	0.2	Skyline Drive mp 21.1	R, P	3,350'	1,237.5	
955.7	0.1	Hogback Third Peak		3,400'	1,237.3	
955.8	0.2	Skyline Drive mp 20.8	R, P	3,350'	1,237.2	
956.0	0.2	Hogback Second Peak		3,475'	1,237.0	PATC Map 9
956.2	0.1	Spring *(E–0.2m)*	w	3,250'	1,236.8	
956.3	0.7	Hogback First Peak		3,390'	1,236.7	
957.0	0.1	Little Hogback Overlook; Skyline Dr. mp 19.7	R, P	3,000'	1,236.0	
957.1	0.5	Little Hogback Mountain		3,050'	1,235.9	
957.6	1.1	Skyline Drive mp 18.9	R	2,850'	1,235.4	
958.7	0.2	**Gravel Springs Hut** *(E–0.2m) …13.5mS; 10.7mN*	S, C, w	2,480'	1,234.3	
958.9	1.1	Gravel Springs Gap; Skyline Drive mp 17.7	R, P	2,666'	1,234.1	
960.0	0.5	South Marshall Mountain		3,212'	1,233.0	
960.5	0.7	Skyline Drive mp 15.9	R, P	3,050'	1,232.5	
961.2	0.9	North Marshall Mountain		3,368'	1,231.8	
962.1	0.6	Hogwallow Spring	w	2,950'	1,230.9	
962.7	1.7	Hogwallow Gap; Skyline Drive mp 14.2	R	2,739'	1,230.3	
964.4	0.9	Jenkins Gap; Skyline Drive mp 12.3	R	2,400'	1,228.6	
965.3	0.4	Compton Springs	w	2,700'	1,227.7	
965.7	0.8	Compton Peak		2,909'	1,227.3	
966.5	0.3	Compton Gap; Skyline Drive mp 10.4	R, P	2,550'	1,226.5	
966.8	1.5	Indian Run Spring *(E–0.3m)*	w	2,350'	1,226.2	

Miles from Springer	Miles to Next Point	Features	Services	Elev	Miles from Katahdin	M A P
968.3	0.2	Compton Gap Horse Trail; Trail to Chester Gap		2,350'	1,224.7	
		North–0.5m to Terrapin Station Hostel	H, M, f			
968.5	0.7	Possums Rest Overlook; self-registration at kiosk for SNP camping permits; SNP northern boundary		2,300'	1,224.5	PATC Map 9
969.2	1.0	**Tom Floyd Wayside** *...10.7mS; 8.1mN*	S, w	1,900'	1,223.8	
970.2	0.5	Northern Virginia 4-H Swimming Pool *(W–0.3m)*		1,350'	1,222.8	
970.7	1.4	Va. 602	R	1,150'	1,222.3	
972.1	3.3	U.S. 522	R, P	950'	1,220.9	
		East–120 yds. to Mountain Home B&B	L			
		West–3.2m to **Front Royal, Va., P.O. 22630**	all			

+Fee charged, mp=milepost

Shenandoah National Park, with 96 miles of well-graded Appalachian Trail, is memorable for its many vistas and abundant wildlife. Skyline Drive, which you will cross 28 times, has many waysides and concessions for resupply stops. *Backcountry permits are required when camping in the park.*

U.S. 250, I-64/Rockfish Gap—Where the A.T. crosses U.S. 250, it is **west** 500 yards to the Rockfish Gap Visitors Center (on the hill next to the Inn at Afton), (540) 943-5187. Open daily 9–5, provides an information packet specifically for hikers that notes area volunteers who provide free shuttles between Rockfish Gap and downtown. (See list at the visitors center, YMCA, and various other locations.) If closed, you can download the info packet from <www.visitwaynesboro.net>; click on "Appalachian Trail." ■ *Lodging:* Yurt, (434) 882-1587, $50s/D, single bed/futon, wood stove, large deck on 70 acres, bath/shower in main house with private entrance; B available. Call Mary to arrange for pick-up, but must book through Airbnb, <www.airbnb.com/rooms/17677894>. No smoking, well-behaved pet-friendly; some limitations; see Web site. ■ *Food:* Kings Kettle Corn, snacks, drinks, info; open seasonally. ■ *Outfitter:* Rockfish Gap Outfitters, (540) 943-1461, located on U.S. 250 on the way to town; fuel by the ounce, backpacking gear, ATC publications, large footwear selection, minor gear repairs, and warranty assistance.

West 1 mile to *Lodging:* Colony House Motel, (540) 942-4156, $58.80, ask for hiker rates, pets $10, pool, laundry, can shuttle back to Trail if asked and available.

West 4.5 miles to **Waynesboro, Va. [P.O. ZIP 22980: M–F 9–5, closed Sa (hikers have gotten mail by knocking on the back door); (540) 942-7320]**, a large, hiker-friendly town with most services. ■ *Hostels:* Grace Evangelical Lutheran Church, 500 South Wayne Ave., open May 28–Jun 22, closed Su nights, check-in 5–9 p.m., check-out 9 a.m., but will store packs for those staying another night. Lounge with big-screen TV, a/c, Internet, showers, cots, kitchen, snacks, and continental breakfast. Members of the congregation host a Th night supper for hikers (max. 15) followed by an optional vespers service. No pets, drugs, smoking, alcohol, firearms, foul language. Maximum 15 hikers; 2-night limit. Donations accepted. Stanimal's 328 Hostel, (540) 290-4002, 1333 West Main St., owner Adam Stanley AT'04, PCT'10; $30PP includes pick-up/ return to Trail, bunk mattress with clean linens, shower with towel, soap and laundry. Large private area, sunroom, computer for guest use, WiFi, DVDs, full-sized fridge, microwave, hiker box. Snacks, drinks, and ice cream for sale. Slackpacking discounts for multinight guests. ■ *Camping:* Waynesboro Parks and Recreation offers tent and hammock sites on a grassy area at the foot of 14th St. near the South River. The ALDHA Hiker Pavilion has a solar charging station for devices. *Free 3-day-max permits with restrictions, available at Y, tourist office, library, and outfit-*

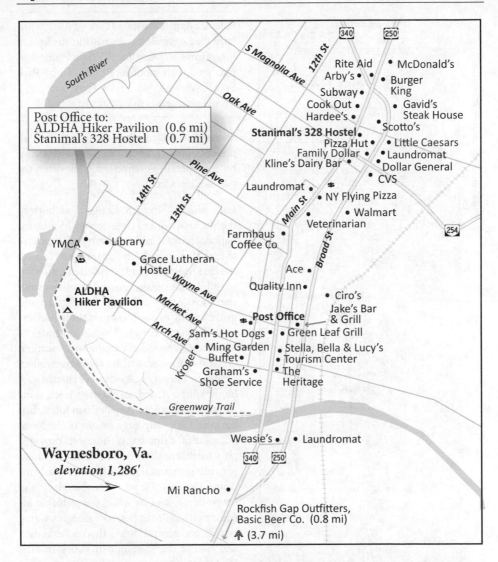

Post Office to:
ALDHA Hiker Pavilion (0.6 mi)
Stanimal's 328 Hostel   (0.7 mi)

South River

S Magnolia Ave

12th St

340   250

Rite Aid   • McDonald's
Arby's • • • • Burger
Subway •   King
Cook Out •   • Gavid's
Hardee's •   Steak House
              • Scotto's
Stanimal's 328 Hostel •
            Pizza Hut • • Little Caesars
        Family Dollar • • Laundromat
Kline's Dairy Bar • • Dollar General
                    • CVS

Oak Ave

Pine Ave

Laundromat • $
              • NY Flying Pizza

14th St

13th St

Main St

          • Walmart
Veterinarian

254

YMCA •   • Library
            Farmhaus •
            Coffee Co

Broad St

• Grace Lutheran
  Hostel

Wayne Ave

          Ace •

Quality Inn •

ALDHA
• **Hiker Pavilion**

Market Ave

          • Ciro's
          Jake's Bar
$ •Post Office & Grill

Arch Ave

Kroger

Sam's Hot Dogs • • Green Leaf Grill
• Ming Garden • Stella, Bella & Lucy's
  Buffet •   • Tourism Center
Graham's • • The
Shoe Service   Heritage

Greenway Trail

Weasie's • • Laundromat

Waynesboro, Va.
elevation 1,286'
→

340   250

Mi Rancho •

Rockfish Gap Outfitters,
Basic Beer Co. (0.8 mi)
(3.7 mi)

ters, *now required for this area.* The YMCA, (540) 942-5107, on South Wayne Ave., offers showers, restroom, and gym; check in at desk M–F 5:15 a.m.–10 p.m., Sa 8–5, Su 1–5; donations appreciated. ■ *Lodging:* Quality Inn, (540) 942-1171, $67.99S, $75.99D, $10EAP, pets in smoking rooms only $10. ■ *Groceries:* Kroger (long-term resupply). ■ *Restaurants:* Ming Garden, AYCE L/D; Gavid's Steaks; Scotto's Italian; Ciros Pizza; Pizza Hut; The Heritage; Free Press; Jakes; Sam's Hotdogs; Benny Stivales Pizza and Beer Garden; N.Y. Flying Pizza; Mister Jamison's; Stella, Bella & Lucy Café; Weasie's Kitchen, B/L/D with AYCE pancake B anytime, open M–Sa 5:30 a.m.–8 p.m., Su 7–2; Greenleaf Grill; Jalisco Mexican Grill & Cantina; Basic City Brewing Co., hot showers and cold craft beer; and many fast-food outlets. ■ *Internet access:* Waynesboro Public Library, M–F 9–9, Sa 9–5, WiFi (24 hours); Grace Church during times of hostel operation (see above). ■ *Other services:* cobbler, coin laundry, pharmacy, ATM, doctor, dentist, veterinarian, barber, massages, Western Union, one-hour photo service. Basic City Beer Co. offers showers for thru-hikers.

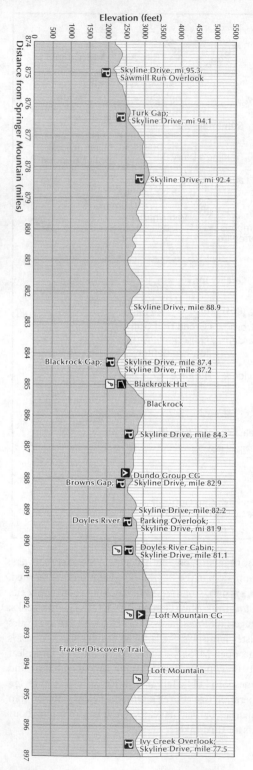

Elevation (feet)

Distance from Springer Mountain (miles)

Skyline Drive, mi 95.3;
Sawmill Run Overlook

Turk Gap;
Skyline Drive, mi 94.1

Skyline Drive, mi 92.4

Skyline Drive, mile 88.9

Blackrock Gap;   Skyline Drive, mile 87.4
                 Skyline Drive, mile 87.2
                 Blackrock Hut
                 Blackrock

Skyline Drive, mile 84.3

Dundo Group CG
Browns Gap;   Skyline Drive, mile 82.9

Skyline Drive, mile 82.2
Doyles River   Parking Overlook;
                Skyline Drive, mi 81.9

Doyles River Cabin;
Skyline Drive, mile 81.1

Loft Mountain CG

Frazier Discovery Trail

Loft Mountain

Ivy Creek Overlook;
Skyline Drive, mile 77.5

Potomac Appalachian Trail Club—PATC maintains the 240.5 miles between Rockfish Gap and Pine Grove Furnace State Park in Pennsylvania. Send correspondence to PATC, 118 Park St. SE, Vienna, VA 22180; (703) 242-0693; <www.patc.net>; <info@patc.net>.

Shenandoah National Park—Although the SNP presents some significant ascents and descents, hikers generally will find the Trail within the park well-graded.

Park history—In 1926, Congress authorized the Shenandoah and Great Smoky Mountains national parks. Unlike western parks, most of today's Shenandoah land was privately owned; the Blue Ridge here had been dotted with communities and isolated groups of settlers since the 1750s. Areas had long been farmed and grazed. Out-of-state corporations had exploited some areas for timber and mineral ores. Three resorts provided Victorian-era vacationers with cool mountain breezes and recreation.

By the 1910s, conditions were changing. A blight killing American chestnut trees, some 30–40 percent of the Appalachian forest, had destroyed not only large swaths of the forest but a way of life for many. Those trees provided nuts that were shipped by railroad to cities, providing mountain families with cash income. The chestnut was strong, straight, and rot-resistant, and its wood was valuable for fence posts, railroad ties, roof shingles, siding boards, and general lumber that residents used and sold in the Shenandoah Valley and the Piedmont.

In 1927, Virginia authorized condemnation of all private property within the boundary of the proposed park. More than 4,000 tracts were surveyed, and 1,081 were purchased and given to the federal government, uprooting most of the 465 families who lived on the land. Virginia resettled the majority and evicted those unwilling to move. Approximately 45 elderly residents were allowed to spend their last years in their homes.

In 1931, four years before Shenandoah was established, construction of Skyline Drive began. First built as a second entrance to Presi-

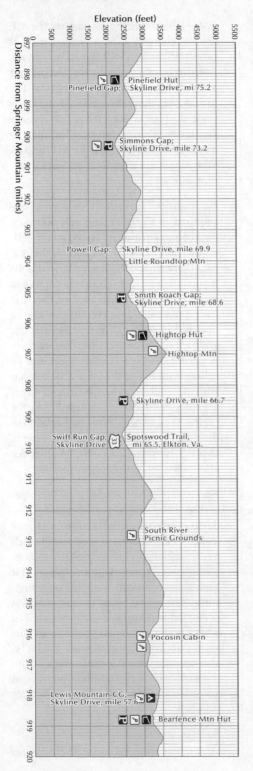

Elevation (feet)

Distance from Springer Mountain (miles)

Pinefield Hut
Pinefield Gap; Skyline Drive, mi 75.2

Simmons Gap;
Skyline Drive, mile 73.2

Powell Gap; Skyline Drive, mile 69.9
Little-Roundtop-Mtn

Smith Roach Gap;
Skyline Drive, mile 68.6

Hightop Hut

Hightop-Mtn

Skyline Drive, mile 66.7

Swift Run Gap; Spotswood Trail,
Skyline Drive mi 65.5, Elkton, Va.

South River
Picnic Grounds

Pocosin Cabin

Lewis Mountain CG;
Skyline Drive, mile 57.6

Bearfence Mtn Hut

dent Herbert Hoover's summer White House, Rapidan Camp, the road was only to go from the camp to Skyland. State leaders successfully lobbied for congressional appropriations to extend the highway north to Thornton Gap (U.S. 211), on to Front Royal, and then south to Rockfish Gap. But, until the park was established in December 1935, Skyline Drive existed only as a 100-foot right-of-way within privately held land that basically coincided with the route of the A.T. In 1933, President Franklin D. Roosevelt's CCC "boys" established camps along the route and built many of the facilities, overlooks, rock walls, and gutters seen there today. They planted hundreds of thousands of trees and shrubs, creating the landscape that draws millions of visitors to the park, and built a new route for the A.T. ATC Chair Myron Avery's acceptance of this disruption, after years of simmering disagreements, produced an open schism between the organization's leadership and founder Benton MacKaye and his allies in New York and New England.

Today, 95 percent reforested, the park is home to wild turkey, white-tailed deer, black bears, and shelter mice. Hundreds of migrating birds and butterflies summer or stop over in this central Appalachian biome. Nearly one million visitors a year come to watch wildlife, get back to nature, view the Shenandoah Valley to the west and the foothills to the east, or visit land on which their ancestors lived.

Ranger Programs—From Memorial Day into Oct, rangers present a organized hikes, programs and events highlighting the natural and human history of the park. The visitors' guide, available at entrances and visitors centers, has the schedule.

Forest Damage—Hurricane Isabel (2003) and fires before it damaged thousands of acres. Coupled with the floods, Tropical Storm Fran in 1996, a severe ice storm in 1998 and 2006, a 2012 derecho, and gypsy-moth and woolly adelgid infestations, the park has been hit hard in recent years. Be mindful of trees and branches that have been weakened by those events and could still fall.

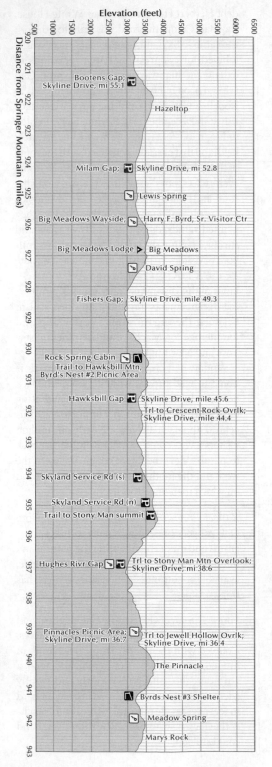

Elevation (feet)

Distance from Springer Mountain (miles)

Bootens Gap; Skyline Drive, mi 55.1

Hazeltop

Milam Gap; Skyline Drive, mi 52.8

Lewis Spring

Big Meadows Wayside, Harry F. Byrd, Sr. Visitor Ctr

Big Meadows Lodge Big Meadows

David Spring

Fishers Gap; Skyline Drive, mile 49.3

Rock Spring Cabin
Trail to Hawksbill Mtn,
Byrd's Nest #2 Picnic Area

Hawksbill Gap Skyline Drive, mile 45.6
Trl to Crescent Rock Ovrlk;
Skyline Drive, mile 44.4

Skyland Service Rd (s)

Skyland Service Rd (n)
Trail to Stony Man summit

Hughes Rivr Gap Trl to Stony Man Mtn Overlook;
Skyline Drive, mi 38.6

Pinnacles Picnic Area; Trl to Jewell Hollow Ovrlk;
Skyline Drive, mi 36.7 Skyline Drive, mi 36.4

The Pinnacle

Byrds Nest #3 Shelter

Meadow Spring

Marys Rock

Fee—Hikers entering the park *via* the A.T. are not charged a fee; hikers entering at other trailheads in SNP may incur a $15 fee. Entering by vehicle, the fee is $30/vehicle for a stay of 1-7 days. During the spring (mid-Feb to mid-Apr), the park occasionally conducts prescribed burns along the A.T. to manage vegetation. During burns, a hut may be closed up to 3 days. Check the ATC or park Web sites or ask at any NPS station for current information.

Backcountry Permits—Free permits are **required** of all thru-hikers and overnight backcountry travelers. Backcountry self-registration kiosks are located on the A.T. near the north and south boundaries of SNP. If you fail to register or can't show proof of registration when rangers ask for it, they may issue a citation or fine. Permits may also be obtained at Skyline Drive entrance stations and park visitors centers when they are open. A permit can be acquired in advance by calling (540) 999-3500, M–F 8-4. Be familiar with the regulations, have your exact itinerary ready, and allow 5–7 business days for the permit to be mailed. Write to: Superintendent, ATTN: Backcountry Camping Permit, 3655 U.S. Hwy. 211 East, Luray, VA 22835. See also <www.nps.gov/shen/planyourvisit>.

Backcountry Accommodations—Two types of three-sided structures are near the A.T.— day-use (called "shelters") and overnight-use (called "huts"). Camping at or near the shelters is prohibited. Huts are available to long-distance hikers (those with an itinerary of at least three consecutive nights) on a first-come, first-served basis. Tenting at huts is permitted in designated campsites marked with a post and a tenting symbol; all huts within the park have campsites. The PATC also operates several locked cabins within the park that require advance reservations and other arrangements. Contact PATC for details.

Backcountry Regulations
• Campfires are prohibited in SNP, except at

the commercial campgrounds and established fireplaces at shelters, huts, and cabins. Use a backpacking stove.

- Camping is prohibited within 10 yards of a stream or other natural water source; within 20 yards of a park trail or unpaved fire road; within 50 yards of culturally historic sites, other campers, or no-camping signs; within 100 yards of a hut, cabin, or day-use shelter (except designated sites); within 0.25 mile of a paved road, park boundary, picnic area, visitors center, or commercial facility. Several zones have been designated "noncamping areas," including Limberlost, Hawksbill Summit, Whiteoak Canyon, Old Rag summit, Big Meadows clearing, and Rapidan Camp.
- Camping is permitted almost everywhere else. New regulations encourage hikers to seek "preexisting campsites" in legal locations that show signs of use and are not posted with no-camping signs. Camping at those sites is limited to two consecutive nights. If necessary, dispersed camping at undisturbed sites is permissible, but they must be left in pristine condition; use such sites only one night.
- Maximum group size is 10 people.
- Food must be stored so that wildlife cannot get it—hang food from a tree branch at least ten feet from the ground and four feet away from a tree's trunk. Alternatively, overnight huts feature food-storage poles or bear boxes, which are to be used instead of the familiar "mouse hangers." Park-approved, bear-resistant food-storage canisters are also permissible.
- Solid human waste should be buried in accordance with Leave No Trace ethics, under 6 inches of soil, more than 200 feet from trails, water sources, or roads. In moldering privies, add a small handful of wood chips.
- Carry out all trash from the backcountry, and dispose of it properly.
- Glass containers are discouraged.
- Pets must be leashed at all times and are prohibited on certain side trails.

Commercial Facilities—Campgrounds, restaurants, lodges, waysides, and small stores are normally open spring through fall and are located strategically near the A.T. and Skyline Drive. Long-distance hikers may be able to save pack weight by resupplying or taking meals at these facilities. Call the park for the precise dates and times of operation. More details can be found at <www.nps.gov/shen>. Campground reservations: (877) 444-6777 or <www.recreation.gov>. Site rates range from $17 to $20.

Calf Mountain Shelter (1984)—Sleeps 6. Privy. Featuring two skylights, this shelter is not a part of the hut system, so SNP rules don't apply here. Water source is a piped spring on the access trail. From here to Blackrock Hut, the A.T. usually is without reliable water sources; plan accordingly.

Blackrock Hut (1941)—Sleeps 6. Moldering privy. Designated tentsites nearby. Water source is a piped spring 10 yards in front of the shelter.

Loft Mountain Campground—Open mid-May to late Oct. The A.T. skirts the campground, but several short side trails lead to campsites and the camp store (short-term resupply). Campsites $15, subject to change; showers $1, laundry, restroom, and soda machine. Loft Mountain Wayside and Grill serves B/L/D, short-order menu, soda machine. From the camp store, follow the paved road 1.0 mile downhill to Skyline Drive or continue north on the A.T. 0.9 mile and take the Frazier Discovery Trail 0.5 mile west (steep descent) to Skyline Drive.

Pinefield Hut (1940)—Sleeps 6. Moldering privy. Designated tentsites nearby. Water source is a spring behind the shelter 50 yards that tends to fail during dry seasons. Northbounders can get water from

---

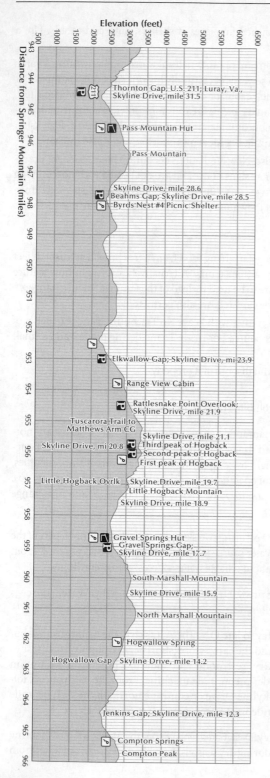

Ivy Creek or Loft Mountain Campground; southbounders, an outdoor spigot at the Simmons Gap ranger station.

Simmons Gap—Simmons Gap ranger station is down the paved road 0.2 mile east from where the A.T. crosses Skyline Drive. Frost-free pump.

Hightop Hut (1939)—Sleeps 6. Moldering privy. Designated campsites nearby. Water source is a usually reliable piped spring 0.1 mile from the shelter on a side trail. An alternative water source is a boxed spring 0.5 mile north on the Trail.

U.S. 33/Swift Run Gap/Spotswood Trail—West from Skyline Drive to water. Backcountry self-registration station located at SNP entrance station, north of U.S. 33 bridge.

On U.S. 33—West 2.9 miles to *Lodging:* Country View Motel, 19974 Spotswood Trail, Elkton, VA 22827, (540) 298-0025, <www.countryviewlodging.com>, $75–$85 room rate, cabin rate $80, no pet fee, shuttle possible back to Trail and Elkton $10, mail drops accepted for guests.

West 3.2 miles to ■ *Camping:* Swift Run Camping, (540) 298-8086, $20 campsite, laundry, pool, and snack bar. ■ *Groceries:* Bear Mountain Grocery, with a deli, daily 6–9.

West 7.5 miles to **Elkton, Va. [P.O. ZIP 22827: M–F 8:30–4:30, Sa 9–11; (540) 298-7772].** ■ *Groceries:* Food Lion, O'Dell's Grocery (both long-term resupply). ■ *Restaurants:* fast-food places. ■ *Other services:* pharmacy, bank, and ATM.

South River Picnic Area—Water, picnic benches, restrooms with sinks.

Lewis Mountain Campground and Cabins—Open early May to Nov; reservations, (540) 999-2255, <goshenandoah.com/lodging>. The A.T. passes in sight of the campground, and several short side trails lead to campsites and the camp store. Campsites $15; hiker special only for cabins available. Lewis Mountain Camp Store (short-term resupply), open 9–7 in summer. Showers $1, laundry, restroom, and soda machine.

Bearfence Mountain Hut (1940)—Sleeps 6. Privy. Designated tentsites nearby. Located on a blue-blazed trail off a fire road. Water source is a piped spring in front of the shelter; prone to fail during even moderately dry spells.

Big Meadows Lodge, Campground, and Wayside—The A.T. passes within sight of the campground, and short side trails lead to the lodge, which also houses a restaurant and tap room and has Internet access. ■ *Lodging:* hiker special (includes B, taxes, B gratuity) available by calling (877) 847-1919; rooms available in main lodge; also cabins, suites, and motel-type accommodations. A few pet-friendly rooms. Reservations required. Lodging and restaurant open late May–late Oct. ■ *Camping:* Open early Apr–late Nov, campsites $20, reservations recommended. Walk-ins are possible, but the campground is often full; showers $1, laundry. ■ *Restaurant:* Dining room open daily for L/D; tap room, with nightly entertainment and light fare, open daily from late afternoon to late evening. From the lodge, follow the paved entrance road 0.9 mile to Big Meadows Wayside and Grill, B/L/D, open late Mar–late Nov, with short-order menu. ■ *Groceries:* Wayside has a good selection (short-term resupply) and camping supplies, and soda machine. Next door is the Harry F. Byrd, Sr., Visitors Center, with exhibits and videos on area history.

Rock Spring Hut (1940, updated 1980)—Sleeps 8. Privy. Designated tentsites nearby. Located on 0.2-mile blue-blazed trail. Water source, down a steep trail in front of the hut, flows from beneath a rock.

Skyland Service Road/Skyland—Skyland was originally a 19th-century mountain summer resort owned by A.T. pioneer George Freeman Pollock, who pushed hard to evict surrounding small landholders and create a national park and then, ironically, was forced to sell and give up management of the resort. Cross the road at the stables, and follow the A.T. north, passing a water tank on your right and the junction marked by a post, which points to Skyland and dining room.

West 0.2 mile to ■ *Lodging:* Skyland, (877) 847-1919, late Mar–late Nov; hiker special available; also motel-type accommodations and suites, reservations required. A few pet-friendly rooms. ■ *Restaurant:* Pollock Dining Room serves B/L/D; limited hours. Tap room, light fare, nightly entertainment.

Pinnacles Picnic Area—Restrooms, covered area, picnic tables, fireplaces. Uphill from picnic pavilion is a frost-free pump for year-round water.

Byrds Nest #3 Hut—Sleeps 8. Moldering privy. A picnic shelter converted to overnight use. A spring is 0.3 mile east, down the fire road.

U.S. 211/Thornton Gap/Panorama—A short side trail, on the southern side of Thornton Gap, leads to Panorama area. The restaurant and backcountry-permit office were torn down in 2008; new restrooms, water source, and a parking area have been installed at "east" end of lot. Park entrance station is north of U.S. 211, east of where the Trail crosses Skyline Drive, with water. *Until further notice, treat or boil water from both those locations due to contamination.*

On U.S. 211—**West** 4.6 miles to **Lodging:** Brookside Cabins, (540) 743-5698, <www.brooksidecab-ins.com>, luxury cabins $85–$200; full-menu restaurant featuring home-style foods and daily AYCE L/D buffet, weekend B buffet, open Su–Th 8–8, F-Sa 8–8:30. Closed early Dec–Mar.

West 5.6 miles to ■ *Lodging:* Days Inn, (540) 743-4521, $90–$250, pets $15/night, seasonal outdoor pool, continental B; Skyline Inn & Suites, (540) 743-3623. ■ *Camping:* Yogi Bear's Jellystone Park, (540) 743-4002, <www.campluray.com>, tentsites $37–$84 2-night minimum, cabins $63–$248,

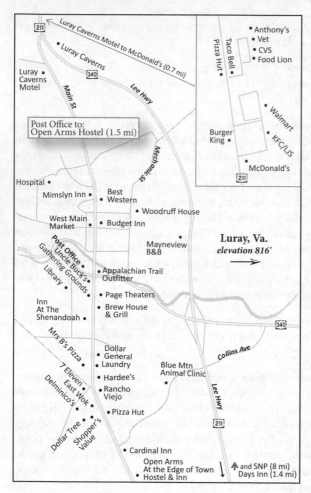

Luray, Va.
elevation 816'

3-night minimum, campstore (short-term resupply), seasonal outdoor pool, laundry, pets allowed (free) only at sites.

West 8.0 miles to the town of **Luray, Va. [P.O. ZIP 22835: M–F 8:30–4:30, closed Sa; (540) 743-2100]**. Luray–Page County Chamber of Commerce, 18 Campbell St., (540) 743-3915, <www.luraypage.com>, M–Sa 9–5, Su 12–4. ■ *Hostel:* Open Arms at the Edge of Town Hostel & Inn, 1260 East Main St., (540) 244-5652, owned by Alison Coltrane, <www.openarmsluray.com>; call or text for availability/pick-up from Thornton Gap; twin bed/linens/shower/kitchen access $30PP; tent-site/shower/kitchen access $15PP; B, soda, and snacks; WiFi; laundry $5; nonguest shower with towel/soap $3; pet-friendly; mail drops free to guests. ■ *Lodging:* Cardinal Inn, (540) 743-5010, $75 and up, no pets; Mimslyn Inn, (540) 743-5105; Best Western Motel, (540) 743-6511; Budget Inn, (540) 743-5176, call for rate, dogs $10/night; Luray Caverns Motels East and West, (540) 743-4531, 20% discount coupon for food/merchandise at Luray Caverns, no dogs; Inn of the Shenandoah, (540) 300-9777, 138 East Main St., includes B; Woodruff House B&B and Cabins, 330 Mechanic St., and Mayne View B&B, 439 Mechanic St., both (540) 843-3200, $109 and up, includes B. ■ *Groceries:* Shopper's Value, Food Lion, Walmart (all long-term resupply). ■ *Restaurants:* Anthony's Pizza, L/D; East Wok, L/D and AYCE L; Gathering Grounds, espresso, sandwiches, meals; 55 East Main Brew House & Grill, brew pub, coffee, burritos; Uncle Buck's, all-day B, Southern comfort food; West Main Market & Deli, soups and sandwiches; The Speakeasy at the Mimslyn Inn, sandwiches and D M–Th 3–10, F–Sa 3–11, Su 2–10, full bar; Hawksbill Brewery; and several fast-food restaurants. ■ *Internet access:* Page Public Library, no WiFi. ■ *Outfitters:* Appalachian Outfitters, 2 W. Main St., (540) 743-7400, full-service outfitter, M–Sa 10–6, Su 1–5. ■ *Other services:* veterinarian, Blue Mountain Animal Clinic, (540) 743-PETS; laundromats; hospital; ATMs; and 5-screen Page Theatres.

Pass Mountain Hut (1939)—Sleeps 8. Privy. Known for the "kissing trees," shelter is located on a blue-blazed trail. Designated campsites nearby. Water source is a piped spring 15 yards behind the shelter.

 Elkwallow Wayside and Grill—Open 9–7 early Apr–early Oct. Visible from where the A.T. crosses Skyline Drive in Elkwallow Gap, the wayside includes a grill, gift shop, and restroom.

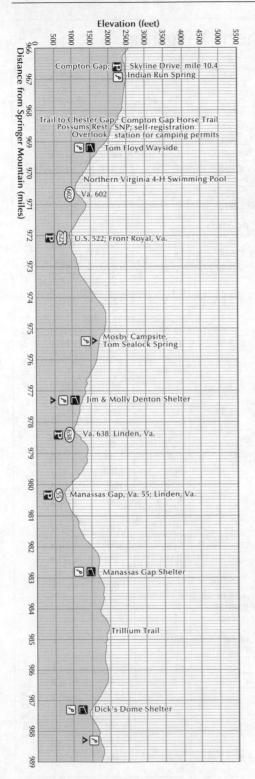

Elevation (feet)

Compton Gap; Skyline Drive, mile 10.4
Indian Run Spring

Trail to Chester Gap / Compton Gap Horse Trail
Possums Rest / SNP; self-registration
Overlook / station for camping permits
Tom Floyd Wayside

Northern Virginia 4-H Swimming Pool
Va. 602

U.S. 522; Front Royal, Va.

Mosby Campsite,
Tom Sealock Spring

Jim & Molly Denton Shelter

Va. 638; Linden, Va.

Manassas Gap, Va. 55; Linden, Va.

Manassas Gap Shelter

Trillium Trail

Dick's Dome Shelter

Grill, B/L/D. Last chance in SNP for north-bounders to get a blackberry milkshake. Gift shop offers limited groceries, camping supplies, soda machine outside. Frost-free pump at picnic area south of wayside.

Mathews Arm Campground—West 0.9 mile from the A.T., 0.3 mile south of the Hogback Parking Area *via* the Tuscarora and Traces trails. Signs lead to nearby primitive campground, open mid-May–late Oct, campsites $15/night, rate subject to change. This junction is the southern end of the 260-mile Tuscarora Trail; the northern is on the A.T. south of Darlington Shelter in Pennsylvania.

Gravel Springs Hut (1940)—Sleeps 8. Moldering privy. Designated tentsites nearby on a blue-blazed trail. Water source is a boxed spring found on side trail near the shelter.

Southbound Registration Station—0.7 mile south of Tom Floyd Wayside.

Tom Floyd (Wayside) Shelter (1980s)—Sleeps 6. Privy. Tentsites. Shelter has an overhanging front deck with storage space above, a railed deck with benches. Outside the SNP boundary, so SNP rules don't apply. Water source 0.2 mile on a blue-blazed trail to the right of the shelter often stops flowing. Next closest water source is a stream crossing about 1.5 miles north on the A.T. near Va. 602.

Northern Virginia 4-H Swimming Pool—Blue-blazed side trail 0.9 mile north of Tom Floyd Wayside leads 0.3 mile **West** to the swimming pool. It is open to the public, including hikers, Su–Th 12–7, M–W 12–2:30 & 5–7 (Memorial Day–Labor Day), $4.50 admission ($2 after 5), swimsuits required. Shower only, $1. Inquire at 4-H office, (540) 635-5029, about multiday parking availability (advance arrangements required).

Virginia—Part 4 (Northern Virginia)

Miles from Springer	Miles to Next Point	Features	Services	Elev	Miles from Katahdin	M A P
972.1	3.3	U.S. 522 *East–120 yds. to* Mountain Home B&B *West–3.2m to* **Front Royal, Va., P.O. 22630**	R, P L all	950'	1,220.9	
975.4	1.9	Mosby Campsite, Tom Sealock Spring	C, w	1,800'	1,217.6	
977.3	1.1	**Jim and Molly Denton Shelter** ...*8.1mS; 5.5mN*	S, C, w	1,310'	1,215.7	
978.4	1.9	Va. 638 *West–1.1m to* **Linden, Va., P.O. 22642** *West–2.5m to* Apple House *West–7m to* **Front Royal, VA., P.O. 22630**	R, P g G, M all	1,150'	1,214.6	
980.3	2.5	Va. 55, Manassas Gap *West–1.1m to* **Linden, Va., P.O. 22642**	R, P g	800'	1,212.7	
982.8	1.9	**Manassas Gap Shelter** ...*5.5mS; 4.7mN*	S, w	1,655'	1,210.2	
984.7	2.6	Trillium Trail		1,900'	1,208.3	
987.3	1.0	**Whiskey Hollow Shelter** *(E–0.2m)* ...*4.7mS; 8.8mN*	S, w	1,230'	1,205.7	
988.3	1.2	Campsite and spring	C, w	1850'	1,204.7	
989.5	2.6	+Sky Meadows State Park side trail *(E–1.7m)*	C, w	1,780'	1,203.5	
992.1	3.6	Ashby Gap, U.S. 50, U.S. 17 *East–1.1m to* Paris, Va.	R, P L, M	900'	1,200.9	PATC Map 8
995.7	0.6	**Rod Hollow Shelter** *(W–0.2m)* ...*8.8mS; 7.1mN*	S, C, w	840'	1,197.3	
996.3	2.7	"Roller Coaster" ...*north to Blackburn Trail Center*		860'	1,196.7	
999.0	0.4	Morgans Mill Stream ...*footbridge*	C, w	780'	1,194.0	
999.4	1.2	Va. 605, Morgans Mill Road ...*gravel*	R, P	1,140'	1,193.6	
1,000.6	0.5	Spring	w	1,150'	1,192.4	
1,001.1	1.5	Buzzard Hill ...*view*		1260'	1,191.9	
1,002.6	1.3	**Sam Moore Shelter**; Sawmill Spring ...*7.1mS; 11.2mN*	S, C, w	990'	1,190.4	
1,003.9	1.2	Stream		715'	1,189.1	
1,005.1	0.5	Stream and campsite ...*footbridge*	C, w	800'	1,187.9	
1,005.6	0.6	Bears Den Rocks, Bears Den Hostel *(E–0.2m)*	P, H, L, C, g, cl, sh, f	1,350'	1,187.4	
1,006.2	2.2	Snickers Gap, Va. 7, Va. 679 *East–1.6m to* Bluemont General Store *East–1.7m to* **Bluemont, Va., P.O. 20135** *West–0.3m to* Horseshoe Curve Restaurant *West–0.9m to* Pine Grove Restaurant *West–8.9m to* **Berryville, Va., P.O. 22611**	R, P G M M G, L, M, cl	1,000'	1,186.8	
1,008.4	0.3	Spring	w	1,083'	1,184.6	
1,008.7	0.1	Virginia–West Virginia State Line		1,140'	1,184.3	
1,008.8	0.6	Crescent Rock		1,312'	1,184.2	PATC Map 7
1,009.4	0.1	Sand Spring	w	1,150'	1,183.6	
1,009.5	2.9	Devils Racecourse ...*boulder field*		1,200'	1,183.5	
1,012.4	1.2	Wilson Gap		1,380'	1,180.6	
1,013.6	3.2	Trail(s) to **Blackburn Trail Center** *(E–0.2m)* ...*11.2mS; 3.5mN*	R, P, C, S, w	1,650'	1,179.4	

Miles from Springer	Miles to Next Point	Features	Services	Elev	Miles from Katahdin	M A P
1,016.8	3.0	**David Lesser Memorial Shelter** *(E–0.1m S; 0.3m spring) …3.5mS; 15.8mN*	S, C, w	1,430'	1,176.2	PATC Map 7
1,019.8	1.5	Keys Gap, W. Va. 9 *East–0.3m to* Sweet Springs Country Store *East–5.5m to* Stoney Brook Organic Farm & Hostel *West–0.3m to* Torlone Mini Mart and Restaurant	R, P, w G H G, M, w	935'	1,173.2	

+ Fee charged

Higher rates of Lyme disease occur from northern Virginia into New England. Take precautions.

This 48-mile section follows a long, low ridge rich in American history and home to the infamous "roller-coaster" south of Snickers Gap.

 U.S. 522—East 120 yards to *Lodging:* Mountain Home B&B, (540) 692-6198, 3471 Remount Rd., Front Royal, VA 22630; first driveway east of the Trail; open year-round, owned by Scott "Possible" (AT '12) and Lisa "Anything" Jenkins, <mountainhomeat@gmail.com>. Cabin (sleeps 6-8) is first small red brick building, $30PP includes bed with fresh linens, B, shower, WiFi, shuttles to town, and mail drops. Snacks, pizza, ice cream, and fuel available; laundry with loaner clothes ($5); dogs 1 max. $5/night; parking for non-guests $3/night. Private rooms with bath; call for availability and rates. All welcome to lemonade, cookies, and water, tours of National Register home.

West 3.2 miles to **Front Royal, Va. [P.O. ZIP 22630: M–F 8:30–5, Sa 8:30–1; (540) 635-7983].** The post office is 1.0 mile farther. The town of Front Royal offers trolley services from the U.S. 522 Trailhead into town from mid-Apr until Jul 31. The large town offers all major services, but they are spread out over a wide area. Except for the post office, most services are located near the U.S. 522 and Va. 55 intersection as you come into town from the A.T. ■ *Lodging:* Front Royal is the gateway to Shenandoah National Park, with motel rates that vary considerably according to season; be sure to specify you are a hiker, as most have special rates. Parkside Inn, (540) 631-1153, <reservations@parksideinnfrontroyal.com>, 4 hostel-style rooms, each sleeps up to 3 ($50S or $25PP when 2-3 people/room), other rooms $50–$80, Trailhead shuttle possible, call ahead, laundry facility on site, hiker box, dogs $5 based on availability; Skyline

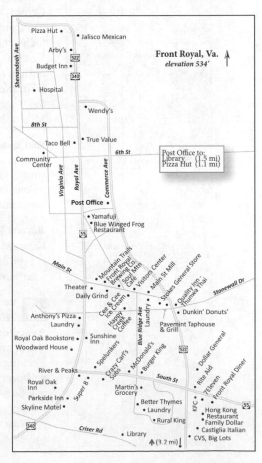

Front Royal, Va.
elevation 534'

Pizza Hut
Jalisco Mexican
Arby's
522
Budget Inn
340
Hospital
Wendy's
8th St
Taco Bell
True Value
6th St
Community Center
Post Office to:
Library (1.5 mi)
Pizza Hut (1.1 mi)
Shenandoah Ave
Virginia Ave
Royal Ave
Commerce Ave
Post Office
Yamafuji
Blue Winged Frog Restaurant
55
Main St
Mountain Trails
Front Royal Brewing Co.
Soul Mtn. Café
Visitors Center
Main St Mill
Stokes General Store
Quality Inn
Thunwa Thai
Stonewall Dr
Theater
Daily Grind
Cee & Cee Ice Cream
Dunkin' Donuts'
Anthony's Pizza
Laundry
Happy Creek Coffee
Blue Ridge Ave
Laundry
Pavemint Taphouse & Grill
Royal Oak Bookstore
Woodward House
Sunshine Inn
Spelunkers
Crazy Carl's Subs
McDonald's
Burger King
522
Dollar General
River & Peaks
South St
Rite Aid
Front Royal Diner
Royal Oak Inn
Super 8
Martin's Grocery
7Eleven
Parkside Inn
Skyline Motel
Better Thymes
Laundry
Rural King
KFC
Hong Kong Restaurant
Family Dollar
Castiglia Italian
55
340
Criser Rd
Library
CVS, Big Lots
(3.2 mi)

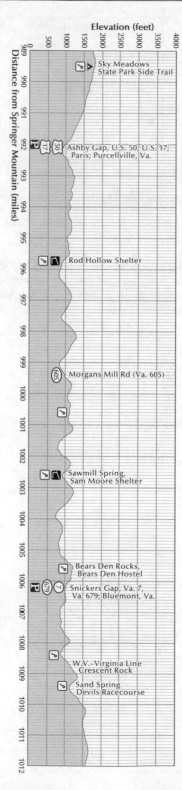

Elevation (feet)

Distance from Springer Mountain (miles)

Sky Meadows State Park Side Trail

Ashby Gap, U.S. 50, U.S. 17; Paris; Purcellville, Va.

Rod Hollow Shelter

Morgans Mill Rd (Va. 605)

Sawmill Spring, Sam Moore Shelter

Bears Den Rocks, Bears Den Hostel

Snickers Gap, Va. 7, Va. 679; Bluemont, Va.

W.V.–Virginia Line Crescent Rock

Sand Spring Devils Racecourse

Resort Motel, (540) 635-5354, office open 8:30–3:30, no dogs; Royal Inn Motel, (540) 636-6168, dogs $10; Super 8 Motel, (540) 636-4888, 10% hiker discount, free B, dogs $10 (based on availability), accepts mail drops; Quality Inn, (540) 635-3161, free B, laundry on site, outdoor pool, dogs $15, Trailhead shuttle 10 a.m. M–F; Woodward House B&B, (540) 635-7010, includes full B, no dogs, shuttle to and from nearby Trailheads. ■ *Groceries:* Martin's, Better Thymes natural foods, Big Lots, Walmart Supercenter (all long-term resupply). ■ *Restaurants:* Front Royal Brewing Company, 122 E. Main St., (540) 631-0773, full menu, closed Tu; Happy Creek Coffee, 18 High St., (540) 660-2133, open daily, WiFi, gluten-free foods, accepts mail drops; Virginia Beer Museum, 16 Chester St.; and many other food outlets. ■ *Outfitters:* Mountain Trails, 120 E. Main St. (540) 749-2470; River and Peak Outfitters, 7 South St., (540) 692-8941, fuel by ounce, canister fuel, open daily except Tu. ■ *Internet access:* Samuels Public Library, M–Sa; Warren County Community Center, daily. ■ *Other services:* Front Royal Brewing Company, 122 E. Main St., (540) 631-0773, base camp for hikers includes free showers, lockers, and laundry; Visitors Center, 414 E. Main St., (800) 338-2576, open daily 9–5, hiker box, WiFi, accepts mail drops. ■ *Shuttles:* A1 Taxi, (540) 636-8294; Yellow Cab, (540) 622-6060; Sharon's Shuttles, (703) 615-5612; Mobile Mike's Shuttles, through Jun, (540) 539-0509.

Smithsonian Conservation Biology Institute—Next to U.S. 522 is the Smithsonian Conservation Biology Institute. On the north side of the highway, the Trail follows one of the center's fences. Exotic animals are sometimes visible.

Jim and Molly Denton Shelter (1991)—Sleeps 8. Privy. Enlarged front porch for extra sleepers. Water source is a spring on the A.T. near the sometimes-functional solar shower; small picnic pavilion.

Va. 638—West 1.1 mile to **Linden, Va. [P.O. ZIP 22642: M–F 8–12 & 1–5, Sa 8–12; (540) 636-9936].** A small outpost on Va. 55, Linden has a post office, farm stand, and convenience store; it's an alternative to hitching into Front Royal to pick up a mail drop. ■ *Groceries:* Monterey Service Station, M–F 4–9, Sa 7–9, Su 8–8; Giving Tree, W–M 10–6; both short-term resupply, hiker-friendly, accepts credit cards.

    West 2.5 miles to ■ *Restaurant:* Apple House, (540) 636-6329, B, fresh-baked pies, doughnuts, sandwiches,

BBQ, buffalo burgers, deli foods; M 7–5, Tu–Su 7–8; credit cards accepted, ATM. ■ *Groceries:* 7-Eleven (short-term resupply), (540) 635-1899, open 24 hrs., deli sandwiches, ice cream; Apple Mountain Exxon, (540) 636-2960, large store, open 24 hrs., ATM, fresh pies, deli sandwiches.

West 7 miles to Front Royal on Va. 55 (see above).

 Va. 55, Manassas Gap—West 1.1 miles into Linden (see above). This is a busier road, parallel to I-66, which leads east to Washington.

Manassas Gap Shelter (1933/2002)—Sleeps 6. Privy. Bear pole. Water source is a reliable spring near the shelter on a side trail.

Whiskey Hollow Shelter (2016)—Sleeps 8. Privy. Bear pole. Water source (which hikers should treat) is Whiskey Hollow Creek in front of the shelter.

Sky Meadows State Park Side Trail—Look for the resting bench at path that leads **East** 1.7 miles to the park's visitors center in Mt. Bleak Mansion, built in the 1840s, (540) 592-3556. Now one of Virginia's finest parks, open daily 8–7:30/dusk. Cultural events are scheduled on summer weekends. Water fountain, soda machine, and rest rooms at the visitors center. Hike-in primitive camping (15+ sites) 1.25 mi from A.T., $15PP, on the way to the visitors center; non-potable water spigot, pit toilet, firewood for sale. Registration encouraged, (800) 933-7275, and hikers must arrive before 4 p.m. or hike another 2 miles round-trip to/from registration office.

 U.S. 50, U.S. 17/Ashby Gap—East 0.8 mile on U.S. 50/17, then 0.3 mile south past barrier on Va. 759 to community of Paris. *Lodging:* The Ashby Inn, (540) 592-3900, restaurant serves L W–Sa 12–2, Su 12–2, D W–Sa 5:30–9, Su 5–8, rooms $160 and up (10% thru-hiker discount), includes B; reservations recommended.

Rod Hollow Shelter (1986)—Sleeps 8. Privy. Bear pole. Tent pads. Located on a blue-blazed trail. Water source is a spring or the streams just south of the shelter. Dining pavilion rebuilt in 2010.

The "Roller Coaster"—Northbounders leaving the Rod Hollow Shelter will enter the "roller coaster," a 13.5-mile section with ten ascents and descents. Southbounders have just completed their ride. The Virginia corridor is narrow here, leaving Trail crews very little choice other than to route the path up and over each of these viewless and rocky ridges.

Sam Moore Shelter (1990)—Sleeps 6. Privy. Bear pole. Constructed of materials salvaged from the old Keys Gap Shelter. Named for maintainer Sam Moore, who gave 55 years of volunteer service to the A.T. Water source is Sawmill Spring in front of shelter or spring to left of shelter.

Bears Den—Bears Den Rocks provide a fine view of the Shenandoah Valley to the west. **East** 0.1 mile to Bears Den Hostel, owned by ATC, operated by PATC; 18393 Blue Ridge Mountain Rd., Bluemont, VA 20135; (540) 554-8708, <www.bearsdencenter.org>. Hiker Special $30 includes bunk, shower, laundry, pizza, soda, and a pint of Ben & Jerry's ice cream; bunk & shower, $20; camping $12 (with shower and indoor-cooking privileges); shower only $3. Hiker room with phone, TV, Internet, and soda is accessible all day with mileage code. The lodge, kitchen, store, and office opens at 5 p.m. daily; check-out is at 9 a.m. Mail drops accepted. Shuttles and slackpacking.

Bear Chase Brewing Co., across from Bears Den entrance, (540) 554-8210, taproom w/ food opens at 11 a.m. daily; lodging.

 Va. 7, Va. 679/Snickers Gap—East 1.6 miles to Bluemont General Store, 6:30 a.m.–7 p.m., (540) 554-2054, short-term resupply, pizza by the slice, sandwiches, ice cream, pies (0.9 mile to Va. 734, turn right, 0.7 mile to store).

East 1.7 miles to **Bluemont, Va. [P.O. ZIP 20135: M–F 10–1 & 2–5, Sa 8:30–12; (540) 554-4537]**. Follow

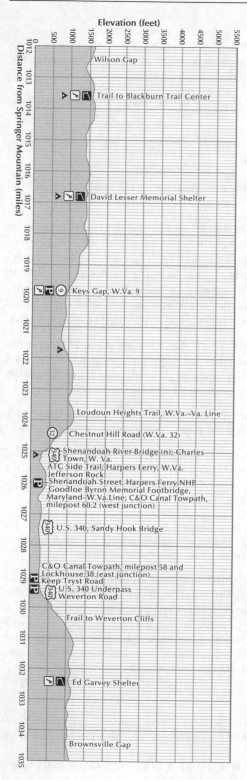

Va. 7 **east** 0.9 mile over Snickers Gap to the Snickersville Turnpike (Va. 734) sign, turn right, and continue 0.8 mile to the post office on Va. 760.

West off Va. 7 on Va. 679 (Pine Grove Rd.) 0.3 mile to *Restaurant:* Horseshoe Curve Restaurant, 1162 Pine Grove Rd., (540) 554-8291, Tu–W 5–9, Th–Su 12–9. Excellent portions. Live music F–Sa.

West 0.9 mile to *Restaurant:* Pine Grove Restaurant on Va. 679, (540) 554-8126, open M–Sa 7 a.m.–8 p.m., Su 7 a.m.–2 p.m.

West 8.9 miles to **Berryville, Va. [P.O. ZIP 22611: M–F 9-5, Sa 9–12:30; (540) 955-2667]** small town with most services. ■ *Groceries:* Food Lion, Circle K, Dollar General, Family Dollar, Market Basket. ■ *Lodging:* The Waypoint House B&B, 211 Church St., (540) 955-8218, shuttle provided, pets permitted; Smithfield Farm, 568 Smithfield Lane, (540) 955-4389, shuttle provided, no pets; AirBnB, (540) 336-9631, shuttle provided, no pets. ■ *Other services:* Bee'Ville Wash-N-Go, Clarke County Public Library (540) 955-5144

Blackburn Trail Center—East 0.2 mile *via* either of two blue-blazed trails, (540) 338-9028. Owned and operated by the Potomac A.T. Club, its mission is to support the Appalachian Trail by housing trail crews, offering facilities for training, meetings, and seminars, and providing trailhead parking, information, and general services to hikers. Trail hikers are welcome. The center offers a hiker cabin with 4 double bunks and a picnic pavilion built with an ALDHA donation in memory of Edward B. Garvey. Six tentsites and a tent platform are located below the cabin. A group campground with tentsites, picnic tables, and a privy is on the north blue-blaze trail. Water is available from an outside spigot. A solar shower is located on the lower lawn. Donations are appreciated. Resident caretakers meet and greet visitors. On a clear day, looking east, you might be able to see the Washington Monument and the National Cathedral in the far distance.

David Lesser Shelter (1994)—Sleeps 6. Privy. Bear pole. An engineering feat. Water source is a spring located 0.4 mile downhill.

West Virginia

Miles from Springer	Miles to Next Point	Features	Services	Elev	Miles from Katahdin	M A P
1,019.8	1.5	Keys Gap, W. Va. 9 *East–0.3m to* groceries *East–5.5m to* Stoney Brook Organic Farm & Hostel *West–0.3m to* Torlone Mini Mart and Restaurant	R, P, w G H g, M, w	935'	1,173.2	
1,021.3	0.4	Powerline		920'	1,171.7	
1,021.7	2.0	Campsite	C, nw	1,120'	1,171.3	
1,023.7	0.7	Loudoun Heights Trail; Virginia–West Virginia State Line		1,200'	1,169.3	
1,024.4	0.7	Chestnut Hill Road, W. Va. 32	R	820'	1,168.6	
1,025.1	0.3	U.S. 340, Shenandoah River Bridge (N end) *East–20m to* Frederick, Md. *West–0.1m to* Econo Lodge *West–1.3m to* Clarion Inn *West–5.6m to* **Charles Town, W. Va. 25414** *West–20m to* Martinsburg, W. Va.	R all L L all all	312'	1,167.9	PATC Map 7
1,025.4	0.5	Appalachian Trail Conservancy side trail *West–0.2m to* **Harpers Ferry, W. Va., P.O. 25425**	ATC, P, B, g, L, w, f	394'	1,167.6	
1,025.9	0.1	Jefferson Rock		425'	1,167.1	
1,026.0	0.1	Shenandoah Street; Harpers Ferry National Historical Park *West–0.1m to* The Outfitter at Harpers Ferry	R, P g, M, O, f	315'	1,167.0	
1,026.1	0.2	Potomac River, Goodloe E. Bryon Memorial Footbridge, West Virginia–Maryland State Line		250'	1,166.9	

Camping and fires are prohibited one-half-mile south of Keys Gap to the powerline 1.5 miles north of the gap (W.Va. 9). An established campsite (no water) is 0.4 mile north of the powerline.

Camping also is prohibited in Harpers Ferry National Historical Park, which begins on the ridgetop 0.5 mile south of the junction with the Loudoun Heights Trail and extends north 3 miles to the Potomac River.

W.Va. 9/Keys Gap—East 0.3 mile to *Groceries:* Sweet Springs Country Store, 34357 Charles Town Pike, Purcellville, VA 20132; (540) 668-7200, M–Sa 4–11, Su 7–11, deli, ATM, accepts hiker packages.

East 5.5 miles to Stoney Brook Organic Farm & Hostel, operated by the Twelve Tribes Spiritual Community, (540) 668-9067 or (540) 668-7123, 37091 Charles Town Pike, Hillsboro, VA 20132. Bunk cabins, tent camping, meals, shower, laundry, dogs okay, mail drops. Call for details and pick-up and drop-off from Bears Den, Blackburn Trail Center, Keys Gap, Harpers Ferry.

West 0.3 mile on Old W.Va. 9 to ■ *Groceries:* Torlone Mini-Mart (short-term resupply), (304) 725-0916, M–Th 8–9, F–Sa 8–10, Su 8–8, shirts and shoes required. ■ *Restaurant:* Torlone Pizza, Pasta & Subs, open T–Th 12–9, F–Sa 11–10, Su 12–8, ATM, recharge devices, refill water containers.

Harpers Ferry National Historical Park—On June 30, 1944, President Franklin D. Roosevelt signed legislation designating part of the town a national monument. Gradual land acquisition in the town and surrounding ridges led to designation as a national historical park in 1963. It saw extensive

Civil War action, especially before the bloody battle at nearby Antietam, Md., but is probably best known for the raid of John Brown, an abolitionist from Kansas who attempted to capture the federal arsenal here in 1859. The arsenal was to be the staging point for a slave uprising. A U.S. colonel named Robert E. Lee crushed the raid in less than 36 hours, and historians point to the event as a steppingstone to the war, which began 16 months after Brown was hanged for treason in nearby Charles Town. But, the history of Harpers Ferry is more than one event, one date, or one individual. It is multilayered, involving a diverse number of people and events that influenced the course of American history. Harpers Ferry also witnessed the first successful application of interchangeable manufacture, the arrival of the first successful American railroad, the largest surrender of federal troops during the Civil War, the education of former slaves in one of the earliest integrated schools in the United States, and the first organized civil rights movement in the country. The park's visitors center (west of town along U.S. 340) offers parking and a free shuttle to the historic district. *Note: Hikers parking in lot must register at the visitors center, open 8–5.* Parking-lot gates open at 8, close at dusk. Entrance fee is $10 per vehicle for 3 consecutive days or park for up to 2 weeks. Today, the Park Service runs many interpretive exhibits in renovated buildings dating back to the mid-19th century. More information on the historic town is available at ATC headquarters, (304) 535-6331, as well as the park's visitors center.

U.S. 340/Shenandoah River—*Traffic can be extremely heavy at this Trailhead, and it is neither safe nor legal to hitchhike here; local police often are nearby, watching for speeders.*

Signs on U.S. 340 say "Appalachian Trail Visitor Center"—that's the ATC visitors center and headquarters.

East 20 miles to Frederick, Md., with all services, including The Trail House, an outfitter, 17 South Market St., (301) 694-8448, 10% hiker discount.

West 0.1 mile to *Lodging:* Quality Inn, (304) 535-6391, ask for hiker rate (10% discount), usually full on holiday weekends, WiFi, no pets, hot B, laundry, vending machines; refrigerator, microwave, and coffee and tea in rooms.

West 1.2 miles to ■ *Camping:* Harpers Ferry KOA (short-term resupply), (304) 535-6895, cabins, tentsites, and lodges; call for rates.. Snack bar, pizzeria, campstore with fuel, pool, laundry $5; leashed pets welcome $2, except Rottweillers, pit bulls, Dobermans, or any mix of those breeds. ■ *Lodging and Restaurant:* Clarion Inn Conference Center, 4328 Wilson Freeway (U.S. 340), Harpers Ferry, WV 25425, (304) 535-6302, bar & grill, call for rates (10% hiker discount), microwave and refrigerator in rooms, WiFi with computer access for hikers, pets allowed (call for rates and conditions), laundry, indoor pool, fitness center, holds and mails guest packages, long-term parking for guests. Shuttle possible F–Sa, as available. White Horse Tavern, L/D M–Th 11–9, F–Sa 11–midnight, Su 12:30–9.

West 5.6 miles to **Charles Town, W.Va. [P.O. ZIP 25414: M–F 8:30–5, Sa 9–12:30; (304) 725-2421].** ■ *Lodging:* Motel 6, (304) 725-1402, call for rates, smoking and nonsmoking rooms, pets under 50lbs. okay with prior approval and deposit; America's Best Value Inn, (304) 725-2041, prices vary, call for rates, smoking and nonsmoking rooms, coin laundry; Hampton Inn, (304) 725-2200, call for rates, nonsmoking rooms only, laundry, hot B, no pets, indoor pool/hot tub, fitness center, business center; Holiday Inn Express, (304) 725-1330, call for rates, nonsmoking rooms only, hot B, laundry, fitness center, business center, outdoor pool; Rodeway Inn and Suites, (304) 725-2081, call for rates, smoking and nonsmoking rooms available, some rooms with Jacuzzi tubs, hot B, dogs okay at $50/day (in some rooms). ■ *Groceries:* Super Walmart, 24/7; Food Lion Food Market, 7–11; 7-Eleven, 24/7; Sheetz; Aldi Supermarket, M–Sa 9–8, Su 9–7; Martin's, 6–midnight. ■ *Other services:* Jefferson Memorial Hospital, (304)-728-1600; Jefferson Urgent Care, M–F 8–8, Sa–Su & holidays 8–5, (304) 728-8533; WVU Medicine University Urgent Care, (304) 725-2273, M–F 8-8, Sa noon-8, closed Su; Kams Taxi, (304) 279-5822; Community Taxi Service, LLC, (304) 725-3794.

West 20 miles (U.S. 340 to W.Va. 9) to Martinsburg, W.Va., with all services, including theaters, malls, as well as many restaurants. For bus service to those towns, see Harpers Ferry entry below.

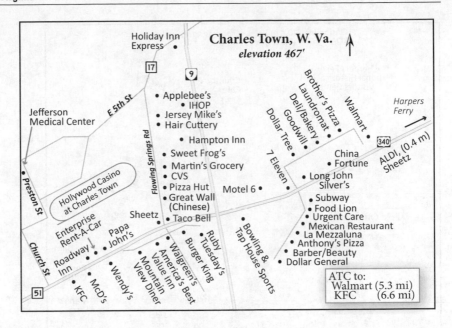

Charles Town, W. Va.
elevation 467'

Holiday Inn Express
17
9
Jefferson Medical Center
E 5th St
Flowing Springs Rd
Preston St
Applebee's
IHOP
Jersey Mike's
Hair Cuttery
Hampton Inn
Sweet Frog's
Martin's Grocery
CVS
Pizza Hut
Great Wall (Chinese)
Taco Bell
Hollywood Casino at Charles Town
Enterprise Rent-A-Car
Papa John's
Sheetz
Roadway Inn
Church St
51
KFC
McD's
Wendy's
America's Best Value Inn
Mountain View Diner
Walgreen's
Burger King
Ruby Tuesday's
Motel 6
7 Eleven
Bowling & Tap House Sports
Brother's Pizza
Deli/Bakery
Laundromat
Goodwill
Dollar Tree
Walmart
China Fortune
Long John Silver's
Subway
Food Lion
Urgent Care
Mexican Restaurant
La Mezzaluna
Anthony's Pizza
Barber/Beauty
Dollar General
Harpers Ferry
340
ALDI, (0.4 m)
Sheetz

ATC to:
Walmart (5.3 mi)
KFC (6.6 mi)

Note: Hitchhiking is illegal on state-maintained roads in West Virginia. That includes U.S. 340 and the main street through Harpers Ferry and adjacent Bolivar.

Harpers Ferry, W.Va. [P.O. ZIP 25425: M–F 8–4, Sa 9–12; (304) 535-2479]. The post office and most services are available above the old town *via* the 0.2-mile blue-blazed trail to ATC headquarters (see below). The A.T. itself leads through the historic district at the bottom of the hill along the riverfronts, with museums, stores, and restaurants. In winter, many businesses in the historic district are closed or open only on weekends. The national historical park is open 7 days a week year-round (park trails close sunset to sunrise), but its visitors center closes Thanksgiving, Christmas, and New Year's Day. ■ *Hostel & Lodging:* The Town's Inn and Hostel, (304) 932-0677, 175 High St., <karantownsend@gmail.com>, located in historic lower town, private rooms (with reservation, pets allowed in one room; contact for details), hostel $35 (walk-ins only, no advance reservations; call for rates), microwave, fridge, WiFi, and coffee/tea in all rooms, country café, full-service restaurant, hiker resupply (snacks and trail food), laundry $5, and shuttles $1/mile (when available); Ledge House B&B; LightHorse Inn and Harpers Ferry Vacation Rentals, (877) 468-4236, 10% hiker discount, call for availability and rates. Information on several other B&Bs can be found at <www.historicharpersferry.com>. ■ *Groceries:* The Outfitter at Harpers Ferry (short-term resupply, including freeze-dried food and hiker favorites), 0.5 mile **east** of ATC, open M–Sa 10–6, Sun 11–5, except Jan–Feb when it's F–Su (hours) only; 7-11 convenience store (snacks, short-term resupply), 1 mile **west** of ATC; supermarkets and Walmart (long-term resupply) in Charles Town, 5 miles **west**. ■ *Restaurants.* **West** of ATC: 0.1 mile, Mena's Pizzeria & Italian Restaurant, (304) 535-6362, 10% hiker discount, L/D, closed M, T–Th 11–9, F–Sa 11–10, Su 12–9; 0.3 mile, Guide Shack Café, (304) 995-6022, open M–F 5–7, Sa–Su 7–7; 0.4 mile, Canal House, closed W, L/D; 0.5 mile, Anvil Restaurant, W–Su 11–9; 1 mile, Country Café, (304) 535-2327, B/L, closed M, Tu–Su 7:30–3. **East** of ATC 0.5 mile in lower town: The Town's Inn Restaurant, (304) 535-1860, 6 a.m.–10 p.m. daily, B/L/D; Potomac Grille, (304) 535-1900, M–Sa 12–5, Su 12–7 (winter hours vary); Cannonball Deli, (304) 535-1762, 10% hiker discounts, M–Su 11:30–5:30 (winter, weekends only). ■ *Outfitter:* The Outfitter at Harpers Ferry, 106 Potomac St., (304) 535-2087 or (888) 535-2087, <www.theoutfitteratharpersferry.com>, full-service outfitter (gear, first aid, footwear), shuttle refer-

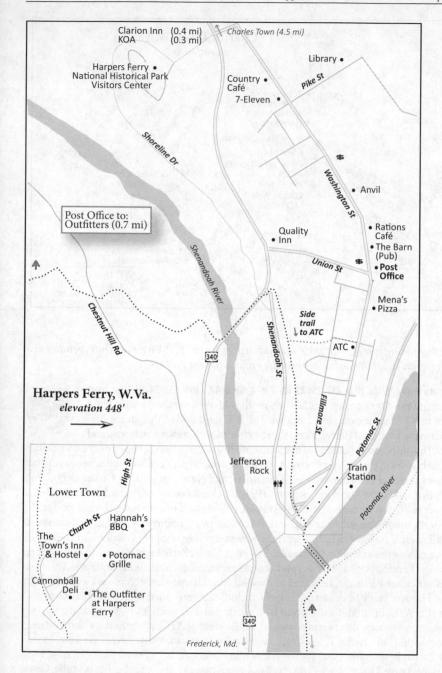

Clarion Inn   (0.4 mi)
KOA   (0.3 mi)

Charles Town (4.5 mi)

Library •

Harpers Ferry •
National Historical Park
Visitors Center

Pike St

Country •
Café
7-Eleven •

Shoreline Dr

$

Washington St

• Anvil

Post Office to:
Outfitters (0.7 mi)

Shenandoah River

Quality •
Inn

• Rations
Café
• The Barn
(Pub)
• **Post
Office**

Union St

Mena's
• Pizza

Chestnut Hill Rd

**Side
trail
↓ to ATC**

ATC •

340

Shenandoah St

Harpers Ferry, W.Va.
elevation 448'
→

Fillmore St

Potomac St

Jefferson
Rock   •

Train
Station   •

Potomac River

Lower Town

High St

Hannah's
BBQ   •

Church St

The
Town's Inn
& Hostel •

• Potomac
Grille

Cannonball
Deli
•

• The Outfitter
at Harpers
Ferry

340

Frederick, Md. ↓

↓

rals, open daily 10–6, Jan–Feb F–Su only. ■ *Internet access:* Bolivar–Harpers Ferry Public Library, (304) 535-2301, M, Tu, F, Sa 10–5:30, W, Th 10–8; ATC. ■ *Other services:* ATC maintains a list of supporters in its A.T. Community program that provide special services or discounts for hikers and ATC members. Banks with ATM; dentist; Caring Hands Chiropractic and advanced massage therapy, Dr. Jenny Foster, a hiker (located near Middletown, Md.), (301) 371-3922, call ahead for possible pick-up (schedule permitting); bicycle rental and supplies at The Outfitter at Harpers

Ferry, (304) 535-2296. Rafting, tubing, canoeing, fishing, and horseback riding opportunities nearby; check <www.historicharpersferry.com>.

Appalachian Trail Conservancy (ATC)—Reached *via* 0.2-mile blue-blazed trail 0.3 mile north of the junction of U.S. 340 and Shenandoah Street, before northbounders reach the historic section of Harpers Ferry; at the corner of Washington Street and Storer College Place.

ATC was formed in 1925 by private citizens to make the dream of an Appalachian Trail a reality. After the initial Trail route was pieced together in 1937 (much of it on roads and across private land), ATC continued to work to identify better routes for the Trail and worked with Congress, the National Park Service, the U.S. Forest Service, states, and others to ensure a continuously protected corridor. Today, ATC is the primary organization responsible for the stewardship of the footpath and 250,000 acres of public land surrounding it. Working with more than 6,000 volunteers in four ATC-run Trail crews and 31 affiliated local clubs and multiple public agencies, ATC leads the efforts to maintain and improve the footpath and protect the natural and cultural resources of the Trail corridor, engage communities along the A.T. to support it, and guard against encroachments. Much of the behind-the-scenes work that continues to makes the A.T. experience possible takes place out of sight in offices upstairs and the connected annex. The single largest source of ATC's funding is individual membership dues and small contributions. If you're not already an ATC member, consider joining here to help support continued protection of the Trail.

ATC publications and merchandise are for sale at the information/visitors center. A.T. exhibits include a 10-foot-long raised-relief map of the A.T. Volunteers or staffers Dave Tarasevich (Pop Tart of '02) and Jeff Metzger can answer your Trail questions. The office accepts donations for Coleman fuel and denatured alcohol and holds packages sent USPS to P.O. Box 807 or FedEx and UPS to 799 Washington St., Harpers Ferry, WV 25425. All hikers are encouraged to stop at ATC headquarters to sign the register. Those hiking the entire Trail, whether in sections or at once, are photographed for an official registry that allows ATC to track the number and demographics of 2,000-miler hopefuls year to year. The same photo can be purchased as a postcard for $2 (postage and tax included; first one is free for ATC members).

The ATC Visitors Center, (304) 535-6331, is open daily 9–5 except Thanksgiving, Christmas, and New Year's Day. Frost-free faucet is on west (Storer College Place) side of building. Drinks for sale inside. Benches and picnic tables in side yard. Phone, WiFi, and Internet access for hikers. Ask for ATC's often-updated "Guide to Harpers Ferry Hiker Services," with more details on area services. Driving directions are available at <www.appalachiantrail.org/locations>.

Jefferson Rock—White blazes take you past this Harpers Ferry viewpoint that overlooks the confluence of the Potomac and Shenandoah rivers. Named in honor of Thomas Jefferson, who was inspired by the beautiful view in 1783. Several large shale slabs originally rested naturally but not securely atop each other. "Jefferson Rock" now rests securely on a set of short pillars erected in the 1850s.

Area Transportation Options—■ *Vehicle rental:* Enterprise, (304) 724-6605 (be sure to key through to direct access to branch), will pick up at ATC headquarters and take you to Charles Town branch next to Rodeway Inn; allow 1-hour advance notice; enter code: W15509 to get ATC discount. ■ *Bus service:* EPTA bus to Charles Town (Walmart) and Martinsburg operates M–F; flag the bus from the ATC office or anywhere along the main Washington/High St. (stand at least 200 feet from the crest of the hill). The charge is $2.50 one-way; exact change required. Tickets can also be purchased online at <www.eptawv.com>. Bus departs at 6:41 a.m., 9:11 a.m., 11:18 a.m., 1:03 p.m., and 4:34 p.m. Leaves Walmart in Charles Town for Harpers Ferry at 6:59 a.m., 9:20 a.m., 11:36 a.m., 12:48 p.m., 1:21 p.m., and 4:52 p.m. No dogs; packs OK unless driver believes one may be suspicious. Times subject to change. ■ *Shuttles:* Half App Shuttlers, (304) 919-0595, (304) 596-1911, Harpers Ferry area only. ■ *Trains to Washington, D.C.*—Amtrak, (800) USA-RAIL, <www.amtrak.com>: Train No. 30 (Capitol Limited) departs Harpers Ferry at 11:25 a.m., 7 days a week and arrives at D.C.'s Union Station at 1:10 p.m. Note that this train frequently runs late coming from Chicago; check status on line.

Train No. 29 is scheduled to leave D.C. daily at 4:05 p.m., arriving in Harpers Ferry at 5:16 p.m. Coach fares are $14 one way (cost may be more if coach is not available). Fares and schedules are subject to change. *Harpers Ferry station is not staffed.* Tickets **must** be purchased in advance at <www.amtrak. com>. Backpacks allowed. A roll-on service for bicycles is available on this route for $20. **Maryland Rail Commuter Service (MARC)**, (301) 834-8360; <www.mtamaryland.com>. Three scheduled commuter trains on the Brunswick line leave Harpers Ferry for D.C. on weekdays, departing at 5:25 a.m., 5:50 a.m. and 6:50 a.m., arriving at Union Station at 7:09 a.m., 7:35 a.m. and 8:32 a.m. Trains leave D.C. Union Station for Harpers Ferry on weekdays, departing at 4:25 p.m., 5:40 p.m., and 6:20 p.m., and arrive at 6:05 p.m., 7:18 p.m., and 7:54 p.m. Fares are $12 one way, seats are not reserved, and tickets must be purchased on board (cash only, no bills larger than $20). More trains are available at the Brunswick, Md., station (8 miles east).

Maryland

Miles from Springer	Miles to Next Point	Features	Services	Elev	Miles from Katahdin	M A P
1,026.1	0.2	Potomac River, Goodloe E. Bryon Memorial Footbridge, West Virginia–Maryland Line		250'	1,166.9	
1,026.3	1.1	C&O Canal Towpath mp 60.2 *(A.T. west jct.)* *West–2.7m to* C&O Huckleberry Hill Campsite	C, w	290'	1,166.7	
1,027.4	1.5	U.S. 340, Sandy Hook Bridge *(overhead)*	R	290'	1,165.6	
1,028.9	0.1	C&O Canal Towpath mp 58 *(A.T. east jct.)*, Lockhouse 38		290'	1,164.1	
1,029.0	0.2	Keep Tryst Road; railroad tracks *East–2.5m to* **Brunswick, Md., P.O. 21716**	R, P g, M	320'	1,164.0	
1,029.2	0.2	U.S. 340 *...underpass*	R	400'	1,163.8	
1,029.4	0.9	Weverton Road	R, P	420'	1,163.6	
1,030.3	2.1	Trail to Weverton Cliffs *...Potomac River view, U.S. Rep. Goodloe E. Bryon plaque*		780'	1,162.7	
1,032.4	2.0	**Ed Garvey Shelter** *(E–0.1m S; 0.5m spring)* *...15.8mS; 4.5mN*	S, C, w	1,100'	1,160.6	
1,034.4	0.3	Brownsville Gap *...dirt road*		1,140'	1,158.6	
1,034.7	1.4	Glenn R. Caveney Memorial Plaque		1,150'	1,158.3	
1,036.1	0.4	Crampton Gap, Gathland State Park, Gapland Road, Md. 572 *...frost-free faucet* *West–0.4m to* Maple Tree Campground	R, P, w C, g, f	950'	1,156.9	
1,036.5	2.6	**Crampton Gap Shelter** *(E–0.3m)* *...4.5mS; 5.5mN*	S, C, w	1,000'	1,156.5	
1,039.1	0.6	Trail to Bear Spring Cabin *(locked) (W–0.5m spring)*	w	1,480'	1,153.9	
1,039.7	0.2	White Rocks Cliff *...view*		1,500'	1,153.3	
1,039.9	1.1	Lamb's Knoll *...antenna tower*		1,600'	1,153.1	
1,041.0	0.5	Tower Road	R	1,300'	1,152.0	
1,041.5	0.5	**Rocky Run Shelters** *(W–0.2m)* *...5.5mS; 7.8mN*	S, C, w	970'	1,151.5	
1,042.0	0.5	High-tension-powerline clearing		950'	1,151.0	
1,042.5	0.5	Reno Monument Road, Fox Gap *East–2m to* South Mountain Creamery	R, P M	910'	1,150.5	
1,043.0	0.3	Powerline		940'	1,150.0	
1,043.3	0.2	Dahlgren Backpacker Campground	C, sh, w	980'	1,149.7	
1,043.5	1.4	Turners Gap, U.S. Alt. 40 *West–2.4m to* **Boonsboro, Md., P.O. 21713** *West–3.8m to* Weis Supermarket	R, P, M g, M, D, V, cl G	1,000'	1,149.5	
1,044.9	0.2	Monument Road	R	1,350'	1,148.1	
1,045.1	0.4	Washington Monument Road *...frost-free faucet*	R, P, w	1,400'	1,147.9	
1,045.5	2.1	Washington Monument *...view*	R, P	1,500'	1,147.5	
1,047.6	0.3	Boonsboro Mountain Road	R, P	1,300'	1,145.4	
1,047.9	0.5	Bartman Hill Trail to Greenbrier State Park *(W–0.6m)*	C, sh, w	1,380'	1,145.1	

Miles from Springer	*Miles to Next Point*	Features	Services	Elev	Miles from Katahdin	MAP
1,048.4	*0.6*	1-70 Footbridge *(north end)*, U.S. 40, blue-blaze to Greenbrier State Park *(W–1.4m)*	R, P	1,200'	1,144.6	PATC Map 5-6
1,049.0	*1.6*	Pine Knob Shelter *(W–0.1m) . . . 7.8mS; 8.3mN*	S, C, w	1,360'	1,144.0	
1,050.6	*1.0*	Trail to Annapolis Rock *(W–0.2m C; 0.4m spring)*	C, w	1,820'	1,142.4	
1,051.6	*0.6*	Black Rock Cliffs		1,800'	1,141.4	
1,052.2	*4.8*	Pogo Memorial Campsite *(east)*, spring *(W–30 yds.)* on Thurston Griggs Trail *(W–0.9m parking)*	C, w, P	1,500'	1,140.8	
1,057.0	*0.2*	Md. 17, Wolfsville Road *West–1.8m to* shopping center *West–2m to* **Smithsburg, Md., P.O. 21783** *West–2.7m to* **Cavetown, Md., P.O. 22509**; supermarket and restaurants	R, P G, D, V G, M, D, cl G, M, f	1,400'	1,136.0	
1,057.2	*0.2*	Ensign Cowall Shelter *. . . 8.3mS; 5.1mN*	S, C, w	1,430'	1,135.8	
1,057.4	*1.3*	Powerline		1,440"	1,135.6	
1,058.5	*1.2*	Md. 77, Foxville Road	R	1,450'	1,134.5	
1,059.7	*0.6*	Spring	w	1,300'	1,133.3	
1,060.3	*0.8*	Warner Gap Road *. . . two board bridges across stream*	R, P, w	1,150'	1,132.7	
1,061.1	*1.0*	Raven Rock Hollow, Md. 491 *. . . rock-hop stream*	R, w	1,190'	1,131.9	
1,062.1	*1.8*	**Raven Rock Shelter** *(E–0.1m spring) (W–0.2m S) . . . 5.1mS; 9.8mN*	S, C, w	1,480'	1,130.9	
1,063.9	*2.9*	Trail to High Rock *. . . view*	R, P	1,950'	1,129.1	
1,066.8	*0.2*	Pen Mar County Park *. . . picnic area* *East–1.4m to* **Cascade, Md., P.O. 21719** *West–1.8m to* **Rouzerville, Pa., P.O. 17250**	R, P, w G, L, M, sh, f G, L, M, D, cl, f	1,300'	1,126.2	
1,067.0	*0.1*	Mason-Dixon Line; Maryland–Pennsylvania State Line	R	1,250'	1,126.0	

Overnight camping in Maryland is allowed only at designated campsites: Ed Garvey Shelter, Crampton Gap Shelter, Rocky Run Shelters, Dahlgren Back Pack Campground, Pine Knob Shelter, Annapolis Rocks, Pogo Memorial Campsite, Ensign Cowall Shelter, and Raven Rocks Shelter. Please obey camping regulations in this heavily used section. Alcoholic beverages are prohibited on all Appalachian Trail lands in Maryland. Report emergencies and illegal activities to ***Park Watch****, (800) 825-7275.*

This section boasts easy terrain, the C & O Canal towpath along the Potomac River, a free on-trail hot-water shower, Civil War history, the War Correspondents Monument, the first monument to George Washington, and the Mason-Dixon line.

C&O Canal Towpath—The southernmost 2.8 miles of the Trail in Maryland follow this path from which until 1924 mules towed barges, between what's left of the canal on one side and the Potomac River on the other. Stretching 185 miles from Washington, D.C., to Cumberland, Md., it was rescued from highway development by a 1954 protest hike led by Supreme Court Justice William O. Douglas, an A.T. 2,000-miler. Now, it is part of a national historical park, accessible to both hikers and bicyclists. Blazes are scarce, but the points at which the Trail enters and leaves it are hard to miss. The Maryland state line is the southern shore of the Potomac, which you cross above when leaving Harpers Ferry National Historical Park.

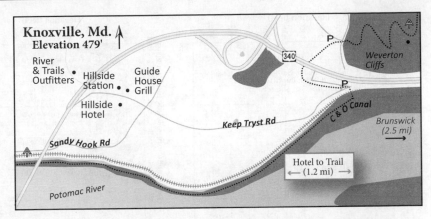

Keep Tryst Road—West 1.13 mile (left on Sandy Hook Road) to ■ *Lodging:* Hillside Hotel, 19105 Keep Tryst Rd., Knoxville, Md. 21758, (301) 660-3580, call for rates, continental B (6–9 a.m.), refrigerator, microwave, no pets or smoking, credit cards only. ■ *Groceries:* Hillside Station, (301) 969-5013; deli hot food, pizza, ice cream, hot wings; ATM; M–F 5 a.m.–9 p.m., Sa 6–9, Su 7–9. ■ *Restaurant:* Guide House Grill, (301) 655-3663, <www.guidehousegrill.com>, W 11–8, Th–Sa 11–9, Su 11–7, closed M–Tu. ■ *Other services:* River and Trails Outfitters, 604 Valley Rd., Knoxville, Md. 21758, (301) 834-9950, <www.rivertrail.com>; zipline; canoe, kayak, tube, and bike rentals, shuttles for C&O Canal, A.T., Potomac and Shenandoah rivers. Brunswick Family Campground; cabins, tent and RV sites. ■ *Shuttles:* Hostelhiker.com, (304) 885-9550, <hostelhiker.com>, from Swift Run Gap in SNP to Boiling Springs, Pa.; also to D.C., Baltimore, *etc.*

East 2.5 mile to **Brunswick, Md. [P.O. ZIP 21716: M–F 8:30–4:30, Sa 9–12; (301) 434-9944]** *via* U.S. 340 and Md. 478 at Knoxville exit or stay on the C&O towpath to milepoint 55. ■ *Groceries:* Dollar General, (301) 834-4024; Family Dollar, (301) 834-5386; Rite Aid & Pharmacy, (301) 834-8100; Weis Supermart, on Md. 17 just east of U.S. 340 junction (long-term resupply); Sheetz; McDonald's, Papa John's. ■ *Restaurants:* Smoketown Brewing Station, (301) 834-4828; MiniDip and TowPath Creamery, (301) 969-6480; Beans in the Belfry, (301) 834-7178; Potomac Street Grill, (301)969-0548; A Better Choice Bakery, (301) 712-4137; King's Pizza, (301) 834-9999; Roy Rogers, (301) 834-8022 (Soulder Rd.); Subway, (301) 834-7940; Domino's, (301) 834-3000; Wing N Pizza Shack, (301) 834-5555; New China, (301) 834-8888. ■ *Internet access:* library, 915 N. Maple Ave., (301) 600-7250, open M–Th 8–10, F–Sa 10–5, closed Su. ■ *Other services:* Ace Hardware, (301) 969-0107; PNC and BB&T bank with 24-hour ATM; Dr. Benjamin Weiser, DDS, (301) 834-6700; Brunswick Heritage Museum, (301) 834-7100 (local history, model railroad); Brunswick Laundromat, (301) 606-8075; Whale of a Wash, (304) 876-0088; barber shop.

Ed Garvey Shelter (2001)—Sleeps 12. Composting privy. Two tentsites north and south of shelter. Water source is found at the end of a 0.5-mile, steep side trail in front of the shelter.

Gathland State Park—Located in Crampton Gap, the state-run facility has water (frost-free faucet), restroom (with electrical outlet), covered picnic pavilion, parking. No camping. Two museums—Civil War and War Correspondents, along with Gath's tomb—are open 9–5 weekends May–Sep. The War Correspondents Monument is the only one of its kind. Constructed in 1896, it stands 50 feet high, 40 feet broad, with plaques relating Battle of South Mountain history. Southbounders may want to pick up water here before heading to Ed Garvey Shelter.

Gapland Road—West 0.4 mile on Gapland Rd., right on Townsend Rd. to *Camping:* Maple Tree Campground, 20716 Townsend Rd., Gapland, MD 21779, (301) 432-5585, <www.thetree-housecamp.com>; tentsites, treehouses, cottages; Hobbit House, ask for rates. All with picnic table,

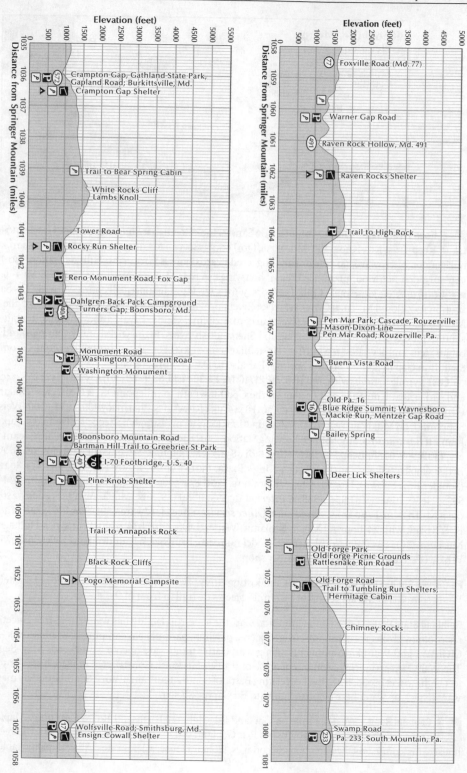

Elevation (feet)

Distance from Springer Mountain (miles)

Crampton Gap; Gathland State Park,
Gapland Road; Burkittsville, Md.
Crampton Gap Shelter

Trail to Bear Spring Cabin

White Rocks Cliff
Lambs Knoll

Tower Road
Rocky Run Shelter

Reno Monument Road, Fox Gap

Dahlgren Back Pack Campground
Turners Gap; Boonsboro, Md.

Monument Road
Washington Monument Road
Washington Monument

Boonsboro Mountain Road
Bartman Hill Trail to Greebrier St Park
I-70 Footbridge, U.S. 40

Pine Knob Shelter

Trail to Annapolis Rock

Black Rock Cliffs

Pogo Memorial Campsite

Wolfsville Road; Smithsburg, Md.
Ensign Cowall Shelter

Elevation (feet)

Distance from Springer Mountain (miles)

Foxville Road (Md. 77)

Warner Gap Road

Raven Rock Hollow, Md. 491

Raven Rocks Shelter

Trail to High Rock

Pen Mar Park; Cascade, Rouzerville
Mason-Dixon Line
Pen Mar Road; Rouzerville, Pa.

Buena Vista Road

Old Pa. 16
Blue Ridge Summit; Waynesboro
Mackie Run, Mentzer Gap Road

Bailey Spring

Deer Lick Shelters

Old Forge Park
Old Forge Picnic Grounds
Rattlesnake Run Road

Old Forge Road
Trail to Tumbling Run Shelters,
Hermitage Cabin

Chimney Rocks

Swamp Road
Pa. 233; South Mountain, Pa.

fire ring, grill. Short-term resupply; white gas, canisters; mail drops accepted; dogs on leashes okay, no extra fee; Internet access.

Crampton Gap Shelter (built by CCC, 1941)—Sleeps 6. Privy, deck with cooking table. Water source is an intermittent spring 0.1 mile south on the A.T. that may go dry in June. Northbounders may want to get water from faucet at Gathland State Park, 0.25 mile south on the A.T.

Rocky Run Shelters (CCC–1941, sleeps 6; PATC–2008. Sleeps 16)—Older shelter is on blue-blaze to piped spring just south of the new shelter. Composting privy at new shelter; pit privy at old. Tent platforms and benches on the ridgeline. Tent and hammock sites near both shelters.

Reno Monument in Fox Gap marks the spot where Union Maj. Gen. Jesse Lee Reno and Confederate Gen. Samuel Garland, Jr., were wounded mortally in the Battle of South Mountain, antecedent to the bloody Battle at Antietam a few miles to the west. (General Robert E. Lee issued Special Order 191 in nearby Frederick before Antietam, a copy of which was subsequently lost and recovered by Union forces, providing valuable information.) Near the monument is the Gen. Garland Trail that leads to the stunning N.C. South Mountain monument; across the road is the Stonewall Regiments Monument, erected by the 17th Michigan Volunteer Infantry Regiment. **East** 2 miles to South Mountain Creamery, 8305 Bolivar Rd., (301) 371-8665, ice cream, fresh all-natural dairy products.

Dahlgren Backpack Campground—Bathhouse with hot showers and flush toilets. Operated by the state at no charge, the bathhouse with electrical outlets (open Apr–Oct), campsites with gravel tentpads, fire rings, bear poles, hammock sites, and utility sink (behind building). A frost-free faucet is about 100 yards up the gravel road toward the inn.

U.S. 40-A/Turners Gap. ■ *Restaurant:* Old South Mountain Inn, (301) 432-6155, Tu–F 5 p.m.–close, Sa 4–close, Su brunch 10:30–1:30, Su D 2–close. This is one of the oldest public houses on the A.T. and reportedly was once a brothel. It has quite a bit of history (see ATC's book, *Hiking through History*). Across the highway is the Gothic, stone Dahlgren Chapel (yes, related to the Dahlgren cannon of Civil War fame). Hikers staying at Dahlgren Campground can literally shower and shave before an elegant dining experience, then walk back to camp in minutes. (Take your pack with you.) ■ *Other services:* chiropractic and therapeutic massage, Dr. Jenny Foster, (301) 371-3922, can pick up along the Maryland A.T., schedule permitting.

West 2.4 miles to **Boonsboro, Md. [P.O. ZIP 21713: M–F 9–1 & 2–5, Sa 9–12; (301) 432-6861].** ■ *Groceries:* Cronise Market Place (short-term resupply), (301) 432-7377, M–F 10–7, Sa 9–7, Su 10–6; My MiniMart & Deli, (301) 432-4646, short-term resupply, M–Th 6–9, F 6–10, Sa 9–10, Su 8–8. ■ *Restaurants:* Crawford Restaurant, (301) 432-2903, cash only; Subway, (301) 432-0100; Mountainside Deli, (301) 432-6700; Vesta Pizzeria & Restaurant, (301) 432-6166, will deliver to parking lot at South Mountain Inn; Potomac Street Creamery, (301) 432-5242, ice-cream shop; Dan's Tap House Restaurant, (301) 432-5224; Domino's, (301) 349-3300; Stone Werks Coffee & Sweets, (678) 749-2158; Rasco N.Y. Pizza, (301) 799-5080. ■ *Internet access:* library, (301) 432-5723, 401 Potomac St., has computers and WiFi, M–Th 10:30–7, F 10:30–6, Sa 10:15–3; Turn the Page Bookstore Café, (301) 432-4588, with A.T. books and maps and expresso coffee bar, owned by Bruce Wilder, who is married to novelist Nora Roberts, so her books (and fans) dominate. ■ *Other services:* Marcy's Laundry, (301) 491-5849, 5:30 a.m–10 p.m. daily; banks with ATM; barber shop; doctor; dentist [(301) 432-4322]; veterinarian; and pharmacy.

West 3.8 miles to ■ *Groceries:* Weis Supermarket & Pharmacy (long-term resupply), (301) 432-3950. ■ *Other services:* dentist, (301) 432-4322.

Washington Monument State Park—A state park built around the first monument to George Washington. The bottle-shaped structure is more modest than the one in Washington, but impressive for small-town Marylanders in 1827. When open, the observation deck on top provides views of the surrounding countryside. South of the monument, on the A.T., are picnic shelters and restroom (with electrical outlets) near the museum. Air-conditioned museum is usually open daily Jun–Aug and weekends during the off-season. No camping permitted in the park. Frost-free faucet on trail above main parking lot. Overnight parking permitted in lot after registration at kiosk.

 U.S. 40/Greenbrier State Park—North of the I-70 footbridge, the A.T. crosses U.S. 40. **West** 0.4 mile to the park entrance.

West 1.4 miles to *Camping:* Greenbrier State Park, (301) 791-4767, open Apr–Oct, pets on leash allowed on some sites. Visitors center, restroom with showers, concession stand, paddle-boat rental and swimming in Greenbrier Lake. Tentsites with hot showers $27.50. Reservations recommended on the weekends; two-night minimum until Labor Day. Walk-in hikers may be allowed a one-night stay if a site is available; day-use-only fee may apply; access *via* Bartman Hill Trail

Pine Knob Shelter (1939)—Sleeps 5. Privy. Shelter is located on a blue-blazed trail. Tent and hammock sites. Water source is a piped spring on north side of the shelter.

Annapolis Rock Campsite—13 tentsites and two privies at this popular area; caretaker on site. Tentsites are near an outstanding overlook popular with climbers. No fires. Spring location is marked.

Pogo Memorial Campsite—The campsite is immediately east of the Trail; 5 individual tentsites, 2 group sites, composting privy, bear pole, and two nearby springs: one on the A.T., the other 30 yards on the blue-blazed Thurston Griggs Trail to the west.

 Md. 17/Wolfsville Road—West 1.7 miles on Wolfsville Road and then left 0.1 mile on Md. 64 to a small shopping center. ■ *Groceries:* Phil & Jerry's Meats & More (short-term resupply), (301) 824-3750, M–Th 8–6, F–Sa 8–8; Dollar General Store, (301) 824-6940. ■ *Other services:* veterinarian, (301) 416-0888; medical clinic, (301) 824-3343; pharmacy, (301) 824-3900; two banks with ATM, near shopping center.

West 2.0 miles *via* Wolfsville Road and Md. 77 to **Smithsburg, Md. [P.O. ZIP 21783: M–F 8:30–1 & 2–4:30, Sa 8:30–12; (301) 824-2828].** ■ *Restaurants:* Vince's New York Pizza, (301) 824-3939; Dixie Eatery, (301) 824-5224, Tu–F 7–8, Sa–Su 7–2, closed M, WiFi; The Wolfe's Den Bar & Grill, (301) 824-3911, L/D, WiFi; Railroad Café, (303) 824-2171, M–Sa 7:30– 9 p.m., Su 10–6. ■ *Internet access:* library, (301) 824-7722, 66 W. Water St., computers and WiFi, Tu 12:30–9, M, W, Th–F 10:30–7, Sa 10–2. ■ *Other services:* coin laundry; dentist; and banks with ATM.

West 1.7 miles *via* Wolfsville Road and south on Md. 64 1.0 mile to **Cavetown , Md. [P.O. ZIP 21720: M–F 12:30-4:30, Sa 8:15-11:15; (301) 824-5230].** ■ *Groceries:* Martin's, (301) 824-5160; Mountain Valley Orchard, (301) 824-2089; High's; and Exxon. ■ *Restaurants:* China 88, (301) 824-7300; Subway, (301) 824-3826; Debbie's Soft Serve, (301) 824-4051; Rocky's New York Pizza, (301) 824-2065, will deliver to Trail. ■ *Other services:* Rite Aid Pharmacy & Food Mart, (301) 824-2211; Smithsburg Pharmacy, (301) 824-1111; Sunnycrest Farm Store (hardware), (240) 734-1102, M–F 7–6, Sa 7–3, fuel, camping supplies; Dolly's Thrift Shop, (240) 734-1112.

Main St.
Water St.
64
The Wolfe's Den ● Dixie Eatery
Library ●
Vince's NY Pizza ●
Laundromat ●
Railroad Café
● Post Office
Jefferson Blvd
Veterinarian, Dollar General, Phil & Jerry's Meats and More, Medical Center
● Ace Hardware
Post Office
Cavetown Church Rd
● High's
77
Federal Lookout Rd
Exxon Mtn Valley
Subway Orchard
Wolfsville Rd
Martin's (0.3 mi)
China 8
Rite Aid
Debbie Soft Serve
Rocky's N.Y. Pizza
Post Office to:
Post Office   (1.3 mi)
Trail /Rt 17 (2.0/2.3 mi)
Smithsburg / Cavetown, Md.
elevation 785'
17

Ensign Cowall Shelter (1999)—Sleeps 8. Privy. Five tent pads, hammock sites, picnic table, fire ring with grill, bear pole. Water source is a boxed spring south of the shelter 0.2 mile on the A.T.

Raven Rock Shelter (2010)—Sleeps 16. Composting privy. Bear cables. Tent and hammock sites, picnic table. Water is a spring 200 feet east of the A.T. (on trail to former Devils Racecourse Shelter).

High Rock—"A Rock with View" and lots of graffiti was the site of an old hang-gliding platform that was destroyed years ago. Be watchful, and notice where the blue blazes are located. Both sets will get you back to the Trail but can be confusing. Shoulderless Pen Mar High Rock Road leads 1.7 miles to Pen Mar Park. State police are usually on site, and the road is closed from dust to dawn.

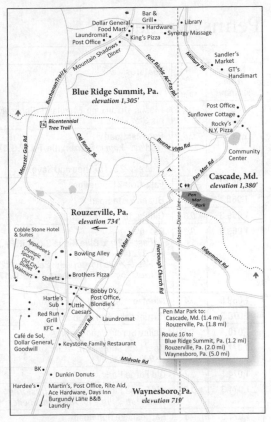

Pen Mar County Park—Open from first Su in May to last Su in Oct. No camping in the park (campsite at Falls Creek 0.9 mile north). Dogs must be leashed (pack out poop). The pavilion provides views of the countryside to the west. Museum (pay phone inside, electrical outlet) open Sa and Su. Restroom locked in the evening. No alcohol, smoking, or vaping is permitted in the park. Parking pass available for lot across the street from the gate.

  East 1.4 miles to the small community of **Cascade, Md. [P.O. ZIP 21719; M–F 10–1 & 2–5, Sa 8–12; (301) 241-3403]**. To reach town from the park entrance, turn left on High Rock Road to Pen-Mar Road, go straight at intersection, pass under a railroad trestle, turn right at the stop sign onto Md. 550. To reach the post office, continue 0.1 mile, and turn left on Ft. Ritchie Road across from entrance to former Ft. Ritchie. ■ *Lodging:* Sunflower Cottage, 25210 Elhuff Ct.; (240) 469-7609, cottage-style home with rooms to rent, $25PP/night includes B; call for pick-up from nearby Trailheads; accepts mail drops. ■ *Restaurants:* Bobby D's, (717) 762-0388; Rocky's New York Pizza, (301) 241-3470; and Brother's Pizza, (717) 765-8808, all will deliver to the park. ■ *Groceries:* GT's Handimart (short-term resupply), (301) 241-3434, 4 a.m–11 p.m. daily, ice cream, sandwiches, hot bar, ATM; Sanders Market (long-term resupply), (301) 241-3612, open M, W, Th, F 8:30–9, Tu, Sa 8:30–8. ■ *Other services:* Ft. Ritchie Community Center, (301) 241-5085, <www.thefrcc.org>, showers and computer access (donations accepted), M–Th 6–9, F 6–6, Sa 9–5, call for Su hours. ■ *Shuttles:* Dennis Sewell, (301) 241-3176 or (717) 446-7436 (Uber).

Mason-Dixon Line—This site—with a stone monument, register, and mailbox constructed by Boy Scouts—signifies the historical survey line, important again in the Civil War, that separates Maryland from Pennsylvania. When Mason and Dixon surveyed this line in 1763–67, they placed at one-mile intervals limestone blocks 3 to 5 feet long, weighing between 300 and 600 pounds, from an English quarry. Every fifth mile, a "Crown" stone was laid with the Penn coat of arms on the Pennsylvania side and the Calvert coat of arms on the Maryland side.

Pennsylvania

Miles from Springer	Miles to Next Point	Features	Services	Elev	Miles from Katahdin	M A P
1,067.0	0.1	Mason-Dixon Line; Maryland–Pennsylvania State Line	R	1,250'	1,126.0	
1,067.1	0.6	Pen Mar Road *West–1.5m to* **Rouzerville, Pa., P.O. 17250** *West–2.3m to* Shop and Save	R, P G, L, M, D, cl, f	1,240'	1,125.9	
1,067.7	0.4	Falls Creek footbridge	C, w	1,100'	1,125.3	
1,068.1	1.2	Buena Vista Road	R	1,290'	1,124.9	
1,069.3	0.3	Old Pa. 16	R	1,350'	1,123.7	
1,069.6	0.2	Pa. 16 *East–1.2m to* **Blue Ridge Summit, Pa., P.O. 17214** *West–2m to* **Rouzerville, Pa., P.O. 17250** *West–5m to* **Waynesboro, Pa., P.O. 17268**	R, P M, D, cl, f G, L, M G, L, M, D, V, cl, f	1,200'	1,123.4	
1,069.8	0.4	Mentzer Gap Road, Mackie Run	R, P	1,250'	1,123.2	
1,070.2	0.2	Rattlesnake Run Road	R, P	1,370	1,122.8	
1,070.4	1.3	Bailey Spring *...box spring*	w	1,300'	1,122.6	
1,071.7	2.4	**Deer Lick Shelters** *(E–0.2m spring)* *...9.8mS; 3.6mN*	S, w	1,420'	1,121.3	
1,074.1	0.2	Old Forge Park	R	890'	1,118.9	
1,074.3	0.2	Old Forge Picnic Grounds *...frost-free water tap-source for Antietam Shelter*	P, w	900'	1,118.7	
1,074.5	0.6	Rattlesnake Run Road	R, P	900'	1,118.5	
1,075.1	0.2	Old Forge Road	R, P	1,000'	1,117.9	
1,075.3	1.3	**Tumbling Run Shelters** *...3.6mS; 6.8mN*	S, w	1,120'	1,117.7	
1,076.6	2.6	Buzzard Peak; Trail Chimney Rocks; Trail to PATC Hermitage Cabin *(locked)*		1,900'	1,116.4	
1,079.2	0.7	Snowy Mountain Road	R, P	1,680'	1,113.8	
1,079.9	0.3	Swamp Road	R	1,560'	1,113.1	
1,080.2	1.7	Pa. 233 *East–1.2m to* **South Mountain, Pa., P.O. 17261**	R, P M, sh	1,600'	1,112.8	
1,081.9	3.0	**Rocky Mountain Shelters** *(E–0.2m S; 0.5m spring)* *...6.8mS; 5.8mN*	S, w	1,520'	1,111.1	
1,084.9	1.9	U.S. 30, Caledonia State Park, Thaddeus Stevens Museum *East–14m to* Gettysburg, Pa. *West–0.3m to* Bonfire Restaurant & Ice Cream *West–0.8m to* Trail of Hope Outreach Ministries Church Hostel *West–3.5m to* **Fayetteville, Pa., P.O. 17222**	R, P, C, M, sh, w all M H G, L, M, D, cl	960'	1,108.1	
1,086.8	0.7	Quarry Gap Road	R	1,250'	1,106.2	
1,087.5	1.5	**Quarry Gap Shelters** *...5.8mS; 7.4mN*	S, w	1,455'	1,105.5	
1,089.0	2.6	Stillhouse Road, Sandy Sod Junction	R	1,980'	1,104.0	
1,091.6	0.5	Middle Ridge Road	R	2,050'	1,101.4	
1,092.1	0.4	Ridge Road, Means Hollow Road	R	1,800'	1,100.9	

PATC Map 4

PATC Map 2-3

Miles from Springer	Miles to Next Point	Features	Services	Elev	Miles from Katahdin	M A P
1,092.5	2.4	Milesburn Road, Milesburn Cabin *(locked)*	R, w	1,600'	1,100.5	
1,094.9	1.3	**Birch Run Shelter** ...*7.4mS; 6.2mN*	S, C, w	1,795'	1,098.1	
1,096.2	0.6	Shippensburg-Arendtsville Road, Big Flat Fire Tower	R, P	2,040'	1,096.8	
1,096.8	1.3	2018 A.T. Midpoint		2,000'	1,096.2	
1,098.1	1.9	PATC Michener Cabin *(locked) (E–0.2m spring)*	w	1,850'	1,094.9	
1,100.0	1.1	Woodrow Road	R	1,850'	1,093.0	
1,101.1	0.3	**Toms Run Shelter** ...*6.2mS; 11.1mN*	S, C, w	1,300'	1,091.9	
1,101.4	1.1	2011 A.T. Midpoint Sign		1,300'	1,091.6	
1,102.5	0.4	Michaux Road	R, P	1,320'	1,090.5	
1,102.9	1.6	Halfway Spring ...*signed*	w	1,100'	1,090.1	PATC Map 2-3
1,104.5	0.3	Pa. 233	R, P	900'	1,088.5	
1,104.8	0.2	Pine Grove Furnace State Park, Ironmasters Mansion **Appalachian Trail Museum**	R, P, H, C, g, w, sh	850'	1,088.2	
1,105.0	2.3	Fuller Lake ...*beach, swimming*		850'	1,088.0	
1,107.3	3.3	Side trail to Pole Steeple		850'	1,085.7	
1,110.6	1.0	Lime Kiln Road	R	1,080'	1,082.4	
1,111.6	0.4	Spring *(signed) (W–0.1m)*	w	750'	1,081.4	
1,112.0	0.5	**James Fry at Tagg Run Shelter** *(E–0.2m)* ...*11.1mS; 8.5mN*	S, w	805'	1,081.0	
1,112.5	0.9	Pine Grove Road *(W–0.4m to Cherokee CG)*	R, C, M	750'	1,080.5	
1,113.4	1.8	Pa. 34, Hunters Run Road, Gardners, Pa. *(E–0.2m to Green Mountain Store and Deli)*	R, P, G, f	670'	1,079.6	
1,115.2	0.4	Pa. 94 *West–2.5m to* **Mt. Holly Springs, Pa., P.O. 17065**	R, P G, L, M, D, cl	880'	1,077.8	
1,115.6	2.4	Sheet Iron Roof Road *West–0.4m to* Deer Run Camping Resort	R, P C, M, L, g, sh, cl, f	680'	1,077.4	
1,118.0	2.1	Whiskey Spring Road, Whiskey Spring	R, P, w	830'	1,075.0	
1,120.1	0.9	**Alec Kennedy Shelter** *(E–0.2m)...8.5mS; 18.4mN*	S, C, w	850'	1,072.9	
1,121.0	1.9	Center Point Knob, White Rocks Trail		1,060'	1,072.0	
1,122.9	0.6	Leidigh Drive	R, P	560'	1,070.1	
1,123.5	0.2	Backpackers' Campsite ...*railroad tracks nearby*	C, w	500'	1,069.5	PATC Map 1
1,123.7	0.1	Mountain Road, Yellow Breeches Creek *West–1.5m to* McConnell Hostel and Campsite	R H, C, sh	500'	1,069.3	
1,123.8	0.2	Bucher Hill Road	R, P	500'	1,069.2	
1,124.0	2.0	Pa. 174, **Boiling Springs, Pa., P.O. 17007** On A.T.–A.T.C. Mid Atlantic Regional Office *East–0.8m to* Allenberry Inn & Playhouse *West–0.1m to* restaurants, Gelinas B&B, Food Mart *West–1m to* Karn's Store *West–2.5m to* Red Cardinal B&B	R, P, O, sh w, f L, M G, L, M G, D, V L	500'	1,069.0	
1,126.0	1.1	Pa. 74, York Road	R, P	580'	1,067.0	
1,127.1	0.6	Lisburn Road	R, P	550'	1,065.9	

Miles from Springer	Miles to Next Point	Features	Services	Elev	Miles from Katahdin	M A P
1,127.7	0.4	Boyer Road	R	550'	1,065.3	
1,128.1	1.1	Pa. 641, Trindle Road	R, P	540'	1,064.9	
1,129.2	0.6	Ridge Drive	R	460'	1,063.8	
1,129.8	0.7	Old Stonehouse Road	R	470'	1,063.2	
1,130.5	0.3	Appalachian Drive	R	510'	1,062.5	
1,130.8	0.6	I-76 Pennsylvania Turnpike ...*overpass*	R	495'	1,062.2	
1,131.4	0.6	Norfolk Southern Railroad Tracks		470'	1,061.6	

1,132.0	0.9	U.S. 11 ...*pedestrian footbridge*
		    West–0.5m to motels, restaurants, travel plaza
		    West–5m to Carlisle, Pa.
			R
			G, L, M, sh
			
			all
				490'	1,061.0	

1,132.9	1.4	I-81 ...*overpass on Bernhisel Bridge Road*	R, P	480'	1,060.1	
1,134.3	1.1	Conodoguinet Creek bridge, ATC Scott Farm Trail Work Ctr *(privy, water, picnic table)*	R, P, w	480'	1,058.7	
1,135.4	0.9	Sherwood Drive	R, P	420'	1,057.6	
1,136.3	1.0	Pa. 944, Donnellytown, Pa. ...*pedestrian tunnel*	R	480'	1,056.7	
1,137.3	0.9	Spring at Wolf Trail Junction	w	650'	1,055.7	
1,138.2	0.1	Tuscarora Trail *(northern terminus)*, Darlington Trail		1,390'	1,054.8	
1,138.3	2.0	**Darlington Shelter** ...*18.4mS; 7.3mN*	S, w	1,250'	1,054.7	
1,140.3	0.3	Millers Gap Road ...*paved*	R	700'	1,052.7	
1,140.6	5.0	Pa. 850, Valley Road	R, P	650'	1,052.4	
1,145.6	1.9	**Cove Mountain Shelter** ...*7.3mS; 8.3mN*	S, w	1,200'	1,047.4	
1,147.5	1.2	Hawk Rock ...*view of Duncannon*		1,140'	1,045.5	
1,148.7	0.1	Inn Road	R, P	360'	1,044.3	
1,148.8	0.4	Sherman Creek bridge	R	360'	1,044.2	
1,149.2	0.5	U.S. 11 & 15, Pa. 274 ...*underpass* *West–0.5m on Pa. 274 to* Mutzabaugh Market	R, P G	385'	1,043.8	
1,149.7	1.0	Market St.; **Duncannon, Pa., P.O. 17020**	R, g, L, M, D, cl, f	385'	1,043.3	
1,150.7	0.2	Pa. 849, Newport Road, Juniata River	R, C, O, sh	380'	1,042.3	

1,150.9	0.6	Susquehanna River, Clarks Ferry Bridge (west end)
		    West–0.1m to Truck Travel Plaza
		    West–2m and 3.6m to motels
			R
			
			G, M, sh
				380'	1,042.1	

1,151.5	0.4	U.S. 22 & 322, Norfolk Southern Railway *(E–16m to Harrisburg, Pa.)*	R, P, all	400'	1,041.5	
1,151.9	1.7	Susquehanna Trail *(1m)* rejoins A.T. north		650'	1,041.1	
1,153.6	0.1	Susquehanna Trail *(1m)* rejoins A.T. south		1,150'	1,039.4	
1,153.7	0.2	Campsite ...*spring*	C, w	1,160'	1,039.3	
1,153.9	3.9	**Clarks Ferry Shelter** ...*8.3mS; 6.7mN*	S, w	1,260'	1,039.1	
1,157.8	2.0	Pa. 225 ...*footbridge*	R, P	1,250'	1,035.2	
1,159.8	0.8	Table Rock ...*view*		1,200'	1,033.2	
1,160.6	1.0	**Peters Mountain Shelter** ...*6.7mS; 18.3mN*	S, w	970'	1,032.4	
1,161.6	0.6	Victoria Trail *(E–1.1m to Pa. 325)*	R, P	1,300'	1,031.4	
1,162.2	1.1	Whitetail Trail		1,310'	1,030.8	
1,163.3	1.4	Kinter View		1,320'	1,029.7	
1,164.7	2.3	Shikellimy Trail *(E–0.9m to Pa. 325)*	R, P	1,250'	1,028.3	

PATC Map 1

KTA Map: Sections 7-8

Miles from Springer	Miles to Next Point	Features	Services	Elev	Miles from Katahdin	M A P
1,167.0	0.3	Spring ...on blue-blaze	w	700'	1,026.0	
1,167.3	0.1	Pa. 325, Clark's Valley, Clark Creek	R, P, w	550'	1,025.7	
1,167.4	0.3	Water Tank Trail		570'	1,025.6	
1,167.7	0.1	Spring	w	620'	1,025.3	
1,167.8	2.8	Henry Knauber Trail	w	680'	1,025.2	
1,170.6	3.2	Stony Mountain; Horse-Shoe Trail		1,650'	1,022.4	
1,173.8	0.2	Yellow Springs Trail		1,380'	1,019.2	
1,174.0	2.1	Yellow Springs Village Site ...trail register		1,450'	1,019.0	KTA Map Secs 7-8
1,176.1	0.2	Sand Spring Trail ...The General Excavator		1,380'	1,016.9	
1,176.3	2.3	Cold Spring Trail		1,400'	1,016.7	
1,178.6	0.5	**Rausch Gap Shelter (E–0.3m)** ...18.3mS; 13.7mN	P, S, w	980'	1,014.4	
1,179.1	0.1	Rausch Creek ...stone arch bridge	w	920'	1,013.9	
1,179.2	0.3	Raush Gap Village ...sign		920'	1,013.8	
1,179.5	1.2	Haystack Creek ...wooden bridge	w	840'	1,013.5	
1,180.7	2.0	Second Mountain		1,350'	1,012.3	
1,182.7	0.6	Greenpoint School Rd then 150 ft. to Pa. 443	R	570'	1,010.3	
1,183.3	1.4	Pa. 443, Green Point, Pa. ...underpass West–2.6m to Twin Grove KOA	R, P C, M, cl, sh	550'	1,009.7	
1,184.7	0.1	Swatara Gap, Pa. 72 East–2.4m to Lickdale, Pa.	R, P C, G, L, M, sh	480'	1,008.3	
1,184.8	0.3	Swatara Creek, Waterville Iron Bridge, Swatara Rail Trail		460'	1,008.2	
1,185.1	6.9	I-81 ...underpass	R	450'	1,007.9	
1,192.0	2.2	**William Penn Shelter** (E–0.1m); Blue Mountain Spring (W–225 yards) ...13.7mS; 4.2mN	S, w	1,300'	1,001.0	
1,194.2	1.8	Pa. 645 ...electrical outlet behind building	R, P	1,250'	998.8	
1,196.0	0.1	Kimmel Lookout		1,330'	997.0	
1,196.1	0.5	Pa. 501, **501 Shelter** (W–0.1m) ...4.2mS; 15.5mN East–2m to **Bethel, Pa., P.O. 19507** West–3.7m to **Pine Grove, Pa., P.O. 17963**	R, P, S, w V G, L, M, D, V, cl	1,460'	996.9	KTA Map: Sections 1-6
1,196.6	2.6	Pilger Ruh Spring Trail (east), Applebee Campsite (west)	C, w	1,450'	996.4	
1,199.2	2.0	Round Head, Trail to Shower Steps	w	1,500'	993.8	
1,201.2	0.5	Shikellamy Overlook		1,390'	991.8	
1,201.7	0.1	Hertlein Campsite	C, w	1,200'	991.3	
1,201.8	3.3	Shuberts Gap		1,200'	991.2	
1,205.1	0.3	Fort Dietrich Snyder Marker, spring (W–0.2m)	w	1,440'	987.9	
1,205.4	0.5	Pa. 183, Rentschler Marker	R, P	1,440'	987.6	
		West–1.6m to Rock and Sole Hostel	H			
1,205.9	0.8	Service Road to Pa. 183	P	1,490'	987.1	
1,206.7	3.8	Black Swatara Spring (W–0.3m)	w	1,510'	986.3	
1,210.5	0.7	Sand Spring Trail ...walled spring (E–0.2m)	w	1,510'	982.5	

Miles from Springer	Miles to Next Point	Features	Services	Elev	Miles from Katahdin	M A P
1,211.2	1.9	**Eagle's Nest Shelter** *(W–0.3m) ...15.5mS; 15mN*	S, w	1,510'	981.8	
1,213.1	2.7	Shartlesville Cross–Mountain Road; Shartlesville, Pa.	R	1,450'	979.9	
1,215.8	0.9	Phillip's Canyon Spring	w	1,500'	977.2	
1,216.7	0.6	Marshall's Path		1,370'	976.3	
1,217.3	2.2	Auburn Lookout		1,400'	975.7	
1,219.5	0.1	John Bartram–Schuylkill River Trail, Railroad Tracks	R, P	420'	973.5	
1,219.6	0.2	Schuylkill River		400'	973.4	
1,219.8	0.7	**Port Clinton, Pa., P.O. 19549** *West–0.3m to* pavilion	R, P, PO, L, M, w S, C	400'	973.2	
1,220.5	2.6	Pa. 61, Port Clinton Avenue *...underpass* *East–1.5m to* Cabela's, motel, restaurants East–3.5m to **Hamburg, Pa., P.O. 19526**	R, P B, G, L, M, O, f B, G, L, M, D, V, cl	490'	972.5	
1,223.1	2.6	Pocahontas Spring	w	1,200'	969.9	
1,225.7	0.2	Windsor Furnace, Reservoir Road, Hamburg Reservoir *(E–0.5m)*	R, P, C, w	900'	967.3	
1,225.9	1.1	**Windsor Furnace Shelter** *...15mS; 9.3mN*	S, w	940'	967.1	
1,227.0	0.5	Trail to Blue Rocks Campground *(E–1.5m)*	S, C, G, cl, sh, f	1,000'	966.0	
1,227.5	1.8	Pulpit Rock *...observatory, overlook*		1,582'	965.5	
1,229.3	0.4	Trail to Blue Rocks Campground *(E–1.5m)*	S, C, G, cl, sh, f	1,150'	963.7	
1,229.7	1.7	The Pinnacle *...overlook*		1,615'	963.3	
1,231.4	0.3	Furnace Creek Trail		1,440'	961.6	
1,231.7	0.6	Gold Spring *(W–30 yds.)*	w	1,580'	961.3	
1,232.3	0.9	Blue-blazed trail to A.T. at Windsor Furnace *(W–1.5m)*		1,420'	960.7	
1,233.2	1.8	Panther Spring *(west)*	w	1,070'	959.8	
1,235.0	1.7	Hawk Mountain Road, **Eckville Shelter** *(E–0.2m) ...9.3mS; 7.6mN*	R, P, S, w, sh	600'	958.0	
1,236.7	1.1	Hawk Mountain Sanctuary Trail *(W–2m to visitors center)*		1,330'	956.3	
1,237.8	3.3	Dans Pulpit *...trail register, view*		1,600'	955.2	
1,241.1	1.3	Tri-County Corner		1,560'	951.9	
1,242.4	1.9	**Allentown Hiking Club Shelter** *(E–0.2m spring) ...7.6mS; 10mN*	S, w	1,350'	950.6	
1,244.3	2.2	Fort Franklin Road *...gravel*	R, P	1,350'	948.7	
1,246.5	1.8	Pa. 309, Blue Mountain Summit B&B	R, P, L, M, w	1,360'	946.5	
1,248.3	1.0	New Tripoli Campsite *(W–0.2m) ...powerline*	C, w	1,400'	944.7	
1,249.3	0.7	Knife Edge, "The Cliffs"		1,525'	943.7	
1,250.0	1.4	Bear Rocks		1,604'	943.0	
1,251.4	0.4	Bake Oven Knob Road *...dirt*	R, P	1,450'	941.6	
1,251.8	0.6	Bake Oven Knob		1,560'	941.2	
1,252.4	2.4	**Bake Oven Knob Shelter** *...10mS; 6.8mN*	S, w	1,380'	940.6`	

KTA Map: Sections 1-6

Miles from Springer	Miles to Next Point	Features	Services	Elev	Miles from Katahdin	M A P
1,254.8	1.1	Ashfield Road, Lehigh Furnace Gap, Ashfield, Pa. ...radio tower (E–0.7m spring)	R, P, w	1,320'	938.2	
1,255.9	1.1	South Trail (1.1m) (southern jct.)		1,580'	937.1	
1,257.0	0.6	South Trail (1.1m) (northern jct.)		1,575'	936.0	
1,257.6	1.5	North Trail (2.5m) (southern jct.) ...Lehigh Valley Tunnel of Pa.Turnpike is underneath A.T.		1,570'	935.4	
1,259.1	0.1	North Trail (2.5m) (northern jct.)		1,550'	933.9	
1,259.2	0.6	**George W. Outerbridge Shelter** ...6.8mS; 16.8mN	S, w	1,000'	933.8	
1,259.8	0.1	Lehigh Gap, Pa. 873 East–2m to **Slatington, Pa., P.O. 18080**	R, P B, G, M, D, cl, f	380'	933.2	
1,259.9	0.2	Lehigh River Bridge (east end), Pa. 873	R, P	380'	933.1	
1,260.1	0.0	Pa. 145 East–2m to **Walnutport, Pa., P.O. 18088**	R B, G, M, D, V	380'	932.9	
1,260.1	5.0	Pa. 248 ...blue-blaze to Palmerton, locked gate after 4:30 p.m. (W–2m) West–2m to **Palmerton, Pa., P.O. 18071**	R, P G, L, M, D, cl, f	380'	932.9	
1,265.1	4.8	Little Gap, Blue Mountain Road East–1.5m to **Danielsville, Pa., P.O. 18038**	R, P G, L, M	1,100'	927.9	
1,269.9	1.8	Delps Trail (E–0.25m) ...unreliable spring	w	1,580'	923.1	
1,271.7	0.7	Stempa Spring (E–0.6m)	w	1,510'	921.3	
1,272.4	3.5	Smith Gap Road ...paved (W–1m to water spigot, cold shower)	R, P	1,540'	920.6	
1,275.9	3.6	**Leroy A. Smith Shelter** (E–0.1m S; 0.2m, 0.4m, 0.6m springs) ...16.8mS; 13.8mN East–0.9m on Katellen Trail to Old Grade Rd	S, w R, P	1,410'	917.1	
1,279.5	0.3	Hahns Lookout		1,450'	913.5	
1,279.8	0.4	Lookout Rock		1,480'	913.2	
1,280.2	0.3	Powerline		1,100'	912.8	
1,280.5	2.0	Pa. 33 East–1m to **Wind Gap, Pa., P.O. 18091**	R, P G, L, M, D, V, cl	980'	912.5	
1,282.5	4.4	Private Road, Blue Mtn. Water Co.	R	1,580'	910.5	
1,286.9	0.5	Wolf Rocks Bypass Trail (south end) ... signed spring	w	1,550'	906.1	
1,287.4	0.3	Wolf Rocks		1,620'	905.6	
1,287.7	1.3	Wolf Rocks Bypass Trail (north end)		1,510'	905.3	
1,289.0	0.6	Pa. 191, Fox Gap	R, P	1,400'	904.0	
1,289.6	0.8	**Kirkridge Shelter** ...13.8mS; 31.4mN	S, w	1,500'	903.4	
1,290.4	1.1	Lunch Rocks ...views		1,515'	902.6	
1,291.5	2.0	Totts Gap ...gravel road, gated	R	1,300'	901.5	
1,293.5	1.0	Mt. Minsi		1,461'	899.5	
1,294.5	0.8	Lookout Rock ...views		800'	898.5	
1,295.3	0.5	Council Rock		600'	897.7	
1,295.8	0.2	Lake Lenape	R, P	510'	897.2	

KTA Map: Sections 1-6

Miles from Springer	Miles to Next Point	Features	Services	Elev	Miles from Katahdin	M A P
1,296.0	0.2	Pa. 611 *West–0.1m to* **Delaware Water Gap, Pa., P.O. 18327** *West–0.4m to* services *West–5m to* East Stroudsburg and Stroudsburg, Pa.	R, P H, L, M B, G, L, M, O, f B, G, L, M, O, D	400'	897.0	KTA Map: 1-6
1,296.2	1.0	Delaware River Bridge (west end); Pennsylvania–New Jersey State Line		350'	896.8	

Camping regulations vary depending on the type of public land. Be aware of posted notices, and check maps for boundaries. Most water sources are unreliable in summer.

Pen Mar Road—West 1.5 miles to **Rouzerville, Pa. [P.O. ZIP 17250: M–F 8:30–1 & 2–4:30, Sa 8:30–11:30; (717) 762-7050]**, with most major services (*see map on page 125*). *Lodging:* Cobblestone Hotel, (717) 765-0034, hiker discount, laundry, pool, hot tub, free B.
    West 2.3 miles to *Groceries:* Walmart (long-term resupply) and Dollar General.

Pa. 16—East 1.2 miles to **Blue Ridge Summit, Pa. [P.O. ZIP 17214: M–F 8–12 & 1–4:00, Sa 9–11:30; (717) 794-2335]**. ■ *Restaurants:* Mountain Shadows, daily, B/L/D; Chapin Gray's Grill; King's Pizza; Unique Bar and Grill; and fast-food options. ■ *Internet access:* Blue Ridge Summit Library, M–Th 3–8, Sa 10–2. ■ *Other services:* hardware store, denatured alcohol; bank with ATM; JJ's Coin laundry; barber; Synergy Massage, (877) 372-6617, <www.synergymassage.com>, massages, pick-up/ return to Trail, free use of outdoor shower, hot tub, and pool; Blue Ridge Summit Medical Center, M, Tu, Th 8–5, W, F 8–1; Dollar General.
    West 2 miles to **Rouzerville, Pa.** See above.
    West 2.3 miles to *Groceries:* Walmart (long-term resupply).
    West 5 miles to **Waynesboro, Pa. [P.O. ZIP 17268: M–F 8:30–5, Sa 9–12; (717) 762-1513; pick-up window only, M–F 6–5, Sa 6–12:15]**, with all major services. The Annual Mason–Dixon Appalachian Trail Outdoor Festival will be held Jun 13, 2020, in Red Run Park, 12143 Buchanan Trail East; <www.waynesboroatc.org>. ■ *Lodging:* Burgundy Lane B&B, (717) 762-8112, phone for shuttle from Trailhead, Internet access, laundry, local shuttles, and slackpacks; Days Inn, (717) 762-9113, call for current rates. ■ *Groceries:* Martin's (long-term resupply); 7–11 (short-term resupply). ■ *Internet access:* library, M–F 9:30–8, Sa 9–4. ■ *Other services:* Waynesboro Walk-in Clinic, (717) 762-1700, 11050 Buchanan Trail East, M–F 2–7, Sa-Su 10–5; YMCA, (717) 762-6012, 810 Main St., showers; hospital; pharmacies; veterinarian; dentist; and UPS Store.

Deer Lick Shelters (1940s)—Two shelters, each sleeps 4. Privy. Water source is a spring 0.2 mile on a blue-blazed trail to the east of the shelter area (seasonal) or stream 50 feet north of shelter.

Tumbling Run Shelters (1940s)—Two shelters, each sleeps 4. Privy. Located on a short, blue-blazed trail. Water source is 100 yards to the west of the shelter.

Pa. 233—East 1.2 miles to **South Mountain, Pa. [P.O. ZIP 17261: M–F 12–4, Sa 8:30–11:30; (717) 749-5833]** on South Mountain Rd. *Restaurant:* South Mountain Hotel (no lodging), (717) 749-3845, grill-type menu, bar, M–Sa 9 a.m.–2 a.m., Su 11 a.m.–midnight, with patio and outside shower.

Rocky Mountain Shelters (1989)—Two shelters, each sleeps 4. Privy. Located 0.2 mile on a steep, downhill, blue-blazed trail; for water, continue on side trail down to a road, then right 75 yards to spring.

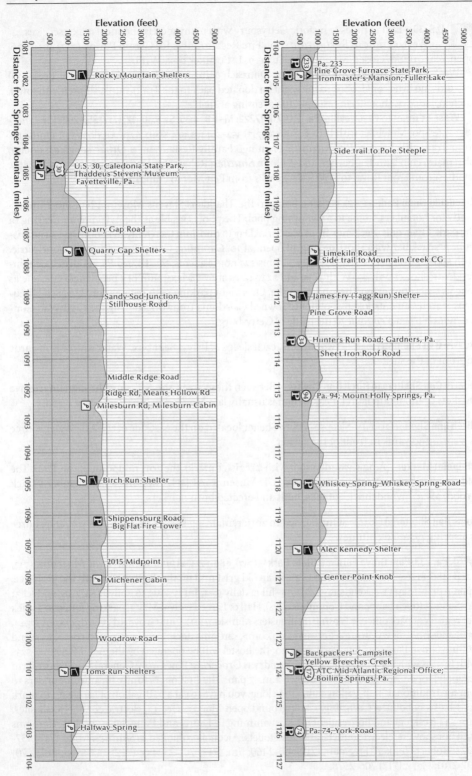

Elevation (feet)

Distance from Springer Mountain (miles)

Rocky Mountain Shelters

U.S. 30, Caledonia State Park,
Thaddeus Stevens Museum;
Fayetteville, Pa.

Quarry Gap Road

Quarry Gap Shelters

Sandy Sod Junction;
Stillhouse Road

Middle Ridge Road

Ridge Rd, Means Hollow Rd
Milesburn Rd, Milesburn Cabin

Birch Run Shelter

Shippensburg Road,
Big Flat Fire Tower

2015 Midpoint
Michener Cabin

Woodrow Road

Toms Run Shelters

Halfway Spring

Elevation (feet)

Distance from Springer Mountain (miles)

Pa. 233
Pine Grove Furnace State Park,
Ironmaster's Mansion; Fuller Lake

Side trail to Pole Steeple

Limekiln Road
Side trail to Mountain Creek CG

James Fry (Tagg Run) Shelter

Pine Grove Road

Hunters Run Road; Gardners, Pa.

Sheet Iron Roof Road

Pa. 94; Mount Holly Springs, Pa.

Whiskey Spring; Whiskey Spring Road

Alec Kennedy Shelter

Center Point Knob

Backpackers' Campsite
Yellow Breeches Creek
ATC Mid-Atlantic Regional Office;
Boiling Springs, Pa.

Pa. 74; York Road

U.S. 30—**East** 14 miles to historic Gettysburg with many motels and most major services.

West 0.3 mile to *Restaurant:* Bon Fire Restaurant & Ice Cream Parlor, (717) 401-6106, open year-round, closed M, open Tu–Su 11–9, L/D, hiker box, WiFi.

West 0.8 mile to *Hostel:* Trail of Hope Outreach Ministries Church Hostel, Pastor Beal (410) 984-0105, no drugs or alcohol, $22PP/night ($1 donated back to the Trail), bunk, shower with towel, kitchen, laundry, short-term resupply, fuel. Tenting available.

West 3.5 miles to **Fayetteville, Pa. [P.O. ZIP 17222: M–F 8–4:30, Sa 8:30–12; (717) 352-2022].** ■ *Lodging:* Rite Spot Motel/Scottish Inns & Suites, (717) 352-2144, $49S, $59D, $20EAP, dogs $15; shuttle to/from Trail, call ahead. ■ *Restaurants:* Flamingo Family Restaurant. ■ *Other services:* doctor, pharmacy, coin laundry, barber, and ATM. ■ *Shuttles:* Robert "Junker" Freeman, (717) 491-2460, shuttles from Front Royal to DWG, slackpacks from Pen Mar to Duncannon.

Caledonia State Park—(717) 352-2161, home to the Thaddeus Stevens Museum, but, more importantly for hot hikers, home to a swimming pool. The pool is visible as the A.T. enters a clearing in the park. Open only weekends from Memorial Day to mid-Jun, then daily to Labor Day; $4 admission. A snack bar with short-order grill opens at 10. *Camping:* Campsites, electric & nonelectric, with showers, no pets: F–Sa, $23 Pa. residents/$25 nonresidents; Su–Th, $19 Pa. residents/$21 nonresidents; shower only $3. With pets, add $2 to rates above. Maximum of 5 people/tents per site as long as tents don't extend beyond campsite. Overnight parking with registration. U.S. Sen. Thaddeus Stevens, an outspoken abolitionist, owned Caledonia Ironworks during the Civil War. Confederates burned it *en route* to the battle of Gettysburg.

Quarry Gap Shelters (1935)—Two shelters, each sleeps 4. Privy. Bear box. Water source is 10 yards in front of the shelter.

Quarry Gap Shelters to Birch Run Shelter—Between these areas, the A.T. runs through impressive thickets of mountain laurel. Peak bloom is usually late May–early Jun.

Birch Run Shelter (2003)—Sleeps 8. Privy. Shelter located on the east side of the A.T. Water source is a spring 30 yards in front of the shelter.

Midpoint Marker—A new wooden sign with a register marks the 2011 midpoint of the Trail. The old one has been retired to the nearby A.T. Museum. ALDHA honorary life member Chuck Wood, a.k.a. "Woodchuck" of 1985, built and erected both markers.

Toms Run Shelter(s) (1936)—One burned in 2013; remaining shelter sleeps 4. Privy. Water source is a spring near old chimney.

Pa. 233/Pine Grove Furnace State Park—(717) 486-7174. *Appalachian Trail Museum,* (717) 486-8126, <www.atmuseum.org>, in an old grist mill on the Trail, well worth the visit; free, open Apr 4–May 3 weekends 12–4, May 4–Jul 12 daily 9–4, Jul 13–Aug 16 daily 12–4, Aug 19–Oct 31 W–Su 12–4 (open Labor and Columbus days); Hall of Fame Festival May 2; parking for up to a week but register at park office. ■ *Hostel:* Ironmasters Mansion, 1212 Pine Grove Rd., Gardners, PA 17324, (717) 486-4108, <www.ironmastersmansion.com>, <ironmasterspinegrove@gmail.com>, west end of Pine Grove Furnace State Park. In 2020, the hostel will be operated by the A.T. Museum; $25S with B; $30S with B, D (pizza); has WiFi, laundry. ■ *Groceries:* Pine Grove General Store (short-term resupply), open Apr 15–mid-Nov, daily 8 a.m.–7 p.m. The first opportunity for northbounders to join the traditional "half-gallon club." To belong, you have to eat a half-gallon of ice cream to mark your halfway point. ■ *Camping:* Campground open Mar 27–Dec 12, electric & nonelectric sites, $19–$34 (resident and nonresident rates), swimming in Laurel and Fuller lakes; heated restrooms with hot showers, electric outlets, and flush toilets. Alcohol prohibited. ■ *Shuttles:* Mike, (717) 437-6022; Robert "Junker" Freeman, (717) 491-2460; Jim, (717) 701-2324 or (717) 343-8955; Bill, (570) 997-2701; Gary, (717) 706-2578.

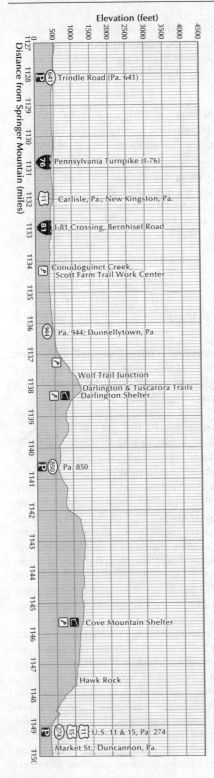

Elevation (feet)

Distance from Springer Mountain (miles)

1127
1128 — Trindle Road (Pa. 641)
1129
1130
1131 — Pennsylvania Turnpike (I-76)
1132 — Carlisle, Pa.; New-Kingston, Pa.
1133 — I-81 Crossing, Bernhisel Road
1134 — Conodoguinet Creek,
       Scott Farm Trail Work Center
1135
1136 — Pa. 944; Donnellytown, Pa
1137
1138 — Wolf Trail Junction
       Darlington & Tuscarora Trails
       Darlington Shelter
1139
1140
1141 — Pa. 850
1142
1143
1144
1145
1146 — Cove Mountain Shelter
1147
1148 — Hawk Rock
1149 — U.S. 11 & 15, Pa. 274
1150 — Market St., Duncannon, Pa.

Mountain Club of Maryland—MCM maintains the 16.2 miles from Pine Grove Furnace State Park to Center Point Knob and the 12.6 miles from the Darlington/ Tuscarora Trail junction to the Susquehanna River. Correspondence should be sent to 7923 Galloping Circle, Baltimore, MD 21244; <paulives2@aol.com>.

James Fry Shelter at Tagg Run (1998)—Sleeps 9. Tentsites. Privy (composting). Called "Tagg Run" in some sources, after the 1930s-vintage shelters it replaced. Water source is 0.4 mile east of the A.T. on a blue-blazed trail; may run dry in drought times.

Pine Grove Road—West 0.4 mile to Cherokee Family Restaurant and Campground, (717) 486-8000; tentsites with shower $16D, $5EAP. **West** 1.5 miles to **Mountain Creek Campground**, 349 Pine Grove Rd., Gardners, PA 17324; (717) 486-7681, <www.mtn-creekcg.com>; mid-Apr–Oct, tenting, cabin, hot showers, call for rates; pool, camp store, camp supplies, snack shack; pets must be kept on a leash. **East** 0.6 mile to Twirly Top, ice cream and grill, closed Su.

Pa. 34—East 0.2 mile to the Green Mountain Store and Deli (short-term resupply), M–Sa 7–8, Su 9–6, hiking supplies, ATM, fuel canisters, Coleman by the pint. For southbounders, the first opportunity to join the Half-Gallon Club.

Pa. 94—West 2.5 miles to **Mt. Holly Springs, Pa.** **[P.O. ZIP 17065: M–F 8–1 & 2–4:30, Sa 9–12; (717) 486-3468].** ■ *Lodging:* Holly Inn and Restaurant, 31 S. Baltimore St., Mt. Holly Springs, PA 17065, (717) 486-3823, call for pick-up; <www.hollyinn.com>; $55S/D $10EAP includes continental B and ride back to the Trail; L/D M–Th Su 11:30–9, F-Sa 11:30–10; Internet; mail drops accepted. ■ *Restaurants:* Cassell's Grill, 5 West Pine St., (717) 486-8800, Tu–Su 11–9; Laura's Family Restaurant; Sicilia Pizza and Subs. ■ *Internet access:* library. ■ *Other services:* Uni-Mart, Dollar General, and Family Dollar (short-term resupply); coin laundry; pharmacy; dentist; optometrist; and bank with ATM.

Sheet Iron Roof Road—West 0.4 mile to Deer Run Camping Resort, (717) 486-8168, www.deerrun-campingresort.com, $10 tent camping, short-term resupply, laundry, showers, WiFi, pool, fishing pond, snack bar on weekends, cabins with hiker discount.

Alec Kennedy Shelter (1991)—Sleeps 7. Privy (composting). Built by the MCM and Tressler Wilderness School.

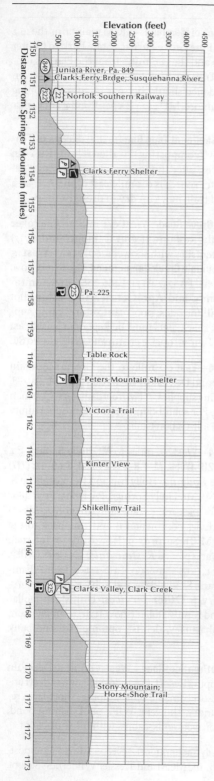

The shelter is 0.2 mile east on a blue-blazed trail. Water source is a spring located on a side trail behind the shelter; prone to go dry during the summer. A second source is a small stream 0.5 mile south of the shelter on the A.T.

Center Point Knob—In 2012, the Mountain Club of Maryland replaced the missing Center Point Knob bronze plaque with a replica on the original boulder.

Cumberland Valley Appalachian Trail Club—CVATC maintains the 17.2 miles between Center Point Knob and the Darlington/Tuscarora Trail junction. Correspondence should be sent to P.O. Box 395, Boiling Springs, Pa. 17007; <www.cvatclub.org>; <wbohn@ paonline.com>.

No fires in the valley—Between Alec Kennedy and Darlington shelters, the Boiling Springs campsite (see next entry) is the only place where camping is allowed.

Mountain Road at Yellow Breeches Creek—**West** 1.5 miles to Lisa's Hostel, (717) 226-8390, $20pp bunk (1 night), shower, laundry, AYCE hot dogs & grilled cheese; call for details.

Boiling Springs, Pa. [P.O. ZIP 17007: M–F 9–12, 1–4:30, Sa 9–12; (717) 258-6668]—Home to ATC's mid-Atlantic regional office, (717) 258-5771. When open to the public, staff members and volunteers can provide information on Trail conditions, weather forecasts, and water availability. Coleman fuel and denatured alcohol are available for a donation; A.T. maps and books for sale. Picnic table and hiker bulletin board are located on the porch. Bursting-at-seams office cannot accommodate packages sent to hikers; please use P.O. across street. *No camping at the office.* Limited parking at opposite end of lake in township parking lot; obtain permit from ATC office during regular office hours (overnight parking is only allowed with permit that you display on your dashboard; call ahead if arriving late). Lodging is limited in Boiling Springs, but a year-round campsite with a portable toilet in season is south of town, before the railroad tracks (toilet Memorial Day–Labor Day). The trains do run past here all night long. The water source for the campsite is a spigot behind the ATC office, next to the oil tank, and might not be available during winter months. Check the hiker-information board for post-

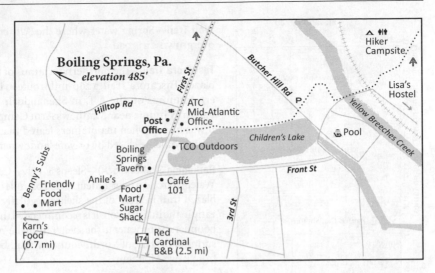

ings of additional camping possibilities in the area. Annual Appalachian Trail Music Festival on Father's Day. ■ *Restaurants:* Anile's Ristorante & Pizzeria, (717) 258-5070, L/D; Boiling Springs Tavern, L/D; Caffe 101, B/L; Benny's Subs, (717) 258-6522. ■ *Groceries:* Karn's Store (long-term resupply), open daily 7–10; Lakeside Food Mart and Friendly Food Mart (both short-term resupply). ■ *Other services:* TCO Outdoors, small outfitter, might have a few hiker items; bank with ATM next to post office; doctor; dentist; veterinarian; Boiling Springs pool, (717) 258-4121, open Memorial–Labor Day, $12 admission, $7 seniors or evenings, $2 hot shower, check ATC hiker bulletin board for coupons; barber; Jumpers Shoe Service, (717) 766-3422, in nearby Mechanicsburg. ■ *Shuttles:* Mike Gelinas, (717) 497-6022.

West 2.5 miles on Pa. 174—*Lodging:* Red Cardinal B&B, (717) 245-0823, <redcardinalbandb@aol.com>, call for reservations and a ride.

Cumberland Valley—Water is scarce between Boiling Springs and Darlington Shelter, as the A.T. winds along hedgerows and through Pennsylvania farmland. Thanks to an ambitious land-acquisition program, most of the Trail has been taken off roads through this heavily developed area, but it is still a hot walk on steamy summer days. Water can be obtained at one of the restaurants on U.S. 11 (see below).

U.S. 11—West 0.5 mile to various facilities spread along this busy highway. ■ *Lodging:* America's Best Inn, (717) 249-7775 or (800) 445-6715, dogs extra, laundry, WiFi; Quality Inn, (717) 245-2242, hiker rate $54.99; Super 8, 1800 Harrisburg Pike, Carlisle, PA 17013, (717) 249-7000, laundry, pool, WiFi; Econo Lodge, (717) 249-7775, continental B, pets extra and only in smoking rooms, laundry, pool, WiFi; Holiday Inn, (717) 245-2400, pets okay ($10 nonrefundable fee), laundry, pool, Duffy's Restaurant and Pub, WiFi; Pheasant Field B&B, (717) 258-0717, Su–Th $88D, F–Sa $105–$185D, pet-friendly room may be available, laundry, free phone, shuttle to and from Trail with stay; Hotel Carlisle, (717) 243-1717, heated indoor pool, sauna, hot tub, WiFi. Other options beyond I-81: Travel Lodge, Rodeway Inn, Howard Johnson, Quality Inn. ■ *Restaurants:* Trailside Restaurant (limited hours), 24-hour Middlesex Diner, Bob Evans, Dunkin' Donuts, and fast-food restaurants on the other side of I-81. ■ *Other services:* The Flying J Travel Plaza has a restaurant, showers $11.50 (includes refundable $5 towel deposit), laundry, and a store (short-term resupply).

West—5 miles to Carlisle, a large town with all major services.

Conodoguinet Creek Bridge—An old ATC-managed farmhouse, known as the Scott Farm, is located next to the bridge where the Trail U-turns, passes under the bridge, and heads north. Open May–Oct, the farm has a privy and a picnic table. *No camping.*

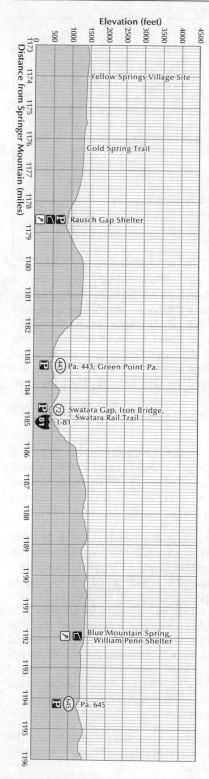

Wolf Trail—Spring water where the A.T. crosses an overgrown dirt road.

Tuscarora Trail—The northern terminus of the blue-blazed Tuscarora Trail, a 260-mile route to its southern terminus on the A.T. in Shenandoah National Park in Virginia near Matthews Arm Campground. It was blazed when maintainers feared that the A.T. route would be closed by private landowners.

Darlington Shelter (2005)—Sleeps 8. Privy. Campsites. Water source, an intermittent spring 0.2 mile on a blue-blazed trail in front of the shelter, regularly dries up early in the hiker season. It is recommended that northbounders bring water to the shelter from the Wolf Trail spring at the base of North Mountain; southbounders, from Cove Mountain.

Cove Mountain Shelter (2000)—Sleeps 8. Privy. Bear box. Built with the help of the Timber Framers Guild using timber salvaged from a barn, some pieces more than 100 years old. Water source is a spring 125 yards away on a steeply graded trail near the shelter.

U.S. 11/Duncannon, Pa. [P.O. ZIP 17020: M–F 8–11, 12–4:30, Sa 8:30–12:30; (717) 834-3332.] P.O. has a hiker box with snacks. *ID required for mail drops.* The A.T. passes through the center of town, and all services are within a short walk. ■ *Camping:* Riverfront Campground (south of the Clarks Ferry Bridge), (717) 834-5252, tentsites and shower $5PP in designated hiker area (*must register first*), shuttle service, canoe and kayak rentals. ■ *Lodging:* Doyle Hotel, 7 North Market St., Duncannon, PA 17020, (717) 834-6789, open 11 a.m.–8 p.m., one of the original Anheuser-Busch hotels, more than 100 years old, $25S, $7.50EAP, pets allowed, shower only $7.50 (includes towel), fuels (denatured, white gas, canister), will hold mail drops (ID required). On U.S. 11/15, 2 miles **north** of the truck stop, Stardust Motel, call first, (717) 834-3191, Su–Th $45S, F–Sa $53S, $5EAP, laundry, no dogs, free shuttles to and from town when available; Red Carpet Inn, 3.6 miles **north** on U.S. 11, (717) 834-3320, shuttles to/from town when available, hiker-friendly. ■ *Groceries:* **West** of town 0.5 mile on Pa. 274, Mutzabaugh Market and pharmacy (long-term resupply), (717) 834-3121, M–Sa 6–10, Su 7–10, *a dangerous walk, take green-blazed trail* or call for possibleshuttle; Quick Mart Convenience Store (short-term resupply), daily 6–10. ■ *Restaurants:* Doyle Hotel, L/D full menu and bar; Goodie's Café, B, closed M; The Pub, L/D; Riviera Tavern, L/D; Sorrento's Pizza and Subs, L/D;

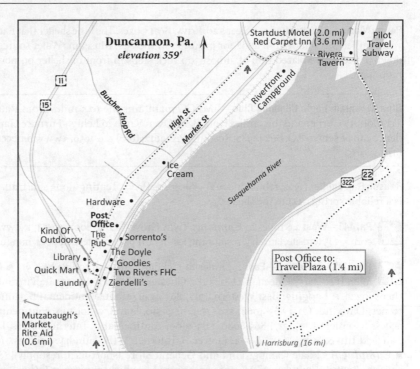

Zeiderelli's Pizza, L/D, 3 B's Ice Cream Stand; Nancy's Soft Pretzels, Th–Su L/D, 16 varieties of pretzels, cotton candy, popcorn, meals on Su; Pat's, a little taste of Italy, L/D, 11–8; Sheetz made-to-order. ■ *Other services:* Mary Parry (Trail Angel Mary), (717) 834-4706, can shuttle and help with any hiker needs; laundry on Market St.; All-American Truck Plaza (short-term resupply), $8 shower, ATM, Subway; coin laundry; banks with ATM; dentist; bank; veterinarian; Duncannon Community Library and Education Center at Duncannon Presbyterian Church, 3 N. High St., open W 1–3, Sat 10–12, Internet, a/c, cold drinks & snacks, hiker box, all hikers welcome; Christ Lutheran Church, 1 block **west** of High St., serves pasta dinners W night 5–7 in Jun–Jul. ■ *Outfitter:* Kind of Outdoorsy, 9 S. Market St., (717) 596-0016, hiker lounge, showers available ($5).

York Hiking Club—YHC maintains the 6.9 miles from the Susquehanna River to Pa. 225. Correspondence should be sent to YHC, 2684 Forest Rd., York, PA 17402; (717) 244-6769; <president@yorkhikingclub.com>.

Earl V. Shaffer—Almost all hikers recognize Earl "Crazy One" Shaffer (1918–2002) from York, Pa., as the first A.T. thru-hiker. In 1948, he completed a northbound thru-hike; in 1965, he did a southbound thru-hike, becoming the first to record both northbound and southbound hikes. To celebrate the 50th anniversary in 1998 of his first hike, Earl did a northbound thru-hike at the young age of 79. ATC's first "corresponding secretary," he was active in Trail work and promoting trails for the YHC and Susquehanna Appalachian Trail Club for many years.

Clarks Ferry Shelter (1993)—Sleeps 8. Privy. Bear box. A blue-blazed trail leads 100 yards to the shelter and 100 yards farther to a reliable piped spring.

Susquehanna Appalachian Trail Club—SATC maintains the 20.8 miles from Pa. 225 to Rausch Creek. Correspondence should be sent to <hike-hbg@satc-hike.org> or SATC Box 61001, Harrisburg, PA 17106-1001.

Peters Mountain Shelter (1994)—Sleeps 20. Privy. Bear boxes. The little shelter that Earl Shaffer built years earlier was removed in 2008 for inclusion in the A.T. Museum. Water source for shelter is down a steep, blue-blazed trail of almost 300 rock steps in front of shelter on north side of the mountain.

Blue Mountain Eagle Climbing Club—BMECC maintains the 62.5 miles from Rausch Creek to Tri-County Corner and the 3 miles from Bake Oven Knob to Lehigh Furnace Gap. Correspondence can be sent to P.O. Box 14982, Reading, PA 19612; (610) 326-1656; <www.bmecc.org>; <info@bmecc.org>.

Rausch Gap Shelter (1972, rebuilt in 2012)—Sleeps 6. Privy. Tenting along side trail. Water source is a reliable spring next to the shelter.

 Pa. 443—West 2.6 miles to *Camping:* Twin Grove KOA, (800) 562-5471, <www.twingrove.com>, $45 tentsite, laundry, restaurant, ice-cream parlor, Internet, pool, nonguest shower $5.

 Pa. 72/Swatara Gap—East 2.4 miles to Lickdale, adjacent to I-81 Exit 90. ■ *Restaurants:* Wendy's, Dairy Queen, McDonald's, Chester's Chicken, Sbarro Italian, Subway, Godfather's Pizza. ■ *Lodging:* Best Western, (717) 865-4234, $109D, continental B, laundry, pool, Internet; Days Inn, (717) 865-4064, $50–$99, pets $10, laundry, hot tub, continental B, Internet access; Comfort Inn, (717) 865-8080, $65–$109, continental B, Internet access, laundry, pool; Fairfield Inn & Suites, (717) 865-4234, free B, Internet/WiFi, laundry, pool, ask for hiker rate. ■ *Camping:* Lickdale Campground and General Store (short-term resupply), (877) 865-6411, $26–$30/tentsite, laundry, ATM, store with rotisserie chicken, pizza. ■ *Other services:* Love's (showers $9, ATM), BP, and Exxon all have stores (short-term resupply).

William Penn Shelter (1993)—Sleeps 16. Privy. With second-floor loft and windows, 0.1 mile east of the A.T., often visited by summer camping groups. Water source is 200 yards on a blue-blazed trail to the west of the A.T.

 Pa. 501—East 2 miles to **Bethel, Pa.** [P.O. ZIP 19507: M–F 8–12 & 1:15–4:30, Sa 8:30–10:30; (717) 933-8305]. ■ *Other services:* Bethel Animal Clinic, (717) 933-4916. ■ *Internet access:* Bethel Library, M–Th 10–8, F 10–5, Sa 9–4. ■ *Shuttle:* Joyce and Lance Carlin, (570) 345-0474 or cell (570) 516-3447, <smtownqn@yahoo.com>; 8 a.m.–10 p.m.; call for rates.

West 3.7 miles to **Pine Grove, Pa.** [P.O. ZIP 17963: M–F 8:30–4:30, Sa 9–12; (570) 345-4955]. Most major services but spread out over three miles. ■ *Lodging:* Hampton Inn, (570) 345-4505, indoor pool, laundry, WiFi, hot continental B, 10% hiker discount; Season's Inn, (570) 345-4505, weekdays $45–$60, dogs $10, nonsmoking rooms, continental B; Comfort Inn, (570) 345-8031, $60–$109D, nonsmoking rooms, pets $10, includes continental B, pool, Internet access, laundry. ■ *Groceries:* Turkey Hill Market with ATM (short-term resupply); BG's Market (long-term resupply), daily 7–9. ■ *Restaurants:* O'Neals Pub, L/D W–Su; McDonald's; Arby's; the Original Italian Pizza Place, L/D; Do's Pizza, L/D, closed Su; Dominick's Pizza, L/D, closed M; Buddy's Log Cabin Restaurant; Burke's Dairy Bar; The Diner, 7 a.m.–11 p.m.; Subway; Auntie Anne's Pretzels. ■ *Other services:* coin laundry (7 a.m.–10 p.m.), barber, bank with ATM, doctor, podiatrist, dentist, veterinarian, pharmacy (closed Su), theater, and community pool ($9.50).

501 Shelter (1980s)—Immediately north of paved Pa. 501, go west on the blue-blaze 0.1 mile; always open, no fee. Shelter is fully enclosed, with 12 bunks, table, chairs, skylight (a potter once had her wheel underneath), privy, and solar shower. Tentsites off woods road uphill, beyond fire ring. Water from faucet at adjacent house of BMECC caretaker. No smoking inside shelter; no alcoholic beverages allowed. Pets allowed (on leash only) if other shelter guests are willing to share and owner takes care of sanitary needs. Shuttles and motoring visitors park in public lot on paved 501 and walk in *via* blue-blaze. Some Pine Grove restaurants might deliver (see above).

Eagles Nest Shelter (1988)—Sleeps 8. Privy. Shelter is 0.3 mile from A.T. on a blue-blazed trail. Intermittent Yeich Spring is crossed *en route* to the shelter.

Port Clinton, Pa. [P.O. ZIP 19549: M–F 12:30–4:30, Sa 8–11; (610) 562-3787]—Port Clinton allows hikers to camp free under the roof of its pavilion. The pavilion, with outhouse, located 0.3 mile west of the A.T. on Penn Street, is a drug- and alcohol-free area. Permission is required for a stay of more than two nights [call LaVerne Sterner, (570) 366-0489]. No car camping. Water can be obtained from a spigot outside the Port Clinton Hotel. ■ *Lodging:* Port Clinton Hotel, (610) 562-3354, <www.portclintonhotel.net>, $65PP, $10 deposit for room key and towel, shower only $5, closed M, limited rooms available, laundry, no reservations, WiFi. ■ *Restaurants:* Port Clinton Hotel, L/D, closed M; 3-C's Restaurant, B/L, M–F 5–3, Sa–Su 6–2; Union House B&B, D. ■ *Other services:* The Port Clinton Peanut Shop, open M–Th 10–7, F–Sa 10–8, Su 10–6, with home-made goodies and snacks, cold drinks, ATM; Port Clinton Barber Shop, hiker-friendly, has music jams, may be able to provide local shuttles.

East on Pa. 61 1.5 miles to ■ *Lodging:* Microtel Inn, <www.microtelinn.com>, (610) 562-4234, $84–$159D, continental B, pet-friendly ($10 nonrefundable fee), free long-distance phone, laundry, WiFi. ■ *Restaurants:* Cabela's Restaurant, B/L/D; Wendy's; Burger King; Cracker Barrel; Starbucks; Cigars International; Pappy T's in Microtel Inn, L/D; Dunkin' Donuts–Baskin Robbins; Shell with food mart (short-term resupply); Subway; Taco Bell/Long John Silver's; McDonald's; Pizza Hut/Wings Street, (610) 562-3619. ■ *Outfitter:* Cabela's Superstore, <www.cabelas.com>, (610) 929-7000, M–Sa 8–9, Su 9–8, shuttles available to/from Port Clinton, camping department, fuel (Esbit, propane/butane, Coleman Powermax), A.T. maps, ATM. ■ *Groceries:* Walmart, Aldi. ■ *Bus service:* M–Sa from Cabela's to Hamburg to Reading with connections to Philadelphia; (610) 921-0601, <www.barta-bus.com>.

East on Pa. 61 3 miles, then left (0.5 mile) on State Street to **Hamburg, Pa. [P.O. ZIP 19526; M–F 9–5, Sa 9–12; (610) 562-7812]**. ■ *Lodging:* American House Hotel near center of town, (610) 562-4683. ■ *Groceries:* Weis Supermarket, open daily 6–11, one block east of the town center. ■ *Other services:* St, Luke's Health Center Care Now, (610) 628-7200; coin laundry; pharmacy; movie theater; doctor; dentist; bakery; medical center; veterinarian; banks with ATM. Near Pa. 61 are Redner's Market Warehouse (open 24 hrs., long-term resupply), Dollar General, Family Dollar, Rite Aid, Arby's, Xiang Shan (Chinese food), Loue's Pizza, Subway.

Hamburg Reservoir—A parking area 0.3 mile **East** of the A.T. requires free permits for overnight parking. Call the Borough of Hamburg, (610) 562-7821, for permission.

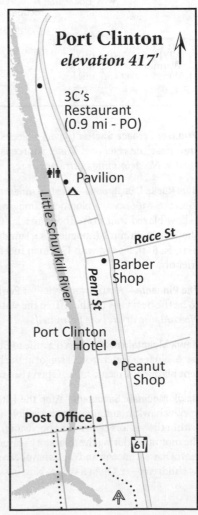

Port Clinton ↑
elevation 417'

3C's Restaurant (0.9 mi - PO)

Pavilion

Little Schuylkill River

Race St

Penn St

Barber Shop

Port Clinton Hotel

Peanut Shop

Post Office

61

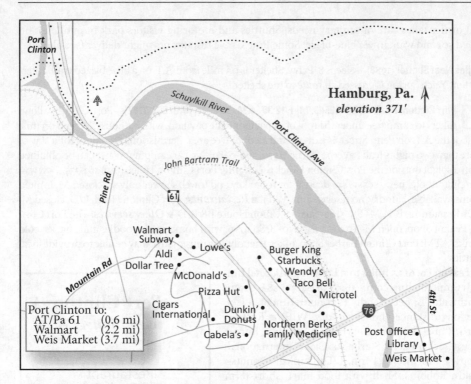

Windsor Furnace Shelter (1970s)—Sleeps 8. Privy. Tentsites. Shelter is located on a blue-blazed trail near the reservoir. Water source is the creek south of the shelter. *No campfires except at shelter. No swimming in streams or reservoir.*

Blue Rocks Campground— East 1.5 miles to campground, 341 Sousley Rd., Lenhartsville, PA 19534; (610) 756-6366, <www.bluerockscampground.com>; *via* a blue-blazed trail from Pulpit Rock and a yellow-blazed trail from The Pinnacle. Tentsites $32 M–F, 50% discount for thru-hikers M–Th, showers, swimming (nonguest) $4, laundry, WiFi. Camp store (short-term resupply), M–Th 9–7, F 9–11, Sa 8–11, Su 8–7, with Coleman fuel and limited hiker supplies. Mail drops accepted. Hiker-friendly.

The Pinnacle—A panoramic view of Pennsylvania farmland from an elevation of 1,635 feet, said to be the best view on the A.T. in the state. Below the viewpoint lies a sheer cliff and a few caves. *No camping or fires are permitted.*

Hawk Mountain Road—East 0.2 mile to Eckville Shelter, an enclosed bunkroom that offers space for 6. No fee. Water from a spigot at the back of the caretaker's house. Solar shower, flush toilet, tent platforms, picnic table. Open year-round; privy and shower are winterized.

Hawk Mountain Sanctuary—Atop the Kittatinny Ridge sits the Hawk Mountain Visitors Center, <www.hawkmountain.org>, accessible *via* a 2.5-mile blue-blazed trail from the A.T. Located within the visitors center are a bookstore, gift shop, and interpretive exhibits on raptors that fly by the mountain during the migratory seasons. Several species other than raptors can be seen; 16 species of hawks, falcons, and eagles have been spotted over the mountain. Daily fee $10 adults, $7 seniors, $5 children 6–12. Open 8–5 Sep–Nov, 9–5 Dec–Aug.

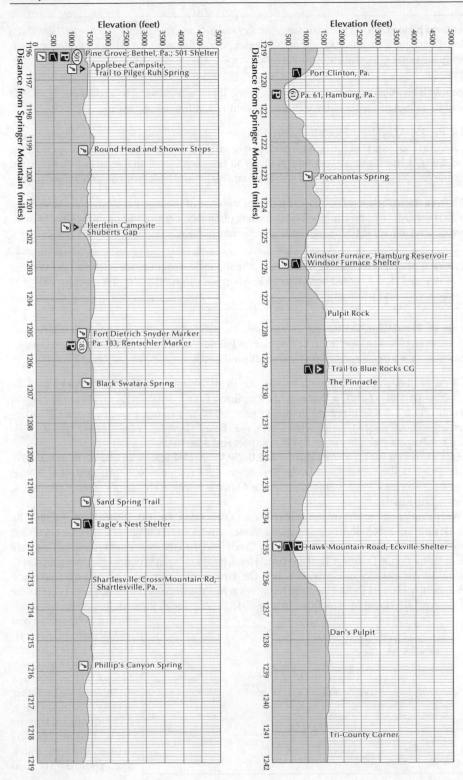

Elevation (feet)

Distance from Springer Mountain (miles)

Pine Grove; Bethel, Pa.; 501 Shelter
Applebee Campsite,
Trail to Pilger Ruh Spring

Round Head and Shower Steps

Hertlein Campsite
Shuberts Gap

Fort Dietrich Snyder Marker
Pa. 103, Rentschler Marker

Black Swatara Spring

Sand Spring Trail
Eagle's Nest Shelter

Shartlesville Cross-Mountain Rd;
Shartlesville, Pa.

Phillip's Canyon Spring

Elevation (feet)

Distance from Springer Mountain (miles)

Port Clinton, Pa.

Pa. 61, Hamburg, Pa.

Pocahontas Spring

Windsor Furnace, Hamburg Reservoir
Windsor Furnace Shelter

Pulpit Rock

Trail to Blue Rocks CG
The Pinnacle

Hawk Mountain Road; Eckville Shelter

Dan's Pulpit

Tri-County Corner

Allentown Hiking Club—AHC maintains the 10.7 miles from Tri-County Corner to Bake Oven Knob. Correspondence should be sent to P.O. Box 1542, Allentown, PA 18105; <www.allentown-hikingclub.org>; <info@allentownhikingclub.org>.

Allentown Hiking Club Shelter (1997)—Sleeps 8. Privy. Tentsites. First water source is a spring 0.2 mile downhill in front of shelter; if dry, continue downhill 0.1 mile to second spring.

Pa. 309—*Lodging:* Blue Mountain B&B, (570) 386-2003, <www.bluemountainsummit. com>, $95–$125/ night; new owners, please call first to confirm. Restaurant open Th–Sa 11–10, Su 11–8; live music all year on F 7–10, on Su Jun–Sep Su 5–8 on the patio; hiker register. Possible camping near restaurant if you ask first. Water available from outside spigot.

Bake Oven Knob Shelter (1937)—Sleeps 6. No privy. One of the original Pennsylvania shelters. The first water source on the blue-blazed trail is often dry; continue 200 yards to the second, more dependable spring, although both may be intermittent.

Keystone Trails Association—KTA maintains the 10.3 miles from Lehigh Furnace Gap to Little Gap. Correspondence should be sent to 46 E. Main St., Mechanicsburg, PA 17055, or call (717) 766-9690; <www.kta-hike.org>.

George W. Outerbridge Shelter (1965)—Sleeps 6. No privy. The surrounding area suffers from heavy-metal contamination from the zinc plant at Palmerton (see Superfund entry on next page). Water source is a piped spring north 150 yards on the A.T.

Pa. 873/Lehigh Gap—**East** 2 miles on Pa. 873 to **Slatington, Pa. [P.O. ZIP 18080: M–F 8:30–5, Sa 8:30–12; (610) 767-2182].** ■ *Restaurants:* The Shack, L/D; Mama's Pizza; Sal's Pizza; Slatington Diner B/L/D. ■ *Internet access:* Slatington Library, M, W 9–7, Tu 9–3, F 9–5, Sa 8–2. ■ *Other services:* coin laundry, ATM, convenience stores, A.F. Boyer Hardware store, doctor, dentist, pharmacy, bowling alley, and bus service to Walnutport and Allentown.

East 2 miles on Pa. 145 to **Walnutport, Pa. [P.O. ZIP 18088: M–F 8:30–5, Sa 8:30–12; (610) 767-5191].** ■ *Groceries:* Dollar General and Dollar Tree (short-term resupply). ■ *Restaurants:* Great Wall Chinese; D'Sopranos Pizza; fast-food options. ■ *Other services:* ATM, doctor, dentist, pharmacy, veterinarian, Kmart.

West 2 miles on Pa. 248 or 2-mile blue-blaze to **Palmerton, Pa. [P.O. ZIP 18071: M–F 8:30–5, Sa 8:30–12; (610) 826-2286].** *Blue-blaze directions:* **West** 1.5 miles from the gravel lot on the northwest side of the Lehigh River over the Aquashicola Creek Bridge to the back road leading to Delaware Ave. in Palmerton. ■ *Lodging:* The Palmerton Hotel, (610) 826-5454, $55S, $65 efficiency unit. Bert's Steakhouse has a bunkroom, pets allowed in the garage; call Tracy, (610) 597-2020. ■ *Groceries:* IGA, Country Harvest (both long-term resupply). ■ *Restaurants:* Bert's Steakhouse, B/L/D; One Ten Tavern, L/D, closed M; Simply Something Café, B/L/D; Tony's Pizzeria; Joe's Place, deli sand-wiches; Palmerton Pizza and Restaurant; Subway; Hunan House Chinese. ■ *Internet access:* library M 10–8, T–F 10–5, Sa 9–4 (Sa Jul–Aug 9–1). ■ *Other services:* coin laundry; ATM; shuttle back to the Trail, Duane Mason-heimer, (610) 767-7969; Shea's Hardware and

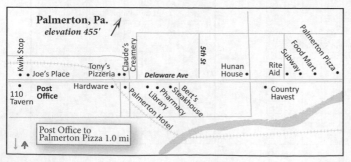

Palmerton, Pa.
elevation 455'

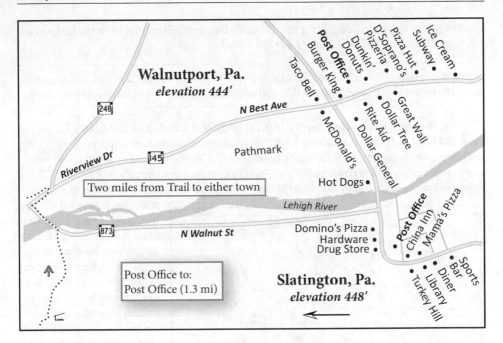

Walnutport, Pa.
elevation 444'

Two miles from Trail to either town

Post Office to:
Post Office (1.3 mi)

Slatington, Pa.
elevation 448'

Sporting Goods, Heet, Coleman fuel, and denatured alcohol; bowling alley; pharmacy; doctor; dentist; and hospital.

Palmerton EPA Superfund Site—The devastation along Blue Mountain near Lehigh Gap is the result of nearly a century of zinc smelting in Palmerton. In 1980, the Environmental Protection Agency shut down the furnaces and, in 1982, put the affected area on the Superfund clean-up list. Revegetation efforts are underway, and the mountain is slowly coming back to life. The scramble up the denuded rocks is among the most challenging on the A.T. south of New Hampshire. Major Trail work and a relocation will soon be in the works here.

Appalachian Mountain Club–Delaware Valley Chapter—AMC–Delaware Valley maintains the 15.4 miles from Little Gap to Wind Gap. Correspondence should be sent to 1180 Greenleaf Dr., Bethlehem, PA 18017; <www.amcdv.org>.

Little Gap, Blue Mountain Drive—**West** 2.5 miles to Little Gap and *Restaurant:* Covered Bridge Inn. **East** 1.1 miles to Blue Mountain Drive-in & Family Restaurant, (610) 767-6379, Tu–F 9–9, Sa–Su 8–9.
  East 1.5 miles to **Danielsville, Pa. [P.O. 18038: M–F 9:30–12 & 2–4:30, Sa 8–12; (610) 767-6822].** ■ *Lodging:* Filbert B&B, (610) 428-3300, <www.filbertbnb.com>, starting at $100D (cash only), reservations required; full, hearty, country B; pay laundry; will pick up and drop off hikers and possibly shuttle; mail drops accepted only for guests, but call first; use of dining room. ■ *Groceries:* Millers Market & Deli, (610) 767-6671.

Smith Gap Road—**West** 3.4 miles to **Kunkletown, Pa. [P.O. ZIP 18058: M–F 8–11:30, 12:30–5, Sa 8–12; (610) 381-3062.]** *Restaurants:* Kunkletown Pub, (610) 895-4255, Tu–Su 12–9; Penny's Place, (610) 381-5350, open daily 11 a.m.–2 p.m.

Leroy A. Smith Shelter (1972)—Sleeps 8. Privy (composting). Shelter is 0.2 mile down a blue-blazed trail. Water sources are said to be reliable; the first, 0.2 mile down the blue-blazed trail; a second, on a yellow-blazed trail 0.2 mile farther; a third, even farther, may be running when the first two are not. *Note: Water pump might be out at Kirkridge Shelter.*

Batona Hiking Club—BHC maintains the 8.5 miles from Wind Gap to Fox Gap (Pa. 191). Correspondence can be sent to BHC, 6651 Eastwood St., Philadelphia, Pa. 19149; <www.batonahikingclub.org>.

Pa. 33—**East** 1 mile to **Wind Gap, Pa. [P.O. ZIP 18091: M–F 8:30–5, Sa 8:30–12; (610) 863-6206].** ■ *Lodging:* Gateway Motel, (610) 881-6045, newly renovated, $60 weekdays, $90 weekends, dogs OK ($20), hiker friendly; Travel Inn, (484) 408-9475, $65S, $90D, nice pets OK. ■ *Groceries:* Giant Food Store located in Kmart Plaza (long-term resupply, 24 hrs.); Turkey Hill Mini Market, Sunoco Mini Mart (both short-term resupply).

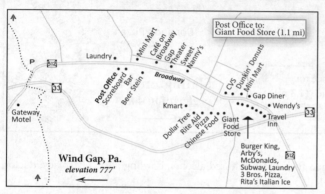

Post Office to: Giant Food Store (1.1 mi)

Mini Mart · Cafe on Broadway · Gap Theater · Sweet Nanny's

Laundry ·

P [512]

Broadway

Post Office · Scoreboard Bar · Beer Stein

[33]

Gateway Motel

Kmart ·

Dollar Tree · Rite Aid · Pizza · Chinese Food · Giant Food Store

CVS · Dunkin' Donuts · Mini Mart

· Gap Diner
· Wendy's

· Travel Inn [33]

Burger King, Arby's, McDonalds, Subway, Laundry 3 Bros. Pizza, Rita's Italian Ice [512]

Wind Gap, Pa.
elevation 777'
←

■ *Restaurants:* Sal's Pizza; Beer Stein; Hong Kong Restaurant; diners serving B/L/D; Rita's Ices; other fast-food options. ■ *Other services:* Sweet Nanny's, ice cream and treats; coin laundry; Kmart; hardware store; doctor (24-hour clinic); dentist; pharmacy; veterinarian; bank with ATM; Jaid's Lounge; and movie theater.

Wilmington Trail Club—WTC maintains the 7.2 miles from Fox Gap to the Delaware River Bridge. Correspondence should be sent to P.O. Box 1184, Wilmington, DE 19899; <www.wilmingtontrailclub.org>.

Kirkridge Shelter (1948)—Sleeps 8. Privy. Shelter is on a blue-blazed trail with excellent views south. Water source, an outside tap to rear of shelter before the Kirkridge Retreat facility parking lot, is turned off in winter months.

Pa. 611/Delaware Water Gap, Pa. [P.O. ZIP 18327: M–F 8:30–12 & 1–4:45, Sa 8:30–11:30; (570) 476-0304]—The A.T. doesn't go through the town center, but services are within a mile of where it crosses Pa. 611. ■ *Hostel:* The Presbyterian Church of the Mountain Hiker Center, (570) 992-3924, director David Childs, with overflow lean-to in backyard; please respect the good-will of Pastor Sherry Blackman and parishioners. Space with shower limited to long-distance hikers—no car or van parking or support vehicles permitted in

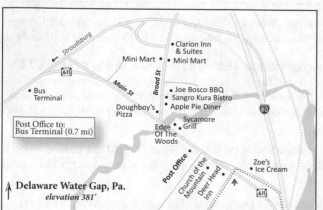

Stroudsburg

[611]

· Bus Terminal

Main St

Broad St

· Clarion Inn & Suites
Mini Mart · · Mini Mart

· Joe Bosco BBQ
· Sangro Kura Bistro
Doughboy's · · Apple Pie Diner
Pizza

[80]

Sycamore
Edge · · Grill
Of The
Woods

Post Office to: Bus Terminal (0.7 mi)

Post Office

Church of the Mountain · Deer Head Inn

Zoe's · Ice Cream

[611]

Delaware Water Gap, Pa.
elevation 381'

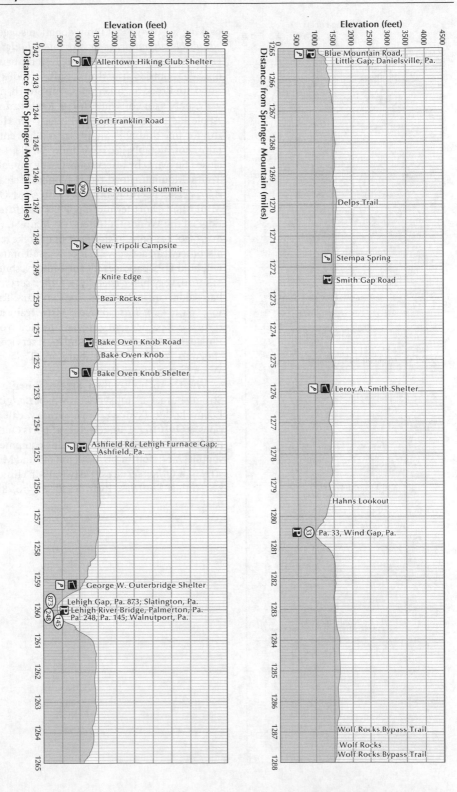

Elevation (feet)

Distance from Springer Mountain (miles)

Allentown Hiking Club Shelter

Fort Franklin Road

Blue Mountain Summit (309)

New Tripoli Campsite

Knife Edge

Bear Rocks

Bake Oven Knob Road

Bake Oven Knob

Bake Oven Knob Shelter

Ashfield Rd, Lehigh Furnace Gap;
Ashfield, Pa.

George W. Outerbridge Shelter

Lehigh Gap, Pa. 873; Slatington, Pa.
Lehigh River Bridge; Palmerton, Pa.
Pa. 248, Pa. 145; Walnutport, Pa.
(873) (248) (145)

Elevation (feet)

Distance from Springer Mountain (miles)

Blue Mountain Road,
Little Gap; Danielsville, Pa.

Delps Trail

Stempa Spring

Smith Gap Road

Leroy A. Smith Shelter

Hahns Lookout

Pa. 33, Wind Gap, Pa. (33)

Wolf Rocks Bypass Trail

Wolf Rocks
Wolf Rocks Bypass Trail

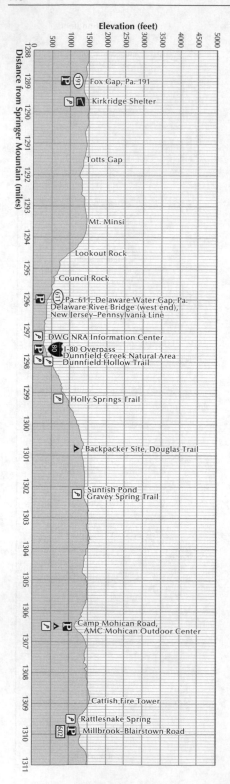

Elevation (feet)

Distance from Springer Mountain (miles)

Fox Gap, Pa. 191

Kirkridge Shelter

Totts Gap

Mt. Minsi

Lookout Rock

Council Rock

Pa. 611, Delaware Water Gap, Pa.
Delaware River Bridge (west end),
New Jersey–Pennsylvania Line

DWG NRA Information Center

I-80 Overpass
Dunnfield Creek Natural Area
Dunnfield Hollow Trail

Holly Springs Trail

Backpacker Site, Douglas Trail

Sunfish Pond
Gravey Spring Trail

Camp Mohican Road,
AMC Mohican Outdoor Center

Catfish Fire Tower

Rattlesnake Spring
Millbrook–Blairstown Road

parking lot. Two-night limit, donation suggested, *absolutely no drugs or alcohol.* ■ *Lodging:* Deer Head Inn, (570) 424-2000, restaurant and upscale rooms; Clarion Inn & Suites, (570) 476-0000, 101 Broad St., hiker rates $79D Su–Th, may vary, pets $50, coin laundry. ■ *Restaurants:* Apple Pie Diner; Doughboy Pizza; Deer Head Inn for fine dining F–Su, pizza, and live entertainment, notably jazz; Sycamore Grille, L/D, closed Su–M, D by reservation; Castle Inn, near Trail at Mountain Road, old-fashioned ice cream. ■ *Groceries:* Fuel On Mini Mart with ATM, Gulf Mini Mart (short-term resupply). ■ *Outfitters:* Edge of the Woods Outfitters, 110 Main St. (Rt. 611), (570) 421-6681, hiking gear, maps, bike rentals, outerwear, active wear, footwear, all brands, will hold UPS packages for thru-hikers, shuttle $1.50/mi, very hiker-friendly. ■ *Other services:* hair salon, run by Paulette, (570) 421-8218, Tu–F 10–7, Sa 10–3. ■ *Bus service:* Martz Trailways, (570) 421-4451 or (570) 421-3040, to New York, Philadelphia, and Scranton, and local service on "Pocono Pony" to Stroudsburg and Delaware Water Gap National Recreation Area.

West 5 miles to East Stroudsburg and Stroudsburg, Pa., full-service towns. ■ *Lodging:* Econo Lodge, (570) 424-1771, laundry, call for rates. ■ *Outfitter:* Dunkelberger's Sports Outfitter, (570) 421-7950, with backpacking equipment, supplies, and clothing, is located at 6th and Main streets. ■ *Other services:* 7-day walk-in clinic at hospital. ■ *Shuttles:* Ryan Rickley, (570) 801-0348, Pa.–N.Y.

New Jersey

Miles from Springer	Miles to Next Point	Features	Services	Elev	Miles from Katahdin	M A P
1,296.2	1.0	Delaware River Bridge (west end); Pennsylvania–New Jersey State Line		350'	896.8	
1,297.2	0.4	Delaware Water Gap National Recreation Area Kittatinny Point Visitors Center	R, P, w	350'	895.8	
1,297.6	0.1	I-80 ...underpass	R	350'	895.4	
1,297.7	0.1	Dunnfield Creek Natural Area ...water pump at northern end of parking area	R, P, w	350'	895.3	
1,297.8	1.4	Dunnfield Creek Trail to Dunnfield Creek Falls (E–0.25m)	w	350'	895.2	
1,299.2	1.6	Holly Springs Trail (E–0.2m)	w	950'	893.8	
1,300.8	1.3	Backpacker Campsite, blue-blazed Douglas Trail West–1.8m to Worthington State Forest CG	C, nw C, w, sh	1,300'	892.2	
1,302.1	0.1	Sunfish Pond ...glacial pond, No Camping		1,382'	890.9	
1,302.2	4.4	Garvey Springs Trl (W–600ft.) ...orange-blazed	w	1,400'	890.8	ATC N.Y.–N.J. Map 4
1,306.6	2.4	Camp Mohican Road ...dirt road West–0.3m to AMC Mohican Outdoor Center	R, P, w C, L, M, g, sh, f	1,150'	886.4	
1,309.0	0.6	Catfish Fire Tower	C, nw	1,565'	884.0	
1,309.6	0.4	Rattlesnake Spring (W–50ft.) ...on dirt road	w	1,260'	883.4	
1,310.0	3.9	Millbrook–Blairstown Rd–County Road 602 West–1.1m to Millbrook Village Picnic Area	R, P w	1,260'	883.0	
1,313.9	1.8	Blue Mountain Lakes Road (Flatbrookville Stillwater Road) (E–0.1m piped spring)	R, P, w	1,350'	879.1	
1,315.7	1.2	Crater Lake Trail (E–0.3m) ...view 150 ft. E	R, P, w	1,560'	877.3	
1,316.9	1.8	Buttermilk Falls Trail West–1.5m to waterfall	C R, P	1,560'	876.1	
1,318.7	2.2	Rattlesnake Mountain ...open ledges	C, nw	1,492'	874.3	
1,320.9	3.6	Brink Road Shelter (W–0.2m) ...31.4mS; 6.9mN	S, w	1,110'	872.1	
1,324.5	0.3	Culvers Gap, U.S. 206 East–0.8m; 1m; 1.6m; 2.5m East–3.4m to Branchville, N.J., P.O. 07826 West–1.8m to Forest Motel	M C, G, L, M M L	935'	868.5	
1,324.8	1.7	Sunrise Mountain Road	R	970'	868.2	
1,326.5	1.1	Culver Fire Tower		1,550'	866.5	
1,327.6	2.4	Gren Anderson Shelter (W–0.1m) ...6.9mS; 5.9mN	S, w	1,320'	865.4	
1,330.0	0.8	Sunrise Mountain ...picnic pavilion	R, P, nw	1,653'	863.0	
1,330.8	2.6	Crigger Road ...dirt	R	1,400'	862.2	ATC N.Y.–N.J. Map 3
1,333.4	0.2	Mashipacong Shelter ...5.9mS; 3mN	S, nw	1,425'	859.6	
1,333.6	2.4	Deckertown Turnpike ...paved	R, P	1,320'	859.4	
1,336.0	1.8	Rutherford Shelter (E–0.4m) ...3mS; 5.1mN	S, w	1,345'	857.0	
1,337.8	1.1	Blue Dot Trail (W–0.4m to Sawmill Lake CG)	C, w	1,600'	855.2	
1,338.9	1.0	N.J. 23; High Point State Park HQ East–1.5m to High Point Mountain Motel East–2.9m to Elias Cole Restaurant West–0.7m to State Park Day Use Area West–4.4m to Shop Rite West–7.1m to Port Jervis, N.Y., P.O. 12771	R, P, w L, M M M, sh G, M G, L, M, D, T	1,500'	854.1	

Miles from Springer	Miles to Next Point	Features	Services	Elev	Miles from Katahdin	M A P
1,339.9	0.2	Observation platform		1,680'	853.1	
1,340.1	0.5	Side trail to High Point Monument		1,600'	852.9	
1,340.6	1.3	**High Point Shelter** *(E–0.1m) ...5.1mS; 12.5mN*	S, w	1,280'	852.4	
1,341.9	0.8	County Road 519 ...*paved (E–2.5m to High Point Mountain Motel)*	R, P, L	1,100'	851.1	
1,342.7	1.2	Courtwright Road ...*gravel*	R	1,000'	850.3	
1,343.9	0.6	Ferguson Road	R	900'	849.1	
1,344.5	0.7	Gemmer Road ...*paved*	R	740'	848.5	
1,345.2	0.3	Stream	w	710'	847.8	
1,345.5	0.2	Goodrich Road ...*paved*	R	610'	847.5	
1,345.7	0.2	Concrete Dam *(outlet of pond)*		700'	847.3	
1,345.9	0.1	Road to Jim Murray property *(W–0.2m)*	S, C, w, sh	660'	847.1	
1,346.0	0.2	Goldsmith Road ...*gravel*	R	600'	847.0	
1,346.2	0.6	Vernie Swamp *(northern end) ...puncheons*		590'	846.8	
1,346.8	0.3	Unionville Road, County Road 651	R, P	610'	846.2	
1,347.1	0.6	Quarry Road	R, P	605'	845.9	
1,347.7	1.0	Lott Road, Jersey Avenue *West–0.4m to* **Unionville, N.Y., P.O. 10988**	R C, G, M	590'	845.3	
1,348.7	0.5	N.J. 284	R, P	420'	844.3	
1,349.2	1.0	Oil City Road	R	400'	843.8	
1,350.2	0.3	Wallkill River	R	410'	842.8	
1,350.5	2.0	Wallkill National Wildlife Preserve		410'	842.5	
1,352.5	0.5	Lake Wallkill Road (Liberty Corners Road)	R, w	440'	840.5	
1,353.0	1.5	**Pochuck Mountain Shelter** *...12.5mS; 11.6mN*	S, nw	840'	840.0	
1,354.5	1.2	Pochuck Mountain		1,200'	838.5	
1,355.7	1.5	County Road 565 *West–1.1m to* **Glenwood, N.J., P.O. 07418**	R, P C, G, L, w	720'	837.3	
1,357.2	0.7	County Road 517 *West–1.1m to* **Glenwood, N.J., P.O. 07418**	R, P C, G, L, w	440'	835.8	
1,357.9	0.7	Pochuck Creek ...*boardwalk, bridge*		410'	835.1	
1,358.6	0.9	Canal Road	R, P	410'	834.4	
1,359.5	1.4	N.J. 94 *East–1.4m to* Appalachian Motel *East–2.4m to* **Vernon, N.J., P.O. 07462** *West–0.1m to* Heaven Hill Farm and Deli *West–2.5m to* Mom's Homestyle Deli *West–6.1m to* **Warwick, N.Y., P.O. 10990** *West–7.4m to* Meadowlark Farm B&B	R, P L G,M,D,V,f G, M, w M B, G, M, D, cl C. L	450'	833.5	
1,360.9	1.7	Wawayanda Mountain ...*Pinwheel's Vista*		1,340'	832.1	
1,362.6	1.1	Barrett Road, New Milford, N.Y.	R, P	1,140'	830.4	
1,363.7	0.6	Iron Mountain Road ...*bridge* *East–1.6m to* Wawayanda Lake	R M, w	1,060'	829.3	
1,364.3	0.2	Wawayanda Road	R	1,150'	828.7	
1,364.5	0.1	**Wawayanda Shelter** *(W–0.1m) ...11.6mS; 12.2mN*	S	1,200'	828.5	
1,364.6	0.4	Hoeferlin Trail ...*water for Wawayanda Shelter (E–0.2m)*	w	1,200'	828.4	

Miles from Springer	Miles to Next Point	Features	Services	Elev	Miles from Katahdin	M A P
1,365.0	1.4	Warwick Turnpike *West–2.7m to* Shop Rite, grill, brew pub	R, P G, M	1,140'	828.0	N.Y.–N.J. Map 3
1,366.4	1.1	Long House Road (Brady Road)	R, P	1,080'	826.6	
1,367.5	1.1	Long House Creek		1,085'	825.5	
1,368.6	0.4	New Jersey–New York State Line; State Line Trail; Hewitt, N.J. *(E–1m to Lakeside Road, P)*		1,385'	824.4	

Bear boxes are provided at several New Jersey shelters; please use them! Bears are extremely active in this area. One bear destroyed a hiker's tent. Never feed bears or leave food unattended. Do not bury or scatter excess food; avoid eating or preparing food in your tent.

Campfires are prohibited in New Jersey. Camping in areas other than those designated by signs also is prohibited in New Jersey. Hitchhiking is illegal in New Jersey.

Venomous snakes are active throughout the area during warmer months. Be cautious when hiking at night, and pay attention near rocky ledges.

New Jersey has the highest population of bears per square mile. Southbounders are at the end of their deli-to-deli hike, whereas northbounders hungrily look forward to theirs. Thru-hiker legs are pumping at machine level now, which is good, because you may have to walk farther to find water.

New York–New Jersey Trail Conference—The NY–NJ TC maintains the 162.4 miles from Delaware Water Gap to the New York–Connecticut state line. Correspondence should be sent to NY–NJ TC, 600 Ramapo Valley Rd., Mahwah, NJ 07430; (201) 512-9348; <www.nynjtc.org>; <info@nynjtc.org>.

Delaware Water Gap National Recreation Area—The Kittatinny Point Visitors Center, (908) 496-4458, visible from the Trail, has restrooms and a picnic area. Open daily Memorial Day weekend–Labor Day and 3 days a week in early Sep. Water is available from a spigot to the left of the building. The Trail on Kittatinny Ridge runs through the NRA and state parks and forests, where regulations are different. The history of the recreation area is linked to a controversial 1960s plan to dam the Delaware, defeated by local opponents and the Trail community. Thru-hikers (defined by DWG as those hiking for two or more consecutive days) are permitted to camp along the Trail in the NRA with the following restrictions: one night per campsite, no more than ten persons per site, hiker camping allowed only within 100 feet of the A.T., no camping within 0.5 mile of an established roadway, no camping within 200 feet of another party, no camping from 0.5 mile south of Blue Mountain Lakes Road to the junction with the Buttermilk Falls Trail, no camping within 100 feet of any water source. Ground fires and charcoal stoves and grills are prohibited. Pets must be on a 6-foot leash at all times.

Holly Spring Trail—Holly Spring is 0.2 mile east of the A.T.; may fail during dry weather.

Worthington State Forest—Camping in Worthington State Forest is only permitted at Backpacker Campsite 2 at the junction with the Douglas Trail 4.6 miles north of I-80 on the A.T. and at the state-forest campground on Old Mine Road (see below). Rangers patrol the area and issue fines for those violating camping restrictions. Worthington State Forest Campground, (908) 841-9575, offers riverside camping and showers. From the A.T., take the blue Douglas Trail west 1.1 mile, then turn left onto the green Rock Cores Trail for another 0.7 mile to forest office; $25/site + $5 walk-in fee, max. 6 people; no pets or alcohol.

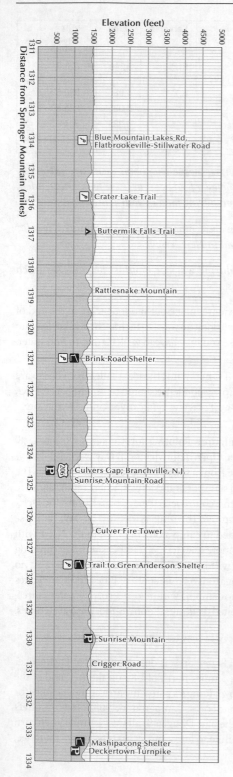

Sunfish Pond—The southernmost glacial pond on the A.T. and one of seven protected natural areas in New Jersey. *No camping or swimming is allowed at the pond.*

Garvey Spring Trail—A seasonal spring is located 600 feet west of the A.T. May fail in dry weather.

AMC Mohican Outdoor Center—West, on a dirt road, 0.3 mile; 50 Camp Mohican Rd., Blairstown, NJ 07825; (908) 362-5670, operated by the Appalachian Mountain Club (AMC). Thru-hikers, ask for rates in a shared cabin with bunk, stove, or tent camping with shower. Shower only, $5. Meal service available, ask for rates. Camp store with deli (mid-Apr to mid-Oct), sodas, ice cream, candy, and limited hiker supplies, including Coleman fuel and denatured alcohol by the ounce. The center accepts packages marked "Hold for A.T. Hiker" (with name) and sent *via* USPS, UPS, or FedEx; it cannot send packages. Check in at the visitors center, entrance on the left. Water available there or from a seasonal spigot near the garage across the road.

Catfish Fire Tower—Several campsites are located just north of the tower, along east side of the A.T. with good views across the valley. Get water at Mohican Outdoor Center or Rattlesnake Spring (below).

Rattlesnake Spring—Located 0.6 mile north of the Catfish Fire Tower on a dirt road about 50 feet west of the A.T. Spring may fail during drought times.

Millbrook–Blairstown Road, CR 602—West 1.1 miles to Millbrook Village, a historical park with flush toilets and picnic area. From Oct to May, the water supply in the picnic area is cut off, and the restrooms are closed except for a unisex, handicap-accessible bathroom.

Blue Mountain Lakes Road/Flatbrookville Stillwater Road—No camping from 0.5 mile south of this road to the junction with the Buttermilk Falls Trail. Several grassy areas for tenting are available 0.5–0.7 mile south of the road. The water pump no longer works, but water is available at a piped spring 100 yards east of the A.T. crossing: Follow the road downhill and 20 yards past the gate; spring is on the right side of the road.

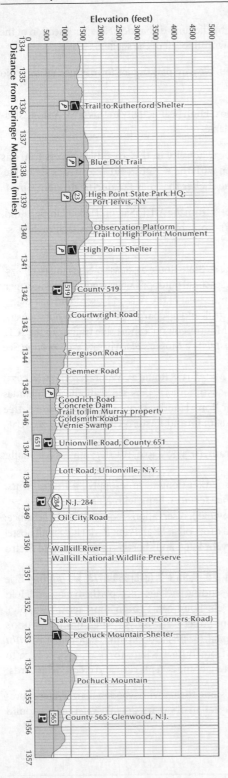

Crater Lake—The A.T. crosses the orange Crater Lake Trail twice. From the second junction (0.4 mile north of the first), the orange trail leads east 0.3 mile to a parking area and beach; west, 0.5 mile to Hemlock Pond, which offers good swimming.

Buttermilk Falls Trail—Several campsites here, but water source is 1.5 miles west down the steep blue-blazed trail to New Jersey's highest waterfall. No camping allowed south of this point to 0.5 mile south of Blue Mountain Lakes Road.

Brink Shelter (2013)—Sleeps 8. Composting privy. Built by NY–NJ TC volunteers and Stokes State Forest staff members using trees downed by Hurricane Irene. Bears and rattlesnakes are especially active here. Water source is across the road at a spring 100 yards northeast of the shelter.

U.S. 206/Culvers Gap—*Restaurant:* Gyp's Tavern, (973) 948-5013, located on nearby Kittatinny Lake, open daily 9 a.m.–1 a.m., serves L/D (cash only); Mountain House Tavern & Grille, (973) 250-3300, open daily 11:30–9.

 East 0.8 mile to Culver Lake Farm Market with fresh baked goods, fruit, and vegetables.

 East 1 mile to *Restaurant:* Jumboland, B/L/D.

 East 1.6 miles to ■ *Groceries:* Dale's Market with ATM (long-term resupply). ■ *Restaurants:* Dairy Queen, Jimmy's Pasta and Pizza.

 East 2.5 miles to ■ *Groceries:* Yellow Cottage Deli & Bakery (short-term resupply), closed M. ■ *Restaurants:* Riviera Maya Mexican, open daily, L/D; Firehouse Bagel Co., open daily, B/L. ■ *Camping:* Harmony Ridge Campground, (973) 948-4941, $18PP for thru-hikers. Showers and small camp store with limited supplies, including canister fuel. Call from U.S. 206 for a ride to/from the campground.

 East 3.4 miles to **Branchville, N.J. [P.O. ZIP 07826: M–F 8:30–5, Sa 8:30–1; (973) 948-3580].** ■ *Restaurants:* Most within 1 block of P.O.: Hatzi's Place; A&G Pizza; Victoria Diner; Third Base Pub; China One (take-out), (973) 948-8882, on U.S. 206. ■ *Shuttle:* George Lightcap, (201) 906-3556, <beatnikhiker@gmail.com>. ■ *Other services:* bank, ATM, drugstore.

Gren Anderson Shelter (1958)—Sleeps 8. Privy. Built by the now-disbanded New York section of the Green Mountain Club. Water source is a spring downhill to left of the shelter.

Sunrise Mountain—*No camping allowed at pavilion.* Nearby parking lot for day-use visitors. No water.

Mashipacong Shelter (1936)—Sleeps 8. Privy. Bear box. High bear activity in this area. A stone shelter with wooden floor. Camping, but no water available.

Rutherford Shelter (1967)—Sleeps 6. Privy. High bear activity in this area. Blue access trail has been relocated 0.5 mile south of the old intersection with the A.T. to avoid a steep rock scramble. Water source is a small stream 25 yards behind the shelter that may fail during drought times.

Blue Dot Trail—**West** 0.4 mile to *Camping*. Steep descent from the A.T. to Sawmill Lake Campground, (973) 875-4800, open Apr 1–Oct 31, flush toilets and potable water, no showers, $25/night + $5 walk-in fee, 6/site, no pets or alcohol.

N.J. 23—High Point State Park Headquarters, 1480 State Route 23, Sussex, NJ 07461; (973) 875-4800 On the A.T., has indoor restrooms and a seasonal outdoor water spigot. Offices are open year-round; mail drops accepted. Day-use area 0.7 mile west of the A.T. on Kuser Road has swimming at spring-fed Lake Marcia, a concession stand, grill, and no charge to walk-ins for hot showers; open Memorial Day–Labor Day, 10–6. High Point Monument, on a short side trail from the A.T., marks the highest point in the state, 1,803 feet. ■ *Hostel:* See Mosey's Place below. ■ *Camping:* See Blue Dot Trail above.
    East 1 mile to ■ *Lodging:* High Point Mountain Motel, 1328 Route 23, Wantage, NJ 07461, (973) 702-1860, <www.highpointmountainmotel.com>, $95D, $10EAP, pets $10 (call ahead), includes shuttle to/from Trail, other shuttles $2/mile (ask for Ron), laundry service $7, soda machine, free WiFi. ■ *Restaurants:* Annabel's Pizza, (973) 875-1886; Grand Eastern Chinese, (973) 702-1138; both deliver to inn.
    East 2.6 miles to *Restaurant:* Elias Cole Restaurant, (973) 875-3550, B/L/D, 7 a.m.–8 p.m. daily, cash only, home-made pie, bread, country food.
    West 4.4 miles to ■ *Groceries:* Shop-Rite supermarket (long-term resupply). ■ *Restaurants:* Village Pizza, Dairy Queen, and McDonald's. ■ *Other services:* bank with ATM.
    West 5.6 miles to *Hostel:* Mosey's Place, (845-239-3028), reservations required, call in advance; $30 includes bunk, shower, laundry, and pick-up and drop-off at High Point Park HQ. Small hostel with 6 bunks owned by Mosey (AT '15). Near grocery for long- and short-term resupply and Metro North train (see below).
    West 7.1 miles to **Port Jervis, N.Y. [P.O. ZIP 12771: M–F 9–5, Sa 9–3; (845) 858-8173].** ■ *Lodging:* Erie Hotel and Restaurant, (845) 858-4100, $69. Call before sending packages; accepts them marked "Hold for Hiker" (with name). ■ *Groceries:* Woogie's Deli, Food Mart (both short-term resupply). ■ *Restaurants:* All within two blocks of P.O.: Front Street Café, Burger King, Brother Bruno's Pizza, Ming Moon. ■ *Other services:* pharmacy; hospital, (845) 858-7000; bank; laundromat. ■ *Train service:* Metro-North Railroad/NJ Transit (across from Burger King), (973) 275-5555, service to Harriman, New York City, and Secaucus, N.J. Ticket machine accepts cash and credit/debit cards.

High Point Shelter (1936)—Sleeps 8. Privy. CCC-built stone shelter with wooden floor. Water sources are two streams on the trail to the shelter; both may fail in dry years. Potable water may be found 1.5 miles south at High Point State Park headquarters.

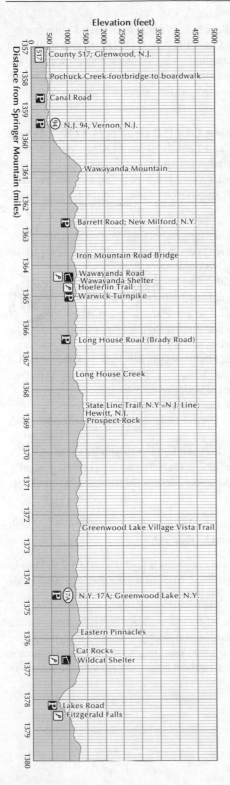

Elevation (feet)

Distance from Springer Mountain (miles)

| 0 | 500 | 1000 | 1500 | 2000 | 2500 | 3000 | 3500 | 4000 | 4500 | 5000 |

1357 — 517 — County 517; Glenwood, N.J.

1358 — Pochuck Creek footbridge to boardwalk

1359 — 🅿 Canal Road

1360 — 🅿 (94) N.J. 94, Vernon, N.J.

1361 — Wawayanda Mountain

1362

1363 — 🅿 Barrett Road; New Milford, N.Y.

1364 — Iron Mountain Road Bridge

— 🅿🛏 Wawayanda Road
— Wawayanda Shelter
— 🅿 Hoeferlin Trail
1365 — 🅿🅿 Warwick Turnpike

1366

— 🅿 Long House Road (Brady Road)
1367

— Long House Creek
1368

1369 — State Line Trail, N.Y.–N.J. Line;
— Hewitt, N.J.
— Prospect Rock

1370

1371

1372 — Greenwood Lake Village Vista Trail

1373

1374

1375 — 🅿 (17A) N.Y. 17A; Greenwood Lake, N.Y.

1376 — Eastern Pinnacles

— Cat Rocks
1377 — 🅿🛏 Wildcat Shelter

1378 — 🅿 Lakes Road
— 🅿 Fitzgerald Falls

1379

1380

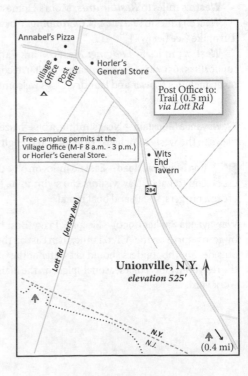

County Road 519—East 2.5 miles to *Lodging:* High Point Mountain Motel (see above).

Road to Jim Murray Property (0.4 mile north of Goodrich Road)—**West** 0.2 mile. For the past 28 years, Jim Murray (AT '89), (845) 986-0942, <backpack@warwick.net>, has cordially allowed long-distance hikers year-round use of the small hiker cabin (sleeps 5), with outdoor shower and privy, on his property adjacent to the Trail. Tenting allowed; no groups. Follow the "well water" sign. This is a privately owned cabin. Be responsible, and please do not abuse this privilege.

Lott Road—West 0.4 mile to the town of **Unionville, N.Y. [P.O. ZIP 10988: M–F 8–11:30 & 1–5, Sa 9–12; (845) 726-3535].** Lott Road is also known as Jersey Avenue. ■ *Camping:* Hikers can use Unionville Memorial Park for tenting, with water and toilet facility. ■ *Groceries:* Horler's Store with ATM (short-term resupply), (845) 726-3110, M–Sa 6–9, Su 7–7. ■ *Restaurants:* Wit's End Tavern, (845) 726-3956, Su–Th 12–12, F–Sa noon–4 a.m.; Annabel's Pizza & Italian Restaurant, (845) 726-9992, open daily 11–9.

Annabel's Pizza

Horler's
General Store

Village Office
Post Office

Post Office to:
Trail (0.5 mi)
via Lott Rd

Free camping permits at the
Village Office (M–F 8 a.m. - 3 p.m.)
or Horler's General Store.

Wits
End
Tavern

284

Lott Rd (Jersey Ave)

Unionville, N.Y.
elevation 525'

N.Y.
N.J.

(0.4 mi)

Pochuck Mountain Shelter (1989)—Sleeps 6. Privy. Bear box. Water is available 0.6 mile (steeply downhill) south of the shelter from a spigot (off late Oct–early Apr) on the north side of a vacant white house at the foot of Pochuck Mountain. No camping is allowed at the house (owned by the N.J. Department of Environmental Protection). A side trail 150 feet north of the Liberty Corners Road crossing leads 200 feet to that source. Southbounders can find water at a stream south of Sussex County Route 565.

County Roads 517 or 565—**West** 1.1 miles to **Glenwood, N.J. [P.O. ZIP 07418: M–F 7:30–5, Sa 10–2; (973) 764-2616].** ■ *Lodging:* Apple Valley Inn and B&B, (973) 764-3735, $150–$160, $25EAP, includes full B. ■ *Groceries:* Pochuck Valley Farm Market & Deli (short-term resupply), (973) 764-4732, with outside water spigot, ATM, and restroom. Open M–F 6–6, Sa–Su 6–5. No smoking. ■ *Camping:* Pochuck Valley market allows limited camping for customers only; ask permission, be responsible, and please respect this privilege.

N.J. 94—**East** 1.4 miles to *Lodging:* Appalachian Motel, 367 N.J. 94, Vernon, NJ 07462; (973) 764-6070, Su–Th $85D, F–Sa $110–$140D, $10EAP, no pets, laundry $10, call for possible pick-up from Route 94. Accepts packages for customers only. No smoking.

   East 2.4 miles to **Vernon, N.J. [P.O. ZIP 07462: M–F 8:30–5, Sa 9:30–12:30; (973) 764-9056].** *See map on next page.* ■ *Groceries:* ACME Market and Healthy Thymes Market (both long-term resupply). ■ *Restaurants:* Mixing Bowl, B/L; Paesano Pizza; Tomato Garden Pizza; see map for other options. ■ *Shuttle:* Ron Meyer, Vernon Taxi, (973) 632-2005. ■ *Other services:* bank with ATM, dentist, veterinarian, and CVS.

   West 0.1 mile to *Groceries:* Heaven Hill Farm and Pitchfork Deli, B/L, baked goods, fresh fruit and ice cream (short-term resupply), water spigot, (973) 764-5144, M–Sa 9–7 Su 9–6, Mar–Dec. Hikers are requested to keep packs outside on left side of building.

   West 2.5 miles to *Restaurants:* Mom's Homestyle Deli, The Grange.

   West 6.1 miles to **Warwick, N.Y.** *Camping:* Warwick Drive-In, 1.9 miles south of town on Warwick Turnpike (see below).

   West 7.4 miles to *Lodging:* MeadowLark Farm B&B, 180 Union Corners Rd., Warwick, NY 10990, (845) 651-4286, <www.meadowlarkfarm.com>, rooms $85–$120 +tax, tent camping on lawn, $15PP includes shower and laundry. Dogs welcome. Accepts packages. Shuttles $1/mile round-trip. Car can be left here.

Wawayanda Mountain—Near summit, a blue-blazed side trail leads 0.1 mile to Pinwheel's Vista, with views to the west of Pochuck Mountain and High Point Monument.

Iron Mountain Road—**East** 1.6 miles on blue trail to Wawayanda Lake. From Memorial Weekend to Labor Day, visitors can swim 10–6. Restrooms, first-aid station, food concession (ice cream, burgers, soda), and boat rental.

Wawayanda Shelter (1990)—Sleeps 6. Privy. Bear box. Water is available at the park office, reached by going north on the A.T. 0.1 mile, then east on the blue-blazed Hoeferlin Trail 0.2 mile; pay phone outside. Southbounders should get water at the office before reaching the shelter. Water source is the restroom faucet or a seasonal spigot on the maintenance building near entrance to the fenced-in work yard.

Warwick Turn-pike—West 2.7 miles to ■ *Camping:* Warwick Drive-In, (845) 986-4440, family-owned, multiscreen drive-in theater allows tenting for hikers, with access to cold running water, restrooms, cell phone charging station, and snack bar. Hikers may watch movies for free. ■ *Groceries:* Shop-Rite (long-term resupply); Pennings Farm Market (short-term re-supply), (845) 986-1059, with fresh fruit, vegetables, ice cream, bakery; grill and brew pub.

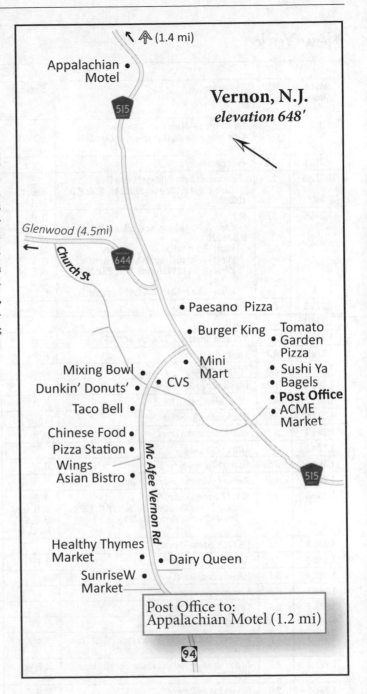

New York

Miles from Springer	Miles to Next Point	Features	Services	Elev	Miles from Katahdin	M A P
1,368.6	0.4	New Jersey–New York State Line; State Line Trail; Hewitt, N.J. *(E–1m to Lakeside Road, P)*		1,385'	824.4	
1,369.0	3.5	Prospect Rock		1,433'	824.0	
1,372.5	2.1	Greenwood Lake (Village) Vista Trail *East–0.9m to* **Greenwood Lake, N.Y., P.O. 10925**	B, G, L, M, f	1,180'	820.5	
1,374.6	1.2	N.Y. 17A *East–2m to* **Greenwood Lake, N.Y., P.O.10925** *West–0.1m to* Bellvale Creamery *West –1.6m to* Bellvale Market and Deli *West–4.6m to* **Warwick, N.Y., P.O. 10990** *West–10m to* Meadow Lark Farm B&B	R, P B, G, L, M, f M, w G, M B, G, M, D, cl C, L	1,180'	818.4	
1,375.8	0.6	Eastern Pinnacles		1,294'	817.2	
1,376.4	0.3	Cat Rocks		1,080'	816.6	
1,376.7	1.5	**Wildcat Shelter** *...12.2mN; 14.3mS*	S, w	1,180'	816.3	
1,378.2	0.3	Lakes Road	R, P	680'	814.8	
1,378.5	2.0	Fitzgerald Falls	w	800'	814.5	
1,380.5	1.2	Mombasha High Point		1,280'	812.5	
1,381.7	0.9	West Mombasha Road	R, P	980'	811.3	
1,382.6	0.8	Buchanan Mountain		1,142'	810.4	
1,383.4	0.7	East Mombasha Road	R, P	840'	809.6	
1,384.1	0.7	Little Dam Lake		720'	808.9	
1,384.8	0.6	Orange Turnpike	R	780'	808.2	
1,385.4	1.2	Arden Mountain, Agony Grind		1,180'	807.6	
1,386.6	0.2	N.Y. 17, Arden Valley Road *East–2.1m to* **Southfields, N.Y., P.O. 10975** *West–3.7m to* Harriman, N.Y.	R, B B, G, L, M B, G, L, M, cl, T	550'	806.4	
1,386.8	0.1	I-87 N.Y. State Thruway *...overpass*		560'	806.2	
1,386.9	1.5	Arden Valley Road	R, P	680'	806.1	
1,388.4	0.5	Island Pond Outlet	w	1,350'	804.6	
1,388.9	0.6	Lemon Squeezer		1,150'	804.1	
1,389.5	0.6	Long Path Trail Junction		1,160'	803.5	
1,390.1	1.1	Surebridge Mountain		1,200'	802.9	
1,391.2	1.1	**Fingerboard Shelter** *(E–0.5 m on Hurst Trail to water spigot) ...14.3mS: 5.3mN*	S, nw	1,300'	801.8	
1,392.3	2.2	Arden Valley Road *...to Lake Tiorati Circle (E–0.3m)*	R, P, w, sh	1,196'	800.7	
1,394.5	0.8	Seven Lakes Drive	R, P	850'	798.5	
1,395.3	1.2	Goshen Mountain		1,180'	797.7	
1,396.5	1.4	**William Brien Memorial Shelter** *(W–0.4m spring) ...5.3mS; 3.8mN*	S, w	1,070'	786.5	
1,397.9	0.7	Black Mountain		1,160'	795.1	
1,398.6	0.2	Palisade Interstate Parkway *...divided highway (W–0.4m to visitors center)*	R, w	680'	794.4	

N.Y.–N.J. Map 3

ATC N.Y.–N.J. Map 2

Miles from Springer	Miles to Next Point	Features	Services	Elev	Miles from Katahdin	M A P
1,398.8	1.1	Beechy Bottom Brook	w	660'	794.2	
1,399.9	1.8	**West Mountain Shelter** *(E–0.6m on Timp-Torne Trail)* ...*3.8mS; 32.8mN*	S, nw	1,240'	793.1	
1,401.7	0.5	Seven Lakes Drive	R	610'	791.3	
1,402.2	1.8	Perkins Drive	R	950'	790.8	
1,404.0	1.6	Bear Mountain, Perkins Tower	R, P	1,305'	789.0	
1,405.6	0.7	Bear Mountain Inn, Hessian Lake *East–0.3m to* **Bear Mountain, N.Y., P.O. 10911**	R, P, B, L, M, w	155'	787.4	
1,406.3	0.1	Bear Mountain Museum and Zoo		130'	786.7	
1,406.4	0.7	U.S. 9W, Bear Mountain Circle Bear Mountain Bridge, Hudson River *West–0.9m to* **Ft. Montgomery, N.Y., P.O. 10922**	R B, G, L, M	150'	786.6	ATC N.Y.–N.J. Map 2
1,407.1	0.7	N.Y. 9D	R, P	230'	785.9	
1,407.8	1.0	Camp Smith Trail to Anthony's Nose *(E–0.6m)*		700'	785.2	
1,408.8	0.2	Hemlock Springs Campsite	C, w	550'	784.2	
1,409.0	3.4	Manitou Road, South Mountain Pass	R, P	460'	784.0	
1,412.4	0.2	U.S. 9, N.Y. 403 *East–4.5m to* **Peekskill, N.Y., P.O. 10566** *West–6.3m to* **Cold Spring, N.Y., P.O. 10516**	R, G, M G, L, M, D, V, T, cl G, L, M, O, T	400'	780.6	
1,412.6	0.3	Old Highland Turnpike ...*paved*		440'	780.4	
1,412.9	0.1	Graymoor Spiritual Life Center–Franciscan Way ...*blue blazes to ball-field*	R, C, sh, w	520'	780.1	
1,413.0	1.9	Old West Point Road	R	550'	780.0	
1,414.9	0.8	Denning Hill		900'	778.1	
1,415.7	1.7	Old Albany Post Road–Chapman Road	R	607'	777.3	
1,417.4	1.0	Canopus Hill Road *(E–1.6m Putnam Valley Market)*	R, G, M	420'	775.6	
1,418.4	2.7	South Highland Road	R, P	570'	774.6	
1,421.1	1.6	Dennytown Road ...*water faucet on building*	R, P, C, w	860'	771.9	
1,422.7	2.1	Sunk Mine Road	R	800'	770.3	
1,424.8	4.2	N.Y. 301 *East–1m to* Clarence Fahnestock State Park *West–7.2m to* **Cold Spring, N.Y., P.O. 10516**	R, P C, sh, w G, L, M, O, T	920'	768.2	
1,429.0	0.4	Shenandoah Mountain		1,282'	764.0	
1,429.4	1.1	Long Hill Road	R, P	1,100'	763.6	ATC N.Y.–N.J. Map 1
1,430.5	1.3	Shenandoah Tenting Area *(W–0.1m)*	C, w	900'	762.5	
1,431.8	0.3	**RPH Shelter**, Hortontown Road ...*32.8mS; 9mN*	R, S, w	350'	761.2	
1,432.1	3.2	Taconic State Parkway ...*underpass*	R	650'	760.9	
1,435.3	1.6	Hosner Mountain Road *West–2.5m to* S & J Deli, Gian Bruno, & Hong King Kitchen *West–3.1m to* Inn at Arbor Ridge, Smoke Haus, & Blue Hill Deli / Food Mart	R, P G, M, V G, L, M	500'	757.7	

Miles from Springer	Miles to Next Point	Features	Services	Elev	Miles from Katahdin	M A P
1,436.9	1.4	N.Y. 52 *East–0.3m to* Mountain Top Market Deli & Pizzeria *West–1.8m to* **Stormville, N.Y., P.O. 12582**	R, P G, M, w G, M	800'	756.1	
1,438.3	2.4	Stormville Mountain Road; I-84 overpass	R, P	950'	754.7	
1,440.7	0.1	Mt. Egbert		1,329'	752.3	
1,440.8	1.1	**Morgan Stewart Shelter** ...*9mS; 7.8mN*	S, w	1,285'	752.2	
1,441.9	1.9	Depot Hill Road	R, P	1,230'	751.1	
1,443.8	0.3	Old Route 55	R, P	750'	749.2	
1,444.1	1.2	N.Y. 55 *West–1.5m to* Pleasant Ridge Pizza & A&A Deli *West–2.1m to* **Poughquag, N.Y., P.O. 12570** *West–3.3m to* Verona Pizzeria & Restaurant	R, P B, M B, G, M, V G, M	720'	748.9	
1,445.3	3.0	Nuclear Lake ...*outlet*		750'	747.7	
1,448.3	0.3	West Mountain		1,200'	744.7	
1,448.6	0.7	**Telephone Pioneers Shelter** ...*7.8mS; 8.8mN*	S, w	910'	744.4	
1,449.3	2.4	County Road 20, W. Dover Road, *Dover Oak* *East–3.1m to* **Pawling, N.Y., P.O. 12564** *East–5m to* Hannaford	R, P B, C, G, L, M, D, T, cl B, G	650'	743.7	
1,451.7	0.2	N.Y. 22, Metro–North Railroad, A.T. Train Platform; Native Landscapes & Garden Ctr *East–0.6m to* Tony's Deli *East–2.6m to* **Pawling, N.Y., P.O. 12564** *East–4.1m to* Hannaford *West–2.6m to* Ben's Deli, Big W's, Dutchess Motor Lodge *West–4m to* **Wingdale, N.Y., P.O. 12594**	R, P, M, T, sh, w, f C, G, M B, C, G, L, M, D, T, cl G, M, L B, G, M, L T, f	480'	741.3	
1,451.9	0.6	Hurds Corners Road	R	480'	741.1	
1,452.5	1.9	Pawling Nature Preserve ...*trail register*		675'	740.5	
1,454.4	2.6	P.N.R. Green Trail *(W– 0.9m to Ben's Deli, Dutchess Motor Lodge)*	G, M, L	960'	738.6	
1,457.0	0.4	Leather Hill Road ...*dirt*	R	750'	736.0	
1,457.4	0.2	**Wiley Shelter** ...*8.8mS; 4mN*	S, C, w	740'	735.6	
1,457.6	1.0	Duell Hollow Road	R, P	620'	735.4	
1,458.6	0.7	New York–Connecticut State Line; Hoyt Rd *West–3.3m to* **Wingdale, N.Y., P.O. 12594** *West–4.7m to* Dutchess Motor Lodge and restaurants	R, P B, G, M, T, f B, G, L, M	400'	734.4	

ATC N.Y.–N.J. Map 1

In New York, campfires are prohibited except in designated fire rings and fireplaces at established campsites and shelters. Camping itself is limited to designated sites.

The first miles specifically intended for the A.T. were built here through Harriman–Bear Mountain state parks in 1922–23. With many parks, roads, and a railroad station right on the Trail, many hikers are thinking, you may find this stretch to be a uniquely multicultural experience. The Trail drops to its lowest elevation point—124 feet—after, or just before, you pass through the Trailside Museum and Zoo at Bear Mountain. Hydration becomes an issue in this area. Don't pass up an opportunity for water.

Prospect Rock—At 1,433 feet, this is the highest point on the A.T. in New York (Bear Mountain is 1,305 feet). This and other rock faces along this ridge provide views of Greenwood Lake to the east.

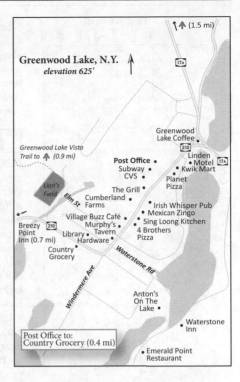

Greenwood Lake, N.Y.
elevation 625'

Greenwood Lake Vista
Trail to (0.9 mi)

Lion's
Field

Post Office
Subway
CVS

The Grill

Cumberland
Farms

Village Buzz Café

Breezy
Point
Inn (0.7 mi)

Library

Murphy's
Tavern

Hardware

Country
Grocery

Greenwood
Lake Coffee

Linden
Motel
Kwik Mart

Planet
Pizza

Irish Whisper Pub
Mexican Zingo
Sing Loong Kitchen
4 Brothers
Pizza

Waterstone Rd

Anton's
On The
Lake

Waterstone
Inn

Post Office to:
Country Grocery (0.4 mi)

Emerald Point
Restaurant

(1.5 mi)

Greenwood Lake Vista Trail—This blue-blazed trail leads **East** 0.9 mile to Greenwood Lake without the fast traffic of N.Y. 17A; from the vista, you can see Lion's Field below, the terminus of the trail. A small, green building next to the softball field has public restrooms and an outside seasonal water spigot hikers can use. **Greenwood Lake, N.Y. [P.O. ZIP 10925: M–F 8–5, Sa 9–12; (845) 477-7328].** ▪ *Lodging:* Linden Motel, (845) 477-0851, hiker-rate $80 room with kitchenette, WiFi, pool, no laundry; Anton's on the Lake, 7 Waterstone Rd., (845) 477-0010, no smoking, no pets, call for rates; The Breezy Inn & Restaurant (1 mile south of town), 620 Jersey Ave. Greenwood Lake, NY 10925, (845) 477-8100, new owners, renovated rooms $125D + tax, no smoking or pets, ATM, WiFi, call for possible pick-up from Trail, accepts packages marked "Hold for Hiker (with name)." ▪ *Groceries:* Country Grocery; Kwik Mart; and Cumberland Farms, with deli sandwiches (all short-term resupply). ▪ *Restaurants:* Planet Pizza; Murphy's Tavern, L/D weekdays, B Sa–Su; Village Buzz Café, B/L; Mexican Zingo; The Grill, B/L; Sing Loong Kitchen; Irish Whisper Pub; Subway. ▪ *Other services:* True Value, fuel; CVS; Chase Bank; Night Owl Taxi, (845) 662-0359, and Greenwood Lake Taxi, M–Th, (845) 477-0341 (call ahead); N.J. Transit buses to New York City.

N.Y. 17A—Hot Dogs Plus, cash only. **East** 2 miles to **Greenwood Lake**.
      West 0.1 mile to Bellvale Creamery, daily Apr–Oct 12–9 (closes earlier in spring/fall), ice cream, water, and device charging.
      West 1.6 miles to Bellvale Market & Deli, T–F 8–7, Sa 8–6, Su 8–4.
      West 4.6 miles to the larger town of **Warwick, N.Y. [P.O. ZIP 10990: M–F 8:30–5, Sa 9–4; (845) 986-0271].** Hitchhikers have been cited leaving Warwick on N.Y. 17A. ▪ *Groceries:* Kwik Mart, CVS (both short-term resupply); Price Chopper, open 24 hours, is 1.7 miles south of town on N.Y. 94; ShopRite is 1.9 miles south of town on N.Y. 94 (both long-term resupply). ▪ *Camping:* Warwick Drive-in Theater allows hikers to camp overnight; restrooms, water, picnic tables. See page 157. ▪ *Other services:* NJ Transit buses run frequently in the area from Warwick to New York City; hospital; restaurants; drug store; coin laundry; bank/ATM; and hardware store. ▪ *Shuttle:* Josie's Taxi, (845) 986-8073.
      West 10 miles to *Lodging:* Meadow Lark Farm B&B (*see* N.J. 94).

Wildcat Shelter (1992)—Sleeps 8. Privy. Water source is a spring 75 yards downhill and left from the shelter that might fail in dry periods.

Mombasha High Point—On a clear day, you can see the New York City skyline, including the Empire State Building.

Sterling Forest—Between Greenwood Lake and Arden, 6 miles of the A.T. cross the northern portion of a 20,000-acre tract called Sterling Forest. It was the center of a decade-long struggle between a corporate private landowner and a coalition of conservation groups, state agencies in New York and

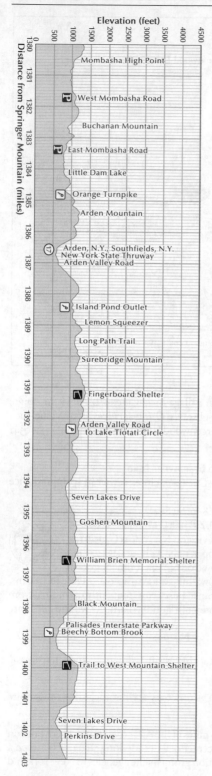

New Jersey, and such organizations as the NY–NJ TC and ATC. All told, more than 30 environmental groups, along with foundations, individuals, states, and Congress, combined to contribute more than $55 million toward the purchase and protection of 14,500 acres. *Note:* Hunting is allowed in season outside of the A.T. corridor.

N.Y. 17—East 2.1 miles to **Southfields, N.Y. [P.O. ZIP 10975: M–F 10–12 & 1–5, Sa 8:30–11:30; (845) 351-2628]**. ■ *Lodging:* Tuxedo Motel, (845) 351-4747, 985 N.Y. 17S, Southfields, NY 10975, $54S, $60D, $10EAP, WiFi, laundry available, no pets, mail drops accepted. ■ *Restaurant:* Steve's Pizza, (845) 915-3022, and take-out Chinese delivered ($20 minimum, cash only) to Tuxedo Motel, (845) 351-4428. ■ *Groceries:* Valero (short-term resupply), snack bar closes at 3 p.m., ATM. ■ *Shuttle:* Deborah Taxi, by advance appointment, text (845) 300-0332 or e-mail <deborahtaxi@gmail.com>. ■ *Other services:* ShortLine (Coach USA) buses from New York City/Tuxedo/Southfields to Harriman with a flag stop at the A.T. crossing of N.Y. 17 and from New York City to Fort Montgomery with a regular stop at Bear Mountain Inn.

West 3.7 miles to the town of **Harriman,** for lodgings, groceries, restaurants, and coin laundries.

Bear Mountain/Harriman State Parks—Home to the first completed section of the A.T. Dry conditions and forest fires have forced the closure of the A.T. in the park for days or even weeks in the summer. In 1994, Harriman State Park instituted a policy under which, even if other trails in the park are closed, the A.T. remains open to thru-hikers.

Bear activity in the area has increased recently. Be sure to store your food carefully when camping in the park. Never feed bears or leave food unattended. Do not bury or scatter excess food; avoid eating or preparing food in your tent. See page xiii.

Fingerboard Shelter (1928)—Sleeps 8. No privy. A stone structure with internal fireplace. *Due to aggressive bears stealing hikers' food near the shelter, hikers are advised to camp here only if using a bear-resistant canister to store food.* The closest dependable water is at Lake Tiorati, 0.5 mile downhill from the shelter going east on the blue-blazed Hurst Trail. Southbounders can get water at Tiorati Circle, 1.1 miles north of the shelter.

Arden Valley Road—East 0.3 mile to Tiorati Circle at the intersection of Seven Lakes Drive. Near the traffic circle are a public beach on Lake Tiorati and a picnic area. Restroom; free showers in bath house for walk-ins when beach is open; open Memorial Day to

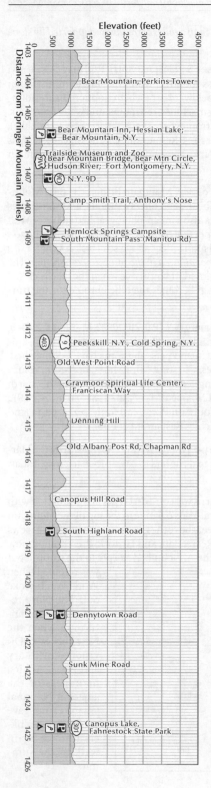

Elevation (feet)

Distance from Springer Mountain (miles)

Bear Mountain, Perkins Tower

Bear Mountain Inn, Hessian Lake;
Bear Mountain, N.Y.

Trailside Museum and Zoo
Bear Mountain Bridge, Bear Mtn Circle,
Hudson River; Fort Montgomery, N.Y.

N.Y. 9D

Camp Smith Trail, Anthony's Nose

Hemlock Springs Campsite
South Mountain Pass (Manitou Rd)

Peekskill, N.Y., Cold Spring, N.Y.

Old West Point Road

Graymoor Spiritual Life Center,
Franciscan Way

Denning Hill

Old Albany Post Rd, Chapman Rd

Canopus Hill Road

South Highland Road

Dennytown Road

Sunk Mine Road

Canopus Lake,
Fahnestock State Park

Labor Day (weekends only through third weekend in Jun), M–F 10–5:45, Sa–Su 11–6:45; vending machines, ice-cream sandwiches, candy, water.

William Brien Memorial Shelter (1933)—Sleeps 8. No privy. A stone shelter built by the CCC. Water source is a spring-fed well that is prone to go dry, 80 yards downhill from the right of the shelter. Water might be available from a stream 0.4 mile west of the A.T. on the yellow-blazed Menomine Trail, although it's unreliable in dry seasons. An alternative for northbounders is to stop at Tiorati Circle, cook at one of the picnic tables, and hike to the shelter for the evening. Southbounders can get water at the park visitors center 0.4 mile west, on the Palisades Interstate Parkway.

Palisades Interstate Parkway—West 0.4 mile to park visitors center, (845) 786-5003, with water from outside seasonal spigot, restroom, maps, soda and snack machines, open 8–5 daily, closed major holidays. From here, it is a mere 34 miles to NYC on the Palisades Interstate Parkway. Hikers may want to pick up water here, as many area streams can be unreliable in dry seasons.

West Mountain Shelter (1928)—Sleeps 8. No privy. Located 0.6 mile east on the blue Timp-Torne Trail. Water might be available at a stream 0.7 mile south of the junction to the shelter or sometimes at an unreliable seasonal stream 0.2 mile before the shelter. Views of the surrounding countryside and the NYC skyline.

Bear Mountain—At 1,305 feet, this is one of the highest points on the Trail in New York and offers views of the Hudson River Valley and the New York City skyline. In the early 1900s, the state was considering a site near the base for a prison, but Mary Averell Harriman, widow of railroad magnate Edward Harriman and primary landholder in the area, had other plans. In 1910, she agreed to donate 10,000 acres for the development of a park with the condition that the state discontinue its plans for a prison. What was then known as Sing Sing Prison was eventually built on the Hudson River 20 miles south of the A.T., its location giving birth to the phrase, "sent up the river." No water available at the summit. Do not rely on the seasonally stocked soda vending machine.

More than 2 million people visit Bear Mountain each year, making this original section of the A.T. the most heavily used along the entire Trail. In September 2018, the NY-NJ Trail Conference and ATC completed a 14-year project to reroute and rebuild the A.T. near Bear Mountain because of this high volume. The finished Trail, almost all of which was built by volunteers, fea-

tures more than 1,000 hand-hewn granite steps and more than 2 miles of treadway supported by stone cribbing.

Bear Mountain, N.Y.—[P.O. ZIP 10911: M–F 9–11, closed Sa; (845) 786-3747]. P.O. may close early; call ahead. Located 0.3 mile east of the A.T. across the street from the park administration building on Seven Lakes Drive. Fort Montgomery (see below) may be a better option. Bear Mountain State Park offers seasonal concession stands, vending machines, restrooms, and water fountains. ■ *Lodging & Restaurant:* Bear Mountain Inn (visible from where the A.T. meets Hessian Lake), (845) 786-2731, $159–$269; Hiker's Café, M–F 11–3, Sa–Su 10–5; Restaurant 1915 and Blue Roof Tapas Bar, M–F 11–8, Sa–Su 11–9. ■ *Other services:* Coach USA runs buses daily from the Bear Mountain Inn to New York City; <www.coachusa.com>.

Trailside Museums and Zoo—North of the inn and south of Bear Mountain Bridge, the Bear Mountain Zoo contains many native species, including black bears, and offers a unique, and sometimes emotional, experience for thru-hikers. Within the park is also a much-photographed statue of Walt Whitman. Admission $1; A.T. hikers admitted free. The portion of the A.T. leading through the zoo to the bridge—an original section from 1923—descends to 124 feet above sea level; it's the Trail's lowest elevation between Maine and Georgia. *Dogs are not allowed in the museum/zoo section.* The southern gate opens at 10 a.m.; at 4:30 p.m., the gate is closed. If you arrive when the gate is closed or are hiking with a dog, hike around on U.S. 9w, which becomes the official route for the time period/circumstances.

Bear Mountain Circle—West 0.9 mile to **Ft. Montgomery, N.Y. [P.O. ZIP 10922: M–F 8–1 & 2:30–5, Sa 9–12; (845) 446-8459]**. ■ *Lodging:* Bear Mountain Bridge Motel, 1041 Route 9w, (845) 446-2472, $85+tax (higher during special events), laundry ($10), no pets, all rooms have 1 double bed, shuttle to/from the Trail, accepts mail drops. ■ *Groceries:* Chestnut Mini Mart (short-term resupply), open 24 hours, free WiFi. MyTown Marketplace (long-term resupply) is 2.8 miles farther north in Highland Falls. ■ *Restaurants:* Bagel Café with ATM, open M–F 5:30–4, Sa–Su 5:30–3, B/L; Country Deli, with ATM, M–Sa 5:30–3:30, B/L; Bear Mountain Pizza, cash only, pizza, pasta, and ice cream, T–Su 11–9; Barnstormer BBQ & Pub, L/D; Richies Restaurant & Pub.

Bear Mountain Bridge—Built at a cost of $5 million in 1923–24 by a private company run by the Harriman family. When Earl Shaffer arrived at the bridge in 1948, he had to pay a nickel to cross. Today, only vehicles must pay.

Anthony's Nose—A half-mile **north** of N.Y. 9D, the A.T. turns west on a dirt road, at the junction with the blue-blazed Camp smith Trail. Going east on this trail leads 0.6 mile to the top of the mountain known as Anthony's Nose. This rock outcropping, 900 feet above the river, offers outstanding views of the Hudson River Valley. The state Office of Parks, Recreation, and Historic Preservation now owns the property; please stay on the trail. Originally, the A.T. climbed steeply to the summit but was rerouted when World War II broke out. The Nose remained closed until 1993, when the New York State Division of Military and Naval Affairs, managers of the adjacent National Guard camp, gave permission for hikers to once again walk to the summit.

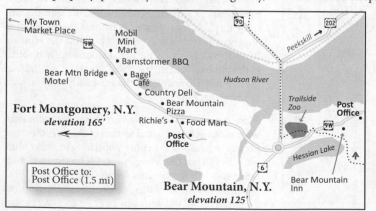

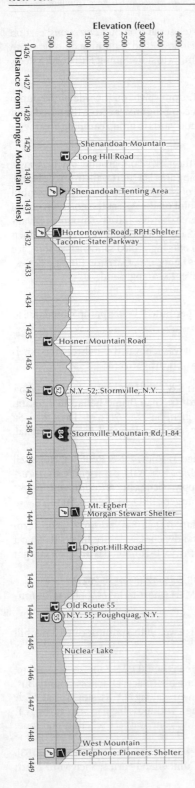

Hemlock Springs Campsite—No privy. Tenting areas just east of the trail. Water source is a small spring that may fail in dry periods. *Do not get water from Copper Mine Brook, which is 0.2 mi. north of campsite next to Manitou Road, due to possible heavy-metal contamination.*

 U.S. 9—*Groceries:* Appalachian Market Deli, (845) 424-6241, Shell station/convenience store just to west at U.S. 9/N.Y. 403 junction, full-service, deli, grill, pizza, open 24 hours.

East 4.5 miles to **Peekskill, N.Y. [P.O. ZIP 10566: M–F 9–5, Sa 9–4; (914) 737-6437].** If you plan to go into Peekskill, take Highland Avenue into town, rather than U.S. 9, where the two roads fork about 3 miles from the A.T. Highland Ave. leads directly to downtown. Services are spread out over a large, bustling area, with several motels and restaurants, supermarkets, pharmacy, laundry, banks with ATM, hospital, doctor, dentist, and veterinarian. The post office is on South St., 4.5 miles from the A.T. Free Internet access at the Field Library, 4 Nelson Ave., M, Tu, Th 9–9, W 11–9, F 9–5, Sa 10–2. *Train service:* Metro–North train to New York City, <www.mta.info/mnr>.

West 6.3 miles *via* Route 403 to N.Y. 9D to **Cold Spring, N.Y. [P.O. ZIP 10516: M–F 8:30–5, Sa 9–12; (845) 265-3486].** ■ *Lodging:* Countryside Motel (5.4 miles **north** of town), 3577 Route 9, Cold Spring, NY 10516, (845) 265-2090, $75 one bed, $85 two beds, $10EAP, WiFi; Pig Hill Inn, (845) 265-9247, $160 and up, includes full B, no pets, no smoking; Cold Spring B&B, (845) 264-0824, room with queen bed and private bath, WiFi, no B included, $152+tax. ■ *Restaurants:* Cold Spring Pizza, Whistling Willies, Foundry Café, Rincon Argentino, Hudson Hil's. ■ *Groceries:* Food Town Supermarket (long-term resupply). ■ *Outfitter:* Old Souls Outfitter, (845) 809-5886, <www.oldsouls.com>, daily 10–6, small outfitter with boots, packs, fuel, clothing, *etc.* ■ *Shuttle:* Highland Transit Taxi, (845) 265-8294; Village Taxi, (845) 265-2200. ■ *Train:* Metro North service to New York City, <www.mta.info/mnr>.

Graymoor Spiritual Life Center—Hikers are permitted to sleep at the monastery's ball-field picnic shelter, which has water, a cold-water shower Apr 1–Nov 1, and a privy. The shelter is open all season. *Directions:* North of U.S. 9, the A.T. climbs uphill and crosses a second paved road leading to the center. Here, northbounders should follow the blue blazes: Turn east on Franciscan Way, left on St. Anthony Way, and left on St. Joseph Drive to the ballfield. Southbounders will cross unpaved Old West Point Road onto the Graymoor driveway; continue straight on driveway, then north where the driveway forks. Garrison Pizza Café, (845) 424-6447, and local deli delivery to the picnic shelter.

 Canopus Hill Road—**East** 1.6 miles to the Putnam Valley Market (short-term resupply), (845) 528-8626, with pizza, hot food from the grill, ATM. Open daily 6–9 (closes at 7 on Su). *Directions:* east on Canopus Hill Road 0.3 mile to intersection with Canopus Hollow Road. Continue 0.1 mile south on Canopus Hollow Road, turn west on Sunset Hill Road 1.2 miles to store. Sunset Hill Road, a steep, winding road, climbs 400 feet from Canopus Hill Road.

Dennytown Road—Water available 50 feet west of A.T. from spigot on the side of the pump building. Opens third F of Apr, closes last Su of Oct. A camping area is across the paved road directly opposite the pump building; go uphill on dirt road 200 yards to group camping areas with picnic tables, trash cans, and portable toilet.

N.Y. 301/Clarence Fahnestock State Park—**East** 1 mile to the park's campground, (845) 225-7207. Camping mid-Apr to Nov; free designated hiker camping area is a short walk from the beach. The beach area can be reached from the A.T. 2.3 miles north of N.Y. 301 *via* an unmarked downhill gully trail that begins a quarter of a mile south of the viewpoint on the A.T. at the northern end of Canopus Lake. The beach area is visible from the overlook. Free showers and a bathroom are available at the beach, with concession stand (open Su–F 9–5, Sa 9–6 Memorial Day–late Jun, then daily through Labor Day) and grill (closes one hour earlier) offering grilled sandwiches, soda, ice cream, first-aid supplies, and toiletries. The beach area closes Labor Day. Garrison Pizzeria & Restaurant, (845) 265-3344, with Italian and Latin food, will deliver to campground.

West 7.2 miles to Cold Spring (see U.S. 9 above).

Shenandoah Tenting Area—0.1 mile west. Group camping is permitted. Water pump closed due to contamination.

RPH Shelter (1982)—Sleeps 6. Privy. Formerly a closed cabin, it was renovated as a three-sided shelter with a covered front porch. Water source is a hand pump or nearby stream.

Hosner Mountain Road—**West** 2.5 miles to ■ *Groceries:* S & J Deli Superette, (845) 227-4697, short-term resupply, M–Sa 7–6, Su 7:30–3. ■ *Restaurants:* Gian Bruno Italian Restaurant, (845) 227-9275, W–Th 11–9, F–Sa 11–10, Su 2–9; Hong King Kitchen, (845) 227-6773, M–Th 11–10, F–Sa 11–11, Su 12–10; Dunkin Donuts, daily 5 a.m.–10 p.m. ■ *Other services:* Hopewell Animal Hospital, (845) 221-PETS (7387).

West 3.1 miles *via* N.Y. 52 to ■ *Lodging:* Inn at Arbor Ridge, 17 Route 376 & Route 52, Hopewell Junction, NY 12533, (866) 767-0285, $87–$110; smoke-free hotel, spa tub, WiFi, pet-friendly. ■ *Groceries:* Blue Hill Deli & Food Mart, (845) 592-2373, short-term resupply, open 24 hrs. ■ *Restaurant:* Smoke Haus & Deli, (845) 221-9195, all-day B, specialty sandwiches, burgers, BBQ, M–Sa 6–6, Su 7–3.

N.Y. 52—**East** 0.3 mile to ■ *Groceries:* Mountain Top Market Deli, (845) 221-0928, (short-term resupply), daily 6 a.m.–8 p.m., daily specials and hot sandwiches, water for hikers on faucet at side of building. ■ *Restaurant:* Danny's Pizzeria, open at 11:30 T–F, noon Sa–M, hikers might have to wait/eat outside.

West 1.8 miles to **Stormville, N.Y. [P.O. ZIP 12582: M–F 8:30–5, Sa 9–12; (845) 226-2627].**

West 2.5 miles *via* Old N.Y. 52 to ■ *Groceries:* Shell Food Mart (short-term resupply). ■ *Restaurant:* Stormville Pizza, M–Sa 11–9:30, Su 12–9.

Morgan Stewart Shelter (1984)—Sleeps 6. Privy. Water source is a well with a pump located downhill and in front of the shelter.

N.Y. 55—**West** 1.5 miles to ■ *Restaurant:* Pleasant Ridge Pizza, L/D, M–Sa 10:30–10, Su 11–9; A&A Deli, M–F 6–7, Su 8–3. ■ *Other services:* Total Care pharmacy; Dutchess County Bus, (845) 473-8424, Route E runs M–Sa from Poughkeepsie to Pawling along N.Y. 55, stopping at A&A Deli (juntion of Route 216) and Stop & Shop (see Poughquag), with possible flag stop at the A.T. crossing of N.Y. 55 near the Nuclear Lake parking area (fare $1.75 one-way; see schedule and route map at <www.dutchessny.gov>).

West 3.1 miles to **Poughquag, N.Y. [P.O. ZIP 12570: M–F 8:30–1 & 2–5, Sa 8:30–12:30; (845) 724-4763].**
■ *Groceries:* Stop & Shop, daily 7–9 (long-term resupply); Cumberland Farms; Shell Mini-Mart;

Clove Valley Deli (short-term resupply). ■ *Restaurants:* Beekman Square Diner, Brothers Trattoria, Great Wall Chinese, Ramblers Roost Irish Bar & Restaurant, Dunkin' Donuts. ■ *Other services:* Beekman Animal Hospital, (845) 724-8387.

Nuclear Lake—The site of a nuclear fuels-processing research facility until 1972. After the Park Service acquired the lands, the buildings were razed, and the area was tested and given a clean bill of health, allowing the Trail to be rerouted along the shore.

Telephone Pioneers Shelter (1988)—Sleeps 6. Privy. Built with the assistance of the White Plains Council of the Telephone Pioneers of America. Water source is the stream crossed by the side trail leading to the shelter.

County 20/West Dover Road—East 3.1 miles to **Pawling, N.Y. [P.O. ZIP 12564: M–F 8:30–5, Sa 9–12; (845) 855-2669].** Northbounders might want to hike 2.4 miles more to N.Y. 22 for easier access. ■ *Lodging:* Station Inn, (845) 266-6262, <www.stationinnpawling.com>, 7 Memorial Ave., Pawling, NY 12564, $219–$219 for room with queen or king bed and private bath, free Netflix, WiFi. ■ *Camping:* The town allows hikers to camp in its Edward R. Murrow Memorial Park, 1 mile from the town center on West Main. The park offers lake swimming, restroom. No dogs permitted. Two-night maximum. ■ *Groceries:* Hannaford, 2 miles south from town center on Rt. 22 (long-term resupply); La Guadalupana Mini-Mart and CVS (both short-term resupply). ■ *Restaurants:* Vinny's Deli & Pasta, Village Pizza, Gaudino Pizzeria, Great Wall Chinese, Tap House Tavern, McKinney & Doyle, Corner Bakery. ■ *Other services:* Pawling Taxi, (845) 855-8585; doctor; dentist; coin laundry; banks with ATM; pharmacy; Pawling Animal Clinic; Metro-North train service to NYC, <www.mta.info/mnr> or call (877) 690-5114 for fare and schedule; Dutchess County Bus, (845) 473-8424, Route E runs M–Sa from Poughkeepsie to Pawling and Wingdale along N.Y. 55, stopping at Pawling Chamber of Commerce and Hannaford, $1.75 one way (see schedule and route map at <www.dutchessny.gov>). ■ *Internet access:* Pawling Free Library, 11 Broad St., Tu–Th 12–8, F 12–5, Sa 10–4, Su 12-4 (except Jul–Aug). *Please leave packs and poles outside or in the hallway.*

Edward R. Morrow Memorial Park

Lakeside Dr

Pawling, N.Y.
elevation 461´

Station Inn
La Guadalupana
Corner Bakery
Tap House Tavern
McKinney & Doyle
Cleanery Laundry
Great Wall II
Vinny's Deli
CVS

W Main St

Post Office
Library

Post Office to:
Memorial Park (1.2 mi)

Hannaford (2.0 mi)

Dover Oak—On the north side of West Dover Road, reportedly the largest oak tree on the A.T. Its girth 4 feet from the ground is more than 20 feet, 4 inches; estimated to be more than 300 years old.

N.Y. 22/Appalachian Trail Railroad Station. *Other services:* Native Landscapes & Garden Center; 991 Route 22, Pawling, NY 12564, (845) 855-7050; owner Pete Muroski, a hiker and hiker-friendly offers free outdoor shower, use of restrooms; mail drops accepted. Snacks, cold drinks, and limited hiker supplies, including canister fuel. Open Apr 1–Dec 24 9–5; limited access other months.

East 0.6 mile to *Camping and Groceries:* Tony's Deli (short-term resupply), open M–Sa 4 a.m.–midnight, Su 5 a.m.–midnight, offers camping ($2PP), water, and 24-hour bathroom.

East 2.6 miles to Pawling (see County 20/West Dover Rd. above).

West 2.6 miles to ■ *Lodging:* Dutchess Motor Lodge, (845) 832-6400, 1512 N.Y. 22, Wingdale, NY 12594, $90S/D including weekends, max. 2 hikers/room, $7 laundry, no pets, WiFi, possible free pick-up from Trail and shuttles for fee (call for availability), accepts packages marked "Hold for Hiker" with name and ETA. ■ *Groceries:* Ben's Deli (short-term resupply). ■ *Restaurants:* Big W's Roadside BBQ, W–Su, 12–8; Pizza Express, Su–Th 11–9, F–Sa 11–11. ■ *Other services:* Dutchess County Bus, (845) 473-8424, Route E runs M–Sa from Poughkeepsie to Pawling and Wingdale along

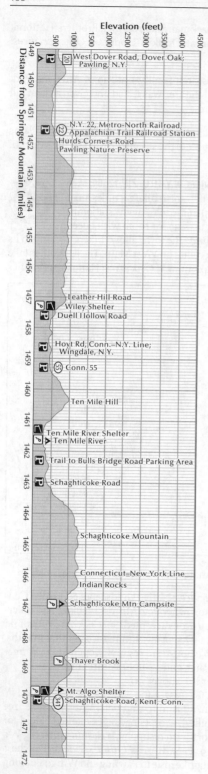

Elevation (feet)

Distance from Springer Mountain (miles)

West Dover Road, Dover Oak; Pawling, N.Y.

N.Y. 22, Metro-North Railroad; Appalachian Trail Railroad Station Hurds Corners Road Pawling Nature Preserve

Leather-Hill-Road
Wiley Shelter
Duell Hollow Road

Hoyt Rd, Conn.–N.Y. Line; Wingdale, N.Y.

Conn. 55

Ten Mile Hill

Ten Mile River Shelter
Ten Mile River

Trail to Bulls Bridge Road Parking Area

Schaghticoke-Road

Schaghticoke Mountain

Connecticut–New York Line
Indian Rocks

Schaghticoke Mtn Campsite

Thayer Brook

Mt. Algo Shelter
Schaghticoke Road, Kent, Conn.

N.Y. 55/N.Y. 22, stopping at Big W's BBQ and Cousin's Café (see Hoyt Road below). Fare is $1.75 one-way; see <www.dutchessny.gov>.

West 4 miles to Wingdale (see Hoyt Road below).

Commuter Train—On the south side of N.Y. 22, the Trail passes the A.T. station of Metro-North, a New York City commuter train, (877) 690-5116, <www.mta.info/mnr>. Trains leave the platform on Sa and Su at 2:35 p.m., 4:35 p.m., and 6:35 p.m. and arrive at Grand Central Terminal 2¼ hours later. Trains leave Grand Central at 7:10 a.m. and 9:10 a.m. on Sa and Su and arrive at the A.T. platform 2¼ hours later. Fares vary, peak/off-peak, one-way/round-trip, and range from $18 one way to $46 round-trip. Weekday, additional weekend services available to New York City from stations in nearby Pawling and Harlen Valley–Wingdale.

Pawling Nature Reserve Trails—**West** 0.9 mile to ■ *Lodging:* Dutchess Motor Lodge. ■ *Groceries:* Ben's Deli. ■ Restaurants: Big W's Roadside BBQ, Pizza Express (See N.Y. 22 above). The A.T. meets the Green Trail of the Pawling Nature Reserve 2.5 miles north of Hurds Corners Road. Follow the Green Trail 0.9 mile to its end (with the final 0.1 mile blazed orange) at Furlong Road. Go 1 block west to reach N.Y. 22; turn right for lodging, deli, and restaurants. Continue north 1.7 miles to reach Wingdale (below).

Wiley Shelter (1940; renovated 2014)—Sleeps 6. Privy. Renovated as part of an Eagle Scout project. Water source is a pump 0.1 mile north of the shelter on the A.T. beyond tent platform; treat the water.

Hoyt Road—**West** 3.3 miles *via* Hoyt Road and N.Y. 55 to **Wingdale, N.Y. [P.O. ZIP 12594: M–F 8–12:30 & 1:30–5, Sa 8–12:30; (845) 832-6147]**. To reach Harlem Valley–Wingdale Metro-North Train Station, continue south on N.Y. 22 for about one mile. ■ *Groceries:* Wingdale Super Market with ATM and deli (short-term resupply). ■ *Restaurants:* Cousin's Pizza; Peking Kitchen; Cousin's Café; Dunkin Donuts. ■ *Other services:* Dover Plains Library, M–F 10–8, Sa 10–4, Internet access; Wingdale Hardware, limited fuel and camping supplies; Dutchess County Bus, (845) 473-8424, Route E runs M–Sa from Poughkeepsie to Pawling and Wingdale along N.Y. 55/N.Y. 22, stopping at Big W's BBQ and Cousin's Café; $1.75 one way (see <www.dutchessny.gov>).

West 4.7 miles to ■ *Lodging:* Dutchess Motor Lodge. ■ *Groceries:* Ben's Deli; ■ *Restaurants:* Big W's Roadside BBQ, Pizza Express.

Connecticut

Miles from Springer	Miles to Next Point	Features	Services	Elev	Miles from Katahdin	M A P
1,458.6	0.7	New York–Connecticut State Line; Hoyt Road *West–3.3m to* **Wingdale, N.Y., P.O. 12594** *West–4.7m to* Dutchess Motor Lodge and restaurants	R, P G, M, T, f L, M	400'	734.4	
1,459.3	1.1	Conn. 55 *East–2.5m to* **Gaylordsville, Conn., P.O. 06755**	R, P G, M	580'	733.7	
1,460.4	1.0	Ten Mile Hill		1,000'	732.6	
1,461.4	0.2	**Ten Mile River Shelter** ...*4mS; 8.4mN*	S, w	290'	731.6	
1,461.6	0.7	Ten Mile River ...*footbridge*	C, w	280'	731.4	
1,462.3	0.7	Bulls Bridge Road; side Ttrail to Bulls Bridge parking area *(E–0.2m)* *East–0.5m to* Country Market	R, P G	450'	730.7	
1,463.0	1.7	Schaghticoke Road	R, P	320'	730.0	
1,464.7	1.2	Schaghticoke Mountain		1,331'	728.3	
1,465.9	0.4	Connecticut–New York State Line		1,250'	727.1	
1,466.3	0.6	Indian Rocks		1,290'	726.7	ATC Mass.–Conn. Map 4
1,466.9	1.9	Schaghticoke Mountain Campsite	C, w	950'	726.1	
1,468.8	1.0	Thayer Brook	w	900'	724.2	
1,469.8	0.3	**Mt. Algo Shelter** ...*8.4mS; 7.3mN*	S, C, w	655'	723.2	
1,470.1	2.8	Conn. 341, Schaghticoke Road *East–0.8m to* **Kent, Conn., P.O. 06757** *East–3.3m to* Cooper Creek B&B	R, P G, L, M, D, f, sh L	350'	722.9	
1,472.9	0.7	Skiff Mountain Road	R	850'	720.1	
1,473.6	0.7	Caleb's Peak		1,160'	719.4	
1,474.3	0.5	St. Johns Ledges		900'	718.7	
1,474.8	2.3	River Road ...*southern jct.*	R, P	480'	718.2	
1,477.1	0.4	**Stewart Hollow Brook Shelter** ...*7.3mS; 10mN*	S, C, w	400'	715.9	
1,477.5	2.0	Stony Brook Campsite	C, w	440'	715.5	
1,479.5	0.8	River Road ...*spring*	R, P, w	460'	713.5	
1,480.3	0.9	Silver Hill Campsite ...*swing, water pump*	C, w	1,000'	712.7	
1,481.2	0.1	Conn. 4 *East–0.9m to* **Cornwall Bridge, Conn., P.O. 06754** *East–1.9m to* Housatonic Meadows State Park	R G, L, M, O, V, f C, sh	700'	711.8	
1,481.3	0.1	Guinea Brook ...*road bypass in high-water*		650'	711.7	Mass.–Conn. Map 3
1,481.4	1.2	Old Sharon Road	R	750'	711.6	
1,482.6	0.7	Hatch Brook		880'	710.4	
1,483.3	0.4	Pine Knob Loop Trail ...*Housatonic Meadows SP (E–0.9m)*	C, sh	1,150'	709.7	
1,483.7	2.2	Caesar Road, Caesar Brook Campsite	R, C, w	760'	709.3	
1,485.9	0.1	Carse Brook	w	810'	707.1	

Miles from Springer	Miles to Next Point	Features	Services	Elev	Miles from Katahdin	M A P
1,486.0	1.1	West Cornwall Road *East–2.2m to* **West Cornwall, Conn., P.O. 06796** *West–4.7m to* **Sharon, Conn., P.O. 06069**	R, P H, G, L, O G, L, M, D, cl	800'	707.0	
1,487.1	0.9	**Pine Swamp Brook Shelter** *...10mS; 11.8mN*	S, C, w	1,075'	705.9	
1,488.0	0.3	Mt. Easter Road	R	1,150'	705.0	
1,488.3	1.2	Mt. Easter		1,350'	704.7	
1,489.5	0.8	Sharon Mountain Campsite	C, w	1,200'	703.5	
1,490.3	2.0	Hang Glider View		1,150'	702.7	
1,492.3	0.4	Belter's Campsite	C, w	770'	700.7	
1,492.7	0.6	U.S. 7, Conn. 112	R, P	520'	700.3	
1,493.3	0.1	U.S. 7, Warren Turnpike, Housatonic River bridge *East–0.2m to* Mountainside Cafe	R, P M	500'	699.7	
1,493.4	1.8	Mohawk Trail Junction *(E–0.2m to Mountain-side Cafe)*	M	500'	699.6	
1,495.2	0.1	Water Street, Hydroelectric Plant *East–0.5m to* **Falls Village, Conn., P.O. 06031**	R, P, C, w, sh C, M	530'	697.8	
1,495.3	0.3	Iron Bridge *...Housatonic River, picnic area*	R, P	510'	697.7	
1,495.6	0.8	Housatonic River Road *...Great Falls*	R, P	650'	697.4	
1,496.4	1.3	Spring	w	750'	696.6	
1,497.7	0.7	Prospect Mountain		1,475'	695.3	
1,498.4	0.1	**Limestone Spring Shelter** *(W–0.5m) ...11.8mS; 7.9mN*	S, C, w	980'	694.6	
1,498.5	0.5	Rand's View		1,250'	694.5	
1,499.0	0.3	Giant's Thumb *...rock formation*		1,220'	694.0	
1,499.3	2.8	Billy's View		1,150'	693.7	
1,502.1	0.7	U.S. 44 *West–0.4m to* **Salisbury, Conn., P.O. 06088** *West–2.4m to* Lakeville, Conn.	R, H G, L, M, f L, M, cl, f	700'	690.9	
1,502.8	2.2	Conn. 41, Under Mountain Road *West–0.4m to* **Salisbury, Conn., P.O. 06088** *West–2.4m to* Lakeville, Conn	R, P, H G, L, M, f L, M, cl, f	720'	690.2	
1,505.0	0.8	Lions Head		1,738'	688.0	
1,505.8	0.6	**Riga Shelter** *...7.9mS; 1.2mN*	S, C, w	1,610'	687.2	
1,506.4	0.6	Ball Brook Group Campsite	C, w	1,650'	686.6	
1,507.0	0.5	**Brassie Brook Shelter**, Brassie Brook *(south branch) ...1.2mS; 8.4mN*	S, C, w	1,705'	686.0	
1,507.5	0.2	Undermountain Trail, Riga Junction *East–1.9m to* Conn. 41	R, P	1,820'	685.5	
1,507.7	0.3	Bear Mountain Road	R	1,920'	685.3	
1,508.0	1.1	Bear Mountain *...rock observation tower*		2,316'	685.0	
1,509.1	0.1	Connecticut–Massachusetts State Line		1,800'	683.9	

ATC Mass.–Conn. Map 3

Campfires are prohibited on the Trail in Connecticut, and camping is permitted only at designated sites. Ridgerunners patrol the state's 51 A.T. miles and serve as caretakers at Sages Ravine campsite.

Southbounders and northbounders pass each other regularly now. Southbounders should consider the hunting seasons and the need to wear bright "blaze" orange. If hiking with a four-footed friend, keep its safety in mind, too.

AMC–Connecticut Chapter—The Trails Committee of the AMC–Connecticut Chapter maintains the 51.2 miles from the New York–Connecticut state line to Sages Ravine, just across the Massachusetts line. The club can be reached at (413) 528-6333; <www.ct-amc.org>.

 Conn. 55—East 2.5 miles to **Gaylordsville, Conn. [P.O. ZIP 06755: M–F 8–1 & 2–5, Sa 8–12; (860) 354-9727].** ■ *Groceries:* Gaylordsville Country Store, (860) 350-3802 (short-term resupply), M–F 6–8, Sa 6–6, Su 6–3, with deli, ATM. ■ *Restaurants:* Alfredo's Restaurant and Pizza, (860) 355-2448; Gaylordsville Diner, (860) 210-1622; The Old Oak Tavern, (860) 355-1100.

Ten Mile River Shelter (1996)—Sleeps 6. Privy. Tentsites at nearby campsite. Water source is a hand pump 100 feet south and west of the shelter.

Bulls Bridge Road—East 0.5 mile to Country Market (short-term resupply) with ATM and Internet access.

Indian Rocks—Half a mile north of the only place along the entire A.T. where the Trail (for a short piece) crosses an Indian reservation. Most of the land from here down to the river is claimed by the Schaghticoke tribe, recognized by the state and briefly by the federal government. The tribe, actually the remnants of several tribes, played a unique communications role during the Revolutionary War by transmitting signals along the ridges between Long Island Sound in N.Y. and Stockbridge, Mass., a distance of nearly 100 miles, in about 2 hours.

Mt. Algo Shelter (1986)—Sleeps 6. Privy. Bear box. Water source is on blue-blaze leading to shelter, 15 yards in front of shelter.

Conn. 341—East 0.8 mile to **Kent, Conn. [P.O. ZIP 06757: M–F 8–1 & 2–5, Sa 8:30–12:30; (860) 927-3435].** ■ *Lodging:* Fife 'n Drum Inn & Restaurant, (860) 927-3509, <www.fifendrum.com>, restaurant M–Th (closed Tu) 11:30–9:30, F–Sa 11:30–10, Su 11:30–8:30, $140D plus tax weekdays, $170D plus tax weekends, $25+EAP, no dogs, call for reservations; Starbuck Inn, (860) 927-1788, <www.starbuckinn.com>, $189-$250D plus tax, includes full B, check-in 4 p.m., check-out 11 a.m. ■ *Groceries:* Davis IGA (long-term resupply); Kent Market (short-term resupply), with deli sandwiches, open daily 8–6. ■ *Restaurants:* Kent Pizza Garden, L/D, 11–10; Villager Restaurant, open daily 6 a.m.–11 p.m. ■ *Outfitter:* Sundog Shoe and Leather, <sundogshoe@aol.com>, (860) 927-0009, 10% thru-hiker discount, boots, socks, insoles, M–Sa 10–5, Su 12–5. ■ *Internet*

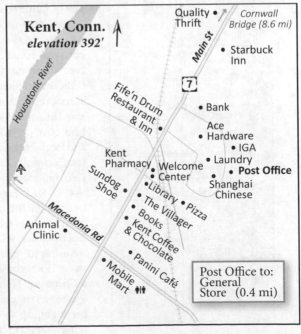

Kent, Conn.
elevation 392'

Housatonic River

Main St

Quality Thrift

Cornwall Bridge (8.6 mi)

Starbuck Inn

7

Bank

Ace Hardware

IGA

Fife 'n Drum Restaurant & Inn

Kent Pharmacy

Welcome Center

Laundry

Post Office

Sundog Shoe

Library

Shanghai Chinese

The Villager

Pizza

Books

Kent Coffee & Chocolate

Macedonia Rd

Animal Clinic

Panini Café

Mobile Mart

Post Office to: General Store (0.4 mi)

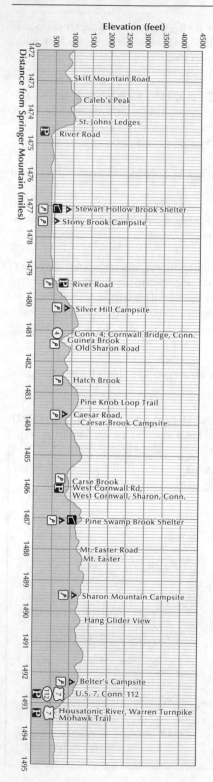

access: Kent Memorial Library, M–F 10–5:30, Sa 12–4. ■ *Other services:* showers (coin-op) and restrooms at the Welcome Center; banks with ATM; doctor; dentist; pharmacy; House of Books, open daily, with guides, maps, fax, UPS and FedEx services.

North 3.3 miles *via* U.S. 7 to *Lodging:* Cooper Creek B&B, (860) 927-4334. Hiker rate Su–Th $95, includes shuttle to Kent and B. No mail drops, no pets; check in at 3 p.m.; shuttle to and from Kent; slackpacking for guests; out-of-area shuttles (Wassaic, N.Y., train station, airports) with advance notice.

Stewart Hollow Brook Shelter (1980s)—Sleeps 6. Privy. Bear box. Water source is reliable Stony Brook, 0.4 mile north of the shelter on the A.T.

Silver Hill Campsite—Campsite, privy, swing, and pavilion sheltering two picnic tables. Water pump.

Mohawk Trail—The former A.T. route starts north of Guinea Brook on the A.T., passes through Cornwall Bridge, and returns near Falls Village.

Conn. 4—East 0.9 mile to **Cornwall Bridge, Conn. [P.O. ZIP 06754: M–F 8:30–1 & 2–5, Sa 9–12; (860) 672-6710].** ■ *Lodging:* Hitching Post Motel, (860) 672-6219, $65D and up weekdays, $85D and up weekends, $15EAP, laundry service $5 and up, shuttle available depending on staffing; Housatonic Meadows Lodge B&B, (860) 672-6067, $110; Cornwall Inn & Restaurant, open year-round, (800) 786-6884, <www.cornwallinn.com>, hiker rate $125D, $150 for 4 in room with 2 queen beds, includes continental B, pool, hot tub, Internet access, restaurant and lounge open Th–Su, L/D $8–$30; The Amselhaus, (860) 248-3155, <www.theamselhaus.com>, $85S, $100D, $50EAP TO 6, includes laundry and local shuttles, longer shuttles available. ■ *Groceries:* Cornwall Country Market (short-term resupply), (860) 619-8199, deli, bakery, coffee, B, and more; M–F 6–5, Sa–Su 7–5. ■ *Outfitter:* Housatonic River Outfitters, 24 Kent Rd., (860) 672-1010, <hflyshop@aol.com>, open 7 days 9–5, limited hiker gear, canister fuel and fuel by ounce, will accept UPS and FedEx but not responsible for packages. ■ *Other services:* hardware store; Housatonic Veterinary Care, (860) 672-4948. ■ *Camping:* Housatonic Meadows State Park, (860) 672-6772, 1 mile north of town on U.S. 7. Campsite $36 per night, up to 6 per site; open mid-Apr to Jan 1, water shut off Oct 15. The park may be self-service in midweek; registration information at the main cabin by the gate. Showers free but check with registration desk; no pets, no alcoholic beverages allowed. Accessible from the A.T. *via* Pine Knob Loop Trail (see below).

Guinea Brook—The AMC Connecticut Chapter installed stepping stones in the brook. In heavy rain, you may want to take the bypass: Northbounders should turn east on Conn. 4 and go downhill to unpaved Old Sharon Road on the north, which rejoins the A.T. on the other side of the stream. Southbounders should turn east on the dirt road that the Trail crosses before the brook, then follow it to Conn. 4, and turn south.

Pine Knob Loop Trail—Housatonic Meadows State Park (see above) can be reached from the A.T. by taking the blue-blazed Pine Knob Loop Trail 0.5 mile to U.S. 7, then following the highway north for 0.4 mile. You can return to the A.T. *via* the Pine Knob Loop Trail.

West Cornwall Road—**East** 2.2 miles to **West Cornwall, Conn. [P.O. ZIP 06796: M–F 8:30–12 & 2–4:30, Sa 9–12; (860) 672-6791]**, site of a historical covered bridge over a whitewater section of the Housatonic River. ■ *Lodging:* Bearded Woods 'One-of-a-Kind' Bunk & Dine, (860) 480-2966, <www.beardedwoods.com>. Hudson and Big Lu mentor hikers and offer accommodations in their home, $50PP cash or PayPal; includes clean bunk with linens, showers with amenities, communal laundry with loaner clothes, a hearty B (D for 5 or more guests, $10PP), and shuttles to/from the Trail and the local P.O. Call or text Hudson for reservations (no walk-ins); 1–6 p.m.. Will pick up from West Cornwall, Falls Village, or Salisbury; ID required. Free slackpacking between those locations with second-night stay; longer shuttles of any distance for a fee. Soda, pizza, snacks, and stove fuel available for purchase. Not a party place, no pets, no mail drops. Open 7 days a week in May, weekends only (F–Su) Jun–Sep; limited services may be available after those dates.

West 4.7 miles to **Sharon, Conn. [P.O. ZIP 06069: M–F 9:30–4:30, Sa 9:30–12:30; (860) 364-5306]**, with a supermarket, restaurant serving B/L/D, laundry, motel, bank with ATM, pharmacy, and hospital.

Pine Swamp Brook Shelter (1989)—Sleeps 6. Privy. Bear box. Water is available on the blue-blazed trail.

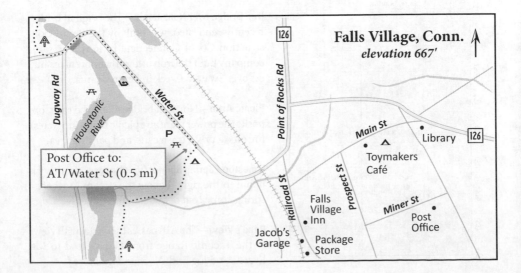

Falls Village, Conn.
elevation 667'

Dugway Rd

Housatonic River

Water St

Point of Rocks Rd

Post Office to:
AT/Water St (0.5 mi)

Main St

Library

Toymakers Café

Railroad St

Prospect St

Falls Village Inn

Miner St

Post Office

Jacob's Garage

Package Store

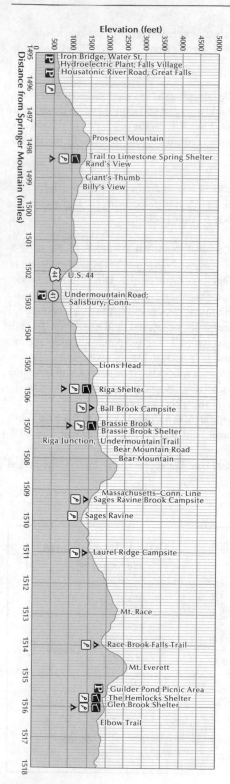

Elevation (feet)

Distance from Springer Mountain (miles)

- Iron Bridge, Water St, Hydroelectric Plant; Falls Village.
- Housatonic River Road, Great Falls
- Prospect Mountain
- Trail to Limestone Spring Shelter
- Rand's View
- Giant's Thumb
- Billy's View
- U.S. 44
- Undermountain Road; Salisbury, Conn.
- Lions Head
- Riga Shelter
- Ball Brook Campsite
- Brassie Brook
- Brassie Brook Shelter
- Riga Junction, Undermountain Trail
- Bear Mountain Road
- Bear Mountain
- Massachusetts–Conn. Line
- Sages Ravine Brook Campsite
- Sages Ravine
- Laurel-Ridge Campsite
- Mt. Race
- Race-Brook-Falls-Trail
- Mt. Everett
- Guilder Pond Picnic Area
- The Hemlocks Shelter
- Glen Brook Shelter
- Elbow Trail

U.S. 7/Warren Turnpike—*Restaurant:* Mountainside Café, (860) 824-7876, 7–3. After crossing Housatonic River and before Trail turns left on Warren Turnpike at high school, cross bridge over railroad tracks, then continue 0.2 mile.

Mohawk Trail—**East** 0.2 mile to Mountainside Café (above).

Water Street—**East** 0.5 mile to **Falls Village, Conn. [P.O. ZIP 06031: M–F 8:30–1 & 2–5, Sa 8:30–12; (860) 824-7781].** ■ *Restaurants:* Toymakers Café, (860) 824-8168, B/L, Th–Su 6:30–2:30, free tentsites, water, power, pizza delivery; Falls Village Inn, upscale but hiker-friendly, L/D but no lodging. ■ *Other services:* Falls Village Package Store, (860) 824-7971, open M–Sa 9–8, Su noon–5; has sodas and hiker snacks, allows hikers to charge phones, get water, and use phone to call area restaurants; bank with ATM at corner of Rtes. 7 & 126.

Hydroelectric Plant—Cold shower and water are available outside the small, vine-covered building past the transformer. Look for silver shower head poking through ivy, with a small concrete pad below. Water faucet is below shower head.

Wheelchair-accessible trail—The A.T. hooks up with the River Trail, converted to create a handicap-accessible loop trail using part of the A.T. and an old racetrack.

Iron Bridge over Housatonic—The original bridge, recently renovated, was built by the Berlin Construction Co. of Connecticut in 1903. The same company built the iron bridge that now takes hikers over Swatara Creek in Pennsylvania.

Picnic Area—North of bridge along the river, opposite the power plant, are picnic tables (no water), fire pits, a privy, trash cans, and parking area.

Limestone Spring Shelter (1986)—Sleeps 6. Privy is uphill to the right. Follow the stream to where a spring comes out of a small limestone cave.

Rand's View—The A.T. passes this vista, with views of the Taconic Range from Lion's Head to Mt. Everett and Jug End. *No camping allowed.*

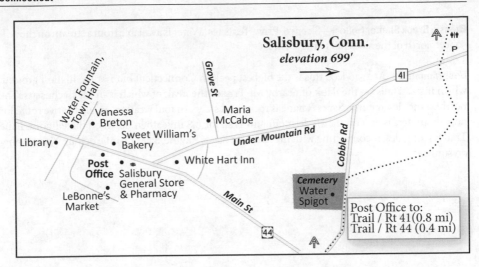

Salisbury, Conn.
elevation 699'

U.S. 44 — West 0.4 mile to **Salisbury, Conn. [P.O. ZIP 06068: M–F 8:30–1 & 2–5, Sa 9–12; (860) 435-5072]**. For northbounders, turn west on U.S. 44 to town. For southbounders, it is best to follow Conn. 41, Under Mountain Road, 0.8 mile into town. Water is available from a fountain at town hall and also from a spigot in the cemetery on Cobble Road (located behind a large cement cross about 200 feet right of the maintenance shed). ■ *Lodging:* Maria McCabe offers rooms to hikers in her home, 4 Grove St., (860) 435-0593, $35PP, includes shower, use of living room, cooking outside, pets outside (no fee), no visitors in home, cash only, shuttle to laundry, mail drops accepted for guests. Vanessa Breton, 7 The Lockup Rd., (860) 435-9577, offers 3 rooms in her home for up to 5 hikers, $40PP, includes shower, laundry $5, use of living room, cooking outside, pets outside (no fee), no visitors in home, cash only, mail drops accepted for guests. Sassafras Bed & Breakfast, 171 Canaan Rd., Salisbury, CT 06068, text (860) 307-3751; guest shuttle service from U.S. 7/Warren Turnpike, Mohawk Trail East, Water Street East, 0.7 mile from U.S. 44W, U.S. 41W on Under Mountain Road. Mail drops accepted for guests; credit cards accepted. Room for 2 or 3 with private shower, laundry, full local B, $65–$100PP; same-day shuttle, indoor shower and laundry with return to Trail, $45. Several other inns and B&Bs in the area. ■ *Groceries:* LaBonne's Epicure Market, (860) 435-2559 (long-term resupply), M–Sa, open 8–7, Su until 6. ■ *Restaurants:* Sweet William's Bakery, (860) 435-8889, baked goods, coffee, 7–5. ■ *Internet access:* Scoville Memorial Library, M–F 9–5. ■ *Other services:* Salisbury General Store and Pharmacy (short-term resupply, including fuel), (860) 435-9388, M–F 8–6, Sa 8–5, Su 8–4 (pharmacy closed Su); bank with ATM; The Auto Shop, Coleman fuel and denatured alcohol. When open, town hall offers restroom and phone inside.

West 2.4 miles to **Lakeville**. ■ *Restaurants:* Mizza's Restaurant and Pizza, (860) 435-6266, free delivery; On the Run Coffee Shop, (860) 435-2007, open every day 5:30 a.m.–2 p.m. ■ *Other services:* hardware store, Washboard laundry open 24 hrs., bank with ATM.

Conn. 41 (Under Mountain Road) — West 0.8 mile to Salisbury (see previous entry).

Riga Shelter (1990) — Sleeps 6. Privy, tentsites, platform. The only shelter in Connecticut with a view. It opens to the east, providing sunrise views. Water is a spring on a blue-blazed trail to the left of the clearing at the A.T. A second source is where the trail to the shelter crosses a small stream. Spring may not run in dry years.

Brassie Brook Shelter (1980s)—Sleeps 6. Privy. Tentsites. Water is available from a stream on the A.T. 50 feet north of the side trail to the shelter.

Bear Mountain—At 2,316 feet, this is the highest peak in Connecticut but not the highest ground, which instead falls on the flank of nearby Mt. Frissel, the peak of which is in Massachusetts. The northbound descent into Sages Ravine is rocky and steep. In foul weather, an alternative route for northbounders is east on the Undermountain Trail for 0.8 mile, then north on the Paradise Lane Trail for 2.1 miles, reconnecting with the A.T. near Sages Ravine, a net 1.7-mile detour. No camping on summit.

Massachusetts

Miles from Springer	Miles to Next Point	Features	Services	Elev	Miles from Katahdin	M A P
1,509.1	0.1	Connecticut–Massachusetts State Line		1,800'	683.9	
1,509.2	0.6	Sages Ravine Brook Campsite	C, w	1,360'	683.8	
1,509.8	1.2	Sages Ravine	w	1,340'	683.2	
1,511.0	1.9	Laurel Ridge Campsite	C, w	1,750'	682.0	
1,512.9	1.1	Mt. Race ...*open ledges*		2,365'	680.1	
1,514.0	0.7	Race Brook Trail, campsite *(E–0.2m)* stream *(E–0.4m)* *East–2.5m to* Mass. 41	C, w R, P	1,950'	679.0	
1,514.7	0.7	Mt. Everett		2,602'	678.3	
1,515.4	0.4	Guilder Pond Picnic Area	R, P	2,042'	677.6	ATC Mass.–Conn. Map 3
1,515.8	0.1	**The Hemlocks Shelter** ...*8.4mS; 0.1mN*	S, w	1,880'	677.2	
1,515.9	0.6	**Glen Brook Shelter** ...*0.1mS; 14.3mN*	S, C, w	1,885'	677.1	
1,516.5	1.7	Elbow Trail		1,750'	676.5	
1,518.2	1.1	Jug End		1,750'	674.8	
1,519.3	0.9	Jug End Road (Curtiss Road) *(E–0.25m spring)*	R, P, w	890'	673.7	
1,520.2	1.8	Mass. 41; Undermountain Road *West–0.1m to* April Hill Conservation Ctr *West–1.2m to* **South Egremont, Mass., P.O. 01258**	R w M	810'	672.8	
1,522.0	1.8	Sheffield–Egremont Road; Shays' Rebellion Monument	R, P	700'	671.0	
1,523.8	0.9	U.S. 7 *East–3.2m to* **Sheffield, Mass., P.O. 01257** *West–1.5m to* Guido's Fresh Marketplace; Big Y *West–1.8m to* **Great Barrington, Mass., P.O. 01230** *West–2.8 to* shopping center	R B, g, L, M G, M all G, cl, f	700'	669.2	
1,524.7	2.0	Kellogg Road, Housatonic River Bridge	R, P	720'	668.3	
1,526.7	1.4	Home Road	R, P	1,150'	666.3	
1,528.1	2.1	East Mountain	w	1,800'	664.9	
1,530.2	1.1	**Ice Gulch; Tom Leonard Shelter** *(E–0.2m stream)* ...*14.3mS; 5.3mN*	S, w	1,540'	662.8	
1,531.3	0.9	Lake Buel Road	R, P	1,150'	661.7	
1,532.2	1.2	Mass. 23 *East–4.3m to* **Monterey, Mass., P.O. 01245** *West–1.6m to* East Mountain Retreat Ctr *West–4m to* **Great Barrington, Mass., P.O. 01230**	R, P H all	1,050'	660.8	ATC Mass.–Conn. Map 2
1,533.4	0.8	Blue Hill Road (Stony Brook Road)	R, P	1,550'	659.6	
1,534.2	0.6	Benedict Pond *(W–0.5m)*, Beartown State Forest	C, w	1,620'	658.8	
1,534.8	0.8	The Ledges		1,820'	658.2	
1,535.6	1.7	**Mt. Wilcox South Shelter** ...*5.3mS; 2.1mN*	S, w	1,720'	657.4	
1,537.3	0.6	**Mt. Wilcox North Shelter** *(E–0.3m)* ...*2.1mS; 14.8mN*	S, w	2,100'	655.7	
1,537.9	3.2	Beartown Mountain Road	R, w	1,800'	655.1	
1,541.1	0.3	Fernside Road/Jerusalem Road	R, P	1,200'	651.9	

Miles from Springer	*Miles to Next Point*	Features	Services	Elev	Miles from Katahdin	M A P
1,541.4	1.5	Shaker Campsite	C, w	1,000'	651.6	
1,542.9	0.5	Tyringham Cobble		1,240'	650.1	
1,543.4	1.1	Jerusalem Road ...*spring* *West–0.6m to* Tyringham, Mass., P.O. 01264	R, P, w, g L, w	930'	649.6	
1,544.5	1.9	Tyringham Main Road *(W–1.1m to town)*	R, P, L, w	930'	648.5	
1,546.4	2.4	Webster Road	R, P, w	1,800'	646.6	
1,548.8	1.9	Goose Pond Road	R, P	1,650'	644.2	
1,550.7	0.5	Upper Goose Pond	w	1,500'	642.3	
1,551.2	0.3	Old chimney and plaque		1,520'	641.8	
1,551.5	1.2	**Upper Goose Pond Cabin** *(W–0.5m)* ...14.8mS; 9.3mN	S, C, w	1,480'	641.5	ATC Mass.–Conn. Map 2
1,552.7	0.1	I-90 Massachusetts Turnpike ...*overpass*	R	1,400'	640.3	
1,552.8	0.3	Greenwater Brook	w	1,400'	640.2	
1,553.1	0.8	U.S. 20 *East–0.1m to* Berkshire Lakeside Lodge *West–5m to* Lee, Mass., P.O. 01238	R, P L all	1,400'	639.9	
1,553.9	0.5	Tyne Road	R, P	1,750'	639.1	
1,554.4	1.8	Becket Mountain		2,180'	638.6	
1,556.2	2.3	Finerty Pond	w	1,900'	636.8	
1,558.5	0.2	County Road	R, P	1,850'	634.5	
1,558.7	1.6	Bald Top		2,040'	634.3	
1,560.3	0.7	**October Mountain Shelter** ...9.3mS; 9mN	S, C, w	1,950'	632.7	
1,561.0	1.5	West Branch Road	R, P	1,960'	632.0	
1,562.5	2.0	Washington Mountain Road, Pittsfield Road *East–5m to* Becket, Mass., P.O. 01223	R, P g, L, D, V	2,000'	630.5	
1,564.5	1.2	Stream	w	1,950'	628.5	
1,565.7	0.7	Blotz Road	R, P	1,850'	627.3	
1,566.4	2.7	Warner Hill		2,050'	626.6	
1,569.1	0.3	**Kay Wood Shelter** *(E–0.2m)* ...9mS; 17.3mN	S, w	1,860'	623.9	
1,569.4	2.1	Grange Hall Road	R, P	1,650'	623.6	
1,571.5	0.1	CSX railroad crossing		1,250'	621.5	
1,571.6	0.5	Depot St. ...*water spigot at "83 Depot St."*	R, H, w	1,240'	621.4	
1,572.1	1.0	Mass. 8, Mass. 9; **Dalton, Mass., P.O. 01226**	R, B, C, G, L, M, D, cl, f	1,200'	620.9	ATC Mass.–Conn. Map 1
1,573.1	3.7	Gulf Road	R, P	1,180'	619.9	
1,576.8	0.4	Crystal Mountain Campsite *(E–0.2m)*	C, w	2,100'	616.2	
1,577.2	2.5	Gore Pond		2,050'	615.8	
1,579.7	0.7	Cheshire Cobbles ...*views*		1,850'	613.3	
1,580.4	0.4	Furnace Hill Road	R	960'	612.6	
1,580.8	0.1	Main St., Hoosic River, Ashuwillticook Rail-Trail	R, P, M	950'	612.2	
1,580.9	0.5	School St., Hiker Kiosk, **Cheshire, Mass., P.O. 01225** *West–75 yds. to* town of Cheshire hiker campsite	R, B, G, M C, w	970'	612.1	

Miles from Springer	Miles to Next Point	Features	Services	Elev	Miles from Katahdin	MAP
1,581.4	*0.8*	Mass. 8 *East–0.8m to* Harbour House Inn *East–2.4m to* Berkshire Outfitters *East–4m to* **Adams, Mass., P.O. 01220** *West–0.2m to* O'Connell's Convenience Store	R L O, f B, G, L, M, D, V, cl g, M	1,000'	611.6	ATC Mass.–Conn. Map 1
1,582.2	*2.7*	Outlook Avenue	R	1,350'	610.8	
1,584.9	*0.9*	Old Adams Road	R	2,350'	608.1	
1,585.8	*0.6*	**Mark Noepel Shelter** *(E–0.2m)...17.3mS; 7.1mN*	S, C, w	2,750'	607.2	
1,586.4	*2.2*	Jones Nose Trail, Saddle Ball Mountain		3,238'	606.6	
1,588.6	*0.5*	Notch Road; Rockwell Road ...*pond*	R, P	3,290'	604.4	
1,589.1	*2.4*	Mt. Greylock, Summit Road; Bascom Lodge, War Memorial	R, P, L, M, sh, w	3,491'	603.9	
1,591.5	*0.8*	Mt. Williams ...*view*		2,951'	601.5	
1,592.3	*0.1*	Notch Road	R, P	2,400'	600.7	
1,592.4	*2.1*	Money Brook Trail to **Wilbur Clearing Shelter** *(W–0.3m)...7.1mS; 10.4mN*	S, C, w	2,310'	600.6	
1,594.5	*0.5*	Pattison Road	R, P, w	900'	598.5	
1,595.0	*0.4*	Catherine Street–Phelps Road	R	670'	598.0	
1,595.4	*0.1*	Mass. 2 ...*Hoosic River, RR tracks overpass* *East–100 yards to* overnight parking *East–0.6m to* West's Variety, Chinese Buffet *East–1m to* YMCA *East–2.5m to* **North Adams, Mass., P.O. 01247** *West–0.4m to* Stop & Shop, motel *West–0.6m to* veterinarian *West–1.4m to* motels, restaurants, groceries *West–2.6m to* **Williamstown, Mass., P.O. 01267**	R, P, B P g, M, cl sh B, G, L, M, D, V, cl G, L V G, L, M, cl, f B, G, L, M, D, sh	650'	597.6	
1,595.5	*1.7*	Massachusetts Avenue *East–0.6m to* Renee's Diner		675'	597.5	
1,597.2	*1.0*	Pete's Spring *(SE)*; Sherman Brook Primitive Campsite *(W–0.1m)*	C, w	1,300'	595.8	
1,598.2	*1.3*	Pine Cobble Trail		2,010'	594.8	
1,599.5	*0.4*	Massachusetts–Vermont State Line; Long Trail *(southern terminus)*...*sign*		2,330'	593.5	

The state line is south of Sages Ravine, near the junction with Paradise Lane Trail. Camping is allowed only at shelters and the following designated campsites: Sages Ravine, Laurel Ridge, Race Brook Falls, Shaker, Crystal Mountain, and Sherman Brook. Ridgerunners employed by the state Department of Conservation and Recreation and the Appalachian Mountain Club (AMC) patrol the trail during the summer months.

From the peak of Mt. Everett to the summit of 3,491-foot Mt. Greylock, the Trail crosses the hills and valleys of The Berkshires, known as a cultural mecca of theater, music, art, and dance and frequented by famous writers and artists since the mid-1800s. The Berkshires have retained much of its rural character, as the Trail winds through agricultural lands and small towns and traverses wilderness forested ridgelines. Juicy, sweet blueberries abound in season.

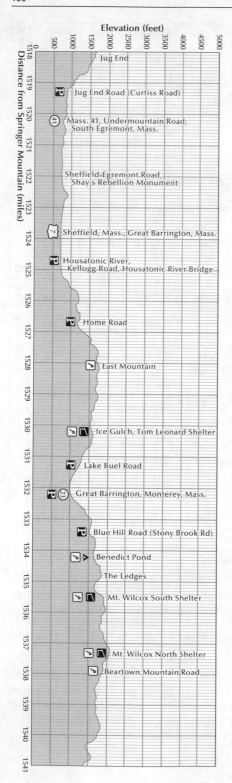

Elevation (feet)
Distance from Springer Mountain (miles)

Jug End
Jug End Road (Curtiss Road)
Mass. 41, Undermountain Road; South Egremont, Mass.
Sheffield-Egremont Road, Shay's Rebellion Monument
Sheffield, Mass., Great Barrington, Mass.
Housatonic River, Kellogg Road, Housatonic River Bridge
Home Road
East Mountain
Ice Gulch, Tom Leonard Shelter
Lake Buel Road
Great Barrington, Monterey, Mass.
Blue Hill Road (Stony Brook Rd)
Benedict Pond
The Ledges
Mt. Wilcox South Shelter
Mt. Wilcox North Shelter
Beartown Mountain Road

Sages Ravine—Two tent platforms and camp-sites with group site, privy. Staffed by Appala-chian Mountain Club ridgerunners who take turns as caretakers. No fires permitted. No fees charged.

Berkshire Chapter of the Appalachian Mountain Club—The A.T. Committee of the AMC–Berk-shire Chapter maintains 89.7 miles from the Sages Ravine area to the Massachusetts–Ver-mont state line. Correspondence should be sent to Berkshire A.T. Committee Box 2281, Pitts-field, MA 02102; <www.amcberkshire.org>; (413) 454-4773.

Berkshire Bus Service—The Berkshire Regional Transit Authority, (413) 499-2782 or (800) 292-2782, <www.berkshirerta.com>, serves the Trail towns of Great Barrington, Lee, Dalton, Cheshire, Ad-ams, North Adams, and Williamstown. The buses run M–F 5:45 a.m.–7:20 p.m. and Sa 7:15 a.m.–7 p.m.; no service Su or holidays. Call for accurate, up-to-date information. The buses can be flagged down anywhere along Mass. 2 or 8 or U.S. 7, but there are designated bus stops. Popular trips for hikers include rides from Dalton west into Pitts-field, the region's hub with all major services, and from Cheshire south to the Berkshire Mall, with numerous shops and a 10-screen cinema. Maxi-mum fare one way is $4.50 ($1.75 two adjacent towns; cash; drivers cannot make change); ask for free transfers. Senior rates available.

Peter Pan Bus Lines—(800) 343-9999, <www. peterpanbus.com>. Buses run daily each way between NYC and Williamstown, Mass., stop-ping at towns near the A.T., including Canaan and Danbury in Connecticut and Sheffield, Great Barrington, Lee, Pittsfield, and Williamstown in Massachusetts. Call for schedules and rates.

Laurel Ridge Campsite—0.1 mile south of Bear Rock Falls, 5 campsites and one group site with 3-tent platform. Privy. Bear box. Water source is a spring off a short side trail south of campsites. *No fires permitted in this area.*

Race Mountain—A spectacular walk on a clear day; spooky when foggy. It's a steep drop-off to the east.

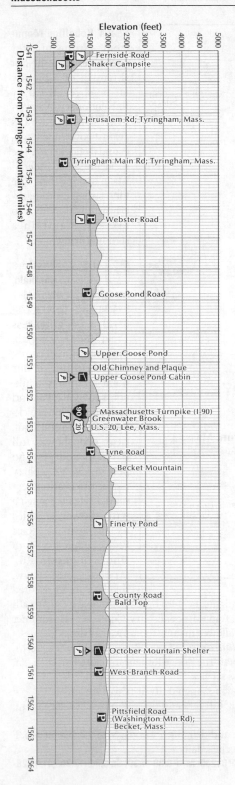

Elevation (feet)

Distance from Springer Mountain (miles)

Fernside Road
Shaker Campsite

Jerusalem Rd; Tyringham, Mass.

Tyringham Main Rd; Tyringham, Mass.

Webster Road

Goose Pond Road

Upper Goose Pond

Old Chimney and Plaque
Upper Goose Pond Cabin

Massachusetts Turnpike (I-90)
Greenwater Brook
U.S. 20, Lee, Mass.

Tyne Road

Becket Mountain

Finerty Pond

County Road
Bald Top

October Mountain Shelter

West-Branch-Road

Pittsfield Road
(Washington Mtn Rd);
Becket, Mass.

Race Brook Falls Campsite—0.2 mile east on the Race Brook Falls Trail. Group camping area, 4 tent platforms, privy, bear box. Water source is stream east of the campsite.

Mt. Everett—This range is the second-highest on the A.T. in Massachusetts.

Guilder Pond—The short side trail to the west leads to this pond in Mt. Everett State Reservation. Picnic table and privy. For conservation reasons, please, no camping or swimming.

The Hemlocks Shelter (1999)—Sleeps 10. Privy. Nestled in a hemlock grove, the shelter offers a sleeping loft with overhang. Water source is on the blue-blazed access trail. If you cannot find water here, Glen Brook crosses the A.T. 50 yards north of the access trail to the shelter.

Glen Brook Shelter (1987)—Sleeps 6. Privy. Two tent platforms and large tenting area. Water source is a reliable stream in front of, and downhill from, the shelter.

Mass. 41 (Undermountain Road)—West 0.1 mile to the April Hill Conservation and Education Center (formerly the Kellogg Conservation Center), now owned by Greenagers, a nonprofit organization that employs teen-agers and young adults in the fields of conservation, sustainable farming, and environmental leadership. No camping or parking, but water from a hose and charging outlets are available. Trailhead parking is available on Sheffield–Egremont Road, 1.8 Trail miles north. For more information, visit <www.greenagers.org>.

West 1.2 miles to **South Egremont, Mass. [P.O. ZIP 01258: M–F 8:15–12 & 12:30–4, Sa 9–11:30; (413) 528-1571].** ■ *Lodging:* ALDHA member Karen Berger has several rooms for rent, call (413) 717-2591 for availability, $35-$45PP includes B, laundry, and pick-up and drop off from trail; The Egremont Village Inn, starting at $125. ■ *Restaurant:* Mom's Country Café, B/L, M–Su 6:30–3, water available from outdoor spigot; Egremont Market (short-term resupply); Old Mill, D, Su Tu–W 5-9, Th–Sa 5–9:30, closed M. ■ *Internet access:* library, M, T & Th 10–6, Sa 9–noon. ■ *Other services:* bank with ATM; Egremont Market (short-term resupply).

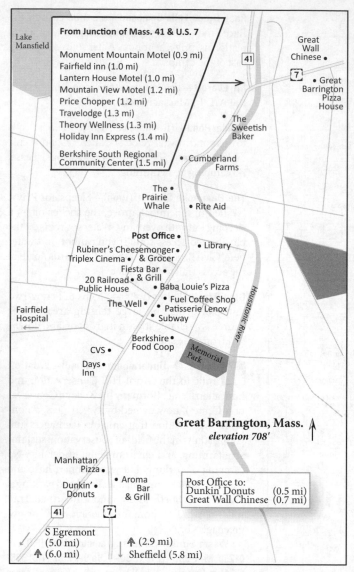

From Junction of Mass. 41 & U.S. 7

Monument Mountain Motel (0.9 mi)
Fairfield inn (1.0 mi)
Lantern House Motel (1.0 mi)
Mountain View Motel (1.2 mi)
Price Chopper (1.2 mi)
Travelodge (1.3 mi)
Theory Wellness (1.3 mi)
Holiday Inn Express (1.4 mi)

Berkshire South Regional
Community Center (1.5 mi)

Lake Mansfield

41

Great Wall Chinese •

7

• Great Barrington Pizza House

• The Sweetish Baker

• Cumberland Farms

The • Prairie Whale

• Rite Aid

Post Office •

Rubiner's Cheesemonger •
Triplex Cinema • & Grocer

• Library

Fiesta Bar •
20 Railroad • & Grill
Public House   • Baba Louie's Pizza

The Well •   • Fuel Coffee Shop
• Patisserie Lenox
• Subway

Fairfield Hospital

Housatonic River

Berkshire •
Food Coop

CVS •

Memorial Park

Days • Inn

Great Barrington, Mass.
elevation 708'

Manhattan Pizza •

Dunkin' Donuts •

• Aroma Bar & Grill

41   7

Post Office to:
Dunkin' Donuts   (0.5 mi)
Great Wall Chinese (0.7 mi)

S Egremont (5.0 mi)
(6.0 mi)

(2.9 mi)
Sheffield (5.8 mi)

Shays' Rebellion Monument—Stone marker commemorates the last skirmish of a bloody farmers' revolt led by Revolutionary War veteran Daniel Shays against government taxes and tactics in 1787. The incident assisted Federalists in making their case for a strong central government with powers to tax and maintain a standing army.

U.S. 7—East 2.8 miles to **Sheffield, Mass. [P.O. ZIP 01257: M–F 9–4:30, Sa 9–12; (413) 229-8772].** ■ *Lodging:* Jess Treat, (860) 248-5710, <jesstrea@gmail.com>, offers rooms in her home for up to 5–6 hikers, $40PP, PayPal and cash only, includes pick-up and drop-off at Trail, clean bed, shower, full B, WiFi, laundry ($5), no pets inside, not a party place, reservations essential, tentsite for $15PP with shower, shuttles usually available; Race Brook Lodge, 864 South Undermountain Rd., (413) 229-2916, <www.rblodge.com>, a restored 1790s barn, A.T.-hiker special $95 for 2 people weeknights includes B, $20 additional for 3rd or 4th person, $10 ride to town, pick-up and drop-off at Jug End Rd. or Salisbury, Conn., regular summer rates Su–Th $120–$260, F–Sa $155–$335, $20EAP, pets allowed in same room $15, mail drops for guests only. Stagecoach Tavern open for D Th–Su. ■ *Restaurants: In town:* Bash Bish Brew & 'Que, M, W 5–9, Th–Su 12–9, closed T. *Along Rt. 7 toward town:* The Bridge Restaurant, closed M, D Tu–Su, opens at 4:30. ■ *Other services:* bank, ATM, and bus service.

West 1.0 mile to Fiddleheads Grille, (413) 644-2999, open daily at 11:30 a.m.

West 1.7 miles to The Bistro Box, (413) 717-5958, burgers and dogs, sandwiches, ice cream; open at 11 a.m., closed W (seasonal).

West 2.3 miles to Guido's, with organic produce and deli; Big Y Foods, M–Th & Sa–Su 7–9, F 7–10; Great Barrington Bagel Co., bagels and sandwiches, daily 7–4.

West 3.4 miles to **Great Barrington, Mass. [P.O. ZIP 01230: M–F 8:30–4:30, Sa 8:30–12:30; (413) 528-**

3670]. ■ *Lodging:* Days Inn, (413) 528-3150, rates $89–$269, $10EAP, max 4/room, no pets, continental B, WiFi; Lantern House Motel, (413) 528-2350, $75 and up, higher on weekends, $15EAP, outdoor saltwater pool, call for reservations, WiFi, continental B, no pets; Travelodge, (413) 528-2340, $55S, $69 and up, higher on weekends and during special events, $10EAP, max 2/room, pets allowed in some rooms for $10 fee, laundry, WiFi, continental B, outdoor pool; Mountain View Motel, (413) 528-0250, $69 and up, no pets, free WiFi, CATV, phone, refrigerator, microwave, continental B; Holiday Inn Express, (413) 528-1810, minimum 20% hiker discount, call for current rates, extended continental B, no pets, WiFi, indoor pool, computer available for guests; Berkshire Marriott Fairfield Inn, (413) 644-3200, <www.berkshiremarriott.com>, call for rates, full hot B, laundry, no pets, indoor and outdoor pools, WiFi and guest's computer; The Briarcliff Motel, (413) 528-3000, <www.thebriarcliffmotel.com>, $175 and up in summer, continental B, WiFi; Monument Mountain Motel, U.S. 7, 247 Stockbridge Rd., (413) 528-3272, <www.monumentmountainmotel.com>, $75 and up, higher on weekends and during special events, no pets, laundry, pool, coffee and tea when office is open, mail drops accepted for guests. ■ *Groceries:* Price Chopper, M–Sa 6–midnight, Su 7–midnight (long-term resupply). ■ *Restaurants:* numerous, in town center and north along U.S. 7. ■ *Other services:* Berkshire South Regional Community Center, 15 Crissey Rd., (413) 528-2810, 1 mile north of the town center on U.S. 7, sells day passes for section- and thru-hikers for $5/person. Day pass entitles guests to the use of the entire facility—showers, saunas, aquatic center, fitness room, and classes. Berkshire South has 6 tent platforms available at no charge on a first-come/ first-served basis; 1 to 2 tents/platform only. No tenting elsewhere on grounds. For more information, please call or visit <www.berkshiresouth.org>. All hikers must check in at the front desk upon arrival. Free community supper served every M 5–6. Smoking, drugs, alcohol, and dogs are prohibited on the center grounds. On Berkshire Regional Transit Bus Route #21, let the driver know, and she/he will take you to Berkshire South; fee 85¢–$1.75 cash; <www.berkshireta.com>. Shopping center 2.8 miles **west** of Trail (1 mile north of town center on U.S. 7) has pharmacy, coin laundry, hardware store, bookstore; Theory Wellness cannabis dispensary, 394 Stockbridge Rd., (413) 650-5527, daily 8–10; taxi, (413) 528-0911. ■ *Bus service:* In front of chamber of commerce in town (buy tickets from driver) and at Fairgrounds Plaza, Barrington Plaza, and Rite Aid.

Tom Leonard Shelter (1988)—Sleeps 10. Privy. Bear box. Located just south of Ice Gulch, a deep cleft in the landscape. Water source is a very cold stream 0.2 mile down a ravine on a blue-blazed trail to the left of the shelter.

Mass. 23—East 4.3 miles to **Monterey, Mass. [P.O. ZIP 01245: M–F 8:30–1 & 2–4:30, Sa 9–11:30; (413) 528-4670].**
    West 1 mile to Lake Buel Road, turn left, first driveway on right, 0.6 mile uphill to *Hostel:* East Mountain Retreat Center, 8 Lake Buel Rd., Great Barrington, MA 01230, or P.O. Box 195 for USPS, (413) 528-6617, <emrc@bcn.net>, open May 15–Aug 15, $10 donation, with shower; use of the cooking facilities and library; 10 p.m. quiet curfew and prompt 8:30 a.m. checkout; will hold UPS/FedEx packages (c/o East Mountain Retreat).
    West 4 miles to Great Barrington.

Benedict Pond, Beartown State Forest—West 0.5 mile on a blue-blazed side trail to a beach with picnic tables, tentsites $14.

Mt. Wilcox South Shelter (1930/2007)—Old shelter sleeps 6. Privy. Bear box. Built as a CCC project; approach trail was part of the original A.T. in Massachusetts. Shelter completed in 2007 is just beyond old one. Water source is the spring crossed *en route* to the shelter.

Mt. Wilcox North Shelter (1930s)—Sleeps 10. Privy. Shelter is on a 0.3-mile blue-blazed trail. Water source, in front of the shelter, may go dry in late summer.

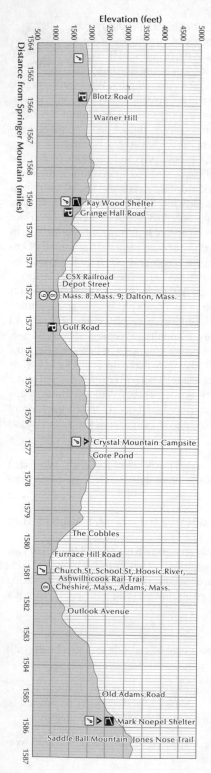

Shaker Campsite—Two tent platforms, privy, bear box. Water is north on the A.T. at stream crossing. Bear sightings have been frequent here.

Tyringham Cobble—Formed by a geological event that separated this hill from the mountain behind it, the cobble rises 400 feet above the village below. The hill and nearly 200 acres around it are owned by a conservation trust.

Jerusalem Road—West 0.6 mile to **Tyringham, Mass. [P.O. ZIP 01264: M–F 9–12:30 & 4–5:30, Sa 8:30–12:30; (413) 243-1225]**. May also be reached from Tyringham Main Road 1.1 mile north on A.T. Water fountain outside post office. Library open T 3–5, Sa 10–12; WiFi and computer available. *Lodging:* Cobble View, (413) 243-2463, call in advance for rates; no pets; across from P.O.

Jerusalem Road Spring—West several yards to short path on left that leads to a piped spring (if you pass the first house on the right, you've gone too far). Opposite spring is the Running Spring Farm stand, with cold beverages, snacks, and eggs for sale. Device-charging outlet, recycling and trash receptacles, and book exchange available.

Upper Goose Pond Cabin—AMC–Berkshire Chapter A.T. Committee maintains this cabin on a 0.5-mile side trail north of the pond. The cabin offers bunks, fireplace, covered porch, privy, bear box, swimming, tentsites, and platforms. Open daily mid-May to mid-Oct. During the summer, the resident volunteer caretaker brings water by canoe from a spring across the pond; otherwise, the pond is the water source. When the caretaker is not in residence or the cabin is closed for the season, hikers may camp on the porch or tent platforms. Privy behind the cabin and near tentsites. No fee is charged for staying at this site; donations appreciated.

U.S. 20—East 0.1 mile to *Lodging:* Berkshire Lakeside Lodge, 3949 Jacob's Ladder Road, Becket, MA 01223; (413) 243-9907, <www.berkshire-lakesidelodge.com>, $60–$165 (call for reservations), use of outside grill, canoes, and kayaks; continental B, WiFi, minifridge and coffee pot in each room; food delivery available; mail drops accepted for nonguests, no fee but call ahead.

    West 5 miles to **Lee, Mass. [P.O. ZIP 01238: M–F 8:30–4:30, Sa 9–12; (413) 243-1392]**. A full-service town with a mile-long downtown area and entrance/exit to the Massachusetts Turnpike (I-90).Nearby Lenox is home of the famous Tanglewood Performing Arts Center and the summer residence of the Boston Symphony Orchestra. Tanglewood also offers other types of concerts in an outdoors setting and spectacular July Fourth fireworks. ■ *Lodging:* Rodeway Inn, (413) 243-0813, Su–Th $59–$79S/D, F–Sa $79–$169, WiFi, continental B, no pets; Pilgrim Inn, (413) 243-1328, Su–Th $79–$95, F–Sa $95–$195, $10 EAP, continental B, coffee in room, pool, WiFi, microwave, fridge, laundry; Super 8, 170 Housatonic St., (413) 243-0143, $59–$205, $10EAP, continental B, WiFi, no pets, accepts mail drops (if staying more than one night); EconoLodge, (413) 243-0501, $59–$79S/D weekdays, $190 weekends, WiFi, microwave, fridge, continental B; Sunset Inn, 150 Housatonic St., (413) 243-0302, $68–$88, fridge, microwave, WiFi. ■ *Groceries:* Price Chopper and Big Y supermarkets (long-term resupply). ■ *Restaurants:* Joe's Diner, Athena's Pizza House, Rose's Restaurant (B/L 7–2), Friendly's, and numerous other restaurants and fast-food chains. ■ *Outfitter:* Arcadian Shop, (413) 637-3010, 91 Pittsfield Rd., Lenox, MA 01230, < www.arcadian.com> full-service outfitter, accepts mail drops.

October Mountain Shelter (1990)—Sleeps 12. Tentsites. Privy, bear box. Loft overhangs picnic table. Water from a stream just south of the shelter on the A.T.

Washington Mountain Road—East 5 miles to **Becket, Mass. [P.O. ZIP 01223: M–F 8–4, Sa 9–11:30; (413) 623-8845]**, where the A.T. ironically is listed as a historical site in a town settled more than 300 years ago and home to the renowned Jacob's Pillow Dance festival and school. ■ *Lodging:* Becket Motel, 29 Chester Rd., Becket, MA 01223, (413) 623-8888, $70–$127, coin laundry, free shuttles to/from Trail, WiFi, mail drops accepted for guests only. ■ *Groceries:* Becket General Store, (413) 623-5700, M–Sa 7-8, Su 8-5, small grocery, deli counter. ■ *Other services:* doctor, veterinarian.

Kay Wood Shelter (1980s)—Sleeps 10. Privy, bear boxes, and tent pads. Shelter is named for Kay Wood, an early Trail angel, long-time Trail maintainer, and 1988–89 thru-hiker who died in 2010 at age 91. Water source is on a blue-blazed trail to the left of the shelter.

Dalton, Mass. [P.O. ZIP 01226: M–F 8:30–4:30, Sa 9–12; (413) 684-0364]—The A.T. goes through the eastern side of town, where most services are available. Depot Street, which the A.T. follows into town from the south, offers a pharmacy, Dewey's Public House and Restaurant, and Sweet Pea's ice cream. Other services are within 0.5 mile of the A.T. ■ *Lodging:* Thomas Levardi, 83 Depot St., (413) 684-3359, cell (413) 212-9691, allows hikers to use a water spigot outside his home and provides the hospitality of his front porch and back yard for tenting (limited space, get permission first); Shamrock Village Inn, (413) 684-0860, S–Th 2 doubles, queen, or a king $80, F–Sa $85, pets $75 deposit, hiker box, WiFi, laundry ($5 nonguests), ask about 10% hiker discount. ■ *Groceries:* Cumberland Farms with

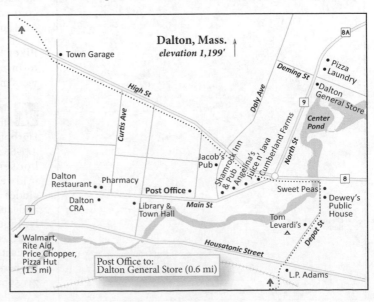

ATM, Dalton General Store with deli (both short-term resupply). ■ *Restaurants:* Jacob's Pub, 51 Daly Ave., (413) 684-9766, L/D M–Sa 11:30–1, Su 12–8, *great* Reubens, very hiker-friendly, hiker box; Angelina's Subs with veggie burgers; Juice 'n' Java, 661 Main St., specialty coffee and sandwiches, M–F 6:30–8, Sa–Su 7–7; Dalton Restaurant, serves B/L/D daily, M–Sa 6–8, Su 6–12:30; Shamrocks Restaurant and Pub, D, Tu–Su 4–11, Su 11:30–8, closed M, WiFi. ■ *Internet access:* library, 1-hour limit. ■ *Other services:* Dalton CRA, 400 Main St., free showers with towel and soap to hikers; Dalton Laundry, closed M Tu–F 8:30–6, Sa 8:30–4, Su 8:30–12; banks; L.P. Adams, 484 W. Housatonic St. (near Trail south of town), provides free denatured alcohol and Coleman fuel outside front entrance 24/7; doctor; dentist; pharmacy. ■ *Bus service:* BRTA connects to shopping centers 2 miles west of Dalton and to the center of Pittsfield, with all major services.

Crystal Mountain Campsite—0.2 mile east. Privy. Bear box. Water is north on Trail; may go dry in summer.

The Cobbles—These outcroppings of marble overlook the Hoosic River Valley and offer views of Cheshire and Mt. Greylock. The Hoosic River, which is crossed south of Cheshire, flows north and empties into the Hudson River in New York.

Cheshire, Mass. [P.O. ZIP 01225: M–F 7:30–1 & 2–4:30, Sa 8:30–11:30; (413) 743-3184]— The Trail skirts the town center to the east and crosses Mass. 8 0.4 mile east of the main stoplight at Church Street. Camping available on town land 75 yards south from Diane's Twist (across Church St.), past the snowplow, on left. Open May 1-Sep 30. Water, electricity, and port-a-potties; two-nights max. No smoking, alcohol, or drugs of any kind. No fires. Sponsored by the Cheshire A.T. Committee. ■ *Restaurants:* Bass Water Grill, closed Tu, Sa–Su B/L/D, M W–F L/D; Diane's Twist, M–Su 11–6, mid-Apr–mid-Oct, deli sandwiches, soda, and ice cream (cash only). ■ *Other services:* bank with ATM. ■ *Bus service:* BRTA stop across from post office, connections to Berkshire Mall and Adams, Mass.

Harbor House Inn (0.8 mi *from trail*)

Convenience Plus, Dunkin Donuts

Dollar General

Cheshire, Mass.
elevation 963'

8

School St

North St

South St

Great Cheshire Cheese

Hiker Kiosk

Diane's Twist

Church St

Town Hall

Post Office

Depot St

8

Ashuwillticook Rail Trail

Cheshire Liquor

Post Office to: Dollar General (0.7 mi) *via Trail*

Bass Water Grill   (0.1 mi)
Whitney's Farm Market (2.8mi)

Hiker kiosk—A detailed town map with hiker services marked.

Mass. 8—East 0.8 mile to *Lodging:* Harbour House Inn, (413) 441-6644, <www.harbourhouseinn.com>, rooms midweek $125. Rate includes B, Internet access, and laundry. Hiker-friendly; inquire about possible shuttles.

East 2.4 miles to *Outfitter:* Berkshire Outfitters, (413) 743-5900, <www.berkshire-

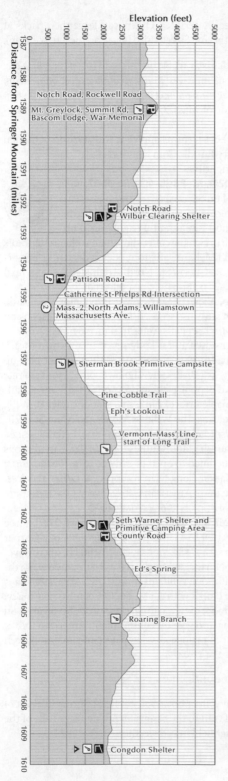

Elevation (feet)

Distance from Springer Mountain (miles)

Notch Road, Rockwell Road

Mt. Greylock, Summit Rd,
Bascom Lodge, War Memorial

Notch Road
Wilbur Clearing Shelter

Pattison Road

Catherine St-Phelps Rd Intersection

Mass. 2, North Adams, Williamstown
Massachusetts Ave.

Sherman Brook Primitive Campsite

Pine Cobble Trail

Eph's Lookout

Vermont–Mass' Line,
start of Long Trail

Seth Warner Shelter and
Primitive Camping Area
County Road

Ed's Spring

Roaring Branch

Congdon Shelter

outfitters.com>, M–Sa 10–6, Th 'til 7, Su 11–4; hiker supplies, minor equipment repairs.

East 4 miles to **Adams, Mass. [P.O. ZIP 01220: M–F 8:30–4:30, Sa 10–12; (413) 743-5177]**, an alternative to the smaller town of Cheshire. Adams is accessible by the BRTA bus service. ■ *Lodging:* Mount Greylock Inn, (413) 743-2665, $129–$199, includes B; Mount Royal Inn, (413) 776-7329, north 2 miles from downtown Adams on Mass. 8, rooms $90. ■ *Groceries:* Adams Hometown Market (long-term resupply). ■ *Restaurants:* AJ's Trailside Pub; Daily Grind, B/L; Coffee Liberation Front, B/L; McDonald's; and Domino's. ■ *Other services:* Thrifty Bundle coin laundry, banks, hardware store, doctor, dentist, Rite Aid, veterinarian, and Western Union.

West 0.2 mile to *Groceries:* Convenience store (short-term resupply), deli sandwiches.

Mark Noepel Shelter (1985)—Sleeps 10. Tentsites (2) and platforms (2), group site, privy, and bear box. Water source is a stream on a blue-blazed trail to the right of the shelter.

Saddle Ball Mountain—At 3,238 feet and located at the A.T. junction with the Jones Nose Trail, Saddle Ball is the A.T.'s first 3,000-footer north of North Marshall in Shenandoah National Park.

Mt. Greylock—Topped by a war memorial, paved road, and Bascom Lodge, Greylock is Massachusetts' highest peak (3,491 feet). A stone tower, crowned by a night-lit globe, is a tribute to the state's war dead. You can climb the 89 steps to the top for views of the Green, Catskill, and Taconic mountains and surrounding towns. *Thunderbolt Shelter on Mt. Greylock is an emergency-only warming hut. No camping or fires on the summit.*

Bascom Lodge—Operated by Bascom Lodge Group, (413) 743-1591, <www.bascomlodge.net>, open daily, B (8–10)/L(11–4:30)/D(7, $30), showers & towel $5, bunk $36, private rooms $125–$190D, $20EAP, open Jun–Oct.

Wilbur Clearing Shelter (1970)—Sleeps 8. Tentsites and platforms. Privy. Bear box. Located 0.3 mile down the Money Brook Trail; very popular during the summer months. Water source is a stream to the right of the shelter that might go dry in late summer.

 Catherine Street/Phelps Road—Joshua Moran of 138 Catherine St., North Adams, provides

3 mountain bicycles for hikers to use to ride to nearby services. Hikers can leave their packs at Moran's property while using the bikes (west on Catherine Street, third house on the left, see map).

Mass. 2/North Adams—BRTA hourly bus service is available on this road (see page 178). *Note: The city of North Adams extends more than one mile west and several miles east of the Trail; the Williamstown line is 1.4 miles west of the Trail. See map on next page.*

East 100 yards to overnight parking on north side of Mass. 2, opposite the Greylock Community Club.

East 0.6 mile to ■ *Groceries:* West's Variety (short-term resupply). ■ *Restaurants:* Oriental Chinese Buffet, AYCE L/D. ■ *Other services:* Thrifty Bundle Coin laundry.

East 1.0 mile to YMCA, free showers, hiker-friendly.

East 2.5 miles to **North Adams, Mass. [P.O. ZIP 01247: M–F 8:30–4:30, Sa 10–12; (413) 664-4554].** ■ *Lodging:* Holiday Inn Berkshires, 40 Main St., (413) 663-6500, $129–$220, pool, fitness center. ■ *Groceries:* Big Y Foods (long-term resupply); Cumberland Farms (short-term resupply). ■ *Restaurants:* Boston Seafood Restaurant, Freight Yard Pub, Capitol Restaurant, Desperado's Fresh Mexican Grill, Brewhaha coffee shop, many other restaurants and fast-food chains. ■ *Other services:* banks with ATM, hardware store, doctor, dentist, veterinarian, and movie theater. ■ *Shuttles:* Dave Ackerson, 82 Cherry St., North Adams, MA 01247, (413) 346-1033, <daveackerson@yahoo.com>; Bill Beattie, (413) 281-9330, text preferred.

West 0.4 mile to ■ *Groceries:* Super Stop & Shop, ATM, pharmacy, Western Union, and bank. ■ *Lodging:* Tourists, (413) 346-4933, rooms starting at $165, also serves B/L/D. A trail and suspension footbridge on the property connects to the A.T. ■ *Other services:* veterinarian, 0.6 mile.

West 1.4 miles to municipal border with **Williamstown** and ■ *Lodging:* Williamstown Motel, (413) 458-5202, $59–89s, $10EAP, continental B, WiFi, Internet, fridge, microwave, call for pick-up from Mass. 2 and Phelps Rd.; Howard Johnson, (413) 458-8158, <www.hojowt.com>, $59–$149 rate based on season and day of week, no pets, continental B, pool, pick-up/drop-off at Trail when available; Maple Terrace Motel, (413) 458-9677, <www.mapleterrace.com>, $75–$160 includes B, WiFi, heated pool, two rooms for pets, all rooms nonsmoking; The Willows Motel, 480 Main St., Williamstown, MA 01267, (413) 458-5768, <www.willowsmotel.com>, Su–Th $69–$119, F–Sa $89–$129, includes continental B, microwave, Internet, free laundry, and shuttles to/from Trail, mail drops accepted for guests only (call first); Fairfield Inn scheduled to open in early 2020. ■ *Restaurants: See map.* ■ *Groceries:* Wild Oats Whole Foods Market (long-term resupply). ■ *Other services:* Williamstown Wash & WiFi, M–F 7:30–9, Sa 9–9, Su 10–9; American Cab & Livery, (413) 662-2000; Silver Therapeutics, cannibis dispensary, 238 Main St., (413) 458-6244, daily 10–8.

West 2.6 miles to **Williamstown, Mass. [P.O. ZIP 01267: M–F 8:30–4:30, Sa 9–12; (413) 458-3707],** home of Williams College, the northern venue for the ALDHA Gathering. ■ *Lodging:* Cozy Corner Motel, (413) 458-8006, <www.cozycornermotel.com>, $49–$89, $10EAP, continental B, microwave/fridge, WiFi, pet-friendly, will pick up and drop off; Northside Motel, (413) 458-8107, <www.north-sidemotel.com>, $69–$159, continental B, fridge, WiFi, pool; Williams Inn, (413) 458-9371, $180–$295 and up. ■ *Restaurants: See map.* ■ *Other services:* banks with ATM; doctor; dentist; pharmacy; movie theater; bookstore; Nature's Closet, (413) 458-7909, <www.naturescloset.net>, M–Sa 10–6, Su 11–5, includes the Gear Den of used outdoor clothing and gear on consignment; American Cab & Livery, (413) 662-2000; Bonanza Peter Pan bus line, (800) 343-9999, <www.peterpanbus.com>; Green Mountain Express bus to Bennington, Vt., M–F, (802) 447-0477.

Massachusetts Avenue—**East** 0.6 mile to Renee's Diner, B/L, M–Sa 7–2, Su 7–1.

Sherman Brook Campsite—Three tent platforms. Privy. Bear box. Water at Pete's Spring just east of the Trail and south of the 0.1-mile loop blue-blazed trail to the campsite. A blue-blaze west of the Trail, north of the campsite, lets you bypass a boulder field in bad weather.

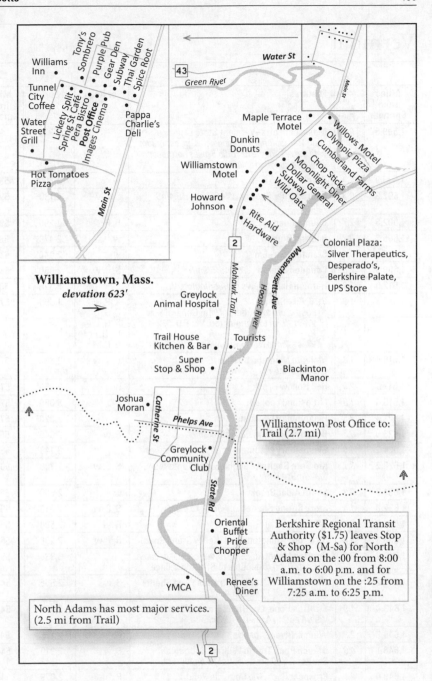

Williams Inn

Tunnel City Coffee

Tony's Sombrero
Purple Pub
Gear Den
Subway
Thai Garden
Spice Root

Water Street Grill

Lickety Split
Spring St Café
Pera Bistro
Post Office
Images Cinema

Pappa Charlie's Deli

Hot Tomatoes Pizza

Main St

Williamstown, Mass.
elevation 623'

Water St

43
Green River

Maple Terrace Motel

Willows Motel
Olympic Pizza
Cumberland Farms

Dunkin Donuts

Williamstown Motel

Chop Sticks
Moonlight Diner
Dollar General
Subway
Wild Oats

Howard Johnson

Rite Aid
Hardware

2

Colonial Plaza:
Silver Therapeutics,
Desperado's,
Berkshire Palate,
UPS Store

Greylock Animal Hospital

Mohawk Trail

Hoosic River

Massachusetts Ave

Trail House Kitchen & Bar
Tourists

Super Stop & Shop

Blackinton Manor

Joshua Moran

Catherine St

Phelps Ave

Greylock Community Club

Williamstown Post Office to:
Trail (2.7 mi)

State Rd

Oriental Buffet
Price Chopper

Berkshire Regional Transit Authority ($1.75) leaves Stop & Shop (M-Sa) for North Adams on the :00 from 8:00 a.m. to 6:00 p.m. and for Williamstown on the :25 from 7:25 a.m. to 6:25 p.m.

YMCA

Renee's Diner

North Adams has most major services. (2.5 mi from Trail)

2

Vermont

Miles from Springer	Miles to Next Point	Features	Services	Elev	Miles from Katahdin	MAP
1,599.5	0.4	Massachusetts–Vermont State Line Long Trail *(southern terminus)...sign, congruent with the A.T. for the next 105.5 miles northbound to Maine Junction at Willard Gap*		2,330'	593.5	
1,599.9	2.4	Brook	w	2,300'	593.1	
1,602.3	0.3	**Seth Warner Shelter** *(W–0.2m)...10.4mS; 7.4mN*	S, C, w	2,180'	590.7	
1,602.6	2.7	County Road	R, P	2,290'	590.4	
1,605.3	3.7	Roaring Branch	w	2,470'	587.7	
1,609.0	0.5	Stamford Stream	w	2,040'	584.0	
1,609.5	2.5	**Congdon Shelter** *...7.4mS; 5.9mN*	S, C, w	2,060'	583.5	
1,612.0	1.8	Harmon Hill *...views of Bennington, Vt.*		2,325'	581.0	
1,613.8	1.6	Vt. 9, City Stream *East–2.5m to* Woodford Mtn General Store *West–5.1m to* **Bennington, Vt., P.O. 05201** *West–7m to* North Bennington, Vt.	R, P, w C, G, L B, G, L, M, D, cl, f G, L, M	1,360'	579.2	ATC N.H.–Vt. Map 8
1,615.4	1.6	**Melville Nauheim Shelter** *(E–250 ft.) ...5.9mS; 8.5mN*	S, C, w	2,330'	577.6	
1,617.0	2.6	Hell Hollow Brook	w	2,350'	576.0	
1,619.6	1.8	Little Pond Lookout		3,060'	573.4	
1,621.4	2.5	Glastenbury Lookout		2,920'	571.6	
1,623.9	0.3	**Goddard Shelter** *...8.5mS; 4.3mN*	S, w	3,540'	569.1	
1,624.2	4.0	Glastenbury Mountain *...observation tower*		3,748'	568.8	
1,628.2	3.7	**Kid Gore Shelter**, Caughnawaga Tentsites *...4.3mS; 4.6mN*	S, C, w	2,795'	564.8	
1,631.9	0.9	South Alder Brook	w	2,600'	561.1	
1,632.8	1.5	**Story Spring Shelter** *...4.6mS; 10.4mN*	S, C, w	2,810'	560.2	
1,634.3	2.1	USFS 71	R	2,500'	558.7	
1,636.4	3.8	Stratton–Arlington Road (Kelley Stand Road)	R, P, w	2,230'	556.6	
1,640.2	3.0	Stratton Mountain *...fire tower, caretaker cabin East–0.8m to* gondola to Stratton Village		3,936'	552.8	
1,643.2	0.2	Stratton Pond Trail to +**Stratton Pond Shelter** *(W–450ft.)...10.4mS; 5.4mN*	S, w	2,565'	549.8	
1,643.4	1.9	Stratton Pond, Lye Brook Trail to +Stratton View Tenting Area *(W–0.7m)*	C, w	2,555'	549.6	ATC N.H.–Vt. Map 7
1,645.3	2.8	Winhall River *...bridge*	w	2,175'	547.7	
1,648.1	0.9	Branch Pond Trail to **William B. Douglas Shelter** *(W–0.5m)...5.4mS; 3.6mN*	S, w	2,210'	544.9	
1,649.0	2.1	Prospect Rock, Old Rootville Road *West–150 ft. to* stream; *2m to* Vt. 11 & 30	R R, P, w	2,079'	544.0	
1,651.1	0.4	**Spruce Peak Shelter** *(W–0.1m)...3.6mS; 4.9mN*	S, C, w	2,180'	541.9	
1,651.5	2.4	Spruce Peak *(W–300 ft.)*		2,040'	541.5	

Miles from Springer	Miles to Next Point	Features	Services	Elev	Miles from Katahdin	M A P
1,653.9	2.0	Vt. 11 & 30 *East–2.1m to* Lodge at Bromley *East–2.5m to* Bromley Market and Deli *East–3.0m on Vt.30 to* Bromley View Inn *East–4.2m to* Hapgood General Store *West–3.6m to* motels and diner; *3.8m to* motel *West–5.5m to* **Manchester Center, Vt., P.O. 05255**	R, P, w L G, M L g, M L, M B, H, G, L, M, O, D, V, cl, f	1,840'	539.1	
1,655.9	1.0	**Bromley Shelter** *(E–110 yards) ...4.9mS; 8.1mN*	S, C, w	2,560'	537.1	
1,656.9	2.5	Bromley Mountain *...ski patrol hut*		3,260'	536.1	
1,659.4	1.6	Mad Tom Notch, USFS 21; Peru, Vt.	R, P	2,446'	533.6	
1,661.0	1.7	Styles Peak		3,394'	532.0	
1,662.7	1.3	Peru Peak		3,429'	530.3	
1,664.0	0.5	**+Peru Peak Shelter** *...8.1mS; 4.7mN*	S, C, w	2,605'	529.0	
1,664.5	0.2	Griffith Lake, +Griffith Lake Tenting Area	C, w	2,600'	528.5	
1,664.7	2.0	Griffith Lake *(north end)*	w	2,600'	528.3	
1,666.7	2.0	Baker Peak		2,850'	526.3	
1,668.7	1.5	**Lost Pond Shelter** *(W–100 ft.) ...4.7mS; 2.8mN*	S, C, w	2,150'	524.3	
1,670.2	0.1	Old Job Trail to **Old Job Shelter** *(E–1.3m)* *...2.8mS; 1.5mN*	S, C, w	1,525'	522.8	
1,670.3	0.1	Big Branch Suspension Bridge		1470'	522.7	
1,670.4	1.3	**Big Branch Shelter** *...1.5mS; 3.3mN*	S, C, w	1,460'	522.6	
1,671.7	2.0	Danby–Landgrove Road, USFS 10, Black Branch *West–3.5m to* **Danby, Vt., P.O. 05739**	R, P, w B, G	1,500'	521.3	
1,673.7	0.1	**+Little Rock Pond Shelter** and Tenting Area *...3.3mS; 5mN*	S, C, w	1,920'	519.3	
1,673.8	0.2	Spring *...water for LRP Shelter*	w	1,854'	519.2	
1,674.0	4.0	Green Mountain Trail to Homer Stone Brook Trail		1,854'	519.0	
1,678.0	0.5	Trail to White Rocks Cliffs *...vista (W–0.2m)*		2,400'	515.0	
1,678.5	0.6	**Greenwall Shelter** *(E–0.2m) ...5mS; 5.3mN*	S, C, w	2,025'	514.5	
1,679.1	0.8	Bully Brook *...cascades*	w	1,760'	513.9	
1,679.9	0.1	Sugar Hill Road	R	1,260'	513.1	
1,680.0	2.1	Vt. 140, Roaring Brook *West–2.8m to* **Wallingford, Vt., P.O. 05773**	R, P, w B, g, L, M	1,160'	513.0	
1,682.1	1.5	Bear Mountain		2,240'	510.9	
1,683.6	2.6	**Minerva Hinchey Shelter** *(E–200 ft.) ...5.3mS; 3.7mN*	S, C, w	1,605'	509.4	
1,686.2	0.1	Clarendon Gorge Wildlife Management Area; Mill River Suspension Bridge	w	800'	506.8	
1,686.3	1.0	Vt. 103 *...railroad tracks* *West–0.8m to* Loretta's Good Food Deli	R, P, B B, g, M	860'	506.7	
1,687.3	0.5	**Clarendon Shelter** *(E–400 ft.) ...3.7mS; 6.1mN*	S, C, w	1,190'	505.7	
1,687.8	0.4	Beacon Hill		1,740'	505.2	
1,688.2	2.0	Lottery Road	R	1,720'	504.8	
1,690.2	0.8	Cold River Road *...paved* *East–2.7m to* Pierce's Store	R, P g, M	1,400'	502.8	
1,691.0	0.8	Gould Brook *...ford*	w	1,480'	502.0	
1,691.8	0.7	Upper Cold River Road *...gravel road* *East–2.5m to* Pierce's Store	R, w g, M	1,630'	501.2	

ATC N.H.–Vt. Map 7

ATC N.H.–Vt. Map 6

Miles from Springer	Miles to Next Point	Features	Services	Elev	Miles from Katahdin	M A P
1,692.5	0.9	Sargent Brook Bridge ...*gravel road*	R, w	1,730'	500.5	
1,693.4	4.3	**Governor Clement Shelter** ...*6.1mS; 4.3mN*	S, C, w	1,900'	499.6	
1,697.7	2.5	**Cooper Lodge** ...*4.3mS; 3mN* Blue-blazed trail to Killington Peak (4,241') *(E–0.2m) ...summit and gondola*	S, C, w M	3,900'	495.3	
1,700.2	1.9	Jungle Jct.; Sherburne Pass Trail to **Pico Camp** *(E–0.5m) ...3mS; 2.5mN*	S, w	3,480'	492.8	
1,702.1	1.9	**Churchill Scott Shelter** *(W–0.1m) ...2.5mS; 12mN*	S, C, w	2,560'	490.9	
1,704.0	1.0	U.S. 4 (west of Sherburne Pass) *East–0.9m to* Inn at Long Trail *West–1.4m to* Mendon Mtn View Lodge *West–8.6m to* **Rutland, Vt., P.O. 05701**	R, P, w B, C, L, M B, L all	1,880'	489.0	
1,705.0	0.9	Maine Junction at Willard Gap, Long Trail to Tucker-Johnson Shelter *(W–0.2m) ...3.2mS; 9.2mN*	S, C, w	2,250'	488.0	
		Caution—Make sure you're on the A.T. and not the Long Trail at this junction				
1,705.9	1.1	Sherburne Pass Trail ...*to Inn at Long Trail (E–0.5m)*	C, L, M	2,440'	487.1	ATC N.H.–Vt. Map 6
1,707.0	0.3	Kent Brook Trail Junction *(E–0.4m to U.S. 4)*	PO, B, G, L, M, O	1,700'	486.0	
1,707.3	0.7	Vt. 100, Gifford Woods State Park *East–0.6m to* **Killington, Vt., P.O. 05751**	R, P, S, C, w, sh B, G, L, M, O	1,660'	485.7	
1,708.0	1.2	Kent Pond, Mountain Meadows Lodge, trail to Base Camp Outfitters *(E–0.3m to U.S. 4)* Thundering Brook Road *(southern jct.)*	L, M, O R	1,450'	485.0	
1,709.2	0.2	Thundering Brook Road *(northern jct.)*	R, P	1,280'	483.8	
1,709.4	0.3	Thundering Falls ...*900-ft. boardwalk*		1,226'	483.6	
1,709.7	0.5	River Road *(E–0.5 to Killington pool)*	R, P	1,214'	483.3	
1,710.2	3.8	Quimby Mountain		2,550'	482.8	
1,714.0	0.8	**Stony Brook Shelter** *(E–250 ft.) ...9.2mS; 10.1mN*	S, C, w	1,760'	479.0	
1,714.8	3.9	Stony Brook Road, Stony Brook	R, w	1,360'	478.2	
1,718.7	0.7	Chateauguay Road	R	2,000'	474.3	
1,719.4	2.1	Lakota Lake Lookout		2,640'	473.6	
1,721.5	2.4	Side trail to the Lookout ...*private cabin (W–0.2m)*	nw	2,320'	471.5	
1,723.9	3.8	**Winturri Shelter** *(W–0.2m) ...10.1mS; 12.6mN*	S, w	1,910'	469.1	
1,727.7	0.9	Vt. 12, Gulf Stream Bridge *East–3.8m to* **Woodstock, Vt., P.O. 05091** *West–0.2m to* On The Edge Farm Store	R, P, w G, L, M, D, V G	882'	465.3	
1,728.6	1.3	Dana Hill		1,530'	464.4	ATC N.H.–Vt. Map 5
1,729.9	1.5	Woodstock Stage Road, Barnard Brook *East–0.9m to* **South Pomfret, Vt. 05067**	R, P, w G, M	820'	463.1	
1,731.4	0.7	Bartlett Brook Road ...*gravel, footbridge, brook*	R, w	1,050'	461.6	
1,732.1	1.8	Pomfret–South Pomfret Road, Pomfret Brook *(E–1.3m to South Pomfret)*	R, P, w	980'	460.9	
1,733.9	2.0	Cloudland Road *(W–0.2m to Cloudland Farm)*	R, P, g	1,370'	459.1	
1,735.9	0.3	Thistle Hill		1,800'	457.1	
1,736.2	1.5	**Thistle Hill Shelter** *(E–0.1m) ...12.6mS; 9mN*	S, w	1,480'	456.8	

Miles from Springer	Miles to Next Point	Features	Services	Elev	Miles from Katahdin	M A P
1,737.7	3.3	Joe Ranger Road	R, P	1,280'	455.3	
1,741.0	0.6	Vt. 14, White River; West Hartford, Vt. *East–7m to* **Hartford, Vt., P.O. 05047** East–8m to White River Jct., Vt.	R, P, C, w B, g H, all	390'	452.0	
1,741.6	0.8	Tigertown Road, Podunk Road	R, P	540'	451.4	
1,742.4	2.1	Podunk Road, Podunk Brook	R, w	860'	450.6	
1,744.5	0.5	Griggs Mountain		1,570'	448.5	ATC N.H.–Vt. Map 5
1,745.0	3.5	**Happy Hill Shelter** *(E–0.1m) …9mS; 7.6mN*	S, C, w	1,460'	448.0	
1,748.5	0.8	Elm Street Trailhead	R, P	750'	444.5	
1,749.3	0.6	U.S. 5, Main Street *West–0.25m to* **Norwich, Vt., P.O. 05055**	R B, G, L, M	537'	443.7	
1,749.9	0.4	I-91; Vt. 10A …*A.T. on sidewalk*	R	450'	443.1	
1,750.3	0.5	Connecticut River; Vermont–New Hampshire State Line	R	380'	442.7	

+ Fee charged

Avoid Vermont trails in "mud season," mid-Apr to Memorial Day. Hiking there in wet, sloppy conditions leads to serious Trail erosion.

Green Mountain Club—GMC maintains the 150.8 miles from the Massachusetts–Vermont border to the Connecticut River on the Vermont–New Hampshire border. Correspondence should be sent to GMC at 4711 Waterbury–Stowe Rd., Waterbury Center, VT 05677; (802) 244-7037; fax, (802) 244-5867; <gmc@greenmountainclub.org>, <www.greenmountainclub.org>.

GMC Shelter Fees—Fees are collected at high-use campsites to help defray the costs of field programs and shelter and Trail maintenance along the A.T. in Vermont. The fee is $5PP per night. This fee applies to anyone camping within 0.5 mile of a fee site. In addition, all hikers who pay the $5 fee in cash at either southern-pond fee site (Stratton Pond or Little Rock Pond) will receive a dated receipt that they can then use for one free night at the other fee site. The receipt must be used within 7 days. No receipt=no free nights=no exceptions. This offer does not extend north of Maine Junction on the Long Trail. This deal only works if you pay cash; it does not apply to folks who promise to pay later.

Stratton Pond	Griffith Lake	Little Rock Pond
Stratton Pond Shelter	Peru Peak Shelter	Little Rock Pond Shelter &
Stratton View Tenting Area	Griffith Lake Tenting Area	Tenting Area

Caretakers are present throughout the season, May–Oct, at several locations. Through conversation and example, caretakers educate hikers about Leave No Trace practices and perform Trail and shelter maintenance. Most importantly, caretakers compost sewage at high-use fee sites and a few no-fee shelter sites in southern Vermont.

Bears—To prevent future problems and costly interventions, please hang all food from tree limbs at least 12 feet off the ground, and practice Leave No Trace camping.

Long Trail—At the Vermont–Massachusetts state line, the A.T. joins the Long Trail (L.T.) for 105.2 miles, to "Maine Junction" at Willard Gap. At Maine Junction, the A.T. leads toward Maine, and the

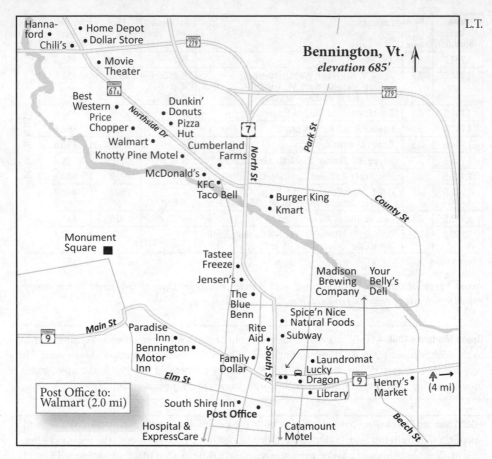

continues north, reaching the Canadian border in another 166.5 miles. Completed in 1930, the L.T. served as one inspiration for the A.T. The L.T. and A.T. are seeing increased traffic in Vermont. Please use only designated shelters and campsites, and make use of privies and wash pits to protect water quality and reduce the visible and permanent impact of greater use of the Trail.

Seth Warner Shelter (1965)—Sleeps 8. Privy. Bear box. Tentsites. Unreliable water source is a brook 150 yards to the west of the shelter.

Congdon Shelter (1967)—Sleeps 8. Privy. Tentsites behind the shelter on the ridge. Small brook east of the shelter. If the brook is dry, follow downstream to larger Stamford Stream.

Vt. 9—East 2.5 miles to ■ *Groceries:* Woodford Mountain General Store (short-term resupply), (802) 442-5222, daily 7–7, deli, Heet. ■ *Camping and Lodging:* Greenwood Lodge and Camp-sites, Prospect Access Rd., 311 Greenwood Drive, Woodford, VT 05201, (802) 442-2547, <www.campvermont.com/greenwood>, open mid-May to late Oct, HI lodging, 20 beds and campsites, call for rates.

West 5.1 miles to **Bennington, Vt. [P.O. ZIP 05201: M–F 8–5, Sa 9–2; (802) 442-2421]**. ■ *Lodging:* Catamount Motel, 500 South St., (802) 442-5977, $55S, $65D, $5EAP, $10 dog, hiker-friendly; Bennington Motor Inn, 143 Main St., (802) 442-5479; Paradise Motor Inn, 141 West Main St., (802) 442-8351. ■ *Groceries:* Henry's Market; Spice and Nice Natural Foods. ■ *Restaurants:* Madison Brewing Company; Iza-

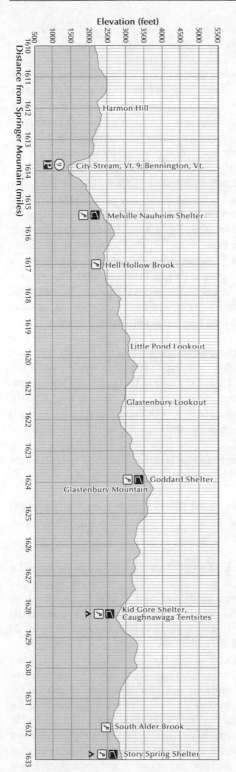

Elevation (feet)

Distance from Springer Mountain (miles)

Harmon Hill

City Stream, Vt. 9; Bennington, Vt.

Melville Nauheim Shelter

Hell Hollow Brook

Little Pond Lookout

Glastenbury Lookout

Goddard Shelter

Glastenbury Mountain

Kid Gore Shelter, Caughnawaga Tentsites

South Alder Brook

Story Spring Shelter

bella's B/L; Blue Benn Diner, B/L/D. ■ *Internet access:* Downtown is a free public WiFi zone; library. ■ *Other services:* Family Dollar; coin laundry; banks with ATM; Express Care, (802) 447-0477, walk-in clinic open daily 8–6 near hospital; shoe repair; doctor; dentist; pharmacy; veterinarian; hardware store; and free showers available at Town Recreation Center on Gage Street. ■ *Shuttles:* Walt's Taxi, (802) 442-9052, $12 Trail to town. ■ *Public transportation:* Bus station at 215 Pleasant St. Green Mountain Express, (802) 447-0477, <www.greenmtncn.org>, use free Emerald Line, M–F to Vt. 9 trail head, with connection on the The Moover, (802) 464-8487, M–F, in Wilmington to Greyhound, (802) 231-2222, and Amtrak, (800) 872-7245, in Brattleboro. Use Purple line M–F to Williams Inn, Williamstown, Mass., to connect to both Peter Pan Bus Lines, (800) 343-9999, to NYC and Boston; or Berkshire Transit, (413) 499-2782 to North Adams and Pittsfield, Mass. Use Orange Line daily service to Manchester. Vermont Translines, (844) 888-7267; morning bus service to Greyhound, Albany, N.Y., and Albany International Airport; afternoon bus service to Burlington, Vt., and Burlington International Airport, with stops in Manchester, Wallingford, Rutland, Brandon and Middlebury. Yankee Trails, (800) 822-2400, <www.yankeetrails.com>, to Greyhound in Albany.

West 7 miles to **North Bennington, Vt.**, Routes 67 and 7A, and ■ *Lodging:* Knotty Pine Motel, 130 Northside Dr., (802) 442-5487, <www.knottypinemotel.com>, $89D, $10EAP, pets accepted on limited basis, continental B, WiFi, pool, holds packages only for guests; Best Western, 200 Northside Dr., (802) 442-6311; Hampton Inn, 51 Hannaford Square, (802) 440-9862. ■ *Groceries:* Price Chopper, Walmart, Hannaford, ALDI supermarkets (long-term resupply). ■ *Restaurants: See map.* ■ *Other services:* movie theater.

Melville Nauheim Shelter (1977)—Sleeps 8. Privy. Tentsites. Water source is a stream on A.T. just north of the shelter side trail.

Vt. 9 to Kelley Stand Road—Please note: *This section of the Trail is receiving heavy use and experiencing resource damage as a result. GMC encourages hikers to use the designated shelters and campsites. If you must camp between shelters, please follow*

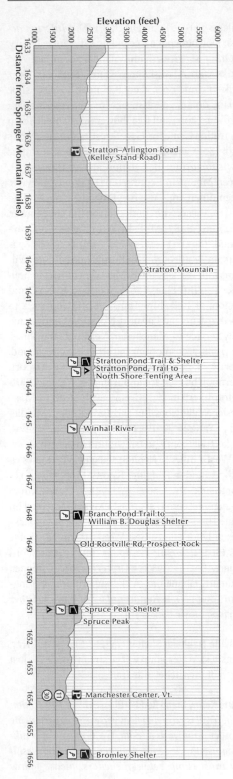

Elevation (feet)

Stratton–Arlington Road (Kelley Stand Road)

Stratton Mountain

Stratton Pond Trail & Shelter
Stratton Pond, Trail to
North Shore Tenting Area

Winhall River

Branch Pond Trail to
William B. Douglas Shelter

Old-Rootville Rd., Prospect Rock

Spruce Peak Shelter
Spruce Peak

Manchester Center, Vt.

Bromley Shelter

Distance from Springer Mountain (miles)

Leave No Trace practices, and camp 200 feet away from the Trail and all water sources.

Goddard Shelter (2005)—Sleeps 12. Privy. Bear box. The shelter has a front porch with a view to the south. Please tent above the shelter, to the west of the A.T. Water source is a spring 50 yards south on the A.T. *To preserve the pristine nature of the spring, no tenting is allowed east of the trail up the mountain.*

Glastenbury Mountain (3,748 ft.). The original fire-tower was built in 1927 and renovated in 2005. The nearby ridges seen from the observation deck are the Berkshires to the south, the Taconics to the west, Mt. Equinox and Stratton Mountain to the north, and Somerset Reservoir, Mt. Snow, and Haystack Mountain to the east. Remains of the old firewarden's cabin and woodstove can be seen to the west of the Trail, south of the summit. Porcupines are active in this area; take precautions with your gear.

Kid Gore Shelter (1971)—Sleeps 8. Privy. Bear box. Ecologically fragile area. Tentsites located north on Trail at the former Caughnawaga Shelter site. Water source is a reliable brook near Caugh-nawaga tentsites. An unreliable spring is 30 yards north of the shelter.

Caughnawaga Tentsites—Tenting only. A 1930s shelter was torn down in July 2008.

Story Spring Shelter (1963)—Sleeps 8. Privy. Bear box. Tentsites. Water source is a spring north on the A.T. 50 yards.

Stratton Mountain—Although he offered a number of variations on the story about how he first thought of the A.T., many believe it was on the slopes of Stratton Mountain that Benton MacK-aye first imagined a long-distance trail that would link the high peaks of the Appalachian Mountains. A firetower tops the summit and is open to hikers. *No camping or fires on the summit.* A side trail at the summit leads east 0.8 mile to a ski gondola at the top of Stratton Ski Area; this hut is not available for hiker use. The gondola ($20 round-trip, usually free for thru-hikers) has operated in past years, allowing hikers to ride down to Stratton Village, which has an outfitter, grocery store, and restaurants. Please check with the GMC summit caretakers, Hugh and Jean Joudry, or Stratton Mountain staff, (802) 297-4000, to see if the gondola is available for hiker use.

Stratton Pond Shelter (1999)—Sleeps 20. Privy. Bear box. Overnight fee. Go 450 feet west *via* Stratton Pond Trail. No tenting at this shelter, but you may tent on platforms at the nearby Stratton View Tenting Area; otherwise, within 0.5 mile of the pond, camping is permitted only at designated sites. Shelter has an open first floor, table, bunks, and an enclosed loft. Water source is an intermittent spring to the right of the Willis Ross clearing at Stratton Pond or the piped Bigelow Spring at Stratton Pond about 0.1 mile down the Lye Brook Trail. *No fires at this shelter*.

William B. Douglas Shelter (1956, renovated 2004)—Sleeps 10. Privy. Tentsites. Go 0.5 mile west *via* the Branch Pond Trail. Water source is a spring located south of the shelter.

Prospect Rock—Views of Manchester and Mt. Equinox. The gravel Old Rootville Road leads steeply downhill 2 miles to Vt. 11 & 30 and another 1.6 miles to the Price Chopper grocery store in Manchester Center.

Spruce Peak Shelter (1983)—Sleeps 16. Privy. This shelter with a covered front porch is 0.1 mile west on a spur trail. Water source is a boxed spring 35 yards to the right (compass south) of the shelter.

Vt. 11 & 30—**East** 2.1 miles to *Lodging:* Lodge at Bromley, 4216 Vt. 11, Peru, VT 05152; (802) 824-6941, $99S/D (includes B; laundry extra), weekends higher, WiFi, Rt. 11 & 30 Trailhead shuttle, and mail drops accepted (nonguest mail-drop fee, $10).

East 2.5 miles *via* Vt. 11 to *Groceries:* Bromley Market, 3776 Vt. 11, Peru, VT 05152; (802) 824-4444, fresh foods, deli open 7–7 7 days, some hiker supplies, mail drops accepted.

East 2.6 miles to Seesaw's Lodge, 3574 Vt. 11, Peru, VT 05152, (802) 824-5533; call for room rates; restaurant M 5–11.

East 4.2 miles to Hapgood General Store, (802) 824-4800, next to Peru P.O., open 7–5, pizza, beer.

West 3.6 miles to ■ *Lodging:* EconoLodge Motel, (802) 362-3333, $100D, $10EAP, higher on weekends; Toll Road Inn, (802) 362-1711, $99D $20EAP. ■ *Restaurants:* Bob's Diner, B/L/D.

West 5.5 miles to **Manchester Center, Vt. [P.O. ZIP 05255: M–F 8:30–4:30, Sa 9–12; (802) 362-3070]**. *See map on next page.* Pick up mail at the post office on the way into town to avoid an extra walk. The Mountain Goat is a good resource for hiker services in town. The Dana Thompson Recreation Area is a short walk from the center and offers showers for long-distance hikers during regular business hours; (802) 362-1439. *Note:* During the Vermont Summer Festival Horse shows, Jul–mid-Aug, affordable lodging will be difficult to find in the area. ■ *Hostel:* Green Mountain House, 2480 Richville Rd., (330) 388-6478, <www.greenmountainhouse.net>; owners Jeff and Regina Taussig, open Jun 7–Sep 15. Space is limited, and reservations are essential. Bed, shower, free laundry, Internet, WiFi, phone, and hiker kitchen, $35PP/night + tax. Visa/MC. Breakfast supplies available. Private room for couples. Call for pick-up from town between 1 and 7 p.m. after resupply. Free shuttle for guests back to the Trail in the morning. Not a party place; no drugs or alcohol. ■ *Lodging:* Sutton's Place, 50 School St., (802) 362-1165, <www.suttonsplacevermont.com>, owner Frank Sutton has hosted hikers more than 15 years, $80s, $95D, $115T plus tax, a/c, WiFi, accepts mail drops and is within walking distance of all services; Palmer House Resort Motel, 5383 Main St., (800) 917-6245, <www.palmerhouse.com>, midweek rate $95S/D, $20EAP, based on availability, weekends higher, light continental B $2.50, no pets, heated outdoor pool with Jacuzzi, accepts mail drops; Carriage House Motel, (802) 362-1706, <www.carriagehousemotel.com>, Jun rate $105D (higher rest of season), $25EAP, no pets, opens end of May, 1 mile east of town on Vt. 7; Hampton Inn,

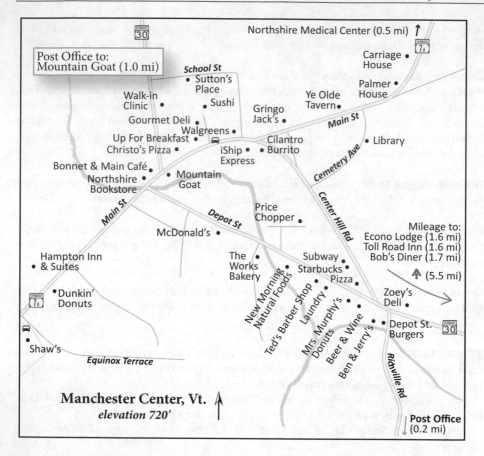

Post Office to:
Mountain Goat (1.0 mi)

School St

Northshire Medical Center (0.5 mi)

Carriage House
Palmer House

Sutton's Place
Walk-in Clinic
Sushi
Gringo Jack's
Ye Olde Tavern

Gourmet Deli
Walgreens
Up For Breakfast
Christo's Pizza
iShip Express
Cilantro Burrito

Main St

Library

Bonnet & Main Café
Northshire Bookstore
Mountain Goat

Cemetery Ave

Main St
Depot St
Price Chopper

McDonald's

Center Hill Rd

Mileage to:
Econo Lodge (1.6 mi)
Toll Road Inn (1.6 mi)
Bob's Diner (1.7 mi)

Hampton Inn & Suites

The Works Bakery
New Morning Natural Foods

Subway
Starbucks
Pizza

(5.5 mi)

Dunkin' Donuts

Ted's Barber Shop
Laundry
Mrs. Murphy's Donuts
Beer & Wine
Ben & Jerry's

Zoey's Deli

Depot St. Burgers

Shaw's

Equinox Terrace

Ridhville Rd

Manchester Center, Vt.
elevation 720'

Post Office
(0.2 mi)

$159 and up, $229 weekends. ■ *Groceries:* Price Chopper with ATM, Shaw's supermarkets (both long-term resupply). ■ *Restaurants:* Manchester Pizza House, Firefly Bar & Grill, Mrs. Murphy's Doughnuts and Coffee Shop, Cilantro's Burrito, Up For Breakfast (7–12:30), Christo's Pizza, Ben & Jerry's Scoop Shop, Zoey's Deli, Starbucks, Subway, and several fast-food outlets. ■ *Internet access:* library, M–F 10–6, Sa 10–4; Northshire Bookstore, M–Th 10–7, F–sa 10–9; I Ship Express (below). ■ *Outfitter:* The Mountain Goat, 4886 Main St., (802) 362-5159, open M–Sa 10–6, Su 10–5, full-service outfitter, fuel by the ounce, custom footbeds and orthotics, mail drops (USPS, UPS & FedEx) accepted. ■ *Other services:* I Ship Express, 5018 Main St., (802) 362-1652, M–F 9:30–5, Sa 9:30–noon, packing and shipping services; coin laundry; bank with ATM; doctor; dentist; pharmacy; veterinarian; Manchester Taxi, (802) 362-4118 and (802) 688-6426; Leonard's Taxi, (802) 362-2620; Green Mountain Express, (802) 447-0477, <www.greenmtncn.org>, $2 bus service between Manchester and Bennington, flag stop across from Walgreens and Shaw's; Marble Valley Regional Transportation, <www.thebus.com>, $2 bus service between Manchester and Rutland/Killington, stops along the U.S. 7 corridor (Danby, Wallingford, North Clarendon); Vermont Translines, see Bennington.

Bromley Shelter (2003)—Sleeps 12. Privy (composting). Tent platforms and campsite are north 0.1 mile. Unreliable spring at the terminus of the spur trail. *No water for next 8 miles.*

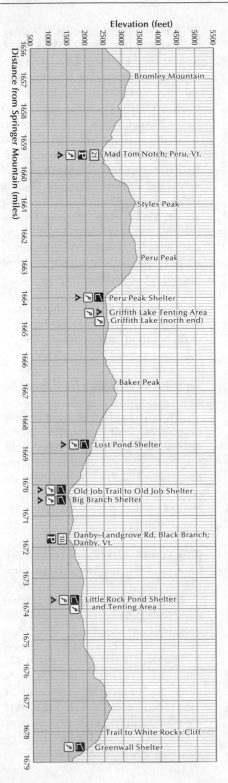

Elevation (feet)

Distance from Springer Mountain (miles)

Bromley Mountain

Mad Tom Notch; Peru, Vt.

Styles Peak

Peru Peak

Peru Peak Shelter

Griffith Lake Tenting Area
Griffith Lake (north end)

Baker Peak

Lost Pond Shelter

Old Job Trail to Old Job Shelter
Big Branch Shelter

Danby–Landgrove Rd, Black Branch;
Danby, Vt.

Little Rock Pond Shelter
and Tenting Area

Trail to White Rocks Cliff
Greenwall Shelter

Bromley Mountain—An observation tower that recently was torn down will be rebuilt, thanks to donations from many, including ALDHA. Ski trails lead to Bromley Base Lodge area. The ski patrol warming hut is open for use; privy on summit; no water.

Peru Peak Shelter/Griffith Lake Tenting Area (1935/1979/2000)—Sleeps 10. Privy. Overnight fee. Camping permitted only at designated tent platforms within 0.5 mile of Griffith Lake. Water source is the pond or a brook near the shelter.

Lost Pond Shelter (2009)—Sleeps 8. Privy. Tentsites. Water source is nearby stream.

Old Job Shelter (1935/2009)—1.3 miles on Old Job Trail. Sleeps 8. Privy. Tentsites. Water source is in front of the shelter at Lake Brook.

Big Branch Shelter (1963)—Sleeps 8. Privy. Tentsites north of shelter. Close to USFS 10 and receives heavy weekend use. Good soaking pools. Water source is Big Branch, located in front of the shelter.

USFS 10, Danby–Landgrove Road—*Light traffic, may be a difficult hitch on weekdays.* **West** 3.5 miles to **Danby, Vt. [P.O. ZIP 05739: M–F 7:15–10:15 & 11:15–2:15, Sa 7:30–10:30; (802) 293-5105].** ■ *Groceries:* Mt. Tabor Country Store, 1072 U.S. 7, (802) 293-5641, M–Sa 5–8, Su 5–7, short-term resupply. ■ *Other services:* Silas Griffith Library, MVRT, (802) 773-3244, <www.thebus.com>, Manchester-to-Rutland commuter, M–Sa $2. Departs for Manchester from the Mt. Tabor Country Store; for Rutland, from Brooklyn Rd.

Little Rock Pond Shelter and Tenting Area (2010)—Sleeps 12. Tent platforms. Privy. Overnight fee. Spring located north on Trail.

Greenwall Shelter (1962/2009)—**East** on side trail 0.2 mile. Sleeps 8. Privy. Tentsites. Water source is a spring, prone to fail in dry seasons, 200 yards along a trail behind the shelter.

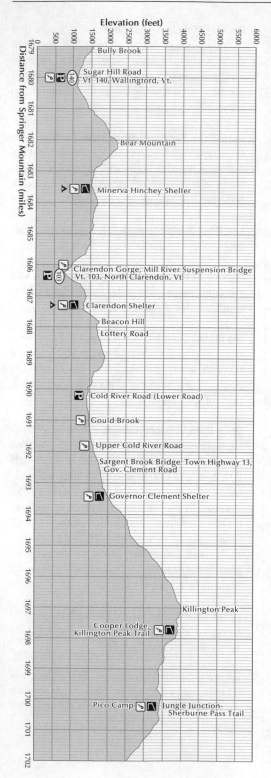

Elevation (feet)

Distance from Springer Mountain (miles)

Bully Brook

Sugar Hill Road
Vt. 140, Wallingford, Vt.

Bear Mountain

Minerva Hinchey Shelter

Clarendon Gorge, Mill River Suspension Bridge
Vt. 103, North Clarendon, Vt.

Clarendon Shelter

Beacon Hill
Lottery Road

Cold River Road (Lower Road)

Gould Brook

Upper Cold River Road

Sargent Brook Bridge, Town Highway 13,
Gov. Clement Road

Governor Clement Shelter

Killington Peak

Cooper Lodge,
Killington Peak Trail

Pico Camp   Jungle Junction-
Sherburne Pass Trail

Vt. 140—West 2.8 miles to **Walling-ford, Vt. [P.O. ZIP 05773: M–F 8–4:30, Sa 9–12; (802) 446-2140].** ■ *Lodging:* Several AirBnBs, $125 and up. ■ *Restaurants:* Sal's South, (802) 446-2935, Italian and pizza, L/D daily 12–9; The Main Street Café, 5 N. Main St., (802) 446-6169, serves B/L daily 6–2 p.m. ■ *Groceries:* Cumberland Farms, Citgo Smart Shop, Family Dollar (all short-term resupply). ■ *Internet access:* Gilbert Hart Library, M, W–Sa. ■ *Other services:* ATM; dentist; Biana Hair Studio; MVRT, (802) 773-3244, <www.thebus.com>, Manchester-to-Rutland commuter, M–Sa $2, departures and arrivals near Cumberland Farms; Vermont Translines (see Bennington, page 192).

Minerva Hinchey Shelter (1969/2006)— Sleeps 8. Privy. Tenting area. Spring 50 yards south of shelter; follow "Wada" signs.

Clarendon Gorge Wildlife Management Area—A suspension bridge 0.1 mile south of Vt. 103 overlooks a favorite swimming hole for residents. Built in 1974, this bridge is dedicated to the memory of Robert Brugmann, who drowned while trying to cross the swollen Mill River. Swimming in the gorge is hazardous during high water. Watch for broken glass. *No camping or fires permitted in the gorge.*

Vt. 103—*Other services:* MVRT, (802) 773-3244, <www.thebus.com>, Bellows Falls to Rutland, $3, flag stop M–F.
    West 0.8 mile to *Groceries:* Loretta's Good Food Deli (short term resupply), 638 Route 103, East Clarendon, VT 05759; (802) 772-7638, M–F 6–6, Sa 10–5, hiker-friendly owners Dennis and Loretta Clark; B/L sandwiches, fresh meats and baked goods, salads, meals-to-go, deli, ice cream, beer, wine, Heet, dog food, first aid, water filters, accepts mail drops (no fee), picnic area. Curbside call stop for The Bus, (802) 773-3144, with service to Rutland, M–F.

A ridgerunner may be found along the Coolidge Range at the these locations, although a fee is not charged: Clarendon Shelter, Governor Clement Shelter, Cooper Lodge, Pico Camp, and Churchill Scott Shelter.

Clarendon Shelter (1952)—Sleeps 10. Moldering privy. Tentsites. Water source is a stream 15 yards east of the shelter.

Cold River Road—East 2.7 miles to Shrewsbury Co-op at Pierces' Store, short-term resupply, sandwiches and daily specials, M–Sa 7–7, Su 8–5. (Distance from Upper Cold River Road is 2.5 miles.)

Governor Clement Shelter (1929/ 2009)—Sleeps 10. Moldering privy. Tentsites. Water source is a brook 63 yards east of the shelter.

Cooper Lodge (1939)—Sleeps 12. Cooper Pooper Privy. Tent platforms. This enclosed stone cabin was built by the Vermont Forest Service and the CCC. Behind the shelter is a 0.2-mile side trail to Killington Peak. Water source is a spring 100 ft. north on the A.T.

Killington Peak—Reached by a steep 0.2-mile side trail from Cooper Lodge. At 4,241 feet, this is the highest point near the Trail in Vermont and the second-highest peak in the state. The open, rocky summit offers panoramic views, and, on a clear day, you can see the White Mountains of New Hampshire and the Adirondacks of New York. At the summit, a short side trail leads to the Summit Peak Lodge, dining and bar service 11–4:30, operated by the Killington ski resort; shops, (800) 621-6867, are located below at the village reached by the gondola. K-1 Gondola ($30) operates from late Jun to fall-foliage season, 10–5. K-1 Base Lodge on the Killington Access Road is on the MVRT Diamond Express bus route to Rutland. A GMC ridgerunner patrols the Coolidge Range (including Killington and Pico) and may be available to answer natural-history and Trail questions.

Jungle Junction–Sherburne Pass Trail—Named after a 1938 hurricane left behind a "jungle" of blowdowns (and essentially broke the A.T. as a continuous footpath a year after it opened as such). The blue-blazed Sherburne Pass Trail (former A.T.) leads 3.1 miles north to Sherburne Pass on U.S. 4, directly to the Inn at Long Trail (opened in 1938, ironically), and continues north of the inn 0.5 mile to reconnect with the A.T. east of Deer Leap.

Pico Camp (1959)—Sleeps 12. Privy. An enclosed shelter located 0.5 mile east on the Sherburne Pass Trail, the former A.T. Water source is 45 yards north on the Sherburne Pass Trail.

Rutland city watershed: The western flanks of the Coolidge Range comprise a major portion of Rutland's watershed. *Fires are not permitted.* Please camp only at designated sites and use facilities provided.

Churchill Scott Shelter (2002)—Sleeps 8. Privy (composting). Tent platform. Water on spur trail downhill behind shelter.

U.S. 4—East 0.9 mile uphill along a busy thoroughfare to ■ *Lodging:* The Inn at Long Trail, 709 Route 4, Sherburne Pass, Killington, VT 05751; (802) 775-7181, <www.innatlongtrail.com>; closed mid-Apr, reopens Memorial Day weekend. The inn offers discounted rooms for hikers with full B; one room designated for hikers with pets, no dogs in the lodge. McGrath's Irish Pub serves L/D 11:30 a.m.–9 p.m. Live Irish music on weekends. Coin laundry, hiker box, outside water spigot, WiFi. Mail drops by UPS or Fed Ex only. Parking, tent camping across the street. Inn opens at 7 a.m., B 7:30–9:30, all meals open to the public. Vermont Translines, (844) 888-7267, <vttranslines.com>, will stop here with advance notice (10:50 a.m. eastbound, 4:55 p.m. westbound), with connections to

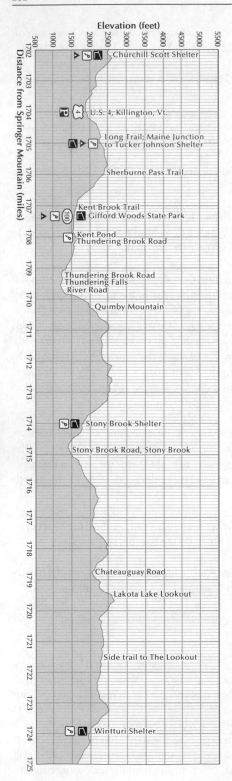

Elevation (feet)

Distance from Springer Mountain (miles)

- Churchill Scott Shelter
- U.S. 4, Killington, Vt.
- Long Trail; Maine Junction to Tucker Johnson Shelter
- Sherburne Pass Trail
- Kent Brook Trail
- Gifford Woods State Park
- Kent Pond
- Thundering Brook Road
- Thundering Brook Road
- Thundering Falls
- River Road
- Quimby Mountain
- Stony Brook Shelter
- Stony Brook Road, Stony Brook
- Chateauguay Road
- Lakota Lake Lookout
- Side trail to The Lookout
- Wintturi Shelter

Burlington, Albany, White river Junction, and Hanover. MVRT Diamond Express bus service daily from inn to Rutland. ■ *Shuttles:* Killington Taxi, (802) 442-9718 (seasonal); Gramps Shuttle, (802) 236-6600; Uber. *A safer alternative to the roadwalk in heavy traffic is to cross Route 4 and continue on the A.T. north 1.9 miles to the northern terminus of the Sherburne Pass Trail, which will lead you 0.5 mile south directly to the inn.*

West 8.6 miles to the city of **Rutland, Vt. [P.O. 05701: M–F 8–5, Sa 8–12; (802) 773-0222]**, with all major services and chain motels; *see map.* ■ *Hostel:* Hikers Hostel at the Yellow Deli (Twelve Tribes), 23 Center St., (802) 683-9378 or (802) 775-9800, <www.hikershostel.org>, located downtown next to the transit center, open year-round, monetary donation or work-trade appreciated but not required, includes B, common room, laundry $2, separate bunk rooms for men and women, possible shuttles, limited resupply, mail drops accepted. ■ *Groceries:* Rutland Food Coop on Wales St., Tops Market, Hannaford and ALDI on U.S. 7, Price Chopper and Walmart on Merchant's Row (all long-term resupply). ■ *Restaurants:* Yellow Deli, L/D, 15% discount to hikers, closed Sa; farmers market (Sa). ■ *Outfitters:* Dick's Sporting Goods at Green Mountain Shopping Plaza can be reached *via* local MVRT bus. ■ *Internet access:* Rutland Free Library. ■ *Other services:* Rutland Regional Medical Center Hospital; Express Care, (802) 773-3386, 215 Stratton Rd., daily 8–8; Clear Choice MD Urgent Care, (802) 772-4165, 173 S. Main St., daily 8–8; veterinarians; Rutland Taxi, (802) 236-3133; Roy's Taxi, (802) 236-1966; All Occasion Transportation, (802) 236-1966. ■ *Public Transportation:* Bus station located at Marble Valley Transit Center, 80 West St. Marble Valley Regional Transit, (802) 773-3244, <www.thebus.com>, Diamond Express $2 daily service in the Rutland–Killington area; M–Sa to Manchester; M–F to Bellows Falls, curbside flag stops along Vt. 103. Vermont Translines (see Bennington above), with additional service along the U.S. 4 corridor, to Greyhound in White River Junction. Daily flights to Boston from the Rutland Airport. Amtrak, from downtown Rutland on Ethan Allen Express to NYC's Penn Station.

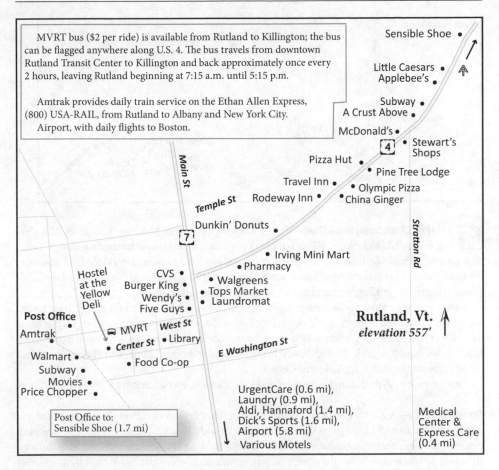

MVRT bus ($2 per ride) is available from Rutland to Killington; the bus can be flagged anywhere along U.S. 4. The bus travels from downtown Rutland Transit Center to Killington and back approximately once every 2 hours, leaving Rutland beginning at 7:15 a.m. until 5:15 p.m.

Amtrak provides daily train service on the Ethan Allen Express, (800) USA-RAIL, from Rutland to Albany and New York City.
Airport, with daily flights to Boston.

Sensible Shoe •

Little Caesars •
Applebee's •

Subway •
A Crust Above •

McDonald's •

4   • Stewart's
       Shops

Pizza Hut •

• Pine Tree Lodge

Travel Inn •   • Olympic Pizza
Rodeway Inn •   • China Ginger

Main St

Temple St

Dunkin' Donuts •

7

Stratton Rd

• Irving Mini Mart
• Pharmacy

Hostel   CVS •
at the   Burger King •   • Walgreens
Yellow   Wendy's •   • Tops Market
Deli   Five Guys •   • Laundromat

Rutland, Vt. ↑
elevation 557'

Post Office •
Amtrak •   ⊟ MVRT   *West St*
              • *Center St* • Library
Walmart •   *E Washington St*
Subway •   • Food Co-op
Movies •
Price Chopper •

UrgentCare (0.6 mi),
Laundry (0.9 mi),
Aldi, Hannaford (1.4 mi),
Dick's Sports (1.6 mi),
Airport (5.8 mi)
Various Motels

Post Office to:
Sensible Shoe (1.7 mi)

Medical
Center &
Express Care
(0.4 mi)

Maine Junction–Willard Gap. The L.T. continues north 166.5 miles to Canada, while the A.T. diverges to the east toward New Hampshire and Maine.

Tucker-Johnson Shelter (2018)—Located on the L.T. 0.4 mile north of Maine Junction. Shelter burned down in 2011; new one sleeps 8. Tenting area. Moldering privy. Water source is Eagle Square Brook, 100 ft. north.

Vt. 100—The A.T. passes through Gifford Woods State Park, (802) 775-5354, ice cream and soda in office, with shelters, tentsites, and bathhouse visible from the Trail. ■ *Camping:* limited primitive sites $6, shelters $27–$29; tentsites $20–$22 up to 4 people, cabin $50 for 4 people, two-night minimum cabin reservation in Jul–Aug, $1/pet/night, coin-operated showers 50¢ (5 mins.), water spigot. Space fills up quickly during the fall "leaf season." ■ *Shuttles:* See U.S. 4 above.

East 0.6 mile to U.S. 4 and **Killington, Vt. [P.O. ZIP 05751: M–F 8:30–11, 12–4:30, Sa 8:30–12; (802) 775-4247].**
■ *Lodging:* Greenbrier Inn, (802) 775-1575, <www.greenbriervt.com>, call for rates, continental B, pool; Killington Motel, (802) 773-9535, call for hiker rates, all rooms nonsmoking, includes B, will pick up hikers as time allows. ■ *Groceries:* Killington Deli & Market Place, (802) 775-1599, <www.killing-tondeli.com>, (short-term resupply), 6:30 a.m.–7 p.m. daily, sandwiches, hot-meal specials, liquor store, and ATM. ■ *Outfitter:* See below. ■ *Other services:* MVRT and VTTRANS bus stops nearby at Welcome Center.

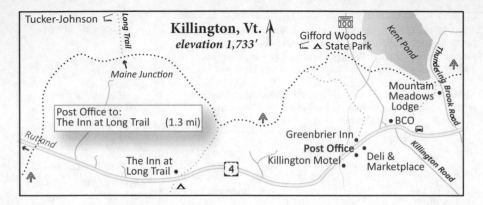

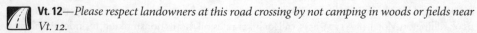 **Kent Pond, Thundering Brook Road**—on A.T. *Lodging:* Mountain Meadows Lodge, 285 Thundering Brook Rd., Killington, VT 05751; (802) 775-1010, <www.mountainmeadowslodge.com>; new owners. If available, hikers not staying at the lodge can have a reasonably priced B/D; kayaking on Kent Pond. Hiker box inside; outdoor water spigot; mail drops accepted. This is not a hostel, but a country inn and wedding venue; please be respectful of nonhiker guests.

East 0.3 mile on side cross-country ski trail (signed marked B.C.O.) to *Outfitter:* Base Camp Outfitters, 2363 U.S. 4, Killington, VT 05751; (802) 775-0166, <www.basecampvt.com>; on bus route to Rutland, open daily 10–5; backpacking equipment, clothing, and supplies, ice cream, freeze-dried food, fuel, disc golf, outside deck area with hiker box and recharging outlets; mail drops accepted. MVRT bus stop to Rutland at Welcome Center.

East 0.6 mile to all the Killington services on U.S. 4 above: *A safer alternative to walking on Vt. 100.*

Thundering Falls—A 2007-8 relocation, which took 30 years from conception to completion, eliminated a road walk and added views of Thundering Falls and the Ottauquechee River. The new path descends through northern-hardwood forest to the base of high Thundering Falls and then through the open Ottauquechee River floodplain. A wheelchair-accessible boardwalk built by the Green Mountain Club and financed by ATC and the National Park Service crosses the river and floodplain.

River Road—**East** 0.5 mile to Killington town offices and Johnson Recreation Center pool ($4 nonresident fee), M–F 12:30–7, Sa–Su 12–7. **East** 0.7 mile to Sherburne Memorial Library, M–Sa.

Stony Brook Shelter (1997)—Sleeps 6. Privy. Tentsites. Brook 100 yards north of shelter on A.T.

Side Trail to the Lookout—One of the few views between Killington Peak and New Hampshire. Follow side trail 0.2 mile west to a private cabin. Use care on ladder that leads up to an observation deck. No water. The owners permit its use by hikers; please be responsible to ensure that this privilege continues.

Wintturi Shelter (1994)—Sleeps 6. Privy. Tentsites. Spring 300 ft. to the north of the shelter.

Vt. 12—*Please respect landowners at this road crossing by not camping in woods or fields near Vt. 12.*

East 3.8 miles to **Woodstock, Vt. [P.O. ZIP 05091: M–F 8:30–5, Sa 9–12; (802) 457-1323].** Home of the Marsh-Billings-Rockefeller National Historical Park. Services include several expensive motels and inns, grocery (long-term resupply), restaurants, bank with ATM, doctor, dentist, pharmacy, and movie theater open F–Su. ■ *Lodging:* The Shire Woodstock Riverview Hotel, 46 Pleasant St., (802) 457-2211, <www.shirewoodstock.com>, WiFi, a/c, all rooms nonsmoking, rates begin at $169D.

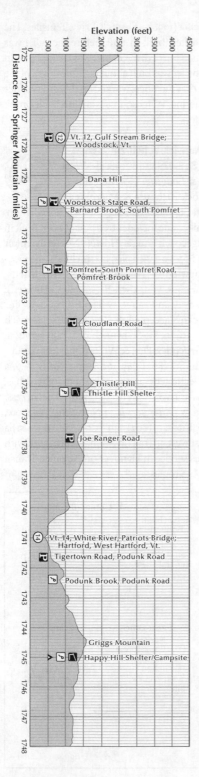

Elevation (feet)

Distance from Springer Mountain (miles)

1725
1726
1727
1728 — Vt. 12, Gulf Stream Bridge; Woodstock, Vt.
1729
1730 — Dana Hill
       — Woodstock Stage Road, Barnard Brook; South Pomfret
1731
1732 — Pomfret–South Pomfret Road, Pomfret Brook
1733
1734 — Cloudland Road
1735
1736 — Thistle Hill
       — Thistle Hill Shelter
1737
1738 — Joe Ranger Road
1739
1740
1741 — Vt. 14, White River, Patriots Bridge; Hartford, West Hartford, Vt.
1742 — Tigertown Road, Podunk Road
       — Podunk Brook, Podunk Road
1743
1744
1745 — Griggs Mountain
       — Happy Hill Shelter/Campsite
1746
1747
1748

Internet access: library, M–Sa.

West 0.2 mile to *Groceries:* On the Edge farm stand, owners Dana and Bill, open daily in summer 10–5:30, Su 10–5; delicious home-made pies, seasonal veggies, fruit, cold drinks, ice cream, cheese, smoked meat, bread rolls, breakfast burritos, jerky, and water.

Woodstock Stage Road—East 0.9 mile to **South Pomfret, Vt. [P.O. ZIP 05067: M–F 12:30–4:30, Sa 8:30–11:30; (802) 457-1147].** ■ *Groceries:* Teago General Store (short-term resupply), M–Sa 7–6, Su 8–4, deli sandwiches and P.O. inside store. ■ *Internet access:* library, WiFi, Tu, Th, Sa.

Cloudland Road—West 0.2 mile to Cloudland Farm Country Market & Restaurant, (802) 457-2599, <www.cloudlandfarm.com>; W 10–3, Th–Sa 10–5, water, cold drinks, beef jerky, cheese, crackers, ice cream. This operating farm is run by Bill and Cathy Emmons.

Thistle Hill Shelter (1995)—Sleeps 8. Privy. Tentsites. The Cloudland privy was moved to Thistle Hill, partly with ALDHA's help. Two nearby streams for water.

Vt. 14—On the A.T., **West Hartford, Vt. [P.O. closed].** ■ *Camping:* "The Hart Family," Randy and Lynda, long-time Trail angels with a home with a big AT on the blue barn, are around to offer water and comfort to the weary. Steve "Capt. Stash" at Hartford Sign Co., 5255 Vt. 14, West Hartford, VT 05084 ("1722" on A.T. sign), (802) 295-6631, allows tenting and mails drops *via* UPS. ■ *Internet access:* library, M–Th, Sa, WiFi.

East 7 miles to **Hartford, Vt. [P.O. ZIP 05047: M–F 8–12, Sa 9–11:30; (802) 295-5511].** Free bus service from Hartford, Vt., to West Lebanon or Hanover, N.H., on Advance Transit Green Route.

East 8 miles to **White River Junction**, a large town with all services and free Advance Transit bus service on the orange route. Near the Greyhound bus station is a super 8 motel and several other major chains, a Chinese Buffet, McDonald's, and Jake's Market. Amtrak provides daily train service on the Vermonter, (800) USA-RAIL. *Hostel:* Hotel Coolidge (Hosteling International), 39 South Main St., White River Junction, VT 05001; (802) 295-3118, (800) 622-1124, <www.hotelcoolidge.com>; $55S, $65D, $10EAP; kitchen, laundry, WiFi; walk to restaurants, banks, and stores.

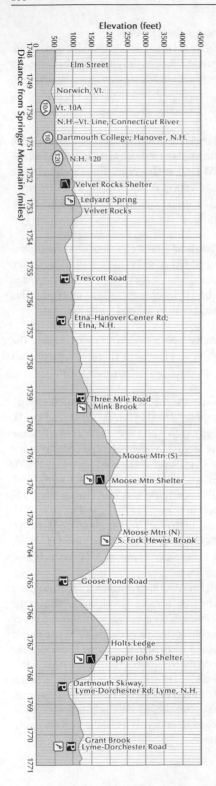

Happy Hill Shelter (1998)—Sleeps 8. Privy. Tentsites. The oldest A.T. shelter (built in 1918, before the A.T.) was torn down, then burned; the debris was carried out. In 1998, a new shelter was built about 0.2 mile north of the original. ALDHA members worked on this project after the 1997 Gathering. Water source is an unreliable brook near the shelter.

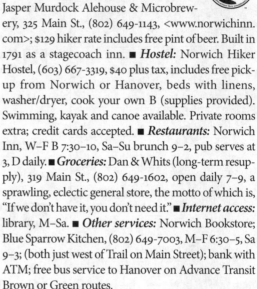

U.S. 5/Norwich, Vt. [P.O. ZIP 05055: M–F 8:30–5, Sa 9–12; (802) 649-1608]—West 0.25 mile to ■ *Lodging:* Norwich Inn & Jasper Murdock Alehouse & Microbrewery, 325 Main St., (802) 649-1143, <www.norwichinn.com>; $129 hiker rate includes free pint of beer. Built in 1791 as a stagecoach inn. ■ *Hostel:* Norwich Hiker Hostel, (603) 667-3319, $40 plus tax, includes free pick-up from Norwich or Hanover, beds with linens, washer/dryer, cook your own B (supplies provided). Swimming, kayak and canoe available. Private rooms extra; credit cards accepted. ■ *Restaurants:* Norwich Inn, W–F B 7:30–10, Sa–Su brunch 9–2, pub serves at 3, D daily. ■ *Groceries:* Dan & Whits (long-term resupply), 319 Main St., (802) 649-1602, open daily 7–9, a sprawling, eclectic general store, the motto of which is, "If we don't have it, you don't need it." ■ *Internet access:* library, M–Sa. ■ *Other services:* Norwich Bookstore; Blue Sparrow Kitchen, (802) 649-7003, M–F 6:30–5, Sa 9–3; (both just west of Trail on Main Street); bank with ATM; free bus service to Hanover on Advance Transit Brown or Green routes.

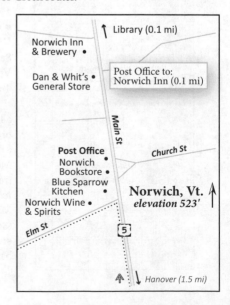

New Hampshire

Miles from Springer	Miles to Next Point	Features	Services	Elev	Miles from Katahdin	MAP	Alt Name
1,750.3	0.5	Connecticut River; Vermont–New Hampshire State Line	R	380'	442.7		
1,750.8	0.7	N.H. 10, Dartmouth College	R, C, G, L, M, O, D, V, B, sh, cl, f	520'	442.2		
		On A.T.–**Hanover, N.H., P.O. 03755** East–2m to Sunset Motor Inn	L, cl				
1,751.5	0.8	N.H. 120	R	490'	441.5		
1,752.3	0.5	**Velvet Rocks Shelter** *(W–0.2m)* *(N–0.2m w) ...7.6mS; 9.7mN*	S, nw	1,040'	440.7		
1,752.8	0.8	Ledyard Spring (W–0.4m) ...*water for Velvet Rocks Shelter*	w	1,200'	440.2		
1,753.6	1.7	Velvet Rocks		1,243'	439.4		
1,755.3	1.4	Trescott Road	R, P	915'	437.7	ATC N.H.–Vt. Map 5	
1,756.7	2.5	Etna–Hanover Center Road *East–0.9m to* Etna, N.H.	R, P, H G, f, sh	845'	436.3		
1,759.2	0.2	Three Mile Road	R, P	1,350'	433.8		
1,759.4	1.6	Mink Brook	w	1,320'	433.6		
1,761.0	0.8	Moose Mountain *(South Peak)*		2,290'	432.0		
1,761.8	1.2	**Moose Mountain Shelter** *...9.7mS; 5.9mN*	S, C, w	1,850'	431.2		
1,763.0	0.7	Moose Mountain *(North Peak)*		2,300'	430.0		
1,763.7	1.3	South Fork, Hewes Brook	w	1,100'	429.3		
1,765.0	2.0	Goose Pond Road	R, P	952'	428.0		
1,767.0	0.5	Holts Ledge ...*peregrine falcon rookery*		1,930'	426.0		
1,767.5	0.9	**Trapper John Shelter** *(W–0.2m)* *...5.9mS; 6.9mN*	S, C, w	1,345'	425.5		
1,768.4	1.9	Dartmouth Skiway, Lyme-Dorchester Rd *West–3.2m to* **Lyme, N.H., P.O. 03768**	R, P G, L, M, V	880'	424.6		
1,770.3	0.1	Grant Brook	w	1,090'	422.7		
1,770.4	3.7	Lyme-Dorchester Road, Smarts Mountain Trailhead	R, P, w	1,100'	422.6		
1,774.1	0.1	Smarts Mountain Tentsite	C, w	3,200'	418.9		LAMBERT RIDGE
1,774.2	3.9	**Firewarden's Cabin**, fire tower *...6.9mS; 5.6mN*	S, w	3,230'	418.8		
1,778.1	0.4	South Jacob's Brook	w	1,450'	414.9		J TRAIL
1,778.5	0.7	Eastman Ledges		2,010'	414.5	ATC N.H.–Vt. Map 4	KODAK TRAIL
1,779.2	0.3	North Jacobs Brook ...*water for Hexacuba Shelter*	w	1,900'	413.8		
1,779.5	1.4	**Hexacuba Shelter** *(E–0.3m) ...5.6mS; 16mN*	S, w	1,980'	413.5		
1,780.9	0.2	Mt. Cube *(south summit)*; Cross Rivendell Trail Junction		2,909'	412.1		MT. CUBE TRAIL
1,781.1	1.5	Mt. Cube, side trail to north summit		2,911'	411.9		
1,782.6	1.8	Brackett Brook ...*ford*	w	1,400'	410.4		
1,784.4	1.6	N.H. 25A ...*beach on lake (E–0.1m)* *East–4.8m to* **Wentworth, N.H., P.O. 03282**	R, P G	900'	408.6		

Miles from Springer	Miles to Next Point	Features	Services	Elev	Miles from Katahdin	M A P	Alt Name
1,786.0	0.6	Cape Moonshine Road (E–1m to Dancing Bones Village)	R, C, sh	1,400'	407.0		ATWELL HILL TRAIL
1,786.6	2.3	Ore Hill Campsite (E–0.1m)	C, w	1,720'	406.4		ORE HILL TRAIL
1,788.9	0.3	Ore Hill		1,850'	404.1		
1,789.2	2.5	N.H. 25C, Ore Hill Brook East–4m to **Warren, N.H., P.O. 03279**	R, P G, M, D, cl	1,550'	403.8		
1,791.7	0.4	Mt. Mist		2,200'	401.3		
1,792.1	0.1	Hairy Root Spring, Webster Slide Trail	w	1,600'	400.9		WACHIPAUKA POND TRAIL
1,792.2	1.9	Wachipauka Pond	w	1,493'	400.8		
1,794.1	1.1	N.H. 25, Oliverian Brook ...ford, road bypass if high water East–0.4m to **Glencliff, N.H., P.O. 03238**	R, P, w H, sh, cl, f	1,000'	398.9		
1,795.2	0.4	**Jeffers Brook Shelter** ...16mS; 6.9mN	S, C, w	1,350'	397.8	ATC N.H.–Vt. Map 4	TOWN LINE TRAIL
1,795.6	0.3	Long Pond Road, USFS 19	R	1,330'	397.4		
1,795.9	0.4	High Street, Glencliff Trailhead	R, P	1,480'	397.1		GLENCLIFF TRAIL
1,796.3	2.6	Hurricane Trail		1,680'	396.7		
1,798.9	0.9	Mt. Moosilauke (south peak), Carriage Rd		4,460'	394.1		
1,799.8	0.4	Mt. Moosilauke (north peak) East–3.7m on Gorge Brook Trail to DOC Ravine Lodge	R	4,802'	393.2		MOOSILAUKE CARRIAGE ROAD
1,800.2	1.5	Benton Trail		4,550'	392.8		
1,801.7	0.4	Asquam Ridge Trail (E–4m to DOC Ravine Lodge)		4,050'	391.3		BEAVER BROOK TRAIL
1,802.1	0.4	**Beaver Brook Shelter** and **Campsite** ...6.9mS; 9mN	S, C, w	3,750'	390.9		
1,802.5	1.1	Beaver Brook Cascades	w	3,000'	390.5		
1,803.6	0.6	Kinsman Notch; N.H. 112 (E–0.3m to Lost River Gorge) East–5m to **North Woodstock, N.H., P.O. 03262** East–6m to **Lincoln, N.H., P.O. 03251**	R, P, w H, G, L, M, cl, f all	1,870'	389.4		
1,804.2	2.7	Dilly Trail		2,650'	388.8		
1,806.9	1.3	Gordon Pond Trail		2,700'	386.1		KINSMAN RIDGE TRAIL
1,808.2	1.9	Mt. Wolf (East Peak)		3,478'	384.8		
1,810.1	0.5	Reel Brook Trail		2,600'	382.9		
1,810.6	0.5	Powerline		2,625'	382.4		
1,811.1	1.4	**Eliza Brook Shelter** and **Campsite** ...9mS; 4.1mN	S, C, w	2,400'	381.9		
1,812.5	1.1	Harrington Pond		3,400'	380.5	ATC N.H.–Vt. Map 3	
1,813.6	0.9	South Kinsman Mountain		4,358'	379.4		
1,814.5	0.4	North Kinsman Mountain		4,293'	378.5		
1,814.9	0.2	Mt. Kinsman Trail		3,900'	378.1		
1,815.1	1.9	Kinsman Pond Trail (south) to +AMC **Kinsman Pond Shelter** and **Campsite** (E–0.1m) ...4.1mS; 15.3mN	S, C, w	3,750'	377.9		
1,817.0	0.9	+AMC Lonesome Lake Hut; Lonesome Lake Trail West–1.7m to Lafayette Place W on I-93	L, M, w R, P, B, C	2,760'	376.0		FISHIN' JIMMY TRAIL
1,817.9	0.5	Kinsman Pond Trail (north)		2,294'	375.1		
1,818.4	1.1	Basin–Cascade Trail; Cascade Brook ...ford	w	2,084'	374.6		

Miles from Springer	Miles to Next Point	Features	Services	Elev	Miles from Katahdin	MAP	Alt Name
1,819.5	0.2	Whitehouse Brook	w	1,610'	373.5		CASCADE BROOK TRAIL
1,819.7	0.2	Pemi Trail		1,520'	373.3		
1,819.9	0.1	Franconia Notch, I-93, U.S. 3 ... *underpass, Pemigawasset River* *East–5.8m to* **North Woodstock, N.H., P.O. 03262** *East–7.3m to* **Lincoln, N.H., P.O. 03251** *West–8m to* Franconia, N.H.	R H, G, L, M, cl, f all B, G, L, M	1,450'	373.1		
1,820.0	0.5	Franconia Notch Bike Path *East–0.2m to* Whitehouse Trail *(follow east 0.8m to hiker parking)* *East–1m to* Flume Visitor Center *West–2.1m to* Lafayette Campground	R, P, B C, B, P	1,450'	373.0		
1,820.5	2.0	Flume Side Trail		1,800'	372.5		LIBERTY SPRING TRAIL
1,822.5	0.3	+AMC Liberty Springs Tentsite	C, w	3,870'	370.5		
1,822.8	1.8	Franconia Ridge Trail ... *Mt. Liberty (E–0.3m)*		4,260'	370.2		
1,824.6	0.7	Little Haystack Mountain; Falling Waters Trail *(W–3.2m to Lafayette Place East on I-93) ...above treeline for next 2.5 miles north on Franconia Ridge*	R, P, B, C	4,800'	368.4		FRANCONIA RIDGE TRAIL
1,825.3	1.0	Mt. Lincoln		5,089'	367.7		
1,826.3	0.8	Mt. Lafayette; Greenleaf Trail *(W–0.2m spring)* *West–1.1m to* +AMC Greenleaf Hut *West–4m to* Lafayette Place E on I-93	w L, M, w R, P, B, C	5,260'	366.7	ATC N.H.–Vt. Map 3	
1,827.1	2.0	Skookumchuck Trail Jct. ...*above treeline for the next 2.5 miles south on Franconia Ridge*		4,680'	365.9		
1,829.1	0.7	Garfield Pond	w	3,860'	363.9		GARFIELD RIDGE TRAIL
1,829.8	0.2	Mt. Garfield		4,500'	363.2		
1,830.0	0.2	Garfield Trail *(W–4.8m to Gale River Loop Road)*	P, R, B	4,180'	363.0		
1,830.2	0.5	+AMC **Garfield Ridge Shelter** and **Campsite** *(W–0.1m) ...15.3mS; 6.4mN*	S, C, w	3,900'	362.8		
1,830.7	1.6	Franconia Brook Trail		3,420'	362.3		
1,832.3	0.6	Gale River Trail *(W–4m to Gale River Loop Road)*	P, R, B	3,390'	360.7		
1,832.9	0.8	+AMC Galehead Hut, Twin Brook Trail	L, M, w	3,780'	360.1		
1,833.7	2.0	South Twin Mtn, North Twin Spur		4,902'	359.3		THE TWINWAY
1,835.7	1.3	Mt. Guyot; Bondcliff Trail to +AMC **Guyot Shelter** and **Campsite** *(E–0.8m) ...6.4mS; 9.8mN*	S, C, w	4,580'	357.3		
1,837.0	1.2	Zealand Mountain		4,250'	356.0		
1,838.2	0.4	Zeacliff Pond Trail *(E–0.1m)*	w	3,800'	354.8		
1,838.6	0.1	Zeacliff Trail (1.4m) ...*rejoins A.T. north*		3,700'	354.4		
1,838.7	1.1	Zeacliff ...*overlook to the east*		3,700'	354.3		
1,839.8	0.1	Lend-a-Hand Trail, Whitewall Brook	w	2,750'	353.2		
1,839.9	0.2	+AMC Zealand Falls Hut	L, M, w	2,630'	353.1		
1,840.1	1.3	Zealand Trail Jct. *(W–2.3m to Zealand Road) ...join former railroad bed*	P, R, B	2,460'	352.9		
1,841.4	0.8	Zeacliff Trail (1.4m) ...*rejoins A.T. south*		2,448'	351.6		
1,842.2	0.5	Thoreau Falls Trail		2,460'	350.8		

Miles from Springer	Miles to Next Point	Features	Services	Elev	Miles from Katahdin	MAP	Alt Name
1,842.7	2.0	Shoal Pond Trail *(E–0.8m)*	w	2,500'	350.3		
1,844.7	1.0	+AMC **Ethan Pond Shelter** and **Campsite** *...9.8mS; 17.4mN*	S, C, w	2,860'	348.3		ETHAN POND TRAIL
1,845.7	0.3	Willey Range Trail		2,680'	347.3		
1,846.0	1.1	Kedron Flume Trail		2,450'	347.0	ATC N.H.–Vt. Map 3	
1,847.1	0.2	Arethusa–Ripley Falls Trail		1,600'	345.9		
1,847.3	0.3	Railroad Tracks, Willey House Station Road, Ethan Pond Trailhead	R, P	1,440'	345.7		
1,847.6	0.1	Crawford Notch, U.S. 302, Presidential Range *East–1.8m to* Dry River Campground *East–3m to* Crawford Notch Cmgrd *East–10m to* **Bartlett, N.H., P.O. 03812** West–1m to Willey House *West–3.7m to* +AMC Highland Ctr	R, P, B C, cl, sh C, sh M, L M B, L, M, sh	1,275'	345.4		
1,847.7	0.1	Saco River *...footbridge*		1,350'	345.3		WEBSTER CLIFF TRAIL
1,847.8	0.1	Saco River Trail *(south) (W–1.2m to Willey House)*	M	1,350'	345.2		
1,847.9	1.6	Saco River Trail *(north) (E–2m to Dry River Campground)*	C, cl, sh	1,400'	345.1		
1,849.5	1.4	Webster Cliffs		3,025'	343.5		
1,850.9	1.4	Mt. Webster		3,910'	342.1		
1,852.3	1.7	Mt. Jackson		4,052'	340.7		
1,854.0	0.8	+AMC Mizpah Spring Hut, +AMC Nauman Tentsite	C, L, M, w	3,800'	339.0		
1,854.8	0.9	Mt. Pierce (Mt. Clinton) *...above treeline for the next 12.7 miles north*		4,312'	338.2		
1,855.7	0.8	Spring	w	4,350'	337.3		
1,856.5	0.5	Mt. Eisenhower Loop Trail *(north)*; Edmonds Path		4,475'	336.5		
1,857.0	0.6	Spring	w	4,480'	336.0	ATC N.H.–Vt. Map 2	
1,857.6	1.0	Mt. Franklin		5,004'	335.4		
1,858.6	0.1	Mt. Monroe Loop Trail *(north)*		5,075'	334.4		
1,858.7	0.8	+AMC Lakes of the Clouds Hut *..."The Dungeon"*	L, M, w	5,125'	334.3		CRAWFORD PATH
1,859.5	0.4	Davis Path; Westside Trail *(south)*		5,625'	333.5		
1,859.9	0.2	Gulfside Trail		6,150'	333.1		
1,860.1	0.2	Mt. Washington, Summit Building, Observatory **Mt. Washington, N.H., P.O. 03589** *(not recommended)* *East–8m on Auto Road to* N.H. 16 Tuckerman Ravine Trail to + AMC **Hermit Lake Shelters** *(E–2m)...17.4S; 7.1mN;* Pinkham Notch at N.H. 16 *(E–4.2m)*	R, P, M R, P S, C, w; R, P, B, G, L, M, sh, f	6,288'	332.9		
1,860.3	0.1	Trinity Heights Connector		6,100'	332.7		GULFSIDE TRAIL
1,860.4	0.1	Cog Railroad Tracks		6,090'	332.6		
1,860.5	0.5	Great Gulf Trail		5,925'	332.5		
1,861.0	0.1	Westside Trail		5,500'	332.0		
1,861.1	0.3	Mt. Clay Loop Trail *(south)*		5,400'	331.9		
1,861.4	0.5	Jewell Trail		5,400'	331.6		
1,861.9	0.1	Greenough Spring *(west)*	w	5,100'	331.1		

Miles from Springer	Miles to Next Point	Features	Services	Elev	Miles from Katahdin	MAP	Alt Name
1,862.0	0.1	Sphinx Col; Mt. Clay Loop Trail (north)		5,025'	331.0		GULFSIDE TRAIL
1,862.1	0.5	Sphinx Trail		4,975'	330.9		
1,862.6	0.5	Cornice Trail; Monticello Lawn		5,325'	330.4		
1,863.1	0.3	Six Husbands Trail		5,325'	329.9		
1,863.4	0.2	Mt. Jefferson Loop (north)		5,125'	329.6		
1,863.6	0.7	Edmands Col; Gulfside Spring (E–50 yds.); Spaulding Spring (W–0.2m)	w	4,938'	329.4		
1,864.3	0.6	Israel Ridge Path to +RMC **The Perch Shelter** and **Campsite** (W–0.9m) ...7.1mS; 2.7mN	S, C, w	5,475'	328.7		
1,864.9	0.5	Thunderstorm Junction West–1.1m to +RMC Crag Camp Cabin West–1.2m on Lowe's Path to Mt. Adams and +RMC **Gray Knob Cabin** ...2.7mS; 23.2mN	S, w S, w	5,490'	328.1		
1,865.4	0.4	Air Line Trail (south)		5,125'	327.6		
1,865.8	0.5	+AMC Madison Spring Hut Valley Way Trail to USFS Valley Way Tentsite (W–0.6m)	L, M, w C, w	4,825' 3,900'	327.2		
1,866.3	0.2	Mt. Madison		5,366'	326.7		
1,866.5	0.3	Howker Ridge Trail		5,100'	326.5		OSGOOD TRAIL
1,866.8	0.7	Osgood Junction; Parapet Trail; Daniel Webster Scout Trail		4,822'	326.2		
1,867.5	1.3	Osgood Ridge ...above treeline for the next 12.7 miles south		4,300'	325.5	ATC N.H.–Vt. Map 2	OSGOOD CUTOFF
1,868.8	0.6	USFS Osgood Campsite; Osgood Cutoff	C, w	2,540'	324.2		
1,869.4	0.2	The Bluff at Parapet Brook; Great Gulf Trail (south)	w	2,450'	323.6		
1,869.6	0.1	Madison Gulf Trail; West Branch of the Peabody River	w	2,300'	323.4		GREAT GULF TRL/ MADISON GULF TRL
1,869.7	1.8	Great Gulf Trail (north)		2,290'	323.3		
1,871.5	0.2	Lowe's Bald Spot ...rock dome		2,875'	321.5		MADISON GULF TRAIL
1,871.7	0.1	Mt. Washington Auto Road	R, P	2,675'	321.3		
1,871.8	0.8	Raymond Path		2,625'	321.2		
1,872.6	0.5	George's Gorge Trail		2,525'	320.4		OLD JACKSON RD TRAIL
1,873.1	0.5	Crew Cutoff Trail		2,075'	319.9		
1,873.6	0.1	Pinkham Notch, N.H. 16, Pinkham Notch Visitor Center, +AMC Joe Dodge Lodge East–16m to Intervale, N.H. East–18m to North Conway, N.H. West–2m to Wildcat Mtn Gondola West–11m to **Gorham, N.H., P.O. 03581**	R, P, B, G, L, M, sh, f M, L, O G, L, M, O, D all	2,050'	319.4		
1,873.7	0.8	Square Ledge Trail		2,020'	319.3		LOST POND TRAIL
1,874.5	0.8	Wildcat Ridge Trail to Glen Ellis Falls		1,990'	318.5		
1,875.3	0.3	Open Ledge, Sarge's Crag		3,000'	317.7		
1,875.6	1.0	Spring (west)		3,250'	317.4		WILDCAT RIDGE TRAIL
1,876.6	1.1	Wildcat Mountain, Peak D ...gondola		4,020'	316.4		
1,877.7	0.4	Wildcat Mountain, Peak C		4,298'	315.3		
1,878.1	0.5	Wildcat Mountain, Peak B		4,330'	314.9		
1,878.6	0.9	Wildcat Mountain, Peak A		4,442'	314.4		

Miles from Springer	Miles to Next Point	Features	Services	Elev	Miles from Katahdin	MAP	Alt Name
1,879.5	0.7	Carter Notch, +AMC Carter Notch Hut *(E–0.2m)* Nineteen Mile Brook Trail *(W–3.6m to N.H. 16)*	L, M, w R, B	3,350'	313.5		
1,880.2	0.5	Spring *(W–60 yards)*	w	4,300'	312.8		
1,880.7	0.4	Carter Dome, Rainbow Trail		4,832'	312.3		
1,881.1	0.4	Black Angel Trail		4,600'	311.9		
1,881.5	0.6	Mt. Hight ...*views*		4,675'	311.5		
1,882.1	0.8	Zeta Pass, Carter Dome Trail *(W–0.8m reliable spring)*	w	3,890'	310.9		
1,882.9	1.3	South Carter Mountain		4,458'	310.1		
1,884.2	0.3	Middle Carter Mountain		4,610'	308.8		CARTER–MORIAH TRAIL
1,884.5	0.3	Mt. Lethe		4,584'	308.5		
1,884.8	1.9	North Carter Mountain		4,539'	308.2	ATC N.H.–Vt. Map 2	
1,886.7	0.7	+AMC **Imp Shelter** and **Campsite** *(W–0.2m) ...23.2mS; 6.3mN*	S, C, w	3,250'	306.3		
1,887.4	1.4	Stony Brook Trail *(W–3.6m to N.H. 16)*; Moriah Brook Trail *(E)*	R, P	3,127'	305.6		
1,888.8	1.2	Carter Moriah Trail to Mt. Moriah *(4,049') (W–0.2m)*		4,000'	304.2		
1,890.0	0.2	Middle Moriah		3,640'	303.0		KEN-DUSKEAG TRAIL
1,890.2	1.1	Kenduskeag Trail		3,300'	302.8		
1,891.3	1.1	Rattle River	w	1,700'	301.7		
1,892.4	0.4	East Rattle River ...*difficult in high water*	w	1,500'	300.6		RATTLE RIVER TRAIL
1,892.8	1.9	**Rattle River Shelter** and **Campsite** *...6.3mS; 13.9mN*	S, C, w	1,260'	300.2		

1,894.7	0.3	U.S. 2, Shelburne, N.H.
		    On A.T.–Rattle River Lodge & Hostel
		    West–1.8m to White Birches Camping Park
		    West–3.6m to **Gorham, N.H., P.O. 03581**
		    West–5.6 to Walmart
		    West–8m to Berlin, N.H.
			R, P
			H, w
			H, C, G, cl, sh
			H, B, G, L, M, O, cl, f
			G
			all, D
				780'	298.3		

1,895.0	0.2	North Road, Androscoggin River	R	750'	298.0		
1,895.2	1.0	Hogan Road ...*unpaved*	R, P	760'	297.8		CENTENNIAL TRAIL
1,896.2	2.1	Brook	w	1,350'	296.8		
1,898.3	2.2	Mt. Hayes, Mahoosuc Trail		2,555'	294.7		
1,900.5	1.1	Cascade Mountain		2,631'	292.5		
1,901.6	1.0	Trident Col Tentsite *(W–0.1m)*	C, w	2,020'	291.4		
1,902.6	0.6	Trident Pass, Page Pond	w	2,240'	290.4		
1,903.2	1.1	Wockett Ledge		2,780'	289.8	N.H.–Vt. Map 1	MAHOOSUC TRAIL
1,904.3	1.5	Dream Lake Inlet, Peabody Brook Trail	w	2,610'	288.7		
1,905.8	0.7	Moss Pond	w	2,630'	287.2		
1,906.5	2.8	Austin Brook Trail Jct. to **Gentian Pond Shelter** and **Campsite** *(E–0.2m) ...13.9mS; 5.7mN*	S, C, w	2,166'	286.5		
1,909.3	0.6	Mt. Success		3,565'	283.7		
1,909.9	1.3	Success Trail *(W–3m to Success Pond Road)*	R, P	3,170'	283.1		
1,911.2	0.5	New Hampshire–Maine State Line		2,972'	281.8		

+ Fee charged   RMC = Randolph Mountain Club

At Hanover, southbounders will have already experienced the White Mountains. Northbounders should gear up for the conditions ahead.

Considered one of the most challenging states, it is also one of the most rewarding. As the trees get shorter and the views get longer, you've entered the krummholz zone, where trees are stunted with flag-like tops due to stress from the wind and cold. Boreal bogs are home to local carnivorous plant species, sundew and pitcher plants. Hardy, yet delicate alpine flowers—Labrador tea, bunchberry, mountain sandwort, and cloudberry—may be in bloom when you pass through. Spruce grouse, winter wren, dark-eyed junco, and the white-throated sparrow will greet you along the way.

Much of the Trail is above timberline, where the temperature may change very suddenly; snow is possible in any season. Snow falls on Mt. Washington every month of the year. High winds and dense fog are common. Most shelters and campsites charge a fee.

Tenting is prohibited within 200 feet of the A.T. from the Connecticut River (Vermont state line) to the summit of Mt. Moosilauke.

Many water sources in southern New Hampshire are not always reliable, including sources at, or adjacent to, shelters.

Dartmouth Outing Club—DOC maintains the 53.3 miles from the Connecticut River to Kinsman Notch in New Hampshire. Correspondence should be sent to DOC Box 9, Hanover, NH 03755; (603) 646-2428; <www.dartmouth.edu/~doc>. The DOC no longer uses orange-and-black paint for blazes, although many are still visible. The DOC does continue to use orange and black on trail signs.

Hanover, N.H. [P.O. ZIP 03755: M–F 8:30–5, Sa 8:30–12, lobby opens at 7 a.m.; (603) 643-5201]—Home of Dartmouth College. The A.T. passes through the center of Hanover, and most services are along the route of the Trail. At the center of town and the Dartmouth Green, a blue-blazed side trail leads (Trail-west) to Robinson Hall and the office of the Dartmouth Outing Club (DOC) in Room 113, (603) 646-2428, <www.dartmouth. edu/~doc/>. DOC has student volunteers (DOC tours), Su–Th 2–6, phone, and Internet access. This is a good place to begin in town. The college does not allow nonstudents to stay in student housing. Dartmouth College security has reported problems with improper use of college facilities and buildings by hikers; hikers must not enter dormitories, offices, laundry rooms, *etc.*, without permission or try to sleep overnight in those locations, including the DOC building. Public (on-street) consumption of alcohol is illegal downtown. ■ *Camping:* Tenting is permitted in the woods, past the soccer fields, *if you are 200 feet from the Trail and on Forest Service land.* ■ *Lodging:* Hanover Inn, (603) 643-4300, <www.hanoverinn.com>, rooms start at $239. ■ *Groceries:* Hanover Food Co-op (long-term resupply), bulk and natural foods; Irving Food Stop, CVS Pharmacy, and Stinson's Village Store (all short-term resupply). ■ *Restaurants:* Ramunto's Pizza; Lou's Bakery & Restaurant, B/L; Thayer Hall, the Dartmouth dining hall, B/L/D; C&A Pizza; Noodle Station; Boloco Burritos; Jewel of India; Dirt Cowboy Café; The Canoe Club Restaurant; Murphy's. ■ *Internet access:* Howe Public Library and DOC. ■ *Outfitters:* Zimmermann's, sells primarily North Face clothing and packs; CamelBak. In West Lebanon: EMS, (603) 298-7716; Omer and Bob's Sport Shop; and L.L.Bean Outlet, (603) 298-6975—take "Orange" bus route, switch to "Red," and ask the driver to let you off at the Powerhouse Mall. ■ *Other services:* Laura's Place, (603) 727-8187, 1 mile out of town near bus line, call for arrangements 8–8; True Value Hardware, Coleman fuel, denatured alcohol; Richard Black Recreation Center, Lebanon and Park streets, shower and laundry for hikers M–F during summer; bookstores; dentist; doctor; hospital; movie theater; optician; banks with ATM; phar-

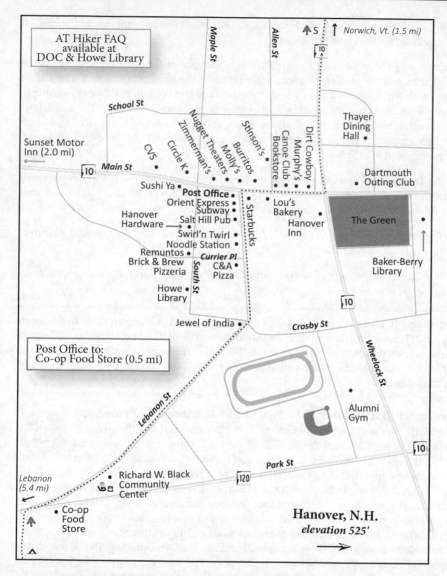

macy; barber shop; Hanover Veterinary Clinic, (603) 643-3313, (603) 643-4829 after hours; Hanover Hot Tubs. ■ *Bus service:* Advance Transit is a local bus service, 6 a.m. to 6 p.m., M–F only. All routes are free; can be picked up outside the Hanover Inn (going north) or in front of Dartmouth Bookstore on Main St. (going south); offers transportation throughout Hanover and to White River Junction, Vt. (where there is an Amtrak station), Lebanon, and West Lebanon, with all major services. Bus schedules available in the bookstore. Bus service to Boston by Dartmouth Coach, (800) 637-0123, and Greyhound, (800) 231-2222. ■ *Long-term parking:* available for hikers in "A" lot, east of campus. Call parking operations, (603) 646-2204, for directions and to make arrangements. ■ *Shuttles:* Stray Kat's A.T. Hiker Shuttle, (603) 252-8295; Trail Head Shuttle, (802) 477-2048; Big Yellow Taxi, (603) 643-8294.

   East (south)—2.0 miles to *Lodging:* Sunset Motor Inn, (603) 298-8721, on N.H. 10, on the "Orange" bus route, $69–$99 through May, $74–$93 Jun–Sep, no pets, no smoking, CATV, continental B, shuttle and laundry may be available if you ask the owners; Super 8 Motel in White River Junction,

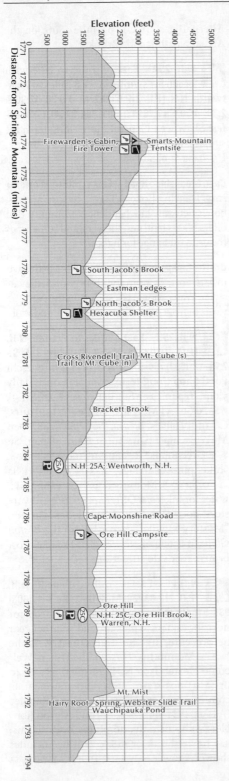

Elevation (feet)

Distance from Springer Mountain (miles)

Firewarden's Cabin; Smarts-Mountain
Fire Tower Tentsite

South Jacob's Brook

Eastman Ledges

North Jacob's Brook
Hexacuba Shelter

Cross Rivendell Trail, Mt. Cube (s)
Trail to Mt. Cube (n)

Brackett Brook

N.H. 25A; Wentworth, N.H.

Cape Moonshine Road

Ore Hill Campsite

Ore Hill
N.H. 25C, Ore Hill Brook;
Warren, N.H.

Mt. Mist
Hairy Root Spring, Webster Slide Trail
Wauchipauka Pond

Vt., (802) 295-7577, on the "Orange" bus route; Days Inn in Lebanon, N.H., (603) 448-5070, on the "Blue" bus route.

Velvet Rocks Shelter (1980s/2006)—Sleeps 6. Privy. On blue-blazed loop trail with access from the north and south. Water source is Ledyard Spring along the northern access trail. During dry periods, hikers may want to bring water from town.

Etna–Hanover Center Road—East 0.9 mile to *Groceries:* Etna General Store (limited resupply), (603) 643-1655, M–F 6 a.m.–7 p.m., Sa 8–7, Su 8–6, snacks, sandwiches, cold drinks, fuels, hot food weekdays, showers, restroom.

Moose Mountain Shelter (2004)—Sleeps 8. Privy. Log shelter built entirely with hand tools by DOC. Water is on the A.T. north of the shelter—follow loop trail to end.

Trapper John Shelter (1990s)—Sleeps 6. Privy uses an old chair. Tentsites. Water source is a brook 15 yards to the left of the shelter.

Lyme–Dorchester Road—West 3.2 miles to **Lyme, N.H. [P.O. ZIP 03768: M–F 7:45–12 & 1:30–5:15, Sa 7:45–12; (603) 795-4421].** ■ *Lodging:* Dowd's Country Inn B&B, 9 Main St., (603) 795-4712, <www.dowdscountryinn.com>; weekdays $75S, $85D; weekends $95S, $115D. One or two rooms are pet-friendly. Internet access and WiFi. Weekend prices may vary depending on availability. Includes full country B and afternoon tea with home-made scones and all N.H. taxes. ■ *Restaurant:* Stella's Italian Kitchen & Market, L/D M–Sa, closed Su. ■ *Other services:* Country store and deli (short-term resupply), open daily; banks with ATM; Lyme Home and Hardware store; veterinarian.

Smarts Mountain Tentsites—Cleared area for three tents. Privy. Water from Mike Murphy Spring (see next entry).

Smarts Mountain Firewarden's Cabin—Sleeps 8. Privy. Panoramic views from the abandoned firetower on Smarts Mountain summit. Water source is Mike Murphy Spring 0.2 mile north of cabin on blue-blazed Daniel Doan Trail.

Hexacuba Shelter (1989)—Sleeps 8. Tentsites. Privy (penta-style). Water source is an unreliable stream at the blue-blaze junction to the shelter.

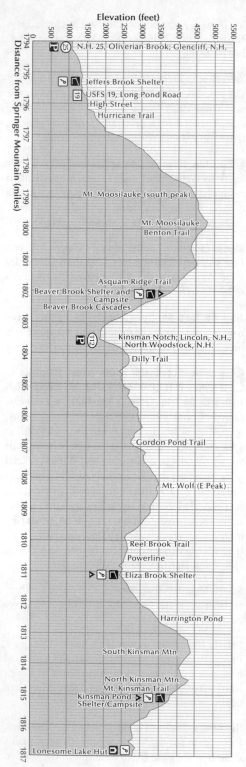

Elevation (feet)

Distance from Springer Mountain (miles)

N.H. 25, Oliverian Brook; Glencliff, N.H.

Jeffers Brook Shelter

USFS 19, Long Pond Road
High Street
Hurricane Trail

Mt. Moosilauke (south peak)

Mt. Moosilauke
Benton Trail

Asquam Ridge Trail
Beaver Brook Shelter and
Campsite
Beaver Brook Cascades

Kinsman Notch; Lincoln, N.H.,
North Woodstock, N.H.
Dilly Trail

Gordon Pond Trail

Mt. Wolf (E Peak)

Reel Brook Trail
Powerline
Eliza Brook Shelter

Harrington Pond

South Kinsman Mtn.

North Kinsman Mtn.
Mt. Kinsman Trail
Kinsman Pond
Shelter/Campsite

Lonesome Lake Hut

Alternative source is 0.3 mile south on the A.T. at North Jacobs Brook.

N.H. 25A—East 0.1 mile to lake with beach for swimming; 4.8 miles to **Wentworth, N.H. [P.O. ZIP 03282: M–F 9:30–12:30 & 2:30–4:30, Sa 7:15–12; (603) 764-9444]**. *Groceries:* Shawnee's General Store (long-term resupply), (603) 764-5553, M–Th 5 a.m.–8 p.m., F 5–9, Sa 6–9, Su 7–8.

Cape Moonshine Road—East 1 mile to *Work for stay:* Dancing Bones Village, <www.dancingbones.net>, an independent community that offers hikers tentsites, showers, and sometimes meals in exchange for light work.

Ore Hill Campsite (2000)—Shelter burned down in late 2011; camping with privy (medieval-style). Water source is a spring on the path 100 yards in front of the former shelter foundation.

N.H. 25C—East 4 miles to **Warren, N.H. [P.O. ZIP 03279: M–F 7:30–9:30 & 3–5, Sa 7:15–12; (603) 764-5733]**. ■ *Groceries:* Tedeschi Food Shop (long-term resupply), open daily 5 a.m.–11 p.m. (7 on Su), deli closes 8 p.m. M–F, 7 Sa, 6 Su, ATM, restrooms. ■ *Restaurants:* Calamity Jane's, B/L/D, (603) 764-5288, open M–W 6 a.m.–2 p.m., Tu–Sa 6 a.m.–8 p.m., Su 8–3; Greenhouse Restaurant, (603) 764-5708, "hiker pizza challenge," M 3–8, Th–F 3–11, Sa 12–10, Su 12–8; Moose Scoops ice cream, WiFi, water for hikers. ■ *Other services:* hardware store, doctor, and coin laundry. See Warren's "Mystery Missile"—according to the *Boston Globe*, it is one of New England's eight most bizarre roadside attractions.

N.H. 25—East 0.4 mile to **Glencliff, N.H. [P.O. ZIP 03238: M–F 12–2, Sa 7–1; (603) 989-5154]**. This is a prudent mail drop for northbounders to pick up cold-weather gear before entering the high country of the White Mountains. *Hostel:* The Hikers Welcome Hostel, 1396 N.H. 25, (603) 989-0040 or (203) 605-9430, <www.hikerswelcome.com>; owned by John "Pack Rat" Robblee (AT '94, PCT '99, CDT '06) and Alyson Robblee; walk-ins only; no phone reservations; $25 hostel/bunk or $18.50 tenting includes shower; shower only $3; laundry ($3 wash, $3 dry); hiker snacks, denatured alcohol and Coleman fuel by the ounce, shuttles and slackpacking, WiFi, and computer. Mail drops *via* USPS (use P.O. Box 25), UPS, and FedEx. Resupply, ATM, and restaurants in Warren (5 miles; see above).

Oliverian Brook—The brook can be a difficult ford after rain. Be careful.

Jeffers Brook Shelter (1970s)—Sleeps 10. Privy. Located on a spur trail. Water source is Jeffers Brook, located in front of the shelter.

The White Mountains—One of the most impressive sections of the A.T., the Whites offer magnificent views with miles of above-treeline travel. Extra caution should be exercised while above treeline, due to rapidly changing weather and the lack of protection from it. Carry cold-weather gear, even in the middle of summer. Winter weather, including sleet, snow, and ice, is possible on these high ridges year-round. Each year, carelessness ends in death for a few visitors to the Whites. Pay close attention at Trail intersections. The Appalachian Mountain Club (AMC) maintains many trails that cross the A.T., and the A.T. route is commonly referred to on signs and in guidebooks by the name of the local trail it follows, such as "Franconia Ridge Trail." The tables beginning on page 206 show those names in the far right column. (And, to add to the confusion, sections above treeline from Mizpah Hut to Madison Hut are often marked with yellow blazes on rock cairns, to stand out in the snow.) When above treeline, stay on the Trail. This alpine zone is home to very fragile plants. One misplaced bootstep can destroy them.

Backcountry regulations—Each summer, AMC serves tens of thousands of backpackers and campers at its backcountry shelters and campsites in the White Mountain National Forest. To prevent the Whites from being "loved to death," the USFS, in conjunction with AMC and the New Hampshire state parks agency, established a strict set of backcountry rules for the White Mountains. Please follow the rules. Hikers should be aware of all pertinent rules and regulations pertaining to camping in these areas and should not be surprised if they are rigorously enforced by ridgerunners and rangers. This especially applies to those who choose to camp immediately adjacent to huts, shelters, caretaker campsites, and road crossings. Hikers who ignore posted warnings may well receive hefty tickets. You will encounter forest protection areas (FPAs), where camping and fires are prohibited. The following regulations apply in those areas: no camping above treeline (where trees are less than eight feet high); no camping within 0.25 mile of huts, shelters, or tentsites except at the facility itself; no camping within 200 feet of the Trail. Groups of 6 or more should contact AMC Group Notification System, <www.outdoors.org>, (603) 466-2721 x8150, so it can effectively manage all large groups that stay at AMC sites. AMC-managed sites can accommodate groups of up to 10. USFS parking fees are established throughout the Whites; be prepared to pay if you park at Forest Service trailheads.

Mt. Moosilauke—The north side of Mt. Moosilauke is slick, particularly in rain. Be careful! Sections use rebar, rock steps, and wooden blocks for footing. For northbounders, it is the first mountain above treeline. For southbounders, the meadow at the base of the southern side is the first pastureland they encounter on the A.T. From the summit, Franconia Ridge, as well as the rest of the Whites, can be seen to the northeast; the Green Mountains are visible to the west. Remnants of the 1860 Prospect House, a tourist spot that burned down in 1942, can still be seen at the summit. The Gorge Brook Trail leads 3.7 miles to the privately owned DOC Moosilauke Ravine Lodge.

Beaver Brook Shelter and Campsite (1980s)—Sleeps 10. Privy (composting). Completed by DOC and ALDHA members, site includes 2 small tent pads and a nice view of Franconia Ridge. Water source is Beaver Brook on the spur trail to the shelter.

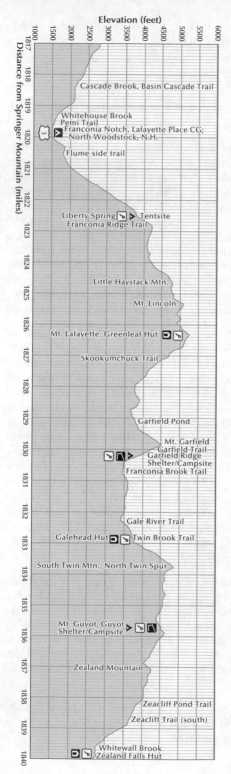

Appalachian Mountain Club—AMC maintains most of the A.T. and many of the surrounding trails between Kinsman Notch and Grafton Notch in Maine, a total of 120 miles; (603) 466-2721; <www.outdoors.org>.

AMC Tentsites, Shelters, and Campsites— "Tentsites" have designated tenting areas and platforms or pads. "Shelters" are three- or four-sided structures. "Campsites" have designated tenting areas *and* a shelter. See below for description of "huts," where reservations are required. Tentsites, shelters, and campsites are on a first-come, first-served basis. Caretakers are in residence at the following tentsites, shelters, and campsites, where an $10 overnight fee is charged: Kinsman Pond Campsite, Liberty Spring Tentsite, Garfield Ridge Campsite, 13 Falls Tentsite, Guyot Campsite, Ethan Pond Campsite, Nauman Tentsite, Imp Campsite, and Speck Pond Campsite (Maine). A caretaker works at those sites due to the locations' popularity and the fragility of their resources. The remaining tentsites, shelters, and campsites, except those operated by the Randolph Mountain Club (see page 224), are available to backcountry travelers at no charge. *All AMC campsites now have metal bear boxes available while a caretaker is on site.*

In 2017, the AMC Campsite Program rolled out an Appalachian Trail Thru-Hiker Pass program. Geared toward any northbounder, southbounder, flip-flopper, or section-hiker, this pass offers a discount through the AMC campsites in the White Mountains. After you spend your first night at one of their sites, every site after that is 50% off at $5 a night. With the purchase of the pass, you will receive a punch card for two free baked goods and a free bowl of soup redeemable at any AMC Hut, as well as 10% off any gear. This pass also is good for discounts at the Pinkham Notch Visitors Center and the Highland Center, as well as 30% off lodging and camping at the Mohican Outdoors Center in New Jersey.

A *work-for-stay option* is possible for thru-hikers at the tentsites and shelter sites that have caretakers. This is at the discretion of the caretaker and may not always be available. A maximum of two thru-hikers per night can be accommodated in that way at each site, and each will be expected to contribute an hour of work.

AMC Huts—These large, enclosed lodges sleep from 36 to 90 people. Rates range from $82 to $167, depending on the day, AMC membership, and the hut. A crew ("croo") staffs these facilities during the full-service season. An overnight stay includes bunk space, pillow, blanket, bathroom privileges (no showers), and potable water. If you plan to stay three consecutive nights, there is a discounted package rate, available all summer. Rates for self-service seasons are significantly less ($28–$51) than full-service seasons. Each hut has trained wilderness first-aid staff, and the facilities' crews give natural- and cultural-history evening programs. The huts also contain excellent libraries and displays on cultural and natural history.

If you plan to pay for a stay in one of the huts, make reservations, (603) 466-2727, especially for the weekends, when bunk spaces fill quickly. *Call AMC or check <www.outdoors. org> to verify the huts' opening and closing dates as well as perhaps-revised 2020 rates and make reservations.* You may also be able to make a reservation by having a caretaker at one of the other huts or campsites radio ahead for you. The huts cater mainly to families and weekend hikers. AMC had wells drilled at all the huts, so you can look forward to water that meets state health standards. During the self-service season, a caretaker is at Lonesome Lake, Zealand, and Carter huts. Schedules vary from hut to hut; check individual listings for specific dates. *Thru-hikers are given member rates as long as they mention that they are thru-hikers.*

Work exchange at the huts—Thru-hikers can sometimes arrange with the croo to work off stays at the full- or self-service huts. Most huts can accommodate one or two working thru-hikers each night—except for Lakes of the Clouds Hut, which takes up to four thru-hikers—but availability of work is never guaranteed. Work-for-stay is at the discretion of the hut croo. When work is available, thru-hikers are asked to put in two hours either at night or in the morning; when work is not available, the full fee may be charged. Please give other thru-hikers a chance to work off their stay, and limit your use of the work-for-stay option to no more than three huts.

The AMC *Thru-Hiker's Guide to AMC-Maintained Trails & Facilities in the White Mountains & Mahoosucs* is a resource written for those who plan to stay at the fee sites (both backcountry and hospitality). It is not a tool for thru-hikers who correctly follow backcountry regulations and camp through this area; see <www.outdoors.org/appalachiantrail>. A free paper map for thru-hikers, with tips and details on hiking the A.T. in the Whites and Mahoosucs is available at AMC huts and shelters and Pinkham Notch Visitors Center.

AMC Shuttle—603-466-2727, <www.outdoors.org/lodging/lodging-shuttle.cfm>, daily late May–late Sep, weekends and holidays only through third week of Oct; $20 AMC members ($24 nonmembers) one way, reservations strongly recommended; walk-ons accepted on a space-available basis, see driver; drop-offs on route between scheduled stops may be arranged with driver. Stops include trailheads at Liberty Spring/A.T. on I-93, Lafayette Place Campground, Old Bridle Path, Gale River, Zealand Falls, Ammonoosuc Ravine, Highland Center at Crawford Notch, Webster Cliff/A.T. at U.S. 302, Pinkham Notch Visitors Center, 19-Mile Brook Trail, Gorham information booth, Valley Way/Appalachia. Check Web site for further details.

N.H. 112/Kinsman Notch—**East** 0.3 mile to Lost River Gorge and Boulder Caves, a series of streams, caves, and waterfalls owned by the Society for the Protection of New Hampshire Forests. Self-guided tour of gorge, ecology trail, and nature garden, $16, daily 9–5, from mid-May to mid-Oct, last ticket sold at 4 p.m. Snack bar. Phone available during business hours, with permission and a phone card.

East 4 miles to *Hostel:* The Notch Hostel, 324 Lost River Rd. (N.H. 112), North Woodstock, NH 03262 ; (603) 348-1483, <www.notchhostel.com>. Lodging in large farmhouse $33PP includes bunk, fresh linens, towel, shower, laundry, coffee/tea, and make your own pancakes in guest kitchen; small campstore offers pizza, ice cream, and soda; Internet/WiFi; rental bikes $5. Beer and wine OK in moderation; no liquor. Trail and town shuttles depart hostel at 7 a.m. and 4 p.m. (Kinsman Notch/N.H. 112 pick-up +5 minutes; Flume visitors center +25 minutes, town +40 minutes) additional midday shuttle during busy season, slackpacking available. Call or text for reservations and shuttles. Mail drops accepted.

East 5 miles to **North Woodstock, N.H. [P.O. ZIP 03262: M–F 9:30–12:30 & 1:30–4:30, Sa 9–12; (603) 745-8134]**, which also is accessible from Franconia Notch (below). ■ *Lodging:* Woodstock Inn, (603) 745-3951 or (800) 321-3985, shared bath $94PP, private bath $112S/D, $25EAP, rates vary on weekends and holidays, no pets, includes B, nonsmoking rooms, pool at Alpine Village, brew pub, restaurant L/D; Autumn Breeze, (603) 745-8549, $72–$90, nonsmoking rooms, no dogs, rooms have kitchenettes; Inn 32, (603) 745-2416, $68–$82, game room, gas grills, picnic tables, pool, hiker box, deli, ATM, laundry. ■ *Groceries:* Wayne's Market (long-term resupply), deli and grinders. ■ *Restaurants: See map.* ■ *Shuttles:* The Hiker Shuttle Connection, (603) 348-7422, 6 a.m.–2 a.m. year-round; Notch Taxi, (603) 991-8777.

East—6 miles to **Lincoln, N.H.** (see below).

Eliza Brook Shelter and Campsite (2010)—Shelter sleeps 8. Privy (composting). Four hardened tent pads. Water source is Eliza Brook.

Kinsman Pond Shelter and Campsite (2007)—Shelter sleeps 15. Privy (composting). Two single and two double tent platforms. Bear box. Overnight fee $10PP, caretaker on site. Water source is Kinsman Pond; treat your water.

Lonesome Lake Hut—This southernmost hut offers swimming in Lonesome Lake. Full service May 28–Oct 17. Self-service the rest of the year except May 24–27 and Oct 18–20.

I-93/U.S. 3/Franconia Notch—*Shuttle:* The Hiker Shuttle Connection, (603) 348-7422, 6 a.m.–2 a.m. year-round; from A.T. in Franconia Notch, follow Rt. 3 south to Exit 34A for shuttle pick-up on Rt. 3.

East on Franconia Bike Path: East 0.2M to Whitehouse Trail then 0.8M to *AMC shuttle* stop and hiker parking on U.S. 3.

East—On Franconia Bike Path: East 1M to Flume Visitor Center, with snack bar/restaurant, and ice cream. Open daily early May to late Oct, 9–5. Call about mail drops; (603) 745-8391. Admission to see The Flume itself is $16.

East 5.8 miles to North Woodstock (see above).

East 7.3 miles to **Lincoln, N.H. [P.O. ZIP 03251: M–F 8–5, Sa 8–12; (603) 745-8133].** *See map.* ■ *Lodging:* Mt. Liberty Lodging, new owners Mike and Susan Izard (A.T. '95), (603) 745-3600, <www.mtlibertylodging.com>, $55–$85D (seasonal), includes shuttle to/from Trail and into town, laundry $5, pool, and river. ■ *Groceries:* Price Chopper (full-service grocery). ■ *Outfitters:* Lahout's Summit Shop, (603) 745-2882, full-service outfitter, Coleman and alcohol by the ounce; Art's Outdoor Outfitter. ■ *Other services:* The Mountain Wanderer, <www.mountainwanderer.com>, guides and maps.

West 2.1 miles to *Camping:* Lafayette Campground, (603) 823-9513, with tentsites $25D, coin-operated hot showers $1, store (short-term resupply), Coleman fuel by the quart, outside soda vending machine. Park rangers hold packages mailed to Franconia Notch State Park, Lafayette Place Campground, Franconia, NH 03580. Write the date you expect to arrive on the package. Open mid-May to Columbus Day. Campground is usually filled by noon on weekends. AMC shuttle stop.

West 8 miles to Franconia; I-93 North at N.H. 18. ■ *Lodging:* Gale River Motel, 1 Main St.,

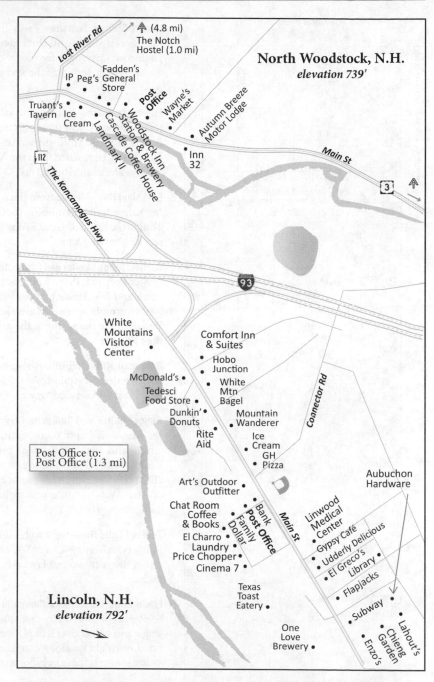

North Woodstock, N.H.
elevation 739'

Lincoln, N.H.
elevation 792'

Franconia, N.H. 03580, (603) 823-5655 or (800) 255-7989, <www.galerivermotel.com>, <info@galeriv-ermotel.com>, $90–$125 Jun–Sep, $95–$220 foliage season, $45–$95 in between and ski season, shuttle to and from Trail when available, seasonal pool, hot tub, Internet access, laundry, call ahead for mail drops; White Mountain Best Western, $90–$110, indoor pool, hot tub, Internet access. ■ *Groceries:* Mac's Market (long-term supply). ■ *Internet access:* library. ■ *Other services:* pizza, restaurant, bank, ATM, Concord Coach bus service.

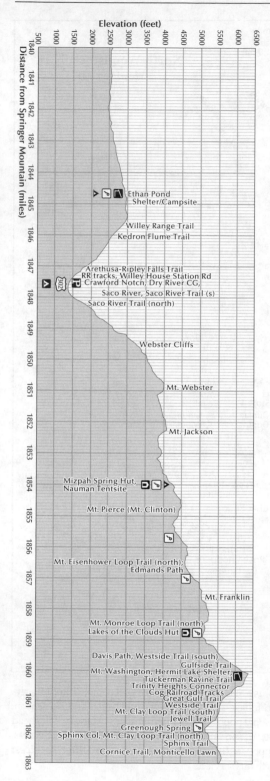

Elevation (feet)

Distance from Springer Mountain (miles)

- ▷ ⬚ ◼ Ethan Pond Shelter/Campsite
- Willey Range Trail
- Kedron Flume Trail
- Arethusa-Ripley Falls Trail
- RR tracks, Willey House Station Rd
- ▷ 302 ⬚P Crawford Notch, Dry River CG,
- Saco River, Saco River Trail (s)
- Saco River Trail (north)
- Webster Cliffs
- Mt. Webster
- Mt. Jackson
- Mizpah Spring Hut, ⬚ ⬚ ▷
- Nauman Tentsite
- Mt. Pierce (Mt. Clinton)
- ⬚
- Mt. Eisenhower Loop Trail (north);
- Edmands Path
- ⬚
- Mt. Franklin
- Mt. Monroe Loop Trail (north)
- Lakes of the Clouds Hut ⬚ ⬚
- Davis Path, Westside Trail (south)
- Gulfside Trail
- Mt. Washington, Hermit Lake Shelter, ◼
- Tuckerman Ravine Trail
- Trinity Heights Connector
- Cog Railroad Tracks
- Great Gulf Trail
- Westside Trail
- Mt. Clay Loop Trail (south)
- Jewell Trail
- Greenough Spring ⬚
- Sphinx Col, Mt. Clay Loop Trail (north)
- Sphinx Trail
- Cornice Trail, Monticello Lawn

Liberty Springs Tentsite—Privy (composting). Seven single and three double tent platforms. Overnight fee $10PP, caretaker on site. Water source is the spring on the A.T.

Franconia Ridge—In any kind of weather, this ridge walk will leave you awestruck. Beautiful views from the summit of Mt. Liberty can be reached from the A.T. south 0.3M on Franconia Ridge Trail.

Greenleaf Hut—Visible from the summit of Mt. Lafayette, it is 1.1 miles on the Greenleaf Trail to the hut. Self-service May 1–24. Full service May 28–Oct 17.

Garfield Ridge Shelter and Campsite (2011)—Shelter sleeps 12. Privy (composting). Two single and five double tent platforms. Bear box. Overnight fee $10PP, caretaker on site. Water source is a spring at the junction to the campsite.

Galehead Hut—Rebuilt 1999–2000, with wheelchair-accessible design. Self-service May 1–24. Full service May 28–Oct 17.

Guyot Shelter and Campsite (1977)—Shelter sleeps 12. Privy (composting). Four single and two double tent platforms. Bear box. Located 0.8 mile east on Bondcliff Trail. Overnight fee $10PP, caretaker on site. Water source is a spring at the campsite.

Zealand Falls Hut—Next to beautiful falls. Full service May 28–Oct 17. Self-service the rest of the year except May 24–27 and Oct 18–20.

Ethan Pond Shelter and Campsite (1957)—Shelter sleeps 10. Privy (composting). Three single and two double tent platforms. Bear box. Overnight fee $10PP, caretaker on site. Water source is the inlet brook to the pond.

🛣 **U.S. 302/Crawford Notch—East** 1.8 miles to ■ *Camping:* Dry River Campground, (603) 374-2272, $25D, tentsites and 3 shelters available ($29); dogs welcome, coin laundry, and showers 25¢. Trail access to A.T. Mail drops accepted at

P.O. Box 177, Twin Mountain, NH 03595 (Crawford Notch State Park). ■ *Shuttle:* AMC shuttle stop at Webster Cliff/A.T. Trailhead.

East 3 miles to *Camping:* Crawford Notch Campground, <www.crawfordnotch.com>, (603) 374-2779; coin-operated shower for guests; dogs; campsites $36D, additional fee for up to 4; cabins $78 for up to 4 people; yurt $68; laundry for overnight guests only.

East 10 miles to the small town of **Bartlett, N.H. [P.O. ZIP 03812: M–F 8:30–10:30 & 11:30–3:30, Sa 8:30–12; (603) 374-2351].**

West 1 mile to the Willey House, with snack bar (ice cream, cold drinks, fudge, sandwiches) and hiker message board, tent repair and seam sealer, open daily early Jun to mid-Oct, 9–5. Mail drops accepted at P.O. Box 177, Twin Mountain, NH 03595 (Crawford Notch State Park).

West 3.7 miles to ■ *Lodging:* AMC's Highland Center, Route 302, Bretton Woods, NH 03575; (603) 278-4453, <www.outdoors.org>, limited hiker supplies, AYCE B $14, 6:30–10; *a la carte* L $8–$15, 10–4; 4-course D $27, reserve seat by 6; bunk room in lodge $65–$110PP, includes B/D; private room in lodge $110–$160PP, includes B/D; Shapleigh Bunkhouse, $46–$83PP includes bunk, shower, towel, and B/D. Facilities generally are for overnight guests only. Mail drops accepted, UPS only. ■ *Shuttle:* AMC shuttle stop. ■ *Other services:* Showers at the Crawford Notch Depot, 9–4 Memorial Day–Columbus Day.

Presidential Range—The highest part of the Trail in New Hampshire, with 25 miles of ridge-walking between Crawford Notch and Pinkham Notch, most of which is above treeline (about 4,400 feet). The A.T. skirts many peaks, which can be reached by short side trails leading to, and often over, the summits.

Saco River Trail—connects the Willey House site to Dry River Campground.

Mizpah Spring Hut and Nauman Tentsite—Self-service May 1–18; full-service May 28–Oct 17. Tentsite, five single and three double tent platforms. Composting privy. Bear box. Overnight fee $10PP. Water source for tentsite is a stream or potable water from hut (if open).

Lakes of the Clouds Hut—Constructed in 1915 at an elevation of 5,050 feet, the highest, largest, and most popular hut. Full-service May 28–Sep 19, with no self-service operation. "The Dungeon," a small basement shelter, is available to thru-hikers for $10, with access to hut restroom and the common area; it sleeps only 6, first-come/first-served, no reservations. "The Dungeon" is an emergency-only shelter when the hut is closed; must not be used as a destination.

Mt. Washington Auto Road/Mt. Washington—The highest peak in the Northeast (6,288 feet). Since it is also accessible by the Auto Road and a cog railroad, more touristy services are here than one might expect. *Note: In 2007, 8 hikers were arrested for mooning said cog railroad; take heed.* The summit building is operated by the New Hampshire Division of Parks and Recreation and houses Mt. Washington Observatory, <www.mountwashington.org>; "Extreme Mt. Washington" ($2 admission); a snack bar; a post office. The state park is open daily 8–8 early May–early Oct, weather permitting. A hiker room is downstairs, with a table, restroom, and a space to rest. (Absolutely no overnight stays are allowed.) Over the years, many buildings have come and gone on the summit, including a 94-bedroom hotel completed in 1873 and destroyed by fire in 1908. The summit is under cloud cover about 55 percent of the time. Average summertime high is 52 degrees, and the average wintertime high is 15 degrees. On April 12, 1934, an on-land wind speed of 231 mph was recorded. If you see a staff meteorologist, ask about the "Century Club." The upper plateau is home to large grassy areas, strewn with rocks but known as "lawns." These lawns hold many species of plants and animals otherwise found only on high mountain peaks and in tundra areas hundreds of miles to the north. Mt. Washington Stage offers a one-way shuttle between the summit and Pinkham

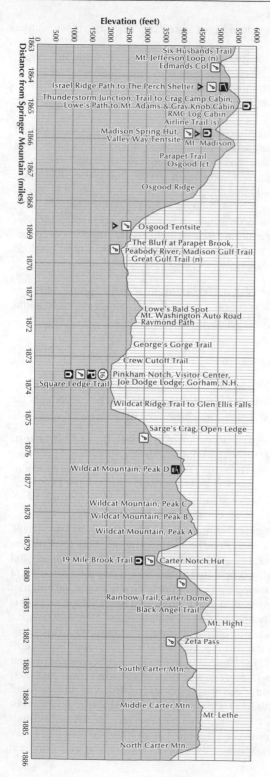

Notch Visitors Center for $31 ($50 after 4 p.m.); make arrangements on the summit or at Pinkham Notch.

Mt. Washington, N.H. [P.O. ZIP 03589: (603) 846-5570]—The post office in the summit building is *not* recommended as a mail drop. Its hours are limited, and it caters to those who visit the summit and desire to have the distinguished Mt. Washington postmark; since there is little space for storing mail drops, they may be redirected to other New Hampshire post offices, well off the Trail.

East 8 miles *via* Auto Road to N.H. 16.

Tuckerman Ravine Trail—A steep, 4.2-mile route from Mt. Washington to Pinkham Notch. In bad weather, you may wish to use this trail to get below treeline and bypass the exposed northern loop of the Presidential Range, but this precarious route is no picnic in icy conditions.

Hermit Lake Shelters—At the base of the Tuckerman Ravine bowl, 2 miles downhill, with steep rock- and boulder-scrambling from the summit; 8 lean-tos, 3 tent platforms, $15PP; pets are not permitted overnight in the shelters; caretaker year-round.

Edmands Col—Just down to the east in the col is a reliable spring and the site of the former Edmands Col emergency shelter. Also, look for a bronze tablet in memory of J. Rayner Edmands, who was instrumental in the construction of most of the graded paths through the northern Presidentials.

Randolph Mountain Club—RMC maintains the 2.2 miles from Edmands Col north of Mt. Washington to Madison Spring Hut; <www.randolphmountainclub.org>.

Randolph Mountain Club (RMC) Cabins and Shelters—Randolph Mountain Club was named an A.T. maintaining club by ATC in Oct 2010. In addition to the 2.2 miles of the A.T. north of Edmands Col, RMC maintains a network of 100 miles of hiking trails, principally on the northern slopes of Mounts Madison, Adams, and Jefferson in the Presidential Range of the White Mountain National Forest and on the Crescent Range in the town of Randolph. The RMC maintains several cabins and shelters below treeline in the Presidential Range that are often used by A.T. hikers seeking shelter from the exposed ridgeline. Crag Camp and Gray Knob are cabins. The Perch is a lean-to. All camps are available to the public on a first-come, first-served basis. If a site is full, the caretaker may ask visitors to move to another RMC facility, if space is available. Groups are limited to 10. To maintain serenity, cellular phones may not be used at any of the camps. Gas stoves at both cabins are available to the public; at all other times, users must bring their own stoves. Year-round, the weather is far harsher and colder here than "below the notches." RMC relies on visitors to carry out their trash and help keep the cabin and woods clean. To support the caretakers' wages and maintain the camps, fees are charged on a per-night basis. If the caretaker is absent, please mail fees to: Treasurer, RMC, Randolph, NH 03570.

RMC The Perch (1948)—Shelter sleeps 8. Privy. Four tent platforms, $10PP fee. Water source is crossed *en route* to the shelter. Accessible *via* Israel Ridge Trail from Mt. Jefferson at Edmands Col, 0.9 mile and a 600-foot descent from the A.T.

RMC Crag Camp Cabin (1909/1993)— Sleeps 20. Water is available from a spring, approximately 0.25 mile west on the Gray Knob Trail. Located 1.1 miles and 1,200-foot descent from the A.T. Caretaker in Jul–Aug; $25PP.

RMC Gray Knob Cabin (1905/1989)—Sleeps 15. Water from a spring, approximately 0.25 mile east on Gray Knob Trail. Resident caretaker year-round; $25PP. Heated in winter; 1.2 miles and 1,200-foot descent from A.T.

Madison Spring Hut—Located in a col 0.5 mile south of the summit of Mt. Madison. Full service May 28–Sep 26, with no self-service operation.

Valley Way and Osgood Tentsites—These two primitive, no-fee U.S. Forest Service tentsites, below treeline on Mt. Madison, are often used by hikers starting or finishing the traverse of the Presidential Range. Valley Way Tentsite is off the A.T., 0.6 mile west of Madison Springs Hut, with two large tent platforms and a privy. Osgood Tentsite is 3 miles north of the hut, along the A.T., and has three tentsites, privy, and spring.

N.H. 16/Pinkham Notch—Pinkham Notch Visitors Center; front desk, (603) 466-2721. AMC's New Hampshire headquarters, located on the A.T., offers a store with limited hiker supplies, restroom, coin-operated showers (open 24 hours), AMC shuttle stop, and Concord Coach bus service (see below). The center holds packages sent to AMC Visitors Center, c/o Front Desk, N.H. 16, Gorham, NH 03581. ■ *Restaurant:* Cafeteria with AYCE $12 B, deli L (not AYCE) 9:30–4, trail L $13, $23 D (thru-hikers get member rates). ■ *Lodging:* Joe Dodge Lodge, (603) 466-2727, $62 includes B/D. Prices can change; contact AMC for the most current rates.
    East 13–16 miles to Intervale, N.H. ■ *Outfitter:* Ragged Mountain Equipment, (603) 356-3042, open daily, backpacking gear and repair service. ■ *Lodging:* Cranmore Mountain Lodge, 859 Kearsage Rd., North Conway, NH 03860; (603) 356-2044, $89D includes B, seasonal heated pool, spa, mail drops accepted. ■ *Other services:* Peter Limmer & Sons Shop, (603) 356-5378, located on N.H. 16A, home of legendary hand-made hiking boots, will repair many brands of boots and hiking gear with priority to thru-hikers; closed Su–M.
    East 18 miles to North Conway, N.H., a tourist town with most major services, including several outfitters, a supermarket, cobbler, coin laundry, bank, ATM, hospital, veterinarian, pharmacy, one-hour photo, movie theater, hotels, and restaurants.
    West 1 mile to the Wildcat Mountain Gondola, daily mid-Jun to mid-Oct, 10–4:45, and

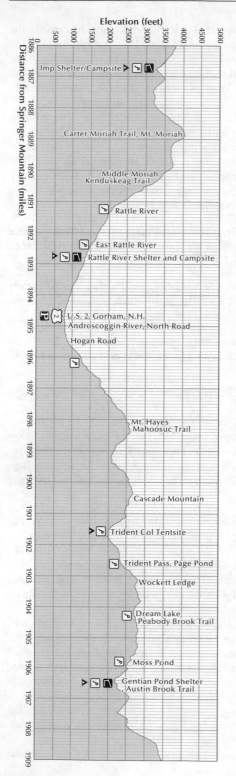

offers rides to and from the A.T. on the top of Wildcat Mountain; $15 round-trip; special round-trip with lunch (deli) available for $25.

West 11 miles to Gorham, N.H. (see below).

Concord Coach Bus Service—Service between Boston and Pinkham Notch, as well as Gorham, Berlin, and Conway, (800) 639-3317, <www.concordcoachlines.com>. Departs Pinkham Notch daily at 8:07 a.m. and arrives at Boston South Station at 12:20 p.m. The bus to Pinkham Notch departs Boston at 4:15 p.m. and arrives at Pinkham Notch at 8:15 p.m. One-way, $35; round-trip, $66.

Carter Notch Hut—The northernmost hut, located on the banks of two small lakes in Carter Notch. It is the original hut, built in 1914. Full service May 28–Sep 19; self-service rest of year except May 25–27 and Sep 20–22.

Imp Shelter and Campsite (1981)—Shelter sleeps 16. Privy (composting). Four single, one double tent platform. Bear box. Overnight fee $10PP, caretaker on site. Water is stream near shelter.

Rattle River Shelter (1980s)—Sleeps 8. Privy. Shelter built by USFS. Water source is Rattle River.

U.S. 2—*Hostel:* On A.T., Rattle River Lodge & Hostel, 592 State Route 2, Shelburne, NH 03581; (603) 466-5049, <www.rattleriverhostel.com>, private rooms starting at $90, bunk rate $37PP. All stays include AYCE B, fresh linens, laundry, shower, WiFi, full kitchen, shuttles to town; free daily Pinkham pick-up 8 a.m., 12, 5 p.m.; slackpacking available, smoking outdoors, credit cards and mail drops accepted ($5), no pets. Non-guest shower and laundry available; parking $10/day.

West 1.8 miles to *Hostel:* The Birches Loft at White Birches Camping Park, owners Bob and Janet Langlands, 218 State Rt. 2, Shelburne, NH 03581; (603) 466-2022, <www.whitebirchescampingpark.com>, <whitebirch131@gmail.com>; May 1–end of Oct, tentsites and hostel $15s per night, private cabins. Hot showers and laundry for guests only, limited resupply, microwave, refrigerator, dogs welcome, local restaurants deliver, swimming pool, mail drops accepted for guests, limited shuttle to town/trailhead for guests only, slackpacking, Visa/MasterCard/Discover.

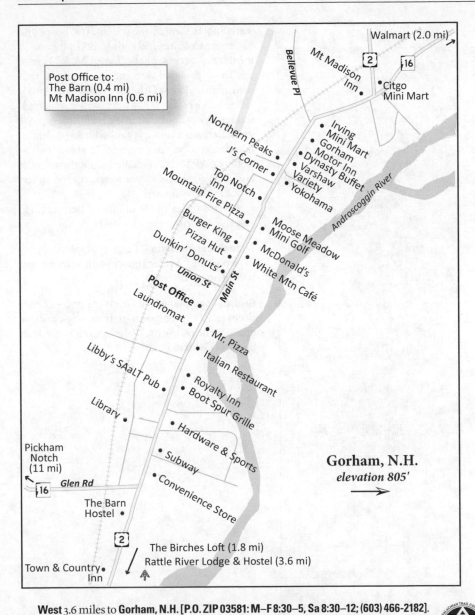

Post Office to:
The Barn (0.4 mi)
Mt Madison Inn (0.6 mi)

Walmart (2.0 mi)

Bellevue Pl

Mt Madison Inn

2   16

Citgo
Mini Mart

Northern Peaks

Irving
Mini Mart
Gorham
Motor Inn
Dynasty Buffet
Varshaw
Variety
Yokohama

J's Corner

Top Notch
Inn

Mountain Fire Pizza

Androscoggin River

Burger King

Pizza Hut

Moose Meadow
Mini Golf

McDonald's

White Mtn Café

Dunkin' Donuts'

Union St

Main St

Post Office

Laundromat

Mr. Pizza

Italian Restaurant

Libby's SAaLT Pub

Royalty Inn
Boot Spur Grille

Library

Hardware & Sports

Pickham
Notch
(11 mi)

Subway

Gorham, N.H.
elevation 805'

16   Glen Rd

Convenience Store

The Barn
Hostel

2

The Birches Loft (1.8 mi)
Rattle River Lodge & Hostel (3.6 mi)

Town & Country
Inn

West 3.6 miles to **Gorham, N.H. [P.O. ZIP 03581: M–F 8:30–5, Sa 8:30–12; (603) 466-2182].** The postmaster requests that all packages include your legal name and ETA; use bold letters/colors and have ID; can knock on door inside lobby to pick up mail drops after hours. ■ *Hostel:* The Barn Hostel, 55 Main St., (603) 466-2271, <libbyhouse@twc.com>. Libby House B&B offers room in the barn hostel, $25PP; WiFi,microwave, TV, shower, shuttles, no pets, $5 laundry; free mail drops for guests ($15 nonguests). ■ *Lodging:* Libby House B&B, (603) 466-2271 or (603) 723-6129, beginning at $70S, $85D, includes continental B, WiFi; Royalty Inn, (603) 466-3312, <www.royaltyinn.com>, $89–$99; Northern Peaks, (603) 466-2288, $65/room (single queen/microwave/minifridge), dogs welcome ($15), a/c, hot tub, hiker box, mail drops for guests; Town & Country Inn, U.S. 2, (603) 466-3315, $100S, $120D, $10EAP, pets welcome ($25), mail drops accepted. ■ *Groceries:* Super Walmart (long-term resupply) located 2 miles north of town on N.H. 16. ■ *Restaurants:* Mr. Pizza, J's Corner, and various fast-food options. ■ *Outfitter:* Gorham Hard-

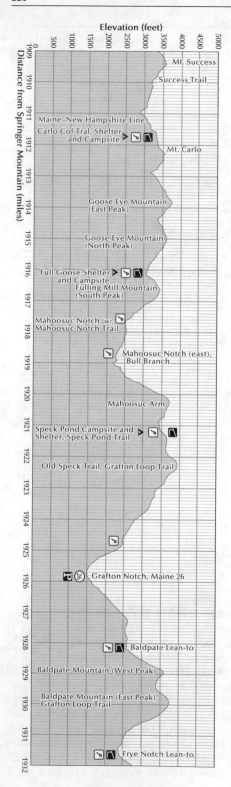

ware/Sports Center, (603) 466-2312, boots and hiker gear, Coleman fuel and alcohol by the ounce. ■ *Internet access:* public library, M, W, F, 10–7, Tu, Th 10–8, closed weekends, located near railroad, nominal fee. ■ *Other services:* Trail Angels Hiker Services, (978) 855-9227, <www.trailangel-shikerservices.com>, shuttles, mail drops, guide service, *etc.*; coin laundry; bank with ATM; dentist; free concerts on the common Tu evenings; Tri-County CAP Transit, local Berlin–Gorham shuttle bus, (888) 997-2020, <www.tccap.org>, no Su service, stops at Walmart.

West 8 miles to small city of Berlin, N.H., and the Androscoggin Valley Hospital.

Trident Col Tentsite—Four tent pads. Privy (composting). Water source is an intermittent spring on a side trail.

Gentian Pond Shelter and Campsite (1974)—Shelter sleeps 14. Privy (composting). Three single and one double tent platform. Water source is the inlet brook of Gentian Pond.

Maine

Miles from Springer	Miles to Next Point	Features	Services	Elev	Miles from Katahdin	M A P
1,911.2	1.3	New Hampshire–Maine State Line		2,972'	281.8	
1,911.7	0.5	Carlo Col Trail Jct. to **Carlo Col Shelter** and **Campsite** *(W–0.3m)* ...*5.7mS; 4.7mN* *West–2.6m to* Success Pond Road	S, C, w R, P	2,945'	281.3	
1,912.1	0.4	Mt. Carlo		3,565'	280.9	
1,913.5	1.4	Goose Eye Trail to Goose Eye Mountain *(West Peak) (W–0.1m)* *West–3.2m to* Success Pond Road	 R, P	3,854'	279.5	
1,913.9	0.4	Goose Eye Mountain *(East Peak)*		3,794'	279.1	
1,915.1	1.2	Goose Eye Mountain *(North Peak)*		3,675'	277.9	
1,916.1	1.0	**Full Goose Shelter** and **Campsite** ...*4.7mS; 5.2mN*	S, C, w	3,030'	276.9	
1,916.6	0.5	Fulling Mill Mountain *(South Peak)*		3,395'	276.4	
1,917.6	1.0	Mahoosuc Notch Trail; Mahoosuc Notch (west end) *West–2.5m to* Success Pond Road	w R, P	2,400'	275.4	
1,918.7	1.1	Mahoosuc Notch *(east end)*, Bull Branch	C, w	2,150'	274.3	
1,920.3	1.6	Mahoosuc Arm Summit, Joe May Cut-off Trail Jct.		3,765'	272.7	
1,920.9	0.6	Speck Pond Brook ...*outlet of Speck Pond*		3,430'	272.1	
1,921.2	0.3	Speck Pond Trail, +AMC **Speck Pond Shelter** and **Campsite** *(W–0.1m)* ...*last water for the next 3.5 miles north* ...*5.2mS; 6.9mN* *West–3.6m to* Success Pond Road	S, C, w R, P	3,500'	271.8	
1,922.3	1.1	Old Speck Trail and Grafton Loop Trail Junction *East–0.3m to* summit and observation tower		3,985'	270.7	
1,924.6	2.3	Eyebrow Trail ...*upper junction*		2,480'	268.4	
1,924.7	0.1	Brook ...*last water for the next 3.5 miles south*	w	2,500'	268.3	
1,925.7	1.0	Eyebrow Trail ...*lower junction*		1,530'	267.3	
1,925.8	0.1	Grafton Notch, Maine 26 *East–5m to* Grafton Notch Campground *East–13m to* Stony Brook Recreation & Camping	R, P C C, g, M, sh, f	1,495'	267.2	
1,926.6	0.8	Table Rock Trail ...*upper junction*		2,125'	266.4	
1,928.1	1.5	**Baldpate Lean-to** ...*6.9mS; 3.5mN*	S, w	2,645'	264.9	
1,928.9	0.8	Baldpate Mountain *(West Peak)*		3,662'	264.1	
1,929.8	0.9	Baldpate Mountain *(East Peak)*; Grafton Loop Trail Junction		3,812'	263.2	
1,930.3	0.5	Little Baldpate Mountain		3,442'	262.7	
1,931.6	1.3	**Frye Notch Lean-to,** Frye Brook ..*3.5mS; 10.5mN*	S, w	2,280'	261.4	
1,932.1	0.5	Surplus Mountain ...*highpoint on NE ridge*		2,875'	260.9	
1,935.3	3.2	Dunn Notch and Falls ...*ford West Branch Ellis River*	w	1,350'	257.7	
1,936.1	0.8	East B Hill Road *East–8m to* **Andover, Maine, P.O. 04216** *East–11m to* East Andover, Maine; "The Cabin"	R, P, C H, G, L, M, f H	1,485'	256.9	
1,937.9	1.8	Burroughs Brook ...*ford, outlet of Surplus Pond*	w	2,050'	255.1	
1,938.0	0.1	Gravel logging road	R	2,050'	255.0	
1,940.8	2.8	Wyman Mountain *(north peak)*		2,945'	252.2	
1,942.1	1.3	**Hall Mountain Lean-to** ...*10.5mS; 12.8mN*	S, w	2,635'	250.9	

Miles from Springer	Miles to Next Point	Features	Services	Elev	Miles from Katahdin	M A P
1,943.5	1.4	Sawyer Notch, Sawyer Brook ...*ford*	w	1,095'	249.5	
1,944.4	0.9	Moody Mountain		2,440'	248.6	
1,946.2	1.8	South Arm Road, Black Brook ...*ford, privy* *East–9m to* **Andover, Maine, P.O. 04216** *East–12m to* East Andover, Maine; "The Cabin" *West–3.5m to* South Arm Campground	R, P, C, w H, G, L, M, f H C, G, cl, sh	1,410'	246.8	MATC Maine Map 7
1,949.0	2.8	Old Blue Mountain		3,600'	244.0	
1,952.2	3.2	Bemis Stream Trail		3,350'	240.8	
1,953.2	1.0	Bemis Mountain *(West Peak)*		3,592'	239.8	
1,954.9	1.7	**Bemis Mountain Lean-to** ...*12.8mS; 8.3mN*	S, w	2,790'	238.1	
1,956.4	1.5	Bemis Range *(Second Peak)* ...*open ledges*		2,915'	236.6	
1,958.5	2.1	Gravel road ...*former rail bed*	R	1,550'	234.5	
1,958.7	0.2	Bemis Stream ...*ford*	w	1,495'	234.3	
1,959.5	0.8	Maine 17 ...*view of Mooselookmeguntic Lake* *West–11m to* **Oquossoc, Maine, P.O. 04964**	R, P G, M, f	2,200'	233.5	
1,960.3	0.8	Spruce Mountain		2,530'	232.7	
1,961.1	0.8	Moxie Pond	w	2,400'	231.9	
1,962.9	1.8	Long Pond ...*sandy beach*	w	2,330'	230.1	
1,963.2	0.3	**Sabbath Day Pond Lean-to** ...*8.3mS; 11.2mN*	S, w	2,390'	229.8	
1,963.7	0.5	Houghton Fire Road		2,300'	229.3	
1,967.8	4.1	Little Swift River Pond Campsite ...*piped spring*	C, w	2,460'	225.2	
1,969.0	1.2	Chandler Mill Stream ...*outlet of boreal bog*	w	2,150'	224.0	
1,970.5	1.5	South Pond	w	2,174'	222.5	
1,972.6	2.1	Maine 4 *West–0.3m to* Hiker Hut *West–9m to* **Rangeley, Maine, P.O. 04970**	R, P L H, G, L, M, O, D, cl, f	1,700'	220.4	MATC Maine Map 6
1,972.7	0.1	Sandy River ...*footbridge*	w	1,595'	220.3	
1,973.3	0.6	Gravel road		1,750'	219.7	
1,974.4	1.1	**Piazza Rock Lean-to** ...*11.2mS; 8.9mN*	S, C, w	2,080'	218.6	
1,975.3	0.9	Ethel Pond	w	2,200'	217.7	
1,975.7	0.4	Saddleback Stream	w	2,350'	217.3	
1,976.3	0.6	Moose and deer pond outlet near Eddy Pond ... *last water for the next 6 miles north*	w	2,616'	216.7	
1,976.5	0.2	Gravel logging road		2,625'	216.5	
1,977.3	0.8	Treeline ...*above treeline for the next 2.9 miles north*		3,700'	215.7	
1,978.3	1.0	Saddleback Mountain		4,120'	214.7	
1,979.9	1.6	The Horn		4,041'	213.1	
1,980.2	0.3	Treeline ...*above treeline for the next 2.9 miles south*		3,620'	212.8	
1,980.6	0.4	Redington Stream Campsite *(W–0.2m spring)*	C, w	3,170'	212.4	
1,981.9	1.3	Saddleback Junior ...*open summit*		3,655'	211.1	
1,982.3	0.4	Brook ...*last water for the next 6 miles south*	w	3,200'	210.7	
1,983.3	1.0	**Poplar Ridge Lean-to** ...*8.9mS; 8mN*	S, w	2,920'	209.7	
1,986.0	2.7	Orbeton Stream ...*ford*	w	1,550'	207.0	
1,986.1	0.1	Gravel road ...*old rail bed; northbound turn Trail* *E–100 ft. to reenter woods*		1,650'	206.9	

Miles from Springer	Miles to Next Point	Features	Services	Elev	Miles from Katahdin	M A P
1,986.8	0.7	Sluice Brook	w	2,145'	206.2	
1,987.5	0.7	Logging road		2,300'	205.5	
1,988.0	0.5	Logging road ...*Perham Stream nearby*	w	2,300'	205.0	
1,989.1	1.1	Lone Mountain		3,280'	203.9	
1,990.2	1.1	Mt. Abraham Trail ...*(E–1.7m to summit; 4,050')*		3,184'	202.8	
1,991.3	1.1	**Spaulding Mountain Lean-to** ...*8mS; 18.6mN*	S, w	3,140'	201.7	
1,992.1	0.8	Trail to Spaulding Mountain *(E–0.1m to summit)*		4,010'	200.9	
1,992.8	0.7	Bronze Plaque ...*1937 completion of the final two miles of the A.T.*		3,500'	200.2	MATC Maine Map 6
1,994.2	1.4	Sugarloaf Mountain Trail *(E–0.3m spring; 0.6m to summit)*	w	3,540'	198.8	
1,996.4	2.2	South Branch Carrabassett River ...*ford*	w	2,100'	196.6	
1,996.5	0.1	Caribou Valley Road ...*gravel (E–4.3m Maine 27)*	R, P	2,220'	196.5	
1,997.5	1.0	Crocker Cirque Campsite *(E–0.2m)* ...*spring*	C, w	2,710'	195.5	
1,998.6	1.1	South Crocker Mountain *(W–150 ft. to summit)*		4,040'	194.4	
1,999.6	1.0	North Crocker Mountain		4,228'	193.4	
2,000.6	1.0	Stream	w	3,300'	192.4	
2,002.7	2.1	Stream ...*in stand of large white birch trees*	w	2,500'	190.3	
2,004.8	2.1	Maine 27 *East–2m to* Mountainside Grocers *East–18m to* Kingfield, Maine *West–5m to* **Stratton, Maine, P.O. 04982**	R, P G G, L, M, D H, G, L, M, cl, f	1,450'	188.2	
2,005.6	0.8	Stratton Brook Pond Road	R, P	1,250'	187.4	
2,005.8	0.2	Stratton Brook ...*footbridge*	w	1,230'	187.2	
2,006.7	0.9	Cranberry Stream Campsite	C, w	1,350'	186.3	
2,008.0	1.3	Bigelow Range Trail, Cranberry Pond *(W–0.2m stream)*	w	2,400'	185.0	
2,009.7	1.7	Horns Pond Trail		3,200'	183.3	
2,009.9	0.2	**Horns Pond Lean-tos** ...*18.6mS; 10.2mN*	S, C, w	3,160'	183.1	
2,010.2	0.3	Spring	w	3,400'	182.8	
2,010.3	0.1	Side Trail to North Horn *(W–0.2m summit)*		3,792'	182.7	
2,010.4	0.1	South Horn		3,831'	182.6	
2,012.5	2.1	Bigelow Mountain *(West Peak)*		4,145'	180.5	MATC Maine Map 5
2,012.8	0.3	Bigelow Col, Fire Warden's Trail, Avery Memorial Campsite	C, w	3,850'	180.2	
2,013.0	0.2	Spring	w	3,900'	180.0	
2,013.2	0.2	Bigelow Mountain; Avery Peak		4,090'	179.8	
2,015.1	1.9	Safford Brook Trail		2,260'	177.9	
2,015.2	0.1	Safford Notch and Campsite *(E–0.3m)*	C, w	2,230'	177.8	
2,017.0	1.8	Little Bigelow Mountain *(west end)*		3,035'	176.0	
2,018.4	1.4	Little Bigelow Mountain *(east end)*		3,040'	174.6	
2,020.1	1.7	**Little Bigelow Lean-to** ...*10.2mS; 7.7mN*	S, C, w	1,760'	172.9	
2,021.5	1.4	East Flagstaff Road	R	1,200'	171.5	
2,021.6	0.1	Bog Brook Road, Flagstaff Lake *(W–0.2m)* ...*inlet*	R, P, w	1,150'	171.4	
2,022.6	1.0	Campsite ...*privy*	C, w	1,210'	170.4	
2,024.3	1.7	Long Falls Dam Road	R, P	1,225'	168.7	

Miles from Springer	Miles to Next Point	Features	Services	Elev	Miles from Katahdin	MAP
2,024.4	0.1	Jerome Brook	w	1,300'	168.6	
2,024.7	0.3	Logging Road ...*gravel*		1,400'	168.3	
2,026.0	1.3	Roundtop Mountain		1,760'	167.0	
2,026.8	0.8	Stream	w	1,360'	166.2	
2,027.1	0.3	West Carry Pond *(west side)*	w	1,320'	165.9	
2,027.8	0.7	**West Carry Pond Lean-to** ...*7.7mS; 10mN*	S, w	1,340'	165.2	
2,028.5	0.7	West Carry Pond *(east side)...side trail west to Arnold Point Beach on Arnold Trail*	w	1,320'	164.5	MATC Maine Map 5
2,030.0	1.5	Arnold Swamp ...*many bog bridges*		1,255'	163.0	
2,030.2	0.2	Long Pond Road	R	1,250'	162.8	
2,030.4	0.2	Sandy Stream, Middle Carry Pond Road ...*bridge*	R, w	1,229'	162.6	
2,031.2	0.8	East Carry Pond Logging Road ...*gravel*	R	1,250'	161.8	
2,031.9	0.7	East Carry Pond *(north end)*	w	1,237'	161.1	
2,033.6	1.7	Scott Road ...*main logging road*	R	1,300'	159.4	
2,034.3	0.7	North Branch of Carrying Place Stream ...*ford*	w	1,200'	158.7	
2,037.8	3.5	**Pierce Pond Lean-to** ...*10mS; 9.7mN*	S, w	1,150'	155.2	
2,038.0	0.2	Wooden dam ...*outlet of Pierce Pond*		1,120'	155.0	
2,038.2	0.2	Trail to Harrison's Pierce Pond Camps *(E–0.1m)*	R, L, M, w	1,100'	154.8	
2,038.5	0.3	Otter Pond Road ...*gravel*		1,080'	154.5	
2,039.2	0.7	Trail to pool at base of waterfalls *(E–0.1m)* ... *Pierce Pond Stream*	w	850'	153.8	
2,039.6	0.4	Otter Pond Stream ...*bridge*	w	900'	153.4	
2,041.5	1.9	Kennebec River ...*ferry*	w	490'	151.5	
2,041.8	0.3	U.S. 201 *East–150 yards to* Caratunk House Hiker B&B *East–0.3m to* **Caratunk, Maine, P.O. 04925** *East–1m to* Sterling Inn *East–16.5m to* Bingham, Maine *West–2m to* Northern Outdoors *West–3.5m to* Three Rivers Trading Post *West–7m to* The Forks, Maine	R, P L, g H, L, g, sh, cl G, L, M, cl C, L, M, sh, cl C,L,M,g C, G, f	520'	151.2	
2,044.5	2.7	Holly Brook	w	900'	148.5	
2,045.9	1.4	Hangtown Road ...*gravel logging road*	R	1,240'	147.1	
2,047.1	1.2	Boise–Cascade logging road	R, P	1,400'	145.9	
2,047.5	0.4	**Pleasant Pond Lean-to** ...*9.7mS; 9mN*	S, w	1,320'	145.5	
2,047.7	0.2	Trail to Pleasant Pond Beach *(E–0.2m)*		1,360'	145.3	MATC Maine Map 4
2,048.8	1.1	Pleasant Pond Mountain		2,477'	144.2	
2,053.7	4.9	Moxie Pond *(south end)*, Joe's Hole, Troutdale Rd	R, P	970'	139.3	
2,053.8	0.1	Baker Stream ...*ford*	w	1,010'	139.2	
2,054.9	1.1	Joe's Hole Brook	w	1,240'	138.1	
2,056.3	1.4	Bald Mountain Brook Campsite	C, w	1,200'	136.7	
2,056.5	0.2	**Bald Mountain Brook Lean-to** ...*9mS; 4.1mN*	S, w	1,280'	136.5	
2,057.9	1.4	Summit bypass trail		2,250'	135.1	
2,058.5	0.6	Moxie Bald Mountain		2,629'	134.5	
2,058.8	0.3	Summit bypass trail		2,490'	134.2	
2,059.5	0.7	Trail to Moxie Bald Mountain *(north peak)(W–0.7m)*		2,320'	133.5	

Miles from Springer	Miles to Next Point	Features	Services	Elev	Miles from Katahdin	M A P
2,060.6	1.1	**Moxie Bald Lean-to** ...*4.1mS; 8.9mN*	S, w	1,220'	132.4	
2,061.1	0.5	Gravel road		1,290'	131.9	
2,062.7	1.6	Bald Mountain Stream ...*outlet of Bald Mtn Pond*	w	1,213'	130.3	
2,064.6	1.9	Bald Mountain Stream Road ...*gravel*	R	1,100'	128.4	
2,066.1	1.5	Marble Brook and "Jeep Road"		990'	126.9	
2,066.4	0.3	West Branch Piscataquis River ...*ford*	w	900'	126.6	
2,069.5	3.1	**Horseshoe Canyon Lean-to** ...*8.9mS; 12mN*	S, w	880'	123.5	Maine Map 4
2,071.8	2.3	East Branch Piscataquis River ...*ford*	w	650'	121.2	
2,072.1	0.3	Old Bangor and Aroostook railroad bed		800'	120.9	
2,072.2	0.1	Shirley–Blanchard Road ...*paved*	R, P	880'	120.8	
2,075.2	3.0	Blue-blaze to Pleasant St., Lake Hebron *East–0.3m to* road, then 1.7m to Monson, Maine	CR, P	900'	117.8	
2,076.3	1.1	Buck Hill		1,390'	116.7	
2,077.1	0.8	Trail to Doughty Ponds		1,240'	115.9	
2,078.5	1.4	Maine 15 *East–4m to* **Monson, Maine, P.O. 04464**; ATC Visitors Center *West–10m to* Greenville, Maine	R, P H, G, L, M, O, cl, sh, f G, L, M, O, D, V, f	1,215'	114.5	
		Enter the "100 Mile Wilderness"				
2,078.6	0.1	Goodell Brook, Spectacle Pond Outlet	w	1,163'	114.4	
2,079.7	1.1	Bell Pond	w	1,278'	113.3	
2,080.4	0.7	Lily Pond	w	1,130'	112.6	
2,081.5	1.1	**Leeman Brook Lean-to** ...*12mS; 7.4mN*	S, w	1,060'	111.5	
2,082.3	0.8	North Pond ...*outlet*	w	1,000'	110.7	
2,082.7	0.4	North Pond Tote Road	R	1,100'	110.3	
2,084.0	1.3	Rim of Bear Pond Ledges		1,200'	109.0	
2,084.8	0.8	James Brook	w	950'	108.2	
2,085.0	0.2	Gravel haul road	R	1,000'	108.0	
2,085.1	0.1	Little Wilson Falls ...*60 ft. high*		850'	107.9	
2,085.3	0.2	Little Wilson Stream ...*ford*	w	750'	107.7	MATC Maine Map 3
2,085.7	0.4	Gravel Road ...*follow for 100 yds.*	R	900'	107.3	
2,087.6	1.9	Big Wilson Tote Road	R	620'	105.4	
2,087.7	0.1	Thompson Brook	w	620'	105.3	
2,088.2	0.5	Big Wilson Stream ...*ford*	w	600'	104.8	
2,088.5	0.3	Montreal, Maine & Atlantic RR Tracks		850'	104.5	
2,088.9	0.4	**Wilson Valley Lean-to** ...*7.4mS; 4.7mN*	S, w	1,000'	104.1	
2,089.5	0.6	Old winter logging road		1,190'	103.5	
2,092.1	2.6	Wilber Brook	w	660'	100.9	
2,092.2	0.1	Vaughn Stream ...*top of 20 ft. waterfall*		670'	100.8	
2,092.7	0.5	Bodfish Farm–Long Pond Tote Road	R	650'	100.3	
2,092.8	0.1	Long Pond Stream ...*ford*	w	620'	100.2	
2,093.5	0.7	Side Trail to Slugundy Gorge and Falls		870'	99.5	
2,093.6	0.1	**Long Pond Stream Lean-to** ...*4.7mS; 4.4mN*	S, w	930'	99.4	
2,096.7	3.1	Barren Mountain ...*abandoned firetower*		2,670'	96.3	
2,097.6	0.9	**Cloud Pond Lean-to** (*E–0.4m*) ...*4.4mS; 7.3mN*	S, w	2,420'	95.4	

Miles from Springer	Miles to Next Point	Features	Services	Elev	Miles from Katahdin	M A P
2,099.7	2.1	Fourth Mountain		2,383'	93.3	MATC Maine Map 3
2,102.2	2.5	Third Mountain, Monument Cliff		2,061'	90.8	
2,102.8	0.6	West Chairback Pond side trail *(E–0.2m pond)*	w	1,770'	90.2	
2,104.1	1.3	Columbus Mountain ...*open ledge*		2,325'	88.9	
2,104.5	0.4	**Chairback Gap Lean-to** ...*7.3mS; 9.9mN*	S, w	2,000'	88.5	
2,105.0	0.5	Chairback Mountain		2,219'	88.0	
2,105.4	0.4	Semiopen ledges ...*views*		2,000'	87.6	
2,107.2	1.8	East Chairback Pond side trail *(W–0.2m)*	w	1,630'	85.8	
2,107.7	0.5	Small stream and spring	w	1,250'	85.3	
2,108.4	0.7	Katahdin Iron Works Road *(E–0.5m parking)* *East–20m to* Brownville Junction on Maine 11 *West–1.5m to* +AMC Gorman Chairback Lodge *West–6.1m to* +AMC Little Lyford Pond Cabins	R, P C, G L L	750'	84.6	
2,108.9	0.5	West Branch Pleasant River ...*ford (E–0.2m parking)*	P, w	680'	84.1	MATC Maine Map 2
2,109.1	0.2	Trail to Pugwash Pond, Pleasant River Campsites, Hay Brook Parking Area *(E–0.7m)*	P, C, w	680'	83.9	
2,109.2	0.1	The Hermitage		695'	83.8	
2,110.2	1.0	Gulf Hagas Trail ...*5.2m loop, rejoins A.T. north*	w	950'	82.8	
2,110.9	0.7	Gulf Hagas Cut-off Trail ...*5.2m loop, rejoins A.T. south*	w	1,050'	82.1	
2,114.4	3.5	Gulf Hagas Brook; **Carl A. Newhall Lean-to** ...*9.9mS; 7.2mN*	S, w	1,860'	78.6	
2,115.3	0.9	Gulf Hagas Mountain		2,683'	77.7	
2,116.2	0.9	Sidney Tappan Campsite ...*spring (E–0.2m)*	C, w	2,425'	76.8	
2,116.9	0.7	West Peak		3,178'	76.1	
2,118.5	1.6	Hay Mountain		3,244'	74.5	
2,119.1	0.6	White Brook Trail		3,125'	73.9	
2,120.2	1.1	White Cap Mountain ...*view of Katahdin*		3,654'	72.8	
2,121.6	1.4	**Logan Brook Lean-to** ...*7.2mS; 3.6mN*	S, w	2,480'	71.4	
2,123.2	1.6	West Branch Ponds Road	R	1,650'	69.8	
2,125.2	2.0	**East Branch Lean-to** ...*3.6mS; 8.1mN*	S, w	1,225'	67.8	
2,125.5	0.3	East Branch Pleasant River ...*ford*	w	1,200'	67.5	
2,127.1	1.6	Mountain View Pond ...*outlet*	w	1,597'	65.9	
2,127.4	0.3	Spring *(east)*	w	1,580'	65.6	
2,128.7	1.3	Little Boardman Mountain *(300 ft. to summit)*		2,017'	64.3	
2,130.1	1.4	Kokadjo-B Pond Road ...*gravel*	R, P	1,380'	62.9	
2,131.0	0.9	Crawford Pond ...*outlet, no camping*	w	1,240'	62.0	
2,133.3	2.3	**Cooper Brook Falls Lean-to** ...*8.1mS; 11.4mN*	S, C, w	880'	59.7	
2,137.0	3.7	Jo-Mary Road *East–6m to* Jo-Mary Lake Campground *East–17m to* Maine 11 and Brownville Junction	R, P, C, w C, G, cl, sh R	625'	56.0	
2,138.3	1.3	Side trail to Cooper Pond *(E–0.2m)*		600'	54.7	
2,139.6	1.3	Gravel logging road ...*snowsled bridge*	R	520'	53.4	
2,139.9	0.3	Mud Brook, Mud Pond outlet ...*bridge*	w	508'	53.1	
2,141.2	1.3	Antlers Campsite	C, w	500'	51.8	
2,142.9	1.7	Lower Jo-Mary Lake ...*sand beach*	w	580'	50.1	

Miles from Springer	Miles to Next Point	Features	Services	Elev	Miles from Katahdin	MAP
2,144.7	1.8	**Potaywadjo Spring Lean-to** ...11.4mS; 4.3mN	S, w	710'	48.3	
2,145.2	0.5	Twitchell Brook ...*bridge*	w	590'	47.8	
2,145.3	0.1	Pemadumcook Lake ...*Katahdin view*	w	580'	47.7	
2,146.5	1.2	Deer Brook		588'	46.5	
2,146.9	0.4	Gravel logging road		580'	46.1	MATC Maine Map 2
2,147.0	0.1	Mahar Trail/Mahar Tote Road *(E–1.2m to White House Landing)*	L, M	580'	46.0	
2,147.1	0.1	Branch of Nahmakanta Stream ...*ford*		580'	45.9	
2,148.2	1.1	Tumbledown Dick Stream ...*ford*		590'	44.8	
2,149.0	0.8	**Nahmakanta Stream Lean-to** ...*4.3mS; 5.8mN*	S, C, w	600'	44.0	
2,150.5	1.5	Tumbledown Dick Trail		625'	42.5	
2,151.6	1.1	Wood Rat's Spring	w	740'	41.4	
2,151.9	0.3	Gravel road	R	749'	41.1	
2,152.2	0.3	Nahmakanta Lake (south end) ...*gravel beach*	R, P, C, w	650'	40.8	
2,153.1	0.9	Prentiss Brook	w	590'	39.9	
2,154.4	1.3	Sand beach 50 ft. east ...*spring*	w	595'	38.6	
2,154.7	0.3	Wadleigh Stream	w	680'	38.3	
2,154.8	0.1	**Wadleigh Stream Lean-to** ...*5.8mS; 8.1mN*	S, w	685'	38.2	
2,156.7	1.9	Nesuntabunt Mountain ...*views*		1,520'	36.3	
2,157.9	1.2	Logging road ...*gravel*	R	1,010'	35.1	
2,159.1	1.2	Crescent Pond *(west end)*	w	980'	33.9	
2,159.5	0.4	Pollywog Gorge ...*views*		1,050'	33.5	
2,160.5	1.0	Pollywog Stream ...*logging road, bridge*	R, P, w	682'	32.5	
2,161.2	0.7	Flume in gorge ...*remains of old logging dam*		1,000'	31.8	
2,162.5	1.3	Murphy Pond outlet stream	w	1,020'	30.5	
2,162.9	0.4	**Rainbow Stream Lean-to** ...*8.1mS; 11.5mN*	S, C, w	1,020'	30.1	
2,164.9	2.0	Rainbow Lake *(west end)* ...*dam on side trail with Katahdin view*	w	1,080'	28.1	
2,166.7	1.8	Rainbow Spring Campsite	C, w	1,100'	26.3	MATC Maine Map 1
2,168.4	1.7	Trail to Rainbow Mountain (E–.75m to summit)		1,100'	24.6	
2,170.1	1.7	Rainbow Lake *(east end)*	w	980'	22.9	
2,170.2	0.1	Trail to Little Beaver and Big Beaver ponds		1,100'	22.8	
2,171.9	1.7	Rainbow Ledges		1,517'	21.1	
2,174.4	2.5	**Hurd Brook Lean-to** ...*11.5mS; 13.7mN*	S, w	710'	18.6	
2,175.1	0.7	Spring	w	740'	17.9	
2,177.8	2.7	Golden Road (Greenville-Millinocket Road)	R	600'	15.2	
2,177.9	0.1	Abol Bridge over West Branch of Penobscot River, junction with International A.T. *On A.T.*–Abol Bridge Campground and Store *On A.T.*–DOC Abol Pines *East–20m to* **Millinocket, Maine, P.O. 04462** *East–27m to* Medway, Maine *East–88m to* Bangor, Maine	R, P C, G, M, sh C, S H, G, L, M, D, O, cl B, L, O all	588'	15.1	
2,178.1	0.2	Junction of Golden Road and Old State Road	R	600'	14.9	
2,178.4	0.3	Gravel pit	R	600'	14.6	
2,178.6	0.2	Abol Stream Trail, Abol Stream, Baxter Park Boundary ...*bridge, ski trail (E–1m to Abol Beach)*	w	620'	14.4	

Miles from Springer	Miles to Next Point	Features	Services	Elev	Miles from Katahdin	M A P
2,178.7	0.1	BSP Hiker Kiosk, registration for The Birches Campsite; Abol Pond Trail, Blueberry Ledges Trail		620'	14.3	
2,179.0	0.3	Katahdin Stream ...*bridge*	w	620'	14.0	
2,179.1	0.1	Foss and Knowlton Ponds Trail		630'	13.9	
2,179.8	0.7	Foss and Knowlton Brook ...*footbridge*	w	625'	13.2	
2,182.0	2.2	Pine Point	w	640'	11.0	
2,182.5	0.5	Lower Fork Nesowadnehunk Stream ...*ford*	w	630'	10.5	
2,183.4	0.9	Upper Fork Nesowadnehunk Stream ...*ford*	w	800'	9.6	
2,183.8	0.4	Rocky Rips ...*below ledge*	w	850'	9.2	
2,184.2	0.4	Big Niagara Falls	w	900'	8.8	
2,184.4	0.2	Spring *(E–150 ft.)*	w	990'	8.6	
2,184.5	0.1	Toll Dam and Little Niagara Falls		1,030'	8.5	
2,185.4	0.9	Daicey Pond Nature Trail		1,090'	7.6	
2,185.5	0.1	+Daicey Pond Campground Road; Ranger Station *(E–0.1m)*	R, P, L, w	1,100'	7.5	
2,186.0	0.5	Tracy and Elbow Ponds Trail		1,100'	7.0	
2,186.8	0.8	Outlet of Grassy Pond	w	800'	6.2	
2,187.7	0.9	Cross Perimeter Road (Tote Road)　　*East–8.7m to* BSP Togue Pond Visitor Center　　*East–10.7m to* Kathadin Forest Cabins　　*East–11.3 to* Penobscot Outdoor Center　　*East–15.7m to* Golden Road　　*East–17m to* Northwoods Trading Post, Big Moose Inns　　*East–23.3m to* Hidden Springs Campground　　*East–25.7 m to* **Millincockett, Maine P.O. 04462**	R L C G, L, M C, sh H, G, L, M, D, O, cl	1,070'	5.3	M A T C M a i n e M a p 1
2,187.8	0.1	+Katahdin Stream Campground, Ranger Station;+**The Birches** Campsite *(E–0.25m)* ...*13.7mS*	R, P, S, C, w	1,070'	5.2	
2,188.8	1.0	The Owl Trail *(W–2.2m to summit)*		1,570'	4.2	
2,188.9	0.1	Katahdin Stream ...*footbridge*	w	1,500'	4.1	
2,189.0	0.1	Katahdin Stream Falls ...*privy*	w	1,550'	4.0	
2,190.5	1.5	"The Cave" ...*small slab cave*		4,500'	2.5	
2,190.6	0.1	Hunt Spur, treeline at base of "The Boulders"		3,400'	2.4	
2,191.4	0.8	Gateway to Tablelands		4,600'	1.6	
2,192.0	0.6	Thoreau Spring	w	4,627'	1.0	
2,193.0	1.0	Katahdin, Baxter Peak ...*sign, plaque, cairn*	northern terminus	5,268'	0.0	

+ Fee charged, ~ Northbound long-distance hikers only at The Birches

Hikers in Maine encounter approximately 282 miles of lakes, bogs, moose, loons, hand-over-hand climbs, and a 100-mile wilderness that is neither 100 miles nor truly a wilderness. It is a mystical, magical place to begin or end your A.T. journey.

No camping is allowed above treeline on the A.T. in Maine.

Carlo Col Shelter and Campsite (1976)—Off Trail 0.3 mile **west** on Carlo Col Trail. Shelter sleeps 8. Privy (composting). Two single and one double tent platforms. Bear box. Water source is a spring left of the lean-to.

Full Goose Shelter and Campsite (1978)—Shelter sleeps 8. Privy (composting). Many hikers choose to stay here before or after Mahoosuc Notch. Three single and one double tent platforms. Bear box. Water source is stream behind shelter.

Mahoosuc Notch—Famous for ice in deep crevices throughout the year. Many call this scramble under, around, over, and between boulders the most difficult mile on the Trail.

Speck Pond Shelter and Campsite (1968)—Off Trail 0.1 mile **west** on Speck Pond Trail. Shelter sleeps 8. Privy (composting). Three single and three double tent platforms. Cookstoves only. Bear box. Overnight fee $10PP. Speck Pond is the highest body of water in Maine. Water source is a spring on the blue-blazed trail behind the caretaker's yurt.

Maine 26/Grafton Notch—Difficult hitch, very light traffic. **East** 5 miles to *Camping:* Grafton Notch Camp Ground, 1472 Bear River Rd., Newry, ME 04261, (207) 824-2292, <www.campgrafton.com>, private campground, 15 wooded sites $28S/D ($7EAP up to 6), with fire pit and picnic table, hot showers and flush toilets, showers only $7, leashed dogs, open mid-May through Columbus Day.

East 13 miles to Stony Brook Recreation, 3036 Main St., Hanover, ME 04237, (207) 824-2836, convenience store & restaurant (summer hours F–Sa open til 10 p.m., Su–Th 9 p.m.); tentsites $30, lean-tos $35, showers, laundry, mini-golf, shuffleboard, zip line, pool (in season), canoe & kayak rentals, shuttles with reservation.

East 19 miles to *Lodging:* Chapman Inn, (207) 824-2657, 2 Church St., Bethel, ME 04217, bunkroom with B $40, private rooms with full B $69-$139, call for reservations.

East 19 miles to *Outfitter:* Adventure to Adventurewear, (207) 824-2201, 196 Walkers Mills Rd., Bethel, ME 04217, full outfitter and resupply. Warranties, swap, repair, boots, gear, food.

Maine Appalachian Trail Club—MATC maintains the 267.2 miles from Grafton Notch to Katahdin. Correspondence should be sent to MATC Box 283, Augusta, ME 04332-0283; <www.matc.org>.

Baldpate Lean-to (1995)—Sleeps 8. Privy. Water source is a spring behind the lean-to.

Frye Notch Lean-to (1983)—Sleeps 6. Privy. Water from Frye Brook in front of the lean-to.

East B Hill Road/Andover— **East** 8 miles to **Andover, Maine [P.O. ZIP 04216: M–F 9:15–12 & 1–4:15, Sa 9–12; (207) 392-4571]**. Andover also can be reached *via* South Arm Road, 9.5 miles north on the A.T. Neither road has much traffic. ■ *Hostel:* Pine Ellis Hiking Lodge, 20 Pine St. (P.O. Box 12), (207) 392-4161, <www.pineellislodging.com>; hiker-friendly hosts Ilene Trainor and friends; located near P.O. and stores; large shared room in house or bunkhouse in backyard $25PP, private rooms $45S, $60D, $75T, all stays include shower, laundry (loaner clothes), morning coffee/muffins, house privi-

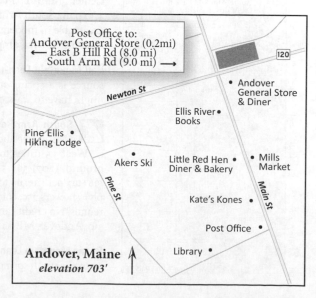

Post Office to:
Andover General Store (0.2mi)
← East B Hill Rd (8.0 mi)
South Arm Rd (9.0 mi) →

120

Newton St

Andover General Store & Diner

Ellis River Books

Pine Ellis Hiking Lodge

Akers Ski

Little Red Hen Diner & Bakery

Mills Market

Pine St

Kate's Kones

Main St

Post Office

Andover, Maine
elevation 703'

Library

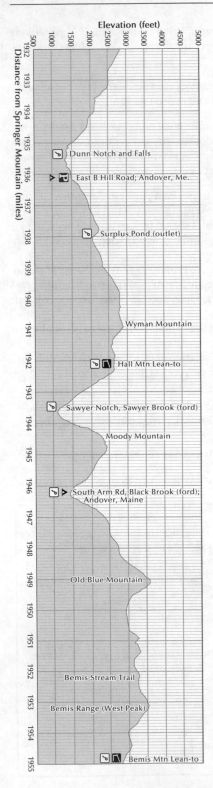

Distance from Springer Mountain (miles) / Elevation (feet)

Dunn Notch and Falls

East B Hill Road; Andover, Me.

Surplus Pond (outlet)

Wyman Mountain

Hall Mtn Lean-to

Sawyer Notch, Sawyer Brook (ford)

Moody Mountain

South Arm Rd, Black Brook (ford); Andover, Maine

Old Blue Mountain

Bemis Stream Trail

Bemis Range (West Peak)

Bemis Mtn Lean-to

leges, WiFi, CATV, and use of kitchen. For a fee: long-distance shuttles to/from Trailhead, slackpacking from Grafton Notch to Rangeley, full resupply, canister fuel, denatured alcohol, and Coleman. Credit cards accepted; mail drops accepted for guests; no dogs. Also, two camping cabins 3 miles from lodge, Paul's A.T. Camp, accommodates up to 4 for $60, EAP extra, includes shower and round-trip shuttles from lodge; dogs allowed, no hard liquor. ■ *Groceries:* Andover General Store & Diner (short-term resupply), open 7 days 5 a.m.–9 p.m., B/L/D, ATM, WiFi; Mills Market, 7 days, 5 a.m.–9 p.m., resupply, deli, pizza; free tenting. ■ *Internet access:* Andover Public Library, 8 computers and WiFi, Tu–Th & Sa 1–4:30, Th also 6–8. ■ *Other services:* Ellis River Books, 12 S. Main St., Th 11–5, F 10–6, Sa–Su 11–6, fuel and such other small items as shoelaces and duct tape; massage therapist Donna Gifford, (207) 357-5686.

East 11 miles to East Andover and *Lodging:* The Cabin, (207) 392-1333, owned by Margie Towne (Honey); log cabin with bunkroom and private room. Reservations only; alumni always welcome. A friend of hikers for more than two decades, does shuttles, takes cash/checks.

East 16.2 miles to Roxbury and *Hostel:* Human-Nature Hostel, P.O. Box 131, Roxbury, ME 04275, (207) 408-8216, <www.humannaturehostel.com>, thru-hiker owner Ryan "Yukon" Holt. Large timber-frame geodesic dome on 42 acres, $30PP includes shuttle, bunk w/ fresh linens, shower w/ towel, laundry w/ loaner clothes, kitchen, WiFi; $5PP coffee/tea & AYCE Maine blueberry pancakes; D available ($10). Free shuttles: Andover Center, 9 a.m., 1 p.m., 5 p.m.; East B. Hill Rd., 8:30 a.m., 4:30 p.m.; South Arm Rd., 8:30 a.m., 4 p.m. Beer, wine acceptable in moderation, no liquor. Thru-hikers only; no vehicles. Mail drops accepted.

Hall Mountain Lean-to (1978)—Sleeps 6. Privy. Water source is a spring south of the lean-to on the A.T.; might have to walk downstream.

 South Arm Road—East 9 miles to Andover, Maine (see above).

West 3.5 miles to *Camping:* South Arm Campground, (207) 364-5155, open mid-May to mid-Sep; $18+tax per site, up to 2. Campstore (short-term resupply); showers 25¢; coin laundry; canoe, kayak, and boat rentals. No credit cards. Packages accepted at P.O. Box 310, Andover, ME 04216.

Bemis Mountain Lean-to (1988)—Sleeps 8. Privy. Water source is small spring to left of lean-to.

Maine 17—West 11 miles to **Oquossoc, Maine [P.O. ZIP 04964: M–F 11:30–3:30, Sa 9–12; (207) 864-3685]**. ■ *Groceries:* Oquossoc Grocery, (207) 864-3662 (short-term resupply), open daily 5 a.m.–8 p.m., with pizza and subs. ■ *Restaurants:* Portage Tap House, local beers on tap, wood-fired oven pizza; Gingerbread House, B/L/D with daily specials, hardy servings, ice cream, desserts.

Sabbath Day Pond Lean-to (1993)—Sleeps 8. Privy. A sandy beach, 0.3 mile south on the A.T., provides an excellent swimming opportunity. Water source is Sabbath Day Pond in front of the lean-to.

Little Swift River Pond Campsite (1975)—Privy. Water from piped spring near pond. Sometimes a canoe is available; be sure to leave it upside-down after use.

Maine 4—West 0.3 mile to the Hiker Hut, (207) 670-8095, <hikerhut@gmail.com>. The Hiker Hut is closed for the 2020 season. Alumni and friends can contact Steve personally. It will reopen for the 2021 season.

West 9 miles to **Rangeley, Maine [P.O. ZIP 04970: M–F 9:30–12:30 & 1:30–4:15, Sa 9:30–12; (207) 864-2233]**, where services are spread along Maine 4. ■ *Hostel:* Fieldstone Cottages, (207) 670-8268, owners Shane and Stacey Vorous, 2342 Main St., Rangeley, ME 04970. Low-density cottages catering to slackpackers and section-hikers; call for reservations. Cottages $100 and up with group rates starting at $40PP, Trailhead pick-up, slackpacking from Andover to Caratunk, airport shuttles; debit/credit cards accepted. ■ *Lodging:* Rangeley Inn & Tavern, (207) 864-3341, $125–$300, ask for hiker discount, WiFi; Rangeley Saddleback Motor

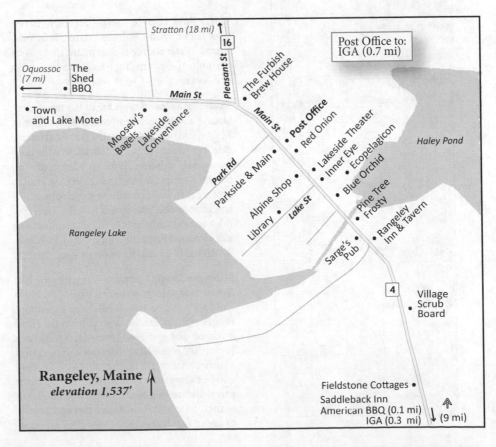

Rangeley, Maine
elevation 1,537'

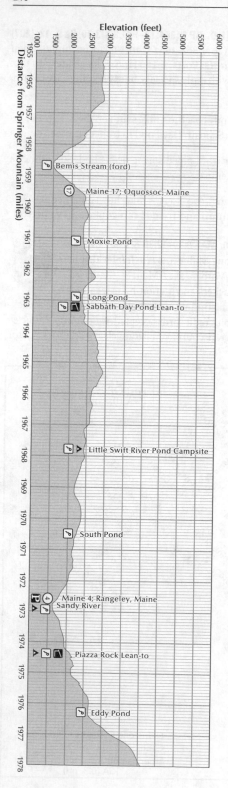

Inn, (207) 864-3434, $110D, WiFi; Town and Lake Motel, (207) 864-3755, $75S, $99D, $10EAP (weekdays only), free kayak and canoe. ■ *Groceries:* IGA Supermarket (long-term resupply). ■ **Restaurants:** Parkside Main Café, L/D; Sarge's Pub & Grub, L/D; Moosely Bagels, Inner Eyes Coffee, WiFi; Red Onion, L/D; Hungry Trout, D 4–9 Tu–Sa; The Shed BBQ, L/D; Blue Orchid, (207) 864-9035; Keeps Corner, café and bakery. ■ *Outfitter:* Alpine Shop, (207) 864-3741, Coleman fuel and alcohol by the ounce; Ecopelagicon, 7 Pond St., (207) 864-2771, freeze-dried meals, backpacker supplies, Leki warranty work; fuel, ATC publications, slackpacking/shuttles, WiFi, mail drops accepted. ■ *Internet access:* Rangeley Public Library. ■ *Other services:* banks with ATM; Village Scrub Board coin laundry; doctor; Rangeley Region Health Center, (207) 864-4397; dentist; bookstore.

West 15 miles to Oquossoc (see entry above).

Piazza Rock Lean-to (1993)—Sleeps 8. Privy; two-seater with cribbage board. Tent platforms. Water source is the stream that passes through the campsite. MATC caretaker in residence.

Saddleback Mountain—One of the most spectacular above-treeline stretches of the Trail in Maine; you may not notice the ski resort on one side. For many years, Saddleback was the controversial "missing link" in Maine during federal attempts to buy lands along the Trail to protect it from encroaching development. In late 2000, a deal was struck to sell a Trail corridor across Saddleback to the government, but it does permit future development of the resort, which has been sold three times since then.

Redington Stream Campsite—0.7 mile north of Saddleback's Horn, at the east base of the Horn (middle peak of the Saddleback mountain range), right where the descent from the Horn levels off and the Trail heads for Saddleback Junior. The blue-blazed side trail leads 1,100 feet to water that might not be reliable. It is about 400 feet along this side trail from the A.T. to the privy. Before you reach the privy, side trails branch off to tent pads, with a current capacity of about two tents each. Open fires are *abso-*

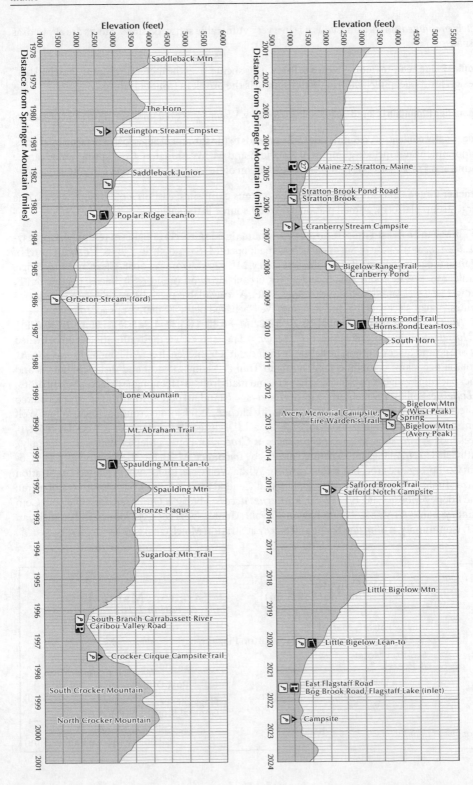

Left chart:

Elevation (feet): 1000 1500 2000 2500 3000 3500 4000 4500 5000 5500 6000

Distance from Springer Mountain (miles): 1978 1979 1980 1981 1982 1983 1984 1985 1986 1987 1988 1989 1990 1991 1992 1993 1994 1995 1996 1997 1998 1999 2000 2001

- Saddleback Mtn
- The Horn
- Redington Stream Cmpste
- Saddleback Junior
- Poplar Ridge Lean-to
- Orbeton Stream (ford)
- Lone Mountain
- Mt. Abraham Trail
- Spaulding Mtn Lean-to
- Spaulding Mtn
- Bronze Plaque
- Sugarloaf Mtn Trail
- South Branch Carrabassett River
- Caribou Valley Road
- Crocker Cirque Campsite Trail
- South Crocker Mountain
- North Crocker Mountain

Right chart:

Elevation (feet): 500 1000 1500 2000 2500 3000 3500 4000 4500 5000 5500

Distance from Springer Mountain (miles): 2001 2002 2003 2004 2005 2006 2007 2008 2009 2010 2011 2012 2013 2014 2015 2016 2017 2018 2019 2020 2021 2022 2023 2024

- Maine 27; Stratton, Maine
- Stratton Brook Pond Road
- Stratton Brook
- Cranberry Stream Campsite
- Bigelow Range Trail; Cranberry Pond
- Horns Pond Trail
- Horns Pond Lean-tos
- South Horn
- Bigelow Mtn (West Peak)
- Spring
- Avery Memorial Campsite; Fire Warden's Trail
- Bigelow Mtn (Avery Peak)
- Safford Brook Trail
- Safford Notch Campsite
- Little Bigelow Mtn
- Little Bigelow Lean-to
- East Flagstaff Road
- Bog Brook Road, Flagstaff Lake (inlet)
- Campsite

lutely prohibited at this campsite as it is in a very vulnerable softwood stand. Stoves are allowed, as usual.

Poplar Ridge Lean-to (1961)—Sleeps 6. Privy. This shelter uses the increasingly rare "baseball bat" design for its sleeping platform. Water source is the brook in front of lean-to.

Spaulding Mountain Lean-to (1989)—Sleeps 8. Privy. Water source is a small spring to right of lean-to.

Sugarloaf Mountain—A 0.6-mile side trail east leads to the summit of Sugarloaf, where, on clear days, panoramic views include glimpses of Katahdin and Mt. Washington. Cool spring water can be found at 0.3 mile. This side trail was the last section of the original A.T. to open, in August 1937.

Crocker Cirque Campsite (1975)—Privy. Numerous campsites; east on a 0.2-mile side trail, one large group platform, 2 small platforms. Water source is the spring.

Maine 27—**East** 2 miles to *Groceries:* Mountainside Grocers (long-term resupply), (207) 237-2248, at the base of Sugarloaf access road; open M–Sa 7:30–8, Su 7:30–6. *Hostel:* Hostel of Maine, 3004 Town Line Rd., Carrabassett Valley, ME 04947, (207) 237-0088. Clean and cozy lodge, bunks $39, private room $110, includes pick-up and drop-off (1 and 4:30), linens, continental B, shower w/ towel, laundry w/ loaner clothes, WiFi. Also available: pizza, beer, wine, ice cream, board games, books, slackpacking, and shipping. Well-behaved pets OK; mail drops accepted.

West 5 miles to **Stratton, Maine [P.O. ZIP 04982: M–F 8:30–1 & 1:30–4, Sa 8:30–11:00; (207) 246-6461]**. ■ *Hostel:* Stratton Motel & Hostel Box 284, (207) 246-4171, <www.thestrattonmotel.com>, owned by Shane and Stacey Vorous; hostel $35PP includes hiker kitchen, free WiFi; motel rooms $80S/D, $10EAP; pets okay; complimentary shuttle to Trail at Maine 27, local and distance shuttles and slackpacking available; pay shuttles, showers, and mail drops ($5) for nonguests; accepts mail drops. ■ *Lodging:* Spillover Motel, (207) 246-6571, $89–$99 (standard double room), $124–$134 for studio suite, pets okay ($15), continental B, community kitchen, WiFi, located south of town; White Wolf Inn, 146 Main St. (P.O. Box 590), (207) 246-2922, L/D, closed Tu (call for room), weekdays $69S/D, weekends $79S/D, dogs $10, accepts packages. ■ *Groceries:* Fotter's Market (long-term resupply), with deli, Coleman fuel and denatured alcohol by the ounce, M–Th 8–7 F–Sa 8–8 Su 9–5; The Coplin Co-op, organic groceries. ■ *Restaurants:* White Wolf Café, L/D, F fish fry (closed Tu); Stratton Plaza, Tu–Sa 11–9, Su 12–8, pizza, L/D; Flagstaff General Store, M–F 5–7, Sa 7–9, Su 7–7 full menu; The Looney Moose Café, B/L, W–Su. ■ *Internet access:* library. ■ *Other services:* Old Mill Coin laundry; bank; ATM; Mt. Abram Regional Health Center, (207) 265-4555, located in Kingfield, an A.T. Community. ■ *Shuttles:* Shane and Stacey at Stratton Motel, (207) 246-4171.

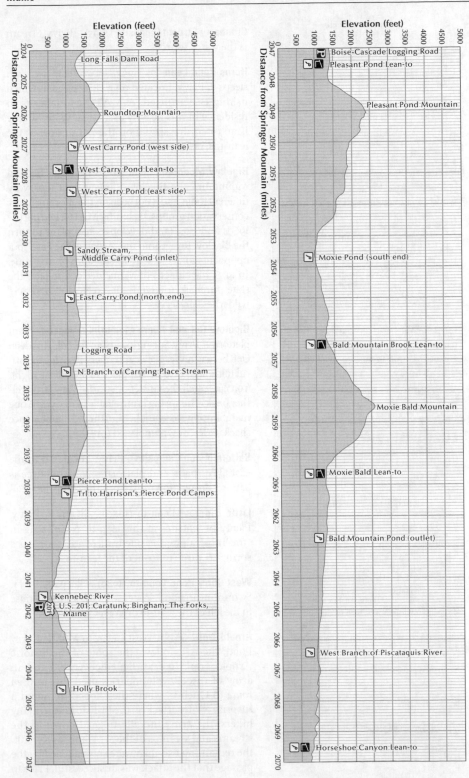

Elevation (feet)

Distance from Springer Mountain (miles)

Long Falls Dam Road

Roundtop Mountain

West Carry Pond (west side)

West Carry Pond Lean-to

West Carry Pond (east side)

Sandy Stream, Middle Carry Pond (inlet)

East Carry Pond (north end)

Logging Road

N Branch of Carrying Place Stream

Pierce Pond Lean-to

Trl to Harrison's Pierce Pond Camps

Kennebec River

U.S. 201; Caratunk; Bingham; The Forks, Maine

Holly Brook

Elevation (feet)

Distance from Springer Mountain (miles)

Boise-Cascade Logging Road

Pleasant Pond Lean-to

Pleasant Pond Mountain

Moxie Pond (south end)

Bald Mountain Brook Lean-to

Moxie Bald Mountain

Moxie Bald Lean-to

Bald Mountain Pond (outlet)

West Branch of Piscataquis River

Horseshoe Canyon Lean-to

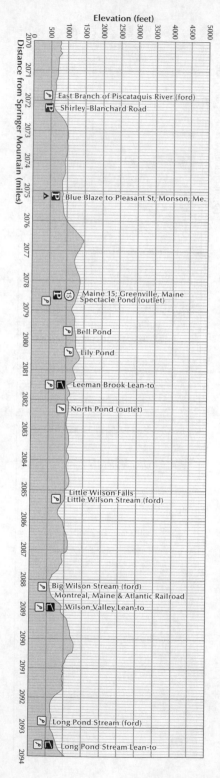

Cranberry Stream Campsite (1995)—Privy. Stream is the water source.

Horns Pond Lean-tos (1997)—Two lean-tos; each sleeps 8. Privy. Located on a clear pond at which fishing is permitted. A MATC caretaker is in residence in this heavily used area. Water source is an often-dry spring on the A.T., north of the lean-tos, or Horns Pond.

Bigelow Mountain—Known as Maine's "Second Mountain," the Bigelow Range might look very different today had it not been for the efforts of many conservation groups, including MATC. During the 1960s and '70s, land developers had plans to turn the Bigelow Range into the "Aspen of the East," but opponents forced a state referendum on the issue. In 1976, the citizens of Maine decided to have the state purchase the land and create a 33,000-acre wilderness preserve.

Bigelow Col and Avery Memorial Campsite—Tent platforms. Privy. Spring located in the col. This deep cleft between West Peak and Avery Peak is a beautiful (although often cold) place to spend the night. You can catch the sunset or sunrise views from either peak. The spring is unreliable in dry years; one maintained water site is behind the red maintenance shack, to left down unblazed trail.

Safford Notch Campsite—Privy. Located 0.3 mile east. Tent pads and platforms. Water source is Safford Brook, downhill from the campsite.

Little Bigelow Lean-to (1986)—Sleeps 8. Privy. Plenty of tentsites at this lean-to. Swimming in "the Tubs" along the side trail. Water source is a spring 50 yards in front of the lean-to.

West Carry Pond Lean-to (1989)—Sleeps 8. Privy. Swimming in pond. Water source is a spring house to the left of the lean-to or West Carry Pond.

Arnold Trail—From West Carry to Middle Carry Pond, the A.T. follows the route of the historic Arnold Trail. In 1775, Benedict Arnold and an army of 1,150 Revolutionaries used this trail *en route* to Quebec, where they hoped to mount a surprise winter attack on the British. Like so many hikers, the army literally bogged down in the streams and swamps of the area, and, as a result, the remaining 650 men were so weakened by the passage that the attack was unsuccessful. Prior to

Arnold's transit, the Abenaki Indians used the route as a portage around rapids on the Dead River, the waters of which now fill artificial Flagstaff Lake.

Pierce Pond Lean-to (1970)—Sleeps 6. Privy (moldering). Located on the east bank of Pierce Pond, with swimming, sunsets, and wildlife. Water source is the pond or stream on a side trail to Harrison's Pierce Pond Camps (see below). If deciding to take a swim, buddy-up and be conscious of the fact that these Maine ponds often have underwater "cells" of 40-degree water. A young 2012 thru-hiker drowned here after diving in to swim off a 20-mile day.

Harrison's Pierce Pond Camps (1934)—Traditional Maine camp on blue-blazed trail across Pierce Pond Stream. Tim Harrison caters primarily to vacationers and anglers; (207) 672-3625. Breakfast with juice, $9–$12; cabin, shower, towel, $40PP with B. If staying at Pierce Pond Lean-to, make reservations for B the night before. Water spigot; no credit cards; pets must be on leash. Hikers may use phone for emergencies.

Kennebec River Ferry—Over the last 30 years, canoes have ferried in excess of 22,000 hikers across the Kennebec River. For the 2020 hiker season, with the financial support of the ATC, HydroFlask, ALDHA, MATC, and the upstream dam operator, Greg Caruso of Maine Guide Service LLC will handle this monumental task. Shuttles possible after the ferry service ends; contact Greg at (207) 858-3627 or <gcaruso@myfairpoint.net> for details. The ferry will operate daily, at no cost to hikers, tentatively (contact MATC) from:

> May 22–Jun 30 9–11 a.m.
> Jul 1–Sep 30 9–2 p.m.
> Oct 1–Oct 12 9–11 a.m.

In off-hours, hikers can schedule a $50 crossing. In early May and late Oct, the ferry also will be available when time and weather allow. Exact hours and dates will be posted at Pierce Pond and Pleasant Pond lean-tos and on line at <www.matc.org>. After the regular season, ferry service is available for a fee of $50 for 1–2 hikers.

Kennebec River—The most formidable unbridged water-crossing on the A.T. Ironically, the Indian word "Kennebec" means "long, quiet water." A thru-hiker drowned in 1985 trying to ford the river, and another hiker drowned as recently as May 2018. Many other hikers have had close calls. Dangers include rocks, strong currents, and unpredictable water levels due to releases from the dams upstream. **ATC and MATC strenuously urge hikers not to attempt to ford the river.** *Purists also should note that a ferry is the official "white-blaze" route,* as well as the original, historical route of the A.T. across the Kennebec. This is a free service funded by ATC, MATC, and ALDHA. Hikers need to arrive a half-hour before the ferry ceases operation. If late, be prepared to wait, and note that camping and fires are prohibited on both banks of the river. You will be required to sign a release form before crossing, wear a life jacket during the crossing, and follow the instructions of the ferry operator; please cooperate in these matters. If river conditions or weather make the crossing dangerous, the service will be discontinued until conditions improve. The ferry is for hiker and pack—the operator will not carry your pack so you can attempt to ford.

U.S. 201—East 0.3 mile on Main Street to **Caratunk, Maine [P.O. ZIP 04925: M–F 2–4, Sa 7:30–11:15; (207) 672-3416].** *Lodging:* Caratunk House Hiker B&B, 218 Main St., P.O. Box 98, (207) 672-4349; 150 yards from Trail, owner Paul "One Braid" Fuller offers twin rooms $20PP, private room $25PP, double bed $35S/$40D, family-style breakfast $7, laundry $3, WiFi, shuttles, and full resupply; mail drops accepted.

  East 1 mile on U.S. 201 to *Lodging and resupply:* The Sterling Inn, 1041 U.S. 201 (P.O. Box 129), (207) 672-3333, <www.mainesterlinginn.com>, reservations recommended. Bunk room $30; private rooms $45 and up (shared rooms from $27PP), includes B and free local shuttle to/from Trailhead,

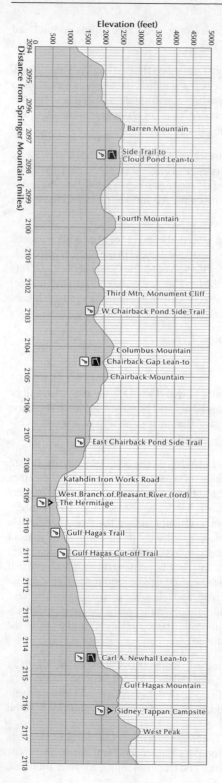

Elevation (feet)

Distance from Springer Mountain (miles)

Barren Mountain

Side Trail to
Cloud Pond Lean-to

Fourth Mountain

Third Mtn, Monument Cliff

W Chairback Pond Side Trail

Columbus Mountain
Chairback Gap Lean-to
Chairback Mountain

East Chairback Pond Side Trail

Katahdin Iron Works Road
West Branch of Pleasant River (ford)
The Hermitage

Gulf Hagas Trail

Gulf Hagas Cut-off Trail

Carl A. Newhall Lean-to

Gulf Hagas Mountain

Sidney Tappan Campsite

West Peak

post office, and area restaurants. Free WiFi, computer, laundry, and LD calling. Call from free phone near PO for pick-up. Debit/credit cards accepted, multiple-night discounts, well-behaved pets okay. Long-term resupply (Caratunk Country Store), showers $3, laundry $6, mail drops, and shuttle service available for nonguests.

East 16.5 miles to the small town of Bingham, with restaurants, coin laundry, pharmacy, and grocery stores (all long-term resupply). *Lodging:* Bingham Motor Inn, (866) 806-6120, <www.binghammotorinn.com>, $62.38S, $80.73D, $89.91T, $99.08Q, plus tax, 10% hiker discount.

West 2 miles to *Lodging:* Northern Outdoors Resort, 1771 U.S. 201, The Forks, ME 04985, (800) 765-7238; Call for rates and hiker discount; lodge rooms (max 4), cabin tents and tentsites; serves B/L/D; coin laundry, hot tub, pool, ATM, no pets, accepts mail drops; Kennebec River rafting trips (class IV); Kennebec River Pub and Brewery on site; free shuttle to/from Trail coincides with ferry schedule; all hikers welcome to the free shuttle, free shower, and free Internet.

West 3.5 miles to *Services:* Three Rivers Trading Post, grocery store open daily 8 a.m.–10 p.m.; restaurant, 4–11; Three Rivers Whitewater, (207) 663-2104, <threeriverswhitewater.com>, campsites $12PP/night, bunk house $27PP/night, showers available.

West 7 miles to ■ *Lodging:* The Inn by the River, 277 U.S. 201, The Forks, ME 04985, (207) 663-2181, <www.innbytheriver.com>; rooms with whirlpools and private porches start at $89–$129, B/L/D, accepts packages for guests. ■ *Groceries:* Berry's General Store and Hardware, (207) 663-4461, open daily 5 a.m.–7 p.m., accepts credit and debit cards; Heet, short-term resupply; in same building as West Forks P.O.

Pleasant Pond Lean-to (1958, renovated 1991)—Sleeps 6. Privy. Sandy beach on Pleasant Pond is 0.2 mile from the lean-to. Water source is a small brook crossed on the path to the lean-to or pond.

Bald Mountain Brook Lean-to (1994)—Sleeps 8. Privy. Water source is Bald Mountain Brook, in front of the lean-to.

Moxie Bald Lean-to (1958)—Sleeps 6. Privy. Many moose in the area. Water source is nearby stream.

West Branch of Piscataquis River—Normally knee-deep, this ford can be dangerous during periods of heavy rain. Do not attempt to cross in high water.

Horseshoe Canyon Lean-to (1991)—Sleeps 8. Privy. Lean-to is located on a blue-blaze. Water source is a spring at the A.T. junction or the river in front of, and below, the lean-to.

East Branch of the Piscataquis River—Like its West Branch, the 50-foot-wide East Branch of the Piscataquis can be tricky fording during periods of heavy rain.

Blue-blaze to Monson—Northbounders have an alternative route to Monson, 3.3 miles south of Maine 15, near Lake Hebron; signs will point you in the right direction. This route leads a short distance to Pleasant St., where you will go left 2 miles into town.

Maine 15—East 4 miles to **Monson, Maine [P.O. ZIP 04464: M–F 9:15–12:15 & 1:15–4:15, Sa 7:30–11; (207) 997-3975].** Post office accepts debit cards with *limited* cash back. ■ *Lodging:* Shaw's Hiker Hostel, 40+ years serving hikers, 17 Pleasant St. (P.O. Box 72), (207) 997-3597, <www.shawshikerhostel.com>; owned by thru-hikers Kimberly and Jarrod Hester ("Hippie Chick and Poet"); open May–Oct, bunks $25PP, private guest rooms $50S $60D, tenting $12PP; credit cards and advance reservations accepted; B $10 daily with regular, gluten-free, and vegan pancakes (outside guests welcome); WiFi, shuttles, slackpacking, and food drops available. Long-term resupply and Poet's Emporium gear shop; guest use of kayak and canoe; dogs welcome. Mail drops free for guests; nonguest mail drops, laundry, and showers are $5 each. Lakeshore House Lodging & Pub, 9 Tenney Hill Rd., Box 215, Monson, ME 04464, (207) 997-7069, (207) 343-5033, <www.thelakeshorehouse.com>, owner Rebekah Anderson Mobile. On Lake Hebron, open year-round, credit cards accepted, ATM. Bunks start at $25PP, semiprivate rooms $35, private

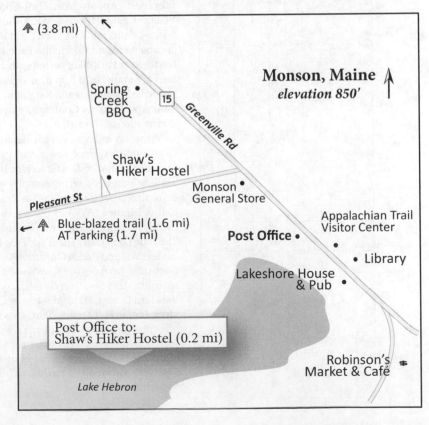

(3.8 mi)

Spring Creek BBQ
15 · Greenville Rd

Monson, Maine elevation 850'

Shaw's Hiker Hostel

Monson General Store

Pleasant St

Blue-blazed trail (1.6 mi) AT Parking (1.7 mi)

Post Office •

Appalachian Trail Visitor Center

• Library

Lakeshore House & Pub

Post Office to: Shaw's Hiker Hostel (0.2 mi)

Robinson's Market & Café

Lake Hebron

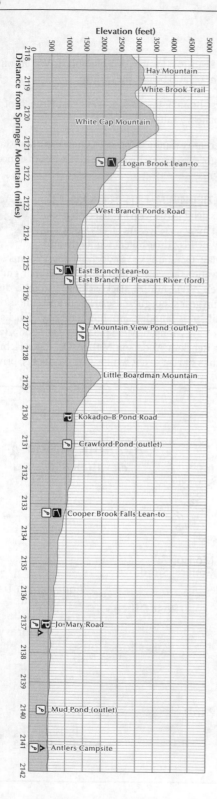

Elevation (feet)

Distance from Springer Mountain (miles)

Hay Mountain
White Brook Trail
White Cap Mountain
Logan Brook Lean-to
West Branch Ponds Road
East Branch Lean-to
East Branch of Pleasant River (ford)
Mountain View Pond (outlet)
Little Boardman Mountain
Kokadjo-B Pond Road
Crawford Pond (outlet)
Cooper Brook Falls Lean-to
Jo-Mary Road
Mud Pond (outlet)
Antlers Campsite

rooms $50; dog-friendly; laundry with loaner clothes; WiFi and loaner laptop and free use of kayaks for guests; free Trailhead pick-up and drop-off; mail drops accepted ($5 nonguests). Pub with full bar, draft beer, home-made food, open mic Th 6–9 p.m., live music Su 3–6 p.m., open Tu–Su 11:30–9, closed M ($5 nonguest services include shuttle to or from Trail, shower, laundry). ■ *Groceries:* Monson General Store, (207) 997-3800, long-term resupply, open daily 7–7, deli, fresh-baked bread and pastries; A.E. Robinson Market, M–Su 5 a.m.–10 p.m., pizzas, calzones, hot sandwiches, ATM; Shaw's Hiker Hostel. ■ *Restaurants:* Lakeshore House Pub, L/D, T–Su 11:30–9, Su 12–8, live music Su 3–6, open mic Th 6–9; Spring Creek BBQ, Th–Sa 11–8, Su 11–4. ■ *Outfitter:* Poet's Emporium gear shop at Shaw's Hiker Hostel, open daily 8–11 a.m. and 2–5 p.m. ■ *Internet access:* Monson Public Library, M–W–F 12–4:30. ■ *Shuttles:* Buddy Ward, cell (207) 343-2564, takes texts, shuttles from Baxter to Mt. Washington; Shaw's; and Lakeshore House. ■ *Other services:* Appalachian Trail Conservancy Visitors Center, (207) 766-7091, 5 Main St., open 8–11, 1–5 daily, Jun–Oct. Long-distance hikers are able to obtain information about the 2020 Baxter State Park hiker permits, which are free. Staff are available to help plan logistics for the 100-Mile Wilderness and Katahdin. Trail conditions posted daily. Community and day-hike information also available.

West 10.3 miles to Greenville, Moosehead Lake's main tourist town and gateway to Maine's North Woods. ■ *Groceries:* Indian Hill Trading Post (long-term resupply), <www.indianhill.com>, (800) 675-4487. ■ *Restaurants:* Kelly's Landing, AYCE B on Su; Auntie Em's Family Restaurant; The Stress-Free Moose Pub; The Blue Loon Café; The Black Frog Pub; Flatlanders Rod and Reel. ■ *Outfitter:* Northwoods Outfitters, (207) 695-3288, <www.maineoutfitter.com>, daily 8–5, Internet (fee), and coffee at the Hard Drive Café inside store. ■ *Other services:* Indian Hill Trading Post, <www.indianhill.com>,(207) 695-2104; banks with ATM; Harris Drug Store, (207) 695-2921; Charles A. Dean Memorial Hospital, 24-hour ER, (207) 695-5200; Greenville Veterinary Clinic, (207) 695-4408.

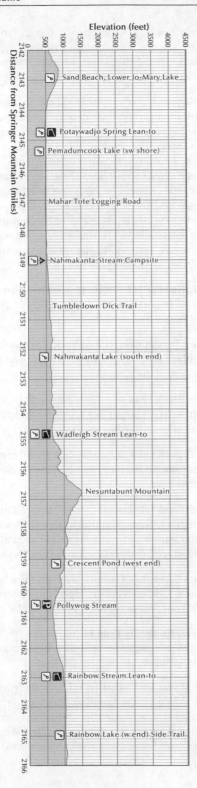

"100-Mile Wilderness"—Signs at each end of this section proclaim this area's remoteness and warn the unprepared hiker to stay away, but don't be intimidated. Hikers should remember to bring cash for Baxter State Park.

Leeman Brook Lean-to (1987)—Sleeps 6. Privy. Water source is the stream in front of the lean-to.

Wilson Valley Lean-to (1993)—Sleeps 6. Privy. Located north of Big Wilson Stream. Water source is a small spring in front of the lean-to, on the opposite side of the A.T.

Long Pond Stream Lean-to (1991)—Sleeps 8. Privy. Swimming in the scenic Slugundy Gorge and falls located 0.1 mile south, on a side trail 150 yards off the A.T. Water source, a small stream to the left of the lean-to, has been unreliable in recent years.

Cloud Pond Lean-to (1992)—Sleeps 6. Privy 0.4 mile east. Water source is Cloud Pond, in front of the lean-to, or a spring to the north of the side trail to the lean-to.

Chairback Gap Lean-to (1954)—Sleeps 6. Privy. Water source, a small spring downhill and north of the lean-to 25 yards, is prone to go dry and is unreliable in drier years.

Katahdin Iron Works (KIW) Road and West Branch of Pleasant River—Just east of the A.T., on the KIW logging road, is a parking lot for Gulf Hagas.

    West on KIW Road to *Lodging:* AMC Gorman Chairback Lodge (0.3 mile to left on Gorman Chairback Camp Rd., 1.2 mile to lodge) and Little Lyford Pond Cabins (4.9 mile to left on Frenchtown Rd., 1.2 mile to lodge), (603) 466-2727; <www.outdoors.org>; $110 for bunkroom space, *possible* two-night minimum, B/L/D included; accepts mail drops at P.O. Box 310, Greenville, ME 04441.

    East 20 miles to Maine 11 and Brownville Junction. *Groceries:* The General Store and More (short-term resupply), (207) 965-8100, deli.

The Hermitage—Camping is not allowed inside this protected area, a national landmark owned by The Nature Conservancy. Look for the plaque to learn the meaning of its name. Home to magnificent old-growth white pines. *Camping:* Maine North Woods, $12 tentsites at Pleasant River Campsites 0.7 mile **east** of the Hermitage area. Maine North

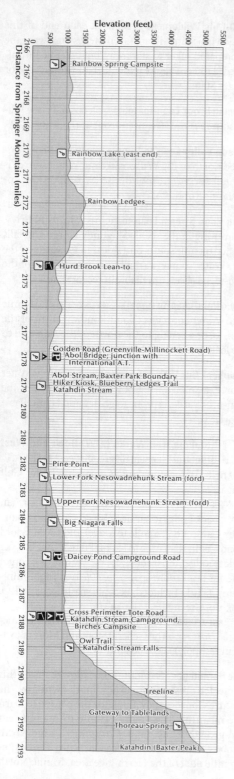

Elevation (feet)

Rainbow Spring Campsite

Rainbow Lake (east end)

Rainbow Ledges

Hurd Brook Lean-to

Golden Road (Greenville-Millinockett Road)
Abol Bridge; junction with
International A.T.

Abol Stream, Baxter Park Boundary
Hiker Kiosk, Blueberry Ledges Trail
Katahdin Stream

Pine Point

Lower Fork Nesowadnehunk Stream (ford)

Upper Fork Nesowadnehunk Stream (ford)

Big Niagara Falls

Daicey Pond Campground Road

Cross Perimeter Tote Road
Katahdin Stream Campground,
Birches Campsite

Owl Trail
Katahdin Stream Falls

Treeline

Gateway to Tablelands

Thoreau Spring

Katahdin (Baxter Peak)

Distance from Springer Mountain (miles)

Woods Box 425, Ashland, ME 04732, (207) 435-6213, <www.northmainewoods.org>; contact it at the gatehouse; advance reservations are strongly recommended.

Gulf Hagas—If you've got the food and the time, you may want to take this side trail. The gulf was formed by water eroding the slate walls of a narrow canyon. The result of this sculpting is a stretch of many spectacular waterfalls nestled in a chasm about 500 feet deep. If you want a taste of the gulf's scenery, Screw Auger Falls is only 0.2 mile from the A.T. on Gulf Hagas Brook. A 5.2-mile loop hike is possible using the Rim and Gulf Hagas trails. MATC stations a ridgerunner in the area, which receives a tremendous amount of day use. *No camping allowed.*

Carl A. Newhall Lean-to (1986)—Sleeps 6. Privy. Lean-to is north of Gulf Hagas Brook, the water source.

Sidney Tappan Campsite—Privy. Follow the blue-blaze 0.2 mile east to water; trail begins just north of the campsite.

Logan Brook Lean-to (1983)—Sleeps 6. Privy. Water source is Logan Brook behind the lean-to; cascades are farther upstream.

East Branch Lean-to (1996)—Sleeps 8. Privy. Water source is the East Branch of the Pleasant River, in front.

Cooper Brook Falls Lean-to (1956)—Sleeps 6. Full-moon privy. Tentsite on trail to lean-to. A waterfront lean-to with numerous pools and falls. Water source is Cooper Brook in front of lean-to.

Antlers Campsite—Campsites are on the edge of Lower Jo-Mary. Fort Relief privy to the west of the Trail. Water source is Jo-Mary Lake.

Potaywadjo Spring Lean-to (1995)—Sleeps 8. Privy. Water source is the 15-foot-wide Potaywadjo Spring, to the right of the lean-to.

Mahar Trail—East 1.2 miles to *Lodging:* White House Landing, (207) 745-5116. Overnight stay is required, reservations recommended. Owners Bill, Linda, and Ben Ware offered bunkhouse $35PP, semiprivate rooms in cabin $45s/$85D, includes shower w/towel, round-trip boat ride, and use of canoe. B with AYCE pancakes/D available. Visa and MasterCard accepted (fee may be applied). Mail drops accepted sent well in advance to: White House Landing, PO Box 1, Millinocket, ME 04462. *Northbound directions:* Follow A.T. 2.8 miles north of Potaywadjo Spring Lean-to to third road north of lean-to, go east 0.2 mile on Mahar Tote Road to Pemadumcook Lake, call or text for boat. *Southbound directions:* Follow A.T. 1.5 miles south of Nahmakanta Stream Shelter, go east 0.2 mile on Mahar Trail to Pemadumcook Lake, call or text for boat.

Nahmakanta Stream Lean-to (2017)—Sleeps 8. Privy. Water is the stream in front of shelter.

Wadleigh Stream Lean-to (1981)—Sleeps 6. Privy. Located 0.5 mile north of Nahmakanta Lake, which has a sandy beach. Water source is a spring on the beach.

Rainbow Stream Lean-to (1971)—Sleeps 6. Privy. Home of the A.T.'s best totem pole; often crowded with hiker groups. Good tenting and hammocking above and behind the lean-to. Water source is Rainbow Stream, in front.

Rainbow Spring Campsite—Privy. Water source is a flowing spring at the shore of Rainbow Lake.

Hurd Brook Lean-to (1959)—Sleeps 6. Privy. During high water, Hurd Brook, 50 feet south of the lean-to, can be deep and swift, and the ford dangerous. Area is frequented by hunters. Water source is Hurd Brook. Southbounders might want to tank up at the spring 0.7 mile north of the lean-to.

"Golden Road" and Abol Bridge. ■ *Camping:* Abol Bridge Campground and Store, (207) 447-5803, <www.abolcampground.com>, open May 15–Oct 1, located along the road on the West Branch of the Penobscot River and Abol Stream, campsites $25PP with B and shower, all visitors must register; Department of Conservation's Abol Pines, seasonal, tentsite or space in one of two six-person lean-tos, $15PP plus tax for out-of-state residents, reached by following a dirt road 75 yards east in front of the camp store. ■ *Groceries:* Abol Bridge Store (short-term resupply), credit cards accepted. ■ *Restaurant:* The Northern Restaurant, (800) 765-7238, daily 11–6, warm food, cold beer.
　　East 20 miles to Millinocket, Maine (near end of chapter).

Baxter State Park—The northern terminus of the Appalachian Trail, hosted by Baxter State Park, is Baxter Peak on Katahdin, Maine's highest mountain. Katahdin, along with the surrounding landscape, is part of a 209,644-acre wilderness sanctuary and forest preserve, Baxter State Park; <www.baxterstateparkauthority.com>. The lands were donated in perpetual trust to the people of Maine by former Governor Percival Proctor Baxter, who served from 1921 to 1924. BSP is self-supporting, in large part due to Baxter's endowment funds and by his design, and is administered separately from any other agency or state park in Maine. Baxter's goal was to place preservation of natural resources as a priority over their recreational use, so some of BSP's regulations and policies are markedly different from what may be encountered elsewhere along the A.T.

Unlike the surrounding landscape south, Katahdin is exposed to extreme weather, including high winds, and has gotten snow during every month of the year. No shelters are located above treeline (north of Katahdin Stream Campground), and all trails to the summit are completely exposed. On humid, unsettled, late-summer days, for example, it is wise to start down by 1 p.m. to avoid electrical storms.

Katahdin—The translation of the Abenaki word is "greatest mountain." Maine's Penobscots considered the mountain a holy place and believed in Pamola, the deity of Katahdin, who purportedly would destroy any man who ventured too close to the mountain. The first recorded ascent of Katahdin by Euroamericans came on Aug 13, 1804, when a party led by Charles Turner, Jr., reached the summit by the same rocks-and-roots route used by the A.T.—the Hunt Trail (named after Irving Hunt, a sporting-camp owner who cut the trail). Since then, the mountain has captured the imagination of many, including Henry David Thoreau, who explored the area in 1846. Thoreau Spring on the Tableland bears his name, although he likely never made it there. From Katahdin Stream Campground, it is a 10.4-mile trip to the summit and back. The ascent packs an elevation gain of 4,000 feet into 5 miles. Backpacks may be left at the ranger station at the campground, where you can borrow a daypack and obtain information on weather conditions. The park posts recommended "cut-off" times for beginning your climb: In Aug, hikers are advised to start by 11 a.m.; in Sep, by 10 a.m.; in Oct, by 9 a.m. Park rules require that you sign in at the campground before your climb and sign out on your return. Don't forget to make your final, or first, register entry on the ranger station's front porch.

Permits—Every A.T. long-distance hiker must register with a ranger upon entering BSP. An information kiosk is located on the A.T. 1 mile north of Abol Bridge. The 12 hikers using The Birches (see below) must sign up at the Abol Stream kiosk and also with the ranger at Katahdin Stream Campground. A Baxter Park "A.T. Steward" patrols the area to help hikers with information on the A.T. and the park.

Camping—Camping is allowed only in designated campsites in the park. Long distance hikers can either stay at the first-come, first-serve Birches campsite or reserve another campsite in the park.

The Birches—Two 4-person lean-tos and tenting space for 4 additional people are available at this site not far from Katahdin Stream Campground. Advance reservations are not required; the fee to stay there is $10PP. Cash only inside park.

The Birches is 9.9 miles from Abol Bridge *via* the A.T. or 4.4 miles from Abol Bridge *via* the Blueberry Ledges Trail. Use of The Birches is limited strictly to 12 long-distance or thru-hikers who have hiked at least 100 contiguous miles up to and including entering the BSP. Stays at The Birches are limited to one night. Park authorities have posted a sign-up sheet for long-distance hikers at the information kiosk just north of Abol Bridge. If all 12 spaces are claimed for the night that you planned to stay at The Birches, you need to stay elsewhere. Your choices include the Abol Bridge private campground; the nearby state-owned Abol Pines site on the West Branch of the Penobscot (both are fee sites); standard-reservation campsites in the park at Katahdin Stream Campground, Foster Field Group Campsite, or any other available site of your choice in the park, if they are not already full; or staying in a campground or motel near Millinocket, if available. In Jul and Aug, and on fall weekends, it is difficult to get a site at Katahdin Stream or anywhere in the park, because sites are often reserved months in advance. However, Labor Day–Oct 22, it is possible (although not certain) that you will find vacant sites at Katahdin Stream during the week.

Reservation campgrounds—The fee is $32 for either lean-to or tentsite (4- to 6-person capacity). A "rolling reservations" policy is available four months in advance of the day you wish to stay within the park. If you want Jun 3, you need to know your reservation will not be processed before Feb 3. The traditional opening day to make walk-in reservations is the closest business day to Jan 15. Please call the park at (207) 723-5140, or check the Web site for updates. More information, and a chart outlining when reservations can be made, is at <www.baxterstateparkauthority.com>. The site provides the many different ways reservations may be secured; you are strongly advised to review those options.

The overnight camping season is May 15–Oct 22 each year. After Oct 22, overnight camping is prohibited anywhere within the park. You may camp at the private Abol Bridge campground or the state-owned Abol Pines Campground downriver and across the road from Abol Bridge. Both charge fees. Your hike to the summit is then 15 miles one way from this area outside the park. Another option when BSP is closed for camping is to stay in Millinocket and hire one of the local shuttle services to transport you in and out of Baxter on the day of your hike. Southbounders should note that the A.T. from Katahdin Stream Campground to Baxter Peak might not be open until early Jun. Northbounders should note that they can check reservation availability by either going on-line or calling. With other mail requests coming in daily, that may not guarantee a spot. Between Jun 16 and Oct 22, campsite reservations may be made with a credit card *via* phone or Internet for any unreserved site in the park for any date.

Northbounders who plan to have family and friends meet them at the park should reserve campsites in advance. Labor Day weekend is especially busy, with a traditional native-American event reserving the entire Katahdin Stream Campground. **If driving into the park, there is a $15 fee at the gate for out-of-state residents.**

Southbound thru-hikers beginning their trek at Katahdin should make reservations for campsites well in advance of their starting dates. During July and Aug, campsites normally are booked to maximum levels. We suggest you reserve a site for the nights before and after climbing Katahdin. For reservations and other information, contact Baxter State Park.

Parking—A day-use parking reservation system is in place at all Katahdin trailheads for users driving into the park. You can make a reservation on line (<www.baxterstateparkauthority.com>) for the Trailhead of your choice for a $5 fee. Out-of-state residents can reserve a spot no earlier than two weeks before arrival; Maine residents can reserve any time after Apr 1. When parking lots fill, visitors will be directed to open lots and alternate trailheads by the rangers at the gatehouse. Families or friends who are picking up hikers are allowed to drive to the Katahdin Stream trailhead, even if it is full, if they arrive in the afternoon and do not plan to hike the mountain.

Weather—Baxter State Park posts daily weather reports and trail-status alerts during the hiking season at 7 a.m. Before Memorial Day and any time after late Sep, it is not uncommon for some trails to be closed for public-safety reasons or to protect the alpine-plant communities. *The "class day" system has been discarded.* Going forward, the mountain either will be open for hiking or it won't. Hikers who choose to hike on closed trails are subject to a court summons, fine, and revocation of park-visitation privileges.

Trail closings on Katahdin—It is advised to plan to hike Katahdin before Oct 15. In this northerly climate, chances are high that you will be unable to successfully finish your hike at Katahdin's summit after this date. Winter hiking season is Dec 1–Mar 31; during that period, you must obtain a permit from the park to climb Katahdin.

In some years, access to the park road and trails up Katahdin can be closed by snowstorms in September and October. On those days, the A.T. up to Baxter Peak is open only when conditions permit (see above). Each day at 7 a.m., park rangers post the weather forecast and trail alerts. Trail closures are not uncommon in late Sep–Oct. When the trails are closed, anyone hiking beyond the designated Trailhead is subject to a court summons and fine and revocation of park privileges. If you must be rescued, assistance will be delayed until the rescuers can proceed safely; you could be found negligent and liable for all costs of search and rescue.

After Oct 22, Baxter State park is open for day use only (sunrise to sunset), conditions permitting. Vehicular access to the park after Oct 22 is at the discretion of the park director and should not be planned on after Nov 1. Call park headquarters if you have questions about road access before May 15 or after Oct 22.

Dogs—Dogs are **not** allowed in the park. See Millinocket and Medway entries for kennels.

Pamphlet—Long-Distance Hiking in Baxter State Park, a pamphlet, is available on request from BSP. It has a map of the A.T. and the Blueberry Ledges Trail, information about the park, and a message from park management.

Mail and Messages—BSP does not accept mail or packages. Mail drops should be arranged through the Millinocket post office.

Pay attention to this: *Park regulations limit hiking groups to no more than 12 individuals; larger groups will be required to separate themselves into separate groups of 12 with at least a mile of trail between them. This regulation is designed to prevent large groups from dominating the experience at Baxter Peak. Public consumption of alcohol is prohibited on the summit.* The park asks, "Please assist us in respecting the spectacular natural setting Percival Baxter generously preserved by complying with this regulation." Plan ahead!

Celebrate Quietly — Save Alcohol for Later — Hike in Small Groups

---

2,000-Miler Certificate Applications—ATC has asked Katahdin Stream Campground rangers to hand out forms to all northbounders who are about to finish the Trail, in an effort to expedite the processing of 2,000-miler certificates. See requirements on page xii.

Reaching Baxter State Park—No public transportation is available to and from BSP. Unless you have someone meeting you at the park, you'll need to arrange for a shuttle or hitch 24 miles from the Trail to Millinocket. Rides are usually easy to find, since almost everyone headed out of the park must go through Millinocket.

Baxter State Park Road—BSP Togue Pond Visitors Center, M–Th 7–3, F–Su 7–6; maps, guidebooks, additional information; beach, and picnic area (no camping).
East 2 miles from the park's south gate to *Lodging:* Maine Timberland Company's Katahdin Forest Cabins, (877) 622-2467, log cabin on Sunday Pond, spectacular view of Katahdin, $97 per night, sleeps 6, with gas heat, stove, and privy; advance reservations necessary.
East 2.6 miles to *Camping:* Penobscot Outdoor Center on Pockwockamus Pond, (207) 723-3580, tentsites, showers, sauna, hot tub, restaurant, and lounge; call for rates.
East 7 miles to Golden Road junction (8 miles from here to Abol Bridge).
East 8.3 miles to ■ *Groceries:* Northwoods Trading Post (short-term resupply), (207) 723-4326, open 7–9, last gas station and ATM before entering BSP. A.T. maps, books, trail guides, patches, and souvenirs. ■ *Lodging:* Big Moose Inn, (207) 723-8391, <www.bigmoosecabins.com>, inn room with shared bath $60; camping $12PP; lean-to $15PP; cabins, call for rates; restaurant and bar open W–Su, B available Sa–Su, no pets.
East 15.6 miles to *Camping:* Hidden Springs Campground, (888) 685-4488 or (207) 723-6337, tentsites $10PP/night, shower without stay $3.
East 17 miles from the park's south gate to **Millinocket, Maine [P.O. 04462: M–F 9–4, Sa 9–11:30; (207) 723-5921]**. BSP Headquarters, (207) 723-5140, is at 64 Balsam Dr.; park reservations, publications, maps, and general information. ■ *Lodging:* Appalachian Trail Lodge, 33 Penobscot Ave., (207) 723-4321, < http://appalachian-traillodge.com, owners Paul (OleMan) & Jaime (NaviGator) Renaud, $25 bunkroom, $55 private room (shared bath), family suite (private bath) $95D (sleeps 4; $10EAP); showers for nonguests $5; WiFi; coin laundry; insured shuttle service to and from bus in Medway, into 100-mile wilderness or Monson, free daily shuttle from Baxter Sep 18–Oct 22 for guests (others $10PP); no pets; accepts credit cards and mail drops for guests (nonguest $1/ package and make arrangements for pick-ups); southbounders special: $70 shuttle from Medway bus stop, bunkroom lodging, B at A.T. Café, shuttle to Katahdin Stream Campground ranger station or Abol Bridge; closes Oct 22, same time as BSP closes for camping. Katahdin

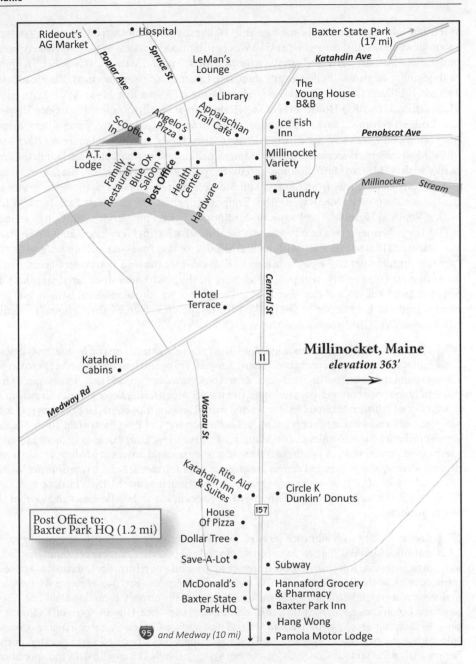

Millinocket, Maine
elevation 363'

Post Office to:
Baxter Park HQ (1.2 mi)

Inn & Suites, (207) 723-4555, $84.99D, $15EAP, dogs $15/night, continental B, indoor pool and hot tub, WiFi, computer access, fitness center, laundry. Baxter Park Inn, (207) 723-9777, call for rates, continental B. Pamola Motor Lodge, (800) 575-9746, (207) 723-9746, <www.pamolalodge.com>, call for best rates, continental B, Internet access, hot tub, lounge, laundry service. Hotel Terrace, (207) 723-4545, call for prices. The Young House B&B, 193 Central Ave., (207) 723-5452, <www.theyounghousebandb.com>, $120, credit cards accepted, WiFi, mail drops accepted. Ice Fish Inn, (207) 723-9999, <www.icefishinn.com>, $120–$135, pet-friendly,

WiFi, hot tub, multiple B options. 100-Mile Wilderness Inn, 96 Oxford St., (207) 731-3537, <100milewildernessinn.com>, owner Gail Wourms, bunks $30, rooms $65–$90 (private, queen, or doubles). Mail drops free for guests. ■ *Restaurants:* Appalachian Trail Café, B/L/D, home of the Sundae Summit Challenge, gift shop, free Internet access, showers $5; Ruthie's Hotel Terrace, B/L/D, AYCE only on weekends; Hang Wong at Pamola Inn, M–Sa AYCE L; Angelo's Pizza Grille, L/D; BBQ House; others shown on map. ■ *Outfitter:* Ole Man's Gear Shop at A.T. Lodge, open 10–4, packs, tents, pads, poles, stoves, fuel, cookware, water filters, maps, head lamps, rain gear, socks, dehydrated/freeze-dried foods, snacks, and more. ■ *Other services:* Most major services are available in town, including supermarkets, coin laundries, and banks with ATM; LanMan's Lounge, 28 Hill St., pack lockers $5/day, TV, snacks, soda, ice cream, restrooms, across from library; Bull Moose Taxi, (207) 447-8079, provides service to the bus station ($18) in Medway, to Abol Bridge ($47), and to Baxter State Park ($57); Millinocket Regional Hospital, (207) 723-5161. Millinocket has no bus service, but Cyr Bus Lines of Old Town, Maine, serves nearby Medway (see below). ■ *Kennel services:* Katahdin Kritters Pet Resort, 20 Dirigo Dr., East Millinocket, ME 04430, (207) 746-8040, Kelly Seile will take care of your furry pet while you're hiking in BSP, call for rates and shuttle services; Connie McManus, (207) 723-6795, will pick up at Abol Bridge and house dogs for thru-hikers. ■ *Shuttle:* Lloyd Kelly, Katahdin Shuttle LLC, (207) 447-0337, to/from Baxter, Bangor, and beyond. Lloyd can help organize your hike with resupply/food drops throughout "100-mile wilderness." Pet-friendly, available May 15 to Oct 15.

Medway— ■ *Lodging:* Rivers Edge Motel, (207) 746-5162, 10 miles east on Maine 157; Gateway Inn, <www.medwaygateway.com>, (207) 746-3193, $59.95 and up, dogs welcome; Pine Grove Campground and Cottages, (207) 746-5172, <www.pinegrovecampgroundandcottages.com>, tentsites, fully equipped cottages, dogs welcome, free use of canoe and kayak for guests, will pick up at bus station. ■ *Outfitter:* Nicatou Outfitter, <www.mainecampingtrips.com>, (207) 746-3253 or (207) 746-3251, call ahead for shuttles or boarding pet. ■ *Bus service:* Cyr Bus Lines of Old Town, Maine, serves northern Maine; 10 miles east on Maine 757, (207) 927-2335, (207) 827-2010, or (800) 244-2335, <www.cyrbustours.com>. A bus departs Bangor at 6:00 p.m. and arrives at Medway at 7:40 p.m.; departs Medway at 9:30 a.m. and arrives at Bangor at 10:50 a.m.; fee $12 one way. ■ *Shuttle:* Maine Quest Adventures, (207) 746-9615, <www.mainequestadventures.com>; Medway bus stop to Baxter SP or Abol Bridge, call for prices; will shuttle to all points in 100-mile Wilderness and to/from all Maine airports.

Bangor—A city with all major services, <www.bangorinfo.com>. For those traveling to or returning from BSP, Bangor has a bus station and airport. The Chamber of Commerce, (207) 947-0307, can provide information as you prepare for your hike or return. For information on local transportation in the Bangor area: BAT Commuter Connection, (207) 992-4670, <www.bangor-maine.gov>. ■ *Lodging:* Many motels and a mall are near the airport, including Days Inn, (207) 942-8272; Econo Lodge, (207) 945-0111; Fairfield Inn, (207) 990-0001; Howard Johnson's, (207) 947-3464; Holiday Inn, (207) 947-0101. ■ *Outfitters:* Epic Sports, 6 Central St., (207) 941-5670, <www.epicsportsgear.com>, M–Sa 9–8, Su 9–5; Dick's Sporting Goods, (207) 990-5932, located in the Bangor Mall. ■ *Bus service:* Concord Coach, (800) 639-3317; Cyr Bus Lines with daily transportation to Medway, (800) 244-2335 (see above).

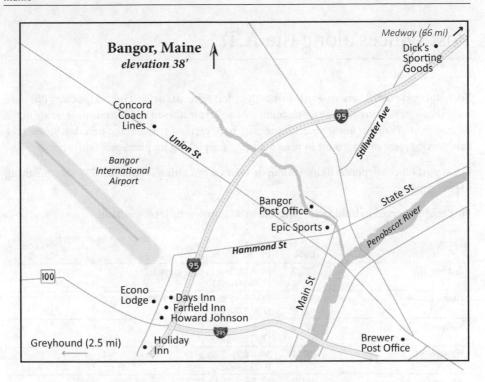

Bangor, Maine
elevation 38'

Medway (66 mi)

Dick's Sporting Goods

Concord Coach Lines

95

Stilwater Ave

Bangor International Airport

Union St

Bangor Post Office

State St

Epic Sports

Penobscot River

Hammond St

95

Main St

100

Econo Lodge

Days Inn

Farfield Inn

Howard Johnson

395

Greyhound (2.5 mi)

Holiday Inn

Brewer Post Office

HIKE IN HARMONY
Appalachian Long Distance Hikers Association

Post Offices along the A.T.

Post offices are listed here in south-to-north order. *Note: Many post offices (perhaps all) have been shaving one hour or more off their daily hours, typically some in the morning, some in the afternoon, and some at lunch time.* Changes we have verified are reflected here, but please take this development into account in your planning for picking up packages—call ahead!

Local post office telephone numbers can be verified by calling (800) 275-8777 or consulting <www.usps.com>.

Post offices printed in **bold** are located on, or within one mile of, the Trail.

Town	ZIP Code	Hours Phone
Suches, GA	30572	M–F 12:15–4:15 p.m., closed Sa (706) 747-2611
Helen, GA	30545	M–F 9–12:30, 1:30–4, Sa 9–12 (706) 878-2422
Hiawassee, GA	30546	M–F 8:30–5, Sa 8:30–12 (706) 896-3632
Franklin, NC	28734	M–F 8:30–5, Sa 9–12 (828) 524-3219
Bryson City, NC	28713	M–F 9–4:30, Sa 10–12 (828) 488-3481
Robbinsville, NC	28771	M–F 9–4:30, closed Sa (828) 479-3397
Fontana Dam, NC	28733	M–F 11:45–3:45, closed Sa (828) 498-2315
Gatlinburg, TN	37738	M–F 9–5, Sa 9–11 (865) 436-3229
Cherokee, NC	28719	M–F 9–4:30, closed Sa (828) 497-3891
Hot Springs, NC	**28743**	M–F 9–11:30 & 1–4, Sa 9–10:30 (828) 622-3242
Erwin, TN	37650	M–F 8:30–4:45, Sa 10–12 (423) 743-9422
Unicoi, TN	37692	M–F 8:45–12 & 1–3:45, Sa 8:30–10:30 (423) 743-4945
Elk Park, NC	28622	M–F 9–12:30 & 1:30–4, Sa 8–11:30 (828) 733-5711
Roan Mountain, TN	37687	M–F 8–12 & 1–4, Sa 7:30–9:30 (423) 772-3014
Hampton, TN	37658	M–F 7:30–11:30 & 12:30–4, Sa 8–10 (423) 725-2177
Shady Valley, TN	37688	M–F 8–12, Sa 8–10 (423) 739-2073
Damascus, VA	**24236**	M–F 8:30–1 & 2–4:30, Sa 9–11 (276) 475-3411
Troutdale, VA	24378	M–F 8–12, Sa 8:30–11:30 (276) 677-3221

Sugar Grove, VA	24375	M–F 8:30–12:30 & 1:30–3:30, Sa 8:15–10:30 (276) 677-3200
Marion, VA	24354	M–F 9–5, Sa 9:30–12 (276) 783-5051
Atkins, VA	24311	M–F 8:45–12 & 12:30–3:15:, Sa 9–10:45 (276) 783-5551
Bland, VA	24315	M–F 8:30–11:30 & 12–4, Sa 9–11 (276) 688-3751
Bastian, VA	24314	M–F 8–12, Sa 9:15–11:15 (276) 688-4631
Pearisburg, VA	**24134**	M–9–4:30, Sa 10–12 (540) 921-1100
Catawba, VA	**24070**	M–F 9–12 & 1–4, Sa 8–10:30 (540) 384-6011
Daleville, VA	**24083**	M–F 8–5, Sa 8–12 (540) 992-4422
Troutville, VA	**24175**	M–F 9–12 & 1–5, Sa 9–11 (540) 992-1472
Buchanan, VA	24066	M–F 8:30–1 & 1:30–4:30, Sa 10–12 (540) 254-2178
Big Island, VA	24526	M–F 8:15–12 & 1–4, Sa 8–10 (434) 299-5072
Glasgow, VA	24555	M–F 8–11:30 & 12:30–4:30, Sa 8:30–10:30 (540) 258-2852
Buena Vista, VA	24416	M–F 8:30–4:30, closed Sa (540) 261-8959
Lexington, VA	24450	M–F 9–5, Sa 10–12 (540) 463-6449
Montebello, VA	24464	M–F 10–2, Sa 10–1 (540) 377-9218
Waynesboro, VA	22980	M–F 9–5, closed Sa (540) 942-7320
Elkton, VA	22827	M–F 8:30–4:30, Sa 9–11 (540) 298-7772
Luray, VA	22835	M–F 8:30–4:30, closed Sa (540) 743-2100
Front Royal, VA	22630	M–F 8:30–5, Sa 8:30–1 (540) 635-7983
Linden, VA	22642	M–F 8–12 & 1–5, Sa 8–12 (540) 636-9936
Bluemont, VA	20135	M–F 10–1 & 2–5, Sa 8:30–12 (540) 554-4537
Berryville, VA	22611	M–F 9–5, Sa 9–12:30 (540) 955-2667
Harpers Ferry, WV	**25425**	M–F 8–4, Sa 9–12 (304) 535-2479
Boonsboro, MD	21713	M–F 9–1 & 2–5, Sa 9–12 (301) 432-6861
Smithsburg, MD	21783	M–F 8:30–1 & 2–4:30, Sa 8:30–12 (301) 824-2828
Cascade, MD	21719	M–F 10–1 & 2–5, Sa 8–12 (301) 241-3403
Blue Ridge Summit, PA	17214	M–F 8–12 & 1–4, Sa 9–11:30 (717) 794-2335

Rouzerville, PA	17250	M–F 8:30–1 & 2–4:30, Sa 8:30–11:30 (717) 762-7050
Waynesboro, PA	17268	M–F 8:30–5, Sa 9–12 (717) 762-1513
South Mountain, PA	17261	M–F 12–4, Sa 8:30–11:30 (717) 749-5833
Fayetteville, PA	17222	M–F 8–4:30, Sa 8:30–12 (717) 352-2022
Mt. Holly Springs, PA	17065	M–F 8–1 & 2–4:30, Sa 9–12 (717) 486-3468
Boiling Springs, PA	**17007**	M–F 9–12 & 1–4:30, Sa 9–12 (717) 258-6668
Duncannon, PA	**17020**	M–F 8–11, 12–4:30, Sa 8:30–12:30 (717) 834-3332
Bethel, PA	19507	M–F 8–12, 1:15–4:30, Sa 8:30–10:30 (717) 933-8305
Pine Grove, PA	17963	M–F 8:30–4:30, Sa 9–12 (570) 345-4955
Port Clinton, PA	**19549**	M–F 12:30–4:30, Sa 8–11 (610) 562-3787
Hamburg, PA	19526	M–F 9–5, Sa 9–12 (610) 562-7812
Slatington, PA	18080	M–F 8:30–5, Sa 8:30–12 (610) 767-2182
Walnutport, PA	18088	M–F 8:30–5, Sa 8:30–12 (610) 767-5191
Palmerton, PA	18071	M–F 8:30–5, Sa 8:30–12 (610) 826-2286
Danielsville, PA	18038	M–F 9:30–1 & 2–4:30, Sa 8–12 (610) 767-6882
Kunkletown, PA	18058	M–F 8–11:30 & 12:30–5, Sa 8–12 (610) 381-3062
Wind Gap, PA	**18091**	M–F 8:30–5, Sa 8:30–12 (610) 863-6206
Delaware Water Gap, PA	**18327**	M–F 8:30–12 & 1–4:45, Sa 8:30–11:30 (570) 476-0304
Branchville, NJ	07826	M–F 8:30–5, Sa 8:30–1 (973) 948-3580
Unionville, NY	**10988**	M–F 8–11:30 & 1–5, Sa 9–12 (845) 726-3535
Glenwood, NJ	07418	M–F 7:30–5, Sa 10–2 (973) 764-2616
Vernon, NJ	07462	M–F 8:30–5, Sa 9:30–12:30 (973) 764-9056
Greenwood Lake, NY	10925	M–F 8–5, Sa 9–12 (845) 477-7328
Warwick, NY	10990	M–F 8:30–5, Sa 9–4 (845) 986-0271
Southfields, NY	10975	M–F 10–12, 1–5, Sa 8:30–11:30 (845) 351-2628
Bear Mountain, NY	**10911**	M–F 9–11, closed Sa (845) 786-3747
Ft. Montgomery, NY	**10922**	M–F 8–1 & 2:30–5, Sa 9–12 (845) 446-8459

Peekskill, NY	10566	M–F 9–5, Sa 9–4 (914) 737-6437
Stormville, NY	12582	M–F 8:30–5, Sa 9–12 (845) 226-2627
Poughquag, NY	12570	M–F 8:30–1 & 2–5, Sa 8:30–12:30 (845) 724-4763
Pawling, NY	12564	M–F 8:30–5, Sa 9–12 (845) 855-2669
Wingdale, NY	12594	M–F 8–12:30 & 1:30–5, Sa 8–12:30 (845) 832-6147
Gaylordsville, CT	06755	M–F 8–1 & 2–5, Sa 8–12 (860) 354-9727
Kent, CT	**06757**	M–F 8–1 & 2–5, Sa 8:30–12:30 (860) 927-3435
Cornwall Bridge, CT	**06754**	M–F 8:30–1 & 2–5, Sa 9–12 (860) 672-6710
West Cornwall, CT	06796	M–F 8:30–12 & 2–4:30, Sa 9–12 (860) 672-6791
Sharon, CT	06069	M–F 9:30–4:30, Sa 9:30–12:30 (860) 364-5306
Falls Village, CT	**06031**	M–F 8:30–1 & 2–5, Sa 8:30–12 (860) 824-7781
Salisbury, CT	**06068**	M–F 8:30–1 & 2–5, Sa 9–12 (860) 435-5072
South Egremont, MA	01258	M–F 8:15–12 & 12:30–4, Sa 9–11:30 (413) 528-1571
Sheffield, MA	01257	M–F 9–4:30, Sa 9–12 (413) 229-8772
Great Barrington, MA	01230	M–F 8:30–4:30, Sa 8:30–12:30 (413) 528-3670
Monterey, MA	01245	M–F 8:30–1 & 2–4:30, Sa 9–11:30 (413) 528–4670
Tyringham, MA	**01264**	M–F 9–12:30 & 4–5:30, Sa 8:30–12:30 (413) 243-1225
Lee, MA	01238	M–F 8:30–4:30, Sa 9–12 (413) 243-1392
Becket, MA	01223	M–F 8–4, Sa 9–11:30 (413) 623-8845
Dalton, MA	**01226**	M–F 8:30–4:30, Sa 9–12 (413) 684-0364
Cheshire, MA	**01225**	M–F 7:30–1 & 2–4:30, Sa 8:30–11:30 (413) 743-3184
Adams, MA	01220	M–F 8:30–4:30, Sa 10–12 (413) 743-5177
North Adams, MA	01247	M–F 8:30–4:30, Sa 10–12 (413) 664-4554
Williamstown, MA	01267	M–F 8:30–4:30, Sa 9–12 (413) 458-3707
Bennington, VT	05201	M–F 8–5, Sa 9–2 (802) 442-2421
Manchester Center, VT	05255	M–F 8:30–4:30, Sa 9–12 (802) 362-3070
Danby, VT	05739	M–F 7:15–10:15 & 11:15–2:15, Sa 7:30–10:30 (802) 293-5105

Wallingford, VT	05773	M–F 8–4:30, Sa 9–12 (802) 446-2140
Rutland, VT	05701	M–F 8–5, Sa 8–12 (802) 773-0301
Killington, VT	**05751**	M–F 8:30–11, 12–4:30, Sa 8:30–12 (802) 775-4247
Pittsfield, VT	05762	M–F 8–12 & 2–4:30, Sa 8:30–11:30 (802) 746-8953
Woodstock, VT	05091	M–F 8:30–5, Sa 9–12 (802) 457-1323
South Pomfret, VT	**05067**	M–F 12:30–4:30, Sa 8:30–11:30 (802) 457-1147
Hartford, VT	05047	M–F 8–12, Sa 9–11:30 (802) 295-5511
Norwich, VT	**05055**	M–F 8:30–5, Sa 9–12 (802) 649-1608
Hanover, NH	**03755**	M–F 8:30–5, Sa 8:30–12 (603) 643-5201
Lyme, NH	03768	M–F 7:45–12 & 1:30–5:15, Sa 7:45–12 (603) 795-4421
Wentworth, NH	03282	M–F 9:30–12:30 & 1:30–4:30, Sa 7:15–12 (603) 764-9444
Warren, NH	03279	M–F 7:30–9:30 & 3–5, Sa 7:15–12 (603) 764-5733
Glencliff, NH	**03238**	M–F 12–2, Sa 7–1 (603) 989-5154
North Woodstock, NH	03262	M–F 9:30–12:30 & 1:30–4:30, Sa 9–12 (603) 745-8134
Lincoln, NH	03251	M–F 8–5, Sa 8–12 (603) 745-8133
Bartlett, NH	03812	M–F 8:30–10:30 & 11:30–3:30, Sa 8:30–12 (603) 374-2351
Mt. Washington, NH	**03589**	M–Sa 10–4, not recommended for mail drop (603) 846-5570
Gorham, NH	03581	M–F 8:30–5, Sa 8:30–12 (603) 466-2182
Andover, ME	04216	M–F 9:15–12 & 1–4:15, Sa 9–12 (207) 392-4571
Oquossoc, ME	04964	M–F 11:30–3:30, Sa 9–12 (207) 864-3685
Rangeley, ME	04970	M–F 9:30–12:30 & 1:30–4:15, Sa 9:30–12 (207) 864-2233
Stratton, ME	04982	M–F 8:30–1 & 1:30–4, Sa 8:30–11 (207) 246-6461
Caratunk, ME	**04925**	M–F 2–4, Sa 7:30–11:15 (207) 672-3416
Monson, ME	04464	M–F 9:15–12:15 & 1:15–4:15, Sa 7:30–11 (207) 997-3975
Millinocket, ME	04462	M–F 9–4, Sa 9–11:30 (207) 723-5921

Mail Drops

Many thru-hikers use "mail drops" to send themselves supplies. The *Companion* lists U.S. Postal Service (USPS) offices and also establishments that accept packages from shippers such as UPS and FedEx. Mail drops can be sent to both types of locations, but it is important to address them differently. Post offices accept only mail; a post office will not accept a FedEx or UPS package, generally speaking (the carriers have arrangements in some areas for this). Only post offices will accept packages addressed to a "General Delivery" address. USPS will forward unopened first-class and "priority" items at no additional fee. **UPS and FedEx packages cannot be sent to "General Delivery"**—you must provide a physical address other than a post office, such as a street number, and (for FedEx) a telephone number for those shipments. Please assist the businesses and post offices by printing legibly and practicing the following labeling instructions:

> Your Full Name (no nicknames or Trail names)
> c/o the business (*General Delivery* if a post office)
> City/State/ZIP Code
> *Please Hold for Thru-hiker or Section-Hiker*
> (and estimated date of arrival)

To obtain prefilled/printed labels for the most frequently used locations, try AT Mailing Labels, <https://aldha.org/at>.

At the post office, be prepared to show a photo ID when you pick up your package. Postmasters are one of a thru-hiker's best friends on the Trail. Help them help you and other hikers by following the labeling instructions above for all your mail. Send a postcard if you leave the Trail for any reason, to let the post office know what to do with your package.

To ensure that your food parcels don't pick up any "unwanted visitors" before you arrive, we suggest that hikers double-bag and securely seal all parcels.

Hostels, Camping & Showers

The first thing that comes to a hiker's one–track mind when she/he hits town is FOOD and lots of it, followed by a good hot shower and affordable accommodations. In the pursuit of just food, shower, and laundry, some hikers want to minimize the town experience and return to the Trail as soon as possible, usually the same day. This list provides low–cost options and will help you to keep the grunge at bay. Campgrounds were chosen for their proximity to the Trail, and consideration was given if they allowed nonguest showers, while keeping in mind travel by foot. There are many other campgrounds listed in the *Companion* that are best reached by car or require a longer walk.

The A.T. Passport program was developed by hostel owner Jeff Taussig as a way for hikers to document their journeys with "stamps" from participating establishments, with any proceeds going to the ATC. The passport can be bought at <www.atctrailstore.org>. More information can be found at <www.atpassport.com>.

Establishments printed in **bold** are located on or within one mile of the Trail.

NA=not available

n/c= no charge

S = shelter; H = hostel; C = camping; L = lodging; B = bunk

State	Miles from Springer	Location; Establishment	Guest Fee	Nonguest Shower–only fee	A.T. Passport
Ga.	0.0	**Amicalola Falls State Park**	C $30		P
Ga.	31.1	Neel Gap; **Walasi–Yi Center**	H $20	$ 4	P
N.C.	105.7	Rock Gap; Standing Indian Campground	C $16	$2	
N.C.	109.4	Winding Stair Gap; Tarlin Hostel Gooder Grove A.T. Hostel	H $20 B $25 C $13		P
N.C.	124.0	Burningtown Gap; Aquone Hostel	H $20		P
N.C.	136.7	Wesser; **Nantahala Outdoor Center**	H $22.14		P
N.C.	166.3	**Fontana Dam Visitors Center**		N/C	P
Tenn.	241.5	Green Corner Rd; **Standing Bear Farm**	H $25		P
N.C.	274.9	Hot Springs; The Sunnybank Inn	L $25		P
	275.3	**The Hostel at Laughing Heart Lodge**	H $20 L $28	$5	P
Tenn.	291.2	Greeneville; **Hemlock Hollow Inn**	L $22–$55 C $15	$4	P
Tenn.	319.7	Sam's Gap; Mother Marian's Natures Inn Hostel	B $30 B		
Tenn.	344.3	Erwin; **Nolichucky Hostel and Outfitters**	H $22 C $10	$5	P
		Candarossa Farm & Apiary	H $30		P
Tenn.	368.6	Greasy Creek Gap; **Greasy Creek Friendly**	H $20 C $7.50	$3	P
Tenn.	395.3	U.S. 19E; **Mountain Harbour B&B/Hostel** **The Station @ 19E**	C $10 B $25 B $30	$4	P
Tenn.	407.4	Roan Mtn; **Vango Hostel**	H $10 L $30s/$40d	$3	P

State	Miles from Springer	Location; Establishment	Guest Fee	Nonguest Shower-only fee	A.T. Passport
Tenn.	420.0	Dennis Cove; **Kincora Hostel**	H $5 C $10		P
		Black Bear Resort	H $25 L $60 C $10		P
Tenn.	428.5	Shook Branch Rd.; **Boots Off Hostel**	H $25 C $12	$5	
Va.	470.7	Damascus; **The Place** **Hiker's Inn** **Broken Fiddle** **Song Peddler Resyt**	H $8 H $25 H $30 H $45		P P P P P
Va.	518.6	**USFS Hurricane Campground**	C $16	$2	
Va.	520.2	Va. 16; Troutdale Baptist Church	H donation	N/C	P
Va.	555.8	Va. 610; **Quarter Way Inn**	H $30 C $18	$5	P
Va.	557.7	Va. 42; Bear Garden Hiker Hostel	H $20		
Va.	576.0	Va. 623; Garden Mountain Hostel	H $15–$30		
Va.	604.9	Va. 608; Lickskillet Hostel			
Va.	610.2	Va. 606; Trent's Grocery Store Weary Feet Hostel	C $6 H $15 C$10	$3 $8	P
Va.	625.4	Sugar Run Rd; **Woodshole Hostel**	H $22 C $16		P
Va.	637.1	Pearisburg; Holy Family Church Hostel Angel's Rest Hiker's Haven	H $10 H $25	$7	P
Va.	704.6	Va. 624; **Four Pines Hostel**	H donation		P
Va.	730.3	U.S. 11; **Pilot Truck Stop**		$10	
Va.	758.5	Va. 614; Middle Creek Campground	C $10 L $65/2	$5	P
Va.	787.3	Glasgow; Glasgow Hiker Shelter Stanimals 328 Hostel	N/C B $30	N/C	
Va.	809.1	Buena Vista; Glen Maury Campground	C $5	N/C	
Va.	825.4	Montebello; Montebello Camping and Fishing	C $15s/$22D		
Va.	834.6	Tye River; Crabtree Falls Campground	C $28D	N/C	
Va.	864.3	Waynesboro; Stanimal's 328 Hostel Grace Evangelical Lutheran Church YMCA/ALDHA Hiker Pavilion	H $30 H donation C donation	N/C N/C	P P
Va.	892.4 918.1 925.9	SNP; **Loft Mountain Campground** **Lewis Mountain Campground** **Big Meadows Campground**	C $15 C $15 C $15	$1 $1 $1	
Va.	944.4	US 211: Luray; Open Arms at Edge of Town Hostel	H $30 C $15	$3	P
Va.	972.1	U.S. 522; **Mountain Home Cabin**	H $30		P
Va.	1,005.6	**Bears Den Hostel**	H $20/$30 C $12	$3	P
Va.	1,013.6	**Blackburn Trail Center**	H, C donations		P
W.Va.	1,025.1	Harpers Ferry; KOA	C $33–$44	$5	
Md.	1,036.1	Gapland Rd. West; **Maple Tree Campground**	C (ask for rate)		
Md.	1,043.3	**Dahlgren Backpack Campground**	C	N/C	
Pa.	1,084.9	U.S. 30; **Trail of Hope Hostel** Caledonia State Park	H $22	$3	P

State	Miles from Springer	Location; Establishment	Guest Fee	Nonguest Shower– only fee	A.T. Passport
Pa.	1,104.8	Pa. 233; **Pine Grove Furnace State Park, Ironmasters Mansion**	H $25		P
Pa.	1,115.6	**Sheet Iron Roof Road; Deer Run Camping Resort**	C $10		
Pa.	1,124.0	Boiling Springs; Lisa's Hostel **Boiling Springs Pool**	B $20	$5 $1	
Pa.	1,132.0	U.S. 11, Carlisle; **Flyin' J Travel Plaza**		$11.50	
Pa.	1,149.7	Duncannon; **Doyle Hotel**	L $25s/ $7.50EAP	$7.50	P
Pa.	1,150.9	Duncannon; **All–American Truck Stop**		$8	
Pa.	1,219.8	**Port Clinton Pavilion**	C N/C		
Pa.	1,235.0	Hawk Mountain Road; **Eckville Hikers Center;** solar shower	B, C N/C	N/C	
Pa.	1,296.0	DWG; **Presbyterian Church of the Mountain Hostel**	H donation		P
N.J.	1,306.6	**Mohican Outdoor Center**	L $35–$40 C $12	$5	P
N.J.	1,337.8	**Sawmill Lake Campground**	C $25 + $5		
N.J.	1,338.9	**High Point State Park** day-use area Mosey's Place	B $30	N/C	P
N.Y.	1,392.3	Arden Valley Rd; Tiorati Circle		N/C	
N.Y.	1,412.9	**Graymoor Spiritual Life Center**	C	N/C	
N.Y.	1,424.8	N.Y. 301; Clarence Fahnestock State Park	C $17.75– $21.75	N/C	
Conn.	1,481.2	Cornwall Bridge; Housatonic Meadows State Park	C $36	N/C	
Conn.	1,495.2	Falls Village; Hydroelectric Plant		N/C	P
		BeardedWoods Hike & Dine	H $50 with meals		
Mass.	1,523.8	U.S. 7; Berkshire South Community Center	C N/C	$5	
Mass.	1,532.2	East Mountain Retreat	H $10		
Mass.	1,571.6	Dalton; **Tom Levardi's 83 Depot St**.	C N/C		P
Mass.	1,595.4	Mass. 2; **North Adams YMCA** Williamstown: Williams Inn		N/C $7	
Vt.	1,653.9	Manchester Center; Green Mountain House	H $35		P
Vt.	1,704.0	Rutland; Hostel at the Yellow Deli	H donation		P
Vt.	1,707.3	Vt. 100; **Gifford Woods State Park**	S $27–$29 C $20–$22/6	50¢	
N.H.	1,786.0	Cape Moonshine Rd; **Dancing Dunes Village**	C work for stay		
N.H.	1,794.1	Glencliff; **Hikers Welcome Hostel**	H $25 C $18.50	$3	P
N.H.	1,803.6	N.H. 112/Kinsman Notch; The Notch Hostel	H $33		P
N.H.	1,819.9	I–93, U.S. 3, Franconia Notch; Lafayette Place Campground	C $25D	$1	
N.H.	1,847.6	U.S. 302, Crawford Notch; Dry River Campground Crawford Notch Campground AMC Highland Center	C $25D C $36D	25¢	
N.H.	1,873.6	N.H. 16; **Pinkham Notch Visitors Center**		coin	

State	Miles from Springer	Location; Establishment	Guest Fee	Nonguest Shower– only fee	A.T. Passport
N.H.	1,894.7	U.S. 2, Shelburne; **Rattle River Lodge & Hostel**	H $37		P
		The Birches Loft at White Birches Camping Park	H $15 C $15		P
N.H.	1,894.7	Gorham; The Barn at Libby House	H $25		P
Maine	1,925.8	Grafton Notch Campground	C $25	$5	
Maine	1,936.1	Andover; Pine Ellis Hiking Lodge Roxbury; Human Nature Hostel	B $25 B $30		P
Maine	1,946.2	East Andover; The Cabin South Arm Campground	donation	25¢	P
Maine	2,004.8	Stratton; Stratton Motel & Hostel	H $35	$5	P
Maine	2,041.8	U.S. 201; **Caratunk Hiker House** **Sterling Inn**	B $20 B $30	$3	
Maine	2,078.5	Monson; Lakeshore House Shaw's Hiker Hostel	B $25 B $25 C $12	$5	P P
Maine	2,177.9	Golden Road; **Abol Bridge Campground** **Abol Pines**	C $25PP C $15PP	coin	
Maine	2,187.7	Millinocket; A.T. Lodge	B $25	$5	P

Among the additional lodging and service providers included in the A.T. Passport program are:

A.T. Kick-Off, Amicalola Falls State Park, Ga.

Survivor Dave's Trail Shuttles, Atlanta, Ga.
Len Foote Inn, Amicalola Falls State Park, Ga.
Blood Mountain Cabins, Blairsville, Ga.
Budget Inn, Hiawassee, Ga.
Ron's Appalachian Trail Shuttle, Hiawassee, Ga.
Holiday Inn Express, Blairsville, Ga.
Three Eagles Outfitter, Franklin, N.C.
Outdoor 76 Outfitter, Franklin, N.C.
First Baptist Hiker Breakfast, Franklin, N.C.
Currahee Brewery, Franklin, N.C.
Lazy Hiker Brewery, Franklin, N.C.
Nantahala General Store, Bryson City, N.C.
Fontana Dam Visitors Center, Fontana Dam, N.C.
Bluff Mountain Outfitter, Hot Springs, N.C.
Hiker's Ridge Ministry Center, Hot Springs, N.C.
Spring Creek Tavern, Hot Springs, N.C.
Smoky Mountain Diner, Hot Springs, N.C.
Hot Springs, N.C., Library
Bob's Dairyland, Roan Mountain, Tenn.
Montgomery Homestead Inn, Damascus, Va.
Mt. Rogers Outfitters, Damascus, Va.
MoJo's Trailside Café, Damascus, Va.
Mt. Rogers Visitors Center, Marion, Va.
Settlers' Museum, Atkins, Va.
Trent's Grocery, Bland, Va.
Holiday Lodge, Pearisburg, Va.
MacArthur Inn, Pearisburg, Va.
The Captain's, Stony Creek, Va.
Howard Johnson Express Inn, Daleville, Va.
Outdoor Trails Outfitter, Daleville, Va.
Three Li'l Pigs, Daleville, Va.
Devils Backbone Brewery, Roseland, Va.
Appalachian Trail Conservancy Headquarters,
    Harpers Ferry, W.Va.
Mena's Pizzeria, Harpers Ferry, W.Va.
Guide Shack Café, Harpers Ferry, W.Va.
Burgundy Lane B&B, Waynesboro, Pa.

Appalachian Trail Museum, Gardners, Pa.
Pine Grove General Store, Gardners, Pa.
Appalachian Trail Conservancy, Boiling Springs, Pa.
TCO Outdoors, Boiling Springs, Pa.
Pheasant Field B&B, Carlisle, Pa.
Port Clinton Hotel, Port Clinton, Pa.
Port Clinton Barber Shop, Port Clinton, Pa.
Port Clinton Peanut Shop, Port Clinton, Pa.
John Stempa, Kunkletown, Pa.
Mohican Outdoor Center, Blairstown, N.J.
High Point State Park, Sussex, N.J.
Native Landscapes, Pawling, N.Y.
Upper Goose Pond Cabin, Mass.
Mountain Goat Outfitter, Manchester Center, Vt.
The Inn at Long Trail, Killington, Vt.
Mountain Meadows Lodge, Killington, Vt.
The Hart Family, West Hartford, Vt.
Dancing Bones Community, Wentworth, N.H.
Moose Scoops Ice Cream, Warren, N.H.
Chet's One Step at a Time, Lincoln, N.H.
Caratunk House B&B, Caratunk, Maine

Annual ALDHA Gathering

Equipment Manufacturers & Distributors

Most manufacturers and distributors stand behind their products. Companies will often replace or repair equipment while you are on the Trail. Usually, it is best to deal directly with the manufacturer rather than going through an outfitter along the Trail (except where noted below). A few telephone calls can save lost time and prevent a lot of headaches.

AntiGravity Gear	(910) 794-3308 www.antigravitygear.com
Arc 'Teryx	(866) 458-BIRD www.arcteryx.com
Asolo	(603) 448-8827, ext. 105 www.asolo.com
Backcountry Gear	(800) 953-5499 www.backcountrygear.com
Campmor	(800) 226-7667 www.campmor.com
Camelbak	(877) 404-7673 www.camelbak.com
Cascade Designs/MSR	(800) 531-9531 www.cascadedesigns.com
Cedar Tree Industry	(276) 780-2354 www.thepacka.com
Columbia	(800) 622-6953 www.columbia.com
Eastern Mountain Sports	(888) 463-6367 www.ems.com
Eureka	(888) 6EUREKA www.eurekacampingctr.com
Ex Officio	(800) 644-7303 www.exofficio.com
Feathered Friends	(206) 292-2210 www.featheredfriends.com
Frogg Toggs	(800) 349-1835 www.froggtoggs.com
Gossamer Gear	(512) 374-0133 www.gossamergear.com
Granite Gear	(218) 834-6157 www.granitegear.com
Gregory Mountain Products	(877) 477-4292 www.gregorypacks.com
Hi-Tec Sports, USA	(800) 521-1698 www.us.hi-tec.com
Hyperlite Mountain Gear	(800) 464-9208 www.hyperlitemountaingear.com
Jacks 'R' Better Quilts	(757) 643-8908 www.jacksrbetter.com
Katadyn	(800) 755-6701 www.katadyn.com
Kelty Pack, Inc.	(866) 349-7225, (800) 535-3589 www.kelty.com
Leki	(800) 255-9982, ext 150 www.leki.com
L.L.Bean	(800) 441-5713 www.llbean.com

Lowe Alpine Systems	(303) 926-7228 www.lowealpine.com
Marmot	(888) 357-3262 www.marmot.com
Merrell	(800) 288-3124 www.merrell.com
Mont-bell	(303) 449-5331 www.montbell.com
Montrail	(855) 698-7245 www.montrail.com
Moonbow Gear	(603) 744-2264 www.moonbowgear.com
Mountain Hardwear	(877) 927-5649 www.mountainhardwear.com
Mountainsmith	(800) 426-4075, ext. 2 www.mountainsmith.com
The North Face	(855) 500-8639 www.thenorthface.com
Osprey	(866) 284-7830 cs@ospreypacks.com
Outdoor Research	(888) 467-4327 www.outdoorresearch.com
Patagonia	(800) 638-6464 www.patagonia.com
Primus	(888) 546-2267 www.primusstoves.com
Princeton Tec	(609) 298-9331 www.princetontec.com
REI	(800) 426-4840 www.rei.com
Royal Robbins	(800) 587-9044 www.royalrobbins.com
Salomon	(800) 654-2668 www.salomonsports.com
Sierra Designs	(800) 736-8592 www.sierradesigns.com
Six Moon Designs	(503) 430-2303 www.sixmoondesigns.com
Speer Hammocks	(252) 619-8292 www.tttrailgear.com
Suunto	(855) 258-0900 www.suunto.com
Tarptent by Henry Shires	(650) 587-1548 www.tarptent.com
Teva/Deckers Corporation	(800) 367-8382 www.teva.com
ULA-Equipment	(435) 753-5191 www.ula-equipment.com
Vasque	(800) 224-4453 www.vasque.com
Western Mountaineering	(408) 287-8944 www.westernmountaineering.com
Zpacks	www.zpacks.com
ZZManufacturing (Zipztove)	(800) 594-9046 www.zzstove.com
Complete list of major and cottage gear manufacturers	**www.aldha.org/at/gear**

ALDHA 2020 Membership/Registration Form

Membership open to all ◆ No prerequisites or requirements ◆ No need to be a hiker to join

Name(s)

Current ALDHA member? ☐ Yes ☐ No

Address

City, State, ZIP Code

Telephone *(with area code)*

E-mail

Trail name(s)

Trails completed and years they were hiked

Membership (choose one)
(includes four newsletters & the membership directory):

☐ Enclosed is $10 for my renewal or 2020 annual membership in ALDHA.

☐ Enclosed is $20 for my 2020 and 2021 annual memberships in ALDHA.

☐ Enclosed is $200 for a lifetime membership in ALDHA. *(Membership is for life but **does not include** the Gathering fee each year.)*

☐ **2020 Gathering registration fee**

(It's $20 per person) _____ registrants X $20 = _____

☐ $_____ tax-deductible donation to ALDHA, a 501(c)(3) nonprofit organization

How would you like to receive your newsletters and directory? ☐ e-mail (color; default) ☐ paper (black & white)

Send completed form with payment (payable to ALDHA) to:

ALDHA, 10 Benning St., PMB 224, West Lebanon, NH 03784

or join on-line with debit or credit card at <www.aldha.org>.

Message to the Class of 2020

2020 THRU-HIKER & 2,000-MILER AWARD CEREMONY FEB 2 6 2020

ALDHA and ATC will be working together at the 2020 Gathering to recognize both thru-hikers and section-hikers who finish their journeys this year. You will be called up to the stage at the Friday-night meeting during the Class Years Event to receive an end-to-end certificate and a "I Hiked ALDHA Way" patch from ALDHA. The application for the official Appalachian Trail Conservancy certificate is on line at <www.appalachiantrail.org/about-the-trail/2000-milers/2000-miler-application>. **Special notice to 2020 thru-hikers and 2,000-Milers: Bring your Trail-worn *A.T. Thru-Hikers' Companion* (or the Maine section in its entirety) and a completed-trail form to the registration desk, and your Gathering fee is on ALDHA!**